Contracts and the Legal Environment for Engineers and Architects

---

SIXTH EDITION

McGraw-Hill Series in Construction Engineering and Project Management

Consulting Editor
Raymond E. Levitt, Stanford University

Barrie and Paulson: *Professional Construction Management: Including CM, Design-Construct, and General Contracting*
Bockrath: *Contracts and the Legal Environment for Engineers and Architects*
Callahan, Quackenbush, and Rowlings: *Construction Project Scheduling*
Griffis and Farr: *Construction Project Planning*
Hinze: *Construction Contracts*
Jervis and Levin: *Construction Law: Principles and Practice*
Koerner: *Construction and Geotechnical Methods in Foundations Engineering*
Oberlender: *Project Management for Engineering and Construction*
Oglesby, Parker, and Howell: *Productivity Improvement in Construction*
Paulson: *Computer Applications in Construction*
Peurifoy, Ledbetter, and Schexnayder: *Construction Planning, Equipment, and Methods*
Peurifoy and Oberlender: *Estimating Construction Costs*
Schuette and Liska: *Building Construction Estimating*
Shuttleworth: *Mechanical and Electrical Systems for Construction*
Stevens: *Techniques for Construction Network Scheduling*

CONTRACTS AND THE LEGAL ENVIRONMENT FOR ENGINEERS AND ARCHITECTS

SIXTH EDITION

Joseph T. Bockrath, A.B, J.D.
Member of the Louisiana and Supreme Court Bar
R. Gordon Kean Professor of Law
Louisiana State University

Boston   Burr Ridge, IL   Dubuque, IA   Madison, Wl   New York   San Francisco   St. Louis
Bangkok   Bogotá   Caracas   Lisbon   London   Madrid
Mexico City   Milan   New Delhi   Seoul   Singapore   Sydney   Taipei   Toronto

McGraw-Hill Higher Education

*A Division of The **McGraw-Hill** Companies*

CONTRACTS AND THE LEGAL ENVIRONMENT FOR ENGINEERS AND ARCHITECTS

This book is printed on acid-free paper.

1 2 3 4 5 6 7 8 9 0 F G R / F G R 9 0 9 8 7 6 5 4 3 2 1 0 9

ISBN 0-07-039363-X

Vice president/Editor-in-chief: *Kevin T. Kane*
Publisher: *Thomas Casson*
Executive editor: *Eric M. Munson*
Editorial coordinator: *Michael Jones*
Senior marketing manager: *John T. Wannemacher*
Project manager: *Susanne Riedell*
Senior production supervisor: *Heather D. Burbridge*
Freelance design coordinator: *Pam Verros*
Supplement coordinator: *Rose M. Range*
Compositor: *Lachina Publishing Services*
Typeface: *10/12 Times Roman*
Printer: *Quebecor Printing Book Group/Fairfield*

Library of Congress Cataloging-in-Publication Data

Bockrath, Joseph T.
   Contracts and the legal environment for engineers and architects /
Joseph T. Bockrath. — 6th ed.
      p.   cm — (McGraw-Hill series in construction engineering and
project management)
   Includes index.
   ISBN 0-07-039363-X (alk. paper)
   1. Engineering contracts—United States. 2. Architectural
contracts—United States. 3. Construction contracts—United States.
I. Title. II. Series.
KF902.D8   2000
   343.73'078624—dc21   99-15562

http://www.mhhe.com

ABOUT THE AUTHOR

JOSEPH T. BOCKRATH is R. Gordon Kean Professor of Law at the Louisiana State University Law Center, where he has taught Contracts, Constitutional Law, and several other subjects since 1976. Prior to his arrival at LSU he was Assistant Professor of Marine Studies at the University of Delaware.

A graduate of Hastings College of Law of the University of California in San Francisco, he is the author of *Concepts in Environmental Law for Engineers, Scientists, and Managers,* also published by McGraw-Hill, the third, fourth, and fifth editions of *Dunham and Young's Contracts, Specifications, and Law for Engineers,* and numerous journal articles.

An inveterate traveler, Professor Bockrath has found his way through more than 60 countries in all parts of the world, particularly favoring Southern Asia, and has lectured at Universities in India and Sri Lanka.

CONTENTS

PREFACE

The sixth edition of *Contracts and the Legal Environment for Engineers and Architects* has been written for students of engineering and architecture and for practicing design professionals. The material has been divided into three parts. Part 1 explains the basic principles of the law of contracts. Part 2 is a discussion of the application of contract principles to construction contracts, together with data on the preparation of specifications and other documents that form an essential part of construction contracts. Part 3 considers fields of law that are of special interest to engineers, architects, and contractors in their professional lives.

As engineers and architects gain experience and progress in a leadership capacity, they will often need to acquire a knowledge of basic legal principles, particularly in the area of contracts and specifications. I hope to introduce the reader to some legal problems that are likely to arise, to the end that he or she will be able to recognize the occasions when a lawyer's aid is needed and will be in a position to cooperate with attorneys with whom he or she is working. I have not tried to teach the law to those who read these pages, but rather create an awareness and appreciation of more or less typical questions that arise when engineering and law interact.

In an effort to minimize difficulties arising from the use of unfamiliar terminology, I have included a glossary of legal terms, which should be consulted when the technical word or phrase employed is not immediately defined, and have attempted to state legal principles simply and clearly, rather than to quote extensively from court decisions or complicated documents. Court cases have been used as references, and, to a much greater extent in this edition, points are clarified by means of illustrations gathered from engineering practice and from actual construction contracts. Fictitious names have been used in factual cases.

Apart from source material acknowledged as such, it is conceivable that an occasional statement or passage in the text will appear to have been taken directly from another publication. Any such circumstances are entirely unintentional. It can readily be appreciated from the nature of the subject that it is virtually impossible to avoid defining some technical terms, or once in a while describing a rule of law, in language that closely resembles that employed by other writers in the field. There are, after all, a limited number of ways in which to discuss the basic legal principles that have been known, applied, and talked about for many years.

This edition has been completely updated in recognition of the dynamic changes in the law in recent years, and every effort has been made to provide current and accurate information. One must be aware, however, that the changes continue, that rules vary from state to state, and that every rule has exceptions. Thus, neither this nor any other text is a substitute for a lawyer's help. My expectation is that a study of this text will enable the reader to recognize when that help is needed.

Technology such as CAD, fax machines, and biotechnology advance much more quickly than does the law, and their exact impact on law is impossible to predict. To the extent possible the sixth edition attempts to incorporate such advances in the chapters ranging from contract formation principles to contract drawings and intellectual property. Readers are encouraged to speculate on the law's likely evolution in the future as technology advances.

ACKNOWLEDGMENTS

This sixth edition benefitted greatly from the research assistance of law student Willa LeBlanc, technical and administrative assistance from Gladys Dreher, and the secretarial help of Linda Duplessis and Madelyn Babin, all of the LSU Law School. The comments of reviewers Robert P. Carnahan, University of South Florida; Fred R. Bennett, Walla Walla College; Frederick L. Plotnick, Drexel University; and Neil Eldin, Oregon State University, were of great help and are deeply appreciated.

Joseph T. Bockrath

CODE OF ETHICS FOR ENGINEERS

PREAMBLE

Engineering is an important and learned profession. The members of the profession recognize that their work has a direct and vital impact on the quality of life for all people. Accordingly, the services provided by engineers require honesty, impartiality, fairness, and equity, and must be dedicated to the protection of the public health, safety, and welfare. In the practice of their profession, engineers must perform under a standard of professional behavior which requires adherence to the highest principles of ethical conduct on behalf of the public, clients, employers, and the profession.

I. FUNDAMENTAL CANONS

Engineers, in the fulfillment of their professional duties, shall:

1. Hold paramount the safety, health and welfare of the public in the performance of their professional duties.
2. Perform services only in areas of their competence.
3. Issue public statements only in an objective and truthful manner.
4. Act in professional matters for each employer or client as faithful agents or trustees.
5. Avoid improper solicitation of professional employment.

II. RULES OF PRACTICE

1. Engineers shall hold paramount the safety, health and welfare of the public in the performance of their professional duties.

   a. Engineers shall at all times recognize that their primary obligation is to protect the safety, health, property and welfare of the public. If their professional judgment is overruled under circumstances where the safety, health, property or welfare of the public are endangered, they shall notify their employer or client and such other authority as may be appropriate.

   b. Engineers shall approve only those engineering documents which are safe for public health, property and welfare in conformity with accepted standards.

c. Engineers shall not reveal facts, data or information obtained in a professional capacity without the prior consent of the client or employer except as authorized or required by law of this Code.

d. Engineers shall not permit the use of their name or firm name nor associate in business ventures with any person or firm which they have reason to believe is engaging in fraudulent or dishonest business or professional practices.

e. Engineers having knowledge of any alleged violation of this Code shall cooperate with the proper authorities in furnishing such information or assistance as may be required.

2. Engineers shall perform services only in the areas of their competence.

   a. Engineers shall undertake assignments only when qualified by education or experience in the specific technical fields involved.

   b. Engineers shall not affix their signatures to any plans or documents dealing with subject matter in which they lack competence, nor to any plan or document not prepared under their direction and control.

   c. Engineers may accept an assignment outside of their fields of competence to the extent that their services are restricted to those phases of the project in which they are qualified, and to the extent that they are satisfied that all other phases of such project will be performed by registered or otherwise qualified associates, consultants, or employees, in which case they may then sign the documents for the total project.

3. Engineers shall issue public statements only in an objective and truthful manner.

   a. Engineers shall be objective and truthful in professional reports, statements or testimony. They shall include all relevant and pertinent information in such reports, statements or testimony.

   b. Engineers may express publicly a professional opinion on technical subjects only when that opinion is founded upon adequate knowledge of the facts and competence in the subject matter.

   c. Engineers shall issue no statements, criticisms or arguments on technical matters which are inspired or paid for by interested parties, unless they have prefaced their comments by explicitly identifying the interested parties on whose behalf they are speaking, and by revealing the existence of any interest the engineers may have in the matters.

4. Engineers shall act in professional matters for each employer or client as faithful agents or trustees.

   a. Engineers shall disclose all known or potential conflicts of interest to their employers or clients by promptly informing them of any business association, interest, or other circumstances which could influence or appear to influence their judgment or the quality of their services.

b. Engineers shall not accept compensation, financial or otherwise, from more than one party for services on the same project, or for services pertaining to the same project, unless the circumstances are fully disclosed to, and agreed to, by all interested parties.

c. Engineers shall not solicit or accept financial or other valuable consideration, directly or indirectly, from contractors, their agents, or other parties in connection with work for employers or clients for which they are responsible.

d. Engineers in public service as members, advisors or employees of a governmental body or department shall not participate in decisions with respect to professional services solicited or provided by them or their organizations in private or public engineering practice.

e. Engineers shall not solicit or accept a professional contract from a governmental body on which a principal or officer of their organization serves as member.

5. Engineers shall avoid improper solicitation of professional employment.

a. Engineers shall not falsify or permit misrepresentation of their, or their associates', academic or professional qualifications. They shall not misrepresent or exaggerate their degree of responsibility in or for the subject matter of prior assignments. Brochures or other presentations incident to the solicitation of employment shall not misrepresent pertinent facts concerning employers, employees, associates, joint ventures or past accomplishments with the intent and purpose of enhancing their qualifications and their work.

b. Engineers shall not offer, give, solicit or receive, either directly or indirectly, any political contribution in an amount intended to influence the award of a contract by public authority, or which may be reasonably construed by the public of having the effect or intent to influence the award of a contract. They shall not offer any gift, or other valuable consideration in order to secure work. They shall not pay a commission, percentage or brokerage fee in order to secure work except to a bona fide employee or bona fide established commercial or marketing agencies retained by them.

III. PROFESSIONAL OBLIGATIONS

1. Engineers shall be guided in all their professional relations by the highest standards of integrity.

a. Engineers shall admit and accept their own errors when proven wrong and refrain from distorting or altering the facts in an attempt to justify their decisions.

b. Engineers shall advise their clients or employers when they believe a project will not be successful.

c. Engineers shall not accept outside employment to the detriment of their regular work or interest. Before accepting any outside employment they will notify their employers.

d. Engineers shall not attempt to attract an engineer from another employer by false or misleading pretenses.

e. Engineers shall not actively participate in strikes, picket lines, or other collective coercive action.

f. Engineers shall avoid any act tending to promote their own interest at the expense of the dignity and integrity of the profession.

2. Engineers shall at all times strive to serve the public interest.

a. Engineers shall seek opportunities to be of constructive service in civil affairs and work for the advancement of the safety, health and well-being of their community.

b. Engineers shall not complete, sign, or seal plans and/or specifications that are not of a design safe to the public health and welfare and in conformity with accepted engineering standards. If the client or employer insists on such unprofessional conduct, they shall notify the proper authorities and withdraw from further service on the project.

c. Engineers shall endeavor to extend public knowledge and appreciation of engineering and its achievements and to protect the engineering profession from misrepresentations and misunderstanding.

3. Engineers shall avoid all conduct or practice which is likely to discredit the profession or deceive the public.

a. Engineers shall avoid the use of statements containing a material misrepresentation of fact or omitting a material fact necessary to keep statements from being misleading; statements intended or likely to create an unjustified expectation; statements containing prediction of future success; statements containing an opinion as to the quality of the Engineers' services; or statements intended or likely to attract clients by the use of showmanship, puffery, or self-laudation, including the use of slogans, jingles, or sensational language or format.

b. Consistent with the foregoing, Engineers may advertise for recruitment of personnel.

c. Consistent with the foregoing, Engineers may prepare articles for the lay or technical press but such articles shall not imply credit to the author for work performed by others.

4. Engineers shall not disclose confidential information concerning the business affairs or technical process of any present or former client or employer without his consent.

a. Engineers in the employ of others shall not without the consent of all interested parties enter promotional efforts or negotiations for work or make arrangements for other employment as a principal or to practice in connection with a specific project for which the Engineer has gained particular and specialized knowledge.

b. Engineers shall not, without the consent of all interested parties, participate in or represent an adversary interest in connection with a specific project or proceeding in which the Engineer has gained particular specialized knowledge on behalf of a former client or employer.

5. Engineers shall not be influenced in their professional duties by conflicting interests.

   a. Engineers shall not accept financial or other considerations, including free engineering designs, from material or equipment suppliers for specifying their product.

   b. Engineers shall not accept commissions or allowances, directly or indirectly, from contractors or other parties dealing with clients or employers of the Engineer in connection with work for which the Engineer is responsible.

6. Engineers shall uphold the principle of appropriate and adequate compensation for those engaged in engineering work.

   a. Engineers shall not accept remuneration from either an employee or employment agency for giving employment.

   b. Engineers, when employing other engineers, shall offer a salary according to professional qualifications and the recognized standards in the particular geographical area.

7. Engineers shall not compete unfairly with other engineers by attempting to obtain employment or advancement or professional engagements by taking advantage or a salaried position, by criticizing other engineers, or by other improper or questionable methods.

   a. Engineers shall not request, propose, or accept a professional commission on a contingent basis under circumstances in which their professional judgment may be compromised.

   b. Engineers in salaried positions shall accept part-time engineering work only at salaries not less than that recognized as standard in the area.

   c. Engineers shall not use equipment, supplies, laboratory, or office facilities of an employer to carry on outside private practice without consent.

8. Engineers shall not attempt to injure, maliciously or falsely, directly or indirectly, the professional reputation, prospects, practice or employment of other engineers, nor indiscriminately criticize other engineers' work. Engineers who believe others are guilty of unethical or illegal practice shall present such information to the proper authority for action.

   a. Engineers in private practice shall not review the work of another engineer for the same client, except with the knowledge of such engineer, or unless the connection of such engineer with the work has been terminated.

b. Engineers in governmental, industrial or educational employ are entitled to review and evaluate the work of other engineers when so required by their employment duties.

c. Engineers in sales or industrial employ are entitled to make engineering comparisons of represented products with products of other suppliers.

9. Engineers shall accept personal responsibility for all professional activities.

a. Engineers shall conform with state registration laws in the practice of engineering.

b. Engineers shall not use association with a nonengineer, a corporation, or partnership, as a "cloak" for unethical acts, but must accept personal responsibility for all professional acts.

10. Engineers shall give credit for engineering work to those to whom credit is due, and will recognize the proprietary interests of others.

a. Engineers shall, whenever possible, name the person or persons who may be individually responsible for designs, inventions, writings, or other accomplishments.

b. Engineers using designs supplied by a client recognize that the designs remain the property of the client and may not be duplicated by the Engineer for others without express permission.

c. Engineers, before undertaking work for others in connection with which the Engineer may make improvements, plans, designs, inventions, or other records which may justify copyrights or patents, should enter into a positive agreement regarding ownership.

d. Engineers' designs, data, records, and notes referring exclusively to an employer's work are the employer's property.

11. Engineers shall cooperate in extending the effectiveness of the profession by interchanging information and experience with other engineers and students, and will endeavor to provide opportunity for the professional development and advancement of engineers under their supervision.

a. Engineers shall encourage engineering employees' efforts to improve their education.

b. Engineers shall encourage engineering employees to attend and present papers at professional and technical society meetings.

c. Engineers shall urge engineering employees to become registered at the earliest possible date.

d. Engineers shall assign a professional engineer duties of a nature to utilize full training and experience, insofar as possible, and delegate lesser functions to subprofessionals or to technicians.

e. Engineers shall provide a prospective engineering employee with complete information on working conditions and proposed status of employment, and after employment will keep employees informed of any changes.

"By order of the United States District Court for the District of Columbia, former Section 11(c) of the NSPE Code of Ethics prohibiting competitive bidding, and all policy statements, opinions, rulings or other guidelines interpreting its scope, have been rescinded as unlawfully interfering with the legal right of engineers, protected under the antitrust laws, to provide price information to prospective clients; accordingly, nothing contained in the NSPE Code of Ethics, policy statements, opinions, rulings or other guidelines prohibits the submissions of price quotations or competitive bids for engineering services at any time or in any amount."

STATEMENT BY NSPE EXECUTIVE COMMITTEE

In order to correct misunderstandings which have been indicated in some instances since the issuance of the Supreme Court decision and the entry of the Final Judgment, it is noted that in its decision of April 25, 1978, the Supreme Court of the United States declared: "The Sherman Act does not require competitive bidding."

It is further noted that as made clear in the Supreme Court decision:

1. Engineers and firms may individually refuse to bid for engineering services.
2. Clients are not required to seek bids for engineering services.
3. Federal, state, and local laws governing procedures to procure engineering services are not affected, and remain in full force and effect.
4. State societies and local chapters are free to actively and aggressively seek legislation for professional selection and negotiation procedures by public agencies.
5. State registration board rules of professional conduct, including rules prohibiting competitive bidding for engineering services, are not affected and remain in full force and effect. State registration boards with authority to adopt rules of professional conduct may adopt rules governing procedures to obtain engineering services.
6. As noted by the Supreme Court, "nothing in the judgment prevents NSPE and its members from attempting to influence governmental action."

Note:

In regard to the question of application of the Code to corporations vis-à-vis real persons, business form or type should not negate nor influence conformance of individuals to the Code. The Code deals with professional services, which services must be performed by real persons. Real persons in turn establish and implement policies within business structures. The Code is clearly written to apply to the Engineer and it is incumbent on a member of NSPE to endeavor to live up to its provisions. This applies to all pertinent sections of the Code.

Courtesy of the National Society of Professional Engineers.
Publication #1102. As revised, July 1993.

1

LAW OF CONTRACTS

Chapter 1 provides a basic introduction to the American legal system. The purpose of Chapters 2 to 7 is to explain the basic principles of law applicable to contracts. The discussion has been condensed so that the reader can secure an overall view of what is involved without having to read too extensively or be burdened with an undue number of details. Illlustrations have been given and cases cited in order to convey the ideas as clearly and in as interesting a manner as possible. For a more comprehensive treatment of the subject or any aspect thereof, one may consult any of the standard legal treatises in the field of contracts.

1

INTRODUCTION

1.1 LAW AND ENGINEERING

Dramatic increases in government regulation and increased liability exposure in the past few decades have made it imperative that engineers be at least conversant with the basics of law.

Law is a learned profession, and even a modest mastery of it requires years of concentrated study. Of course, mastery is unnecessary for those not going into the profession. What is necessary for engineers who want to expand their interests is an elementary understanding of how law works. Law is a dynamic discipline, and even lawyers have fewer answers than the public might believe. What they do have are the questions. Learning to answer the questions would require years of study and a restructuring of the thought process, but it is unnecessary; developing a sensitivity for potential legal problems is a relatively short-term and attainable goal. If an engineer, after a study of this work, can recognize situations which give rise to legal questions, the book will have succeeded.

An engineer ordinarily uses a logical method to solve problems, trying generally to identify and control variables and eliminate guesswork from the final equation. Objectivity is important. The result of the process generally has few subjective components or disregards them in the interest of maintaining the integrity of the scientific process.

In law, however, the logic of the process is secondary to the fact of the result. The life of the law, said Holmes, has not been logic; it has been experience. Experience and analogy are most important in the process of legal thought. This ability to analogize and to know when not to do so is critical to the lawyer's training. While many legal analogies may seem absurd to those to whom factual variables are items to be controlled or eliminated, the facts may be legally similar to those in the question at issue. It is result rather than method with which the lawyer must be concerned. Lawyers, rather like engineers, must please clients rather than themselves. It has been said that "the client cares little for a beautiful case." A favorable outcome is what is sought.

Much of the difficulty in this area is inherent in the adversary process. Unlike the engineer, the lawyer is engaged not to find a truth but to present his or her client's position and counter, if possible, the arguments of the opponent. Although a lawyer should not subvert the truth, concern with the correct or "just" resolution of the issue is beyond the province of the individual lawyer. The legal process is one devoted to the resolution of conflicts. Particular laws may be either arbitrary or based on historical irrelevancy or error, but they serve a utilitarian purpose if everyone (at least the lawyers) knows what they are and that they will be applied in like circumstances in the future.

To achieve a result in a reasonable time and with at least a semblance of right reason, the law regularly utilizes a device that science may find anathema and akin to putting up the solution of a mathematical problem to a vote: compromise. This method of resolving conflicts may be utilized in the law either for expediency or in recognition of the fact that rarely is the side of righteousness easily discernible or all with one party. A jury's finding of guilt based on marginal evidence may be balanced by a light sentence. Likewise, although negligence may in theory be a yes or no question and completely separate from damages, a jury unsure of the liability but sympathetic to the victim may compromise its unsureness by finding for the victim but with lower damages. Similarly, the plaintiff's lawyer may settle for less than full compensation if the liability issue is unclear.

The idea of balancing interests in determining a result is deeply rooted in all areas of the law. Injunctions are issued after a balance of equities; custody litigation weighs the interests of the child, the parent, and the community. The "right" answer from the law's view is often not fully satisfactory to either party. The scientist's effort to tolerate if not accept this aspect of legal methodology may determine his or her usefulness as a participant in the making and implementation of policy decisions with a scientific component. It is not rare for the engineer studying law to be appalled at the impotence of the judicial system with respect to seemingly unwise or foolish legislative or administrative action. This view, however, is myopic in two respects.

The legislature, in theory if not in fact, does not have a license to act other than that granted by the voters. The voters' recourse, should they choose to exercise it, is obvious, however slowworking it may be. To think that judges are not subject to political pressures and prejudices is to be naive. Many judges are elected, and most of those appointed are politicians or party loyalists. Appointment to the bench, even for life, cannot displace one's political and social views acquired over a lifetime.

Most significant, however, is the simple fact that judges and lawyers are human, subject to the same prejudices, lapses, and foibles as any citizen. Referring to oneself as "the court" rather than "Judge Smith" does not obscure the fact that a person is deciding questions within the confines of a system designed, or at least accumulated, by human beings.

As Cardozo phrased it:

> It is often through these subconscious forces that judges are kept consistent with themselves, and inconsistent with one another. All their lives, forces which they do not recognize and cannot name have been tugging at them—inherited instincts, traditional beliefs, acquired convictions; and the resultant is an outlook on life, a con-

ception of social needs, a sense in James's phrase of "the total push and pressure of the cosmos," which, when reasons are nicely balanced, must determine where choice falls. Deep below consciousness are other forces, the like and dislikes, the predilections and prejudices, the complex of instincts and emotions and habits and convictions, which make the man, whether he be litigant or judge.

Speaking of the process of judicial decision making, it has been suggested that "one wills at the beginning the result; one finds the principle afterwards; such is the genesis of all judicial construction." While this is probably an exaggeration when applied to persons schooled in the value of precedent and continuity, it is true in one degree or another of all persons who face choices. It would be less or more than human for persons not to tailor their logic or procedure in some manner to compel the desired result.

Law should be thought of as a process rather than a set of rules: a process by which disputes are resolved. Oftentimes the dispute has no right or wrong but rather is a contest between competing interests, both of which are legitimate. Rules exist, to be sure, but economic and political pressures and considerations are a part of the process, as are the personalities of the litigants, judges, and attorneys. To expect perfect justice from a process of human intervention and administration is to seek disappointment.

1.2   THE LAW IN GENERAL

The *Law* is such a broad term that it is difficult to define. The following statements convey some of the meanings associated with the term:

1.   Law means a rule of civil conduct; it commands what is right and prohibits what is wrong.

2.   Law constitutes the rules under which civilized individuals and communities live and maintain their relationships with one another. It includes all legislative enactments and established controls of human action.

3.   *Webster's* dictionary gives the definition "A binding custom or practice of a community: a rule of conduct or action prescribed or formally recognized as binding or enforced by a controlling authority."[1]

4.   "Law is that which is laid down, ordained, or established. A rule or method according to which phenomena or actions co-exist or follow each other. That which must be obeyed and followed by citizens, subject to sanctions of legal consequences."[2]

5.   Law denotes those rules, standards, and principles which are applied by courts in the decision of controversies.

[1] *Webster's New Collegiate Dictionary*, G.&C. Merriam Company, Springfield, Mass., 1977.
[2] *Black's Law Dictionary*, 6th ed., West Publishing Co., St. Paul, Minn., 1990, p. 884.

6.   Law relates to such rules as are declared and published by government as a means of developing and maintaining order in society.

Law includes court decisions as well as legislative acts, and it is these applications of rules to facts that often serve as the cutting edge of legal change.

1.3   BASIC DIVISIONS OF LAW

International law has to do with relations among the countries of the world. It embraces the obligations one nation owes to another and also the conduct of a nation's citizens toward other nations and their citizens.

Substantive law creates, defines, and regulates duties, rights, and obligations. *Procedural law,* on the other hand, prescribes methods of enforcing rights and of obtaining redress in case of their invasion.

Constitutional law has to do with the organization of government, the interpretation of constitutions (which represent the fundamental law of the state and nation), and the validity of statutory enactments when measured against constitutional provisions.

Administrative law deals with rules and regulations established by the executive branch of government through its various agencies, commissions, and the like.

Criminal law defines and prohibits the several types of crimes and provides for their punishment.

Maritime law (or *admiralty law*) includes jurisdiction of all transactions and proceedings relating to commerce, navigation, and injuries and damages sustained upon the sea. It is a distinct group of traditional practices and rules. The Constitution of the United States has placed this separate jurisprudence in the federal realm, rather than in that of the states. Any nation of the world may adopt the precept of the maritime law as its own, but each nation is free to incorporate whatever modifications and restrictions it deems advisable.

Commercial law refers to the various rules established, more or less on a worldwide basis, for the control of commercial transactions. The general commercial law is said not to be circumscribed within purely local limits but rather to partake of an international character. Although the laws of civilized countries are in substantial agreement on many questions affecting the property rights and the relations of persons engaged in commerce, it is also true that commercial law cannot truly be separated from the domain of the particular state or nation whose authority makes it effective.

1.4   STATUTE LAW

A *statute* is a rule of conduct enacted by the duly authorized legislative authority. According to common usage, the term "statute" applies to acts of Congress and to laws passed by the legislative bodies of the states. Enactments at the municipal level are referred to as "ordinances." A statute represents the express written will of the lawmaking power and is rendered authentic by promulgation in accordance with certain prescribed formalities. Court decisions implementing and interpreting a given statute are of great importance, as will be discussed in the section on Common Law (Section 1.5).

The Constitution of the United States is the supreme law of the land, and state and federal statutes that contravene it may be declared unconstitutional by the judiciary. In addition to conforming to the U.S. Constitution, state statutes cannot contravene the constitution of the state in which they are enacted, or conflict with federal legislation. Apart from constitutions, statutes, and ordinances, the written law in this country includes (1) international treaties (trade agreements and the like), (2) orders and decrees of the executive branch of government, and (3) regulations and rulings by state and federal administrative agencies.

An enormous quantity of published material is required to handle the ever-increasing volume of written law. The *United States Code,* whose preface declares that the work "contains a consolidation and codification of all the general and permanent laws of the United States," is subdivided for convenient reference into fifty titles (for example, Title 35, Patents; Title 49, Transportation; Title 41, Public Contracts). In addition, there is a wealth of miscellaneous published material embracing such works as administrative regulations, law dictionaries, treatises, and textbooks on various subjects in the law. Although the foregoing publications are the special province of the attorney, the engineer may have occasion to assist the attorney in researching technical matters.

1.5   COMMON LAW

The *common law* comprises those doctrines that have their origin in court decisions and are not founded upon statute. The rules established through the judicial process are not inflexible but are modified as particular facts or situations warrant. Many common-law rules, however, have been codified and are now part of the statutory law of the United States or one of the several states.

A New Jersey case[3] explains the nature of the common law as follows:

> The common law is described by Blackstone as the unwritten law (lex non scripta) as distinguished from the written or statute law (lex scripta), i.e., enacted law . . . Kent says it includes "those principles, usages and rules of action applicable to the government and security of persons and property, which do not rest for their authority upon any express or positive declaration of the will of the Legislature" (*Kents Com.,* 471).

Recent cases admit the existence of federal common law that has expanded into matters of federal concern where no applicable federal statute exists. However,

---

| [3]*In re Davis' Estate,* 134 N.J. Eq. 393, 35 A.2d 880, 885 (1944).

there is no such thing as a national common law applicable in the state courts of each of the states of the United States.[4]

The United States has primarily a common-law system of jurisprudence,[5] much of it originating in England. The English common law, in turn, drew heavily upon the old Roman law. In addition to its English heritage, our common law has developed in line with our own usages and customs, and a number of civil-law principles, such as that of community property, have had widespread adoption.

As circumstances change and the need arises, statutes are enacted that result in modifying or in obviating entirely some particular aspect or rule of the common law. For example, there is a general principle in common law known as *caveat emptor* ("let the buyer beware"). However, continued abuses in the manufacture and sale of food and drugs eventually led to passage of the Pure Food and Drug Act, which was designed to safeguard the public health and welfare. Similarly, questionable practices in the promotion and sale of securities dictated enactment of the so-called blue-sky laws, aimed at protecting the investor.

To illustrate the operation of judicial precedents and the role of the common law, assume that a dispute arises between an owner and a contractor regarding the meaning of the words "subsurface construction" in a contract. The question is whether this term refers to all construction below ground level or merely to any construction that is to be finally covered with earth. The dispute is taken to court. The court decides that, under the particular wording of the contract and considering the intent of the parties, justice demands that the dispute be settled in a certain way and that the contractor and the owner fulfill their respective obligations accordingly. This official decision acquires a name and citation by which it may readily be located in the published reports of the cases. Henceforth, if other litigation arises in which all significant circumstances are analogous to those in this previously settled dispute, the prior decision (unless it has been since reversed by a higher court or criticized in other cases) will be treated as a precedent of considerable weight.

It sometimes happens that a particular point in dispute is decided one way by a court in state *A* and otherwise by a court of equal rank in state *B*. It is obvious that these two conflicting decisions may lead to confusion in the future. The lawyer for one side in some subsequent case (in a third state) involving the same point will cite whichever of the prior decisions tends to support his or her side of the argument, while the opposing attorney will cite the contrary holding. The court must then determine whether or not there were any fine points of difference, either legal or factual, between the two cited cases and whether or not either (or both) is truly applicable to the dispute at hand. Assuming that both prior decisions are relevant and that there is no factual basis for distinguishing between them, the court must choose whichever line of reasoning it thinks superior. Note that three separate states are involved. If, however, the court in the third case happens to sit in state *A* or in state *B*, it would be expected to follow the determination arrived at in that state.

---

[4]*Fiddler v. Rundle,* 497 F.2d 794 (3d Cir. 1974).

[5]The state of Louisiana is a notable exception in that most of its law has as its basis the Louisiana Civil Code, patterned after the Civil Code of France and certain laws of Spanish origin.

A reported judicial decision normally gives the pertinent facts involved, explains the applicable law, and states the court's conclusions. The accumulation of published court decisions from throughout the country is vast. Engineers normally have little need to read the text of an opinion; however, when the occasion does arise, the librarian of a law library can be of assistance in finding the decision.

1.6   EQUITY

Literally, *equity* means fairness or equality in dealing, but the term has been employed in a variety of ways. Thus, on the one hand, it is used to refer to a unique system of jurisprudence, but it is also applied to the special doctrines and remedies characterizing that system. The supplementary body of maxims, rules, and forms of action composing equity grew up as a means of filling certain voids in the common law. Suits in equity would be entertained where plaintiffs could show that plain, adequate, and complete remedies at law were not available in respect to their particular grievances. For many years this collateral system of jurisprudence was administered by separate courts of equity. These courts exercised broad discretionary powers in granting relief to aggrieved parties where justice seemed to dictate. The equity court decided what rights the respective litigants had and how such rights could be enforced. Like courts of law, the equity courts were not empowered to create rights, nor could they disregard applicable statutes or constitutional provisions.

Today in the federal court system of this country and in nearly all the states separate equity tribunals do not exist, and the ancient and confusing procedural distinctions between actions at law and suits in equity have largely been removed. In today's typical jurisdiction, legal and equitable principles and remedies have been commingled in one form of action, and litigants are thereby given comprehensive relief in a single suit.

The origin and the rather limited role of equity are well described in the following passage from a 1933 Texas case[6] wherein plaintiff unsuccessfully sought the equitable remedy of injunction:

> The equity system in England grew out of the rigidity and inflexibility of the common law as interpreted by the English judges, and, as modified through the centuries, it has come to America, and its principles, more or less modified, have been adopted in all American courts. Equity, as administered in America at least, is for the purpose of giving aid to the execution of the law according to the principles of justice. It cannot be used to supplant or circumvent the law, but only to give aid and assistance to its higher and better principles. Hence the rule that equity will not interfere when the law provides an adequate remedy for any wrong. Of course, a writ of injunction is an equitable remedy and should not be used except in the execution of law and in the protection of the rights of the individual. It cannot take the place of the law or be made a substitute for it, but must be used in upholding and aiding in the due execution of the law.

| [6]*Hinds et al. v. Minus,* 64 S.W. 2d 1093, 1095 (Tex. Civ. App. 1933).

Some of the fundamental principles of equity jurisprudence are embodied in the familiar "maxims of equity," a few of which are set forth below:

"He who comes into equity must come with clean hands." In other words, a litigant seeking relief at equity will be denied such if his own conduct has been improper.

"Where one of two innocent parties must suffer, he through whose agency the loss occurred must bear it."

"Equity aids the vigilant" and will deny relief to one who has slept on his rights and has been dilatory in prosecuting his cause of action. The undue delay is technically known as *laches*.

The remedies and courses of action which equity makes available are many. Some of the more prominent include (1) injunction, (2) specific performance,[7] (3) subrogation, (4) accounting, (5) rescission of a contract for fraud, and (6) reformation of instruments.

Issuance of an injunction creates no rights but merely protects those already in existence. A preventive injunction requires that the party to whom it is directed refrain from taking certain action. The acts that the injunction is designed to prevent may be only in the stage of anticipation, or they may already have started, in which event their continuation or repetition will be precluded. Whether the injunction sought is temporary or permanent, plaintiff must show that irreparable injury to his or her legitimate interests is threatened unless defendant is restrained.

1.7   OUR SYSTEM OF COURTS

Court systems in the United States and the kinds of matters they handle are as follows:

1. The federal courts deal with those civil and criminal cases which involve (a) federal laws or the Constitution, (b) disputes between two or more states, or (c) disputes between citizens of different states:

   a. *Supreme Court of the United States.* This court, as its name indicates, has the most authority of any in the country and all courts must follow precedents set by it. Virtually all its business lies in reviewing decisions of lower courts.

   b. *Circuit courts of appeals.* There are twelve of these courts in addition to the Court of Appeals of the District of Columbia. These "intermediate" courts, sitting in various cities across the country, hear such cases as are appealed from federal district courts. The decisions of the circuit courts of appeals may go to the Supreme Court for review.

   c. *District courts.* There are over a hundred of these courts in the United States, one or more located in each state. These trial-level tribunals exercise a broad original jurisdiction of federal matters; appeals may be carried to the proper circuit court or, in unusual circumstances, directly to the Supreme Court.

---

[7]For further discussion of the remedy of specific performance, see Section 6.32.

d. *Special courts.* Examples of such courts, which are generally created by Congress as the need arises, are the Court of Claims, the Court of Customs and Patent Appeals, and the Tax Court of the United States.

2. The state courts have concurrent jurisdiction with federal courts in most instances and also deal with disputes not within the jurisdiction of federal courts. California will serve as a typical example. The California system includes the following:

a. *Supreme court.* This is the highest judicial forum in the state and hears appeals from lower state courts.

b. *District courts of appeal.* As in the federal system, these "intermediate" courts hear cases on appeal from the superior court.

c. *Superior courts.* These are trial-level courts of general jurisdiction, located in each county of the state. Their jurisdiction is both civil and criminal, and their workload may include the trial of felonies, divorce, contract and tort cases, and the like.

d. *Municipal and justice courts.* Administered on a county basis, municipal and justice courts have jurisdiction over misdemeanors and civil cases involving small amounts.

1.8 CONTACTS WITH LAWYERS

An engineer's involvement with the law or, more specifically, with lawyers may occur in a variety of situations:

1. Preparing contract documents and specifications.

2. Conducting contractual relationships and the handling of claims and payments.

3. Interpreting contract clauses and the settlement of disputes arising therefrom.

4. Educating attorneys regarding engineering matters and customs.

5. Preparing material for use as trial evidence.

6. Settlement of disputes out of court.

7. Giving assistance in tax and valuation problems.

8. Handling engineering matters connected with the purchase and sale of property and goods.

9. Preparing reports on zoning, environmental, and other matters involving governmental agencies or organizations.

Also, various legal proceedings often require an engineer's participation, usually as an expert witness. For example:

1. Regular jury trials.

2. Cases heard before one or more judges.

3.   Hearings before special commissions (such as the Interstate Commerce Commission).

4.   Councils of review (for example, special hearings regarding a city's building code or zoning ordinances).

5.   Mediation and arbitration of disputes.

1.9   LICENSING

In addition to being conversant with certain aspects of the law in general, it is necessary for design and other professionals to be aware of various legal requirements specific to their profession. All fifty states have legislatively established licensing or registration boards whose function is to regulate the practice of architects or engineers, as well as other professionals, in their state. In all states professional practice is prohibited without approval of the appropriate board.

Although licensing requirements vary among the states, generally education, training, and successful completion of an examination are required. The trend is toward more stringent educational requirements, usually a professional degree from an accredited university. States whose requisite education is less demanding generally have more extensive training requirements.

In addition to licensing residents, most boards have some provision, such as reciprocity, for granting a license or temporary certification to professionals who are licensed in another state. Increased professional mobility has contributed to an impetus for uniform requirements, and virtually all states work with national professional organizations in formulating their policies.

There is less consistency in the licensing of contractors. A majority of the states do license construction contractors, although in many states this is limited to commercial and not residential construction. Some states require licensing only for public works contracts.

Almost all licensing or registration boards have the authority to revoke or suspend a license on a variety of grounds. Conviction of a felony, for example, is usually a basis for revocation or suspension, as is gross negligence or incompetence. In addition, most boards promulgate rules, the violation of which provides a basis for suspension or revocation. As a practical matter on professional issues these boards form a level in our system of courts below those discussed in Section 1.7, and their decisions are usually appealable to a superior court. Although many times issues of professional liability are first raised in a trial, it is possible to successfully defend a lawsuit and still be subject to sanctions from the licensing board.[8]

---

[8]For a graphic account of a license revocation proceeding, see *Duncan v. Missouri Board for Architects, Professional Engineers and Land Surveyors*, 744 S.W.2d 524 (Mo. App. 1988). This case, involving the collapse of walkways in the Hyatt Regency Hotel in Kansas City, is discussed further in Chapter 20, Section 20.15.

1.10   DEFINITIONS

The following definitions will serve for the chapters to follow.

Drawings are sketches or finished line drawings, as well as any notes of explanation or instruction thereon. Prints and other reproductions of drawings are generally deemed to be the equivalent of the originals from which they are made.

Owner denotes the individual or organization for whom something is to be built or furnished under contract. The owner is thus the purchaser, who pays for the goods or services.

Engineer refers to the architect or the engineer (or both) who acts for the owner in the transaction. The term may denote an organization as well as an individual. Sometimes it happens that an individual or organization will occupy the dual role of owner and engineer.

Contractor is the party who undertakes to supply goods or to perform a construction job or other project for the owner. In the practice of architecture and construction the contractor not only controls the work of construction but also acts as intermediary between the engineer or architect, who designs the work, and the artisans, who execute it.

The term *engineering* will be used in an extremely broad sense to include the work of all those engaged in design and related activities having a necessary connection with construction contracts.

1.11   A GENERAL PICTURE OF ENGINEERING

The field of engineering involves much more than the utilization of materials and machines. As the engineer advances toward top executive and managerial positions he or she must work effectively with business people, architects, lawyers, economists, and personnel managers, as well as with other engineers.

Much of an engineer's work involves the drawing of construction and other contracts, often with the assistance of a lawyer. He or she must know how to cooperate with others, how to weigh the advice given and the data produced by research, how to make important decisions without inordinate delay, and how to see to it that such decisions are carried out promptly.

In college the principal categories of engineering are necessarily separated from one another. The usual departmentalization is chemical, civil, electrical, mechanical, and industrial, perhaps together with other areas made specialties by particular institutions. In engineering practice these artificial dividing lines tend to disappear. As the engineer gains experience, he or she gradually acquires useful information in fields of endeavor allied to a particular job, becoming a "professional engineer" in the comprehensive sense of the term. Although an adequate college course in a given engineering subject helps tremendously in getting a start in the desired direction, the student must perforce continue study and preparation on the job.

1.12   RESPONSIBILITY OF THE ENGINEER

An engineer may be engaged by the owner (and placed temporarily on the latter's payroll) to handle all the engineering work, including preparation of the contract, for one specific job. Or the engineer may perform all these duties on a fee basis in the capacity of an outside consultant, using his or her own personnel and facilities. Or the engineer may be one of the owner's regular staff members, handling whatever engineering work comes along in the course of business. Whatever the nature of the relationship, the engineer owes the owner a duty of good faith and loyalty.

1.13   PHASES OF THE DEVELOPMENT OF CONSTRUCTION PROJECTS

The engineering endeavors that precede the physical phase of a construction project may be divided into the following stages:

Preliminaries   The first steps to be taken are making preliminary studies and cost estimates, selecting a site, preparing a project feasibility report, and justifying the proposed expenditure. After the project is approved and authorization to proceed is obtained, there is arranging for the financing and securing of property, rights-of-way, and permits. Next comes organizing an engineering staff or contracting with an engineering firm to handle the project.

Planning   The next essential phase is the making of property and topographic surveys and subsurface explorations, establishing the broad principles and general character of the various parts of the project, and making preliminary layouts of the main features involved.

Designing   In a broad sense this phase constitutes the further developing of the general layout and determining just what is wanted. This includes settling of the details of the flow sheet (sequence of operations of an industrial plant); locating the structures exactly; adapting the project to suit the topography; planning the transportation facilities; determining the sizes and types of structures to be built, together with the materials to be used for construction; choosing the architectural features; investigating methods and facilities to be used for construction; deciding upon any provisions for future expansion; and determining many other general features.

Dimensioning   This phase includes developing the detailed plans for all parts of the project, the dimensioning of all elements of the structure, and preparing the drawings.

Preparing the Contract Documents   This phase includes completing the contract drawings, specifications, and all other papers containing data needed to enable contractors to bid on the job. Included also should be preparing the engineer's estimate of the cost of the project.

Securing Proposals The next phase is advertising for bids and furnishing plans and specifications to prospective contractors.

Awarding the Contract Included in this phase are receiving proposals from the contractors, comparing these proposals, determining the successful bidder, and signing the contract by both the owner and the builder.

Proceeding with Construction During this phase plans are converted into reality. Keys to the success of the project are sound management and organization, including the utilization of special skills and know-how and the proper handling of personnel, materials, and machines. A knowledge of the law of contracts and of the general conduct of business is also very important.

QUESTIONS

1. Define "law."
2. Briefly define each of these terms: *(a)* municipal law, *(b)* substantive law, *(c)* constitutional law, *(d)* international law, *(e)* criminal law, *(f)* administrative law, *(g)* maritime law, *(h)* commercial law.
3. Define and illustrate "statute law."
4. Define and illustrate "common law."
5. What constitutes the written law of the United States?
6. What is the United States Code?
7. Explain the effect of court decisions upon both statute law and common law.
8. Can statute law change a common-law principle?
9. Describe the setup and general operation of the federal courts and of state courts.
10. Define "equity."
11. List several of the remedies available in equity.
12. What is the supreme law of the land?
13. Is the common law uniform throughout the United States? Explain.
14. Under what circumstances may an engineer or architect have occasion to deal with lawyers?
15. In what kinds of legal proceedings might an engineer be involved?
16. Define "owner," "engineer," and "contractor" as used in contract documents.
17. What are the engineer's responsibilities in handling contract work for the owner?
18. Why may some knowledge of the law be helpful to an engineer?

TYPES OF CONTRACTS

For the practicing engineer, contract law is an important field of study. An in-depth study of the entire field and its ramifications is incompatible with the purpose of this book and discussion will be limited to the various kinds of contracts and their interpretation, modification, rescission, performance, and breach.

The law of contracts undergoes a constant process of evolution because of changing customs and practices. Broad contract principles are subject to exceptions and modifications, but the rules and principles discussed here are, for the most part, those that have received general acceptance.

The definitions of "contract" put forth over years of slowly changing usage and convenience are legion. Section 1549 of the Civil Code of California (West 1982) defines a contract as "an agreement to do or not to do a certain thing." The American Law Institute, in its *Restatement of Contracts*, second edition, 1981, section 1, declares that "a contract is a promise or a set of promises for the breach of which the law gives a remedy, or the performance of which the law in some way recognizes as a duty."

Basically a *contract* is an understanding enforceable at law, made between two or more persons, by which rights are acquired on the one side to acts or forbearance on the other. To make an agreement that results in a contract, there must be an offer and an *acceptance*; and to the promises which stem from the offer and acceptance the law attaches a binding force of *obligation*. The contractual arrangement must involve competent parties and be based upon a legal *consideration*. (These concepts will be developed more fully in Chapter 3.)

2.1   EXPRESS CONTRACTS AND CONTRACTS IMPLIED IN FACT

These terms are used to indicate a variation in the character of the evidence by which the contract is proved. The same basic elements are essential in both types.

Technically, an *express contract* is one whose terms are declared by the parties, either orally or in writing, at the time the agreement is made. An express contract involves an actual promise, while an *implied* contract is inferred or deduced from facts and circumstances showing a mutual intention to contract. An implied contract is an *actual* contract, circumstantially proved. The difference between an express contract and one implied in fact is that in the former all the terms are set forth by the parties themselves, while in the latter the law must imply the terms from the conduct of the parties. For example, where one performs for another with the other's knowledge a service that in the ordinary course of events receives compensation and the recipient of the service expresses no dissent or avails himself of the benefits, a promise to pay the reasonable value of the service is implied.

Both express and implied contracts are usually founded on the agreement of the several parties and require a *meeting of the minds.* But, if all of the requisite elements of a contract are present, a contract may exist even if one of the parties was joking or otherwise did not intend to be contractually bound.[1] An objective approach is used and, if given all of the circumstances, a reasonable person in the position of the person seeking to enforce would be warranted in believing that the other party intended to be bound, that party is bound, regardless of his subjective intent to the contrary.

Of interest to the engineering profession is the fact that, unless specifically required by statute to be in writing, a contract for construction or repair work may be implied. Where, however, a contractor sublets the contract, the law will not imply any agreement on the part of the owner to compensate the subcontractor for the work performed. The implied obligation of the owner to make compensation to one who improves his or her property is deemed taken away by the special contract between the contractor and the subcontractor.

2.2   UNILATERAL AND BILATERAL CONTRACTS

In a *unilateral contract* only one of the parties makes a promise, and he or she is the only party under an enforceable legal duty. Perhaps the most typical example of a unilateral contract is the *option*, common to real estate transactions. The option is in essence a contract to give another the right to buy, and the party granting the option thereby agrees to sell the property at a certain price at any time within a stipulated period, leaving the prospective purchaser with a clear choice in the matter

---

[1] *Lucy v. Zehmer,* 84 S.E. 2d 516 (Va., 1954).

and (having paid something for the option) under no further contractual obligation. A *bilateral contract* comprises mutual promises, with each contracting party playing the dual roles of promisor and promisee. The legal effects of a bilateral contract are reciprocal duties and obligations. To put the distinction another way, the exchange for the promise in a unilateral contract is something *other than* a promise, while in a bilateral contract promises are exchanged and there is something on both sides to be done or forborne. If a contract cannot be clearly classified as bilateral or unilateral, the law presumes it to be bilateral.

Suppose Lewis offers to sell Martin a load of topsoil for payment of $12, an offer for a unilateral contract exists. If Lewis had asked for a *promise* of $12 and Martin had given such a promise, the contract would be bilateral. If a baseball fan purchases a reserved-seat ticket for a certain game at Yankee Stadium, the baseball club promises to hold that particular seat for the fan and to let him or her occupy it at the game in question. The foregoing constitutes a unilateral contract, since the baseball club is the only party with a promise outstanding. On the other hand, if the Yankees contract with General Electric for 500 bulbs for the stadium floodlights at a specified price, the arrangement is bilateral since the company promises to deliver the bulbs and the Yankees promise to pay for them.

2.3 JOINT AND SEVERAL CONTRACTS

Whether the rights and duties created by a particular contract are intended to be (1) joint or (2) several or (3) joint and several is sometimes a difficult question of interpretation.[2] Promises of a number of persons (which promises appear in a single instrument) are presumed to be joint unless a contrary intention is evident from the inclusion of obvious words of severance. Some states have laws declaring that contracts in the joint form shall be joint and several.

Where a contract is *joint,* the various obligors must all be joined as parties to any action brought upon the agreement, and release by plaintiff of one obligor discharges the others as well. Suppose several stockholders employ Y on a commission arrangement to procure a purchaser for their aggregate holdings in a certain corporation. Y's services are being retained for the joint advantage of all the stockholders involved and not for the particular benefit of any one of them. The contract is joint in the sense that each of the obligor-stockholders is potentially liable for the entire commission. If Y, having performed her part of the bargain, needs to bring suit to recover the stated compensation, she must join as defendants all of the obligor–stockholders. Should any one of the latter group be obligated to satisfy the judgment, he would have available a right of contribution against the other stockholders.

In a *several* contract each obligor is liable for only a portion or pro rata share of the obligation. Typically the contract will read "we agree," and all of the signing

---

[2]To simplify the consideration of this concept, we shall refer only to the duty aspect of the agreement. It should be borne in mind, though, that rights under a contract may likewise be joint or several.

parties will be presumed to owe an equal portion of the whole obligation. However, the contract may specify a certain portion owed by each obligor in other than equal shares. In the event that one or all of the obligors fail to perform, each nonperforming party will have to be sued separately, and only for the portion of the obligation for which he was liable.

Agreements that are joint and several require all or any one of the obligors to render the entire obligation as in a joint contract. However, in enforcing the contract, each of the obligors may be sued separately for the entire obligation. Of course, the complaining party may only recover the obligation once. All the defendants may be joined in one suit, and if they are they may not also be sued separately by the party bringing suit.

2.4   ENTIRE AND SEVERABLE CONTRACTS

A contract is *entire* when full and complete performance by one party is a condition precedent[3] to the right to require performance by the other party. In such contracts there is no liability for part performance, and failure of one party to perform fully relieves the other of any obligations. Where the drilling of a well is to be performed as a whole and the compensation for such work is to be paid as a whole, the contract is entire, even though the payment is expressed as a stipulated amount per linear foot. Similarly, a contract for the purchase and sale of 1,000 head of cattle for delivery within sixty days is entire, although deliveries of 50 or 100 were to be made on various occasions within the time set in the agreement. And where one party agrees to furnish the other a certain quantity of crushed stone for a fixed price per cubic yard at a stated rate per day, the contract is entire, requiring full performance before payment of the consideration is due.

In a case involving modern construction technology,[4] a contract to deliver and assemble a modular home was also held to be entire, rather than severable, where the contract set a fixed price but provided for periodic partial payments that were not made. A property owner borrowed $18,500 from a bank to finance the purchase of a double-width modular home and procured a fire insurance policy designating the bank as beneficiary. The contract provided that partial payments not to exceed 60 percent of the value of the work in place, less the aggregate or previous payments, would be made at intervals of construction based upon estimates by the contractor of the value of the work in place and approved by the bank. The contractor delivered the two halves of the modular home to the lot for assembly but the home was destroyed by fire the next day. The contractor contended that the contract was severable and that he had provided labor and materials with the value of $17,785.

---

[3]This concept will be discussed in Chapter 4, Section 4.2.
[4]*LDA, Inc. v. Cross*, 279 S.E.2d 409, (W.Va. 1981).

The property owner contended that the contract was entire and, since construction was not complete, the contractor could have no recovery based on the contract.

The court declared that whether a contract is entire or severable is a determination to be made by the court according to the intention of the parties. Such intention should be ascertained from a consideration of the subject matter of the contract, a reasonable construction of the terms thereof, and the conduct of the parties during the negotiations, all of which should be viewed in light of the surrounding circumstances. With these principles in mind, the court found that, the provision for partial payment notwithstanding, the record indicated that the parties intended that the contractor would construct the modular home for a fixed price, $18,500.[5]

A contract is *severable* or *divisible* when the part to be performed by one party consists of a number of distinct and independent items and the price to be paid by the other party is apportioned, or is susceptible of apportionment, to each item. An agreement to pay a certain price for every bushel of wheat supplied that corresponds to a given sample is a typical illustration of a severable contract. Another is an agreement to build six houses for a stated sum; a proportionate recovery will be permitted for the actual completion of one or more of the six dwellings. In this severable contract, a breach by one party in respect to any one item does not justify the other in repudiating the whole agreement; the latter is still bound to perform, but if he has sustained any injury as a result of the breach, he has a right to recover for such injury in a damages action.

The primary criterion in determining whether a contract is entire or severable is the intention of the parties in regarding the various items as a whole or each contract item as a separate unit. An example of this is an omnibus insurance policy covering different classes of property, with each class separated from the others and insured for a specific amount. The contract, to reflect the apparent intent of the parties, should be treated as severable and not entire; thus breach of the contract conditions for one class of the insured property will not disturb the remainder of the coverage.

2.5 VOID AND VOIDABLE CONTRACTS

Void contracts are null from their inception and may not be ratified by the parties. The parties may go to court to have the nullity judicially recognized. Illegal agreements and agreements against public policy are examples of void contracts. Contracts properly called *voidable* are fully effectual until affirmatively avoided by some act. Such contracts are prima facie valid but are subject to certain defects of

---

[5]*See also In re Ferguson,* 183 B.R. 122 (Bkrtcy. N.D. Texas 1995) in which a contract for "The removal and installation of 10,000 feet of bordering for a price of $12,894.02 and installation of carpet on 69 stairs at a price of $345" was entire and not devisable.
But see also St. John v. Barker, 638 S.W. 2d 239 (Tex. App. 1982) aff. as mod., *Durham v. St. John,* 645 S.W.2d 261 (Tex. 1983) where the court found that a contract for a major home remodeling, by its very nature, is susceptible to division (in this case the job of building and installing cabinets from the remainder of the job.)

which one party can take advantage and avoid the legal relations that the contract creates. Conversely, by ratifying the contract, that party may extinguish the power of avoidance. Ordinarily, the power in question is confined to one party to the contract, but such is not invariably the case.

Typical instances of voidable agreements are those involving a party without the capacity to contract such as minors or incompetents, or those that are induced by fraud, mistake, or duress.

2.6   EXECUTORY AND EXECUTED CONTRACTS

In the *executory contract* a party is bound for the future to do or expressly refrain from doing a particular thing—as where an agreement is made to build a garage in three months. A fully *executed contract,* on the other hand, is one in which the object of the agreement has been performed and nothing remains to be accomplished by either party, for example, where an article is sold, handed over, and paid for on the spot.

2.7   SUBCONTRACTS

Where a person has agreed to perform certain work, for example, to erect a building, and in turn engages a third party to handle all or part of that which is included in the original contract, for example, to install the plumbing fixtures, the agreement with such third person is called a *subcontract.* Subcontracts are subject to the same formal and other requisites as other contracts.[6]

2.8   QUASI CONTRACTS

Obligations created by law for reasons of justice are variously termed *constructive contracts, contracts implied in law,* or, perhaps most popularly, *quasi contracts.*

Quasi contract is a convenient term for a class of legal relations that possess this common feature: without agreement—expressed or unexpressed—and sometimes without delict or breach of duty on either side, party *A* has been compelled to pay or provide something for which party *X* ought to have paid or made provision, or *X* has received something that *A* ought to have received. The law in such cases imposes a duty upon *X* to compensate *A.* Such "contracts" are not real contracts at

---

[6]See, for example, *Anderson Construction Col., Inc. v. Lyon Metal Prod.,* 370 So.2d 935 (Miss. 1979) holding a subcontract for the supply of lockers for a school construction subject to the statute of frauds. On the statute of frauds, see Chapter 3, Section 3.10.

all but fictions of the law, based on principles of unjust enrichment and without regard to any actual or presumed intent of the party held to be bound—often, indeed, in the face of the party's dissent. There is no "agreement" whatever involved, but these quasi-contractual obligations are considered contracts for the purpose of setting up the remedy. The key difference between quasi contract and true contract is that in the former, the duty defines the contract; in the latter, the contract defines the duty.

QUESTIONS

1. Why may one wish to have work done under a contract rather than hire laborers to perform the work?

2. Distinguish between *(a)* "formal" and "informal" contracts, *(b)* "implied" and "express" contracts, *(c)* "executory" and "executed" contracts.

3. What are some essential elements of a valid contract?

4. What is a "quasi contract"?

5. Define "unilateral contract" and "bilateral contract." Illustrate each.

6. Distinguish between "joint" and "several" contracts.

7. Distinguish between an "entire" contract and a "severable" contract.

8. When is a contract voidable? When is it void?

9. Under what circumstances may a contract be unenforceable?

10. What is a subcontract? Illustrate.

c h a p t e r

3

FORMATION PRINCIPLES

3.1 THE ESSENTIALS OF CONTRACT

An agreement, in order to constitute a binding contract, must be entered into by competent parties who express definite assent in the form required by law. Furthermore, such an agreement must be supported by a proper "consideration" (see Section 3.29), must not at the time it is made be obviously impossible of performance, and must not so contravene principles of law or public policy as to be entirely devoid of legal effect. The present chapter will analyze the prerequisites to the formation of a valid contract.

3.2 MEETING OF THE MINDS

An essential in the formation of a valid contract is mutual assent to the terms of the agreement, a circumstance variously termed *offer and acceptance,* or a *meeting of the minds.* The manifestation of mutual assent usually takes the form of an exchange of oral or written words, though occasionally the assent is indicated in some other fashion. It should be remembered that an actual expression of mutual assent, rather than the mere existence of the assent, is essential.[1]

3.3 DEFINITENESS

An important feature of any contract is that it describe what is to be done or what materials are to be furnished with sufficient clarity and enough detail to make evi-

---

| [1]Quasi contracts, discussed in Chapter 2, Section 2.8, are an exception.

dent what is wanted. Courts can neither enforce nor award damages for the breach of contractual agreements which are lacking in certainty. The terms of a contract must be complete, and the various obligations must be described with sufficient definiteness to enable a court to determine whether or not these obligations have been performed.

COMPETENT PARTIES

3.4 THE CONTRACTING PARTIES

There must be a definite promisor and a definite promisee, each of whom is legally capable of playing the intended part in the proposed contractual arrangement.

Although any greater number may be involved, a contract requires a minimum of two parties since it is not possible under existing law for one to contract with oneself. It is possible, nonetheless, for an individual to act in several roles at the same time, such as those of trustee and partner. Regardless of the capacities in which a person may act, he can never contract with himself nor maintain an action against himself.

Moreover, a contract cannot obligate someone who has not the legal capacity to incur at least voidable contractual duties. Certain persons are by law incapable of binding themselves by a promise. Such incapacity may stem from one of several causes, the most significant of which are infancy and lack of mental capacity.

3.5 CONTRACTS OF INFANTS

For contract purposes a person is considered an infant until he reaches 18 years of age, although there are a few states where the age of majority is 21. Under common law, the contracts of a minor[2] are not void but are voidable, except those for "necessaries" and those authorized by statute. An infant is presumed by the law to lack the capacity to understand contractual rights and obligations and thus has the right to disaffirm his contracts. The contracts are legally binding on the other party, however, and a party contracting with a minor does so at his own peril. Lack of knowledge of the minor's age is generally not a defense, even when the minor has intentionally misrepresented his age.

Necessaries are such things as food, shelter, and clothing that are supplied to the minor on his credit when the minor's parents or guardians are unable or unwilling to provide him with such items and he is in need of them. What constitutes "necessaries" is an issue of fact to be determined by a judge or jury, depending on the circumstances of the case.

---

[2]The terms "infants" and "minors" are generally used interchangeably in the law.

In addition to recognizing obligations incurred by a minor in obtaining items found to be necessary, the courts recognize obligations authorized by statute when the statute is expressly directed to minors—for example, the New York statute which follows—or provides legal requirements in circumstances in which the minor is engaged and for which there is no express exemption for minors—for example, requirements for posting a bond.

Section 3-101 of the New York General Obligations Law[3] states:

1. A contract made on or after September first, nineteen hundred seventy-four, by a person after he obtained the age of eighteen years may not be disaffirmed by him on the ground of infancy.

2. A contract made on or after April thirteenth, nineteen hundred forty-one, and before September first, nineteen hundred seventy-four, by a person after he has obtained the age of eighteen years may not be disaffirmed by him on the ground of infancy, where the contract was made in connection with a business in which the infant was engaged and was reasonable and provident when made.

3.6   CONTRACTS OF MENTAL INCOMPETENTS

It is essential to the validity of a contract that the parties possess the mental competence to consent. There is no binding contract where one of the parties was, by reason of mental deficiency, incapable of understanding and appreciating the force and effect of the agreement made. But mere mental weakness, falling short of inability to appreciate the business at hand, will not invalidate the contract. Furthermore, the mental incapacity that affects the validity of a contract is that which exists at the very time the transaction occurs, and prior or subsequent insanity is not relevant. Accordingly, a contract is normally held to be binding if it was entered into during a lucid interval. In any event, an insane person, just as a minor, may be liable for the reasonable value of necessaries supplied in good faith.

While the contracts of insane persons are voidable and may be expressly disaffirmed by that party on returning to sanity or during a temporary rational period, the other party does not have this option. However, where there has been no judicial determination of mental incompetence and where the sane party did not at the time of contracting have knowledge of the other person's insanity, there are decisions to the effect that the contract is binding upon the incompetent if it has been so far executed that the respective parties cannot be restored to their original positions.

| [3]*McKinney's Consolidated Laws of New York*, 1989.

3.7   CONTRACTS OF INTOXICATED PERSONS

A contract made by an intoxicated person is invalid if the intoxication has rendered that person incompetent, that is, unable to appreciate the nature and extent of the contract, or if it is accompanied by fraudulent behavior on the part of the other contracting party. The mere fact that one is under the influence of liquor or other drugs at the time of contracting does not of itself nullify the agreement.

The enforceability of contracts made by intoxicated persons depends primarily upon the degree of intoxication and whether or not the person was capable of understanding the nature and consequences of the transaction. As is the case with infants and insane people, intoxicated persons will be liable for the value of necessaries received.

PROPER SUBJECT MATTER

A valid contract must have a definite and lawful subject matter. The subject matter should be clearly defined and sufficiently certain to enable a court to determine an appropriate remedy for failure to perform. All things not prohibited as unlawful may properly become the subject of contracts. The possible subject matter thus includes such things as future rights and liabilities, pending causes of action, and goods not yet in existence.

3.8   ILLEGAL BARGAINS

It is a basic principle that a contractual undertaking must have a lawful purpose and that transactions in violation of law cannot be the foundation of a valid contract. An illegal agreement cannot form the basis for a contract, and such an agreement is void and therefore unenforceable. The taint of illegality may manifest itself in the consideration for the agreement, in a promise expressed in the agreement, or in the purpose to which the agreement is applied. Broadly speaking, a bargain is deemed illegal if either its formation or its performance is expressly prohibited by statute or seeks to accomplish a purpose which is contrary to law, morality, or public policy. It is not necessary that there be any corrupt intention on the part of the contracting parties in order to render illegal an agreement in violation of law.

There is no absolute rule by which to determine what contracts are against *public policy*. The term does not lend itself to precise definition, but it may be said that an agreement is against public policy if it is injurious to the welfare of the general public or impinges upon some established interest of society. Examples are: an agreement which contemplates procuring personal or political influence to secure acceptance of a bid on a public contract being let by a governmental department, a contract that will inevitably result in stirring up litigation, and a contract that tends to disturb family relations.

In one case[4] a married man promised to marry a second woman, who was the mother of his illegitimate daughter, as soon as he divorced his wife. Later, asserting that his wife was terminally ill, he again promised marriage as soon as his wife died. The promise to marry was held invalid, even in a state where a breach of promise to marry action was recognized, because the woman knew or should have known that the man was already married. The court said that it would not enforce a contract contravening the public policy favoring stability in marriage, and therefore a promise contingent on divorce or death of a known spouse was not enforceable.[5] On the other hand, in a case involving a contract between a man and woman living together without marriage an agreement to support has been upheld.[6]

The mere fact that the promisor was married has been held not to void a contract to support a third party; while an agreement to exchange sexual favors for support is void, where the agreement does not cast to either party the responsibility to perform illegal activity, the agreement is enforceable.[7]

Illegal contracts are infinite in number and variety, but a representative list of such would include an agreement to commit a criminal act, an agreement to commit a tort, an agreement to defraud individuals or the public in general, an agreement in restraint of trade,[8] an agreement clearly ignoring a fiduciary duty, and an agreement made in obvious violation of a statute or one which cannot be performed without necessarily violating a statute.

Ordinarily an illegal contract cannot be directly or indirectly enforced by either party, and there can be neither damages for breach nor return of benefits through rescission. The illegality referred to must inhere in the contract itself, rather than merely being collateral to the arrangement. Of real importance from a procedural standpoint is the fact that illegality is one defense a party to the contract is never prevented from pleading, even when the party asserting the defense was aware of the illegality at the time of contracting. The defense of illegality is always available and cannot be effectively waived, even by means of a written agreement of the parties.

---

[4]*Thorpe v. Collins,* 245 Ga. 77, 263 S.E.2d 115 (1980).

[5]On a similar note, see *Rogers v. Webb,* 558 N.W. 2d 155 (Iowa 1977), where a married woman and a man she was involved with entered into a contract whereby the man would help the woman procure a divorce in return for 25 percent of the marital assets secured by the woman in the dissolution. Finding preservation of the marital relation to be fundamental public policy, the court refused to enforce the agreement. See also *Hoffman v. Boyd,* 698 So.2d 346 (Fla. App. 1997) where a contract between two persons, both married to others, that the man would support the woman if he did not marry her was void.

[6]*Byrne v. Laura,* 60 Cal. Rptr. 2nd 908 (1997).

[7]*Boot v. Beelen,* 480 S.E. 2d 267 (Ga. App. 1997).

[8]There are instances of contracts that clearly restrain trade and yet are held to be perfectly valid; in such cases the restraint involved is either partial or is otherwise limited in its operation (for example, in time or place).

3.9   DURESS AND UNDUE INFLUENCE

An agreement made under compulsion or threat is not binding upon the person whose assent was involuntarily given. The threat must be sufficiently grave to induce a reasonable person to assent against his will. Generally, duress has been established when there is a threat to do an unlawful act that will cause serious harm to the person, property, or family of the victim.

Similarly, undue influence may result in lack of volition sufficient to render a contract voidable. When a person takes advantage of mental weakness, near relationship, or special confidence in order to coerce another to agree to an unfair bargain, the resultant contract may be attacked on the grounds of undue influence.

3.10   THE STATUTE OF FRAUDS

By statute, some contracts must be written. An English law (passed in 1677), entitled "An Act for the Prevention of Frauds and Perjuries," served as the forerunner and model for similar statutes enacted in the various states in this country. Such statutes in the several states differ from one another and from the original English version, but all regulate the contract formalities necessary to render the agreement enforceable under the judicial process.

There are many parts to a typical statute of frauds. The following classes of contracts, however, should be noted as representative of those agreements that will not be enforceable unless, in the words of one case, "the same, or some note or memorandum thereof, be in writing and subscribed by the party to be charged, or by his agent":

1. Contract for the sale of goods valued above a stated amount.

2. Contracts for the sale of interests in land.

3. Contracts not to be performed within one year.

Where the contract is not explicit about the time within which performance is expected to be complete, courts supply a liberal construction and hold that the test is the "shortest possible" and not the "probable" time required for performance. Thus, if the contract *might* be performed in less than a year, it is not within the statute. Contracts that do not fall within the categories to which a statute of frauds applies are, of course, equally binding whether oral or reduced to writing.

OFFER

3.11   THE NATURE OF OFFER

An *offer* may be defined as the signification by one person of willingness to contract with another on certain specified terms. It is a statement by the offeror of what will be given or done in return for some desired promise or act on the part of the offeree. By means of such an offer the offeror confers upon the offeree the power to create a binding contractual relation merely by acceptance.

An operative offer must be more than an expression of desire or hope that a contract can be effectuated. Preliminary negotiations, invitations to deal, advertisements, and acts evidently done in jest cannot be regarded as offers because the requisite intent to contract is lacking. An invitation to enter into negotiations may be just a suggestion advanced with the purpose of inducing offers by others. Similarly, a quotation of price should be distinguished from a real offer. The question of whether a given communication naming a price is meant to be a quotation or an offer depends upon the prospective vendor's intention as manifested by the facts and circumstances of the particular case or the custom of the trade.

Extravagant terms advanced under circumstances of considerable excitement may reveal the absence of any serious intent to make a firm offer. Not what the apparent offeror actually said but how the recipient of the proposal reasonably interprets the intent provides the key to the situation. On occasion the courts have been known to treat a "joke contract" seriously. In *Plate v. Durst*,[9] the defendant had promised the plaintiff $1,000 and a diamond ring if she would continue certain services rendered in promoting his business. At the trial he admitted these promises, but claimed they were made in jest. The court stated:

> Jokes are sometimes taken seriously by the young and inexperienced in the deceptive ways of the business world, and if such is the case, and thereby the person deceived is led to give valuable services in the full belief and expectation that the joker is in earnest, the law will also take the joker at his word, and give him good reason to smile.

3.12 COMMUNICATING THE OFFER

Communication of an offer is necessary so that the intended offeree is cognizant of the proposal and may take appropriate action with respect to it. An acceptance will not convert an offer into a contract unless the existence of the offer is known to the offeree at the time of such acceptance. That is, an offeree cannot accept an offer (of which he has not been apprised) merely by happening to take certain action which, unknown to him, is prescribed in the offer as the mode of acceptance.

In a typical case of the sort just mentioned, Boyle offered by newspaper advertisement a $100 reward for return of her horse. McAdams, without knowledge of the offer, returned the missing horse and took the magnificent sum of $2 for his efforts. Later he learned of the advertised reward, but the court denied him any contractual rights in the matter since there had been no timely communication to him of the offer in question. In other words, there had been no agreement.

---

[9] 42 W. Va. 63, 24 S.E. 580 (1896). See also the often cited case of *Lucy v. Zehmer*, 196 Va. 493, 84 S.E.2d 516 (1954), in which a contract to sell a farm (which contract was written on a napkin in a bar) was upheld.

3.13   IMPERFECTLY TRANSMITTED OFFERS

With respect to errors occurring in the transmission of offers, it should be noted that, where a person makes use of the mails to send an offer, the post office will be regarded as the agent. The offer is not deemed to have been made when the letter is posted but rather when it is received, and the offeror must suffer any consequences which may arise from delay or mistake on the part of the postal authorities.

3.14   DURATION OF OFFERS

The offeror may fix any time as that within which acceptance must be made. If no time limit is specified in the proposal the offeree may assume that a "reasonable" time is contemplated. What constitutes a reasonable time is purely a question of fact depending on the individual circumstances of the case and on any pertinent business customs involved. For instance, an offer in connection with speculative stock will be assumed to have a shorter duration than an offer to sell an old rug or an item of used furniture.

Once an offer lapses, it is incapable of being accepted. Similarly, once an offer is rejected, it ceases to exist and cannot later be accepted without an express renewal by the offeror.

3.15   REVOCATION OF OFFERS

In the absence of independent consideration binding the offeror, the rule in most jurisdictions permits him to withdraw his offer prior to an unqualified acceptance and prior to the time fixed for its automatic termination. The offeror must, however, give notice of revocation to the offeree, either expressly or impliedly. An exception to this rule is when an offer has been made through a public medium. In such an instance, revocation is effective if given the same degree of publication as the offer itself, even though such revocation does not actually reach all those in the position of offerees.

A sale to *X* of property covered by a previous offer to *Y* amounts to a revocation of such offer, provided knowledge of the sale reaches *Y* before any attempted acceptance on his part.

In addition revocable offers are generally terminated by the death or insanity of the offeror or offeree prior to acceptance, through outright rejection or counteroffer by the offeree, and where, after the making of the offer and before acceptance, the proposed contract becomes illegal.

ACCEPTANCE

3.16   THE NATURE OF ACCEPTANCE

An offer, until terminated by lapse of time or withdrawn, gives to the offeree power to create a legally enforceable contract by his acceptance. This acceptance is necessarily irrevocable, once it is communicated to the offeror. Such acceptance should be unambiguous and conform to the terms of the offer. If the offeree attempts to effect any material changes in the terms presented, it constitutes a counteroffer rather than an acceptance, and a contract is not formed.

3.17   WHO MAY ACCEPT OFFERS

An offer addressed to a particular person may be accepted by that person only. A general offer to the public may be accepted by anyone, and an offer to a class or group of persons may be accepted by any individual in the class described.

3.18   FORM AND NOTICE OF THE ACCEPTANCE

The offer in a unilateral contract may call for the performance of an act or for forbearance. In a bilateral contract the offer demands a counterpromise, and that is what the acceptance must provide. In case of doubt, the law construes an offer as anticipating a bilateral contract. The explanation for this interpretation lies in the fact that there is mutuality of obligation as soon as a bilateral contract is created. With a unilateral contract, however, the offeror generally can revoke even after part performance by the offeree. Because of the inherent unfairness in this situation, the courts are currently moving toward the position of considering the contract bilateral once performance is begun.

Where a bilateral contract is contemplated and acceptance is to be in the form of a promise, notice of the acceptance must be afforded the other party. But where acceptance of the offeror's proposal is by an act, the performance of the act—without notice—concludes the contract (always assuming that the offeror has not expressly stipulated that some notice independent of the actual performance be given).

If a particular mode of acceptance is prescribed and the offeree nevertheless elects some other method, the offeror may treat the purported acceptance as a nullity. If, however, the text of the offer (or the manner of its communication) *suggests* a mode of acceptance, the offeree is not strictly limited to such means as the offeror has mentioned. Some other form will be effective if it does not cause undue delay and if it successfully brings the acceptance to the knowledge of the offeror. In the last analysis, the propriety of the means adopted to communicate the acceptance, where such method differs from that utilized by the offeror in transmitting the proposal, depends upon what would reasonably be expected by persons in the position of the respective contracting parties in view of the prevailing business usages and other surrounding circumstances.

3.19   SILENCE AS ACCEPTANCE

The silence of an offeree, unaccompanied by other circumstances (such as exercise of dominion over any of the offeror's property involved in the proposal), is not an acceptance. Indeed, it has been held that silence alone does not operate as acceptance even though the offeror prescribes it as the desired mode of acceptance, and the offeree, knowing this, *intends* his silence as an acceptance. Where, however, the relation of the parties, their previous business dealings, or other circumstances are such as to impose an obvious duty to speak, the offeree's failure to do so resulting in harm to the other party can preclude him from later arguing that he never intended by silence as acquiescence.

A famous case illustrating this exception to the general rule is *Hobbs v. Massasoit Whip Co.*[10] This was an action to recover the price of a consignment of eelskins sent by plaintiff and kept by defendant for several months without communicating acceptance or rejection. Plaintiff had made several prior shipments to defendant (which the latter had accepted and paid for) and there was a vague standing order from defendant for skins of a certain length and quality. It was argued by defendant that one person may not "impose a duty upon another, and make him a purchaser, in spite of himself, by sending goods to him, unless he will take the trouble, and bear the expense, of notifying sender that he will not buy." But the court held that the history of prior dealings created an exception to the general rule advanced by defendant and that, under the circumstances, silence on defendant's part—coupled with a retention of the skins for an unreasonable time—warranted plaintiff in assuming acceptance. The "proposition stands on the general principle that conduct which imports acceptance or assent is acceptance or assent, in the view of the law, whatever may have been the actual state of mind of the party."

3.20   CONDITIONAL ACCEPTANCE, OR COUNTEROFFER

Qualified (conditional) acceptance or acceptance that varies the terms of the original offer is actually a counteroffer. A *counteroffer* expresses willingness to negotiate the subject matter of the original offer and operates in effect as an offer. There is no liability on the part of the initial offeror with respect to his original proposal, nor legal necessity for him to continue negotiations.

[10]158 Mass. 194, 33 N.E. 495 (1893).

On the other hand, mere inquiry or request by the offeree for more detailed information about certain of the terms of the proposal does not have the effect of rejecting the offer. Similarly, when the offeree embodies in the acceptance terms that were not spelled out in the offer but that the law will imply anyway, the acceptance is not conditional and will effectively bring the contract into being. For instance, an acceptance reading, "I accept your offer if you can convey good title to the house" is effective since the offer to sell the property implicitly included a promise to convey valid title.

3.21 POINT AT WHICH CONTRACT IS MADE

When an offer is sent by mail and the offeree is expressly or implicitly invited to reply in kind, the contract is deemed effective as of the time when the letter of acceptance is mailed. This is so even if in the meantime a letter of revocation has been mailed by the offeror but has not reached its destination before the mailing of the acceptance. (The proliferation of electronic mail, voice mail, and fax transmissions will doubtless prove a challenge to such traditional common law rules.)

PROBLEMS IN THE FORMATION PROCESS

3.22 MUTUAL MISTAKE

The situations in which mistake affects the contract are the infrequent exceptions to an almost universal rule that a person is bound by an agreement to which he or she has expressed a clear assent uninfluenced by fraud or duress. In many instances where mistake is given as the reason for invalidating a contract, the trouble is really caused by the act of a third party, or perhaps by the dishonesty of one of the contracting parties. There are relatively few cases of genuine *mutual mistake*—where parties might contract for a thing which has ceased to exist or are in error about the identity of one another or about the subject matter of the purported agreement. An English case, often cited to illustrate a perfectly innocent misunderstanding of the parties, is *Raffles v. Wichelhaus*.[11] The defendant in that action had agreed to buy from the plaintiff a cargo of cotton "to arrive *ex Peerless* from Bombay." It seems that there were two ships of that name, and both sailed from Bombay—but Wichelhaus meant the *Peerless* that arrived in October, while Raffles had in mind the *Peerless* that arrived in December. Each party took his respective position in good faith, and neither acted in a negligent or unreasonable manner in arriving at his particular understanding of the matter. The court held that in the light of the varying interpretations no actual agreement had been reached, and hence there was no enforceable contract in existence.

| [11]Hurl. & C., 906 (Ct. Ex. 1864).

3.23   UNILATERAL MISTAKE

A mistake on the part of one of the contracting parties, or unilateral mistake, in most cases will not allow the mistaken party to avoid the contract. Mistake in a legal sense is erroneous belief about an existing or past fact and does not include a "mistaken" prediction of future events, either anticipation of contingencies that fail to materialize, or failure to consider contingencies that do arise. A person is expected to exercise diligence in contracting and the courts will not undertake to relieve a party of the consequences of error caused by his negligence or poor judgment to the detriment of a party relying on the agreement in good faith.

Mistakes caused by errors in mathematical computations in preparing bids for construction jobs are a frequent source of litigation seeking to rescind a contract on the basis of unilateral mistake. In many states it is a matter of public policy to favor holding contractors to mistaken bids based on a theory of negligence. However, deviations from the rule refusing rescission of contracts on the basis of unilateral mistake exist in bidding as well as other contract situations.

Factors the courts will consider in determining whether to allow recision of a contract for unilateral mistake are: whether the mistake was "material," or concerned a matter of such importance to the object of the contract that the mistaken party would not have agreed to the contract had he been aware of it; whether the other party knew or should have known of the mistake and acted in good faith to avoid damage to either party; whether the mistaken party exercised reasonable diligence but the mistake was induced by misrepresentation or ambiguity by the other party in presenting the terms of agreement; whether enforcement of the contract would place an unconscionable burden on one party and the other party could be returned undamaged to his former position.

The courts also will not allow a party to avoid a contract by claiming it was signed by mistake. One who signs an agreement is held bound by its contents in keeping with a basic legal duty to read and understand documents before signing them. Therefore, absent fraud, all terms of a contract will be binding on the parties who sign it.

3.24   MISTAKES OF LAW

What has been said up to this point relates to mistakes of fact. A mistake of law is completely different. As a general rule an erroneous conclusion about the legal effect of known facts does not destroy the validity of a contract when there is no concurrent mistake of fact.

3.25   CLERICAL ERRORS

Where there is an agreement between the parties and the sole difficulty is that a clerical error was made in committing the understanding to writing, the mistake will not vitiate the contract. In the occasional instance where the parties cannot correct such an error by common consent and one party unfairly seeks to take advantage of the situation, the other may by court action have the contract enforced in accordance with the actual intent and original understanding of the parties. Courts freely exercise the power to correct clerical mistakes when the available proof leaves no doubt that the contract was meant to be something at variance with what appears in the writing.

3.26   FRAUD AND MATERIAL MISREPRESENTATION

Fraud is (1) a reckless or intentional misstatement of a material fact, (2) made with intent to deceive, (3) resulting in misleading the innocent party to contract, (4) to his detriment. Acting as a reasonable person, the defrauded party must have been entitled to rely on the truth of the assertions made. Whether the victim is considered reasonable in his reliance will depend on the circumstances of the particular case (such as the precise form of the representation), the relations of the parties, and their respective means of knowledge.

An intentionally false statement of a past or existing fact is the basis for a claim of fraud. Such factual representations should be distinguished from an expression of opinion about the future. A misrepresentation may be created by concealment or suppression of material facts as well as by affirmative misstatement. It is not necessary for the misrepresentation to be intentional. Misrepresentation that is perfectly innocent may, if it constitutes a material inducement, render a contract voidable.

3.27   REMEDYING FRAUD

Apart from a tort action, the party deceived by *fraud* has available to him a choice of remedies in contract litigation. If he permits the contract to stand he may sue to recover any damages he suffered. If he chooses to rescind the contract, he may recover all consideration paid by him, provided that he is prepared to restore to the wrongdoer anything received pursuant to the contract he is electing to abrogate. Some courts may, in the same action, award damages resulting from the fraud to the rescinding party. Generally speaking, the defrauded party may not pursue inconsistent remedies and will be bound by an election once made. Also, he must act promptly in repudiating the contract once he has discovered the fraud.

3.28   WAIVER OF FRAUD

A contract induced by fraud is not absolutely void, but only voidable. The fraud may therefore be *waived* and the contract ratified. Ratification is established when the innocent party, having acquired knowledge of the true situation subsequent to date of the agreement, by acts of commission or omission evidences a clear intent to affirm the contract despite the fraud.

CONSIDERATION

3.29   MEANING AND IMPORTANCE

Although competent contracting parties may have agreed with reference to a common purpose, and the other prerequisites thus far discussed may have been fulfilled, the agreement will not be a legal and binding contract unless supported by consideration.

Consideration is something of value received by or given at the request of the promisor in reliance upon and in exchange for his or her promise. The consideration may be furnished by the promisee or by some other person. Similarly, it may go to the promisor or to a third party. However, nothing is deemed to be consideration unless it was so regarded by the contracting parties. It must be something actually bargained for, that they looked upon as an inducement.

By way of illustration, assume that Smith offers to sell Jones certain property for a stated sum, and, when Jones asks for two weeks' time in which to consider the offer, Smith promises not to sell to anyone else during that period. Under these circumstances, Smith may nevertheless dispose of the property to a third party, since his promise to Jones was unsupported by any consideration. If, however, Jones pays for Smith's promise, there is a contract duly supported by a consideration, and Smith must keep the offer to Jones open for the stipulated period. The payment by Jones is known in law as a consideration.

Consideration, given in exchange for a promise by the other party, may be either (1) a present act, forbearance, or sufferance or (2) a promise to do, forbear, or suffer sometime in the future. In the first case, the consideration is present, or *executed,* and the contract is unilateral; in the second case, it is future, or *executory,* and the contract is bilateral. The fact that the promise given for a promise may be conditional in nature does not affect its efficacy as a consideration. Not every promise, however, is sufficient consideration for a return promise. Generally, though, where doing of a certain thing will be good consideration, a *promise* to do that thing will be so too.

When mutual promises serve as consideration one for the other, the law requires that there is real substance to each promise. Those without substance are deemed illusory and of no effect. For instance, an agreement to agree is unenforceable. Similarly, a promise to do what is obviously a physical or legal impossibility is not a true consideration and will not support a binding return promise.

Consideration must be lawful, definite, and certain. A promise which purports to be consideration must not be too vague and unsubstantial to be enforced. For example, a commitment to pay "such remuneration as shall be deemed right" throws upon the courts a responsibility of interpretation which they are not prepared to assume.

The consideration for a contract differs from the motive in that the latter is the underlying cause for entering into the agreement whereas the former is the thing given by one party in exchange for and in reliance upon the other party's promise.

3.30   FORBEARANCE AS CONSIDERATION

It is well settled that forbearance from exercising a legal right, without being asked to do so, is not consideration which will support a promise. When requested, however, forbearance may be sufficient consideration.

In some cases the form of the consideration is such that there is no apparent benefit to anybody but merely a detriment to the person furnishing the consideration in question. Such detriment exists where the party affording consideration agrees to give up something to which he has undoubted right (for example, the use of intoxicating beverages).

An old but still cited case[12] provides an illustration of this type of forbearance as consideration. An uncle promised his nephew $5,000 if the boy refrained from smoking until reaching age twenty-one. The nephew did as his uncle wished and, when the promised $5,000 was not forthcoming, sued for breach of contract. The defense claimed there was not consideration for a binding promise, since the uncle received no actual benefit. The court, however, held that the nephew had given up legal rights and was entitled to recover.

Forbearance to exercise a legal right also covers situations where a person refrains from exercising his right to sue on an enforceable claim. In order to serve as consideration for a promise it must be requested, and, presumably, of benefit to the requesting party. In these cases, the forbearance is sufficient consideration even when there is no waiver or compromise of the right of action, and even though forbearance is for a short time only.

The actual compromise of a suit can without question serve as consideration. The law has always favored any conduct between disputants that will preclude litigation and, accordingly, looks with great favor on the compromise of suits.

3.31   ADEQUACY OF CONSIDERATION

If the parties intended some thing as consideration, its apparent "inadequacy," relative to the value of the promise for which it is exchanged, is of no consequence. If a party gets what has been contracted for, the courts will not question whether such consideration was of a value equivalent to that of whatever the party was obliged to give in return.

It is the duty of the court to interpret and not to redraft the contracts which come before it in litigation. A shrewd business person is entitled to the fruits of his bargain, and the commercial world must be able to rely upon the stability of contracts. Accordingly, a court of law will act on the presumption that parties capable of contracting are likewise capable of regulating the terms of their contracts, and judicial relief is granted only when obvious unfairness in the bargain is shown to have arisen from mistake, or fraud. Occasionally, the inadequacy or inequality of consideration is so gross as to amount to proof of undue influence of some sort.

---

[12]*Hamer v. Sidway*, 124 N.Y. 538 (1891).

3.32   PERFORMANCE OF EXISTING DUTY

If a promisor gets nothing in return for his promise but that to which he is already entitled, the consideration will not support the promise. For instance, where there is an existing contractual obligation to perform certain services for a stated fee, any promise to pay additional compensation for such obligated performance is made without a valid consideration and will not bind the promisor. But where one party refuses to complete his contractual duties by reason of having encountered substantial performance difficulties unanticipated by the parties at the contract's inception and casting an additional and totally unexpected burden upon the performer, a promise by the other party of extra compensation to induce completion of the project is generally regarded as supported by a valid consideration. The presumption in the latter case is that the parties by their subsequent actions waived their respective rights and obligations under the original agreement and substituted the new arrangement.

Instead of having a *contractual* duty, a person might be under a preexisting duty imposed by law to do the thing he promises to do. In such circumstances, the promise is of no value whatever and is not a proper consideration for a return promise. For example, when an ordinary witness is subpoenaed to appear at a trial, there is no consideration for any promise to pay anything beyond expenses, since there is a legal duty to come and give evidence. On the same principle, a promise not to do what one cannot lawfully do is an insufficient consideration.

The undertaking or doing of anything surpassing what one is already bound to do, though of the same kind and in the same transaction, provides a good consideration. Thus a public officer cannot recover a reward if the services performed come strictly in the line of her official duty, because a contract to award additional compensation for the performance in question would be both without consideration and against public policy. But it is also true that a contract to grant a public officer special remuneration or reward for services rendered outside, and not inconsistent with, their official duty is valid.

3.33   THE DOCTRINE OF *FOAKES V. BEER*[13]

From one of the most famous contracts cases of all time comes the proposition that, because "a lesser sum of money cannot be a satisfaction of a greater," part payment of a liquidated and undisputed debt already overdue is not valid consideration for a promise of the creditor to accept such payment as in full. The debtor, in rendering the part payment, has suffered no detriment he was not already bound to suffer and has surrendered no legal right he was not already obligated to surrender. The end result of the rule in *Foakes v. Beer*—a doctrine which, despite growing criticism, prevails in a great many jurisdictions—is that a creditor can effectively extinguish a $50 debt by accepting in its stead a canary, but he cannot accomplish the same thing

---

[13]L.R. 9 App. Cas. 605 (House of Lords, 1884).

by promising to take $49.50 in lieu of the full $50. It is obvious that there are many situations in which application of this rule leads to ludicrous results.

The rule in *Foakes v. Beer* has been repudiated by court decision in several states and by statute in a few more. The modern trend seems clearly away from the *Foakes* proposition. Since the *Foakes* rule is not favored, the courts often exercise ingenuity to avoid application of the doctrine. Seemingly, they have refused to apply the rule whenever they could discover some circumstance which could be regarded as a technical legal consideration. Thus, an agreement to give a smaller sum of money for a greater, if the time of payment is sooner, is binding. One court indicated its reasoning in this connection in rather expressive language: "Peradventure parcel of the sum, before the day, would be more beneficial than the whole sum on the day."[14] Similarly, the giving of a negotiable instrument for a money debt or the giving of virtually anything other than money itself will be deemed sufficient consideration to support a release of the entire debt.

Where the amount due is itself open to dispute between the parties, the rule in *Foakes v. Beer* has no bearing. Under such conditions, if the debtor sends the creditor a check marked "in full payment of my account," which check is for a smaller sum than the amount claimed by the creditor, the entire debt, according to majority opinion, is discharged (by what is technically known as an *accord and satisfaction*) when the creditor negotiates the check without protest.[15] Let us assume that White owes Black $500 and that the debt is past due. White promises that in thirty days she will turn over her speedboat to Black if the latter will accept same in full payment. Black agrees, but the debtor then fails to deliver as scheduled. Under these circumstances, Black can elect to sue for either the $500 or the speedboat. Black's agreement to accept delivery of the speedboat within the stipulated thirty days constituted what is known as an *accord executory*. If White had turned over the boat as promised, there would have been an accord and satisfaction acting as a bar to any attempt on Black's part to get the $500 as well. It should be noted that White's promise to deliver the boat did not of itself operate to discharge the $500 debt, because Black is deemed to have agreed to take the boat in satisfaction, not merely the *promise* respecting the boat. This is clearly a distinction of significance.

Moreover, cases in various states have held that the payment of only part of a liquidated debt is a good discharge of the whole where the creditor agreed to accept it as such if it were advanced for the purpose by some person other than the debtor. Such payment by a third party of a portion of the debt gives the creditor something different from what that recipient was entitled to demand and therefore operates as a valid consideration for this promise to release the actual debtor from the entire obligation.

---

[14]*Chicaro Fertilizer Co. v. Dunan*, 91 Md. 144, 46 A. 347, 351 (1900).

[15]*See Nassoiy v. Tomlinson*, 148 N.Y. 326, 42 N.E. 715 (1896). It is interesting to note that at least in Georgia a notation on the check is not necessary. *See Souchak v. Close*, 132 Ga. App. 248, 207 S.E. 2d 708 (1974); and *Hodson Gas System, Inc. v. Atlanta Airlines Terminal Corp.*, 408 S.E. 2d 454 (Ga. App. 1991).

3.34   PAST CONSIDERATION

It is a general principle that past consideration is insufficient to support a promise. That is, an act or forbearance rendered antecedently and not as the agreed equivalent for a subsequent promise is normally to be regarded as in the nature of a gift and not consideration. For example, where a father promises to buy his college student son a car next year because the son was admitted to Harvard last year, the father's promise is supported only by past consideration.

Where, however, an act is done upon definite request, under such circumstances that the law would imply a promise to pay therefor, and an express promise is actually made after the performance has been accomplished, the promise is generally held valid, being supported by what is often called an *executed,* or *past, consideration.* Even in the absence of the express promise, a suit may be brought to recover reasonable value of the requested services. When an actual promise is made subsequent to the performance, it serves as confirmation of the fact that the promisee's act was completed with the understanding that it was not intended to be gratuitous. A *subsequent promise* (that is, one which follows the other party's performance to which it relates) is binding only when the request, the consideration, and the promise form substantially one transaction. The request can be thought of as the offer of a promise, the precise extent of which becomes apparent only when the promise is actually given, some time after the requested consideration—for example, performance of a personal service—is forthcoming from the promisee.

3.35   MORAL CONSIDERATION

As a general rule a moral obligation will not of itself furnish consideration for an executory promise. Thus, if Smith rescues Jones from drowning, the latter is under some measure of moral compulsion to tender at least a nominal reward, particularly if Smith sustained any loss as a result of his act. But, even if Jones, temporarily overcome with gratitude, were to promise to pay a fixed sum as a reward for Smith's valiant efforts, there could be no legal recovery against Jones for breach of that promise. Such an offer could also fail, as the consideration, or act of saving in this case, is past. By the same token, promise or executory contracts made on the basis simply of love and affection—unsupported by a material benefit for which payment might reasonably be expected—create at most moral obligations, and a breach of such promises presents no basis for redress by the courts.

But a moral obligation arising from what was once a legal liability—the latter since barred or suspended by operation of some positive rule of law—will furnish a proper consideration for a subsequent executory promise. Where, for example, a person under a legal obligation to pay a sum of money is released by the running of a statute of limitations and afterward promises the creditor that the sum will nonetheless be paid, the creditor can recover. Some courts reach this result on the theory that the renewed promise is valid without a new consideration, since a moral obligation sufficient to support the promise survives. Other courts, while likewise recognizing the validity of the "released" debtor's subsequent promise, enforce it rather on the ground that the particular circumstances obviate the necessity for a consideration in that the statute of limitations is merely a defense the law has given the debtor to use or not at his pleasure.

We have seen that at common law the contracts of a minor cannot be enforced against him if he claims the defense of infancy. Upon reaching majority the infant may decide to validate previously made contracts, and any new promise to perform in accordance with the original agreement will effectively bind him without the necessity of any new consideration.

As in the case of infancy, contracts induced by fraud or duress are regarded as voidable and not entirely void. If, with knowledge of the fraud, the wronged party elects to ignore the obvious defense and makes a new promise to perform in accordance with the antecedent contract, such promise will be enforceable even though there is no consideration given specifically in return for it.

3.36 MUTUALITY OF OBLIGATION

It is often asserted that in executory bilateral contracts there must be *mutuality of obligation*; that is, both parties must be bound, or neither will be. Actually, of course, there are many situations where only one side is really bound, as for instance, where one party is an infant or where one party is guilty of fraud or undue influence.

The proposition which requires mutuality of obligation regarding those contracts to be performed in the future, where the promise of one party constitutes the sole consideration for the promise of the other, stems from the obvious unfairness of enforcing any contract which would require performance without question by one of the parties while leaving the other party a free choice in the matter. Thus, where one party alone has an arbitrary right to cancel or terminate the contract at any time, mutuality is absent.

Mutuality of obligation, a most difficult and controversial concept, involves primarily a question of consideration. If the promises which are to serve as consideration for one another are each binding, there is no lack of mutuality, and nonperformance of one of these enforceable promises does not constitute want of consideration nor lack of mutuality.

3.37 ILLEGAL CONSIDERATION

An *illegal consideration,* which may be defined as a performance or promise which runs counter to law or public policy, will not support an agreement. Despite some difference of opinion on the point, it is ordinarily said that even partial illegality of the consideration will vitiate the accompanying contract in its entirety.

3.38   FAILURE OF CONSIDERATION

Some courts subscribe to a doctrine which they characterize as *failure of consideration.* Such failure is deemed to result when for some reason or other, the anticipated consideration cannot be supplied or performed, and this unexpected state of affairs renders the contract unenforceable. The failure of consideration is predicated upon the happening of events which materially change the respective positions of the parties and which were not within their contemplation at the time of execution of the contract.

3.39   ESTOPPEL

A promisor is, under certain circumstances, precluded from asserting that a valid consideration is lacking. The classic doctrine is that the promise and the consideration must be given as the contemplated exchange one for the other. From this traditional theory of consideration, the idea of *promissory estoppel* represents a departure in that it renders a promise binding if the promisee has taken action or suffered some detriment in reliance thereon, even though such detriment was not requested as consideration for the promise. A typical example might be the situation where a mortgagee, following a default in payments, promises not to foreclose for a certain period of time. The mortgagor relies upon such freely given promise and, with the mortgagee's knowledge, makes expensive repairs to part of the property concerned. Under these conditions, the mortgagee's promise, despite the absence of consideration and other normal contract essentials, will be enforced as the logical means of avoiding injustice to the mortgagor.

A long and constantly increasing line of decisions in the United States has established the binding character of most charitable-subscription agreements. It is clearly understood that a subscription—rather than being part of a bargain that provides for the exchange of agreed equivalents—is a donation, an outright gift; and yet promises of this kind are now almost universally enforced. The reason most commonly advanced is that the promisee has given consideration by acting in reliance on the subscription and by proceeding to carry out the purposes for which the pledge was solicited and given. For example, perhaps the beneficiary has expended money in building construction before the subscriber makes any attempt to revoke the promise.[16] In some cases different reasons have been given for the enforcement of the subscription obligation. Occasionally, a court will find an implied promise by the trustee of the charity to execute the work contemplated, such promise operating as a consideration. Or it has been held that the promises of several subscribers mutually support each other. Under this last theory, the subscription agreement amounts to a bilateral contract between or among subscribers, of which contract the charitable organization is a donee-beneficiary. A charitable

---

[16]*See,* for example, *Estate of Timko v. Oral Roberts Evangelistic Association,* 215 N.W.2d 750 (Ct. App. Mich. 1974).

pledge may also be made enforceable when the charity relies on it. Thus, in one case a $3,000,000 pledge to create a Holocaust Museum was held enforceable when the charity commenced construction and used its pledges as collateral for a loan.[17] In any event, regardless of the theory adopted, the courts of this country will usually treat the ordinary charitable-subscription promise as clearly enforceable at law.

QUESTIONS

1. How many parties constitute the minimum needed to form a contract? Why?

2. What feature distinguishes a "minor"?

3. Under what conditions can a minor be released from his or her contract?

4. If a 50-year-old business person contracts to sell an automobile to a minor, can the promise of the former be subsequently avoided? Can the minor avoid his or her part of the bargain? Why?

5. In contract law, what significance has (a) mental weakness of one of the contracting parties? (b) actual mental incompetence of one of the parties?

6. Under what conditions will a person be bound by a promise which was made when intoxicated?

7. Illustrate a case in which the subject matter or promise would be illegal or against public policy and therefore would void a contract involving same.

8. A agreed to pay B $5,000 for certain diamonds which B was to smuggle into the country. When B delivered the jewels, A refused to accept them. What can B do about it? Why?

9. A called a builder, B describing in considerable detail an additional room which she planned to build on her house, and she asked B how much he would charge to build it. After lengthy discussion, B said, "I think it will cost you $3,000." A said, "That will be satisfactory." The next day B called A and said that, after making a careful estimate of the job, he found the addition would cost $3,400. A claimed that B had already contracted to do the work for $3,000. Is A correct? Why?

10. X sent Y the plans and specifications for the complete electric lighting system for a new factory. Y replied that she would do the work for $4,500. X announced that he "hereby" awarded the contract to Y but that certain fixtures were to be changed and relocated and other revisions made in the plans. Is Y bound to go through with the project?

---

[17] *In re Park Avenue Associates, Inc.,* 182 Bankruptcy Rptr. 690 (50 NY 1995). *See also, King v. Trustees of Boston Univ.,* 647 N.E. 2d 1196 (Mass. 1995) in which a pledge of his papers after his death by Dr. Martin Luther King, Jr. to Boston University was held binding on his estate.

11. Black told White that she would sell all her "do-it-yourself" tools for $300. White replied: "Unless you hear otherwise from me before April 15, I shall accept your offer." On April 12 White wrote Black that she could not afford to purchase the tools, and she gave the letter to Jones to mail. Jones forgot to do so until April 16, whereupon she posted the letter. Is White obliged to purchase the tools? Explain.

12. X sold his automobile to Y with the statement that all four tires were practically new. Y discovered next day (before paying for the car) that all tires were retreads. Can Y rescind the contract and avoid any payment whatever? If not, what recourse does Y have?

13. A had a nephew, B, to whom, when B was seventeen years and two months old, A loaned $2,000 for his educational expenses. In return B gave A a promissory note calling for repayment (without interest) two years from the date of the note. One year later, B quit school and joined the army. Two months after B's nineteenth birthday, on the due date, A demanded payment. B refused. Can A collect? Explain.

14. Murray wrote to Giegler stating that he would install a completely new heating system in Giegler's house, in accordance with the latter's specifications, for $1,200. Giegler was away on vacation when the letter arrived at his home, and he had left no forwarding address. The next day, Murray discovered that he had made an error in his estimate. He therefore wrote Giegler another letter, repudiating the first one, and stating that the cost would be $1,400. Giegler received both letters simultaneously upon his return home. Can Giegler hold Murray to the latter's first quotation? Explain.

15. Mrs. S was hit by a car, and her ankle was broken. Three days later, a paper was mailed to her by the representative of the insurance company who asked her to sign and return it. She did so without reading the paper carefully, believing it to be an initial payment of $500. Later, she discovered that the paper was a release of the company from all liability upon payment of $500. What can she do about the matter?

16. Explain the effect of duress or undue influence upon contractual relationships.

17. Carlson, a builder, promised Pratt that she would engage the latter to install all the hot-air furnaces in houses to be built by Carlson during the year 1984. Pratt ultimately sued Carlson for loss of anticipated profits because Carlson changed all of her house plans and installed hot-water heating systems instead of hot air. Can Pratt collect? Explain.

18. What is the meaning of "consideration" as the term is used in contract law?

19. A told B that, if the latter would take him along on a ten-day fishing trip in Maine, he would take care of B's yard and flower beds all summer free of charge. B accepted the offer. Is there a binding contract? Explain.

20. Can an agreement not to do something be a proper consideration for a return promise?

21. Brown was interested in buying Gray's secondhand truck and happened to tell his (Brown's) daughter that he was willing to pay $1,000 for it. Gray called at Brown's house when the latter was away, and Gray told Brown's daughter that he would sell the truck for $1,000, whereupon the daughter accepted the offer and arranged for delivery next day. Is Brown obligated to pay? Why?

22. A had agreed to sell his house to B for $20,000 and stated that he would confirm his offer by letter the next day. When A wrote the letter, he made a typographical error, stating that the selling price was $2,000. What are the rights of the parties?

23. Black agreed to sell certain secondhand machinery to Green for $20,000, and Green accepted the offer. The following week Black learned that the machinery was actually worth $40,000 and thereupon refused to sell at the lower figure. Was Black's position sound? What can Green do?

24. X told Y that he would buy Y's old tractor at a "proper" figure as soon as Y received delivery of a new machine which was on order. Have the parties made a contract? Elaborate.

25. X owed Y $500 but was unable to pay on the due date. He told Y that he could pay only $300 in cash but that he would let Y have two pointer pups in addition if I would "call it square." If Y accepts, what is the status of the $500 debt?

26. X promised to buy Y's house and lot for $25,000 and made a deposit of $1,000 to bind the bargain. She was to receive transfer of title on August 10. On August 6 the house burned down. What happens to the contract? What happens to the $1,000 deposit?

CONDITIONS AND THIRD PARTY BENEFICIARIES

4.1   DEFINITION AND CLASSIFICATION

A *condition* is a proviso upon which the rights and duties of the parties depend. A condition in a contract operates to suspend, rescind, or modify the principal obligation under given circumstances.

Conditions may be *express, implied in fact,* or *implied in law.* A certain fact may operate as a condition because the parties intended that it should and indicated as much in so many words; it is then an express condition. Or it may operate as a condition because the parties' intention that it should is a matter of reasonable inference from conduct other than words; it is then a condition implied in fact. Or it may operate as a condition because the court believes that the parties would have intended it to operate as such if they had thought about it or because the court believes that justice requires that it should so operate; it is then a condition implied in law. Implied conditions include: the continued life of both parties in employment contracts; the continued existence of the subject matter in a contract to sell specific goods; and the continued legality of any contract. When a contract is made in reliance upon the happening of a particular event, the actual occurrence of that event is an implied condition of the contract.

Although courts are reluctant to enforce obligations beyond the express written intent of the parties they will recognize as implied provisions anything considered indispensable to effectuate the intent of the parties. For example, a contract to paint the interior of a home implies a provision that the performing party will be allowed reasonable access to the home. Similarly, the law in every state implies a covenant of good faith and fair dealing in every contract and will require that each contracting party refrain from doing anything to impair the right of the other to receive the benefit of the agreement. For example, it was held in a case involving a franchise that unless the contract expressly provided otherwise, the franchise could only be terminated for good cause.[1] But, where the contract does "unmistakably" express the parties' rights, the obligation of good faith does not override the express contract terms.[2]

4.2   CONDITION PRECEDENT

Conditions are further classified as *precedent, concurrent,* or *subsequent.* A condition precedent arises where a promise is predicated on the happening of a certain event. There is no obligation to fulfill the promise unless and until the specified event actually does take place. The employment of such contract terminology as "when," "if," or "as soon as" normally points to the inclusion of a condition precedent. Generally in contracts for services, performance is a condition precedent to payment.

A court may also find that a condition precedent is implicit when a contract is read as a whole, even though a specified condition is not referred to. For example, in *Handley v. Ching*[3] the plaintiff and defendant entered into a joint venture to develop a residential condominium project. The plaintiff, a real estate developer, and the defendant entered into an agreement under which a new Hawaii corporation was to be formed that would own and operate the condominium. The agreement contained a provision under which the defendant was obligated to reimburse the plaintiff for funds expended if the defendant defaulted. The defendant did default and the new corporation was never formed. Defining a condition precedent to call for the performance for some act after a contract is entered into, upon the performance of which the obligation to perform immediately is made to depend, the court said that a necessarily drawn implication from the language of the agreement was that the formation of the corporation contemplated by the parties was a condition precedent to any obligation to perform the provisions of the agreement. Specifically, the court observed that the agreement stated "whereas, Handley and the Allens desire to form a new Hawaii corporation for the purpose of developing the subject property" and that nearly every subsequent section of the agreement referred to rights and duties of the parties in terms of the existence of the new corporation.

---

[1]*Dayan v. McDonald's Corp.,* 466 N.E.2d 958 (Ill. App. 1st Dist., 1984). In this case the termination of a franchise for a McDonald's in Paris was upheld for failure to maintain quality and cleanliness standards.
[2]*Bertera Chrysler Plymouth, Inc. v. Chrysler Corp.,* 992 F.Supp.674 (D.C. Mass. 1998) (applying Mich. law).
[3]2 Haw. 166, 627 P.2d 1132 (1981).

4.3 CONDITION CONCURRENT

Where performance by both parties is designed to be simultaneous, performance by one is often termed a *condition concurrent* to performance by the other. For example, a city may specify in a contract for sewer construction that, when the contractor installs the sewer in Maple Street, the work shall be done one block at a time and that each block will be closed to traffic while work is progressing in it. The closure is then a condition concurrent.

4.4 CONDITION SUBSEQUENT

A *condition subsequent* is one that relieves the promisor of a liability that has already attached. If such a condition is violated, the promisor's liability will be annulled. Conditions subsequent are matters of defense to be proved by the party seeking release from the obligation. One example would be a fire insurance policy clause reciting that no suit may be brought on the contract unless within a stated period of time following a loss. The same sort of time limit may be prescribed for claims of a contractor for extra costs occasioned by changes ordered during the course of a job.

Many conditions that appear to be subsequent in nature are in fact conditions precedent. For instance, the recital of obligation in a surety bond will indicate that the obligation attaches only in the event the principal fails in the specified performance. Default by the principal is therefore to be actually a condition precedent to the surety's liability on the bond.

4.5 PERSONAL-TASTE CONTRACTS

In contracts involving personal taste, an agreement by *A* to perform to the satisfaction of *B* places the latter in a dominant position, and *A* cannot recover his fee until *B* is in fact satisfied. Any dissatisfaction which *B* might express, though it may be capricious by ordinary standards, requires only good faith to be effective. A typical case is the situation where one party undertakes to paint a portrait or to design clothing for another; in such instances the customer's standard of taste is the test.

Where personal satisfaction is not involved quite so directly, as in a building contract that contains the common provision that no payments are to be made except on certificate of the architect or engineer, the fact that the building was erected in a workmanlike manner and precisely according to specifications will be evidence that the architect was acting in bad faith in withholding the certificate.

4.6   CONDITIONS ABOUT TIME OF PERFORMANCE

As in the case of contractual provisions generally, stipulations about time will be construed in accordance with the intent of the parties as shown by the fair import of the language employed. Completion of a contract within a "reasonable" time is sufficient if no exact time limit has been stipulated. Thus, an agreement to take certain action "as soon as possible" or "forthwith" has been held to require merely that performance be made within a reasonable time under the circumstances of the particular case. The rule is somewhat more strict in connection with those contracts where time is deemed to be "of the essence," as, for instance, agreements for the payment of money. In such cases, where no precise time is set, the assumption is normally that the money is payable immediately. Where a contract to render services is silent regarding the time of payment, remuneration is due as soon as the services have been rendered.

4.7   CONDITIONS ABOUT PLACE OF PERFORMANCE

Where the place of performance has been named by the parties their expression prevails. If, however, the contract is silent in this respect and there are no circumstances showing the parties' intended performance to be elsewhere, the place of performance is deemed to be the place where the contract was made.

4.8   CONDITIONS ABOUT AMOUNT OF THE COMPENSATION

A complete absence of price in a contract will usually render it invalid, although price may occasionally be inferred from previous dealings between the parties. Where, for instance, the amount of compensation is not specified in an oral contract for work similar to that done under a previous written contract between the same parties wherein the compensation was specified, it may be presumed that payment under the new agreement was intended to be the same.

When there is a contract to perform certain work according to a schedule and that schedule provides for doing the work under the direction of an engineer, the cost of variations and additional work ordered by the engineer may be recovered. However, when a designer directs extra work to be done and the designer's sole authority is to see that materials and workmanship are in accordance with the specifications, the contractor probably cannot—in the absence of ratification by the owner—recover for the extra work.

4.9 FAILURE OF CONDITION

The nonfulfillment of a *promise* is called a *breach of contract* and creates in the other party to the agreement a right to damages. On the other hand, nonfulfillment of a condition simply excuses the other party from performing his side of the original bargain but creates no right to damages unless fulfillment of the condition has been expressly guaranteed.

4.10 WAIVER OF CONDITION

A condition precedent to a contract duty of performance can be waived by a voluntary act of the party who is undertaking the duty. Thus the party is free to carry out the terms of the contract despite failure of the condition upon which the obligation was grounded. For example, when an insured submits a claim for a fire loss on other than the form stipulated by the carrier but the latter ignores this circumstance in replying and simply notifies the policyholder that it disclaims liability on the ground that the fire had been deliberately set by the insured, the contract condition prescribing definite claim forms is waived.

4.11 ESTOPPEL

If the promisor is himself the cause of the failure of a condition on which his liability hinges, he will be precluded from alleging such failure. His conduct in such a case has made it inequitable for him to insist upon fulfillment of the condition.

For example, in a case where defendant hired plaintiff to find a joint venturer to invest in coal properties and where plaintiff was to receive a finder's fee of 5 percent upon conclusion of the joint venturer agreement, it was held that the finder's fee is payable, even if the agreement is never concluded, when the failure results from bad faith negotiations on the part of the defendant.[4]

---

[4]*Nuvest S.A. v. Gulf and Western Industries, Inc.,* 649 F.2d 943 (2d Cir. 1981). This problem, and the same result, also often occurs between real estate brokers and clients. See, for example, *Green v. Bowers,* 493 S.E. 2d 709 (Ga. App. 1997).

4.12   THE REQUIREMENT OF PRIVITY

A binding promise may, of course, be enforced by the recipient thereof, and his rights also encompass promises made for the benefit of some third person. Subject to a very significant exception in the case of certain third-party-beneficiary contracts, generally only one who is a party to the contract or someone in *privity* with him may enforce the obligation. Otherwise a person's responsibility for failure to carry out his agreement with another would have no reasonable limits. *Privity of contract* is a term denoting mutual or successive relationship to the same right of property or to the same subject matter. Thus, the assignee is in privity with his assignor, the donee with his donor, and the lessee with his lessor. There is privity of contract between an owner and the general contractor who is erecting a building for him, but generally not between the owner and a subcontractor on the job. An obvious corollary to the rule rendering contracts enforceable only by parties thereto or their *privies* is that an action on a contract cannot be maintained *against* a person who is not a party to the agreement.

There are several variations from this general proposition, one being that a principal is bound by the contract made for him by his agent (if the latter acted within the scope of his authority), even though the principal is not actually named in the contract nor his interest disclosed. On the other hand one who contracts in a representative capacity is not individually liable where, from the manner in which the instrument is executed, it is apparent that it is intended as the obligation of the person represented and that the principal (and not the agent) is the real contracting party.

THIRD-PARTY BENEFICIARIES AND ASSIGNMENT

4.13   RIGHT TO SUE

One of the controversial subjects in contracts has been whether the common-law rule that only the promisee can enforce a promise should be applied to cases in which the promise clearly was made for the benefit of a third person. The right of a beneficiary who furnishes the consideration to realize the fruits of the contract in which he has invested has long been acknowledged—often on the theory that the promisee acted as agent for the beneficiary in dealing with the promisor—but there has been considerable diversity of opinion about the rights of a beneficiary who is a complete stranger to the contract he seeks to enforce.

The common law recognized these types of third party beneficiaries: (1) creditor beneficiaries, (2) donee beneficiaries, and (3) incidental beneficiaries, but allowed only the first two to maintain an action on the contract.

Where two parties enter into an agreement in which one promises to pay the other's debt to a third party, that third party is a *creditor beneficiary* and may recover against the promisor as well as against his debtor. A typical example of a creditor beneficiary is where a mortgagor who is himself personally indebted sells his interest in the mortgaged property to a grantee who assumed payment of the mortgage debt. The mortgagee is a creditor beneficiary and is almost universally allowed to sue the grantee to secure a personal judgment against him for the amount of the debt.

A third-person beneficiary under a contract is a *donee beneficiary* if the purpose of the promise in obtaining a commitment from a promisor is to make a gift to the beneficiary or to confer on him a right against the promisor to some performance neither due nor asserted to be due from the promisee to the beneficiary. The donee beneficiary's ratification of the contract is presumed from the fact of benefit without burden, and his rights arise immediately upon formation of the contract. In life insurance the beneficiary is a donee beneficiary, and in all jurisdictions he can maintain suit on the policy.

Recovery in donee beneficiary situations formerly was limited to cases where the third party was a close blood relative of the promisee, but the modern tendency is to permit any donee beneficiary to recover against the promisor when the contracting parties intend to confer a benefit upon him.

An *incidental beneficiary* is neither a creditor beneficiary nor a donee beneficiary but is one who happens to have found in some contract a provision which would inure to his advantage. The incidental beneficiary has no enforceable rights under such a contract since the contracting parties had no intention of benefiting him, and it is the intention rather than the effect that governs. To permit recovery on his part, the intent to benefit the third person must clearly appear from the language of the agreement as a whole, construed in the light of the surrounding circumstances.

While these categories still find their way into court decisions in some jurisdictions, today most states have adopted a version of the *Restatement of Contracts 2nd,* which recognizes only two categories of third-party beneficiaries: intended and incidental. The *Restatement* says:

Intended and Incidental Beneficiaries

(1) Unless otherwise agreed between promisor and promisee, a beneficiary of a promise is an intended beneficiary if recognition of a right to performance in the beneficiary is appropriate to effectuate the intention of the parties and either

(a) the performance of the promise will satisfy an obligation of the promisee to pay money to the beneficiary; or

(b) the circumstances indicate that the promisee intends to give the beneficiary the benefit of the promised performance.

(2) An incidental beneficiary is a beneficiary who is not an intended beneficiary.

Thus, prevailing view in this country now permits a third person for whose benefit an agreement was made to sue on it even though he is a stranger to the contract and to the consideration involved.

The liberal view permitting the beneficiary to sue makes a great deal of sense because it should make no difference to the promisor—who has received his consideration—whether the enforcement be brought by the promisee, with whom he dealt directly, or by a third party, who is the intended beneficiary under the contract.

The contract upon which the third-party beneficiary seeks to recover must be a valid and binding one. The beneficiary's rights against the promisor derive from the contract as it was made, and if it was void in its inception for lack of any essential element the third party has no rights. Furthermore, one who sues on a contract made for his benefit must accept the contract as it is. His rights are affected by any infirmities of the contract as between the contracting parties themselves. The rights of a third-party beneficiary are analogous to those of an assignee. Therefore, the promisor may interpose against the beneficiary any defenses that would have been available were the action brought by the promisee. Where the contract is void or voidable, as against the promisee, on grounds of fraud, mistake, infancy, or insanity, it is so likewise against the third party; or, if the duty of the promisor is subject to a condition precedent, the correlative right of the beneficiary is likewise conditional.

Identification of Beneficiary   It is not essential that the person to be benefited by the contract be named therein as long as he is otherwise sufficiently designated. In fact, he may be one of a class of persons if the *class* is adequately described. Moreover, in order to enable a third person to elect to enforce a contract made for his benefit, it is not necessary that he be aware of the existence of the contract at the time it was made.

4.14   RESCISSION OF THIRD-PARTY-BENEFICIARY CONTRACTS

After the third-party beneficiary has become aware of the contract made for his benefit and has taken action in reliance on it, the promisee no longer has power to release the promisor from the latter's duty to the beneficiary. This is true whether the beneficiary involved is a creditor or a donee. On the other hand, there is divided opinion among courts regarding the power of the contracting parties to rescind *before* the intended beneficiary acquires knowledge of the existence of the agreement and changes his position as a consequence thereof. The weight of authority seems to be that the rights of a donee beneficiary become indefeasible upon formation of the contract, while those of a creditor beneficiary may be lost or qualified by prompt action of the contracting parties before the beneficiary can bring suit or otherwise materially alter his position in reliance on the promise. A life insurance beneficiary presents something of a special case. Unless said beneficiary has been irrevocably designated as such by the policy owner (who is typically the insured person), the beneficiary may be changed through exercise of a power normally reserved to the owner by the policy contract itself.

4.15 THE NATURE OF ASSIGNMENT

An *assignment* by the holder of a right introduces a new party (the assignee) in his place. Duties cannot ordinarily be assigned, but the expression of intention to pass a right on to someone else is generally given effect. When such is the case, the assignment extinguishes the right of the assignor against the obligor and substitutes a similar right in the assignee.

A contract to assign in the future does not qualify as an assignment, since the term assignment has no pertinence if any further action on the assignor's part will be necessary to complete the right of the assignee.

Any contractual duty can be extinguished with the consent of the party who holds the right. If the party agrees to the substitution of a new party as the one bound to perform, this is a novation rather than an assignment. A novation is the substitution of a new obligation for an existing one and requires (1) a previous valid contract; (2) an agreement between parties to abide by a new contract; (3) a valid new contract; and (4) extinguishment of the old contract by substitution of the new one.[5] For example, a court found a valid novation where a lawyer and client agreed to terminate a contingent fee agreement and substitute in its place an agreement whereby the client would pay the attorney $1,000.[6] It is not an "assignment," because the latter term is used to denote a substitution brought about by the action of one party without procuring the assent of the other.

4.16 WHAT MAY BE ASSIGNED

Assuming the parties themselves have not expressly stipulated otherwise, all contract rights are assignable in the absence of a statute to the contrary or unless the contract is of such a nature as to cause an assignment to conflict with public policy or to increase materially the burden imposed upon the obligor. A contract clause purporting to forbid assignment is almost invariably taken as having been intended to prevent the delegation of performance rather than to affect assignment of rights arising under the agreement. Thus, if Smith contracts with Jones to have the latter paint the Smith garage and the instrument states that "this contract shall not be assignable," it should be held to mean that Jones must personally do the work and not that Jones is prevented from assigning his right to the agreed compensation. The right of an assignee under these circumstances would be conditioned upon the satisfactory rendering by Jones of the stipulated personal performance.

An assignment is not ineffective because it is conditional or is revocable by the assignor. Generally speaking, an operative present assignment may be made of rights dependent upon a performance not yet due or rendered.

---

[5]*Phoenix Power Partners, L.P. v. Colorado Public Utilities Comm.*, 952 P.2d. 359 (Colo. 1998).
[6]*People v. Metcalf*, 79 Cal. App. 3d 1, 144 Cal. Rptr. 657 (1978). For other illustrations of novation and discussion of the principle, *see United Security Corp. v. Anderson Aviation Sales, Inc.*, 23 Ariz. App. 273, 532 P.2d 545 (1975) and *Hemisphere Nat. Bank v. District of Columbia*, 412 A.2d 31 (D.C. Cir. 1980).

4.17   THE DELEGATING OF DUTIES

Generally rights may be assigned but not liabilities. A promisor cannot escape a contractual duty by assigning it to another or by delegating another to perform it. However, a particular duty can often be performed by a person other than the promisor, and the promisee ordinarily cannot prevent the discharge of his contract right and the promisor's correlative contract duty by such a vicarious performance. If *Y* undertakes to do work for *Z* which requires no special skill, and it does not appear that *Y* was selected with reference to any personal qualification, *Z* cannot complain if *Y* has the work done by an equally competent person. But *Y* is still liable should the work be poorly done, and *Y* is the only one who can sue for payment unless he has effectively assigned his right to the compensation stated in the contract.

There are a number of situations in which the promisor cannot delegate performance of his duty because the promised performance by its specialized nature necessitates his personal attention. If Caruso had promised to sing on a given program, he could not have delegated performance to another tenor. The artistry contracted for was that of Caruso, and the work of a substitute would neither discharge Caruso's duty nor create a right to payment of the agreed compensation. Instead, Caruso would be liable in damages for breach of the agreement.

4.18   THE EFFECT OF AN ASSIGNMENT

The assignment of a bilateral contract really consists of two phases: (1) a *delegation* of the power to perform the assignor's contractual obligations, assuming such are not purely personal in nature, and (2) an *assignment* of such present or future rights as the assignor may have under the terms of the agreement. As we have seen, delegation of performance does not of itself relieve the assignor of responsibility for seeing to it that the stipulated functions are properly accomplished. If the assignee should fail to perform or should perform in an unsatisfactory manner, the assignor will be liable unless (by novation) the promisee has permitted the assignee to take the place of the assignor as party to the original contract.

With respect to the assignment of rights, assignee's rights can be no greater than those originally contracted for, and if the assignor's claim was voidable or conditional, the assignee's is also; that is, the assignee's claim is subject to all defenses which would have been available against the assignor. The assignee may (and usually by statute must) sue in his own name, since he, and not the assignor, is the real "party in interest." Where, however, the assignment was merely as security for the payment of a previous debt due from assignor to assignee, the former retains an interest, and it has been held that in such circumstances suit can be maintained in his name.

QUESTIONS

1. Define and illustrate *(a)* an express condition in a contract, *(b)* a condition precedent, *(c)* a condition concurrent, *(d)* a condition subsequent.

2. Sullivan, an architect, contracted to make the plans for Russell's new warehouse in accordance with the latter's wishes and to meet with the latter's approval. When the plans were finished, Russell did not like them. Sullivan refused to revise the plans unless paid extra for doing so. Can Russell compel her to make the revisions without extra payment? Explain.

3. On April 2, Conners contracted to deliver 50 cubic yards of topsoil to Buck for grading the latter's lawn. In spite of Buck's telephoned requests, Conners had not delivered the soil by May 15, whereupon Buck purchased the topsoil from Perkins (without notifying Conners) and had the job finished by May 21. A week later Conners started delivery and insisted that Buck go through with the bargain. If litigation ensues, what result can be expected?

4. What is the meaning of "privity of contract"?

5. Ferris bought a secondhand motor boat from Lewis, to be delivered to Ferris's son on June 1 in return for $500. Just prior to June 1, the elder Ferris died. Can the son force Lewis to deliver the boat for the stated sum?

6. An expert sculptor contracted to make a bust of a movie star. She tried to sublet the job to another sculptor, but the actor refused to permit this. Did the latter have this right? Why?

7. Can *X* who has a contract with *Y* assign his rights under the contract to *Z*? His duties? Is *Y*'s approval of the assignee *(Z)* necessary?

8. *A* promised *B* to build a small bridge for $48,000, constructing and maintaining in the meantime a detour that would be satisfactory to the state highway department. Later on, *A* discovered that the detour would cost her so much that she would lose heavily on the job. She therefore tried to annul the contract on the ground of inadequate consideration. What are her chances of success?

9. Brown, a consulting engineer, agreed to sublet the making of the design drawings for bridge approaches to Black—provided that Brown secured the contract for designing this certain large bridge project. Assuming that Brown would get the job, Black contracted to employ White at a salary of $800 per month for one year. Brown failed to get the award. Is Black nonetheless obligated to hire White?

10. Does a third-party beneficiary of a contract have the right to demand enforcement of the contract? Explain.

11. Differentiate intended beneficiary from incidental beneficiary.

12. *A* sent a check to *B* in payment for a certain list of lumber but gave *B* no instructions as to time for delivery. What time for delivery can *A* demand? Why?

13. *A* ordered 100 pieces of hemlock two-by-fours 16 feet long. *B* had only seventy-six such pieces so she sent them and included thirty-two pieces 12 feet long, giving the same total length. What may *A* do about it?

14. On October 3 Smith sent a check to Jones in payment for a TV set to be delivered to his son on December 24 as a Christmas present. He told his son about the arrangement. On November 15, Smith was killed in an auto accident. What action can Smith's son take if Jones fails to deliver the TV set? Explain.

15. *X* claimed to be in the business of mowing lawns for suburbanites. *X* contracted with *Y* to mow the latter's lawn for $50 for the season. When *X* appeared at *Y*'s place, he claimed that *Y* had to furnish the power mower to perform the work. Discuss *Y*'s possible course of action.

CONSTRUCTION AND INTERPRETATION

5.1   GENERAL RULES OF CONSTRUCTION

The words of a contract are to be given their commonly accepted meaning in the absence of some evidence of a contrary intent. But technical terms will be construed in a technical sense, and words having special meaning, widely adopted in a trade, will be so defined in contracts involving that trade. Moreover, in construing technical terms utilized in an agreement, a court will ascribe considerable importance to the meaning given those particular terms in the course of any prior dealings between the parties.

A court will interpret a contract by giving a reasonable meaning to all the contract provisions rather than leaving portions of the agreement useless or absurd, and whenever possible will construe a contract so as to uphold its legality and validity.[1] Likewise, a court will often make some attempt at a construction equitable to each of the parties, but it cannot ignore or change harsh or even seemingly unreasonable terms that are clearly written into the contract, for passing upon the folly or wisdom of a contractual undertaking is not within the province of the court.

5.2   PARTIES' INTENT IMPORTANT

Perhaps the cardinal rule in the interpretation of contracts is that the court must ascertain and give effect to the intention of the parties as far as this may be accomplished without contravention of legal principles or public policy. The Supreme Court of Georgia recently stated that "a cardinal rule of construction of contracts is

---

[1] *Allendale Mutual Insurance Co. v. Excess Insurance Company, Ltd.*, 992 F. Supp. 271 (S.D. N.Y. 1997).

to ascertain the intention of the parties. This intention must be enforced unless it contravenes some rule of law." The court then went on to find that a separation agreement entered into by a husband and wife for payment of 50 percent of the net income of an investment was not intended to be alimony but rather a division of property, and therefore was unaffected by the subsequent remarriage of the wife.[2]

Generally a court will not disregard contract terminology employed by the parties or insert words that the parties have not themselves utilized. In other words, judicial interpretation of a contract does not include its modification or the creation of a new or different contract.

When preliminary negotiations are consummated by a written agreement or when an oral contract is evidenced by a subsequent agreed memorandum, the latter supersedes any previous understandings, and the intent of the parties must be derived from the writing. In case of real doubt about the contract's meaning, however, all the preliminary negotiations between the parties will be taken into account in giving the final contract a proper construction.

5.3   CONTRACT TO BE CONSIDERED AS A WHOLE

It is a fundamental rule of construction that a contract must be interpreted as a whole, with the meaning taken from the entire context rather than from a consideration of only particular portions or clauses of the agreement. A court will not isolate a certain phrase of a contract to garner the intent of the parties but will read it as a whole to ascertain the paramount and guiding intent of the parties.

Similarly, when several instruments are drawn up as part of a single transaction, they will read each with reference to the other or others. Marginal notes on the contract document or matters contained in separate writings referred to in the contract (when clearly intended as a part of the agreement) may properly be considered in the interpretation of the contract. For example, a performance bond will be construed in connection with the underlying contract.

5.4   CONSTRUING VAGUE TERMINOLOGY AGAINST THE DRAFTER

Ambiguous language[3] in an agreement will be interpreted against the party who employs it.[4] The explanation for this is that the drafter is the one responsible for

---

[2]*Head v. Hook*, 285 S.E.2d 718 (Ga. 1982).

[3]A contract is not ambiguous merely because the parties disagree as to its proper construction. *Betz v. Fagan*, 926 S.W. 2d 432 (Mo. App. 1998); *Beiger Heritage Corp. v. Montandon*, 691 N.W. 2d 1334 (Ct. App. Ind., 1998).

[4]*See Transit Casualty Co. in Receivership v. Certain Underwriters at Lloyd's of London*, 963 S.W.2d 392 (Mo. App. 1998).

the uncertainties and must suffer any difficulties occasioned thereby. This is most often applied where the contract is on a *printed* form prepared by one of the parties. This principle is especially important to engineers who produce plans and specifications that become contract documents. If the engineer's work is open to two different interpretations, the contractor's interpretation does not have to be the best one; it only needs to be a reasonable one to prevail.

5.5   PARTIES' OWN INTERPRETATION

When the parties to an ambiguous agreement have given it a practical construction by their conduct, as by acts in partial performance, such construction will be considered by the court in determining what mutual intention was as of the critical time of contracting.[5]

An excellent example of this point is afforded by the case of *Wiebener v. Peoples*,[6] in which there was a contract for the construction of a building that called for the contractor to furnish all materials and labor to erect the structure according to plans and specifications. One rather nebulous clause read: "Excavations and foundations complete to joist line; will be completed to joist line by owners." The litigation dealt primarily with the responsibility for supplying a stairway and an iron railing required by the contract to be placed above the joist line on an outer retaining wall of a light and air space outside the basement. The builder argued that such outside railing was part of the basement and, as such, came within the exception quoted. In the course of its opinion, the court took special notice of the parties' mutual understanding of contract language, and said:

> It appears that in the construction of the building the parties to this contract mutually understood and construed it as requiring the defendants [owners] to make the excavation and foundations and to complete the entire basement of the building as required by the plans and specifications to joist line; and, in view of such construction by the parties themselves, . . . we hold that the expression "excavation and foundations complete to joist line," as used in this contract, refers to and means all that portion of the building within the excavations and below the joist line, i.e., the entire basement below that line, *although we might be disposed to hold otherwise but/for such construction by the parties* as there is no other evidence of a technical or special meaning of the language used in this exception and it would not otherwise seem to include stairways leading to and from the basement.

| [5]The parol evidence rule, discussed in Chapter 25, would preclude the introduction of any oral evidence to *contradict* the terms of the written agreement.
[6]44 Okla. 32, 142 P. 1036 (1914).

5.6   IMPLIED TERMS

A contract includes not only what is expressly stated but also what is *necessarily* to be implied from the language used. However, courts proceed with considerable caution in supplying by implication provisions omitted from written contracts and will imply an unexpressed term only where the implication arises automatically from the terminology employed in the instrument or is indispensable to effectuate the apparent intention of the parties.[7]

A common example of an implied contract term is the case of persons who present themselves as specially qualified to perform work of a particular character. In such instances there is an implied understanding that their product will prove to be of adequate workmanship and possess reasonable fitness for its intended use. Moreover, those who undertake to accomplish a certain result agree by implication to supply all the means necessary to enable them to perform their bargain.

As a general rule no implied covenants are recognized in a contract in relation to any matter that is specifically covered by the written terms of the agreement itself. There is a familiar maxim, *Expresso unius est exclusio alterius,* that the expression in a contract of one or more things of a certain class implies the exclusion of all things of that class *not* expressed. Similarly, the fact that a condition is set forth in one of the clauses of a contract is regarded as excluding the idea that the same condition—this time unexpected—was intended to be declared in another clause as well.

5.7   GENERAL VERSUS SPECIFIC TERMS IN THE CONTRACT

In an agreement where there are both general and special provisions relating to the same thing, the special will prevail. That is to say, the specific language will take precedence over the more general wording. Thus, where a contract of reinsurance contained a clause in which the reinsurer agreed to submit to the jurisdiction of any court of competent jurisdiction in event of its failure "to pay an amount claimed to be due," and also an arbitration clause stating that "All disputes . . . arising out of this agreement shall be submitted . . . " to arbitration, the court, applying the specific-over-general rule, found the consent to court jurisdiction in cases of failure to pay amounts claimed to be due to prevail over the more general "all disputes" clause.[8] Where, however, both the general and special provisions may be given reasonable effect, both are to be retained.

---

[7]See discussion of conditions, Chapter 4, Section 4.1.

[8]*Transit Casualty Company in Receivership v. Certain Underwriters at Lloyd's of London,* 963 S.W. 2d. 392 (Mo. App. 1998).
   See also, U.S. v. Pielago, 135 F.3d 703 (11th Cir., 1998) where the same principle was applied to a proffer and plea agreement in a criminal case.

5.8 WRITING VERSUS PRINTING

When a contract is partly printed or typed and partly handwritten, and the printed portion cannot be reconciled with the handwritten portion, the latter will prevail. The reason behind this particular rule of construction (which is resorted to only where absolutely necessary) is that the handwritten words are the immediate language and terms chosen by the parties themselves for the expression of their meaning, and should be of greater weight than printed terminology intended for general use without reference to particular objects and aims. Similarly, and for the same reason, typewritten language ordinarily prevails over preprinted language,[9] and added language prevails over boilerplate language.[10]

5.9 WORDS VERSUS FIGURES

In the event of an inconsistency between words and figures appearing in a contract, the words will govern.

5.10 CLERICAL ERRORS

Obvious clerical errors or omissions, which are revealed by a perusal of the instrument as a whole, can be discounted in determining the intent of the parties. In fact, the court will strike out an improper word or even supply an omitted word if from the entire context it can readily and definitely ascertain what terminology was intended and should have been used.

QUESTIONS

1. *A* contracted to furnish certain bridge steelwork "complete and delivered to the site" for $30,000. He fabricated all the steel members properly and deposited them at the designated location, but he refused to erect the structure. Was he obligated to erect it? Explain.

2. Black contracted to deliver to storekeeper Brown three hogs per month for twelve months at a stated sum per pound; that was all the contract stipulated. Black delivered the first two months' allotments dressed, and Brown paid for them. Then Black brought the next three hogs butchered but not dressed and

---

[9] *Silver Dollar City, Inc. v. Kitsmiller Construction C., Inc.*, 931 S.W. 2d. 909 (Mo. App. 1996).

[10] *In re Kevin W. Emrick Farms, Inc. v. Firstar Bank Burlington, N.A.*, 201 B.R. 790 (U.S. Bankrpcy Ct. Ill. 1996); *In re Grove Rich Realty Corp.*, 200 B.R. 502 (U.S. Bankrpcy Ct. E.D. N.Y., 1996).

claimed payment based on their "live" weight. Was Brown correct in refusing to pay for more than the dressed weight?

3. Will vague terms in a contract be construed against the one who composed them? Elaborate.

4. *A* contracted to deliver "200 pairs of Firestone tires of assorted sizes" to *B* by January 1. *B* intended to send *A* a list of the desired sizes but did not make this fact clear. *A* promptly shipped 200 pairs of tires, determining on his own the several sizes and the number of pairs of each. *B* refused to pay, and *A* brought suit. Will *B* have to accept and pay for the tires in the assortment tendered?

5. In quoting her price on some concrete construction, *A* listed the proposal as follows: "500 cubic yards at ninety-eight dollars ($98.00) per cubic yard." How is *A*'s bid price to be determined?

6. Distinguish between "written" and "printed" information.

6

PERFORMANCE OR BREACH OF CONTRACT OBLIGATIONS

PERFORMANCE

6.1 PERFORMANCE AS CONDITION PRECEDENT TO RECOVERY

When the contractual duties of parties to an agreement are supposed to be performed concurrently, neither party can recover (for breach by the other) without a showing that he has himself performed, has a valid excuse for nonperformance, or has made an effective *tender of performance*—that is, has given timely notification to the other party that he is ready, willing, and able to accomplish whatever the agreement may have required of him.

When a contract has been fully performed on one side, the other party's obligation to do his part is apparent. But when a contract is yet completely executory, much depends—as far as the obligation to proceed with performance is concerned—upon the nature of the respective promises involved. When these are independent of one another, a party must undertake timely performance of his particular obligation, regardless of what has been done on the other side. Should the promise of *A* be so constituted as to depend upon performance by *B, A* is not obligated to discharge his contractual duty unless and until *B* has accomplished his part of the bargain.

6.2   SUBSTANTIAL PERFORMANCE

Generally speaking, performance of a contract must be strictly in accordance with its terms, and a party cannot be compelled to accept performance at variance with that for which he bargained. This is so even though a tendered substitute might prove more valuable in a strictly pecuniary sense.

Nevertheless, there is a trend in judicial decisions toward requiring substantial performance in lieu of absolutely literal compliance with precise contract requirements. The equitable doctrine of substantial performance stems from a desire of the courts to protect those who have faithfully and honestly endeavored to perform their contractual duties in all material respects and to preserve the rights of such persons to compensation despite some defects in the performance involved. (But, if a failure to perform in a workmanlike manner is a material breach, then substantial performance has not occurred.[1])

Substantial performance may be defined as the accomplishment of all things essential to the fulfillment of the purpose of the contract, although there may be insignificant deviations from certain contract terms or specifications which do not detract from required performance standards. While courts will enforce the rights of one who has thus substantially performed, it is equally logical that the other party, who has received something less than what he should have, is entitled to some consideration.

In determining this amount, the party receiving the defective performance will generally have to submit evidence of the value of which he was deprived, or of the cost of remedying the deficiencies.

Building contracts obviously present situations most susceptible to a claim of "substantial performance," and they have been the basis for extensive litigation. The extent of performance necessary to constitute "substantial performance" is dependent on the facts of each case and is a matter to be determined by the court. The doctrine was not intended, however, to allow a party to freely deviate from the contractual undertaking or to substitute some material, or type of operation that he prefers for that which was called for in the contract.

The Supreme Court of North Dakota's statement of substantial performance[2] with regard to building contracts is representative of the general position of courts throughout the country:

> To entitle a building contractor to recover upon a building contract, which has not been fully complied with by him, under the doctrine of substantial performance, it must appear, not only that he endeavored to perform it in good faith, but also that he has done so, except as to unimportant omissions or deviations, which are the result of mistake or inadvertence, and were not intentional, and which are susceptible of remedy, so that the other party will get substantially the building he contracted for.

---

[1]*J.P. Stravens Planning Associates, Inc. v. City of Wallace,* 928 P.2d 46 (Idaho App. 1996).

[2]*Dittmer v. Nokleberg,* 219 N.W. 2d 201, (N.D.1974). This case involved a verbal contract for construction of a dwelling, a poor idea in any case, made worse by sketchy blueprints and the lack of complete specifications or a materials list. Nevertheless, the project was 95 percent complete when the dispute arose.

While the tradition has been that where any deviation from the contract is willful or made in bad faith the offending party is not entitled to recover at all, this is not uniformly enforced. The supreme court of Connecticut held in a 1982 case[3] that an adverse conclusion on the issue of good faith is not decisive but should be weighed with other factors in determining the relative performance of the contract.

The doctrine of substantial performance also may be available in construction contract situations where the contractor is prevented from completing the work by the property owner. Thus, the failure to completely perform a contract for the erection of a prefabricated luxury home has been held not to bar recovery for the contract price less appropriate allowances where the defects resulted from the purchaser's incessant efforts at varying the prefabricated home as designed and where the contractor was eventually ordered off the premises.[4]

6.3   PARTIAL PERFORMANCE

Partial performance is performance which, while sufficient to confer appreciable benefit on the recipient, falls short of the concept of substantial, or virtually complete, performance.

Partial performance of an "entire" contract will not generally support a recovery on the contract. This is not the case, however, with respect to those contracts classified as severable (or divisible).[5] Thus, complete, or at least substantial, performance by one party is a prerequisite to his right to compel performance by the other party, unless the promises of the respective parties are independent of each other.

While the foregoing represents the general rule, there have been a number of cases that have permitted recovery of the fair value of the benefit afforded by the partial performance, particularly when the benefit is of such a nature that it cannot be returned. Naturally, a party who has performed part of his obligation and is prevented or excused by action of the other party from completing the work is entitled to compensation for material supplied and for that portion of the work done. Similarly, if completion of performance is obviated by the intervention of an act of God or is prevented by governmental authority, an equitable recovery for the part performance may be had.

---

[3]*Vincenzi v. Cerro*, 442 A. 2d 1352, (Conn. 1982), where a builder sued an owner for breach of a contract to construct a three-family home and the owner defended contending that the house was not complete and that some work was defective.
  But see, *National Constructors, Inc. v. Ellenberg*, 681 So.2d 791 (Fla. App. 1996), a case involving a home repair in the wake of hurricane Andrew, in which the traditional approach was reiterated.
[4]*Pilgrim Homes and Garages, Inc. v. Fiore*, 75 A.D. 846, 427 N.Y. Supp.2d 851 (1980).
[5]For a consideration of the difference between entire and severable contracts, see Chapter 2, Section 2.4.

6.4   **THE TIME ELEMENT**

Unless the characteristics of a given contract are such as to render of extreme and obvious importance the performance thereof at the precise time designated or unless the contract itself emphasizes the vital nature of the time element, failure of a promisor to fulfill his particular obligation within the stipulated period will not automatically discharge the other party's duty of performance. Some contracts will expressly provide that "time is of the essence of this agreement." When the parties have agreed to the inclusion of such language, a failure to perform expeditiously represents a material breach of contract. Although any unwarranted delay will normally subject the delinquent party to damages, it is possible that the delay may be waived by the promisee or otherwise excused.

Without a contract provision to the contrary, it seems that time will not be regarded as of the essence where a typical building contract is concerned. Most construction contracts call for a projected completion date and a specified amount per day as liquidated damages, to be deducted from the total price in the event the job is not finished on schedule.

Obviously, it would be unfair to penalize a contractor for delays in performance occasioned through the fault of the other party. In such circumstances, the contractor is usually held entitled to recover damages. Where, however, the contract expressly precludes the recovery of damages by the contractor for delay caused by the fault of the owner, that provision will be given full effect.

6.5   **APPROVAL OF PERFORMANCE**

The authorities are far from unanimous regarding the effect of a contract provision whereby one party agrees to perform to the satisfaction of the other. It is reasonably clear that the latter must exercise good faith in evaluating the performance; the difficult question is whether or not his decision must be reasonable.

A distinction is frequently drawn between cases where personal taste is a factor and those involving only mechanical utility or operative fitness. In contracts of the former type, where approval depends upon a matter of personal feelings it has usually been held that the party to be satisfied may, simply because of some whim, effectively reject what would appear to be a perfectly good performance.

(But, at least one court has held that even in contracts which involve matters of "fancy, taste or judgment," and in which the promisor is the sole judge of his satisfaction, the promisor must assert his dissatisfaction in good faith.[6])

Where no obvious question of personal taste is concerned, courts have disagreed on whether or not the party whom the contract says shall be satisfied has an absolute right to pass on the character of the performance. A number of cases have

---

[6]*Lock v. Warner Bros. Inc.*, 66 Cal. Rptr. 2d 921 (Cal. App. 1997), a case involving a suit between actors Sondra Locke and Clint Eastwood and a movie studio, in which Locke claimed that the studio acted with bad faith when it declined to develop her proposed film projects or hire her to direct.

held that a promise by one party to perform to the satisfaction of the other will be interpreted literally and that approval may be arbitrarily withheld as long as any dissatisfaction is bona fide and not merely feigned for purposes of avoiding payment.[7] The difficulties of proof of what constitutes good-faith dissatisfaction are obvious. On the other hand, many courts have held that a performance that would be satisfactory to a reasonable person suffices.[8] If a contract aims at a fixed mechanical result or at operative fitness—about which other persons can judge as well as could a party to the contract—and especially if the tests of performance are fully set out in the contract the tendency is to hold (in spite of the typical stipulation for satisfaction) that performance is successful if it attains the intended result. Under such circumstances, dissatisfaction professed is treated as unreal.

6.6   SATISFYING THIRD PERSONS; ARCHITECT'S CERTIFICATE

Contracts of any sort may, and construction contracts normally do, stipulate that all work is subject to the approval of some third person, typically an architect or engineer with expert knowledge in the field. When a contract requires the certificate of an architect as a prerequisite to payment, in order to get paid, the contractor must show (1) that such a certificate has indeed been issued or (2) that the designated architect has withheld his approval fraudulently or in bad faith or (3) that the owner has somehow waived his right to insist upon presentation of the architect's written acceptance of the performance.

Where the contracting parties have thus duly constituted an architect, engineer, or some other third person as sole judge of the proper performance of the contract, the ultimate approval or disapproval given is conclusive in the absence of fraud or bad faith.[9] This qualification is an important one. If the architect or engineer fails to exercise his judgment honestly or makes such gross mistakes as to imply bad faith, his decision about issuance of the certificate will not bind the parties.[10] Refusal to execute a certificate of approval is justified only when there is real and substantial failure by the builder to fulfill his contract duties. The architect or engineer is not authorized to reject work which complies with contract plans and specifications. The power of approval vested in the third person does not entitle him to exact from the builder performance beyond the prescriptions of the contract. Also, the usual certificate of satisfactory performance is binding as regards visible or readily ascertainable defects in the work completed, but not as regards latent flaws.

---

[7] *Stone Mountain Properties Limited v. Helmer*, 229 S.E. 2d 779, (Ga.1976).

[8] *Meredith Corp. v. Design and Lithography Center*, 614 P.2d 414 (1980); *Aztec Film Production, Inc. v. Prescott Valley, Inc.*, 128 Ariz. 402, 626 P.2d 132 (1981).

[9] *Laurel Race Course, Inc. v. Constr. Co., Inc.*, 274 Md. 142, 333 A.2d 319 (1975). *Lincoln Construction, Inc. v. Thomas J. Parker and Assoc.*, 617 P.2d 606 (Or. 1980). See also, *Global Const. v. Missouri Hwy. and Trans. Comm.*, 963 S.W. 2d 340 (Mo. App. 1998), finding this rule to apply even if the engineer is connected to one of the parties to the contract.

[10] *Gold v. National Savings Bank*, 641 F.2d 430, applying Tenn. law, *cert. denied*, 102 S.Ct. 116, (1981). *Savin Bros., Inc. v. State*, 62 A.D.2d 511, 405 N.Y.S.2d 516 (1978).

6.7   ARBITRATION AND/OR MEDIATION CLAUSES

Often building contracts will outline the procedure to be followed in arbitrating disputes which may arise during progress of the work or after its completion. The decision of the named arbitrators, where they act within the authority conferred by the contract, is conclusive unless these supposedly neutral persons have, in making their determination, been guilty of fraud, misconduct, or such gross mistake as would imply bad faith.[11]

When the arbitrators undertake to pass upon a matter not contemplated by the contracting parties to be within the arbitrator's province, that is, when they exceed their authority as it is prescribed in the contract, any action taken by them under such circumstances is not binding, regardless of the motives involved in the taking of that action.[12]

6.8   WAIVER OF IMPERFECTIONS IN PERFORMANCE

Frequently an owner will consent to certain deviations from contract plans and specifications and will accept incomplete or defective performance as though it were in strict compliance with the terms of the agreement. Whether or not work has been expressly or impliedly accepted and any imperfections waived are questions of fact which often prove difficult to resolve. If the defects are obvious or if circumstances are such that knowledge of the imperfections may be imputed to the owner, his acceptance of the work will obligate him to pay for it. Furthermore, unless he promptly objects to the shortcomings in the work, he will have no right to damages (for instance, an offset against the contract price) for such defects in the performance.

Where the deficiencies in a contractor's work are not such as could reasonably have been ascertained when the owner took possession of the structure and made payment under terms of the contract, the latter is clearly entitled to damages upon subsequent discovery of these imperfections within a reasonable time. What constitutes "a reasonable time" will vary widely with the type and size of structure involved and with other facts of the case.

Apart from latent defects, acceptance does not always act as a waiver of imperfections entitling the performing party to remuneration. In the absence of substantial performance, acceptance of work for which a contractor seeks recovery must be something beyond merely "keeping and using," where the situation provides no opportunity for the owner to return whatever has been received. For example, acceptance of a house as substantially completed has been held not to be a

---

[11]*Delta South Co., Inc. v. Louisiana and Arkansas Railway Co.,* 394 So.2d 1299 (La. 1981).
[12]See Chapter 27 for further discussion of arbitration, and Chapter 27, Section 27.14 for mediation.

waiver of claims against the contractor where a list of defects was attached to the acceptance by the owner.[13]

EXCUSES FOR DELAY OR NONPERFORMANCE

6.9   IMPOSSIBILITY

Definition and Types   The term *impossibility,* when used in connection with excuses for nonperformance of contractual obligations, refers not only to literal impossibility but also to impracticality owing to some extreme difficulty encountered.

Impossibility may be characterized as either subjective or objective. *Subjective impossibility* is due to incapacity of the party who has undertaken the performance; *objective impossibility* is that which is attributable to the nature of the thing to be done.

Subjective Impossibility   When impossibility of fulfilling a contractual commitment is due entirely to inability of the promisor himself—perhaps because of physical handicap or lack of skill—the nonperformance will not be excused.

Objective Impossibility   This type may be present at the time the contract is entered into or may occur subsequently. Where the impossibility of performance arises from circumstances in existence when the promise was made, performance is excused in the absence of evidence that the promisor intended to assume the risk of impossibility.

There is a notable lack of consensus about whether performance of an unqualified contract is excused where, by an unavoidable accident or some unforeseen contingency, it becomes impossible to accomplish what a party has promised. Some cases have taken the position that, in the absence of an express manifestation to the contrary, a contract will be regarded as subject to an implied condition that, if something necessary in connection with the promised performance goes out of existence through some act of God or other unforeseen occurrence not the fault of the promisor, nonperformance is excused. Even these liberal decisions recognize that a release from contractual obligation by reason of impossibility is necessarily subject to several qualifications. First, the impossibility involved must be bona fide and not simply a question of hardship or inconvenience. Second, the promisor seeking to be excused must not have assumed the risk of impossibility. Third, the performance will never be excused if the impossibility stems from negligence or want of diligence on the part of the promisor.

A second line of decisions has adopted a completely different approach, much less pleasing to promisors caught unaware by supervening objective impossibility. These cases have held that one who unconditionally obligates himself for a certain performance will not be excused by subsequent impossibility brought on by an act of God or other unforeseeable emergency. In other words, a positive commitment

---

| [13]*Lofton v. Don Trahan, Inc.,* 399 So.2d 818 (La. 1981).

to do something possible of accomplishment as of the time of contracting will bind the promisor despite effective interference by some superior agency over which the promisor had no control but against which interference he might have provided, through exception or reservation, in his contract. Where one of two innocent parties must sustain a loss, the law will leave the burden where the contract has left it. However, where performance is prevented by the negligent or wrongful action of the other contracting party, the promisor's nonperformance is automatically excused.

Finally, there has emerged a sort of compromise position. Cases which take this third viewpoint have excused performance when it has become impossible by an act of God (such as a great storm or an earthquake) but have refused to afford similar relief when the impossibility is occasioned by any lesser accident or unavoidable circumstance. These decisions take the position that a promisor is presumed, in the absence of an express contrary provision, to have assumed the risk of unforeseen contingencies arising during the course of the work, unless performance is rendered impossible by operation of law, by the other contracting party, or by a true act of God.

Intentions Manifested in Contract   A determination of whether an act of God or an unavoidable mishap will discharge a contract duty often depends upon an interpretation of the contract itself. Frequently, contracts are so written that it is evident a promisor intended to bind himself to do certain things (or to pay damages for nonperformance thereof) notwithstanding the possibility, or even the likelihood, that the promised performance might subsequently become impossible. There is no doubt that a person may contract to do the impossible as well as the difficult and be liable for failure to perform.

On the other hand, many contracts provide that such things as fire, war, accident, or "other causes beyond the control" of the promisor will obviate the necessity for performance. Where such a provision is not present, courts are likely to answer a promisor's plea of impossibility or extreme impracticality with the assertion that emergency situations could have been provided for by appropriate stipulation in the contract.

Parties to construction contracts should insert clauses designed to impose upon one side or the other (or perhaps to apportion in some desired fashion) responsibility for loss resulting from accidental destruction of the building before its completion.

Financial Recovery for Defaulting Promisor   Where, after partial performance, subsequent impossibility is deemed to excuse completion of the undertaking, the party benefitting from the partial performance will be obliged to return what has been received or to pay reasonable value for the benefit conferred unless the contract clearly provides otherwise. In this respect, cases recognizing impossibility as an excuse for noncompletion of a promised performance are true quasi-contract cases embodying the principle of unjust enrichment.

Take, for example, a contract for all the plumbing work in a building under construction; a fire destroys the structure before the plumber has finished the work or received any payment. The plumber could normally recover in *quantum merit* for the value of such work as had been done before the fire. Literally, *quantum merit* means "as much as he deserved." An action in *quantum merit* is based on a promise imputed to the defendant (in the absence of an express promise) to pay the plaintiff reasonable value for services rendered or materials furnished.

6.10 DEATH OR ILLNESS OF PARTY

Closely allied to the subject of impossibility as an excuse for nonperformance is death or disabling illness of the would-be performer. Where contracts for strictly personal services are involved, the death, insanity, or incapacitating illness of the party obligated will prevent his failure to perform from operating as a breach.[14] In other words, absent the spelling out of a contrary intention in the agreement itself, contracts of such a nature as to require for performance the continued existence of a particular person will be treated as including an implied condition that the death of such party (before any breach on his part) will excuse nonperformance of his undertaking.

The above rule is not applicable where the service involved is of such a character that it may be performed as well by someone other than the promisor or where the contract language indicates that performance by others was contemplated. In an ordinary building contract, the law takes the position that a personal representative of the contractor could perform the contractor's duties. Should death or incapacity of such contractor intervene before the job is finished, the executor or representative will be obliged to ensure that the work is completed.

6.11 DESTRUCTION OF SUBJECT MATTER

The general rule is where an obligated performance is such that accomplishment thereof absolutely depends upon the continued existence of a specific thing, the contract must be regarded as implying that, should the aforementioned thing become unavailable (before time for performance and without fault of the promisor), the duty in question will be discharged. This rule assumes, of course, that the promisor has not expressly agreed to be responsible for the continued existence of the subject matter involved. For instance, if a contractor undertakes to repair or remodel an existing building, the agreement is deemed to carry with it an implied condition that destruction of the building before the work can be done will discharge the contractor's duty, as long as he is not to blame for the mishap.[15]

The terms of a contract may, of course, foreclose any doubt by stipulating that a promisor is bound by his undertaking notwithstanding the untimely destruction of the subject matter through some unavoidable accident. It is not particularly

---

[14]The involuntary dissolution by governmental authority of a corporate promisor presents a similar situation.

[15]*Fowler v. Insurance Co. of North America*, 155 Ga. App. 439, 270 S.E.2d 845 (1980). *See also, LeRoy v. Sayers*, 635 N.Y.S.2d 217 (N.Y. App. Div. 1995), in which the court found a sufficient issue of fact to bar summary judgment when a summer rental house in the Hamptons was damaged by fire, repaired, and the tenant repudiated the lease claiming severe allergies to the smoke and the new paint.

unusual to find a provision, for example, making a contractor responsible for repairing or re-erecting the building under construction at his own expense should fire, storm, or other named causes of damage intervene before completion.

6.12   **H**ardship or **I**nconvenience

In its normal connotation, *hardship,* or *severe inconvenience,* will not provide release from performance. A party may contract to do a difficult piece of work, and the fact that the undertaking proves more burdensome than anticipated will not make the contract invalid or relieve the promisor of his obligation. If he wishes to be relieved of the necessity of performing should various contingencies arise, a contractor should assume only a qualified duty, expressly exempting himself from responsibility in certain events.

Almost any contract involves a measure of risk, and in many instances unforeseen difficulties or expense will result in a considerable loss for one party and perhaps for both. A contractor submitting a bid on a construction job has to protect himself against, among other things, possible adverse changes in the cost of labor and materials. If he underestimates these items and unfavorable circumstances arise, he must nevertheless perform his obligation according to its terms and absorb any resultant loss. Even if the promised performance is found to be extremely burdensome to one party or the other, the function of the courts is not to make the contract more equitable but to enforce it as it stands.

Excavation contracts typify agreements whose breach the promisor attempts to justify on the grounds of hardship.[16] Often the contractor runs into solid rock where gravel or sand was expected, but this occurrence will not excuse failure to perform.

While not serving as an excuse for nonperformance, severe difficulties that are unforeseen by the parties at the time of contracting and that impose upon one an additional burden not contemplated by either may support a promise of extra compensation made in order to ensure completion of the contract. Thus, courts have usually held that such a promise is adequately supported by consideration and will therefore be enforceable. Likewise, where one party extends time for performance by the other in view of hardship conditions unanticipated by either party, the promise of extra time is generally regarded as supported by consideration.

6.13   **S**trike and **L**abor **T**rouble

Unless a contract clearly provides otherwise, delay or nonperformance is not excused because progress has been impeded by strikes or labor trouble. These are considered part of a contractor's calculated risk, and his means of protection is to

[16]*McKee v. City of Atlanta,* 414 F.Supp. 957 (N.D.Ga. 1976).

insert in the contract a stipulation relieving him from the obligation of timely performance if a strike should occur. Agreements that do not contain clauses of this type are not construed as if they did.

6.14   SUPERVENING ILLEGALITY

Apart from the infrequent instance where there is a contract provision to the contrary, an agreement is normally regarded as carrying with it the implied condition that a promisor's duty will be discharged if, through no fault of his, performance is prevented or prohibited by statutory enactment subsequent to the date of the contract. In other words, frustration of contract by governmental action is a good defense to a claim for breach, and nonperformance will create no right to damages when performance was rendered impossible by a change in the law. As a practical matter, supervening illegality has to be treated by the courts as a complete excuse for nonperformance of affected contractual obligations, because to hold parties as bound to anticipate future legislation would be most unrealistic.

Denial of a necessary license or permit will not discharge a contractor's obligation even though performance is illegal without such governmental permission. It is presumed that the contractor was aware of the necessity for the permit and had assumed the risk of obtaining it.

6.15   FRUSTRATION OF OBJECT

Where parties contract with obvious reference to some activity governed by outsiders and that activity fails to develop as anticipated by the contracting parties, nonperformance of their respective duties may be excused. To effect a discharge, the activity must have been so thoroughly the basis of the contract that both parties agree that without it their entire contract was meaningless.

6.16   WAIVER BY OTHER PARTY

It is well established that strict performance of a contract duty may be dispensed with, or waived, by the other party. Sometimes the waiver, which may be conditional in nature, amounts to an outright dispensation of any performance whatever of the obligation involved, but more often it takes the form of acceptance of performance that differs materially from that called for by the contract. *Waiver* requires both knowledge and intention, and is the voluntary surrender of a right. A waiver must be manifested is some definite fashion, though meaningful conduct will be as acceptable as an oral or written declaration.

6.17   MATERIAL ALTERATION OR FRAUD BY OTHER PARTY

In the event one of the contracting parties, without consent of the other, substantially changes the terms of a written agreement, the other party at his option may regard the contract as terminated and his duties as extinguished. Fraud by the party otherwise entitled to performance will excuse the other party's failure to perform.

6.18   REPUDIATION OR BREACH BY OTHER PARTY

Where contractual promises have been exchanged, a material breach on the part of one party will, unless occasioned by conduct of the adverse party, clearly justify the other's refusal to perform and will entitle the latter party to any provable damages resulting from that breach. If one party is unable or unwilling to perform his part of the contract such failure will discharge the obligation of the other party. The breach must be substantial if it is to result in excusing subsequent nonperformance by the injured party. An "immaterial" breach will not terminate the arrangement, and the adversely affected person must fulfill his promise, though he retains the right to recover for any loss which the partial breach occasions. The standards of materiality vary widely, and it is often a close question whether a given breach will justify the other party in treating the contract as terminated.

Prospective failure of consideration is as effective as actual failure in excusing the injured person from performing. Thus, where one party to an executory agreement repudiates his own contractual obligations, the other party, upon being apprised of this, will no longer be obliged to render whatever performance he had promised. While outright repudiation obviates the necessity of performance (or tender thereof) by the other party, the repudiation must be definite and must go to the essence of the contract. Moreover, the repudiator may nullify the effect of his statement by a timely retraction before the other person has accepted the refusal as final and has acted in reliance thereon.

In the event of repudiation before performance by the other party is complete, such other party cannot, by continuing to perform regardless, enhance the measure of damages that the breach has entitled him to recover.

6.19   PREVENTION BY OTHER PARTY

Every contract contains an implied covenant by each party not to hinder performance of the other: therefore, where wrongful conduct of one party has prevented performance by the other, the latter's duty is discharged. Moreover, the wrongdoer has by inference committed an actionable breach of contract and will find himself liable in damages. The general rule is that suit to recover these damages may be instituted even before arrival of the time fixed for performance by the guilty party of his own contract duties.

It follows that a building contractor who is delayed or stymied completely by the owner (or by an architect or engineer acting on the job for the owner) cannot be held responsible for failure to complete the work on time, or for outright nonperformance, as the case may be.

Similarly, where one party has by act or word unequivocally indicated his unwillingness to accept the obligated performance of the other party if and when tendered, the latter will be excused from performing. The party who is ready and willing to satisfy his contractual obligation cannot force the adverse party to accept performance. Therefore, his inability to complete his undertaking is directly traceable to conduct of the other party and is excusable.

6.20   FAILURE OF CONDITION

The terms of a contract may make it apparent that a particular duty of performance is conditioned upon the occurrence, perhaps at a stated time and place, of a given event. Failure of such a condition would, of course, relieve the promisor of the necessity of performing that particular duty.

THE NATURE OF BREACH

6.21   DEFINITION AND FORMS OF BREACH

An actionable *breach of contract* occurs when a promisor, without sufficient excuse or justification, fails to perform in accordance with the terms of his agreement.

While failure to perform an obligation in whole or in part is the most common form of breach, there are several other ways in which a contract may be broken: A party (1) may renounce his duties thereunder or (2) may by his own act make it impossible that he should fulfill them or (3) may prevent or seriously hinder the other party's performance.

6.22   TOTAL BREACH; PARTIAL BREACH

Although every breach of a contractual obligation confers upon the injured party a right of action, it does not follow that every breach will discharge the latter from accomplishing whatever he has committed himself to do under the contract. The agreement may have been broken wholly or only in part. If the breach is merely *partial*, it may or may not be of sufficient importance to terminate the reciprocal duty of the injured party. Where one party is guilty of *total* breach (or of partial breach which, in the particular circumstances, is material in its scope), the other person may cease performance on his part and obtain a judgment for damages as well.

6.23   ANTICIPATORY BREACH

If a party announces, before his performance is due, his definite unwillingness or inability to fulfill the contract, he thereby admits he is guilty of breach and relieves the other party from further obligation, meanwhile affording the latter an immediate right to sue for damages. The repudiation must be positive and unequivocal; a mere threat to abandon the contract will not suffice. A true *anticipatory breach* requires that the repudiation predate the time fixed in the contract for performance by the renouncing party.

Any proceedings culminating in a bankruptcy adjudication are the equivalent of anticipatory breach, apparently on the theory that every contract carries an implied condition to the effect that a promisor will not allow himself (through insolvency, for example) to reach such a condition that he is unable to perform as scheduled.

6.24   VOLUNTARY DISABILITY AS BREACH

It is well settled that a person cannot avoid liability for nonperformance of an obligation simply by so maneuvering as to place performance beyond his power. Put another way, a party who deliberately incapacitates himself or renders impossible the proper performance of his contract duties has broken his agreement and is liable in damages.

An old English case[17] illustrates this point. Franklyn promised to assign to Lovelock all his interest in a certain lease within seven years from the date of the promise. But before the end of the seven years Franklyn assigned his whole interest to a third person. In the course of holding that Lovelock need not wait until the end of seven years to bring suit, the court had these comments:

> The plaintiff has a right to say to the defendant, You have placed yourself in a situation in which you cannot perform what you have promised; you promised to be ready during the period of seven years, and during that period I may at any time tender you the money and call for an assignment, and expect that you should keep yourself ready; but if I now were to tender you the money, you would not be ready; that is a breach of the contract.

---

[17]*Lovelock v. Franklyn*, 8 Q.B. 371 (1846).

6.25   PREVENTION AS BREACH

As mentioned previously, interference by one party rendering performance by the other party impossible will excuse the resulting nonperformance of the innocent party. Such tactics also constitute a breach of contract on the part of the obstructionist and provide the innocent party with a right of action. Thus, where owner without justification prevents performance by contractor, the latter's duty is discharged, and the owner is liable for breach of contract.

WAIVER OF BREACH

6.26   DEFINITION; ALTERNATIVES FOR INNOCENT PARTY

Waiver is voluntary abandonment of a known right, and, when the term is employed in connection with breach of contract, it means the giving up of a right to treat the agreement as terminated by reason of the other party's breach of a duty thereunder. Such right is deemed to have been waived when the injured party continues to treat the contract as an existing obligation, as by expressing willingness to accept further performance by the wrongdoer (or by actually insisting upon that performance), notwithstanding the breach.

When a particular obligation has been broken in the course of performance of the contract, the injured party is presented with several alternatives. He may elect to treat the entire contract as discharged outright because of the default, or he may waive the breach and continue to carry out the agreement according to its provisions. Such a waiver does not necessarily preclude the injured party from recovering for any damages occasioned by the partial breach. Acts evidencing an intent to adopt the waiver alternative will operate to deprive the innocent party of any excuse for subsequent failure of performance on his own part. If the breaching party has been induced to carry on with performance or otherwise to alter his position in reliance upon the continued recognition of the contract by the innocent party, the latter cannot subsequently switch signals and assert that the contract was indeed discharged in the first place.

6.27   ELEMENTS OF WAIVER

Courts are careful whenever a claim of waiver arises, since abandonment of a right to insist on performance strictly in line with the contract amounts in a sense to modification of the agreement. To render an alleged waiver binding there must be present something in the nature of consideration or an element of estoppel. Moreover, the party electing to waive must have knowledge of all essential facts surrounding the breach. An Illinois case[18] highlights these essentials to a valid waiver. In recognizing that the acceptance of the work in question was not expected or intended to relieve the defendant from its duty, either to complete the work pursuant to the contract or to repair defects, the court noted:

> A waiver is an intentional relinquishment of a known right and acceptance of a structure does not waive proper performance where the person neither knows nor has reason to know of its defective nature.

Waiver may be accomplished by express words or by conduct that is inconsistent with an intention to abrogate for breach, but mere silence will not amount to waiver where one is not bound to speak. Neither will acknowledgment of project delays by a prime contractor waive a defense based on untimely notice of the delays.[19] Whether there has indeed been a bona fide waiver in a given set of circumstances often presents a close question of fact. For example, in one case[20] a subcontract for installing panes of glass in a building obligated the subcontractor to clean the glass before final inspection. Upon his refusal to do so, it became necessary for the contractor himself to perform the work, since the cleaning was a prerequisite to final approval of the entire construction project by the architect and engineer. Under the circumstances, it was held that the general contractor's conduct did not present a waiver of the duty on the subcontractor.[21]

6.28   MUTUAL DESIRE TO IGNORE REPUDIATION

As previously noted, when one party renounces his contract and refuses to perform, the other party acquires an immediate right to abandon the agreement and to secure legal redress for the harm done him. The innocent party is not entitled to ignore the fact of renunciation and enhance his damages by continuing to perform. However, where there is mutual consent to do so, the respective parties may forget all about the repudiation and may resume fulfillment of the contract. Also, the repudiation may be nullified by timely withdrawal of the "renouncing" declaration before the other party has become aware of the fact of repudiation and changed his position accordingly.

---

[18]*Intaglio Service Corp. v. J.C. Williams and Co., Inc.*, 95 Ill. App.3d 708, 420 N.E. 2d 634 (1981).
[19]*Associated Mechanical Contractors, Inc. v. Martin K. Eby Construction Co., Inc.*, 983 F.Supp 1121 (1997, applying Ga. Law).
[20]*Pittsburgh Plate Glass Co. v. American Surety Co. of New York*, 66 Ga. App. 805, 19 S.E.2d 357 (1942).
[21]Other cases where a continuation of work was held not to be a waiver are Bd. of Regents, *Univ. of Tex. v. S. & G. Constr. Co.*, 529 S.W.2d 90 (Tex. App. 1975); and *John Kubinski & Sons, Inc. v. Dockside Development Corp.*, 339 N.E.2d 529 (Ill. 1975).

REMEDIES FOR BREACH

6.29   GENERAL CONSIDERATIONS

It is axiomatic that persons who violate their agreements to the detriment of others with whom they contract must answer in some appropriate way for the injury done. The contract may, and quite commonly does, provide for the precise consequences that shall follow upon breach. Where the parties have stipulated in advance for a particular remedy, that one will be treated by the courts as the exclusive means of redress.

Apart from express contract provisions that might readily alter the situation, breach normally presents the injured party with a choice of several possible alternatives. His principal option lies between compensatory damages and restitution. Under certain circumstances, a decree of specific performance or an injunction will be an available recourse.

The general rule is that material breach of contract frees the injured party from any further duty to render the performance required of him by the contract. At the same time, he is privileged to seek redress for the wrong done him, and usually this recovery will take the form of an action for money damages, measured, roughly, by the value of the performance he had expected to receive under the terms of the contract. If, on the other hand, he has himself partly performed at the time breach occurs, he may decide to sue for the reasonable value of what he has supplied or accomplished. If he chooses this remedy of restitution and a recovery in quantum merit (reasonable value), courts usually say he has "rescinded" the contract.

While the injured party generally has such an election of remedies at his disposal, it must be remembered that, once he has manifested his choice and the other party has taken any action in reliance upon that manifestation, the choice is binding and will bar recourse to any other alternative.

6.30   DAMAGES

Nominal Damages   A breach of contract invariably creates a right of action in the aggrieved party. Even in those instances where no substantial harm has been done or where no loss whatever is traceable to the breach, and even in those very rare circumstances where the innocent party is actually benefited by the breach, the defaulting party is subject of a judgment for *nominal damages*. This will mean a very small sum fixed by the court more in recognition of the default in performance than in compensation for any bona fide loss.

Compensatory Damages   The most common remedy for breach of a valid contract is the recovery of a sum of money awarded as *compensatory damages*. Since damages for breach are intended as compensation, and not as punishment for wrongdoing, the injured party generally recovers nothing in the nature of punitive or exemplary damages, even if the contract itself prescribes such a consequence for breach.

In determining the proper amount of such damages, the court attempts to place the innocent party in the position he would have occupied had the contract been performed according to its terms, including recompense for losses suffered and gains prevented in consequence of the default. As it has been expressed in a number of decisions,[22]

> One who fails to perform his contract is justly bound to make good all damages that accrue naturally from the breach; and the other party is entitled to be put in as good a position pecuniarily as he would have been by performance of the contract.

However, recovery is not allowed for purely speculative damages or for elements of damage that were not within the contemplation of the respective parties at the time their agreement was signed. The injured party is not entitled to *better* his position from what it would have been had no default occurred. While a builder has no general license to install what, in his judgment, is just as good, where the cost of replacement would be great but the difference in value would be either nominal or nothing, the latter is held to be the proper measure.[23] But, in one case,[24] a homeowner sued a general contractor for a failure to discover that the roof and an overhead dormer did not comply with the architect's drawings, resulting in the roof being centered over the library rather than the living room. Finding that the aesthetic appearance of the custom-built residence was of utmost importance to the owner, the court held the appropriate measure of damages to be the amount necessary to replace the defective construction, rather than the diminution in the value of the house.

Expenses incurred by a party in preparation for performance of a contract before its abandonment by the other party are proper elements of damage occasioned by the breach. If there remain on hand at the time of breach materials that the builder has purchased for the particular job but that can be used by him elsewhere, the value of such supplies should be deducted from the builder's total expense outlay when damages are being measured.

If the contractor is the defaulting party the owner may generally recover the cost of having the job completed. Should the contractor finish the job but it develops that the work is defective, the owner may seek reimbursement of whatever it costs him to make the work conform to the contract.

Duty to Mitigate Damages   A party in default on a contract has the right to expect that the opposite party will do everything reasonably possible to minimize damages, and the latter cannot recover that portion of the loss that he could have avoided once the breach became known to him. For example, the measure of damages for default on a contract to deliver goods is ordinarily the difference between the contract price of goods and the market price at the time when delivery should have been effected. If, however, the injured party might have reduced his loss (as, perhaps, by an immediate purchase at a low price of goods to replace those not

---

[22]See, for example, *Maraldo Asphalt Paving Inc. v. Harry D. Osgood Co., Inc.*, 53 Mich. App. 324, 220 N.W.2d 50 (1974); and *Martin v. Phillips*, 122 N.H. 34, 440 A.2d 1124 (1982).
[23]*Jacob & Young, Inc. v. Kent*, 129 N.E. 889 (N.Y., 1921).
[24]*Lyon v. Belosky Construction, Inc.*, 669 N.Y.S. 2d 400 (App. Div. 1998).

delivered), his failure to do so may be taken in account in assessing his recoverable damages. What constitutes a reasonable effort at mitigation is a question of fact in each case.

Liquidated Damages Contracts in general, and building and construction contracts in particular, often stipulate that a certain sum per day shall be paid by way of *liquidated damages* in the event completion of the work is not accomplished on schedule. Although courts as a rule favor liquidated damages, they are opposed to penalties; therefore, such clauses will not be upheld if the sum provided for greatly exceeds the extent of injury that could reasonably be anticipated and the effect of the provision is compensation for breach rather than exaction of a penalty from the contract breaker.[25] The test is whether the amount fixed bears some reasonable relation to the damages likely to result from breach of the contract.

A Washington court of appeal[26] explained its position as follows:

> A liquidated damage clause must meet certain pre-conditions. The amount of damages stipulated must be a reasonable estimation of compensation for the damages caused by the contractual breach. The scope of the harm caused by the breach must be difficult of accurate estimation. A liquidated damage clause becomes a penalty when a sum is inserted in a contract, not as compensation for its breach, but rather as a punishment for default, or by way of security for actual damages which may be sustained by reason of non-performance. . . . Its essence is a payment of money as *in terrorem* of the offending party, while the essence of liquidated damages is a genuine covenanted pre-estimate of damages.

The *Brower* case is of interest because the contract involved, including the liquidated damages clause, was prepared by the owner's architect. In the ensuing litigation the owner sought to receive compensatory damages for delay in completion in excess of those stipulated for liquidated damages. Although these damages were actually sustained and provable, the court limited recoverable damages to those stipulated in the contract.[27] Finding that the owner was bound by the architect's estimate even though it appeared that the architect did not have complete knowledge as to the damages to be anticipated when the contract was prepared, the court noted that the owner was bound by his agent's (architect's) knowledge and that anticipated damages "looks to the time of contracting, not to some later time."

---

[25]*For example,* see *LeRoy v. Sayers,* 635 N.Y.S. 2d 217 (App. Div. 1995), in which a tenant rented a summer house in East Hampton from July 1, 1992, until September 8, 1992, for $135,000, and the lease set as liquidated damages the $50,000 that was paid at the lease signing. The house then suffered over $740,000 damage in a fire and was repaired, but the tenant, complaining of smoke and paint odors, refused to move in or pay the balance. Despite the difficulty of rerenting in midseason, the court found the clause to be a penalty and unenforceable.

[26]*Brower Co. v. Garrison,* 468 P.2d 469 (1970).

[27]Also applying this general principle is *International Fidelity Ins. Co. v. Country of Chautangua,* 667 N.Y.S. 2d 172 (App. Div. 1997).

6.31   RESTITUTION

Where the aggrieved party in a breach situation does not desire compensatory damages but wants to recover whatever he may have expected in the process of satisfying his own contractual obligations, he seeks the remedy of *restitution.* In a sense, he unilaterally "rescinds" the agreement at the point of breach and demands the return of money he has paid thereunder or the value of goods he has delivered or of such work as he has done. The usual restitution case does not involve the return by the party in breach of a specific item but rather payment of the reasonable value of whatever consideration he has received under the contract up to the time of the default.

In theory, restitution works both ways, and the aggrieved party must himself return or account for any benefits he received before the breach occurred. This requirement is not enforced with unvarying strictness, however, and is presumably not applied so as to make it a shield for wrongdoing. Such restoration by the injured party as is "reasonably possible" and such as "the merits of the case demand" will suffice. For instance, it has been held that the injured party seeking the remedy of restitution need not offer restoration for his own part where what he has received consists solely of money, the amount of which he will be entitled to in any event.

6.32   SPECIFIC PERFORMANCE

Under certain rather well-defined circumstances, courts will enforce by a *specific-performance decree* a contract promise to do a given thing, and by an *injunction* a promise to forbear. In either instance, specific performance or injunction, the promisor is being required to live up to the bargain he has made. This particular form of redress is not available in all breach situations; some of the more significant limitations follow.

Where damages provide an adequate remedy, specific performance will not be granted. In personal property cases, compensating damages will normally suffice. However, there have been a number of instances where specific performance was decreed on the ground that unique chattels of uncertain value were involved, such as a liquor license.[28] Agreements for the sale of interests in real property, on the other hand, are very commonly enforced by specific performance decrees. A specified piece of land is impossible of precise duplication, and money damages in any amount for breach of a contract to sell that particular plot are (in theory, at least) inadequate.

The remedy of specific performance is largely discretionary with the court before which it is sought. Specific performance is seldom decreed unless the contract at issue is fair and just and unless its terms are definite and certain. The court

---

[28]*Tomb v. Lavalle,* 298 Pa. Super. 75, 444 A.2d 666 (1981).

must be in a position to determine with reasonable assurance the contractual obligations of which enforcement is sought and the conditions under which performance is supposed to be rendered. It is not necessary that both parties have identical remedies available in the event of breach; consequently, specific performance may be decreed at the instance of one party even though similar redress would not have been open to the other party had he been the injured one. Suppose that Green agrees to serve as Brown's gardener for the summer in return for Brown's promise to transfer a specified piece of real estate. Green fully performs her part of the contract, but Brown defaults completely. Under the foregoing circumstances, Green would be entitled to specific performance despite the fact that in no event could Brown have secured a similar decree (since obligations to render personal service will not be specifically enforced). Moreover, it has been held that specific enforcement of a contractual undertaking is not precluded by the existence of a liquidated-damages provision.

Since courts have discretion in dealing with petitions for specific performance, they are inclined to exercise their prerogative and refuse to grant the requested relief if it appears that the performance entailed is such that extensive and burdensome supervision would be needed for effective enforcement. If, for example, a court endeavored to enforce an agreement for the supply of goods by installment over a long period of time, this would involve the court in a task of supervision that it could not conveniently undertake. Partly for this same reason of undue supervisory difficulty and partly because their specific enforcement would amount to involuntary servitude, promises to render personal services are not handled by affirmative orders of specific performance. Within limits, however, negative promises respecting personal services are enforceable by injunction; that is, promises not to do the work in question for someone other than the promisee. Thus, a great musician might promise his services to a particular orchestra and at the same time covenant that he would not perform with any other musical organization.

In general, construction contracts are not enforced by specific performance decrees. There are various reasons for this, but the principal one seems to be that damages afford an adequate remedy, regardless of whether the owner or the builder is the party in breach. Also superintending performance of a construction contract would impose upon the court an extremely difficult, if not impossible, burden.

QUESTIONS

1. What is a tender of performance?
2. Illustrate the difference between specific performance and substantial performance.
3. A plumbing contract called for certain "Crane" fixtures, but the contractor installed "standard" fixtures, which she claimed were equivalent to the stipulated type. The owner claimed a deduction because of the substitution. Was he justified in so doing?

4. Lewis contracted with the government to dredge 2 million cubic yards of silt from the ship channel in New Haven Harbor. After excavating 1.5 million cubic yards, he quit the job. Should he be paid anything for partial performance?

5. A particular contract stated that "time is of the essence." What legal significance is there in the quoted wording?

6. Illustrate a contract in which personal taste would determine what constitutes satisfactory performance.

7. What interpretation and effect should be given to a clause stating that all work is to secure the approval of the engineer?

8. *B* ordered a 5-ton truck "on approval" from *C*. When the truck was delivered, *B* objected to the color of the paint and refused to accept the vehicle. Did *B* have a right of refusal?

9. Who has the right to waive imperfections in the quality of performance? What does "waiver" mean?

10. Impossibility may be an effective excuse for nonperformance; inconvenience is not. Explain.

11. Distinguish between subjective and objective impossibility of performance.

12. What is meant by "act of God?" What effect may such an occurrence have upon a contract? Under what conditions may it fail to relieve the contractor of the obligation to perform?

13. If an act of God makes completion of a contract impossible after part of the work has been done, what arrangements should perhaps be made regarding compensation to the contractor?

14. *X* contracted to do personally certain engineering work for *Y* for the sum of $2,000. When the job was 25 percent completed, *X* fell seriously ill. Can *X* avoid her contract? Can she have someone else finish the work?

15. Farmer Clark contracted with Pillsbury to furnish 10,000 bushels of wheat to the latter on September 1. Lack of rain caused a poor crop and Clark was able to raise only 7,000 bushels. Can Pillsbury collect damages from Clark for the shortage of 3,000 bushels? Explain.

16. Douglas contracted to drive a well for Tucker for the sum of $500 and to furnish potable water at a flow of 5 gallons per minute. After spending $800 on the work, Douglas was unsuccessful and quit the job. What payment, if any, is Tucker obligated to make?

17. Explain what is meant by "breach of contract."

18. Name several ways in which a contract may be breached.

19. Can one part of a severable contract be breached without breaching the whole contract? Explain.

20. Define each of the following types of damages: (a) nominal, (b) compensatory, (c) punitive, (d) liquidated.

21. What is meant by "restitution"? Under what contract circumstances does this concept enter the picture?

22. How does interference on the part of the owner affect the question of liquidated damages where the contractor does not finish the job on time because of such interference?

23. What is meant by a "latent defect" in speaking of a contracting party's performance?

24. *B* was constructing a shopping center for *C*. In the midst of the job, *C* was threatened with bankruptcy. Is *B* obliged to continue with his undertaking?

25. Fulton contracted to furnish Mortimer 50 bushels of apples per week during October and November. She did so the first week of October, then failed the following week. Mortimer then contracted with Evans for the needed apples to December 1, notifying Fulton that the latter had broken her contract. Fulton stated that she was sick in bed during the second week of October, that this circumstance excused her failure, and that her contract with Mortimer remained in full force and effect. What are the rights of the parties?

7

TERMINATION OF CONTRACTS

IN GENERAL

7.1 MEANS OF DISCHARGE

Contracts may be terminated in a variety of ways. Full and satisfactory performance by both sides is the usual mode. The second most common way of termination is breach.

A third means of contract termination is mutual agreement, the same process that created the relationship in the first place. Fourth, a contract may be terminated because it has become impossible of fulfillment, under circumstances that completely excuse the respective parties from their obligations and duties. Finally, discharge of the contract may be effected through operation of law as, for example, in a bankruptcy. Contracts "voidable" by reason of fraud, infancy, and the like are discharged through "operation of law" when the party entitled to do so exercises the privilege of terminating the contractual relationship.

TERMINATION THROUGH PERFORMANCE OR EFFECTIVE TENDER

7.2 TYPE OF PERFORMANCE REQUIRED

In order to bring about discharge of the contract in its entirety, the performance must be complete on both sides and in accord with the terms and conditions of the agreement. Obviously, if the contract involved is a *unilateral* one, wherein one party makes a promise in exchange for an executed consideration, fulfillment by the promisor will bring the contract to an end because that was the only obligation outstanding. On the other hand, parties to *bilateral* contracts have exchanged executory consideration—a promise for a promise—and each must do that which is required before the contract can be said to be terminated. Performance by one party only will discharge that particular obligation, but the contractual duty of the other party is still due, and the contract remains in force.

Tender of performance will be as effective as actual performance when performance is prevented by the other party. That is, an unconditional offer to discharge one's contractual duty in accordance with its precise definition in the agreement plus the actual present ability to carry out such offer will, if rejected, relieve the party tendering of any further obligation.

TERMINATION THROUGH BREACH

7.3   REFINEMENTS OF TERMINOLOGY

Material breach can be a means of contract termination. Agreements which have thus been broken are variously spoken of as *abrogated, avoided, terminated,* or *discharged.* These words are used interchangeably and normally are intended to convey the same thought.

7.4   MATERIAL BREACH

Any material default in performance discharges the other party and affords that party the right to treat the contract as at an end.[1] In order for the default, or breach, to justify termination of the contract, it must be substantial, and not minor or technical. Courts use the word "material" as a term of art to designate breach of this magnitude. The determination of whether a breach is "material" is dependent on the facts of an individual case, and may be viewed by courts differently. However, one court decision[2] enumerates the factors that courts will generally use in making this determination. The pertinent part of the decision reads:

> [T]he factors to be considered include the extent to which the injured party will obtain the substantial benefit which he reasonably anticipated, the extent to which the injured party may be adequately compensated in damages, the extent of partial performance, the relative hardship on the parties, and the bad faith of the breaching party.

The court also noted that when both parties have continued substantial performance, any breach is less than material.

---

[1] A material breach of one aspect of a contract has been held to be a material breach of the whole contract. *U.S. v. First Dakota National Bank,* 137 F.3d 1007 (8th Cir. 1998, applying S.D. law). See also, *Cooper v. Brough of Wenonah,* 977 F.Supp. 305 (D.N.J. 1997) where the court said that under New Jersey law, a material breach that concerns the essence of the contract may justify recission.

[2] *Cleveland-Cliffs Iron v. Chicago & N.W. Transport. Co.,* 581 F Supp. 1144, (D. Mich. 1984).

Another 1984 decision[3] provides an informative illustration of "material breach." In this case, suit was brought by a prime contractor on a Corps of Engineers project against a dredging subcontractor for breach of subcontract. In its countersuit, the subcontractor alleged, among other things, defective specifications and differing site conditions, amounting to breach of contract. The contract had specifically addressed those issues in provisions that allowed for equitable adjustments in the price to reflect the increased cost as a result of defective specifications (the specifications had been supplied by the Corps of Engineers) or different site conditions from those ordinarily encountered in such work, provided the subcontractor give notice in writing of the problems.

Extensive shoaling problems were encountered in the dredging operation, and the subcontractor notified the appropriate parties and requested additional payment. When agreement was not reached between the subcontractor and the Corps as to additional payments, the prime contractor notified the subcontractor that it must settle its claims or it would not be permitted to dredge. The subcontractor refused to proceed without assurance that it would be compensated for the additional work, and was terminated by the prime contractor.

The trial court found that the specifications were inaccurate and that the Corps had prepared a design memorandum indicating the true site conditions, but it had not been furnished to the subcontractor. Due to this and the refusal to honor the subcontractor's claims for additional payment in accordance with the terms of the contract, the court held that the prime contractor had materially breached the contract, and the subcontractor's actions rescinding the contract were justified.

7.5 CANCELLATION CLAUSE IN CONTRACT

Subcontracts in connection with construction jobs typically contain language permitting the general contractor to terminate the agreements for cause upon giving some stipulated notice. In a Wisconsin case,[4] a painting subcontract read in part as follows:

> If any time during the prosecution of the work of this contract, the Subcontractor, not being hindered by causes beyond his control, fails to maintain a sufficient working force, or if it shall become evident to the Contractor that the work is not being prosecuted with proper diligence to complete said work so as not to delay the progress of the building, or if the Subcontractor shows gross carelessness or incompetency, or if the Subcontractor fails, refuses, or neglects to comply with the contract . . . [the Contractor may elect to terminate the arrangement].

---

[3] *W.F. Maganon Corp. v. Diamond Mfg. Co., Inc.*, 580 F. Supp. 1299, (D. S.C. 1984). See also, *Community Builders v. Indian Motorcycle*, 692 N.E. 2d 964, (Mass. App. 1998), where a limited partnership's failure to make timely payment of a final $50,000 owed was held to justify a termination of an agreement, which occurred just a few days after the payment became due.

[4] *Valentine et al. v. Patrick Warren Constr. Co.*, 263 Wis. 143, 56 N.W.2d 860 (1953).

During the course of the work, it became apparent to the general contractor that the painting subcontractor was not in a position to supply workers, materials, or equipment sufficient to permit satisfactory completion of the job in a reasonable time. For instance, the subcontracting firm furnished only 5 rolling scaffolds for an undertaking that required at least 12, allowed its accounts for paint to become delinquent, and failed to meet two of its own payrolls. Consequently, the general contractor wrote a letter of cancellation, indicating that, in order "not to delay progress of construction, we are forced to invoke clauses in your contract to complete your work with our own forces." The court determined that the subcontractor's breach of contract was a serious one and that the prime contractor's use of the cancellation provision was justified.

TERMINATION THROUGH AGREEMENT

7.6   MUTUAL RENUNCIATION (RESCISSION) OF THE CONTRACT

Parties to a contract may abrogate it, either wholly or in part, by their mutual consent, if the rights of third persons have not intervened. Some states have laws to this effect. By way of illustration, the Revised Codes of Montana (1997 ed., §28-2-1711) lists four situations (additional to "by consent of all the other parties") in which a party to a contract may rescind:

> (1) If the consent of the party rescinding, or of any party jointly contracting with him was given by mistake, or obtained through duress, menace, fraud, or undue influence, exercised by or with the connivance of the party as to whom he rescinds, or of any other party to the contract jointly interested with such party; (2) If, through the fault of the party as to whom he rescinds, the consideration for his obligation fails in whole or in part; (3) If such consideration becomes entirely void from any cause; (4) If such consideration, before it is rendered to him, fails in a material respect, from any cause; or (5) If all the other parties consent.

If it is the joint will[5] of the respective parties to terminate their arrangement, they may accomplish this aim even though the contract itself might contain a provision purporting to preclude its cancellation within a certain period of time or to restrict in some other fashion the right of the parties to cancel by agreement.[6] The mutual consent to terminate need not be express but may be inferred from a course of conduct of the parties that is obviously inconsistent with any intention of proceeding with the contractual relationship.[7] The question of proof is eliminated

---

[5]Absent agreement by both parties, however, a provision waiving right of recession is valid. See *Abele Tractor and Equipment Company, Inc. v. Varity Corp,* 977 F.Supp. 1252 (D.N.Y. 1997, applying New York law).

[6]*Resource Engineering Inc. v. Siler,* 500 P.2d 836 (Idaho 1972).

[7]*Orange Improvements Partnership v. Cardo, Inc.,* 984 F.Supp. 85 (D. Conn. 1997, applying Conn. law). In *San-ann Service, Inc. v. Bedingfield,* 305 So.2d 374 (Ala. 1975), the Supreme Court of Alabama noted that this rule can be given operative effect only when the conduct of the party is found to be positive and unequivocable. See also *County of Morris v. Fauver,* 707 A.2d 958 (N.J. 1998).

when the understanding of the parties is reduced to writing or expressed orally before disinterested witnesses. Normally, an agreement to end the contract will include provision for restitution, where there has been partial performance on one side or both.

Where it is an entirely executory contract (where there are mutual existing duties as yet unperformed) that is being terminated by agreement the consideration received by each party is the abandonment by the other of his rights under the contract. That is, the release of one party from the obligation to perform is adequate consideration for the corresponding release of the other. Where a contract that the parties jointly consent to cancel has been fully executed by one party, some consideration must be afforded the party who has performed if his waiver of the other party's obligated performance is to operate as a discharge.

7.7 SUBSTITUTION OF NEW CONTRACT

Closely related to termination by mutual consent is termination of an existing contract as a result of the parties making a new contract inconsistent with the former. The new agreement may or may not expressly repudiate its forerunner. The original contract will be discharged if the parties agree to such a substantial alteration in its terms as to amount to the replacement of the original contract with a new one. In a case from Missouri involving an action to recover fees allegedly due under a contract to perform architectural services regarding improvement and expansion of a docking and parking facility, the court said: "Whatever may have been the parties' original agreement, it was competent for them, before any breach of its provisions, to waive, dissolve or abandon that contract and substitute a new oral contract by conduct and imitation, as well as by express words."[8]

Reformation of an existing document may be accomplished without a substitution of contracts. *Reformation* is the correction of defects so as to conform the contract to the actual intent of the parties, when that intent was, through inadvertence, improperly expressed in the instrument as originally drawn. Among the errors that have been held reformable are obvious mistakes of computation in the proposals submitted by building contractors. Also, the parties may agree to modify an existing contract, such as to incorporate an additional provision, without drafting a new document.

7.8 RELEASE; COVENANT NOT TO SUE

A *release* is a discharge, by the party entitled, of the right of action that has become his as the result of default in a contractual promise to him. Release is differentiated from *waiver* in that the waiver usually refers to the abandonment of a

---

| [8]*Pallardy v. Link's Landing Inc.*, 536 S.W.2d 512, 515 (Mo. App. 1976).

stated right before there has been any breach of contract. The release will fully bind its maker, but in accordance with the elementary rule of contracts, only if there is proper consideration. *Conditional releases* are perfectly valid and will be effectuated according to their precise terms.

There is also such a thing as a *covenant not to sue.* Here one party promises the other that he will not, perhaps for a stipulated period of time or, less likely, forever, bring suit to enforce a given contract right.[9]

7.9   ACCORD AND SATISFACTION

The concept of *accord and satisfaction* is similar to that of substituted contract. The principal distinctions are (1) an accord and satisfaction generally starts with an actual default situation, that is, where one party is in breach and a right of action consequently accrues to the other party; (2) the *accord* itself does not ordinarily discharge the original contract right and correlative duty but simply holds these in abeyance pending *satisfaction* of such accord.

Under an accord and satisfaction, the party in default promises to render, and the party who holds the right of action agrees to accept, some performance differing from that which was originally contracted for and which might legally have been enforced. An accord and satisfaction is really a compromise and settlement by the substitution of a new contract, and the several requisites of contract formation must be present. Accordingly, the "party obligated" under the original pact must afford a proper consideration to the "party entitled" in order to support the latter's agreement to accept a different performance in lieu of his previous contract right. Basic contract principles respecting consideration apply here. Thus, where a liquidated, matured, and undisputed sum of money is due and owing under the prior agreement, there is no consideration for the contract creditor's promise to accept a lesser sum in satisfaction thereof.

In an action[10] by a contractor for a breach of contract and for foreclosure of a mechanic's lien, the court said:

> An accord and satisfaction has been defined as . . . a method of discharging a contract, or settling a cause of action arising either from a contract or a tort, by substituting for such contract or cause of action an agreement for the satisfaction thereof and the execution of such substituted agreement . . . An accord and satisfaction must be . . . accompanied by such acts or declarations as amount to a condition that if the money be accepted it is to be in full satisfaction and to be of such character that the creditor is bound so to understand such offer . . . When considering the existence of an accord and satisfaction, we should examine the following elements:

[9]For a case attempting to distinguish a release from a covenant not to sue see *Mercantile National Bank v. Founders Life Assurance Co.,* 222 S.E.2d 368 (Ga. 1976). See also, *Kobbeman v. Oleson,* 574 N.W. 2d. 633 (S.D. 1998).

[10]*Smith Constr. Co. v. Knights of Columbus Council No. 1226,* 519 P.2d 286 (N.M. 1974). See also, *In re Caldor, Inc.,* 217 Bkrtcy. 121 (Bkrtcy. S.D. N.Y. 1998).

1. Did the debtor make an offer in full satisfaction of the debt;

2. Was there an unliquidated or disputed claim which formed the basis of this offer;

3. Was this offer accompanied by acts and declarations which amounted to a condition;

4. Were those acts and declarations such that the offeree was bound to understand them; and

5. Was the offer accepted in full satisfaction of the debt.

Apart from those relatively rare situations where the parties stipulate that the accord itself operates as satisfaction, the right to enforce the original contract duty is merely *suspended* only so long as there occurs no breach of the new accord. Upon performance of the substituted agreement the previously existing duty is fully discharged. Where, however, the accord is not followed in due course by performance the injured party can sue either upon that accord or upon the no-longer-suspended original contract duty itself. Where the applicability of the doctrine of accord and satisfaction is in doubt, it will not be applied.[11]

7.10 NOVATION

In an early Washington decision,[12] the court had occasion to discuss at length the subject of novation, both as regards the several forms it may take and as regards its essential elements. It said:

> The doctrine of novation is so well understood that it hardly seems necessary to cite authorities to define it. Novation means substitution. It may be either the substitution of a new obligation for an old one between the same parties with intent to displace the old obligation with the new, or the substitution of a new debtor for the old one with intent to discharge the old debtor, or the substitution of a new creditor with intent to transfer the rights of the old creditor to the new. The second class is the ordinary case of novation, and is the case involved in the cause on trial. A novation is a new contractual relation. It is based upon a new contract by all the parties interested. It must have the necessary parties to the contract, a valid prior obligation to be displaced, a proper consideration, and a mutual agreement. If *A* owes *B* a sum of money, and *C* agrees to pay the debt of *A* to *B,* and *B* agrees to accept *C* instead of *A* as payor of the debt, and to discharge *A* from his original obligation that is a novation.

It may be seen from the foregoing quotation that substituted contract without change of parties is technically a form of novation but that the ordinary novation arrangement involves a substitution of parties.

---

[11]*Martin v. Elmwood Medical Center,* 707 So.2d 1287 (La. App. 1998).

[12]*Sutter v. Moore Investment Co.,* 70 P. 746 (Wash. 1902). See also, *Phoenix Power Partners v. Colorado Public Utilities Comm.,* 952 P.2d 359 (Colo. 1998), where the Supreme Court of Colorado said that the four requirements for novation are (1) a previous valid contract; (2) an agreement between parties to abide by a new contract; (3) a valid new contract; and (4) extinguishment of the old contract by substitution of the new one.

7.11   EXERCISE OF POWER RESERVED

It is not at all unusual to find that one of the contracting parties has expressly reserved the option of terminating the contract under certain circumstances, such as the nonfulfillment of a condition precedent or the occurrence of a stated condition subsequent, or after a stipulated period of time has elapsed.

TERMINATION THROUGH FRUSTRATION OF OBJECT OR DESTRUCTION OF SUBJECT MATTER

7.12   THEORY OF FRUSTRATION

The doctrine of *frustration* holds that, where the existence of a specified thing, condition, or state of affairs is essential to the performance of the contract, the entire agreement is dissolved when, by reason of circumstances beyond the control of either party, the subject matter is no longer available. When frustration occurs, it does not merely provide one party with a defense in an action brought by the other. It voids the contract by removing its very foundation and discharges both parties automatically. Similarly, where the purpose of a contract is completely defeated and its performance rendered impossible by a supervening event or factor that was not within the contemplation of the parties, the contract is deemed discharged. In this situation the law reads into contracts an implied stipulation designed to regulate a matter that the parties themselves would presumably have taken care of by agreement had the necessity occurred to them.

In dealing with this issue, one court[13] has said that frustration of purpose "focuses on events which materially affect a consideration received by one party for its performance. Both parties can perform but, as a result of unforeseeable events, performance by party *X* would no longer give party *Y* what induced him to make the bargain in the first place. Thus frustrated, *Y* may rescind the contract."

QUESTIONS

1. In what ways may a contract be terminated?

2. *A* contracted to paint *B*'s house for $600. *A* tried twice to make arrangements to start the job, but *B* kept stalling. Then *A* secured another job, and when *B* finally wanted her to start painting, *A* refused, saying that she was already "tied up." Is *A*'s position defensible?

---

[13]*U.S. v. General Douglas MacArthur Senior Village, Inc.,* 508 F.2d 377, 381 (2d Cir. 1974).

3. What are the differences among the following terms as used in referring to a contract: *(a)* abrogated, *(b)* avoided, *(c)* terminated, *(d)* discharged, *(e)* rescinded?

4. Under what circumstances may the right to cancel a contract unilaterally be properly reserved to the owner?

5. Cox had contracted to build an addition to Bollard's factory. A sudden flood virtually destroyed the factory before any work was started. What can Bollard do about the commitment?

6. *C* agreed to purchase from *D* 100 tons of steel sheet piling. Later on, *C* found some secondhand piling that he could buy more cheaply. What can *C* do about the situation?

7. In the preceding case, would *D* have the right to let *C* substitute a contract to purchase 100 tons of reinforcing bars from *D*?

8. *X* made a contract with *Y* for the benefit of a third party, *Z*. Under what conditions can either of the contracting parties release the other?

9. As the term is used in contractual relations, what is the meaning of "accord and satisfaction"?

10. What are the essential elements of "novation"?

11. What is the meaning of "rescission" of a contract?

12. Under what conditions might a contractor have the right to cancel a contract with a subcontractor?

13. Evans contracted to buy 10 acres of Olsen's land for a factory site. Thereafter, the zoning board rezoned the area that included the property site into a "commercial," or business, section. Is Evans nevertheless obliged to go through with the purchase or answer in damages?

14. Brown contracted to build a house for Gray for $32,000, starting May 10. On May 9, Brown brought his equipment for excavating the basement. Gray told him that she had decided to postpone his project for one year, and that Brown should build the house then at the same price. Is Brown under any legal obligation so to do?

15. Abbott contracted to deliver to Olcott 2,000 cubic yards of fill for grading a low area in the latter's property. In return therefor, Olcott was to deliver to Abbott 25 tons of 3/4-inch reinforcing bars. Abbot delivered 500 cubic yards of fill, and that was all. What is Olcott's obligation?

16. When and how may it be desirable to have in the master contract a clause empowering the prime contractor to sublet only a limited portion of the work involved in the contract?

17. Where a contract is rescinded by mutual agreement, the concept of "restitution" is often in the picture. What does it involve?

18. Assume that Long contracted to design the superstructure and building foundations for Short's new factory for a stated percentage of the contract price. After the contract was let, Short asked Long to augment their agreement so as to include thereunder (at 0.5 percent remuneration) all founda-

tions for the machines. Can Long decline and enforce the contract as originally constituted?

19. *B* had a contract with *A* whereby the latter was to furnish *B*'s restaurant with all the baked goods needed for one year at stipulated unit prices. During the year, B sold her restaurant to *C*. Does *A* have to fulfill the remainder of her contract with *B*, and does *B* have to complete her contract with *A*? What if *C* agrees to assume *B*'s obligation but *A* does not want any part of the substitution?

20. Moore contracted to sell 100,000 board feet of 3/4-inch oak flooring to Ralston at a stipulated price and to make delivery not later than April 15. Moore actually delivered the lumber on April 3, and Ralston paid for it on April 10. What is the status of the contract on April 15?

21. Norton, aged seventeen, contracted to buy a sports car from Jones but failed to get the approval of her father for this expenditure. What can Jones do about the matter?

22. *C* contracted with architect *D* to design the structural work of the latter's school project. However, the job was delayed by the city because of financing. The project was finally cleared, but before *C* started any of *D*'s work, *C* obtained two other large jobs. He telephoned *D* and explained that he now had all the work that he could handle, and he asked *D* to get someone else. Can *D* hold *C* to his bargain?

2

APPLICATION TO CONSTRUCTION CONTRACTS

The second portion of this text is designed to show how each of the many facets of the law of contracts bears upon engineering and construction undertakings. This part also covers several other subjects with which construction contracts are customarily concerned.

Probably the first step in preparing construction contracts is arriving at an agreement between the owner and the engineer or architect for the preparation of the contract documents and the rendering of other essential services connected with the project.

The documents prepared for the usual construction job consist of (1) drawings, which portray the structure to be built; (2) specifications, which describe the qualities of materials and workmanship to be provided by the contractor; and (3) clauses setting forth specific features that apply to the work and concern the obligations of the parties.

When the planning of a building project is getting under way, it is necessary to make preliminary layouts and studies in order to determine the general features of the structures, equipment, and other facilities that will be needed. Then follow estimates of cost, research to decide whether the undertaking is economically feasible, and, finally, authorization for the engineer to design the works and prepare the contract documents. It is at this last-mentioned stage of the proceedings that the material included in Part Two enters the picture.

After approval of the project and issuance of orders by the owner for the engineer to proceed come the development of the design and the making of the final drawings that will become a part of the contract. All essential features of the project have to be determined, designed, and developed in sufficient detail for the potential contractors to prepare their cost estimates. We do not try to specify precisely how these drawings should be prepared or how the information on them should be presented, because such considerations will vary widely with the nature of the project. However, some important points to remember in connection with any drawing are mentioned.

The next item on the engineer's agenda, after the contract drawings have been worked in sufficient detail, is the drafting of the specifications describing the materials and workmanship that the contractor is to provide. Various principles and ideas to be borne in mind in the preparation of this portion of the contract documents are described. A number of sample clauses are included so that the student can study the wording used as well as the basic propositions involved.

Then it is necessary to draft, for inclusion in the contract documents, a number of provisions spelling out specific requirements pertaining to the conduct of the work and the obligations of the contracting parties. This is done not for the protection of the owner alone. The provisions constitute rules under which all parties are bound to conduct themselves. The considerable importance of such ground rules is apparent when one recalls that the project may involve the expenditure of vast sums of money.

When the drawings, specifications, and miscellaneous contract clauses are well in shape, the owner and the engineer will determine what type of contract is most desirable from the standpoint of the method of payment: for example, lump sum or unit price. After this decision is made, the engineer prepares the proposal form that is to be used by contractors wishing to submit bids on the work.

Two other important details that must next be settled relate to the bid bond and the performance bond, and there must be incorporated into the contract documents any special requirements affecting the preparation and submission of bids, general information for the guidance of bidders, and a statement about the procedures that will be followed in making the award.

When the contract drawings and all pertinent documents are sufficiently complete to enable the engineer to determine just when such papers may be released to potential bidders, he or she sets a date for receipt of proposals and advertises for bids.

chapter

8

CONTRACTS FOR CONSTRUCTION AND ENGINEERING SERVICES

8.1   APPLICATION TO CONSTRUCTION INDUSTRY

The principles of contracts can be well illustrated by applying them to the construction field because participation in the preparation and execution of construction contracts is among the major endeavors of engineers and architects. A building or construction contract presents the characteristics common to contracts in general. The purpose of a construction contract is to govern the rights, duties, and liabilities of the builder who performs the work, the person or organization for whom the construction is to be executed, and the architects and engineers who design and perform contract administration duties such as inspection.

Organizations that design a project for the owner generally have the duty of compiling the contract documents. The exact wording to be used in any individual case is something that will be dictated by the particular circumstances and subject matter. If the contract is drawn properly, if the specifications are clear and complete, and if the drawings are both comprehensive and sufficiently detailed, trouble with the execution of the contract can be minimized. The contract should be so phrased as to ensure that each party has the right and the power to secure the desired performance. Troubles may develop between contractor and (engineer) or owner when a contract is loosely and poorly written, when the exact scope and character of the work are misrepresented or not shown properly, or when the requirements are unreasonable or injudiciously interpreted.

8.2   DEFINITIONS

For the sake of clarity and in order to avoid repetition in the contract documents, it is advisable to define at the outset of such documents the terms that will be used.

Such definitions are to apply whenever the terms involved appear in any part of the contract. So-called standard clauses are useful in this connection.

Here are some illustrative definitions:

1. "Chief Engineer" shall mean the Chief Engineer of the John Doe Corporation, acting personally.
2. "Engineer" shall mean the Chief Engineer, acting either personally or through duly authorized representatives operating within the scope of the authority vested in them.
3. "Contract" shall mean the entire agreement between the parties, including the Form of Contract of Agreement together with the Specification, the Advertisement, the Information for Bidders, the Contractor's Proposal, the Contract Drawings, and conditions of the Contract both General and Supplementary.
4. "Owner" shall mean the John Doe Corporation.
5. "Contractor" shall mean the individual, corporation, company, firm, or other organization that has contracted to furnish the materials and to perform the work under the Contract.
6. "Work" shall mean all labor, plant, materials, facilities, and other things necessary or proper for or incidental to the contract of ___.
7. "Contract Drawings" shall mean those listed in the Agreement under the title "Contract Drawings" and shall include any future changes and revisions of said drawings.
8. "Inspector" shall mean any representative of the Engineer designated by the latter to act as Inspector within the scope of the authority delegated to him. The Engineer, however, may review and change any decision of an Inspector.
9. "Subcontractor" shall mean anyone (other than the Contractor) who performs work directly or indirectly for or on behalf of the Contractor, but the term "Subcontractor" shall not include one who furnishes only materials not fabricated specifically for the work.
10. "Permanent structure," and words of like import, shall mean all construction, installation, materials, structures, and equipment required to be left by the Contractor at the construction site after the completion of the Contract.

8.3 CONTRACTS FOR ENGINEERING AND ARCHITECTURAL SERVICES

If the owner does not have an engineering or architectural staff, he or she must engage someone to take charge of the design and administer the project. Generally the owner makes a contract with whoever is selected, and the terms can be arranged in whatever manner is acceptable to the parties.[1]

---

[1] The American Institute of Architects, the National Society of Professional Engineers, and the American Society of Civil Engineers have prepared standard contracts for professional services. These have been carefully written and tested by experience. They are intended for use by architects, engineers, and their clients.

In the case of individual houses, stores, apartments, public buildings, landscaping, parks, and other projects where the planning in terms of architectural features is particularly important, an architect may be the one to place in overall charge of the project. The architect often engages and works with engineers in the preparation of the plans and specifications.

In the case of industrial projects, bridges, highways, hydraulic structures, public utilities, waterfront construction, and other structures where the engineering features are predominant, an engineer may be placed in general charge, with an architect in an assisting capacity if necessary. Sometimes an individual is competent in both these fields of professional work and can take charge of all phases directly.

When public work is involved, if the agency concerned does not have sufficient architectural and engineering staff of its own, or if the work is too extensive for it to handle, the agency may notify various consulting firms that it is looking for someone to do the architectural and engineering work of the project. It may ask these firms to send reports or brochures showing the works that each has designed in the past, the experience and capabilities of its stall, the workers that it can devote to the project, and any other data that will show the firm's qualifications for performing the technical work desired. The agency will then choose the firm that seems to be the most desirable.

The law and practices of some states, as well as those of the federal government, require that competitive bids be submitted for architectural and engineering services for public works projects. This procedure forces engineers and architects to state publicly a price (or rate) for their services. Sometimes this means that they may have to skimp on the quality of service rendered if their stated price is so low that hasty performance becomes necessary in order to avoid losing money on the job. The quality of their service and the finished product may therefore suffer. In Europe the various contractors often make designs of their own and present their proposals on the basis of these designs. Thus the competition involves both the engineering and the construction side. This method certainly brings out very keen competition, and varying ideas on the engineering portion of the work are elicited. In the United States the bidding is generally confined to the construction.

In some cases, as for certain architectural services, stated fees have been published for the guidance of all those concerned, the fees varying somewhat with the character and magnitude of the proposed project. For example, the fee may be stated as 6 percent of the "cost" of the structure, 75 percent of this fee being payable to the architect upon completion of the plans and the letting of the contract, and the remainder being payable upon completion of the construction.

The legality of such fee schedules was questioned in *United States v. National Society of Professional Engineers*.[2] The fee schedules were found to constitute price fixing, in violation of federal antitrust statutes,[3] because members of the soci-

---

[2]435 U.S. 679 (1978).

[3]While any extensive antitrust coverage is beyond the scope of this book, attention is directed to the case of *Ehlinger & Assoc. v. Louisiana Architects Assoc. and the American Institute of Architects*, 989 F.Supp. 775 (E.D. La. 1998). This case involves a long and tortuous history of litigation in which an architectural firm unsuccessfully claimed that it had been "blackballed" from lucrative state contracts.

ety were thereby prohibited from entering competitive bids. The trial court noted: "Without the ability to utilize and compare prices in selecting engineering services, the consumer is prevented from making an informed, intelligent choice."

Therefore, any fee schedule that is intended to be mandatory rather than simply a basis from which to estimate prices and which prohibits competitive bidding practices is suspect. The proper fees for the planning and design of engineering works are difficult to determine and so, in many instances, are of architectural services. It is perhaps unwise to attempt to set up schedules for such services. Each case should be left for negotiation between the persons involved.

There are various reasons why it is difficult to estimate correctly in advance the cost of engineering-design work and the preparation of contracts; some of the reasons are:

1. The engineers generally will not have control of the basic requirements that will be presented by the owner. It is therefore practically impossible to foresee all the work that may be necessary.

2. At the start, the basic requirements are usually vague and uncertain.

3. Preliminary engineering studies and the making of alternate plans require an amount of time and cost that is difficult to anticipate. Nevertheless, such studies are usually of extreme importance in determining the best and most economical layout, and they may bring about large savings for the owner. On the other hand, an attempt to minimize engineering costs may result in the adoption of the first design that is reasonable, because the engineers cannot afford to use more time and money on this phase of the work.

4. The owner frequently changes his mind about what he wants as the design progresses, or he finds that he wants or needs various modifications and additions. The engineers cannot predict how much delay and expense these changes will require.

One can see how inadvisable it may be for an engineer to be paid for an engineering job on any lump-sum basis such as a percentage of the cost of the project. If the work is done with painstaking care and thereby produces a design that can be built with a minimum of cost, the engineers receive less compensation for greater exercise of skill than they would for a hastily designed and more costly job.

When a great deal of preliminary planning is to be done, it may be desirable for the owner to engage an engineer or architect on the basis of the cost of labor and materials used in the preparation of the plans, specifications, and other contract documents, plus a percentage fee for overhead and profit. In this manner, adequate studies can be made without an unfair cost to the designers.

An engineer is sometimes required to serve as a consultant in cases where the owner and his staff wish to have the benefit of the knowledge and experience of a specialist in some particular field. This person may contract to do this special work on a per diem basis or may agree to do it for a lump sum that covers all services necessary for the completion of the project. Alternatively, he or she may be retained on the basis of a stipulated monthly or annual salary or fee, with the understanding that specified regular hours will be apportioned to the work. In the latter arrangement the specialist may be engaged with the agreement that he or she will spend whatever time is necessary in assisting the client with the work. In short, the parties can make whatever contract they wish for such special services.

Still another arrangement that may have advantages for the owner and the engineer is the selection of a capable contractor to act as a consultant during the planning and design of the project. This applies primarily to work that involves unusual difficulties of construction. The contractor, having superior knowledge of construction procedures and possibilities, acts as an adviser to the engineer and is generally engaged on either a per diem or a fixed-fee basis. Thus the engineer can have the benefit of the contractor's knowledge during the work on the preliminary studies, the development of the design, and the preparation of the contract documents. In this case, the engineer still retains complete control of the development of the project, but, by securing timely advice, may avoid subsequent revision of the plans because of unanticipated construction difficulties.

Even without a formal contract for their services, many manufacturers and contractors are willing to give their advice about specific points, especially if the advice enhances their chance of getting some or all of the work. For example, during the design of the Bayonne Bridge by the Port of New York Authority, a question arose whether or not any steel company could manufacture the proposed heavy forgings that were planned as a part of the bridge bearings. These forgings were believed to be larger than any that had been made previously. Certain manufacturers were consulted about the possibility of producing these forgings. The final designs were produced upon the manufacturer's affirmative reply.

8.4   COMPONENTS OF A CONSTRUCTION CONTRACT

The contract documents are generally composed of design drawings, specifications, invitations to bid, instructions to bidders, the agreement or form of contract, general conditions, supplementary conditions, addenda, the proposal, the bid bond, the performance bond, and the material and payment bond. These documents delineate and describe the work that is required, the quality of materials and workmanship to be furnished, and the various conditions surrounding the agreement. The design drawings that are prepared are often called the *contract drawings* because they are the ones upon which the contract is based. They may be amplified or even replaced by *supplementary drawings* if the contract drawings alone are not sufficiently extensive and detailed for use in carrying on the contract work. The use of supplemental drawings should not change the quantity, quality, or methods established in the contract without an appropriate change order. In some cases *reference drawings* are used to show the general character of work required, even though they are not part of the contract.

The plans, specifications, and other writings constituting parts of a building or construction contract are to be construed together as integral parts of the whole when any question arises. Generally, what is stipulated in the written documents are of less importance than what is shown on the drawings because the latter are usually made especially for a particular project. One should never forget, however, that if a discrepancy between the written word and a set of drawings exists, the court will give preferences to the written/printed word of the specifications. Ideally, the intent of the specifications and the drawings will match.

The organization of the parts of the contracts and the terms designating them vary. Some persons divide the specifications into two parts: general clauses (covenants or agreements) and technical data. Others place these general clauses, covenants, and agreements under what is typically called general conditions or *contract clauses*; then the technical instructions affecting materials and workmanship are grouped in the *specifications*. However, such details are not of great importance provided that the contract documents contain all the necessary instructions and requirements somewhere, and these are clearly and correctly stated. Lawyers sometimes prepare the general condition or contract clauses with the technical help of the engineers involved, but the most widely used general conditions are those prepared by groups such as the American Institute of Architects (AIA) and the Engineers Joint Contract Documents Committee (EJCDC).

8.5   STIPULATED SUM CONTRACT

A *stipulated sum contract,* commonly called a lump-sum contract, is one in which the contractor agrees to perform for a stated number of dollars. For this compensation he is to fulfill all his obligations under the contract, even though the cost in doing so may prove to be greater than the stipulated payment. The point to be emphasized is that the contractor agrees to do his part for the stipulated fee no matter what trouble and expense are encountered so long as the problem is not the result of a breach by the owner. The remuneration may be made in a series of partial payments as work progresses or in one final settlement after acceptance of the work.

From the owner's (buyer's) standpoint, such a contract has many advantages. The bids tell exactly what the project will cost unless he later decides upon changes. If he is not satisfied with this cost, or if he does not have enough money, he may reject all bids provided that he has reserved this right. Furthermore the owner need not engage a staff to keep account of exactly what work has been done and materials furnished week after week, except as this may be necessary in connection with making partial payments. Of course, the engineer, if designated as the owner's representative for that purpose, has to keep watch to see that the contract is fulfilled in its entirety as called for by its terms.

Everything that is required of the contractor must be made very clear and specific before the contract is let. In the case of a large construction contract, the owner should have all the necessary plans, contract terms, and specifications complete in every respect. If the extent and details of the job are not shown properly, many features may have to be determined and provided for as the work progresses, probably resulting in additional costs for such extras.

A lump-sum contract can be used successfully for the routine construction of schools, mill buildings, warehouses, and similar structures with which the average contractor has had considerable experience. Although these projects involve many different kinds of work, a capable and experienced contractor can generally estimate the total cost and prepare the bid with a fair degree of accuracy.

By contrast, if the work required by the contract is not readily determinable in all its features at the time of bidding, a lump-sum contract should not be used. It would be unfair to the bidders to expect them to bind themselves to the performance of work, significant aspects of which cannot be outlined in advance. If obliged to bid on such an indefinite project, bidders would have to protect themselves by making proposals high enough to cover the cost of whatever increases and uncertainties may materialize.

Some types of work that are unsuited to lump-sum contracts are:

1. Difficult foundations for which no one knows how much excavation will be required, how many piles will have to be driven, how difficult the shoring and unwatering of the excavation will be, and how much time will be required to complete the work.

2. Contracts involving excavation of uncertain quantity and character, the bidder not knowing how much of the work may be the excavation of rock instead of earth.

3. Emergency projects that have to be rushed without time to prepare complete plans prior to obtaining bids.

4. Alteration projects that involve the maintenance of operations while the work is being performed.

5. Projects that are subject to unpredictable hazards, such as floods, cold weather, and the conduct of persons beyond the contractor's control.

From the contractor's point of view, a lump-sum contract may be preferable (unless of course competition or unsound judgments have caused him to make a bid that is too low) because whatever the contractor can gain by meticulous planning and efficient management benefits him, and any legitimate saving that he can devise will add to his profit.

8.6   UNIT-PRICE CONTRACT

A *unit-price contract* is one in which payment for the work is to be made upon the basis of the computed quantities of specifically stated items of work actually performed and materials furnished and used by the contractor in the project, each such quantity being multiplied by the contractor's bid price for that unit. For example, the contract may state that the engineer's estimate of the quantity of reinforced concrete is 10,000 cubic yards. If the contractor's bid on that item is $80 per cubic yard, that is the amount to be paid for each cubic yard of concrete placed in the furnished work whether the actual quantity is 11,000 or 9,000 cubic yards. Notice that the cost of the project depends upon the bid unit prices and the quantities used. The total cost may or may not be less than it would be if a lump-sum form of contract were used and bids were made on that basis. Furthermore, the contractor's profit does not vary with the form of the contract; profit depends upon how much compensation exceeds expenses.

In order to secure unit-price bids it is ordinarily necessary to prepare general designs and drawings together with estimates of quantities so that the bidders may ascertain the magnitude of the project, the character and difficulty of the work, and the probable cost of performing it. Contractors may properly claim adjustments in their compensation if the actual work proves to be considerably different in quantity and quality from that indicated by the data presented for bidding purposes.[4] The fact that contractors will be paid the bid price on whatever quantity of that item they actually furnish or on whatever service they perform is likely to reduce some of the gamble in bidding.

From the owner's standpoint, one disadvantage of such a contract is that he cannot be absolutely sure of the total cost until the job is finished. On the other hand, the owner can avoid the delay and expense that would otherwise be necessary in performing an exhaustive study and making a large number of contract drawings to show in detail everything that will be needed, as should be done in the case of the lump-sum contract. After the contract is let, supplementary drawings can be prepared to enable the contractor to secure all the necessary information in time for obtaining materials, making detailed drawings, and doing the work.

Of course, both the owner (more likely the engineer or his designee) and the contractor will have to do considerable measuring, computation, and bookkeeping during the progress of the unit-price job. It is usual practice for the parties to have their own staff make periodic estimates of the amount of materials furnished and work completed during the preceding period, basing their figures upon field measurements or data obtained from the drawings, shipping bills, and similar information. Their estimates are then compared. If there are discrepancies of importance, the computations are checked, and a set of quantities is usually determined and agreed upon as a basis for payment.

It is not customary to have a unit-price item for absolutely everything that goes into a large project. In the preparation of the contract documents, the engineer selects the payment items that will apply to all major portions of the work, and includes as many of the minor items as necessary or desirable. The list of payment items should be sufficiently complete to avoid being unfair to either contractor or owner but without having the number of unit prices so great that it is unwieldy and difficult to use. Furthermore, the units for payment should be definite and readily measurable.

A contract for the foundations and other concrete work of a large industrial project having steel superstructures will serve as an illustration of the selection of

---

[4]A change in the work ordered by the owner and contemplated in the original contract is called a change order, and, as an adjustment to the original contract, must satisfy the normal formalities.

Even when the original contract grants the owner the right to make changes, those changes must be within the general parameters of the original contract. If they are not they are called cardinal changes and are not covered by the typical changes clause.

Among the cases exploring the scope of change clauses and cardinal changes are *U.S. For Use And Ben. Evergreen Pipeline v. Merritt,* 890 F.Supp. 1213 (S.D. N.Y. 1995); *Roy F. Weston, Inc. v. Halliburton Nus. Env. Corp.* 839 F.Supp 1150 (E.D. Penn. 1993); and *In re Construction Contractors of Ocala, Inc. v. Lathan Construction Corp.,* 196 B.R. 188 (Bankr. M.D. Fla. 1996).

the items that are to serve as the basis for payment. The items used in this contract were the following:

1. Earth excavation, per cubic yard.

2. Concrete, per cubic yard.

3. Cement, per ton.

4. Steel reinforcement, per pound.

5. Clearing the site, grading, disposing of excavated material, and cleaning up the site after completion of the foundations (lump sum).

The computation of the quantity of excavation was to be based upon the theoretical excavation from the original ground surface down to the elevation of the bottom of the structure or part (as shown on the plans) and within vertical planes bounding the outline of whatever the part might be. In determining the unit price for this item the contractor was to include whatever the miscellaneous work (shoring, drainage, and backfilling) would cost. The payment for concrete was to include the cost of all materials, forms, placing, curing, and finishing of concrete. Furthermore, from typical details that were shown on the drawings, the bidder was to make an estimate of the expense involved in cutting, bending, and placing the bars. Detail drawings of the bars were to be furnished by the owner.

The use of a lump-sum bid on item 5, above, illustrates how one portion of a unit-price contract may be treated as a lump-sum item. This is a convenient way to handle work that would be difficult to classify and to keep track of in the field.

Notice that many of the specific hardware items necessary for such a job are not directly measurable in any line of the unit-price contract. For example, all piping and conduits were to be furnished by the owner and placed by the contractor; the same applied to anchor bolts to be set in the concrete. The contractor was supposed to allow for these features. The contract made this clear, and the drawings showed the nature and magnitude of such special arrangements so that the contractor could include their cost in bid prices.

By no means do we intend to convey the impression that unit-price contracts are generally preferable to lump-sum contracts. Take, for example, a small bridge job costing approximately $40,000. It involves a large variety of materials, but each kind will be used in small quantities. Actual increases in volume of work done when the estimated quantities are small may lead to unexpected increases in the total cost. Reduction in quantities may lead to claims for extra compensation. It may therefore be desirable to use a lump-sum type of contract for bidding such a structure. However, it should be recognized that the form of contract is not what determines the owner's cost or the contractor's profit.

8.7 COST-PLUS-PERCENTAGE CONTRACT

There are several reasons that an owner may choose to use a cost-plus contract. The work may be such that the owner fears that the bidders will add large contingencies, or in an emergency situation requiring construction of something without time to develop plans for it, a contractor may not be able to make a proposal on a lump-sum basis. A unit-price basis is equally undesirable because it is difficult to foresee all that is required. In such a situation it is preferable to engage a contractor to do the work on the basis of cost plus some allowance for overhead and profit. One such basis may be for the contractor to be reimbursed the stipulated costs plus a percentage of the cost to be added for overhead and profit.

Materials, labor, rentals of equipment and property, transportation, and everything else except the salaries of the contractor's supervisory staff are generally included in the cost item of such a contract. Sometimes even the wages of the contractor's staff in the field are included as direct costs to which the percentage is to apply, but this depends upon the particular agreement. Ordinarily, the percentage to be paid to the contractor should not be applied to the costs of any portion of the contractor's general office overhead, postage, traveling expenses, insurance (other than that directly applicable to the job), salaries or portions of salaries of company officials who may visit the job, or charges for the use of any equipment that the contractor would not customarily use for the performance of the work. All these points should be made clear in the written agreement.

To make a cost-plus-percentage contract in an emergency, the owner may call in several contractors, find out who can and will tackle the job, make an agreement regarding the percentage to be paid to the contractor, and see that things start moving at once. While the contractor is assembling staff and equipment, the owner will try to determine enough about what is to be done to start the work as soon as the contractor gets the field staff organized; thereafter information is channeled to the contractor on an as-needed basis.

A cost-plus contract may also be useful in situations that are not emergencies, especially when it is uncertain what troubles or difficulties will be encountered in the work. In this way decisions can be made as the work progresses. In the accounting, the contractor generally keeps all records of costs and then presents them to the owner for checking, approval, and payment as the job proceeds.

8.8   COST-PLUS-FIXED-FEE CONTRACT

Another advantageous type of contract for emergency jobs and others involving uncertainties is one based upon the cost of labor and materials plus a fixed fee for the contractor. This overcomes the possible weakness of the cost-plus-percentage type of contract, which is that the more nonproductive and wasteful the contractor is, the more profit he makes. In the cost-plus-fixed-fee arrangement, the contractor receives only the stipulated fixed-fee sum regardless of what the costs of the project and his overhead and profit are. If staff salaries are to be paid out of this fee, the contractor will naturally endeavor to expedite the project so as to make as much profit as possible. Even if staff salaries are to be classed as a part of the general costs of the job, the contractor will still want to rush the work so that his workers can be available for another contract as soon as possible.

Under this cost-plus-fixed-fee arrangement the owner can select a reliable contractor and engage a capable engineer to design and check the work. The gamble is largely removed for both the owner and the contractor. The contractor knows precisely what the profit for the job will be, and the owner has confidence that the job will be handled expeditiously and in an economical manner. In using the term "cost plus" in a contract, one must be sure of its exact meaning. If it states that the compensation is to be on the basis of the cost of labor and materials or on the basis of time and materials plus a percentage or fixed fee, the contractor probably cannot include in the cost such items as overhead. Such points should be clarified before the contract is signed. Also, the scope of the work needs to be reasonably defined as to quantity and complexity in order for the contractor to establish a fixed fee, and should include a provision to increase the fee for expansion of the work. Obviously, if the owner doubles the size of the project, the contractor should not be expected to do twice the work for the same price.

8.9   SUBDIVISION INTO SEVERAL CONTRACTS

It is sometimes advantageous to split a contract into two or more parts if some portion of the project involves many uncertainties. Here is one example. A large industrial corporation was to make extensive additions to and alterations in the structures and equipment of one of its plants. Foundation conditions were known to be poor and to involve considerable difficulty, and many utilities were to be relocated. All this construction work was to be done while maintaining production in the existing facilities, and its cost would be very difficult to predict. However, as soon as the foundations and subsurface work could be completed, the superstructure and installation of new equipment could go ahead without such uncertainties. Therefore the engineer decided that the best way to handle this job was to make all foundation construction, utility alterations, and subsurface work a cost-plus-fixed-fee contract and to make the remainder a separate unit-price contract. Both parts were to be handled by the same contractor, an arrangement that would assure coordination of the work.

Subdivision may also be advantageous in the case of a very large project. This procedure enables the engineer to make the plans, specifications, and other written material for one portion of the project at a time and to let a separate contract for each portion as soon as its design is completed. Subdivision also saves time, keeps the magnitude of each contract within reasonable limits, and spreads the work among various contractors, each of whom may be especially well qualified for a particular part. However, the use of multiple prime contractors requires the coordination of the contractors in much the same way that a single prime has to coordinate its subcontractors. This situation requires the expenditure of effort or funds whether it is done by the owner, the engineer, or a construction manager. For example, the work on the Lincoln Tunnel in New York was subdivided into nearly a hundred separate contracts. Typical of these were the following: The caisson for the ventilation shaft on the New York side of the Hudson River, the New Jersey shaft, the under-river portions of the south and north tunnels, each of the three ventilation buildings, various sections of the tunnel between the river and the portals, each of the two plazas, and a series of sections of the approach in New Jersey.

8.10   CONTRACTS FOR COMBINED ENGINEERING AND CONSTRUCTION

Some organizations make a specialty of both designing and building a project. In other words, they will sign a contract with an owner to prepare all the preliminary studies and the final design and also to build the structures involved. This is sometimes called a *design–build* type of contract. Such a contract may be made on the basis of the cost plus a fixed fee, the cost plus a percentage of the cost, or whatever arrangement is satisfactory to the parties.

Such a combined contract has been used effectively in specialized industrial projects, especially where the design involves proprietary processes. In some cases, specialists may even assist in getting the plant into operation in order to see that everything functions properly. Or a manufacturer may contract to develop the design of an unusual piece of equipment and then to build it. In the field of small buildings, there are some contractors who make a specialty of designing and constructing standard buildings such as prefabricated metal buildings.

The proponents of such contracts claim that they allow work to be expedited because extensive plans and specifications do not have to be prepared and bids do not have to be submitted before work in the field can start. Furthermore, there is no division of responsibility; the contractor prepares the plans and then builds the structures, becoming the final inspector of the initial design work. If handled by a skillful, reputable concern, such methods may be efficient. The owners are, of course, dependent upon the contractor in this situation, just as they are dependent upon the engineer in other cases. Caution is advisable here since contractors, by law, are not allowed to design buildings or structures for personal or public use. The contractor's plans must be "stamped" by a professional engineer or architect.

8.11   PREPARATION OF DOCUMENTS

Obviously great skill and diligence should be exercised when preparing contract documents. The following are some points that will assist in producing a well-written contract.

1. Be sure that the wording is clear and precise. Have it checked carefully by another person. The readers of the documents see only the words that are written. They do not know the thoughts and intentions of the author.

2. Coordinate the written material with the work of those persons who are making the drawings, and have the latter examine all parts relating to their work.

3. Be sure that the grammar and punctuation are correct.

4. Use short simple sentences instead of long involved ones, even if the former do not sound as attractive. You are writing a legal document in which accuracy and clarity are of vast importance. Make sentences complete; do not allow phrases to stand as complete sentences.

5. Do not write on a given point until you are sure of the subject matter. Obtain competent assistance where necessary.

6. Avoid the use of ambiguous words and colloquialisms. Repeat a word as often as necessary rather than using synonyms, because the latter may have slightly different connotations. The vocabulary used should be what is customary in the line of work involved and clearly understood by the readers.

7. Repeat names as often as necessary. Personal pronouns are likely to cause confusion.

8. Remember that you are giving instructions, not suggestions. You need not explain the reasons behind the instructions.

9. Avoid such all-inclusive expressions as "etc."

10. Be very careful to make cross-references clear by using title and paragraph numbers.

11. Be sure that the requirements are fair, reasonable, and practicable.

12. Reveal all known hazards and give all information that may affect contingencies to be provided for by the contractor.

13. Examine all the implications of broad, general statements before using such statements.

14. Make an outline of all parts to be covered before composing the clauses. Divide the documents into whatever sections are appropriate.

15. Avoid omissions, on the one hand, and irrelevant or uselessly repetitious information on the other.

16. Establish some kind of numbering system for the various sections and clauses in the documents so that each can readily be referred to later on. It is often convenient for the reader if titles or labels are added in the margins alongside the various main clauses so that the reader can quickly see the nature of the subject matter contained therein.

17. Prepare a table of contents with page references and also prepare an index.

18. Avoid using standard (sometimes called boilerplate) specifications containing specifications for materials and work that do not apply to the project.

19. Coordinate all drawings with each other and with the specifications to identify inconsistencies and ensure that the information to be conveyed is shown in its proper place.

If revisions of or additions to the contract documents are found to be necessary before the bids are received, issue an addendum to all bidders and demand written acknowledgment of its receipt by all parties who have previously received copies of the contract documents. Be sure that the addendum refers to the specific clauses that are eliminated, revised, or replaced, so that no doubt will remain as to the final instructions. Of course, an addendum takes precedence over the original clause or clauses that it modifies.

8.12   EXAMPLES OF WORDING

The following illustrations, taken from actual documents, are given in order to emphasize the importance of careful writing when preparing contract papers. They show the difference in meaning that may arise from the position of a word, the use or omission of a punctuation mark, the use of a connective, and other seeming trivia. The key words are in italics.

1. "The Chief Engineer *only* has the right to authorize extra work."

   This seems to mean that he has no other right. It would be better to say, "*Only* the Chief Engineer . . . "

2. "Within the area of the foundation, the Contractor shall remove all compressible soils *and* blast out all rock above elevation 110."

   This seems to mean that the contractor is to remove nothing below elevation 110. If this is not the intent it would be better to write. "The Contractor shall remove all compressible soil within the area of the foundation, and shall also blast out and remove all rock above elevation 110 in this area."

3. "The remaining fifteen (15) percent will be *paid* at the *conclusion* of the job *on* the final approval of the Chief Engineer."

   This seems to mean that the chief engineer is to be approved by somebody. It would be better to state that the money will be "paid to the Contractor after the Contractor has completed the Contract, and after the Chief Engineer has approved the completed work."

4. "Brick masonry shall be laid so that all joints are horizontal *and* vertical." This statement really says that the joints within the same course are to be both ways simultaneously. The statement should read, "Brick masonry shall be laid so that the joints between courses are to be horizontal whereas abutting joints within the same course are to be vertical."

5. "If an error in the drawings is discovered by the Contractor he is to suspend work until he can *get hold* of the Chief Engineer."

   Colloquial or slang expressions like "get hold of" are inadvisable in technical writing.

6. "The Contractor is to be notified *what to do in writing* by the Chief Engineer."

   This sentence implies that the contractor will be told what to write about and how to do it. This is primarily a case of improper sequence of words. It is the notification that is to be in writing. The sentence should read, "The Contractor is to be notified in writing by the Chief Engineer regarding what to do."

7. "The Contractor shall make reparation to the Owner *due* to the mistake."

   Reparation is not owed to the mistake. It would be better to say "because of the mistake" or "for damages caused by the mistake." A word like "due" has a variety of meanings, and its use can lead to misinterpretation.

8. "The Contractor is to report any errors discovered *immediately*."

   The meaning of this sentence is ambiguous. The contractor is to report immediately regarding any error that he may discover, whether discovered early or late.

9. "The Contractor *should* make a written report to the Chief Engineer *on the fifteenth of each month* showing the estimated quantities of work completed during the preceding month."

   The word "should" means that the contractor ought to report but is not compelled to do so. It is better to say "shall" or "is to," which means that he is obliged to do so. It would also be better to start the sentence with, "On the fifteenth of each month the Contractor shall . . ." Similarly, the word "may" would be permissive and should not be used when a specific order is intended.

10. "The Contractor shall be compensated for any extra time *or* effort involved."

    This implies that he will be compensated for one or the other, not for both. This situation leads some persons to use "and/or" as a connective in order to cover one or both items. If the statement is " . . . time and effort involved," it probably will be satisfactory because even though one item is omitted the sum will contain the applicable item.

11. "Upon completion of the installation, the Contractor shall leave the premises in an orderly condition."

    This sentence is actually quoted from a contract. A jokester might pretend to wonder whether it is the condition of the contractor or the condition of the premises that is important. The intended meaning is, "Upon completion of this installation, the Contractor shall clean the premises and ensure that they are in an orderly condition."

QUESTIONS

1. Is it desirable to have construction work done under a contract? Why?
2. What party or parties are obligated by a construction contract? Explain.
3. Who prepares the contract documents for a construction project? What is the objective?
4. Who may suffer if a contract is poorly or unwisely prepared? Explain.
5. For what services does the owner have to depend upon the engineer and architect? The contractor?

6. Define the following as applied to the preparation of construction projects: *(a)* planning, *(b)* design.

7. Explain the principal difference between "public work" and "private work."

8. What legal problems arise from the use of fee schedules?

9. Why should carefully prepared definitions be included early in the contract documents? Illustrate one likely definition.

10. It is the purpose of the engineer to prepare the contract so that the work will be done properly, expeditiously, and amicably. Discuss this idea and its application in practice.

11. How is a court likely to interpret an ambiguous clause in the contract documents? Explain.

12. If the requirements of the drawings and the specifications differ, what should be done about it?

13. Discuss the implications of a "reasonable interpretation" of the contract documents in case some statements in the papers are ambiguous.

14. On what basis is it customary to make contracts for engineering and architectural services?

15. What safeguards should be provided if you are planning to contract for rendering your own personal services as an engineer or architect?

16. Explain some reasons that it may be difficult for an engineer to predict accurately the cost of engineering planning and the preparation of contracts.

17. Explain the basic features and advantages of the following types of contract: *(a)* lump-sum, *(b)* unit-price, *(c)* cost-plus-percentage, *(d)* cost-plus-fixed-fee.

18. What sort of contracts are unsuited to lump-sum bidding?

19. Why is it sometimes desirable to have certain items of a unit-price contract bid on a lump-sum basis? Explain. Illustrate possible advantages of this system.

20. Under what circumstances might an owner prefer to have a project built under a lump-sum contract instead of under a unit-price contract?

21. Is the contractor likely to make more profit on a unit-price contract than on a lump-sum contract or a cost-plus-fixed-fee contract? Elaborate.

22. Does a unit-price contract generally have a separate payment item listed for every different kind of material and every bit of work required in such contract? Explain.

23. How is the total payment under a unit-price contract determined? Is such a contract likely to be more economical for the owner than a lump-sum contract? For the contractor? Explain.

24. What are the advantages and disadvantages of cost-plus-fixed-fee contracts from the standpoint of the several parties concerned?

25. When a unit-price contract requires certain minor work to be done and material items to be furnished for which there is no stated payment item in the contract, what will the bidder probably do to obtain compensation therefor? Illustrate.

26. Illustrate a situation in which the subdivision of work into several contracts may be preferable to having the entire project performed under one general construction contract.

27. How does the owner-engineer relationship differ from that of engineer-contractor?

28. What are the pros and cons in the debate regarding *(a)* engineers bidding for engineering work on the basis of price; *(b)* engineers advertising for receipt of bids for engineering services by other engineers on a price basis?

29. Can an owner have the contract documents prepared by engineer *A* reviewed by engineer *B*? Explain the proper steps to be taken by the parties concerned. If *B* discovers errors in the documents prepared by *A*, what should *B* do? Explain.

30. An engineer who was engaged to design a large building made studies of the soil conditions. As a result, he decided to use piles to support the structure. The owner, without notifying the engineer, called in Ms. Doe, a fellow engineer, and asked the latter to make a Separate and secret study of the problem to see if the piles could be eliminated. What should Doe do about it when receiving this request?

31. Upon what logical basis might a contractor determine the percentage to charge in case of a cost-plus-percentage contract?

32. Upon what logical basis might a contractor determine the fee to charge in case of a cost-plus-fixed-fee contract?

33. When and why may it be advantageous for an engineer to have charge of the inspection of work to be performed under contracts that he has prepared?

34. What is an addendum? When and why may one be used?

9

ADVERTISING FOR BIDS

9.1   PURPOSE OF ADVERTISEMENT

Advertising for bids or requests for proposals (RFP) are usually intended to secure the benefit of bidding competition. Advertisements may also be made for the purpose of fulfilling legal requirements, as a matter of policy, or a combination of the foregoing.

If a large construction job is being designed, it is probable that news concerning it will spread by word of mouth and that interested contractors capable of doing the work will be somewhat familiar with the project in advance of formal advertisement. In the case of smaller projects, however, the published notice may be very effective in reaching prospective bidders who might otherwise fail to learn about the job.

In private work the owner need not publicly advertise for bids but has the right to negotiate directly and to contract with whomever he or she chooses. This procedure has much to recommend it in connection with unusual structures, industrial construction, and other work that requires special knowledge and equipment. There are contractors who have built up an excellent reputation for certain specialized kinds of work, and the owner may prefer to trust one of this group to make a good proposal. On the other hand, advertising private work secures the advantages stemming from competition and ensures that no one can accuse those responsible for awarding the contract of favoritism detrimental to the owner's interests.

The law generally requires that federal, state, and municipal contracts be advertised publicly. This method is intended to ensure that the work is done at a minimum cost to the public. A scarcity of bids is most likely to occur when the project involves special work that only a few contractors are equipped to do. If the requisite three bids are not received on certain government projects, special authorization will ordinarily be needed if an award is to be made. In case of war or other emergency, the government may dispense with public advertising and negotiate with someone directly because the public welfare requires that the work be started and executed with all possible speed.

9.2   ADVERTISING MEDIA

Since printed advertisements cost money, expenditures are best utilized by advertising a contract in whatever media are most likely to bring the message to the attention of the greatest number of potential bidders. A large-city daily newspaper reaches many people, but contractors may not be accustomed to reading it for data about prospective contract work. On the other hand, local projects are frequently advertised in small-town newspapers, and those who are interested in such work will look for the advertisements there. Trade journals make a specialty of advertising for proposals on construction contracts, and many contractors look to that source for information.

Before advertising a contract, the nature of the job and the available means of conveying the information to potential bidders should be considered. The object is to get the best results for the minimum cost. The fact that an advertiser's rates are very low is one factor to consider; however, it is equally important that the chosen advertising medium offer the best prospect of success in securing active competition and reasonably low bids.

9.3   TIMING OF ADVERTISEMENT

Another factor is that of timing. An advertisement appearing several days in succession may be desirable for some purposes. In other circumstances, one that is repeated weekly or biweekly for a month or so may be preferable, provided the publication carrying the advertisement appears on a regular time schedule.

In regard to public work, it is important to ensure that no legal requirements are overlooked in selecting the medium and the timing for the advertisement.

9.4   ATTRACTING ATTENTION

The heading of an advertisement should be designed to attract the attention of the readers. The site of the work and the owner for whom the structure is to be built should be disclosed in the heading or immediately following it. A contractor's reaction to the advertised work may depend to some extent upon the owner's identity. The builder may have had some previous experience with the particular owner or may have heard something that will have a bearing upon his desire to do the work in question.

The following title appeared on an advertisement in the *Engineering News-Record,* July 7, 1983:

Bids August 18, 1983

City of San Jose, California, San Jose/Santa Clara Water Pollution Control Plant, Intermediate Term Improvements, Sludge Processing Facilities.

The reader was quickly informed about the general character and location of the project and the date for bids. Those who were interested in doing that type of work and in that locale were then likely to read the full advertisement.

9.5   INFORMATION TO BE GIVEN IN THE TEXT

The body of the advertisement should consist of a brief summary of the proposed project and of the special conditions or requirements that distinguish it—for example, regulations affecting labor rates for personnel working under compressed air during the construction of a subaqueous tunnel. Just what a particular advertisement ought to contain will depend upon the circumstances. In most cases the advertisement is, to a large extent, a condensed version of the instructions for bidders. In a typical construction project, the following points are covered:

1. *The kind of job* (school construction, sewers, etc.). This matter must be thoroughly covered, even if the heading of the advertisement gives the general information.

2. *The location* in which the work is to be performed.

3. *The owner* for whom the job is to be accomplished. From the identity of the owner and the engineer, many contractors can judge the quality of the work that will be required and the extent of the cooperation they can expect. Other things being equal, contractors are likely to make lower bids on work designed by and under the charge of an engineer whom they know personally (and favorably) or concerning whom they have heard good reports than on work handled by an engineer totally unknown to them or in whom they lack confidence for some reason.

4. *The magnitude of the project.* It is usually desirable to avoid stating the engineer's estimate of cost in dollars, although such figures are occasionally included. The engineer's estimate may or may not accurately represent the cost of the project. Publication of the estimate gives the contractors a target figure that tends to preclude an independent assessment of the cost. In lieu of a statement of estimated cost, the size and character of the job are often shown by one or more of these methods:

   a.   Dimensions of width, length, and height.

   b.   General size, number of floors, type of framing, kind of floor and wall construction; for example, "School, 75 by 250 feet; 3 stories, steel frame, brick walls, concrete floors."

   c.   Square feet of floor area (plus general description of the structure).

   d.   Cubic feet of volume (plus general description of the structure).

   e.   Estimated quantities of some major items of material or work; for example, "50,000 cubic yards of earth excavation."

   f.   General capacity and character; for example, "Reinforced-concrete, four-story hospital to accommodate 200 beds."

g.   General scope and scale; for example, "5 miles of concrete pavement for four-lane highway," or "200-foot, two-lane, steel-truss highway bridge."

5. *The type of contract* ("lump sum," "unit price," etc.). This aspect is of particular significance in the case of large projects.

6. *The date, place, and form of receipt of sealed bids.* Note that the date of opening of the bids is the first item appearing in the advertisement example given in Section 9.6.

7. *The procedure that will be followed in opening and reading of bids.* The advertisement should state that the proposals are to be opened and *read aloud publicly*.

8. *The action regarding letting of the contract.* If the contract is to be awarded to the lowest *responsible* bidder (see Section 10.8, 9), that fact should be made clear. Also, a time within which the contract will be awarded after opening of the proposals should be stated—for example, "two weeks after opening of the bids."

9. *The possibility of rejection of any or all proposals.* It is generally advisable to state in the advertisement the fact that the owner has the right to reject "any or all" bids (perhaps because the indicated costs may be too high or because all bidders may be "unsatisfactory").

10. *The type and size of deposit required with the proposal,* as well as the procedure for the return of deposits.

11. *The performance bond.* If such a bond is required, this should be disclosed, together with the amount expressed in dollars or as a percentage of the bid price.

12. *The time set for starting and completing the work.* Any contemplated bonus or liquidated-damage provisions should be mentioned.

13. *The availability of data and forms.* State *(a)* where and from whom the contract papers, drawings, and specifications may be obtained; *(b)* at what cost; and *(c)* whether or not a refund will be made upon their return in satisfactory condition.

14. *The withdrawal of bids.* Indicate whether or not this is permissible. If bids may be withdrawn—which is not customary—state the conditions under which it may be accomplished.

15. *The date for signing the contract.* State any final date by which the selected bidder must sign the contract so that work may progress on schedule.

16. *Special conditions.* If special hazards exist, if restricted or full traffic must be maintained, if particular labor conditions prevail, or if unusual features are involved, these should be mentioned in the advertisement.

17. *Further data.* It may be desirable to *(a)* state that, at a specific date, place, and hour, the prospective bidders may meet with the engineer to examine the site, ask questions about items that need clarification, and familiarize themselves with the problems involved in the work; *(b)* include a statement as to whether or not the contractor is to reflect all federal, state, and local taxes in his bid price; *(c)* give applicable regulations regarding equal opportunity in employment; and *(d)* state requirements relating to workers' compensation, general liability, automobile and public liability, and property damage insurance.

It may seem that much of the foregoing information is too detailed for an advertisement. However, a fairly complete description at this early stage of the proceedings is helpful to all concerned. It aids the engineer by reducing the number of inquiries from persons accustomed to making a full investigation before deciding whether or not a given job is something they can and wish to handle. In many cases, absent a complete advertisement, prospective contractors might conclude too hastily that they are not interested, thus reducing potential competition and presumably working to the disadvantage of the owner. A reasonably detailed advertisement helps, too, by cutting down the number of useless requests for plans. Presumably, only those contractors who are real prospects will bother to apply for supplementary information.

Moreover, a sufficiently comprehensive, accurate advertisement protects the engineer against the possibility of a valid assertion of misrepresentation of the nature and conditions of the proposed contract. In this connection, also, it is advisable to reprint the entire advertisement in the contract documents, particularly when the project involved is a public job.

9.6 EXAMPLES OF ADVERTISEMENTS

The following advertisement has been copied from the *Engineering News-Record* of July 7, 1983. Its content should be compared with the suggestions in the preceding discussion.

Bids: August 3, 1983
City and County of San Francisco
Department of Public Works
Westside Pump Station and Force Mains
Specification No. 1114W

Sealed bids will be received in Room 282, City Hall, San Francisco, California, 94102 between 2:00 and not later than 2:30 PM local time on August 3, 1983, after which time they will be publicly opened and read. Plans, specifications and bidding forms will be available at the office of the City Engineer, Room 353, City Hall, San Francisco 94102, telephone (415) 558-3676. A nonrefundable fee of $180.00 paid by cash or check will be required for each set. Checks should be payable to "Department of Public Works." Bidders may make their own arrangements to pick up the bidding documents, or, if they make a request in writing, and submit the required fee, such documents will be shipped or mailed to them C.O.D. C.O.D. will only cover the shipping and mailing costs.

All Plan Holders on record as of May 18, 1983, will receive Addendum No. 3 including a new bid proposal package at no additional charge.

The bids for the subject project received on May 18, 1983, are hereby rejected. The average bid amounts for Proposition "A" were $17,458,364.00 and for Proposition "B" $17,471,614.00.

This project includes the construction of a sewage pump station with a nominal wet weather capacity of 140 mgd and installation of force mains, 42-inch, 48-inch, 54-inch diameters and gravity pipelines, 54-inch and 84-inch diameter.

The pump station will be located within the boundary of the Great Highway, south of its intersection with Sloat Boulevard, and immediately adjacent to the San Francisco Zoo.

The work shall consist of building the pump station, force mains, gravity pipelines, 160 feet of connecting consolidation sewer, berm embankment, appurtenant electrical, instrumentation and controls, mechanical, structural, landscape, architectural, roadway, and utility work.

Major components of the pump station will include seven submersible sewage pumps (300 hp each); two mechanically cleaned bar screens, diesel generator, dewatering pumps; piping, valves, sluice gates; ventilation and odor control equipment; auxiliary systems; electrical and instrumentation systems.

To accommodate the equipment, all work required to excavate, demolish existing structures and underground encumbrances, backfill, control groundwater, place embankment and dispose of excess and/or undesirable materials, pave and landscape will be included, as well as relocating any existing interfering utility systems.

The work shall include trenching, demolishing part of two pedestrian underpasses, furnishing materials, installing testing, backfilling, restoring the ground surface to original condition and all other effort required for relocation of existing utility interferences, fences, pavement and the like.

Supporting, working around, and protecting certain utility agency and company facilities in conjunction with the work under this contract, and located in the public street areas, shall be done where shown or where required and in accordance with the pink pages in these Special Provisions, except as otherwise specified.

Upon completion of the construction and installation of equipment, all systems will be tested and their adequacy to perform their functions suitably demonstrated as described herein, and, to the satisfaction of the Engineer, the Contractor shall accomplish all other related and incidental work, as shown on the Plans, and in accordance with the Specifications.

Federal and State funds are involved in this project.

Contract will provide for progressive payments for the value of the work done and materials incorporated based on the unit prices bid. Contract will provide for Liquidated Damages, as fixed in the specifications.

Any contract or contracts awarded under this invitation for bids are expected to be funded in part by a grant from the United States Environmental Protection Agency. Neither the United States nor any of its department agencies or employees is or will be a party to this invitation for bids or any resulting contract. This procurement will be subject to regulations contained in 40 CFR 35.936, 35.938 and 35.939.

In order for the City to receive grant assistance, approval to award this contract must be received from the California State Water Resources Control Board prior to date of award. Therefore, Proposals are subject to the condition that the successful bidder will accept the contract as bid up to a period 120 days after receipt of bids.

Bidders on this work will be required to comply with the President's Executive Order No. 11246. The requirements for Bidders and Contractors under this order are explained in the specifications.

A Pre-Bid Conference will be held on July 11, 1983, at 9:00 AM local time in Room 282, City Hall, San Francisco, California. The purpose of the conference is primarily to discuss the required Affirmative Action Programs for equal opportunity in employment and minority entrepreneurship, and any questioned contractual requirements. It is strongly recommended that all bidders attend this conference, but is not mandatory.

Bidders are warned that failure to submit properly completed Affirmative Action Program forms included with the proposal will render the proposal nonresponsive.

A certified check or corporate surety bond of 10 percent of the amount bid must accompany each proposal.

The successful bidder will be required to execute the contract within 10 days after the award of the work to him, and shall furnish bonds to the satisfaction of the City and County of San Francisco for faithful performance and for labor and materials, each in the sum of 100 percent of the amount of the contract as awarded. In case of failure to execute the contract as stated or to furnish bonds the bidder will be considered to have abandoned the contract and the bond or check accompanying the proposal shall be forfeited to the City, not as penalty but as liquidated damages.

Minimum wage rates for this project, as determined by the Secretary of Labor and by the Director of the State of California Department of Industrial Relations, are set forth in the Special Provisions or available for inspection at Room 353, City Hall, San Francisco. If there is a difference among the wage rates predetermined by the Secretary of Labor and those determined by the State of California for similar classifications of labor, the higher wage shall prevail.

Right is reserved to reject any or all bids.

Approved:

Dir. of Public Works & Clean Water Program.

QUESTIONS

1. Why may an engineer advertise for bids on a public project? On a private project?

2. In what ways other than advertising may an engineer request bids?

3. Name an acceptable media for advertising contracts for *(a)* construction, *(b)* machinery.

4. List the kinds of data that should be given in the advertisement for a junior high school. Assume all necessary information.

5. Why should the advertisement specify the procedure to be followed *(a)* for receipt of proposals, *(b)* for opening proposals, *(c)* for awarding the contract?

6. An advertisement for a construction project contained the words "estimated cost is $1,800,000." Is this proper or advisable? Explain.

7. If a project is suddenly canceled after being advertised, what should be done about the request for proposals?

8. Smith's advertisement for bids on the construction of a sewage-disposal plant stated: "$500 per day liquidated damages if not completed in fifteen months after signing of the contract." Reynolds saw Smith, explained the effect upon cost, and secured permission to omit this requirement. Has Smith the right to make this change? What should Smith do about other bidders?

9. Why is it advisable, in a public project, to print a copy of the advertisement in the contract documents?

10. Why might a contractor who reads an advertisement of a construction project be interested in and influenced by *(a)* the location of the project, *(b)* the name of the owner, *(c)* the character of the job?

11. What influence may the magnitude of the job have on whether or not prospective bidders will be interested in preparing proposals for performing the work required?

12. Explain the principles to be followed in giving bidders an idea of the character and magnitude of a construction project when advertising.

13. Why state in the advertisement that the contract will be awarded in a specified time after receipt of proposals?

14. Why state in the advertisement that the successful bidder must sign the contract within a specified time after notice of award of the contract?

15. Why might a private owner prefer to negotiate a construction contract directly with one particular contractor instead of advertising for bids?

10

PROPOSALS

10.1   SIGNIFICANCE OF A PROPOSAL

A *proposal* is made by the bidder as an offer to the owner in which the bidder states that he will furnish all materials and perform all work required by the contract documents except as noted by the contractor on the bid, and that he will do so for the remuneration stated in the proposal. The proposal should be designed so that acceptance by the owner will constitute a binding contract.

The preparation of a proposal by contractors requires a great deal of information. If any of the data given on the design drawings and in the specifications are not clear, definite, and sufficiently comprehensive, the bidders may be unable to estimate the cost properly, and may endeavor to protect themselves against uncertainties by entering bids on the high side. This will probably result in the owner paying more than he should for the job. Uncertain or inadequate information supplied to bidders also increases the likelihood of subsequent disputes between the contractor and the engineer.

From the contractor's point of view, if his estimate fails to properly consider the full extent of the scope and conditions of the project the resultant low bid will have serious consequences.

It takes time and costs money for a bidder to prepare an effective proposal. Typically an owner wants everything done with maximum speed, including preparation of proposals and letting of the contract. It is unwise for the engineer to go along with this urgency and to be unrealistic in setting the date for the receipt of proposals. He should allow adequate time for the prospective bidders to study the work at hand and to make suitable, accurate estimates of the cost. Permitting an unduly limited period for this study will probably cause bidders to increase their quotations in order to cover possible expenses that they have not had time to estimate properly.

10.2   Purpose of Proposal Forms

When soliciting proposals or bids for work, an owner often prepares a proposal form that offers precise guidance to the prospective bidder as to the nature and scope of the work. In construction contracts it is essential for the owner to provide all bidders with the same proposal form. This practice assures that each bid is entered on the same basis. Preferably, the form should be incorporated in the pamphlet that contains the written portion of the contract documents. Use of the same form for all quotations will help to avoid uncertainties regarding what the respective bidders propose to do and will aid in a comparison of proposals.

It should be clearly stated in the contract documents that all proposals not only must be set forth in full on the printed form but also must conform strictly with the instructions for bidding. Deviations, omissions, and errors may constitute cause for rejection. The form should also include any requests for special information—for example, the bidder's available equipment and organization, other projects completed that are comparable to that in prospect, and proposed time schedule for performance of various parts of the job.

In order to make certain that a proposal signed by a corporate officer will properly bind the corporation, it may be desirable to insert in the proposal form (following such signature) a paragraph somewhat as follows:

CERTIFICATE OF AUTHORITY IF BIDDER IS A CORPORATION

I, the undersigned, as Secretary of the corporation submitting the foregoing Proposal, hereby certify that, under and pursuant to the bylaws and resolutions of said corporation, each officer who has signed said Proposal on behalf of the corporation is fully and completely authorized so to do. (SEAL)

10.3   Standard Proposal Forms

Some engineering offices have developed standard proposal forms for general use. If necessary, various items in the form may be modified in accordance with the peculiarities of a given situation.

Standard proposal forms are most widely used in contracts for services and for the purchase of materials, machinery, and some kinds of equipment. However, large construction projects are likely to involve so much specialized work that they may not lend themselves to use of a standardized proposal form.

10.4   Special Forms

Special proposal forms will vary with the type of contract, the character of the work to be done, the materials to be furnished, and a number of conditions that apply to each case. Therefore, the preparation of the form will usually require considerable original composition. In such writing the author should have some other competent person check the final product. It is also desirable for the author to set aside for a few days what has been written, then reexamine it carefully. It is surprising how many times something that has been misstated or overlooked will surface on this second reading. In the preparation of special proposal forms it may be practicable (1) to use parts from some previous contract, combining them with whatever new material is necessary, or (2) to use the forms from former contracts as a general guide. However, any "cut and paste" method is likely to be hazardous. Slight differences or shades of meaning may go unnoticed. There may be possible interpretations of the previously written material that are far from what is currently intended. Moreover, it may prove difficult to coordinate new material with old and maintain the clarity that a consistent style will provide.

Before preparing a proposal form, the engineer must determine the type of contract most suitable for the particular job to be done—a lump-sum, unit-price, cost-plus-fixed-fee, or cost-plus-percentage contract.

10.5 PROPOSAL FORMS FOR LUMP-SUM CONTRACTS

A lump-sum contract is a relatively simple form of proposal. It is basically a statement provided by the owner or engineer, signed by the bidder, indicating that he proposes to complete the prescribed work for the sum of money stipulated by him directly on the form. Frequently, however, other items will be covered by custom, legal requirement, or the designer's personal style. Of course, the proposal must be clearly identified with the drawings, specifications, and other contract documents.

The following is an illustration of a proposal form for a lump-sum contract for a municipal improvement:

CITY OF X-Y-Z, NEW YORK
WAYNE AVENUE BRIDGE

PROPOSAL

INSTRUCTIONS

PARTIES SUBMITTING PROPOSALS SHALL BE VERY CAREFUL TO FOLLOW ALL THE REQUIREMENTS IN CONNECTION THEREWITH.

THE AMOUNT OF THE PROPOSAL SHALL BE WRITTEN IN FULL AND THEN REPEATED LEGIBLY IN FIGURES IN THE SPACE PROVIDED BELOW.

IF A CHECK IS SUBMITTED WITH THE PROPOSAL, IT MUST BE CERTIFIED; IF A BID BOND IS SUBMITTED, IT MUST BE APPROVED BY THE COMPTROLLER AND THE CORPORATION COUNSEL.

ANY PROPOSAL NOT COMPLYING WITH ALL THESE REQUIREMENTS MAY BE REJECTED.

DEPARTMENT OF PUBLIC WORKS
ROOM 10, MUNICIPAL BUILDING

MARCH 12, 2000

PROPOSAL FORM

TO THE COMMISSIONER OF PUBLIC WORKS:

I, THE UNDERSIGNED, HEREBY DECLARE TO FURNISH ALL THE LABOR AND MATERIALS NECESSARY IN CONNECTION WITH THE PERFORMANCE OF THE FOLLOWING NAMED WORK OR IMPROVEMENT:

FOR THE CONSTRUCTION OF A BRIDGE OVER UNCAS RIVER AT WAYNE AVENUE FOR THE SUM OF _____ ($_____) AND TO RECEIVE IN PAYMENT THEREFOR SUCH VOUCHERS ON THE CITY TREASURER AS THE LAWS AND REGULATIONS OF THE CITY PROVIDE.

I HEREBY DECLARE THAT I HAVE CAREFULLY EXAMINED THE PLANS, SPECIFICATIONS, AND CONTRACT PAPERS ON FILE IN THE OFFICE OF THE COMMISSIONER OF PUBLIC WORKS OF X-Y-Z, NEW YORK; THAT I WILL PROVIDE ALL NECESSARY TOOLS AND APPARATUS, DO ALL THE WORK, FURNISH ALL THE MATERIALS, AND DO EVERYTHING REQUIRED TO PERFORM THE ABOVE-MENTIONED WORK OR IMPROVEMENT IN STRICT ACCORDANCE WITH THE PLANS, SPECIFICATIONS, AND CONTRACT PAPERS.

ACCOMPANYING THIS PROPOSAL IS A CERTIFIED CHECK FOR TWENTY THOUSAND DOLLARS ($20,000.00), WHICH SHALL BECOME THE PROPERTY OF THE COMMISSIONER OF PUBLIC WORKS OF X-Y-Z, NEW YORK; THAT I WILL PROVIDE ALL NECESSARY TOOLS AND APPARATUS, DO ALL OF THE WORK, FURNISH ALL OF THE MATERIALS, AND DO EVERYTHING REQUIRED TO PERFORM THE ABOVE-MENTIONED WORK OR IMPROVEMENT IN STRICT ACCORDANCE WITH THE PLANS, SPECIFICATIONS, AND CONTRACT PAPERS.

ACCOMPANYING THIS PROPOSAL IS A CERTIFIED CHECK FOR TWENTY THOUSAND DOLLARS ($20,000.00), WHICH SHALL BECOME THE PROPERTY OF THE CITY OF X-Y-Z, NEW YORK, IF I SHALL FAIL TO EXECUTE A CONTRACT WITH, AND GIVE BOND TO, SAID CITY, WITHIN SEVEN (7) DAYS AFTER THE DATE OF A WRITTEN NOTICE BY THE COMMISSIONER OF PUBLIC WORKS OF THE CITY OF X-Y-Z, NEW YORK, STATING THAT THIS PROPOSAL HAS BEEN ACCEPTED BY THE COMMISSIONER OF PUBLIC WORKS AND THAT SAID COMMISSIONER IS READY TO HAVE THE SAID CONTRACT SIGNED.

PROMPTLY AFTER SIGNING OF THE CONTRACT I PROMISE TO PRESENT TO THE COMMISSIONER OF PUBLIC WORKS OF THE CITY OF X-Y-Z, NEW YORK, A SURETY COMPANY PERFORMANCE BOND IN THE PENAL SUM OF TWENTY-FIVE (25%) PERCENT OF THE AMOUNT OF THIS PROPOSAL, IN CONFORMITY WITH ARTICLE 25 OF THE CONTRACT DOCUMENTS.

I FURTHER DECLARE THAT NO OFFICER OR EMPLOYEE OF THE CITY OF X-Y-Z, NEW YORK, IS OR HAS BEEN DIRECTLY OR INDIRECTLY INTERESTED IN THIS PROPOSAL NOR IN THE LABOR OR MATERIALS TO WHICH IT RELATES NOR IN ANY PORTION OF THE PROFITS THEREOF; THAT SAID PROPOSAL IS MADE AND CONTRACT WILL BE EXECUTED WITHOUT COLLUSION WITH ANY OTHER PERSON OR PERSONS PRE-

SENTING ANY PROPOSAL FOR THE SAID LABOR AND MATERIALS; AND
THAT SAID PROPOSAL IS IN ALL RESPECTS FAIR AND JUST.

_____

_____

ADDRESS _____

It is perfectly acceptable to replace the paragraphs dealing with the examination of data, the certified check, the performance bond, and the employees of the city by a single paragraph that automatically ties the proposal to the remainder of the contract documents in which such information and instructions are given. This paragraph might be as follows: "The Instructions for Bidders, and all papers and things required by it, by the Form of Contract, by the Specifications, by the Drawings, and by any papers made a part thereof, are a part of this Proposal."

10.6   PROPOSAL FORMS FOR UNIT-PRICE CONTRACTS

In unit-price contracts, the engineer will prepare a schedule of items together with a list of estimated quantities for each item. Such data may be incorporated as part of the proposal form or may be located in a separate schedule to which reference is made in the form itself. The bidder is to insert in the schedule (1) each bid unit price, (2) each bid unit price times the applicable estimated quantity, and (3) the total of such products.

The form is similar to that for a lump-sum contract except for the schedule of prices in lieu of a total sum. The aggregate of these estimated quantities multiplied by the pertinent unit prices is treated as a lump-sum bid in determining the bid price for the contract award purposes. Actual payment will be made by applying the bid unit prices to the quantity of each item actually furnished or performed. The computation of such quantities is usually made by both the contractor and the engineer, and both parties must agree on the correct figures to be used in computing the payment due. If the parties cannot agree about the quantities, it may be necessary to have an independent calculation made or to resort to arbitration[1] or other means available for settling disputes.

The following represents part of a hypothetical proposal form for a unit-price type of contract:

CONTRACT NHA-12

TO THE A-B-C CONCRETE PRODUCTS CORPORATION:

THE UNDERSIGNED*

OFFER TO ENTER INTO CONTRACT   HEREBY OFFERS TO ENTER INTO A CONTRACT WITH THE A-B-C CONCRETE PRODUCTS CORPORATION IN ACCORDANCE WITH THE ATTACHED FORM ENTITLED "FORM OF CONTRACT." THE PRICES INSERTED BY THE UNDERSIGNED IN THE CLAUSE OF SAID FORM OF

[1]See Chapter 27, *infra.*

CONTRACT ENTITLED "SCHEDULE OF PRICES FOR CLASSIFIED WORK" FORM A PART OF THIS PROPOSAL.

WARRANTIES AND REPRESENTATIONS

THE UNDERSIGNED HEREBY MAKES EACH AND EVERY REPRESENTATION AND WARRANTY REQUIRED TO BE MADE BY THE BIDDERS IN SAID FORM OF CONTRACT AND AGREES THAT THE ACCEPTANCE OF THIS PROPOSAL SHALL HAVE THE EFFECT PROVIDED IN THE INFORMATION FOR BIDDERS BOUND HEREWITH, AND THAT EFFECT ONLY.

PAPERS FORMING PART OF PROPOSAL

THE INFORMATION FOR BIDDERS, ALL PAPERS REQUIRED BY IT AND SUBMITTED HEREWITH, AND THE FORM OF CONTRACT AND ALL PAPERS MADE A PART THEREOF BY ITS TERMS ARE MADE A PART OF THIS PROPOSAL.

BIDDER'S OFFICE

THE UNDERSIGNED HEREBY DESIGNATES NUMBER _____ STREET, CITY OF _____, STATE OF _____, AS HIS OFFICE TO WHICH NOTICES MAY BE DELIVERED OR MAILED.

THE UNDERSIGNED FURTHER AGREES TO COMPLY WITH ALL CONTRACT REQUIREMENTS ABOUT CONDITIONS OF EMPLOYMENT AND MINIMUM WAGE RATES.

DATED, _____, 20___

BY** _____

_____

_____

_____

*INSERT THE BIDDER'S NAME. IF THE BIDDER IS A CORPORATION, GIVE THE STATE IN WHICH INCORPORATED, USING THE PHRASE "A CORPORATION ORGANIZED UNDER THE LAWS OF . . . . " IF THE BIDDER IS A PARTNERSHIP, GIVE THE NAMES OF ALL PARTNERS, USING ALSO THE PHRASE "COPARTNERS DOING BUSINESS UNDER THE FIRM NAME OF . . . . " IF THE BIDDER IS AN INDIVIDUAL USING A TRADE NAME, GIVE THE INDIVIDUAL'S NAME, USING ALSO THE PHRASE "AN INDIVIDUAL DOING BUSINESS UNDER THE TRADE NAME OF . . . "

**IF THE PROPOSAL IS SIGNED BY AN OFFICER OR AGENT, GIVE HIS TITLE AND ADDRESS.

In one contract for a portion of the New Jersey approach to the Lincoln Tunnel at New York City, there were 54 classified items in the schedule of prices. Many of them contained detailed descriptions that were necessarily lengthy and that had to be prepared with great care. Careful instructions should be given to the bidders, and the several items to be priced should be adequately outlined, as in this sample:

PRICES AND PAYMENTS
SCHEDULE OF PRICES FOR CLASSIFIED WORK

PRICES COVER ALL COSTS

THE FOLLOWING SCHEDULE DOES NOT CONSTITUTE A COMPLETE OUTLINE OF THE WORK TO BE PERFORMED BY THE CONTRACTOR IN ACCORDANCE WITH THE REQUIREMENTS OF THE CONTRACT DRAWINGS AND SPECIFICATIONS IN THEIR PRESENT FORM BUT IS MERELY A LIST OF THE ITEMS OF WORK TO WHICH UNIT PRICES ARE TO BE APPLIED IN COMPUTING THE CONTRACTOR'S COMPENSATION. IT CONTAINS ALL SUCH ITEMS, AND THE COMPENSATION COMPUTED THEREFROM IS TO BE THE FULL COMPENSATION FOR ALL WORK AND MATERIALS WHATSOEVER REQUIRED BY THE CONTRACT DRAWINGS AND SPECIFICATIONS IN THEIR PRESENT FORM, WHETHER OR NOT INDICATED ON SAID SCHEDULE OR PERTAINING TO THE ITEMS OF WORK SHOWN THEREOF.

QUANTITIES NOT GUARANTEED

THE QUANTITIES SHOWN IN THE FOLLOWING SCHEDULE ARE ESTIMATED QUANTITIES AND ARE GIVEN SOLELY FOR THE PURPOSE OF FACILITATING THE COMPARISON OF PROPOSALS. THE OWNER SHALL NOT BE HELD RESPONSIBLE IF THE STATED QUANTITIES ARE NOT EVEN APPROXIMATELY CORRECT. ALL COMPUTATIONS OF THE CONTRACTOR'S COMPENSATION SHALL BE BASED UPON THE QUANTITIES OF WORK ACTUALLY PERFORMED, WHETHER GREATER OR LESS THAN THE ESTIMATED QUANTITIES.

WRITING CONTROLS OVER FIGURES

IN CASE OF DISCREPANCY BETWEEN THE PRICES STATED IN WRITING AND THOSE STATED IN FIGURES, THE WRITING SHALL CONTROL.

COMPUTATION OF PAYMENT

IN COMPUTING THE CONTRACTOR'S COMPENSATION, NONE OF THE PRICES STATED IN THE SCHEDULE OF PRICES FOR CLASSIFIED WORK WILL BE APPLIED TO ANY WORK EXCEPT THAT EXPRESSLY PROVIDED THEREIN. FURTHERMORE, IN ALL CASES WHERE PRICES ARE QUOTED UPON MATERIALS, THEY WILL BE APPLIED ONLY TO MATERIALS INSTALLED BY THE CONTRACTOR AND FORMING A PART OF THE PERMANENT CONSTRUCTION.

APPLICATION TO CONSTRUCTION CONTRACTS

LINCOLN TUNNEL
NEW YORK CITY
NEW JERSEY APPROACH

SCHEDULE

ITEM	ESTIMATED QUANTITIES	ITEMS OF WORK WITH PRICES WRITTEN	DOLLAR AMOUNTS
1	7500 CU YD	**ROCK EXCAVATION PER CUBIC YARD**	

_____DOLLARS

_____CENTS

PAYMENT LINES FOR ROCK EX-CAVATION ARE SHOWN ON THE CONTRACT DRAWINGS. THE ABOVE UNIT PRICE WILL BE AP-PLIED TO THE VOLUME OF ROCK BETWEEN THE SURFACE OF THE ROCK AND SUCH PAYMENT LINES, WHETHER SUCH VOLUME OF ROCK IS GREATER OR LESS THAN THE VOLUME OF ROCK AC-TUALLY EXCAVATED.

IN CASES WHERE THE ENGINEER HEREAFTER ORDERS ROCK EX-CAVATION IN ADDITION TO THAT REQUIRED BY THE CONTRACT DRAWINGS AND SPECIFICATIONS, THE ABOVE UNIT PRICE WILL BE APPLIED ONLY TO THE VOLUME OF ROCK BETWEEN THE SURFACE OF ROCK AND PAYMENT LINES ESTABLISHED SIX (6) INCHES OUTSIDE OF AND PARALLEL TO THE NET LINES ESTABLISHED FOR SUCH ADDITIONAL EXCAVA-TION, WHETHER SUCH VOLUME OF ROCK IS GREATER OR LESS THAN THE VOLUME OF ROCK AC-TUALLY EXCAVATED.

AS USED HEREIN, "SURFACE OF ROCK" DENOTES THE SURFACE OF ROCK EXPOSED AFTER EXCA-VATION OF THE EARTH ABOVE

THE ROCK HAS BEEN COMPLETED, AND "ROCK" MEANS ANY SOLID MATERIAL WHICH NORMALLY CANNOT BE REMOVED BY HAND OR MECHANICAL MEANS AND THE REMOVAL OF WHICH WOULD NORMALLY REQUIRE BOTH DRILLING AND BLASTING.

| 2 | 20,000 CU YD | **EARTH EXCAVATION** |
| | | **PER CUBIC YARD** |

_____DOLLARS

_____CENTS

PAYMENT LINES FOR EARTH EXCAVATION ARE SHOWN ON THE CONTRACT DRAWINGS. THE ABOVE UNIT PRICE WILL BE APPLIED TO THE VOLUME OF EARTH BETWEEN THE SURFACE OF THE GROUND AND SUCH PAYMENT LINES, WHETHER SUCH VOLUME OF EARTH IS GREATER OR LESS THAN THE VOLUME OF EARTH ACTUALLY EXCAVATED.

IN CASES WHERE THE ENGINEER HEREAFTER ORDERS EARTH EXCAVATION IN ADDITION TO THAT REQUIRED BY THE CONTRACT DRAWINGS AND SPECIFICATIONS, THE ABOVE UNIT PRICE WILL BE APPLIED ONLY TO THE VOLUME OF EARTH BETWEEN THE SURFACE OF THE GROUND AND THE NET LINES ESTABLISHED FOR SUCH ADDITIONAL EXCAVATION, EVEN THOUGH A GREATER VOLUME IS ACTUALLY EXCAVATED.

AS USED HEREIN, "SURFACE OF THE GROUND" DENOTES THE NATURAL TOP SURFACE OF THE EARTH PRIOR TO THE COMMENCEMENT OF EXCAVATION OPERATIONS, AND "EARTH" MEANS ALL MATERIALS LYING BELOW THE SURFACE OF THE GROUND OTHER THAN "ROCK" AS DEFINED IN ITEM 1.

3   12,500 CU YD   **CONCRETE, PER
                               CUBIC YARD**

                               _____DOLLARS

                               _____CENTS

                               THE ABOVE UNIT PRICE WILL BE
                               APPLIED TO THE VOLUME COM-
                               PUTED FROM THE CONTRACT
                               DRAWINGS IN ACCORDANCE
                               WITH THE LINES OF THE STRUC-
                               TURE AND/OR THE PAYMENT
                               LINES FOR CONCRETE SHOWN
                               THEREON.

                               NO DEDUCTIONS WILL BE MADE
                               FOR REINFORCING BARS OR ANY
                               ROCK LEFT PROJECTING WITHIN
                               THE PAYMENT LINES, BUT DEDUC-
                               TIONS WILL BE MADE FOR THE
                               VOLUME OF EMBEDDED PIPES,
                               DUCTS, AND CONDUITS TWO (2)
                               INCHES OR MORE IN DIAMETER.

10   9600 SQ YD   **CONCRETE BASE (FOR PAVEMENT),
                               ON SUBGRADE, PER SQUARE YARD**

                               _____DOLLARS

                               _____CENTS

                               IN APPLYING THE ABOVE UNIT
                               PRICE, NO DEDUCTIONS WILL BE
                               MADE FOR THE SURFACE AREA
                               OF MANHOLES, CATCH BASINS,
                               OR OTHER SIMILAR STRUCTURES.

19   1,800,000 LB   **REINFORCING BARS, PER POUND**

                               _____DOLLARS

                               _____CENTS

                               THE ABOVE UNIT PRICE WILL BE
                               APPLIED TO THE WEIGHT OF RE-
                               INFORCING BARS (COMPUTED
                               FROM THE BAR LISTS ON THE AP-
                               PROVED WORKING DRAWINGS)
                               USED IN CONNECTION WITH THE
                               MATERIALS TO WHICH THE UNIT
                               PRICES QUOTED UNDER ITEMS 3,
                               7, 8, 9, 10, AND 11 PERTAIN. IT
                               WILL BE APPLIED IN ADDITION
                               TO SUCH PRICES BUT WILL NOT

BE APPLIED TO ANY OTHER REIN-
FORCING BARS, NOR TO THE
WEIGHT OF FORM TIES, SPACERS,
CHAIRS, CLIPS, WIRES, OR OTHER
DEVICES FOR HOLDING AND SUP-
PORTING THE REINFORCEMENT
OR FORMS.

It is sometimes practicable for the engineer to prescribe that some item or
items of a unit-price contract are to be bid as an individual lump-sum. Such things
as clearing and grubbing of the site, cleaning up and landscaping after other work
is finished, interior decorating, and installation of a septic tank and tile field do not
lend themselves to the devising of satisfactory units of measurement. Any selected
payment items are likely to be either too general or too excessively detailed. However, an experienced contractor can usually estimate the cost of such work fairly
accurately, and the lump-sum bid on the item will cover all the work necessary to
achieve the desired product.

The list of unit prices includes everything that is to be done or furnished under
the contract. Many miscellaneous jobs have to be performed by the contractor;
payment for these is supposed to be made "indirectly," as will be explained in Section 10.13. Payment to the contractor will be made only upon the basis of the
stated items, the bid unit prices, and the quantities as finally approved, in addition,
perhaps, to a lump-sum item or two as above described.

The engineer should carefully evaluate whether the selection of payment items
for inclusion in a unit-price contract represents a wise choice. The items should be
definite, readily measurable, of customary type, and of sufficient scope to cover as
much as is reasonably possible of the total work required.

10.7   PROPOSAL FORMS FOR COST-PLUS CONTRACTS

The proposal form for either a cost-plus-percentage or a cost-plus-fixed-fee contract is similar to that for a lump-sum contract. The form should state clearly what
the contractor is to do; for instance, furnish all labor, equipment, material, transportation, and power. Also, it may indicate the staff he is to provide, the length of
time he is to be in charge, the nature and extent of his authority, and the point at
which his services are to terminate. When the bidder signs this form with all the
necessary data recorded thereon, he has executed a proposal including his compensation, expressed either as a specific percentage or as a lump-sum figure. The proposal for the rendering of engineering services in designing a project or in supervising its construction may be merely a letter stating what percentage of the
construction cost or what lump sum will be satisfactory to the engineer. No special
proposal form is then necessary.

The contract documents that by reference are made a part of the proposal will
cover many details essential to the job. In the case of a cost-plus-percentage con-

tract, the engineer should be careful to clarify what will be included in the cost of the project. Land, easements, taxes, insurance, housing, and the salaries of the owner's supervisory and engineering force are items usually excluded from the list of costs to which the agreed percentage is to be applied.

The contractor, in addition to recouping his costs, receives as compensation the "fee" included in his bid, when the contract is on a cost-plus-fixed-fee basis, or the agreed-upon percentage of the final "contractor's cost" total, when the job is under a cost-plus-percentage arrangement.

10.8 LOWEST RESPONSIBLE BIDDER

It is advisable to state in the contract papers that, if awarded at all, the contract will go to the lowest *responsible* bidder. Of course, the owner wants to get the job completed as economically as possible, but this may not necessarily mean awarding the contract to the *lowest* bidder.[2] As a general proposition, it is preferable to disallow unqualified contractors to bid at all rather than to refuse to award the contract after they have gone to the trouble and expense of putting together proposals. Factors weighed in a decision to reject a low bid should be objectively justifiable and not based on personal feelings. The following are valid considerations.

1. The lowest bidder may not have sufficient finances to handle the project. It may therefore be cheaper in the long run to award the contract to the next-higher bidder rather than to chance the trouble and loss for the owner which might ensue if the low bidder were to get the award and then, by reason of inadequate cash reserves, be unable to finish the work. Even though the posting of a proper bond by the contractor affords the owner a considerable measure of protection[3] (as will be explained in Chapter 21), it is desirable to require the bidder to present a statement of financial condition.

2. The lowest bidder may not have sufficient experience in the particular kinds of work involved. The record of past performance is an excellent, although not infallible, guide. Limited experience does not necessarily mean a bidder is incapable of performing satisfactorily. However, it may be reasonable, for example, to question the ability of the bidder to perform a $500,000 contract when the largest one that was previously handled was in the neighborhood of $50,000.

3. The lowest bidder may have an unsatisfactory reputation. The contractor in question may have been guilty in the past of careless work, of always maneuvering for extras, of being uncooperative, or of making it necessary for the engineer to inspect the construction work with extreme care. Although rejection on this rather nebulous ground of "reputation" may lead to many disputes, it remains a proper course of action when circumstances call for it.

---

[2]For a case analyzing "lowest responsible bidder" in the context of a Public Bid Law, see *Systems Plus, Inc. v. East Jefferson General Hospital*, 638 So. 2d 404 (La. App. 1994).

[3]There are cases holding to the effect that a provision in the advertisement for tenders (stating that the bidders will be required to give security for the performance of the work) may be waived by the owner, and a valid contract will be created by the acceptance of a proposal, although no security is in fact given by the successful bidder.

4.   The lowest bidder's staff and equipment may be inadequate. The engineer may ask the bidder to submit an itemized list of his proposed staff and of the equipment he intends using. Justification for this is obvious, as it is in the best interest of all parties not to award to a small building contractor with limited resources the contract for the construction of a large and difficult project. Though his bid may be in perfectly good faith, such a contractor is not really equipped to do the job and acceptance of his proposal would likely result in misfortune for him as well as for all others involved.

10.9   PREQUALIFICATION OF BIDDERS

To avoid the possibility of having to reject a proposal for reasons such as those just described some engineers have adopted the procedure of *prequalification of bidders*. To accomplish this, an individual or group is empowered to determine whether or not particular general contractors are qualified to handle contracts of a certain size and type. The investigators will generally ask the prospective bidders for the same sort of financial data and performance records as they would supply were they submitting a proposal on the actual job. The details, of course, will vary with the circumstances. Based on the results of such research, a list of contractors who are approved as prospective bidders may be prepared. Compiling such a list is frequently a difficult task because (1) omission of a particular contractor is likely to be criticized as unfair; (2) political pressure may be exerted in favor of one or more concerns; (3) a contractor who is not able to qualify at one time may be able to meet all requirements later, or vice versa; and (4) the ability to accomplish contract work successfully is not always easily determined. The prequalification procedure may prevent some builders from being awarded a contract that, because of its scope and complexity, would likely prove disadvantageous for them, notwithstanding their personal beliefs to the contrary.

Private owners are able to use this principle of selection simply by sending inquiries and data only to those whose qualifications have received advance approval. Likewise, governmental bodies (such as highway and public works departments) may, unless there are statutes forbidding it, use this method to advantage, though claims of partiality may make its use difficult.

Prequalification of subcontractors may also be practiced, and if it is, the general contractors should be given the approved list well before bidding, since this information will affect their advance arrangements with prospective subcontractors. In any case, the owner should retain the right to approve or reject any subcontractor.

10.10   DEPOSIT FOR SECURING PLANS

The bidders will be informed as to how, where, from whom, and for what price copies of the plans, specifications, and other contract documents may be obtained. It is customary to require prospective bidders to make a cash deposit for these documents, the charge representing the estimated cost of printing or an amount that will preclude requests from those who are not seriously interested in bidding. Payment usually must accompany the request for the documents. It is also customary to state that all the deposit (or some stipulated portion of it) will be refunded upon return of the documents in good condition. Sometimes the refund is limited to those who not only return the documents but actually submit bids as well.

10.11   MISCELLANEOUS ITEMS FOR INFORMATION OF BIDDERS

Some information to be given bidders includes:

1. *Familiarity with the work.* It should be made clear that, upon signing the proposal, the bidder thereby gives assurance that he has familiarized himself with *(a)* the conditions at the site, *(b)* the requirements of the contract, *(c)* the character of the work, and *(d)* the content of the plans and specifications.

2. *The size of the "bid" and "performance" bonds,* and any "labor and materials" bond required.

3. *The amount of time allowed between the opening of the proposals and the award of the contract.* This interval is ordinarily from one to four weeks. The purpose of limiting the interval is to avoid undue delay in signing the contract. If the owner decides to reject all proposals, such action should be taken within this one- to four-week period.

4. *The time limit between (a) written notice by the owner to the contractor that the latter's proposal has been accepted and (b) signing of the contract.* A reasonable period is seven days.

5. *Important dates.* It is generally desirable to set a date for the start and for the completion of the contract work.

6. *Liquidated damages.* Data is needed regarding any liquidated damages that will apply in the event of failure to complete the work on schedule. Conversely, any bonus for particularly rapid completion of the work should be mentioned.

7. *Taxes.* There may be special taxes, license, or permit fees that the contractor must pay. If so, this should be made clear. On the other hand, there may be work which, because of its nature, will be exempt from certain taxes. Here, for example, is a clause from the instructions for bidders who were estimating the cost of an extension to a hospital:

   > Sales Tax:
   > The Institution is not subject to the State Sales Tax, and the Contractor shall take advantage of this in his bidding.

8. *Corporate charter.* In the case of corporate bidders, it may be desirable to require that a copy of the corporation's charter, or other proof of its right to conduct business and perform the work indicated be furnished the owner.

9. *Labor.* Any special requirements affecting labor should be given. For example, it may be required in some places that the rates of pay for labor be published in the instructions for bidders. Likewise, any consideration that would compel employment of a particular type of labor should be noted, for instance, that a specified percentage of the workmen on the construction job be residents of the jurisdiction in which the work be performed, or members of a minority.[4]

Upon receipt of a proposal form and related documents the bidder must now prepare his bid. Keep in mind that it is he who is making the offer, even if his bid merely fills in the blanks of the proposal form.

10.12 PREPARATION OF BID ON COST-PLUS CONTRACT

Engineers should understand how the bidder arrives at the figures appearing in the final proposal. The determination of a proper fee or percentage for a cost-plus contract is largely a matter of judgment on the part of the contractor and the engineer. They have to consider the particular problems to be met. These are so special in many cases that it is impractical to attempt to state general rules to govern the proper extent of the contractor's compensation. However, in emergency jobs for the federal government, it is probable that precedents have been established that will afford a worthwhile guide. In some instances involving public work there may be laws or "recommended fees" that govern the compensation. Large private organizations sometimes have a particular contractor to whom they award contracts on a cost-plus-percentage basis in view of excellent work the contractor has done for them in the past.

10.13 PREPARATION OF LUMP-SUM BID BY A CONTRACTOR

A bid for a lump-sum contract for the purchase of materials is generally based largely upon component costs and competitive factors. In many instances the prices of common materials and products are somewhat standardized or at least known to be within a narrow range at any particular time. Prices of some articles are given in catalogs or on price lists—with or without discounts. In such cases, the total cost of a product can be estimated with reasonable accuracy, and bids are not expected to vary widely one from another.

Making a lump-sum proposal on a large construction project is a different matter. Here bidders have to estimate various contributing costs carefully since the work entailed requires the use of many different materials, the labor of large num-

---

[4]For further discussion of minority hiring, see Chapter 28.

bers of employees, and the performance of a wide variety of operations. Estimating the probable overall costs of such work requires considerable time and expense.

Bidders must estimate the quantities of materials involved, then compute their cost. They must calculate the approximate cost of all labor that will be required to perform the work including taxes, workers' compensation, and insurance. Since large construction projects can take a significant time to complete, consideration should be given to possible increases in prices. The best way to provide for this is by an *escalator clause* in the contract that obligates the owner to pay for increases in the costs of materials and labor. This is fair because if no increases occur the owner will not incur this cost. The duration of the job governs the necessity for such a clause, and it is most appropriate in contracts that will require substantial time to perform. In the absence of an escalator clause, a bidder should protect himself against losses caused by rising prices by estimating the anticipated increase and adding it as a cost.

Bidders also have to include many items of cost besides those that are directly associated with materials and labor involved in the construction. Other items of expense that will have to be considered in the estimate are:

1. *Supervisory and office staff* in the field. This includes foremen, bookkeepers, and secretaries. In this item there may also be included such things as office supplies, blueprinting, and postage.

2. *Engineering.* This may be a considerable item if the contractor's staff is to make detail drawings; design special features like cofferdams, shoring, and heavy form work; and do the surveying to establish lines and grades.

3. *Rentals or construction of* office space, field headquarters, and sometimes housing—if the contractor has to provide temporary living accommodations for some of his employees.

4. *Equipment.* This includes depreciation and repair of the contractor's own equipment, possibly a portion of the cost of new equipment (either additional or to replace that which wears out on the job), the cost of tools that may be lost or damaged, and the rental of machines leased from someone else.

5. *Storage facilities.* Sometimes this includes a storage yard and temporary warehousing at a shipping terminal as well as tool houses and storage facilities at the job site.

6. *Power and means of* getting it to the places where it is needed. This may include power lines or small generating plants for the supplying of heat, steam, electricity, or compressed air.

7. *Transportation of all materials and personnel.* This may include the building of access roads, transportation of workers to and from their living quarters, demurrage on freight cars not unloaded promptly, and the cost of transfer from one means of transportation to another.

8. *Contingencies.* This topic covers the miscellaneous odds and ends that the contractor may have to take care of and for which he may not have made specific allowance in his estimate. For example, if delays, construction hazards, and liquidated damages are likely, this contingency item is designed to "reimburse" the bidder should these extra expenditures materialize. This item is

often estimated as a percentage of the cost of the project or of direct materials and labor; it may range from 5 to 15 percent of this sum, or it may be a lesser percentage if the bidder is convinced that the work is shown completely and clearly on the drawings and in the other contract documents and that no unpleasant surprises are likely to develop.

9. *A portion of the general overhead* of the central or home office. This is because the job will require the services of various persons who are not at the site (or who are there only occasionally) and who may be assigned to the inspection and expediting of materials. "Overhead" might also include a figure to represent the cost of making estimates for this job (and perhaps a little extra for other bids that were or will be made by the contractor).

10. *Profit.* This item will vary in accordance with what the contractor thinks is reasonable and can be realized without losing the job.

11. *Interest on money.* The contractor may have to borrow money to finance his operations. If so, he will probably reflect in his bid the estimated cost of interest on loans made to him. He may also wish to take into consideration what his own funds tied up in the job might earn if they were drawing interest at current rates.

12. *Insurance on property and personnel.* This item includes, among other things, fire, theft, vandalism, and public liability insurance protection.

13. *Bonds.* This refers to the cost of procuring the bid bond, the performance bond, and any other bonds required.

14. *Taxes.* Allowance should be made for sales taxes or income taxes and other federal, state, and local taxes that are involved.

15. *Special expenses.* These may include payments for a temporary right-of-way, the cost of permits of various kinds, fees on the use of patents, fees for consultants, legal expenses, and commissions to agents who may perform certain duties.

When the estimated costs of appropriate additional items are added to those for direct labor and materials, the sum is the total estimated expense. This may or may not turn out to be the actual bid price. If, in the contractor's opinion, the total estimated cost is higher than the sum he thinks others will bid on the job, he may *reduce* his own bid figure somewhat, hoping that he can still make a profit by doing the work more economically than the estimated costs indicate. If he is badly in need of work, he may even seek the contract without allowing for any real profit at all.

It may be, on the other hand, that the contractor believes the estimated costs are too low. He may then *round up* the bid price to what he thinks is adequate. If he is already swamped with other work, he may decide that he will not take any serious chances but will set a price such that, if he gets the job, he will be able to augment his staff and organization and still make a profit.

It is important to recognize the difference between an *estimate* and a *proposal*. An *estimate* is not assumed to be an accurate statement of the final cost. It is generally based upon information that is not complete and exact, and it involves the making of assumptions. By nature it is an approximation. A bidder estimates cost and will use this or a modification as the basis for the *proposal* on the job. The proposal becomes a binding contract when accepted, even though the figure quoted does not purport to be an exact mathematical computation of the real cost.

10.14   PREPARATION OF A UNIT-PRICE BID BY A CONTRACTOR

When a contractor is trying to estimate costs on a contract for which a unit-price proposal is required, he will proceed at first substantially as he would if it were a lump-sum contract. However, he may not have to be as careful in estimating the quantities of material and labor involved. He will investigate carefully such things as the nature of the work, the various construction difficulties that may be anticipated, the expected duration of the job, the availability of materials, and the quality of workmanship needed.

As shown in Section 10.6, the list of items in the proposal form usually states the estimated quantities and the units of measurement. The contractor will therefore distribute the estimated total cost of the project among these various items, adjusting the figures until the sum of the bids on all items substantially equals the aggregate number of dollars previously reckoned to be the cost of the job as a whole. Or the contractor may estimate the cost of labor, materials, overhead, profit, and so on for each main item of work if this method seems to be desirable.

As an illustration of this procedure, assume that the following items are given in the proposal form for a construction contract pertaining to a highway and bridge project:

Rock excavation	2,000 cu yd
Earth excavation and fill	5,000 cu yd
Concrete	3,000 cu yd
Reinforcing steel	300,000 lb
Membrane waterproofing	600 sq yd
Structural steel	800,000 lb

Assume further that the contractor estimates that the total bid price with profit included should be about $850,000. Now he may make a trial summary as follows:

Rock excavation	2,000	cu yd at	$ 20.00	$ 40,000
Earth excavation & fill	5,000	cu yd at	5.00	25,000
Concrete	3,000	cu yd at	100.00	300,000
Reinforcing steel	300,000	lb at	.45	135,000
Membrane waterproofing	600	sq yd at	5.00	3,000
Structural steel	800,000	lb at	.40	320,000
Total				$823,000

This is $27,000 less than the desired total. The deficiency has to be made up by various adjustments. The contractor may add to some of the unit prices as follows:

Rock excavation	add $2.00 per cu yd	2,000 × 2 = $ 4,000
Earth excavation & fill	add $1.00 per cu yd	5,000 × 1 = 5,000
Concrete	add $6.00 per cu yd	3,000 × 6 = 18,000
Total		$27,000

Therefore, the final figures recorded on the proposal form may read:

Rock excavation	2,000	cu yd at	$ 22.00	$ 44,000
Earth excavation & fill	5,000	cu yd at	6.00	30,000
Concrete	3,000	cu yd at	106.00	318,000
Reinforcing steel	300,000	lb at	.45	135,000
Membrane waterproofing	600	sq yd at	5.00	3,000
Structural steel	800,000	lb at	.40	320,000
Total				$850,000

Notice that in making the upward adjustments the contractor has added relatively more to the items of work that will be performed early in the course of the contract than those that will be done later. This is *one form of an unbalanced bid*. By so doing, partial payments made in the first few months will yield enough return so that less of the contractor's cash will be needed.

Another type of unbalanced bid may be arrived at by bidding low on an item that the contractor thinks will underrun the quantities listed in the proposal form and by making a high bid on something that is likely to overrun[5] the stated quantity. Remember that the contractor will be paid the bid price per unit multiplied by the number of units actually performed or furnished. Reasonable "unbalancing" is perfectly proper, but it represents something of a gamble by the contractor in most cases.

[5]The word "overrun," as used here, means that the actual quantity of work to be done under some particular item exceeds the quantity stated by the engineer in the list of items; of course, "underrun" means just the opposite. For example, the item for earth excavation in the preceding list states that the unit price is to be applied to 5,000 cubic yards of material when the amount of the contractor's bid is figured. If the contractor thinks that 6,000 cubic yards will actually prove to be necessary, he believes that the work required will overrun the estimated quantity.

In one contract that involved a large amount of both earth and rock excavation the borings had been made about 150 feet on centers. The site was in territory where the rock surfaces often varied greatly in elevation within short distances. One contractor realized this and asked permission to take additional borings at his own expense. This was granted, and the information that he obtained was naturally his own to use. Actually, he found that his own estimates, based on the more complete information, showed much more earth excavation and less rock excavation than stated in the proposal form. He therefore bid a little high on the unit price for the earth excavation and a little low on the rock excavation. He was awarded the contract, and made a good profit when the final computed quantities of earth and rock turned out to be substantially as he had estimated.

10.15   IMPROPER PROPOSALS

If a proposal is not prepared in the manner required, this can be proper cause for rejection. In one case, two steel companies presented nearly equal bids on a contract. The unit prices were supposed to be based upon the "scale weights" of fabricated members—that is, actual weights as the material was loaded on the cars. One contractor added to his proposal a paragraph stating that his bid was based on "calculated weights"—computed from the detail drawings without allowance for beveled cuts, copes, and other reductions from the overall size of each piece before cutting. The contract involved considerable steelwork as to which the calculated weight would considerably exceed the scale weight. This particular contractor's unit price was slightly under that of the other bidder. However, he had failed to quote on the basis stipulated in the invitation for bids, and the contract was let to the company whose bid was in proper form. It may be that a proposal form will contain a statement to the effect that the owner reserves the right to waive any informality or irregularity in the bids received. This provision is intended to be utilized when the bidder makes some minor mistake or is guilty of an oversight that does not materially affect the actual bid.

In another case, a contract called for bids on a project that involved pouring large quantities of concrete during the winter season. The papers stated that enclosures and heating would be required to protect the concrete during setting and curing in freezing weather. The lowest bidder added a paragraph stating that the quotation submitted excluded the cost of this protection, and the proposal was rejected because it deviated from the prescribed pattern. If in the case just cited the engineer had accepted the lowest bid, such action would have been binding on the basis of the terms stated in that proposal, because the bidder had made an offer and the engineer had accepted it. On the other hand, such action by the engineer would have been unfair to the other bidders. They, too, might have submitted lower figures if they had realized that they could violate the specification with respect to the cold-weather protection.

10.16 ALTERNATIVES

In some cases proposals may be requested on the basis of two or more alternatives. One purpose for securing of bid prices on each of several possible arrangements is to make a choice possible after the costs have been set forth in the various bids. A second objective may be that of obtaining bids on a basic contract and, with them, securing additional proposals on special items that the owner may or may not decide to add to such basic contract.

The proposals for the construction of the suspension system of the George Washington Bridge illustrate one function of "alternatives." The Port of New York Authority made two different designs—one for wire cables and another for eyebar chains. This bridge was to have a main span that would be twice as long as the then-longest existing suspension structure—the Philadelphia-Camden Bridge. There were many arguments among engineers for and against each of the two designs. It was ultimately decided that complete designs and specifications would be prepared for both types and that the matter should be settled on the basis of actual bid prices, or, at least, the decision would be made after the costs became known. Roebling's bid on the wire-cable design was lower than any other of its kind and lower than any on the eyebar-chain proposition. The wire-cable design was adopted, and the contract was awarded accordingly.

The use of alternatives for additions or subtractions may be illustrated in this way: Assume that a municipality desires lump-sum proposals on the construction of a large school building for which the appropriation is to be a specific and limited amount. The city wants to have the building constructed in accordance with at least the minimum plan. The estimated cost (as prepared by the engineer) of this minimum structure is well within the appropriation. However, the authorities would like, if financially possible, to include an extension of the wing that is to house shops and manual-training facilities so as to increase their size. Furthermore, although space is provided for a swimming pool in the minimum plan, the pool itself and the locker rooms and equipment are not included in the basic proposition. These items are all desired if their costs will permit their inclusion. The engineer or architect may ask for lump-sum proposals as follows:

1. The basic plan as shown.
2. The extension of the shop wing as one alternative (addition).
3. The swimming pool as a second (separate) alternative.

Assume that the bids received are as shown in Table 10.1 and that the planned appropriation is $2,100,000. All the bids on item 1 are less than this sum, and A is the lowest bidder. For items 1 and 2 together, B is the lowest bidder, and three of the contractors' bids are within the limit. For items 1 and 3, C is the lowest, and the same three proposals are again under the appropriation figure. However, for items 1, 2, and 3 combined, C is low, but all bids are beyond the limit of the available funds.

Table 10.1   Assumed bids on a large school

Item No.	Contractor			
	A	B	C	D
1	$1,950,000	$1,965,000	$1,970,000	$2,050,000
2	125,000	100,000	120,000	95,000
3	100,000	95,000	60,000	75,000
1+2	2,075,000	2,065,000	2,090,000	2,145,000
1+3	2,050,000	2,060,000	2,030,000	2,125,000
1+2+3	2,175,000	2,160,000	2,150,000	2,220,000

Now suppose that the choice of alternatives is open so that the city officials can decide whether to go ahead on the basis of item 1, items 1 and 2, or items 1 and 3. In the first case A would presumably get the contract; in the second instance, the award would go to B; in the third, C would be successful. The combination of items 1, 2, and 3 is automatically eliminated because of prohibitive cost.

It is obvious that if there are several alternative plans available, it may be possible to award the contract to some preferred builder merely by selecting the arrangement on which that total bid was the low one. Operating in that fashion might well lead to abuse, or at least to accusations of unfairness or partiality. It is therefore desirable to determine in advance, and to state in the proposal form, the order of acceptance of any alternatives. In the case of this school, the contract papers might be prepared so as to call for the basic bid on item 1. Then, if one or more alternatives is to be accepted, item 2 is to be first on the list, with item 3 following. With the use of this procedure in the school example given, and with $2,100,000 as the top limit, the authorities must then award the contract to A for item 1 alone or to B if item 2 is to be included. They have no other choice, assuming both A and B are responsible contractors.

The same principles apply in case of subtractions. Again, the sequence of the elimination of items should be specified. In the case of this school, the basic design might cover the entire project, and lump-sum bids might be asked for on the complete structure (including pool, etc.). Then the proposal form might call for the statement of a figure by which the contractor would reduce the bid price if the swimming pool and its accessories are eliminated. Still another figure might be requested in order to show the further reduction in the bid price should both the pool and the extension of the shop wing be removed from consideration. Use of alternates may avoid the difficulty otherwise encountered in revising and readvertising a contract when all bids for the *complete* structure exceed the funds available. The program of reductions, if any, should be clearly described in the proposal form and should be followed in awarding the contract.

10.17 WITHDRAWAL OF PROPOSALS

As a general rule, withdrawal of a proposal will not be permitted, and this prohibition should be publicized in the invitation for bids. In no event should a proposal be withdrawn after the public opening and reading session is under way.

Even where timely withdrawal is allowed, the bidder is expected to give an acceptable reason. One might be the discovery of a numerical error in the figures, (not to be confused with second thoughts about the wisdom of his proposal).[6] It may be that some major quantity of material or some substantial labor item has been inadvertently omitted from the calculations, or the same item may have been included twice. In these relatively rare instances, the engineer must decide whether or not to allow the affected bidder to rectify the situation either by correcting the proposal or by withdrawing it completely.

The engineer should take a course of action that is fair to the owner, the bidders, and himself. If the lowest bidder has made a very serious error, the engineer should not insist upon penalizing him just because a chance to do so presents itself. Fair play in a particular case may demand that the engineer recommend (1) that the contractor be allowed to withdraw the unfortunate proposal, (2) that he enter into a modified agreement satisfactory to him and the owner if allowable, or (3) that his bid be rejected. On the other hand, the mere fact that a contractor makes an error that may cause him to lose some money on the job is not always in and of itself sufficient cause for leniency by the engineer. The decision in any event is to be made by the engineer rather than by the contractor.[7]

The engineer's primary duty is to protect the owner's interests in cases where the contractor's calculations are obviously in error. It may very well not be to the owner's advantage to force the contractor into possible bankruptcy by having him go through with a thoroughly unrealistic proposal and then end up by having to find someone else to finish the work at considerable additional cost. Often, in such cases, it is preferable to accept the next-higher proposal in the first place and to release the erring low bidder from the potentially disastrous commitment.

If a contractor submits proposals on two different contracts that are scheduled for award at approximately the same date and he knows he is not equipped to handle both jobs simultaneously, his limited capacity will not serve as a sufficient excuse for withdrawing either bid without penalty should he be the low bidder on both.

---

[6]See Section 3.23 on Bid Mistakes.

[7]On a large tunnel job, the lowest bid was approximately $1 million (15 percent) under both the next-higher proposal and the engineer's estimate. The engineer called in the low bidder and told him that, if he had made an error, he might withdraw his proposal. The contractor stated that his bid was as he intended, and he revealed that it was based upon the use of certain new, patented equipment. The proposal therefore was accepted. In another case, a contractor forgot to include a $50,000 stack in his proposal for the construction of an industrial plant. The contractor was not allowed to withdraw his proposal without penalty.

10.18   OPENING OF PROPOSALS

Instructions should be given regarding the procedure to be followed after bids are received. It is desirable to specify that each proposal must be contained in a separate, sealed envelope addressed as directed in the instructions. Each envelope should be clearly labeled "Proposal for Contract." The reason for keeping the contents of each proposal secret is to avoid subsequent claims of collusion; not even the owner should know the contents of any proposal prior to the official opening. At the stated hour the sealed proposals are to be opened *publicly and read aloud.* Reading the proposals in silence, even if done in the presence of others, is not sufficient. Usually a representative of each bidder will be on hand to protect his principal's interests. Furthermore, it is desirable to have a disinterested person check the bids as the reading proceeds or promptly after it terminates.

10.19   REJECTION OF PROPOSALS

Information for bidders should state that the owner has the right to reject *any* or *all* proposals. A list of possible reasons for the rejection of a particular proposal was given in connection with the discussion about the lowest responsible bidder. The same objections may apply with respect to the next-higher bidder or to any other one. It may also be desirable to reject any proposal that has not fulfilled all the prescribed requirements and any that seems to contain a flagrant unbalancing of bid unit prices. The owner should have the right to reject all proposals if the lowest proves so high as to make the project unaffordable.

Consider the case where Brown advertised for and received proposals on the modernization of her large warehouse. Before the contract was let she received a very attractive offer from Jones, who wanted to purchase the structure "as is." Being near retirement age, Brown decided to accept this offer and to discontinue her warehousing business. The unexpected opportunity to sell meant that she was no longer interested in the remodeling project; she therefore rejected all the proposals. This case exemplifies the relatively weak position in which bidders find themselves—normally they cannot withdraw their proposals once submitted, whereas the owner is free to abandon the project if he or she decides to do so.

In government work it is generally required that at least three proposals be received on a project before any can be accepted. This rule is designed to assure "adequate competition."

10.20   READVERTISEMENT

If the lowest bid is higher than the amount of money available to pay for the job, the engineer—in the absence of changes in the contract—should not readvertise in the hope of obtaining lower bids the next time around. With the lowest proposal in the original batch known at the time a second set of bids is sought, each bidder is told in effect to beat the figure in order to stand a chance of getting the contract. This "shopping for bids" is a bad practice. If the first group of proposals is to be rejected and the contract readvertised, the entire design or some major feature thereof should be substantially altered, perhaps by reducing the extent or the quality of the performance required so that the new bids will be submitted on an independent basis.

Assume that all the bids received on a proposed large school building are in the vicinity of $2,500,000 whereas the available funds are limited to $2,000,000; the proposals consequently have to be rejected. Perhaps one entire wing will then be eliminated and the job sent out for new proposals. If the one wing that is to be omitted is about one-fifth of the structure as originally contemplated, the total cost will be proportionately decreased, and the bidders on the smaller structure will be influenced by the knowledge obtained in regard to the former proposals. They are thus given a sort of monetary target at which to aim. It will probably be more desirable not only to omit this wing but also to change the framing to a more economical type, to use cheaper materials, or to make other revisions in materials and workmanship extensive enough so the bidders practically have to re-estimate the project in its entirety.

It is possible in such a case to negotiate a revised contract on a lesser structure with the lowest responsible bidder, thereby eliciting a greatly reduced quotation. However, this procedure is somewhat unfair to the other bidders, and the cost to the owner is likely to be greater in the long run than if all bidders are permitted to submit new proposals on the basis of the revised project.

10.21 AWARDING THE CONTRACT

No particular words are necessary to constitute an acceptance of a bid provided the intention of the owner to accept is made evident. However, it is best to have the form that will be signed by the owner and the contractor, constituting part of the official contract, prepared in advance and included among the contract documents so that all data will be available for inspection before the respective parties sign.

When the sealed bids are duly opened in public and read aloud the apparent low bidder is determined at once, absent the extremely improbable circumstance of a tie. Unless prequalification of bidders has been required, however, the determination of the lowest "responsible" bidder must still be made. The engineer must make sure that the successful bid is in order and that the contractor's resources, equipment, experience, and sureties are satisfactory. Thereafter the engineer should give notification that the proposal in question has been accepted and that the contract is to be signed at a specified place and time. This notice should be written and delivered to the successful bidder by messenger, registered mail, or telegram, although proof that it was deposited in an official United States post office or mailbox will suffice.

QUESTIONS

1. Illustrate a situation in which standard proposal forms might be used advantageously. Explain the advantages of the use of such proposal forms.

2. Why may use of the cut-and-paste method of preparing proposal forms be helpful? When would it be inadvisable?

3. Why is the use of a printed proposal form advisable for construction contracts?

4. Is a printed proposal form essential for the making of a construction contract? Why?

5. Describe how a contractor might go about preparing a bid on a school building to accommodate 400 pupils, assuming that it is to be a lump-sum job. List several of the typical work items involved.

6. For the school mentioned in the preceding question, describe how a contractor might prepare the bid if it were to be on a unit-price basis.

7. Who determines the contingency figure in the cost estimates for a construction project?

8. Who ultimately pays the cost of preparing proposals on a contract in the case of *(a)* the successful bidder? *(b)* the unsuccessful bidders?

9. How does a bidder estimate the profit that she hopes to obtain from the performance of a contract on which she makes a proposal (assuming a unit-price contract)?

10. What are "escalator" clauses as used in connection with proposals on construction contracts? Why may they be used?

11. Does the engineer generally make an estimate of the cost of a project before obtaining proposals? How? Why?

12. What is an unbalanced bid? Why might one be used?

13. On what basis is the successful bidder determined in the case of *(a)* a lump-sum contract? *(b)* a unit-price contract?

14. In what respect may a proposal be improper? What should be done by the engineer in such a situation?

15. Should the engineer specify a time limit after receipt of a proposal before it will cease to be binding on the bidder?

16. When a bidder submits a proposal, is that act something that completes a contract?

17. Who should usually determine the type of contract to be used for a given construction project? On what basis should it be determined?

18. For a unit-price contract: *(a)* How are the quantities which are given in the proposal form determined? *(b)* Are these quantities guaranteed to be accurate? *(c)* What are the stated quantities used for? *(d)* Are these quantities the same as the actual quantities that will probably be used in the job? *(e)* What happens if the stated and the actual quantities differ?

19. How are the quantities determined for a lump-sum contract?

20. Does the fact that a proposal for a construction project is on a unit-price basis mean that the cost of a job to the owner will be less than if the proposal were made on a lump-sum basis? Explain.

21. Can a portion of the work in a unit-price contract be listed as a lump sum? Why? Illustrate.

22. If the plans and specifications are vague and incomplete, what can bidders do to protect themselves?

23. How can a bidder determine the percentage or fixed fee to charge in connection with a cost-plus contract?

24. Explain how and when alternatives might be used when one is seeking proposals on the construction of a large building project.

25. Is it wise to have alternatives applied to a main contract as additions? To have them applied as subtractions?

26. Why should proposals for a construction contract be sealed when submitted to the owner?

27. Why forbid withdrawal of any submitted proposal before actual opening of all proposals?

28. What should be done if a bidder changes any portion of the proposal form?

29. Jones's proposal for a building contract was $125,500. After finding that her bid was low, she checked her estimates and found that an item of $25,000 had been incorrectly recorded as $2,500 in making the summary of costs. What can she do about the situation? Explain.

30. What is meant by "lowest responsible bidder" in connection with construction contracts?

31. Under what conditions may the lowest bid be rejected *(a)* in private work? *(b)* in public work?

32. Davis's bid of $542,000 was the lowest on a building job. The cost of the largest construction contract which he had performed previously was $78,000. What should the engineer do to determine whether or not to let the contract to Davis?

33. If, in the case described above, the advertisement says, "The contract will be let to the lowest bidder," must this be done?

34. Explain possible procedures for and advantages of prequalification of bidders.

35. Why and under what conditions should the advertisement state that the owner has the right to reject any or all proposals?

11

CONTRACT CLAUSES— GENERAL CONDITIONS

11.1   INTRODUCTION

The preparation of the contract clauses entails a great deal of painstaking effort. The arrangement and content of the material will depend on the preferences of the writer and the character of the project; the number of clauses to be prepared will also vary with the scope and complexity of the work to be done. Brevity is desirable—but it should not be attained at the expense of adequate coverage of the essential material.

A first step in the writing of the contract clauses is the preparation of an outline of points to be covered. These points then must be organized into some logical arrangement. One way to do this is to prepare a table of contents which will become an essential part of the contract documents. It is also desirable to establish a numbering system for sections and paragraphs in order to have the benefit of the numbers in referring to various items.

This chapter and the next have been written for the purpose of showing many of the contract clauses that should be included in a large construction contract. Others will be needed for particular projects, but those given in these two chapters will illustrate most of the general principles involved and the kind of information that has to go into such clauses.

In the preparation of these papers the engineer should have the help and guidance of competent legal advisors. In large organizations it may be that he or she is to assist the attorneys, who will take the lead in compiling the material.

In studying these clauses, remember that a contract is binding in both directions. Although we generally think of the contract clauses and specifications as a means of binding the contractor, they also serve as a vehicle whereby the contractor can hold the owner and the engineer to their side of the bargain.

11.2   PURPOSE OF WRITTEN CONTRACT PAPERS

It should be emphasized that a construction contract contains so many important general and technical features that it is essential to have all points clearly shown and described in writing or on drawings. All parties concerned will thereby have the same data, and all future interpretations will be based upon that information. In this way misunderstandings are minimized, since no one has to depend upon what was thought to be said or implied.

Perhaps the reader will think that some of the matters discussed subsequently are unnecessary in a contract because the contractor can be expected to perform them without specific instructions to do so. Nevertheless, in preparing the contract documents the engineer should include all provisions that may possibly prove important for the protection of the owner, on the one hand, and the contractor on the other.

11.3   STANDARD CONTRACTS

In some lines of business it is practical to prepare standard contract forms that can be used repeatedly by merely filling in the names, dates, prices, terms of payment, and other information appropriate to the particular fact situation (for example, the purchase of an automobile). It may also be good practice for small construction contracts, such as those for private homes. For example, the American Institute of Architects has prepared "The Standard Form of Agreement between Contractor and Owner for Construction of Buildings." Such standard contracts will generally have been proved by experience to be satisfactory, and any errors will have been found and corrected. In major construction contracts, however, the various projects differ so much that it is generally not feasible to prepare standard contract forms for repeated use.

11.4   STANDARD CONTRACT CLAUSES

Since there are usually individual contract clauses that are used repeatedly in construction contracts, it is advantageous to prepare standard clauses, often called "boilerplate" clauses, especially for specifications, that can be incorporated into different contracts. This plan, to a lesser degree, has the advantages afforded by the use of standard contracts in their entirety. Not only is the saving of time and expense in the preparation of the contract documents an advantage, but it usually aids in avoidance of omissions and mistakes. However, it is important to verify that the standard clause exactly reflects what is required under the proposed contract.

Such care would have proved valuable in the case of a consulting engineer's office that had prepared a clause to describe in considerable detail the contractor's responsibility in the maintenance of water mains, sewers, telephone lines, and electric power lines. This clause was copied verbatim in a subsequent contract involving the maintenance of some gas mains as well as the other utilities just mentioned. No one noticed at the time that reference to the gas mains was not included in the wording of the standard clause. The result was that the contractor in the second case claimed extra compensation for their maintenance.

11.5 CONTRACTOR'S WARRANTIES

It may be that contractors will at some juncture contend that they did not understand a certain portion of the contract, that they did not realize that certain things were to be included in the work, that they did not fully comprehend the local conditions affecting the work, or that they did not realize the extent of the difficulties involved in it.

To avoid subsequent claims based upon such considerations, it is advisable to place in the contract, under the heading "Contractor's Warranties" or "Contractor's Understanding," clauses such as the following:

1. "The Contractor is thoroughly familiar with all requirements of the Contract." Perhaps this appears to be unnecessary or superfluous because a contractor would be foolish to bid on a job with which he did not first become sufficiently familiar. However, addition of the clause should preclude the chance of his subsequently making the lame excuse that he misunderstood what was expected of him.

2. "The Contractor has investigated the site and satisfied himself regarding the character of the work and local conditions that may affect its performance." Again, this is a safeguard and a warning.

3. "The Contractor is satisfied that the work can be performed and completed as required in the Contract." In other words, if something seems to be wrong or some task impossible of performance, it should be brought to the engineer's attention by the contractor *before* the latter signs the contract.

4. "The Contractor accepts all risk directly or indirectly connected with the performance of the Contract." This is stated primarily for emphasis.

5. "The Contractor warrants that there has been no collusion." By this is meant collusion (in preparing the bid) with other contractors, with any of the engineer's staff, or with any other persons.

6. "The Contractor warrants that he has not been influenced by any oral statement or promise of the Owner or the Engineer, but only by the contract documents." This provision is aimed at preventing the contractor from getting special "inside information" from the engineer's staff or anyone else regarding the work and its requirements and from obtaining assurances from the engineer or the owner that certain extracontractual favors will be granted to him.

Other statements that are sometimes required of the contractor include:

1. "The Contractor is financially solvent."
2. "The Contractor is experienced and competent to perform the Contract."
3. "The statements in the Proposal are true."
4. "The Contractor is qualified and authorized to do work in the state."
5. "The Contractor is familiar with all general and special laws, ordinances, and regulations that may affect the work, its performance, or those persons employed therein." These requirements are especially important for out-of-state and even out-of-city contractors to investigate.
6. "The Contractor is familiar with tax, labor, and pay regulations that may affect the work." This warns "foreign" contractors. On large projects it is desirable to publish in the contract any special data regarding wage rates with which the out-of-state contractor may not be familiar. In subaqueous tunneling, for example, state regulations and stipulated wage rates for compressed-air work should be quoted or at least referred to.

11.6   **APPROVAL OF CONTRACTOR'S PLANS AND EQUIPMENT**

The engineer should not allow the contractor to do anything that he wants to do in the name of performance of the contract, even though the contractor is undeniably responsible for performance. If, for instance, the engineer learns that the contractor intends to do something that appears to be unsafe, the contractor should be questioned about the matter and told where the contemplated procedure is unsatisfactory. It may be that the engineer's knowledge of the project enables him to recognize some important consideration that the contractor has failed to realize.

It is therefore advisable to state in the document that the contractor is to submit prints of any special construction accessories that he intends to use to the engineer for approval before undertaking any of the affected work—for example, the falsework for the erection of a large bridge or the cofferdam to be used around the site of a power plant located at the edge of a river. This procedure is designed to give the engineer an opportunity to identify potential difficulties and is usually welcomed, since the avoidance of subsequent trouble is to the contractor's benefit. However, the engineer should not dictate solutions to the contractor because the primary responsibility for the successful completion of the work is the contractor's, and by demanding a certain procedure the engineer subjects himself to liability for its effectiveness. Also, it should be clearly understood that approval of a proposal does not relieve the contractor of his responsibility for its effectiveness.

11.7   DEFECTIVE DRAWINGS

When the engineer prepares the design drawings and specifications, it is taken for granted by the contractor that these are correct and, if carefully followed, will produce the desired results. The engineer is considered to be responsible for the accuracy of contract documents unless it is specifically stated that the drawings are to show general features only and are not in any sense "warranted." If it later develops that the design drawings contain errors, the contractor obviously is not at fault provided he did the work properly and neither knew nor was expected to know of the defects.

It is not the contractor's duty to check the design drawings. In the best interests of all parties, however, the contractor should call to the engineer's attention anything that is apparently incorrect. This action may strengthen the contractor's position if the questioned feature ultimately develops trouble. The contract should state that, if the contractor discovers an error in the drawings or specifications, (1) he is to orally report it promptly to the engineer, (2) he is to confirm it in writing soon thereafter, and (3) he is not to proceed with the affected work until directed to do so by the engineer.

This principle may be carried beyond the range of apparent errors in the drawings to matters which may involve the best interest of the structure or even the safety of the performance of the work. For example, assume that the contractor notices that the plans do not call for shelf angles to be used at upper floors to support the brick facing of the masonry cavity walls of a multistory building, whereas experience shows that such supports are essential. In such a case, the contractor should recommend in writing to the architect or engineer that such angles be used and state actual cases to illustrate the reasons for the recommendation.

11.8   APPROVAL OF CONTRACTOR'S DRAWINGS

The contractor generally has to provide *shop drawings* that, when approved by the architect or engineer, are to be used in the actual construction. The contract should state that these shop drawings are to become the approved workings drawings for any work to which they apply is done, but these drawings should first be checked for concurrence of accuracy by the contractor.

For example, assume that a mining company is building a large plant for the crushing and concentration of copper ore. A contract for a large gyratory crusher is to be let to some manufacturer of heavy equipment. The engineer may specify certain basic requirements for this machine, some of which are the following:

1. Size of feed.
2. Size of discharge.
3. Material for body and liners.

4.   Capacity.

5.   Type of spindle at top.

6.   Arrangement and other details of drive.

7.   Type and position of discharge.

8.   Provisions for maintenance and repairs.

9.   General proportions.

The manufacturer who is awarded the contract will prepare shop drawings to show every detail of the crusher. Then prints of these drawings will be examined by the engineer to make sure that the equipment will be suitable. The engineer will then return a copy of these prints to the manufacturer, having indicated thereon approval or desired corrections. The contractor is to make the corrections unless the engineer, after discussion, agrees to let the drawings remain as they are or to accept substituted details devised by the manufacturer. When the latter thinks that the drawings are in satisfactory form, he will submit new prints for the final approval of the engineer. When this approval is received, the drawings will be ready for release for production.

The important point to be emphasized about this procedure, and to be set forth explicitly in the contract, is that although the shop drawings are to be approved by the engineer, the *contractor is responsible* for the accuracy of the work. A clause similar to the following can be utilized for this purpose.

> The approval by the Engineer of any shop or working drawing, or of any drawing of the Contractor's plant or equipment, shall not in any way be deemed to release the Contractor from full responsibility for complete and accurate performance of the Work in accordance with the Contract Drawings and Specifications; neither shall such approval release the Contractor from any liability placed upon him by any provision in the Form of Contract.

The following two hypothetical cases will illustrate this matter of responsibility for the data shown on various types of drawings:

1.   Assume that one piece of the crusher previously referred to is supposed to be 2 feet 0 inches deep (according to the approved general plan for the equipment) but that the contractor's drafter incorrectly dimensions it 2 feet 1 inch. The checker in the shop misses the error on the shop drawing. The engineer, too, fails to notice it, and he stamps the drawing "Approved." The piece is accordingly made 2 feet 1 inch deep. When the crusher is assembled, the piece obviously will not fit. In this situation the contractor is responsible for the cost of revision or replacement of the incorrect part since he was obligated to create the detailed design and to furnish the equipment.

2.   On the other hand, assume that the engineer shows on his design drawings that the overall depth of the crusher is to be a certain dimension. The contractor makes the machine accordingly. Later it is discovered that the depth should have been 1 inch less in order to assure a fit. This is a mistake in the engineer's basic data. The contractor made the machine the size called for in the design; therefore, he is not responsible for the error. The cost of making the correction is imputed to the owner.

11.9   GUARANTEE BY THE CONTRACTOR

Many contracts require the contractor to guarantee that the materials and workmanship of the job will prove satisfactory for one year after completion of the contract. By that time any defects will probably be discovered, and the contractor will have to correct them or arrange some settlement that is acceptable to the owner.

To illustrate the principle involved, consider the case where a contractor erected a large high-speed forced-draft fan that has a direct-connected drive. The motor was not positioned in exactly the right alignment, and the equipment did not operate properly. Since the trouble was discovered a few weeks after the contractor completed the work, the one-year guarantee required him to remedy the situation.

In another case, a reinforced-concrete underpass or tunnel for a railroad was built under a large embankment. Shortly after the work was completed the engineer discovered that the structure had cracked. The problem then was to ascertain the cause. Considerable study and investigation revealed that the contractor had placed a large amount of fill on one side of the tunnel before placing any fill on the other side, thus causing an imbalance of loads that distorted and overstressed the structure. Such inequality of filling was contrary to the specifications. Although the engineer believed that there would be no collapse of the tunnel, the structure was not what the owner paid for; the contractor was held responsible for damages but was not compelled to replace the entire tunnel.

In general, contractors are responsible for their own work and that of their subcontractors. They are to guarantee that the work is free from defects caused by poor performance of construction, but they are not responsible for faulty plans and specifications or for anything that is done under direct orders of the engineer or owner.

11.10   CONDUCT OF WORK

Although such a course may be ill advised, the owner sometimes may issue instructions directly to the contractor regarding the conduct of work. The engineer is the one who should give all such instructions. If the owner nevertheless persists, and especially if the engineer has advised the owner that his orders will cause defective work or other trouble, neither the engineer nor the contractor is to blame for the unsatisfactory results. Proper procedure requires that if the owner believes that something in the plans or specifications should be changed, he should confer with the engineer, who, if he is in agreement, then issues instructions to the contractor. The contract ought to require that the contractor's operations should be carried on in a workmanlike manner, and it should call for him to expedite the work. He should have a superintendent or other responsible official on duty at all times. The engineer ought to have the power to order that work be speeded up if it is evident that this can and should be done and when the best interests of the project require such action. On the other hand, the engineer must be sure that such action is justified because it may result in overtime work that materially increases the cost of the job.

One occasion upon which the engineer ought to have authority to order that the job be expedited is when there is impending danger. For example, the threat of a flood may imperil completed foundation work of a cofferdam. In some cases, if such orders result in additional costs, the contractor may claim extra compensation, provided there has been no negligence on his part. In most cases of emergency the engineer will be acting in the interest of the contractor as well as of the owner. Remember that the progress and safety of the job are essential and that all parties have a real interest in these matters. When the contractor does not move to assure both progress and safety, the engineer should have the right to compel such action.

While being careful to avoid dictating to the contractor exactly how the work should be done, the engineer may justifiably recommend and even try to persuade the contractor to do certain things and to conduct operations in what seems to the engineer to be a desirable manner. For his part, the contractor may suggest improvements in the job or the work product as originally outlined, but, when all is said and done, the design is the engineer's responsibility.

Circumstances may develop that make it essential for the owner to take over all or a portion of the work from the contractor and to have the job finished by the contractor's forces or by outsiders. In this connection, note the following clause:

> If, in the opinion of the Engineer, the Contractor is or appears to be unable to finish the work, the Owner shall have the right to take over and complete the work as agent of the Contractor. However, the exercise of such right by the Owner shall not release the Contractor or his sureties from any of his or their obligations and liabilities under the Contract or the Performance Bond. The Owner shall also have the right to use or permit the use of any and all plant, materials, and equipment provided by the Contractor for the execution of the Work, and the Contractor shall not remove them from the site without the written permission of the Engineer. The Engineer shall determine the cost of all Work done by the Owner as agent for the Contractor, shall credit the Owner with the cost thereof, and shall credit the Contractor with the compensation which would have been earned thereby; the difference in actual cost above the contract price shall be payable to the Owner.

11.11   D EFECTIVE   W ORK

The contract may contain this clause:

> All material furnished and all work done which, in the opinion of the Engineer, is not in accordance with the plans and specifications shall be removed immediately, and other material which is satisfactory shall be furnished and other work which is satisfactory shall be performed.

On the other hand, it is not always practical or fair to insist upon complete replacement of work that fails to meet the specifications and the requirements of the drawings but is not valueless. Concrete work is a common example of this. The contract may state that test cylinders are to have an ultimate 28-day compressive strength of 3,000 pounds per square inch. What is to be done if, a month after pouring the cylinders, the concrete tests 2,800 pounds per square inch? That particular portion of the structure is now covered by many more cubic yards of concrete, and it would be very costly to remove this later concrete plus that which did not meet the test requirements. To deal with such a situation the contract may contain a clause to the effect that although the engineer has the right to demand removal of defective material and work, he also has the right in lieu of such demand to make a deduction in the contractor's compensation if the tests of the concrete cylinders fail to meet the specified 28-day strength. For example, the contract may specify a reduction of $1 for each 1 percent deficiency multiplied by the number of cubic yards of concrete in the portion of the work to which said test was to pertain. The engineer should be careful to specify that he alone has the power to require that repairs, strengthening, or even complete replacement of the work is to be made at the contractor's expense or, in the alternative, that the contractor is to suffer a reduction in payment.

Suppose that the contractor inadvertently erected a light steel beam where the contract drawings called for a heavy one, and vice versa, and the error went unnoticed until tons of equipment were installed in the building and caused excessive deflection of the light beam. The contractor would be required to bear the expense of making the changes needed, even though the engineer had inadvertently accepted the work. Since safety is involved here, there is no doubt about the necessity for remedial measures.

On the other hand, if the engineer's staff, who designed the beams in the preceding case, had labeled them incorrectly on the design drawing, the contractor could not be expected to notice the error. As long as the work proceeds according to the engineer's plans, the contractor should not bear the expense of any necessary repairs or alterations.

11.12 RELATIONS WITH OTHER CONTRACTORS AND SUBCONTRACTORS

The contract should state whether or not more than one contractor is to work on parts of the project at the same time. It should also specify that the contractor is to cooperate with all others and to avoid interference with their work. The same requirement of cooperation should apply to relations between the general contractor and the subcontractors, even though the former controls the latter and is responsible for the conduct and quality of their work.

Where storage space is required by the general contractor, and by other contractors as well, it is almost essential for the engineer to show on the contract drawings the particular storage areas and the means of access that are to be allotted to each such contractor. A contractor can then arrange with his subcontractors for their use of part of the space reserved for him.

The division of work responsibility should be made clear in advance. It will probably be impossible to delineate everything exactly, but an attempt should be made. For example, in a contract for a large factory building with pile foundations, the project might be divided among three contractors as follows:

1. One contract for all foundations, including piling and concrete work below and including the ground floor.
2. A second contract for all of the superstructure above the ground floor.
3. A third contract for all the mechanical, electrical, and other equipment, including the erection of same.

As far as it can be done practically, the contract documents should clearly allocate the duties of the respective contractors. For example, here are some questions to be settled:

1. Who provides and installs water supply lines, sanitary and storm sewers, and other utilities and within what limits of the building line versus property lines? When will material and data be available for this work?
2. Who is to maintain utility services (lights, etc.) during construction?
3. Who is to be responsible for the protection of the public, and of the property itself, and for how long?
4. Who furnishes and sets the anchor bolts, and when and from whom will information for this work be obtained?
5. Who grouts column bases and bed plates for machinery?
6. Who provides and erects conduits for electric power and light, and when will the material and necessary data be available?
7. Who provides attachments for equipment that is to be connected to the superstructure (including provision of openings for that equipment)?
8. Who is to be responsible for the maintenance of traffic and access, and for how long?
9. If part of the project is to be put to use before completion of the entire project, who is to be responsible for finishing such part?
10. If various articles of equipment are to be furnished under separate contracts, who erects these articles, who provides their supports, and who is responsible for their protection?
11. What is to be the order of construction?
12. When is each contractor to begin and to complete his part of the work?

The following is a paraphrased and abbreviated version of a provision from a contract for a large bridge:

During the time that the Contractor will be performing the Contract, other persons will be engaged in doing work at the site or in the immediate vicinity thereof, among them being the following:

1. Under Contract G-1, the John Jones Corporation will perform the work of excavation, filling, and grading in accordance with the information shown on the

reference drawings and in conformity with the Specifications for said Contract, all of which papers may be examined at the office of the Owner.

2. Future contracts will provide for the construction of foundations and super-structures of the east and west approach spans adjoining the main bridge, together with the building of the connecting roadways.

The Contractor shall therefore plan and conduct his operations so as to work in harmony with all others on the project, and he shall not delay, endanger, or avoidably interfere with the activities of such others; he shall at all times maintain a roadway across the area allotted to him for his operations, so that others may have access to the work in which they will be engaged; and he shall cooperate with other contractors in whatever is, in the opinion of the Engineer, in the best interests of the Owner and the public.

11.13 ORDER OF COMPLETION

It is essential that the contract state specifically any requirements there may be regarding the sequence of construction and the order of completion. This is particularly important for large projects that involve various structures or parts, and especially when two or more contractors may be working simultaneously or in relays. Such information not only obligates a given contractor to cooperate with the others but also affords him the opportunity to plan his work more efficiently and to allow in his bid for the extra costs that may result from delays stemming from the operations of the other contractors or by the effect of the stipulated order of completion.

The following is a common example involving a completion date for a portion of the work. A contract for the steelwork of a large industrial plant covered several buildings and was let directly to a steel fabricator. The general excavation, concrete work, roofing, and siding for all structures were to be done under other contracts. All the contracts stated that the foundations, steel framing, roofing, and siding of one of the major buildings were to be completed by November 15, 2000, so that the difficult work of constructing concrete foundations for machines, erecting machinery, and installing electrical equipment in this building could be accomplished under shelter during the winter.

The engineer must be careful when setting up a schedule and order of completion of the structures. He should be sure that the requirements can be met by the contractors and will not cause unjustified additional expense to the owner through high bids that the contractors are obliged to submit in order to be able to afford to perform the work on time.

Although the engineer is not responsible for the contractor's operations, he may properly require that the contractor prepare an outline of his program showing the contemplated sequence of work. The engineer may also call for the contractor to compose a schedule of expected progress in order to determine whether or not the contractor's plans appear to be adequate in terms of time. The engineer can then use this schedule of operations later on to see whether the work is progressing as anticipated. A clause such as the following may be found in many contracts:

> Within two weeks after the signing of the Contract the Contractor shall submit for approval of the Engineer six (6) black-and-white prints of his proposed construction schedule. This is to show graphically the date on which he expects to start and to complete the various major portions of the project. This schedule is to be so prepared that the *actual* progress of the work can be recorded and compared with the *expected* progress. On the first and fifteenth of each month, and until the job is fully completed, the Contractor shall deliver to the Engineer three (3) prints of the construction schedule with the progress to date shown thereon.

If no time for commencement or completion of the work is specified, a *reasonable* time is to be implied. In other words, the contractor is to begin without unwarranted delay and continue with diligence. When there is no important reason to set a deadline for completion, the contract might properly state that the "Contractor shall expedite completion of the work, and shall conduct his operations in a workmanlike and efficient manner."

The foregoing concept applies as well to contracts for engineering services. Thus, when the engineer is engaged to make plans for a project, if the time for their completion is not stipulated, a reasonable time for this work is implied. Or, the agreement may state that the plans are to be completed "as the Owner may direct." In that case the engineer is entitled to a reasonable time after receipt of the anticipated advices from the owner. Naturally, delays caused by the owner are to be considered in determining what is a reasonable time.

11.14   INSPECTION OF MATERIALS

The purpose of the engineer's inspection of materials to be used in construction is to see that the contract is properly carried out and that the owner's interests are adequately protected. Such activity by the engineer or his representative generally involves inspection of shopwork as well as of the quality of the materials themselves. For example, in a large bridge project involving important steelwork, the engineer may have an inspector at the steel mill to make sure that the material meets the specifications. Often the steel mill will be required to submit test "coupons" from an actual billet sample of the raw material to verify the chemical and structural properties of the material. The engineer may also have an inspector at the fabricating shop for several months to see that all shopwork is satisfactory. In smaller jobs, the engineer may accept the report of the manufacturer's or the contractor's inspector when it is submitted with an affidavit vouching for its accuracy. In any event, the contractor should be obligated to notify the engineer in advance so that the latter can, if he desires, have his inspector on hand when work affecting the contract is to be performed.

A large project might involve so much inspection of materials that a separate department in the engineer's office is designated to handle this work. As an alternative procedure, the engineer may engage a firm of specialists to carry out (1) inspection of materials, (2) inspection of shop fabrication, and (3) any necessary testing.

The contract should make clear what is to be done regarding inspection and exactly what is expected of the contractor. For instance, if test cylinders of concrete are to be made in the field, the bidder should be told in the contract documents what he will have to do in this regard so that he can reflect the cost in his proposal.

11.15   INSPECTION OF FIELD OPERATIONS

In a large job it is common practice for the owner to have the engineer maintain a resident engineer with a staff of inspectors in the field to see that work called for by the plans and specifications is performed satisfactorily. The inspectors often check such things as the dimensions and adequacy of forms for concrete, the arrangements and sizes of reinforcing bars, the grading of the site, the compaction of fill, the erection of structural steel, the quality of riveting or bolting and welding, the location of anchor bolts, and the erection of machinery.

The inspection process is not intended to shift responsibility for the results to the engineer. The contract should be worded so that there is no question that the contractor is responsible for his own work. The resident engineer and his staff should try to help the contractor avoid making errors, but their approval of his work should not relieve him of ultimate responsibility. The inspectors should point out potential problems and assist in finding solutions, but not dictate precisely what the contractor should do or how he should do it.

In one case, some of the footings of a big concrete structure were to be subjected to large overturning moments. The contractor placed the reinforcement in these footings, and an inspector gave his approval. However, in some unexplained manner, only half as many bars as were required by the drawings projected up (from the footings) to withstand the bending moment that would be applied by the future construction. After the concrete of the footings had been poured and set, the men placing the next tier of reinforcement discovered the mistake. The inspector's approval did not relieve the contractor from the very costly task of remedying the error.[1]

In projects of small or medium size it is not usually necessary for the engineer to have an inspector at the site continuously. It may be that the engineer or his representative will visit the job two or three times each week to supervise the work in a general way. Another arrangement might be the scheduling of regular weekly job meetings for inspection and conferences with the contractor and the owner's "clerk of the works." Thus the engineer will be available to discuss any questions with the contractor and see whether or not the work is progressing satisfactorily.

It is generally advisable for the engineer to make inspection trips on a predetermined schedule so that the contractor knows when the engineer will be available for consultation. The contract, if it does not prescribe a schedule for inspections,

---

[1] In *Kaminer Construction Co. v. United States*, 488 F.2d 980 (Ct. Cl. 1973), the court said that "the right to inspect does not imply a duty to inspect."

should provide for the contractor to notify the engineer in advance of starting on a particular phase of the work so that the latter or his representative will have time to arrange to be on hand at the appropriate time. The contractor should be obligated, further, to have his key operatives available and to otherwise do everything necessary to facilitate inspection by the engineer.

Here is the wording of a clause that was prepared to apply to both the inspection of materials and of fieldwork:

> All work, materials, processes of manufacture and methods of construction shall be subject to the inspection of the Engineer (or his duly authorized representative), who shall be the judge of the quality and suitability of them all for the purposes for which they are used. If any of them fail to meet with his approval, same shall forthwith be replaced, corrected, or otherwise made good, as the case may require, by the Contractor at his own expense. Rejected material shall be disposed of as the Engineer may direct. Acceptance of any material or workmanship shall not serve to prevent subsequent rejection by the Engineer if he finds either or both to be unsatisfactory. Unless ordered by the Engineer, no material shall be shipped from its place of manufacture without prior inspection and approval.

11.16   DUTIES OF AN INSPECTOR

The function of an inspector is that of seeing that the work is done *in accordance with the terms of the contract*. If the contract calls for certain things that are incorrect, it is not the inspector's job to change them, nor is he empowered to do so. If something has been overlooked in the plans or specifications, or if an error has been made in them, the inspector may properly assist the engineer in bringing about remedial action under those terms of the contract that cover revisions, extras, and adjustments. The inspector is representing the engineer and the owner through the engineer.

The inspector may have to keep accounts of time spent, materials furnished, and work done by the contractor. He cannot be everywhere at once, and he may not have to be on the job continuously. He has to learn what to watch for and how things should be done. He should be able to detect developing as well as existing troubles and uncertainties. He should report such matters to the engineer at once, so that the latter can make any necessary decisions promptly. He should remember that delay on his part may cause loss for the owner.

Adopting the middle ground between laxity and fastidiousness is a central concern of the inspector. It involves a balanced approach—protecting the owner's rights without unnecessarily antagonizing those executing the job. Here is an example of undue fussiness. In making the shop drawing of the riveted steel girders for a highway viaduct that was to be on a slight grade, the drafter drew the stiffener angles in a vertical position because it was easier for him to do so than to slope them a tiny bit. The fabricator built the girders with the stiffener angles perpendicular to the flanges. This is the practical and customary procedure because the slight skewing needed to make them vertical would prevent the use of efficient multiple punching of the rivet holes in the web plate. When the girders were ready to be shipped to the site, the inspector demanded, without consulting the engineer, that the girders be dismantled and refabricated so as to have the stiffeners truly vertical. The fabricator sent a representative to explain the situation to the engineer, and the latter agreed at once that the girders were fabricated as he intended.

Much practical experience and knowledge are essential for inspection work. A contractor will generally cooperate well with an inspector whom he trusts, who is trying to be fair, and whose knowledge he respects. The inspector who is unreasonable or who does not understand the problems of performing construction work will arouse a contractor's ire immediately; one who operates in a sloppy manner will arouse the contractor's disdain.

The inspector should never fail to protect the owner's interests within the terms of the contract. In a rather extreme case a contractor persuaded an inspector to do otherwise and gave him a share of the "savings." The job consisted of highway and bridge work, one item being timber piling. The contractor drove short pieces of piles a few feet into the ground so that they looked like pile heads. Furthermore, he made the specified eight-inch concrete pavement eight inches thick at the edges but four or five inches thick over the rest of its area. The dishonesty and wrongdoing came to light when the structures and pavement failed. The guilty contractor and inspector received prison sentences.

11.17 LAND AND FACILITIES

Ordinarily it is the owner's responsibility to acquire the property needed, not only for the job site itself but also for whatever use may be necessary during construction. It may be that an easement has to be secured to provide access to the construction area, that a permanent right-of-way must be purchased, or that some land has to be rented for storage and working space. All these land rights and privileges are to be secured by the owner in advance so that full information can be given to the bidders before they submit their proposals. Any arrangement whereby the contractor undertook to secure the necessary rights, etc., would probably prove more costly to the owner in the long run.

Various facilities will have to be provided by the contractor (perhaps on a cost plus basis), if they are not furnished by the owner. The contract should be very specific in all such matters. Facilities that typically are needed include:

1. Electric power.
2. Access roadway.
3. Warehouse or other storage.
4. Contractor's and engineer's offices.
5. Utilities for these offices.
6. Provision for maintenance of traffic and other services.

11.18   PERMITS AND LICENSES

It is generally the duty of the owner to secure any building permits that are required for the construction of the project. He should obtain any other permits that are called for; examples include (1) a permit to close a street temporarily while some particularly dangerous work is being done, (2) a permit to truck heavy steel-work through the streets, (3) a permit to move an existing house to a new location, and (4) a permit to shut off certain utilities for a while when they have to be relocated. However, arrangements for procedures that the contractor chooses to follow in order to complete the work to his own best advantage are to be made by him. For example, if the contractor wishes to build temporary piers for the erection of a bridge and to place them within prescribed "channel limits," it is the contractor who should secure permission to do so.

It may happen that, through inadvertence, a contract contains a clause that directs or permits the contractor to do something contrary to the applicable building code or some other law or regulation. It is the engineer's responsibility to avoid such a situation, and the contractor, in bidding, is entitled to assume that he is to quote upon the contract as it is. If later events reveal that some change must be made to meet legal requirements, the contractor may rightly claim extra compensation for any additional costs.

Some states require that a contractor, and perhaps even a subcontractor, must have a license issued by that jurisdiction in order to do any work within its boundaries. If such a requirement pertains it is desirable that this fact be stated in the information provided for bidders so that unlicensed contractors will not waste their time and money in preparing a bid on the project, or so that they can take immediate steps to obtain the necessary license.

Any contractor who attempts to perform work without a required license may find that he cannot enforce collection of payment for work done by him within the state.[2] The same rule is likely to apply to an individual engineer in respect to services performed without a license. In *United Stage Equipment v. Charles Carter & Company,*[3] the court held that the subcontractor who performed work without a license could not collect on the contract. However, in other cases[4] the courts have allowed a contractor without a license to collect for actual cost incurred on the basis of unjust enrichment.

In one case,[5] a company's unlicensed status was held not to bar recovery for services rendered. A local licensing ordinance defined "home improvement business" as a "business of providing for a profit a home improvement to an owner." An unlicensed painting company had agreed to supply materials and a labor crew

---

[2]*See Schultz v. Lujan,* 948 P.2d 558 (Ha. App. 1997), where a contractor who had a license to do cabinet and fixture work and nonstructural remodeling and repair work was precluded from recovering from homeowners for structural and foundation work outside the scope of his license.
Also, if a contractor's "responsible managing employee" is disassociated, the contractor's license may be automatically suspended and the contractor thus not licensed and unable to bring suit. *Buzgheia v. Leasco Sierra Grove,* 70 Cal. Rptr. 2d 427 (Cal. App. 1997).

[3]342 So. 2d 1153 (La. 1977).

[4]*Alonzo v. Chifici,* 526 So. 2d 237 (La. App., 1988).

[5]*Roth Painting Company, Inc. v. Fishman,* 670 N.Y.S. 2d 681 (1997).

at cost as a courtesy to a long-time friend of its president. When the "friend" refused to pay, the painting company sued and its unlicensed status did not bar recovery since the job was at cost and not for profit.

11.19 LABOR CONSIDERATIONS

It is important to become familiar with federal, state, and local laws regarding eligibility for any conditions affecting employment. There may be statutes regulating the hiring of local personnel, working conditions, and maximum working hours or minimum wage rates that must be complied with.[6]

Especially when the legal and other requirements are not standard practice, the engineer should give bidders any essential data available so that they can make their proposals accordingly. The following samples of contract clauses deal with labor matters:

> No person under sixteen (16) years of age and no convict labor shall be employed by the Contractor in the prosecution of the work.
>
> All laborers except major supervisory personnel shall be residents of the State of New York.
>
> The Contractor shall not employ for the Work any person whose age or physical condition renders his employment dangerous to his health or safety, or to the health or safety of others. However, this provision shall not be construed to prevent the employment of physically handicapped persons who may be employed for work which they are able to perform satisfactorily.
>
> All employees engaged in the Work under this Contract shall have the right to organize and bargain collectively through representatives chosen freely by them. Furthermore, no employee shall be required to join any union or to refrain from joining any union or labor organization of his own choosing.
>
> The Contractor shall not accept more than eight (8) hours of work each day, to be performed within nine (9) consecutive hours, and he shall not employ any person or persons for more than eight (8) hours in twenty-four (24) consecutive hours, except in case of necessity, in which event the pay of employees for time in excess of said eight (8) hours shall be at the rate of time and one-half.

11.20 NOTICES

All notices, instructions, and information sent to the contractor by the engineer should be in writing. It is often necessary to expedite the completion of the work by use of verbal messages given to the contractor in person or by telephone, but these should be promptly confirmed in writing. This procedure avoids many of the

---

| [6]Chapter 28 discusses some of these issues in more detail.

arguments and uncertainties that are likely to develop when messages regarding details of the work are reviewed months later, at which subsequent time the recollections of the parties involved may be dimmed. For the same reason the contractor should, in turn, also put in writing the communications emanating from his office to the engineer.

11.21   WORK DONE BY THE OWNER

Sometimes there are projects in which the owner is to handle part of the job himself or have someone do that part under the direct supervision of the engineer as the owner's representative. Such work should be conducted so as to minimize interference with the general contractors and his part of the overall operations. Naturally, the contractor should likewise cooperate.

   This applies to small projects as well as to large ones. For example, Mrs. A plans to build a house for herself and her family. She intends to perform certain work personally in order to minimize the amount of money paid out. The contract with the builder should clarify any such arrangement and describe in detail what work the owner is to perform. Such a contract may seem to be "small," but it is very important for the prospective householder. She should obtain professional assistance in its preparation unless she has had adequate personal experience in this field.

11.22   LINES AND GRADES

The contract should be specific in its requirements regarding the establishment of lines and grades for a construction project. This function usually falls to the contractor, but some engineers, especially on a large project, prefer to keep direct control by having the establishment of lines and grades handled by their own field organization. If the contract provides for the latter arrangement but further states that the contractor is to check all the lines and grades and any other dimensions determined by the engineer, failure by the contractor to do so will mean that he probably will have difficulty collecting from the owner for additional costs resulting from errors in the engineer's determinations.

   Whether it is desirable for the contractor or the engineer to make these surveys in a particular case depends upon the size of the staff available to the engineer, the character of the job, and the capabilities of the engineer's personnel. Sometimes it is best to have the contractor do this surveying as well as the construction part in order to make him clearly responsible for all phases of the work. In one instance where the engineer was responsible for lines and grades, his men set the elevation of the foundation of a heavy machine one foot too high. The owner had to pay the contractor for all the labor, materials, and incidentals involved in the removal of the concrete and the rebuilding of the foundation.

When the lines and grades are to be established by the engineer, the contract documents ought to stipulate that the contractor is obliged to preserve stakes, bench marks, and the like, and is to conform to all lines and grades. The contractor is expected to cooperate with the engineer's men in all this work by avoiding interference with them and by conducting his operations so as to expedite their work as much as possible. In this connection, the contractor should be required by the contract to give the engineer reasonable advance notice of times and places at which he intends to perform certain work so that the engineer may proceed to establish all necessary lines and grades and so that all measurements required for payment and record purposes may be made at the engineer's convenience but without undue delay for the contractor.

Often, although the engineer establishes the controlling lines and grades, it becomes necessary for the contractor to make many minor and detail measurements. The contract should reflect this eventuality so that the contractor can include the cost of such work in his proposal.

11.23 UNDERPINNING

There are likely to be requirements in municipal ordinances or state laws regarding the procedure and responsibility for underpinning a structure whose safety is likely to be imperiled by a contractor's operations. It is proper, if there are no regulations indicating otherwise, to make the owner of a projected structure responsible for the safety and support of his neighbor's existing building, and sometimes of the adjacent land, when new construction is to be of such a nature that the foundations of existing structures will be endangered.

Underpinning an existing building is both difficult and costly. The owner of the proposed structure should have the engineer design the new structure so that danger to the neighbor's property can be avoided, or at least minimized. If underpinning work is not done well, uneven settlement and cracking of the structure may result, causing the affected property owner to make damage claims against the owner of the building under construction. For protection against unjust claims that his neighbor might advance, the owner of the planned new structure should have a third party make a careful examination of the condition of the neighbor's property before work is started and then again after work has been completed. Photographs taken by a professional photographer in advance of the performance of any building work may be very helpful in establishing the condition of the preexisting structure at the start of the construction operations.

Occasionally, underpinning work can best be handled as a separate contract, with the owner of the new structure absorbing the expense. Contractors are generally reluctant to make a lump-sum proposal on this kind of work because of the uncertainties accompanying it. In general, it is advisable to arrange for such operations on a cost-plus-fixed-fee basis.

The engineer may show the character of the underpinning work to be done and then require the contractor to follow that pattern. The latter, in presenting his proposal, either agrees that the indicated work can be accomplished or proposes modifications of his own. In the alternative, the engineer may ask for proposals in which the contractor is to present both the design of the underpinning and his estimate of the cost.

11.24 ORDER AND DISCIPLINE

The contractor should be made responsible for the maintenance of order and discipline during the performance of the contract. This is true primarily in regard to the supervision of his own workers, but it should include also a subcontractor's workers who are employed on the job. To accomplish this, it may be advantageous if the contract forbids the storage and use of intoxicating beverages at the job site.

> A clause such as the following will establish the contractor's right and responsibility in this regard. In the performance of this Contract, the Contractor shall exercise every precaution to prevent injury to persons or property; he shall erect such barricades, signs, and lights as the Engineer believes to be suitable; he shall adopt and enforce such rules and regulations as may be necessary, desirable, or proper to safeguard the public, all persons engaged in the Work and its supervision, and all traffic on adjacent streets; and he shall be responsible for the maintenance of discipline throughout the conduct of the Work.

11.25 PERFORMANCE

When the contractor has done all that the contract requires, he has performed his part of the agreement. This is naturally a prerequisite to final acceptance and payment by the owner.

Ordinarily, when one makes a contract to perform stipulated services, he is not entitled to the agreed-upon fee until he has done what he said he would. In the case of construction contracts, "substantial performance"[7] of the specified work or services may suffice to render the contractor's compensation due and payable. Perhaps this liberal policy stems somewhat from the fact that there is, as a practical matter, probably no such thing as "perfect performance" of big construction contracts. If the builder has done his job in good faith and with the intent of fully accomplishing what is required of him, even though there may be small defects or omissions, he is generally regarded as entitled to the contract price (minus the cost of remedying any such defects or omissions).

A contract may state that the performance is to be "satisfactory" to the owner, the architect, or the engineer. If the particular subject matter of the contract is something that involves the personal taste or fancy of an individual (as in the case

| [7]Discussed in Chapter 6.

of a contract for interior decorating), the contractor is obliged to satisfy that person before the fee has been earned. In construction contracts as a class, satisfactory performance is normally interpreted to mean performance that should be satisfactory to a "reasonable" man.

11.26 FINAL INSPECTION AND ACCEPTANCE

Upon written notice from the contractor that he believes he has performed all the work required by the contract, the engineer is to inspect the job promptly to see whether everything is satisfactory. Much that has previously been inspected and accepted by him or by his staff need not be reexamined in great detail, but if something needing correction is discovered in the work that was approved earlier, the former acceptance does not prevent the engineer from requiring that it be remedied by the contractor.

The "final inspection" may not disclose hidden defects, and the engineer may not become aware at that juncture of an imperfection. Ordinarily, the *final* acceptance of the work by the engineer releases the contractor unless he has guaranteed his work, in which event, regardless of the approval of the work at the time of the final inspection, the contractor is still bound for the period stated in the contract by his guarantees as to the quality of material and workmanship.

If the engineer finds the job to be satisfactory in all respects, or when any deficiencies have been corrected, he is to notify the contractor in writing that the latter has performed adequately and that the structure is accepted. The engineer will simultaneously advise the owner in writing and will recommend that the owner make the final payment to the contractor. This payment may have retainage amounts withheld especially if warranty conditions acceptance.

The contract should outline these steps and should state that final payment to the contractor will not be made until the engineer has inspected and approved the completed work and has accepted it on behalf of the owner. The following clause is illustrative:

> When notified by the Contractor that, in his opinion, all work required by the Contract has been completed, the Engineer shall make a final inspection of the Work, including any tests of operation. After completion of this inspection and these tests, the Engineer shall, if all things are satisfactory to him, issue to the Owner and the Contractor a Certificate of Final Completion certifying that, in his opinion, the Work required by the Contract has been completed in accordance with the Contract Drawings and Specifications. However, the Certificate shall not operate to release the Contractor or his sureties from any guarantees under the Contract or the Performance Bond.

The general rule is that acceptance of work constitutes a waiver of its defects. Taking possession, however, does not necessarily constitute acceptance. If the final inspection reveals defects or work that does not meet the requirements of the contract, the owner may occupy the building and still maintain a claim for damages.[8]

---

[8]See waiver of imperfections, Chapters 6–8.

11.27 MISCELLANEOUS

It is impossible to list here all the miscellaneous items that should be included in a typical construction contract. However, the considerations mentioned below will serve as a reminder.

Employment The contract should prohibit hiring during the job period of any of the owner's or engineer's employees by the contractor for his own force. This provision is intended to prevent the contractor from raiding and depleting the owner's and engineer's staffs.

Emergencies It may be advisable to specify general procedures to be followed in case of emergencies, giving the engineer the right to order overtime work under stated conditions if he considers that this is necessary. Overtime work requirements do not usually apply to supervisory, administrative, clerical, and other personnel not engaged in manual work.

Minimum-Wage Rates In public work it may be necessary to publish legal requirements. On any job, if applicable rates are clearly stated, it helps to put all bidders on an equal basis in estimating the cost of the work. When given at all, the tabulation of wage rates should be sufficiently extensive to cover all anticipated classifications of work. The tabulation should take into account fringe benefits as well as hourly wage rates.

Domestic versus Foreign Materials and Labor Public works may require restrictions regarding the use of foreign materials or foreign labor. If so, this circumstance should be made clear.

Construction Reports The contract is to specify what periodic reports will be required of the contractor. These might include monthly estimates of the quantities of materials furnished and work done, progress reports showing the percentage of completion of various portions of the project, and periodic communications covering the status of materials in the process of manufacture.

Payroll and Bills for Materials The engineer may require that a copy of the payrolls of the contractor and all subcontractors, together with bills for materials, be made promptly available to him in the case of cost-plus work, extras, and the like.

Cooperation among Contractors In large projects, several contractors may be working simultaneously, or their work times may overlap. The contract should require that each is to conduct his operation so as to cooperate with the others.

Patents Specifying the use of patented devices or materials may be undesirable because this restricts competition and may inflate costs. If such devices or materials are necessary, however, the contract should indicate who is to secure permission to use these devices and materials and who is to pay any royalties or the like.

Schedule of Securities   This is generally a tabulation giving the market value and other data respecting any securities that are posted by the contractor in lieu of a bond. Usually these securities are deposited with the owner.

Guarantee of Equipment   If an equipment guarantee is to be required, the details should be clearly stated in the contract. The contractor may be obliged to keep any machinery and other mechanical equipment, electrical work, power generating plants, and hydraulic structures that he erected or supplied in repair and in good operating condition for a year or some other specified time after completion of the contract. Such a clause might be worded somewhat as follows:

> The Contractor shall guarantee that the material, equipment, and apparatus required by the Contract and Specifications shall be free from all defects in material, design, and workmanship and shall give satisfactory and continuous service under all conditions of service required and specified or that may be reasonably inferred from the Specifications, and that all Work performed by him shall be perfect in material and workmanship. The Contractor shall agree to repair or replace, at his own expense, any part of the material, apparatus, or workmanship proving defective within one year from date of acceptance.

Dredging   This work may require special instructions regarding sequence periods of work, maintenance of traffic, and the handling of obstructions and of any unforeseen difficulties that arise. Government permits to do such work should be secured by the owner unless the dredging is purely for the contractor's convenience, in which case the latter will seek the necessary permission.

Borings   Beyond what the engineer has done, explorations of foundation conditions may be required on the part of the contractor, especially in the case of unit-price and cost-plus contracts. If so, the engineer should have the right to determine the extent of the explorations needed and to approve or reject the contractor's plans for such activity. The method of payment for work of this character should preferably be specified on a cost-plus basis or as a stipulated price per foot of depth of boring, per soil sample taken, and per soil test made.

Spare Parts   These may be needed in the case of electrical and mechanical equipment being supplied by a contractor as his work product, and detailed requirements for such parts should be given in the contract.

Tests   Tests of materials and of mechanisms, if required at all, should be fully described in the contract papers.

Medical Facilities   The contractor ought to be obliged to provide at the site of any sizable construction job medical facilities sufficient for the administration of first aid. Moreover, he should have the means available for removing disabled persons to a hospital.

QUESTIONS

1. Explain the principal powers of the engineer in connection with the conduct of work in the field. What is his responsibility in case of an emergency?

2. Who should be responsible for coordination of work done (a) by the contractor and subcontractors? (b) by two different contractors? (c) partly by the owner and partly by the contractor? Explain.

3. Why should the engineer specify that he is to approve all the contractor's (a) drawings, and (b) equipment?

4. Should the contractor check the engineer's plans? Why? What should the contractor do if he happens to discover an error in the contract drawings?

5. What sort of things are supposed to be covered (a) by a contractor's warranties? (b) by his guarantees? Why should the engineer require him to warrant and to guarantee these things?

6. Who is responsible for the expense resulting from the correcting of defective work?

7. Ordinarily, who should establish the order in which the contractor is to perform various major portions of a large construction project? Explain.

8. Why is it desirable for the contract documents to contain a clause that requires each bidder to visit (or to have one of his men visit) the site of a construction job before submitting a proposal on the project?

9. A contractor was building a highway underpass in an urban area. The contract stated that she was to maintain traffic and to maintain and relocate all utilities. She encountered an old sewer that was not shown on the plans or mentioned in the specifications. (a) Is maintenance and relocation of this sewer her responsibility even though she had visited the site before bidding, as required by the specifications? (b) Can she properly claim extra compensation for this work? Explain.

10. A contract states that the work is to be completed in 30 days. What does this mean? Is the statement proper?

11. A contract states that the work is to be completed promptly. What does this mean legally?

12. If the contractor guarantees a structure for one year, (a) what is the usual starting time of the guarantee? (b) What sort of things would the guarantee usually cover?

13. What is the significance of "substantial performance" in construction contracts?

14. What control (if any) should the engineer have (a) over the conduct of a contractor with respect to other contractors engaged in the same major project? (b) over subcontractors?

15. The contractor designed the falsework for a large bridge, and the engineer approved the drawing. Subsequently one erection bent collapsed. Who is responsible for the resulting damages? Elaborate.

16. A contract called for the building of a large oil tank on silty soil near a wharf—all in accordance with the design. Under one edge of the area to be occupied by the tank the contractor unexpectedly encountered a group of old wooden piles that had been covered by earth and were not shown on the plans. He cut them off just below the future tank bottom, and he covered them with a little dirt. He did not report the situation to the engineer, who knew nothing about the piles. When the completed tank was tested by filling it with water, the greater resistance of the piles (compared with the bearing value of the neighboring soil) caused uneven settlement; as a result, the side of the tank over the piles buckled. Who is responsible for remedying the situation? Explain.

17. Describe some of the duties and responsibilities of and limitations upon an inspector in the field.

18. Who is to do the inspecting of work done by subcontractors—the engineer or the contractor—since the owner has no direct contact with the subcontractors?

19. If an engineer is not able or willing to send someone from her organization to inspect certain products before shipment from the factory, must she accept these products regardless of deficiencies?

20. If the inspector accepts work done by the contractor, does that mean that the contractor is no longer responsible for proper performance and quality of the work which has thus been accepted?

21. Does the inspector in the field have the right to tell the contractor how to perform his work? Explain.

22. Why make a final inspection when all the work has supposedly been inspected and approved before?

23. What are the principal procedures for and significance of final inspection and acceptance of a job? Does this acceptance relieve the contractor of subsequent responsibility for the quality of the work?

24. If defective work done by the contractor cannot practicably be replaced, what can the engineer do about it?

25. In a construction job, who should provide the necessary land, access, power, sanitary facilities, permits, and licenses? If not specified, what can be done about settling these matters?

26. When may it be desirable for the engineer to establish all lines and grades for a large construction project? When undesirable?

27. Why should the contractor be responsible (a) for the protection of the public at a job site? (b) for the maintenance of discipline?

28. Explain why it is important to confirm (in writing) telephoned messages between the engineer and the contractor when these messages relate to the construction project.

29. Does the contractor accept all risk when he takes the contract? Why make him state officially that he does so?

30. Why make the bidders warrant that they are familiar with all laws, ordinances, pay rates, and other regulations affecting the job?

31. Why might the engineer want to specify the order of completion of portions of the contract work? Illustrate a case.

32. Has the engineer the right to require the contractor to prepare a construction schedule? Why may one be desirable?

33. Who should provide the building permit? Why is one necessary in many cases?

34. What sort of contract is best suited for underpinning jobs? Why?

12

CONTRACT CLAUSES RELATING TO FINANCES

12.1 SUSPENSION OF CONTRACT

The contract clauses should give the engineer and the owner the right to suspend the contract if, in their opinion, an emergency or other unexpected development makes this necessary to protect the owner's interests. On the other hand, the right to suspend the contract should not be given to the contractor. The right is intended to protect the owner, but it should not be used in such a fashion as needlessly to injure the contractor.

The suspension clause might read like this:

> If at any time the Engineer considers it impracticable to start or to continue performance of the work or any portion thereof (whether or not for reasons beyond the control of the Owner), the Engineer shall have authority to suspend performance until such time as he may believe it feasible or desirable to proceed. However, should such action suspending the work be taken, the Engineer shall take all appropriate steps to minimize the duration of the suspension of the work, and the Contractor shall be entitled to such compensation for the resultant unavoidable expenses to him as the Engineer may believe to be just and reasonable because of the suspension.

To illustrate the need for such a clause, assume that a textile manufacturing corporation has let a contract to build a new and modern addition to one of the old buildings at its plant in Massachusetts. The foundations of the new structure are partially completed when the old structure is destroyed by fire. Obviously, the complete execution of the contract may now be utterly inadvisable. Under such circumstances the owner should have the right to suspend the work until he can determine what to do. He may want to change the design of the structure or to build an entirely new plant. He may wish to rebuild the destroyed structure so as to utilize fully the addition now under contract. He may not have had sufficient insurance to enable him to proceed with the reconstruction until he can secure more money. This financing may cause considerable delay, so that several weeks will elapse before he is sure he can go ahead. He may even decide to go out of business, or to carry out the expansion at another plant.

In case of a contract with a definite time limit for completion, an extension of time should be granted to the contractor to make up for the time lost because of the suspension. The extension should be a liberal one because a protracted interruption of work will almost always cause considerable further delay before the contractor can get adequate production under way again. He cannot keep his personnel on hold indefinitely nor keep the flow of materials to the site all ready to be resumed at short notice.

12.2   CANCELLATION OR TERMINATION OF CONTRACT

It is possible for circumstances to develop that make it necessary or desirable for the owner to terminate a contract. This right should be definitely stated in the contract clauses. The case described in the preceding article illustrates one way in which the need for the exercise of this right may arise.

The contract might specify the following additional bases on which the owner shall have the right to terminate it:[1]

1. Bankruptcy of the contractor or assignment by him for the benefit of his creditors.

2. Appointment of a receiver or liquidator for the contractor's property (unless such receiver is dismissed within two or three weeks).

3. Failure or refusal of the contractor (after adequate warning by the engineer) to supply enough skilled workers or proper materials to carry on the work in a suitable manner.

4. Failure or refusal of the contractor to prosecute the work diligently.

5. Failure or refusal of the contractor to comply with the instructions of the engineer or with applicable laws and codes.

6. Failure or refusal of the contractor to pay for labor and materials.

The termination of a contract may lead to a great deal of argument and trouble. Therefore, not only should the right to cancel be specifically reserved for the owner but the details of the procedure to be followed should be stated clearly.

The following is one version of a termination or cancellation clause:

> The Owner shall have the right, if the Engineer shall deem the Contractor guilty of a breach of any portion whatsoever of this Contract, to take over and complete the

---

[1] It is customary to require, however, that the contractor be given adequate written notice before the owner acts; for example, ten days.

Work, or any part of the Work, as agent for the Contractor and at the expense of the Contractor, either directly or through the operations of other contractors. Likewise, the Owner shall have the same right if the Contractor shall become bankrupt or if his property and affairs shall be placed under the control of a receiver or trustee.

Whenever the Owner shall be empowered to take over the Work as described in the preceding paragraph, or whenever circumstances or the affairs of the Owner make it necessary for his own financial well-being, the Owner shall have the right to annul, cancel, or rescind the Contract, in whole or in part. If an equitable financial settlement cannot be mutually agreed upon by the Engineer and the Contractor, the settlement shall be arrived at in accordance with the article herein entitled "Settlement of Disputes."

12.3   TRANSFER OF CONTRACT

The owner should determine that the prospective contractor is capable and well-qualified before the contract is awarded. It follows that the successful bidder should not be entitled to transfer the contract to someone else unless such action is first approved by the owner.

A clause to prevent such transfer might be stated this way:

This Contract is made in reliance upon the qualifications and responsibility of the Contractor, and any advance payments made hereunder are intended to assist him in part in the financing of the performance of the Work. Therefore, the Contractor shall not assign or transfer this Contract or any part thereof without the written consent of the Owner. However, the Contractor may subcontract portions of the Work to be performed hereunder to such persons as the Engineer may expressly approve in writing.

Assume that you as the owner plan to build a house. It will be a major investment for you; therefore, you want to make a contract for its design with an architect in whose character and skill you have confidence. Now suppose that, after starting the design of your house, this architect is selected to design two or three large jobs. As a result she wants to transfer your contract to an architect friend of hers whom you do not know. Since you engaged her for her known skills, you want her to do the design work personally, not have someone else do it.

Again, suppose that your house has been designed and that you have negotiated a contract with a particular builder because you trust him and believe that he will provide the best possible structure. Naturally you would oppose transfer of the contract to anyone in whom you do not have equal confidence. There may be conditions, however, in which a transfer of the contract is desirable for the owner as well as for the contractor. Sickness of the contractor, death of some key personnel, financial difficulties, labor trouble that prevents proper prosecution of the work are all examples. Transfers, though, are likely to be accompanied by considerable difficulty in the matter of adjusting payments for work done by the new contractor and the old. Transfers are also likely to result in delays, confusion as to responsibility, and difficulty on the part of the new contractor in picking up the work where the other one left off. Considering the inherent difficulties involved, transfer of responsibility for the completion of a contract should not be allowed unless circumstances absolutely require it.

12.4   REVISIONS

Situations arise in which revisions of plans prove expedient or imperative after a contract has been awarded. Although the engineer would prefer to avoid making revisions, it is important to recognize that they are sometimes necessary, and decisions regarding revisions should be carefully evaluated. A few principles to bear in mind are the following:

1. Any error should be corrected promptly.

2. Matters involving the safety of personnel, structures, and equipment should receive top priority.

3. When something bearing upon satisfactory operation is discovered to be amiss, especially in the case of a moneymaking or self-liquidating project, the indicated changes should be made unless they entail undue hardship or expense. The structure or machine is built once; it is to be used or operated continuously thereafter. Additional trouble and expense in the building of it may be offset many times over by saving in operation.

4. Modifications that are merely the result of differences of opinion and that will have little real consequence are to be avoided unless they can be made early enough to prevent difficulty in execution.

5. Revisions that involve substantial changes in quantity or quality of work should not be effected until the contractor and the owner have agreed upon what is the allowable additional expense involved. This agreement should be confirmed in writing.

6. If a revision constitutes so major a change that it greatly affects the scope or character of the work, the matter may have to be treated as requiring a negotiated modification of the original contract or the preparation of a new and separate contract covering the proposed additional work.[2]

All revisions should be in written form. A telephone call is an expedient way to pass along information, but it should be followed up promptly by written confirmation of the instructions. This confirmation may be in the form of a letter, or it may be the revision of a drawing, which is also a method of recording information.

---

[2]See for example, *Albert Elia Bldg. Co., Inc. v. N.Y. State Dev. Corp.*, 54 A.D.2d 337 (1976), where a contract for the construction of a convention center authorized changes within the general scope of the contract, but the court found that supplemental work of constructing a tunnel to an adjacent plaza, plans for which had not begun at the time of the convention center contract, was a new undertaking requiring a new public bid. This was true even though the entire work was located within the convention center facility.

It is advisable to send a letter of transmittal with any revision of a drawing, calling the contractor's attention to the fact that the drawing has been revised.

Revisions may also be sent by facsimile transmission, or by electronic mail. Drawings may be sent by facsimile transmission or by CAD with a fax confirmation by the recipient.

Regardless of the mode of communication the need to maintain an accurate record of revisions sent and confirmations of their receipt remains unchanged.

It is also desirable for the contract to contain a clause stating that the contractor is not to proceed with the execution of revisions until official data and instructions in writing have been received. Similarly, after having been notified officially that certain revisions are pending, he is not to proceed with work that will be affected thereby because doing so would probably result in even greater cost and trouble in carrying out the revisions later.

Assume that the engineer telephones to a steel fabricator stating that the plates for some coal bunkers in a power plant are to be made 1/2 inch thick instead of 3/8 inch as shown on the original contract drawing. The fabricator should not go ahead with further work on these plates or on parts that will be affected by their change in thickness, nor should he go ahead with work on new 1/2 inch plates until official revisions are received. However, if the engineer telegraphs or faxes this information, this constitutes notice in writing, and the contractor may proceed accordingly. The engineer should still confirm the change by a revision of the drawing.

The contract documents should state that the contractor must carry out all revisions required by the engineer, who is the best judge of their desirability or necessity. However, in the usual case the engineer should not order the contractor to proceed until the extra expense involved, if any, is settled, or until the contractor has informed him that the revised work will be done under the unit prices stated in the contract.

Furthermore, the contractor should be obliged to notify the engineer in writing within a stated period (such as seven days) after receipt of the official revisions if he considers them to require additional compensation. He should submit a statement of how much the extra cost will be and how the amount was calculated, thus allowing the engineer an opportunity to cancel the revision or modify it if the price is not satisfactory.

12.5 EXTRAS IN GENERAL

The contract should make definite and adequate provisions for the handling of "extra" costs, whether the contract is on a lump-sum or a unit-price basis. This matter is especially troublesome in the case of lump-sum contracts. Extra charges may result from ordinary revisions made by the engineer, from a substantial increase in the quantity of work required, or from a real change in the quality of materials and workmanship from what was specified in the contract. Also, something unforeseen may be encountered, and the performance of unanticipated work may become essential. If so, the additional task simply has to be accomplished regardless of extra costs involved.

One way to handle the problem of extras caused by revisions of a lump-sum contract[3] is to specify the procedure in such a way as the following:

> If revisions made by the Engineer cause an increase of the Work to be done under the Contract or in the cost of said Work, the Contractor shall estimate or keep records of the increase in the cost of labor and materials resulting from the revisions. Upon approval of this estimate or record by the Engineer, this computed extra cost plus fifteen (15) percent thereof for overhead and profit shall be payable to the Contractor as extra compensation because of said revisions. On the other hand, if the revisions of the Contract result in a cost reduction, the Contractor shall estimate such reduction in the cost of labor and materials. Upon approval of this estimate by the Engineer, the stipulated sum shall be deducted from the Contractor's bid price, but this deduction shall not include any portion of the original allowance for anticipated overhead and profit.
>
> The preceding paragraph is to apply to Work performed by subcontractors as well as to that performed directly by the general contractor. However, in the case of extra costs because of revisions made by the Engineer in subcontracted Work, the stipulated allowance of fifteen (15) percent of the approved additional estimated cost or approved actual cost of the extra Work is to be paid as an allowance for overhead and profit to the subcontractors only, no additional percentage being payable to the general contractor.

The above provisions are intended to minimize the likelihood of disputes regarding the contractor's claims for extra compensation by reason of changes made in the plans or specifications by the engineer. Provision for extras is not intended to remedy misjudgment, inefficient management, or other shortcomings attributable to the contractor or the subcontractors that may have caused the cost of performance to be greater than originally anticipated.

If the contractor goes ahead with extra work, duly ordered by the engineer with the understanding that extra expense for the owner will be involved but before the receipt of written instructions to do so, there is an assumption that this extra work will be paid for by the owner. The contract requirement of a written order for extras would not seem to bar the contractor from seeking payment in such a situation.

12.6   EXTRAS CAUSED BY SUBSURFACE CONDITIONS

Subsurface conditions on a construction job are a prolific source of trouble. The engineer should be very careful to obtain all the advance information that reasonably can be secured, having adequate explorations made and presenting the results to all bidders. But he should not try to interpret, extrapolate, or guarantee the data given in the logs of the borings, even though he has to prepare his design of the structure on that basis.

In the construction of the caisson foundation for a certain bridge, the record of the borings was given to the bidders. However, boulders caused much more diffi-

[3]A lump-sum contract may contain a clause setting forth unit prices for extra work done and credits for work omitted at the behest of the engineer; such a clause is often called the *additions-and-deductions provision*.

culty than the successful bidder expected. Later he brought suit for recovery of the extra cost over and above his estimate. His claim was rejected by the court because he had been given all the information that the engineer possessed. In glacial territory, such as that involved in this case, boulders are not unusual. Miscalculation on the part of the contractor was adjudged not to be the fault of the engineer.

In another case a contractor was to build a four-story reinforced-concrete building on pile foundations at an old waterfront. The owner had some soil borings made and furnished the logs of these borings to the bidders. Later, when the contractor was driving piles, an old sea wall was encountered, the removal of which caused considerable expense. He claimed extra for this work. The court granted his claim because the owner possessed old plans showing such a sea wall, but he did not show them to the bidders—probably because he had forgotten about the existence of the plans. Nevertheless, the fact remains that he failed to present all the information at his disposal.

In a third situation, the record of the boring taken at the center of the site for a large concrete structure indicated bedrock to be at a given elevation. Later it was discovered that the boring had merely hit a large boulder. The extra excavation to sound rock had to be done under very difficult conditions, and the contractor could not estimate in advance how much the extra expense would be. The engineer therefore approved the contractor's proposal that the additional work be paid for on a cost-plus-percentage basis.

The following paragraph shows one suggested way to phrase a clause about borings:

> Borings have been made at the site for the Owner. The locations of these borings and the information obtained from them are recorded on the reference drawings. Samples of the soils removed and the records made during the boring operations may be examined at the office of the Owner. However, in transmitting information regarding the materials expected to be encountered, the Owner does not guarantee the accuracy or completeness of the data given, and he assumes no responsibility therefor. The Contractor shall draw his own conclusions from whatever information is available, through the Owner or otherwise.

12.7 EXTRAS CAUSED BY ADDITIONAL QUANTITIES OF WORK OR MATERIALS

Additional quantities of work ordered during the progress of operations may entitle a contractor to claim an extra on a lump-sum job. This may not be so for a unit-price contract when the contractor receives proper payment through the application of the unit prices.

The borings at the site proposed for a large industrial building showed that pile foundations would be needed along one side. The plans were made accordingly, and the contract was let on a unit-price basis. It was later discovered that one boring taken near the center of the structure had encountered a knob of sand that was surrounded by an area containing very unsatisfactory soils. This necessitated the use of much more piling. Since it was a unit-price contract, the owner and the contractor agreed that the extra piling, concrete, and so on should be paid for at the bid unit prices. It would have been unfair to penalize the contractor for this unforeseen additional work, even if the contract had been for a lump sum.

As another example, suppose that one unit-price item in a contract covers the payment for 1,000 poured-in-place concrete piles with an assumed length of 60 feet at $10 per foot of pile. The assumed length of piles stipulated in the contract is such that the contractor can use equipment already in his possession. When the driving is started, it is found that in order to attain the specified resistance the piles have to be 10 feet longer than originally expected. Because the piles are too big to be driven by his own equipment, the contractor will have to rent costly equipment. Besides the extra cost represented by the rental, the greater length of the piles will cause the contractor many additional worker-hours of labor, rendering the bid unit price inadequate. Therefore, the contractor should be entitled to extra payment. Where a building or construction contract has been fully performed by the contractor, his subsequent promise to do extra work must, to bind him, be supported by consideration. This further promise is supplemental to the original contractual undertakings.

12.8   EXTRAS CAUSED BY ADDITIONAL DIFFICULTY OF PERFORMANCE

Whether the work is increased in quantity or not, unforeseen difficulty in the way of performance may be a just cause for the contractor to claim extra compensation. An example of this occurred in the construction of a vehicular tunnel at West 178th Street in New York City. The contract was on a unit-price basis. A deep subterranean ravine was found to cross the site between two of the borings. It contained many heavy boulders, and it was the course of an underground stream. The contractor was paid the regular unit prices on all extra excavation, concrete, and such. The work, however, was more difficult than that called for by the contract papers, and a considerable extra sum was paid to compensate the contractor for the additional expense of surmounting the unexpected difficulties.

Concrete construction is another prime source of claims for extra compensation by reason of more difficult work than anticipated, especially in connection with forms and reinforcement. All too often the owner insists that a few general drawings be rushed to "completion" and that unit-price bids for excavation and concrete be secured just as soon as possible. Not only can the engineer not show on the drawings all the ramifications that may ultimately have to be developed, he often cannot predict them at this early stage of the project's development. The contractor therefore makes his bid upon the basis of certain estimated quantities and the expected degree of difficulty. Later on, the owner may be shocked by the extra costs claimed by the contractor for more forms and steel per cubic yard than the owner expected. The engineer's position in such circumstances is difficult, to say the least.

By way of example, a large plant required about 2,000 linear feet of subterranean tunnels for electric power distribution. The drawings used for bidding simply showed these tunnels in plan by dotted lines and portrayed one typical cross section. Later on it was found that many manholes were needed in the top or sides for conduits and that branch tunnels were required. Also needed were a number of stairways for escape hatches and fan houses for ventilation of the tunnels. The contractor presented a claim for additional payment because of this more complicated work. All these extra items were necessary and had to be provided. The contractor's claim was found to be justified.

12.9 EXTRAS CAUSED BY REDUCTION OF WORK

A reduction in the quantity of work may also be a proper basis for an extra under a unit-price contract. Thus, a contract had been entered into for some extensive pile driving at a harbor. The engineer later decided to eliminate about 25 percent of the piles. Because of the resulting loss of profit and of a portion of the allowance for overhead built into the quoted unit price for piles, the contractor was able to collect an extra payment above that made in accordance with the bid itself. The decision to honor a claim for an extra was based upon the fact that the reduction in work was substantial. But few piles more or less (say 5 percent) than the estimated number or the number shown on the drawings generally will not entitle the contractor to an extra if the contract is on a unit-price basis. The contract should state the permissible variation in quantities in order to avoid possible controversy.

Here is a suggested clause dealing with variation in quantities:

> The Contractor's proposal is to be based upon the estimated quantities shown in the "Schedule of Prices." Inasmuch as the quantity of concrete and the number of piles driven may be affected by conditions encountered in the performance of the Work, or by written instructions to be issued by the Engineer as the Work progresses, the quantity of work done under these two items may vary considerably from the estimated quantities. In this event, payment for any overrun of these quantities shall be made to the Contractor at the bid unit prices. However, if the quantities of either or both of these items actually installed are less than ninety (90) percent of the respective estimated quantities stated in the schedule, the Contractor shall be entitled to such adjustment of the bid unit prices for the affected item or items as the Engineer believes will fairly compensate the Contractor for the loss of profit caused by the decreased amount of Work done under the Contract.

12.10 RESPONSIBILITY FOR EXTRA COSTS

It is very important to determine whether the owner and/or engineer are responsible for unanticipated costs or whether these are occasioned by fault of the contractor.

Undoubtedly the owner is obliged to pay when the information given by the contract documents is inadequate to enable the contractor to determine in advance what work he will have to do. The owner is also obligated (1) when inaccurate data are given by the engineer to the bidders, (2) when the extras develop because of improper design and plans in the first place, and (3) when the engineer makes extensive changes after the contract is signed.

If the contractor performs the work as required by the contract but unforeseen conditions arise, through no fault of his, necessitating modifications of the design, and if these modifications are approved or ordered by the engineer, then the extra costs involved are properly to be paid for by the owner. In one case a contractor was to build a 150-foot brick stack at an incinerator. No borings had been taken at the site, and the engineer had designed the footing of the stack as though it were to be supported upon firm ground at the specified elevation. However, under the stack it developed that there was deep clay overlain by a few feet of sand and gravel. The contractor was afraid that the compaction of the clay might cause harmful settlement of the stack. Finally the engineer made an investigation of the soils and decided to support the stack on piles. The new design of the foundation required considerable additional construction. This was obviously to be paid for by the owner as an extra charge.

Conversely, extra costs resulting from the mistakes and ill-advised practices of the contractor are his own responsibility. In one instance a contractor tried to pour some heavy concrete foundations during extremely cold weather without first thawing out the existing concrete. Ice lenses formed at and near the junction of the new and the old work, causing small, open, horizontal cracks after the ice lenses melted, the upper portion of the concrete being supported by the reinforcing bars which acted as tiny columns. The contractor was responsible for the replacement and repairing of this work because the contract stated that no concrete was to be poured against frozen surfaces of any kind.

It may be that extra costs in a given situation are caused by both the owner and the contractor. Such costs should be apportioned by agreement of the parties. Thus, a contract for a large industrial plant could not be completed on time unless at least some of the construction was performed during cold winter weather. This was because of delays in getting started, some of which were attributable to the owner and some to the contractor. The contract had called for discontinuance of work from November 30 to April 1. However, to expedite the project and to enable the contractor to proceed continuously and thus to avoid undue loss (despite expensive winter operations), the owner made a special agreement with him to take certain parts out of the former contract and to place them in the new one, which was to be carried on during the winter. This was a compromise arrangement of sorts between the two parties.

In a cost-plus construction contract dispute, the fact that the price was higher than either of the parties anticipated is not part of the proof, nor is its reasonableness. Absent some claim indicating fraud or gross negligence, it is not incumbent upon the person providing the service to prove that charges for labor and material were reasonable. Thus, in a case where a contractor agreed to construct a residence for cost plus a fixed fee of $10,860, the contractor was held entitled to the full cost of his labor and materials, without proof of reasonableness.[4] The risks of an owner entering into such a contract are self-evident.

---

[4]*Romine v. Rex Darnall Inc.,* 541 S.W.2d 50 (Mo. App. 1976). The converse is also true. See, for example, *Tube Co. v. Dayton Equipment Services Co.,* 123 F.3d 616 (7th Cir, 1997, applying Indiana law), where a contract for installation of a static cast line in a foundry was found to be a time and materials rather than a fixed price contract, and, since the price was not fixed, recovery was for the reasonable value of that provided.

12.11   ERRORS DISCOVERED BY THE CONTRACTOR

The contract should require that the contractor is to report immediately to the engineer any error discovered in the contract drawings or in any other data furnished by the engineer.[5] The contractor should also report at once any detected error made by his own staff and should cease work immediately on the affected part of the job until the engineer can issue instructions regarding what is to be done in the matter.

On a certain job the contract drawings showed the doors of a factory to be hinged so as to open inward, contrary to the applicable building code. The contractor admitted he had timely knowledge that this was an error but had nevertheless hung the doors without notifying the engineer. The contractor was later obliged to absorb the cost of reversing the doors.[6]

The following clause shows fairly standard wording used to prescribe the procedure in this matter of correcting errors:

> If the Contractor discovers any errors or omission in the Contract Drawings of Specifications or in the Work undertaken and performed by him, he shall immediately notify the Engineer and the latter shall promptly investigate the matter. If, knowing of such error or omission and prior to receiving instructions from the Engineer regarding correction thereof, the Contractor proceeds with any Work affected thereby, he shall do so at his own risk and the Work so done shall not be considered as Work done under the Contract and in performance thereof unless and until duly approved and accepted by the Engineer.

12.12   DELAYS

Unless the contract specifically states otherwise, the contractor is generally entitled to recover losses sustained because of delays caused by the owner. The latter is regarded as having an implied obligation to provide all drawings and other information necessary to enable the contractor to complete the job within the specified time. If, on the other hand, the contract states that the "contractor herewith specifically waives claims for damages for any hindrance or delay," it means just that.[7] If such a clause is in the contract, however, the contractor will probably add to the

---

[5] In a government contract, a potential contractor in a roof replacement contract was held to have some responsibility to inquire about major patent discrepancies, but not to seek clarification of any and all ambiguities or doubts. *Beta Construction Co., Inc. v. United States*, 39 Fed. Cl. 722 (U.S. Ct. of Cl. 1997). And see *Hoffman Const. Co. of Oregon v. United States*, 40 Fed. Cl. 184 (U.S. Ct. of Cl. 1998) where an inconsistency in bidding documents in which the information drawings showed duct work and the contract drawings did not was held obvious and thus patent, and resolved against the contractor.

[6] The contractor's knowledge of an error in the plans even prior to signing the contract destroys any reasonable claim for extra compensation for correcting the mistake provided he did not call the error to the engineer's attention at that time. See *Wickham Inc. v. U.S.*, 546 F.2 395 (Ct. Cl. 1976), where the error was an erroneous 1' = 200' scale where the drawing specified the correct 1" = 2' scale. Followed by *Johnson Controls, Inc. v. U.S.*, 671 F 2d 1312 (Ct. Cl 1982) where on a contract to install an energy monitoring system for a hospital, the preliminary drawings showed 67 and 16 control points and the final drawings required 133 and 70 control points.

[7] *S. L. Roland Constr. Co. v. Beall Pipe & Tank Corp.*, 141 Wash. App. 297, 540 P.2d 912 (1975), where delays in the construction of 11 1/2 miles of 51 inch steel pipeline was delayed by changes with respect to the grade and elevation of the pipe installation after the contract was set. And see *Nelse Mortensen & Co. v. Group Health*, 566 P.2d 560 (Wash. App. 1977), where an owner delay clause was held binding on the contractor who claimed 146 owner-caused delays in the remodeling of a hospital.

contingency item in his bid an amount he believes sufficient to cover such eventualities, with a resulting higher bid. Some contracts may contain a clause that prohibits delay damages except those due *solely* to fraud or bad faith on the part of the owner.[8] While tempting, such language reinjects the very uncertainty that the contract was intended to avoid.

A clause in a construction subcontract providing that the subcontractor would bear the risk, even if the delay was caused by the contractor, need not be set forth conspicuously where both parties are experienced and familiar with the industry custom of allocating risk for delay.[9]

A better way to handle this problem may be to state in the contract that, in case of any act or omission on the owner's part causing delay, the contractor will be entitled to just recompense and to an extension of time.[10] However, the contractor should be required to give written notice of his claim for extension and of the cause for it within a stated number of days after such cause arises. Furthermore, the engineer should have the power to grant what he considers to be a reasonable extension.

Delays brought about by the contractor are his responsibility, and he will naturally make every effort to prevent such delays. The engineer should not set an impractical completion date, for if his requirement is unreasonable, the contractor will have to add a sum to his bid to cover foreseen penalties or else will have to include extra expenses for overtime work and other costs that arise when a job is rushed. Before allowing only a marginal amount of time for completion, the engineer should be satisfied that the advantage to be derived from speed of execution is worth the extra charge that may be added in the bid.

Delays caused by "acts of God" are not the fault of the contractor, or the owner, or of any other human being. It is often difficult, however, to establish whether or not a particular event is truly an act of God. For example, assume that a contractor has constructed a cofferdam around the area in which he is building a bridge pier in a river. A flood occurs with water seriously damaging the cofferdam, causing a delay of three weeks for repair. Who is to blame? If the cofferdam was not made sufficiently high and strong to withstand floods that are known to occur in that river at least once in three or four years, the contractor will probably be held responsible. However, if he made the cofferdam strong enough so that it would have withstood the worst flood that had occurred during the preceding 10 or 15 years, he would probably be considered to have taken reasonable precautions and would be relieved

---

[8]See, for example, *Ragan Enterprises, Inc. v. Land B Construction Co., Inc.* 492 S.E. 2d 671 (Ga. App. 1997).

[9]*Green International, Inc. v. Solis,* 951 S.W.2d 384 (Texas 1997).

[10]A contract was let for the construction of a large stack at an industrial plant. It was to be built in the vicinity of a similar stack that emitted sulfurous fumes. The owner realized that work might be delayed by these fumes when the wind carried them across the site of the new structure. Therefore, a clause was inserted stating that any delays resulting from the problem of fumes would mean a corresponding automatic setting back of the scheduled completion date.

of any responsibility for the flood damage. The owner (or his insurance company) would presumably have to pay for the reconstruction in that event.

The contractor is entitled to prompt decisions on the part of the engineer. In a large dredging job in a harbor, the owner decided to make some important changes after the contract was under way. The job had to be stopped until the owner settled various questions concerning the revisions. Each day of delay cost the contractor an estimated sum of $1000 in rentals, overhead, and unavoidable miscellaneous expenses. The contractor should be compensated for the cost entailed by such a delay. If the delay were to continue for a long time, he might also claim the loss of profits that he could have made on some other job.

Here is a sample clause dealing with the subject of delays:

> If the Engineer believes that, on account of any act or omission of the Owner or the Engineer and without fault of the Contractor, any of the plant, equipment or salaried men being used by the Contractor in performance of the Contract are necessarily kept idle for more than seven (7) consecutive calendar days, the Contractor shall be entitled to increased compensation. This increase shall be an amount equal to that which he may pay during such period of idleness for the availability of such idle salaried persons and for other related expenses, plus a sum computed at the rate of fifteen (15) percent per annum on the sum which the Engineer deems to be the actual value of idle plant and equipment, all computations being based upon the total duration of the delay.

In the preceding clause the stipulation of a minimum time of idleness that must elapse before the contractor is allowed to make a claim against the owner for damages caused by delay resulting from an act of the owner may not be entirely wise or warranted. Such a limitation may cause the contractor to increase the contingency item in his bid.

Generally speaking, the contractor or subcontractor should be granted an extension of time not only for delays caused by acts or omissions of the owner or of the engineer but also for delays stemming from occurrences such as the following:

1. Acts of God.
2. Acts of war.
3. Acts of the government.
4. Acts of another contractor over whom the first contractor has no control.
5. Fires.
6. Epidemics.
7. Quarantine restrictions.
8. Freight embargoes.
9. Strikes.

12.13   PARTIAL PAYMENTS

In a large contractual undertaking over an extended period of time, a contractor will generally have to borrow money. Part of the interest on this borrowed money will be added into the contractor's estimated costs and will be included in his bid. Therefore the owner will ultimately have to pay the contractor's borrowing expense.

Consequently, it is a good practice to arrange for partial payments to the contractor during the course of the job. One convenient method is provision for payments once a month, each payment being based upon an estimate of the value of the work or portion of the contract that has been completed during the preceding month. The mechanics for the determination of the size of these payments should be specified in the contract. The idea of partial payments is applicable to lump-sum contracts as well as to unit-price contracts. Of course, cost-plus contracts are financed directly by the owner; hence some of the incentives of making partial payments are lacking.

If the contract states that partial payments are to be made to the contractor as the work progresses, this commitment must be honored.[11] Even when the contract fails to specify such a procedure, it may be utilized if full financing by the contractor alone proves unrealistic.

Partial payments should not be based upon elapsed time alone. If a contract is supposed to be completed in ten months but the contractor inexcusably takes twelve months to complete it, he should not be paid in ten equal monthly installments that really prepay him for tardy work. On the other hand, if he completes the work in eight months, he should be paid on that basis. Partial payments should be related to accomplishments, not to intentions.

Assume that a unit-price contract has been assigned for a reinforced-concrete bridge and its approaches costing an estimated $1 million, to be completed in twelve months. The unit prices cover such items as excavation, concrete, and reinforcement. At the beginning of a given month the engineer and the contractor may make independent estimates of the quantities of work performed during the preceding month, or the engineer may check the contractor's estimates of the work done.[12]

In either case both parties are to agree upon the figures or upon a compromise estimate. The engineer should have the authority to state what estimated figures the payment will be based upon if such decisive action becomes necessary because of disagreement between the parties.

Similarly, if the bridge contract is on a lump-sum basis for $1 million, partial payments might well be determined and made on the basis of work accomplished.

---

[11]*Guerini Stone Co. v. P.J. Carlin Constr. Co.*, 248 U.S. 334, 345 (1919): "As is usually the case with building contracts, it evidently was in the contemplation of the parties that the contractor could not be expected to finance the operation to completion without receiving the stipulated payments on account as the work progressed. In such cases a substantial compliance as to advance payments is a condition precedent to the contractor's obligation to proceed." See also, however, *U.S. for the Use of Bldg. Rentals Corp. v. Western Casualty & Surety Co.*, 498 F.2d 335 (9th Cir. 1974), where a delay or deviation in payments withheld were found not to justify rescission of the contract, when the delay was caused, at least in part, by a request or demand of the party to whom the payment was owed.

[12]These computations of quantities take time. Therefore, the contract might well state that "the Contractor is to submit to the Engineer by the tenth of each month the estimated quantities of the work performed by him during the preceding month."

To do this, the engineer could establish imaginary unit prices, and he might make his own estimates of quantities, and thus of the payment due, practically in the same way as for a real unit-price contract. Or he might specify that, subject to approval of the several segments of the work, the contractor is to be paid as follows:

1. $50,000 upon completion of the excavation and cofferdams or shoring for the foundations.

2. $100,000 upon completion of the river piers.

3. $75,000 upon completion of the abutments.

4. $100,000 upon completion of the two side spans.

5. $375,000 upon completion of the three main spans.

6. $100,000 upon completion of the approaches.

7. $200,000 upon completion and final acceptance of the entire job.

In any case, the procedure for making partial payments is to be specified in detail in the contract so as to avoid future misunderstandings.

It often happens that materials are furnished or delivered but that the construction involving them is not completed. Technically, the bid unit prices may not be applicable to such items, but the engineer should estimate the value of these materials and, in fairness to the contractor, include such in the calculation of the partial payment. By way of illustration, suppose the structural steel for a large building is contracted for at a certain unit price as "erected." At the end of a particular month all the material has been rolled, 50 percent has been fabricated, 25 percent has been delivered, but none has been erected. It is proper and logical to make some partial payment to the contractor who in turn can pay the steel company.

The following clause has been paraphrased from a lump-sum contract and is included here for the purpose of showing a poorly worded clause on partial payments:

> Payments will be made monthly in an amount equal to eighty-five (85) percent of the value of all labor and material incorporated in the work and/or suitably stored on site during the preceding month until eighty (80) percent of the work has been completed. Monthly payments will then be increased to ninety-five (95) percent of work accomplished.

The following relate to this clause:

1. The engineer should specify the day of the month on which the payment is to be made.

2. The clause should state that the quantity of work completed each month (and its assumed value) is to be determined from the estimates made by the engineer.

3. It is unwise to provide that materials "stored on the site" are to be included in the quantities on which partial payments will be determined. Such a provision might cause disputes regarding the value of material simply brought to the site and left there. Also, labor is not "stored."

4. It would be better to let one established percentage apply until the full job is completed and accepted and until the final payment is made.

5. Each time it is employed, the term "monthly payment" should be amplified by adding "to the contractor."

6. Such a phrase as "work accomplished" is altogether too vague. One cannot afford to be ambiguous in these matters.

12.14   WITHHOLDING OF A PORTION OF PARTIAL PAYMENT

It is usually desirable for the engineer to have the right to withhold 10 or 15 percent of the estimated monthly payments otherwise due the contractors, as computed from the quantity of work completed, as a protection for the owner. Often called retainage, this gives the owner leverage in discouraging the contractor from quitting near the end of the job. Also, the withheld funds can be used by the owner toward remedying poor work or finishing up if the contractor fails to complete the contract. When performance under the contract is fully accomplished by the contractor, these withheld funds are to be paid as part of the final settlement. The money withheld from the monthly payments to the contractor is not a substitute for the performance bond.

A unit-price contract might well contain a clause such as the following: "On the fifteenth of each month, the Contractor is to be paid ninety (90) percent of the sum obtained by applying the respective bid unit prices to the approved estimated quantities of work completed by the Contractor during the preceding month."

Under a system of partial payments, the contractor may get little compensation during the first month or two, whereas during the next six or seven months the payments may be relatively large. Finally, during the last month or two, when odds and ends are being cleaned up, the payments may again be small. However, partial payments, large or small, will be of assistance in financing his operations.

12.15   FINAL PAYMENT

Some suggestions in connection with the final payment are illustrated by the following clause:

> Prior to final payment the Contractor shall obtain and furnish to the Owner satisfactory evidence that the Work is fully released from all claims, liens, and demands and shall secure and furnish written consent of his sureties to final payment hereunder. Furthermore, acceptance by the Contractor of final payment shall release the Owner from all claims and liability to the Contractor for all Work done and materials furnished in the execution of the Contract. Final payment (or any other payment), however, shall not itself serve to release the Contractor or his sureties from their obligations under or in connection with this Contract or the Performance Bond.

After the final inspection and approval of the work by the engineer and its acceptance by the owner, a general accounting is usually necessary before the size of the balance due the contractor can be determined. Normally, unless a construction contract specifies otherwise, all the work must be substantially completed before a final payment is due.

When there are no extra claims by the contractor and no credits or deductions to be made in favor of the owner, the amount due the contractor on a lump-sum contract is simply the bid price less the sum of all partial payments that have been made. Use of a unit-price contract makes it necessary, first, to compute the final quantities for each payment item, then to multiply each such quantity by the applicable bid unit price, and from these products to calculate the total cost of the contract. This total, less all partial payments, is the net sum owed to the contractor. Usually the owner and the contractor can agree upon the calculated quantities and the final computed cost. In case of disagreement, the engineer may determine what the computed costs are to be, a third party may make an independent calculation, or the questions may be settled by arbitration. The contract should state which of these three procedures is to be followed.

The general contractor will usually withhold from interim payments to the subcontractors the same percentage as that held back by the owner,[13] making final payment to them only after he has been completely paid off. This practice can be inequitable. Thus, a subcontractor for foundation work may complete his part of the job and have it accepted early in the life of the contract; nevertheless, he may have to wait months before he can collect any withheld percentage that is still due. It would be more equitable if subcontracted work is sufficiently definite and independent to have the master contract state that upon approval and final acceptance of the subcontractor's work, the owner is to pay the contractor therefor and that the latter is to remit promptly to the subcontractor.

Another way to aid the subcontractors would be a statement in the contract to the effect that, when final payment is made by the owner to the contractor, the latter is promptly thereafter to pay the subcontractors any amounts previously withheld from them and properly due to them. Double payee checks may also be used to ensure that subcontractors are paid by the general contractor.

12.16   FAILURE TO MAKE PAYMENTS

If the owner fails to make payments to the contractor as and when provided in the contract, the contractor ought to have the right to suspend the work, but he should be ready to renew his activity if the payment is delivered before the expiration of some prescribed time limit. However, since such a delay almost always causes

---

[13]One contract put it this way: "The Contractor shall pay to each of his subcontractors, not later than the fifth day after receipt of each payment made to him by the Owner, the respective amounts allowed the Contractor on account of the work performed by such subcontractors, to the extent of each such subcontractor's interest therein." With regard to "pay when paid" clauses see *Christman Co. v. Anthony S. Brown Dev. Co.*, 533 N.W. 2d 838 (Mich. App. 1995) *app. den.* 549 N.W.2d 562. There, a subcontractor's claim that a "pay when paid" clause merely postpones payment for a reasonable time, but not indefinitely, was rejected, in a situation where the prime contractor went unpaid by the owner.

additional expense to the contractor, he should be entitled to make a claim for the recovery of all the cost directly chargeable to such interruption. A contractor and all of the subcontractors are well advised to keep appropriate records of costs attributable to those delays which are the fault of the owner.

Continued failure by the owner to make payment ought to entitle the contractor to terminate the contract after a stipulated written notice to the owner of the contractor's intention to do so (assuming payment is not made in the meantime). In the event of such termination, the contractor should be able to recover the cost of all materials actually provided, all work done, and all losses and damages suffered by him as the result of the owner's breach.

12.17   LIQUIDATED DAMAGES

The invitation for bids may contain the words "Time is of the essence," meaning that the time of completion of the project is an important item for the contractor to consider when bidding on the job. The contractor will be bound to meet a designated completion date, or else some specified compensation will have to be made to the owner. Such payments for failure to meet the required date are referred to as *liquidated damages,* not as penalties.

A toll bridge, a factory, an apartment house, a store, or any project that is to be a profit source for the owner will be in the class where relatively quick completion is highly important. Even though the typical owner may have been hesitating for a considerable time before deciding to go ahead with the project, once the decision has been made the work should be completed with the utmost speed. The contractor's desire to minimize interest charges (on money which he has to borrow to finance construction) constitutes one reason for speed in converting the project into a profit-making one as soon as possible.

In setting the dates for starting and completion, the engineer should consult interested contractors about the time necessary to prepare for and to complete the construction. If the time allowed for completion is inadequate, the contractor will have to set a high bid price to cover costs which inevitably accompany overtime work and allow for the possibility of certain liquidated damages if the work does not progress satisfactorily. Perhaps these costs will be included as an indistinguishable part of the bid prices. Nevertheless, they are very real, and the engineer should be sure that the owner realizes that specifying a short period for completion of the work is likely to prove expensive.

The liquidated damages are usually expressed in the form of a stated number of dollars for each day that actual completion of the job extends beyond the date specified in the contract. The amount of this daily figure is supposed to be the owner's estimate of what will be lost in income by reason of the delayed completion.[14] The owner generally will deduct any liquidated damages from the sum due the contractor at the time of final payment.

---

[14]The law disfavors liquidated damages and will not enforce punitive clauses. Liquidated damages cannot be used as a means of making a profit for the owner at the expense of the contractor. Also, it would seem fair to provide that the contractor will be given a bonus if he can conduct his work as to get the structure into service before the time set as the limit. This bonus arrangement is only occasionally provided, however.

In the construction field, the liquidated-damages clause is the primary means of avoiding litigation by settling in advance a figure to be used in computing damages for delay in performance beyond the scheduled completion date. In general, courts have accepted the true liquidated-damages clause so long as it meets the test of reasonableness. An unusually clear recital of what a court will look for in deciding upon the enforceability of a particular damages provision is this extract:[15]

> Where, as the parties here have agreed is the fact, proof of actual damage for delay in performance of a contract is impracticable or difficult, courts look with favor upon reasonable agreements for liquidated damages made by the parties with full understanding of the situation confronting them; and such contract provisions are uniformly enforced as the parties have written them . . . Where, however, the amount stipulated in the contract as liquidated damage for the failure of performance bears no relation to the actual damage which may reasonably be anticipated from such a failure, courts decline to enforce the terms of the stipulation . . . Contracts falling in this latter category are regarded by the courts as contracts for unenforceable penalties. Where the contract for liquidated damages is reasonable in character, it is valid and enforceable although the party complaining of a failure of performance neglects or is unable to prove actual damages by reason of a breach of contract . . . But it is also established that where one seeking to enforce a provision for liquidated damages is responsible for the failure of performance or has contributed in part to it, provision will not be enforced.

Misunderstandings may arise because of uncertainties respecting the date on which payments for liquidated damages are to begin. Assume that the owner of a store signs a contract with an electrical contractor to have the store rewired and to have new lighting fixtures installed. The work is to be done within three weeks after the signing of the contract (after which period liquidated damages of $100 per day are to be imposed) but with the proviso that the owner examine and approve a similar installation that the contractor has completed in a neighboring city. The contract is not intended to be effective until the owner has made this stipulated examination and until he has found the previous job satisfactory as a sample. Receipt by the contractor of the approval notice should signal the start of the three-week period, and it is advisable to make this point clear in the contract. The notice of the official "go-ahead" should be given in writing because oral notification may lead to a misunderstanding.

There may be a conflict over whether the liquidated damages are to be determined from the number of calendar days of delay in completion or from the number of working days in the period of overrun. If the contract states that a job is to be completed in a given number of working days after the signing of the contract or after the specified date for the commencement of work, this is usually interpreted to mean actual days that the contractor can carry on his work. It generally excludes Sundays, holidays, perhaps Saturdays if the job is to be run on a five-day-per-week schedule, days when bad weather prevents the conduct of work, periods of delay caused by the owner and his staff, and periods of delay caused by acts of God. The contract should state just what is intended in this regard.

| [15]*United States v. Kanter*, 137 F.2d 828, 830 (8th Cir. 1943).

When liquidated damages are mentioned in the contract, it is especially important for the contractor to notify the owner promptly and in writing when the former asserts that a delay is being caused by the owner. The contractor should give dates, reasons for the delay, and other pertinent data that will assist in establishing his claim for an extension.

What happens when the contractor quits the unfinished job after the time limit has expired? In one such case[16] the court held that liquidated damages applied from the time fixed for completion until the work was abandoned and for a further period of time reasonably necessary to complete the job. Of course, the owner will not be permitted to increase his recovery either by unreasonable delay in taking over the job or by failure to complete it diligently.

When all parties are at fault, apportionment of fault is appropriate to determine the amount of liquidated damages.[17]

12.18 DAMAGES FOR DEFECTIVE OR INCOMPLETE WORK

The contract should state that the contractor will be held responsible for the quality of the work performed. The owner should make it clear that he has the right to make claims against the contractor for defective work. Any such claims should first be approved by the engineer, but in any case caution should be exercised because the validity of the claims may eventually have to be substantiated before a board of arbitration or a court. The damages that an owner can collect for defective work by the contractor are not unlimited, and the claims should be reasonable and consistent with the circumstances.

Assume that Jones let a contract for a central heating system to be installed in her new house. She specified the type, capacity, and general character of the entire heating system, including the boiler. The contractor warranted the equipment and workmanship to be of top quality. During the first winter of operation the boiler proved to be defective, and it also became apparent that the capacity of the boiler was inadequate. Jones decided to have the old boiler replaced by a larger one that cost $200 more than the original. Although the contractor can be required to replace the defective boiler with a new one of first quality, Jones cannot expect him to furnish and install a larger and more costly article than that for which she initially contracted.[18] The extra cost of the larger unit is not an obligation of the contractor, and Jones should pay him for the excess value of the larger boiler. To reit-

---

[16]*Austin-Griffith Inc. v. Goldberg*, 224 S.C. 372, 79 S.E. 2d 447 (1953).

[17]See *Aetna Cas. & Surety Co. v. Butte Meade Sanitary Water Dist.*, 500 F. Supp. 193 (1980), where liquidated damages for a delay in the completion of a contract for the construction of a pipeline, pump house and water main were required to be apportioned among three parties, the difficulty of so doing not withstanding.

[18]*Temple Beth Shalom and Jewish Center, Inc. v. Thyne Const. Corp.*, 399 So. 2d 525 (Fla. App. 1981). For a variation on this well-established rule, see *North County School Dist. v. Fidelity & Deposit Co. of Md.*, 539 S.W.2d 469 (Mo. App. 1976), in which the court approved a jury instruction to the effect that the measure of damages should be the same whether the case involved a contract or a tort claim.

erate, the contractor should be held to the performance to which he has agreed under the contract, and there should be no attempt to hold him to anything further without proper compensation. Notice that, since Jones had specified in detail the type and capacity of the boiler and the character of the entire plant to be installed, its inadequacy for the intended use was her responsibility. The contractor's responsibility is limited to the execution of the plans unless the contract calls for him to design as well as to construct.

Uncertainty as to the amount of damage need not prevent the recovery of some amount. Section 352 of the *Restatement of Contracts,* 2nd, states that "damages are not recoverable for loss beyond an amount that the evidence permits to be established with reasonable certainty."[19]

Comment A to Section 352 adds "courts have traditionally required greater certainty in the proof of damages for breach of contract than in the proof of damages for tort. The requirement does not mean, however, that the injured party is barred from recovery unless he establishes the total amount of his loss. It merely excludes those elements of loss that cannot be proved with reasonable certainty."

It should not be forgotten, however, that a failure to introduce sufficient evidence to prove that damage has occurred will bar recovery. Failure of proof usually occurs in cases in which the certainty of damage is difficult to establish and where a plaintiff complained that a contractor built a home for him in a totally unworkmanlike manner, recovery was denied as purely speculative when the owner could not prove that the value of the house was diminished.[20]

Where the contractor is clearly to blame but the measure of damages is not controlled by an express provision of the building contract, the decided cases have not followed any single rule in compensating the owner. Many courts have embraced the so-called "cost" rule whereby the expense to the owner of completing or correcting the work upon partial breach or default by the contractor is regarded as the proper measure of damages to be applied,[21] and this expense item would normally be deducted from whatever might be due the contractor for such satisfactory work as has been accomplished. Other decisions have adopted what is often called the "reduction in value" theory, under which the damaged owner, by way of compensation, is credited with an amount that represents the supposed difference in value between the building contracted for and the lesser building that was actually presented,[22] at least where the breach was unintentional and the remediation would result in unreasonable economic waste.[23]

---

[19]See *Hall v. Lovell Regency Homes Limited Partnership,* 708 A.2d 344 (Md. App. 1998), in which purchasers of newly constructed homes were unable to prove a drop in market value of their homes despite evidence of substantial drainage problems after heavy rain or snow.

[20]*Hubbard Brothers Construction Company, Inc. v. Brackner,* 390 So.2d 648 (Ala. App. 1980). And see *Design and Corrosion Engineering Inc. v. Piggly Wiggly,* 408 So.2d 292 (La. App. 1981), where an owner could not prove with required exactness the cost of repairing a contractor's performance in the asphalt overlay of a parking lot.

[21]See *Arch of Illinois v. S.K. George Painting Contractors, Inc.,* 681 N.E.2d 1049 (Ill. App. 1997).

[22]See, for example, *McDonald v. Schwartz,* 706 S.2d 1230 (Ala. App. 1997).

[23]*Lyons v. Belosky Construction, Inc.,* 669 N.Y.S.2d 400 (App. Div. 1998). In this case, however, the proper measure of damages was held to be the cost of replacing a defective roof and overhead dormer that changed the appearance of a house, because of the utmost significance of the aesthetic appearance of the house to the homeowner.

12.19   SPECIAL CLAIMS FOR DAMAGES AGAINST THE CONTRACTOR

Since progress and completion of the work are the objectives of the owner, it may be necessary for him to take special steps to secure the desired results if he believes that they cannot (or will not) be attained satisfactorily by the contractor acting independently. To provide for such a situation, it may be advisable to write the contract in such a way that the owner will have the power to complete any unfinished work himself, but at the expense of the contractor, charging the latter for any losses or extra expenses (damages). Imagine that *A* has a contract to build a store for *B*, but *A* is so busy constructing a shopping center in a nearby town that he has seriously neglected the supervision of *B*'s project. Or, assume that *A* has contracted pneumonia and will be unable to take charge of the work under the contract. In such circumstances, it may be desirable for *B* to take over direct supervision of the work. If so, he should have the right to do so and to charge *A* for any loss entailed.

As another example, assume that the contractor has been paid what is due him but has failed to pay his employees their wages for the past week or two.[24] The engineer learns that the men have threatened to strike or to leave the job if they are not paid promptly. In such an event the owner should have the authority (notwithstanding the fact that the project is still supervised by the contractor) to make direct payment to the contractor's employees of all or part of what is due them and to deduct the amount of such payments from the money owed or to be owed to the contractor, thereby keeping the men at work and the job progressing.

One way for the engineer to deal with the questions of potential claims of laborers or suppliers is to place a clause in the contract stating that the contractor must prove that he has paid all bills for labor and materials in respect of work performed during a given month before any partial payments are made to the contractor for that month's work. This proof may take the form of affidavits, copies of receipts, or whatever method is mutually agreed upon. Thus, if these bills have not been paid by the contractor, the owner can refuse to make further payment to him until the difficulties are remedied, and he can use the withheld funds to pay the creditors himself in a proper case, provided the owner receives a waiver of lien from the person being paid.

12.20   RISK, LIABILITY, AND INDEMNITY

It is usually an advantage to the owner to have the work done by an independent contractor instead of by the owner's employees. This relieves the owner of the bur-

---

[24]Under laws which are very common, unpaid material suppliers and laborers are entitled to the protection of a *mechanic's lien,* which when perfected, is attached to the structure being built (and the land on which it stands) and secures for them a priority toward satisfaction of their particular claims. Such laws are grounded on the principle that the building becomes a part of the realty, enhancing the value thereof, and that persons who have contributed labor and material to the improvement of property should be entitled, if the need arises, to look to that property for their compensation.

den of devising ways and means of performing the desired work. The agreement should make clear that the contractor is to assume all risks directly connected with the work and is to carry adequate property and other insurances until such time as the owner accepts the structure or products and the contract is terminated. It may be advisable to have the types and amounts of the insurance coverages specified in the contract so as to avoid disagreements about what is "adequate." The contractor can include the cost of insurance in his bid.

Further, the contract should state that the builder is to protect not only the owner himself but also the holders of adjacent property from injury arising from the performance of the contract. Construction work is likely to be conducted in places where the general public will be affected. The responsibility for protection of the public should definitely be placed upon the contractor, who is the person in the best position to prevent accidents. Protective measures may involve fencing a site to keep out trespassers, roofing a sidewalk adjacent to a large building operation in a city so as to protect pedestrians, erecting fences or other guards around utilities, such as power ducts or cables, building temporary decking over excavations in streets, and even manually guarding busy construction passageways and areas where blasting or other dangerous operations are being carried on. The contract should require that adequate protective devices be maintained at all times of need. Signs and warning lights alone are generally considered to be insufficient.

As a broad generalization a builder is legally responsible where his negligence during the construction process is the proximate cause of injury to (1) persons rightfully on the scene, (2) persons in lawful use of an adjacent public thoroughfare, and (3) persons who are occupants of premises that abut the project site. If a contractor is known to be careless, incompetent, or inexperienced, he should not be awarded the contract in the first place; the owner could possibly be held liable for resulting injuries to outsiders if he fails to use reasonable care in the selection of a contractor. Similarly, the owner may charge the engineer with negligence if the latter had advised the owner to let the contract to a bidder known to the engineer to be irresponsible.

Frequently construction contracts contain a clause whereby the builder undertakes to indemnify or "hold harmless" the owner against claims for injury resulting from the builder's own negligence. Such clauses vary in scope. Here is a provision, taken from an actual contract, which would be characterized as comprehensive:

> The Contractor shall be the insurer of the Owner and shall render a Certificate of Insurance with the owner as an additionally insured party said insurance shall care for the latter's agents and employees against any and all of the following risks, whether they arise from acts of commission or omission of the Contractor or of third persons, excepting only those risks which result from affirmative, willful acts done by the Owner subsequent to the submission of the Contractor's Proposal:
>
> 1. The risk of loss or damage to the Work prior to the issuance of the Certificate of Final Completion. In the event of any such loss or damage, the Contractor shall promptly replace, repair, and make good the Work without cost to the Owner.

2. The risk of injuries (including wrongful death) and damages, directly or indirectly, to the Owner, his agents, and his employees, and to his or their property, arising out of or in connection with the performance of the Work. The Contractor shall indemnify the Owner and the latter's agents and employees against and from all such claims and demands, and for all loss and expense incurred by them in the defense, settlement, and satisfaction thereof.

Neither the Certificate of Final Completion nor any payment to the Contractor shall release the Contractor from his obligations. The enumeration elsewhere in this Contract or in the Specifications of specific risks assumed by the Contractor or of particular claims for which he is to be responsible shall not be deemed to limit the effect of the foregoing provisions of this numbered clause nor to imply that he assumes and is responsible for only risk or claims of the types enumerated.

Another clause of considerable breadth is the following, as quoted in a Pennsylvania case:[25]

It is understood and agreed that the party of the second part shall be deemed and considered an independent contractor in respect to the work covered by this agreement, and shall assume all risks and responsibility for casualties of every description in connection with the work, except that he shall not be held liable or responsible for delays or damage to work caused by acts of God, acts of public enemy, acts of government, quarantine restrictions, general strikes throughout the trade, or freight embargoes not caused or participated in by the Contractor. Party of the second part shall have charge and control of the entire work until completion and acceptance of the same by party of the first part. Party of the second part shall be alone liable and responsible for, and shall pay, any and all loss and damages sustained by any person or party either *during the performance or subsequent to the completion of the work* covered by this agreement, by reason of injuries to person and damage to property, buildings and adjacent work, that occur either *during the performance or subsequent to the completion of the work* covered by this agreement, or that may be sustained as a result or consequence thereof, *irrespective* of whether or not such injuries or damage be due to negligence or to the inherent nature of the work . . . Party of the second part agrees to fully indemnify, protect and save harmless the City, the Director and his subordinates, from any and all liability and from all suits and actions of every kind and description brought or which may be brought against them or any of them. [italics supplied]

12.21   POWER OF ENGINEER IN SETTLING DISPUTES

Many contracts contain a clause to the effect that the (engineer or the architect) has the power to make final and binding decisions in the settlement of various types of

---

[25]*Keefer v. Lombardi*, 376 Pa. 367, 102 A.2d 695, 696 (1954).

disputes that arise in the execution of the contract. This power should be defined carefully.

The engineer in charge of a construction contract has no *implied* power to bind the parties by his interpretations, but express provisions in the contract that any dispute about the construction of the language used shall be submitted to the engineer (whose decision shall bind the parties) have been upheld. Not infrequently, a contract will stipulate that, in the absence of fraud or other wrongdoing, the decision of the engineer or some other designated person shall be final on any question submitted. An example of such a question is what constitutes "satisfactory" performance.

Since the engineer is representing the owner in the implementation of the contract, it may seem that the engineer is not in a position to make unbiased decisions in disputes between the owner and the contractor. In practice, however, the engineer's reputation is likely to depend upon his fairness as well as upon his technical ability. Except in the case of the engineer's fraud, gross error of judgment, or actions that indicate bad faith, the engineer's decisions are binding provided that the signed contract contains a clause to that effect. It is advisable, however, to make provision for the disposition of certain types of disputes through resort to arbitration[26] or mediation.

QUESTIONS

1. Describe the function of the contract clauses relating to the performance of a construction contract.

2. Differentiate between "standard contracts" and "standard contract clauses." When and how may each be used to advantage?

3. Describe a situation which might justify *(a)* the suspension of a contract; *(b)* its cancellation.

4. Assume that Elkins contracted to build an addition to Cromwell's plant producing cruise missiles just prior to the gulf war. The war ended before Elkins started work, and Cromwell tried to cancel the contract. Can Elkins do anything about the loss of his anticipated profit *(a)* if the contract contained a proper cancellation clause? *(b)* If the contract contained no clause dealing with cancellation?

5. If work under a contract is revised, what procedure should be followed? Is the contractor obliged to follow the revisions?

6. When may claims by the contractor for extra payment be justified in a lump-sum contract? How may these payments be computed?

7. When may claims by the contractor for extra payment be justified in a unit-price contract? How may these payments be computed?

| [26]See Chapter 28.

8. The boring data shown on the drawings for two bridge piers indicated the presence of boulders at the site. The successful contractor included in his bid the cost of cofferdams to surround the piers and to permit removal of these boulders. When work started, the contractor decided to try to get along without the use of cofferdams, and he succeeded. Does the contractor have to make a refund to the owner because of the decrease in the actual cost of doing the work? Explain.

9. What would be the situation if the contractor bid on the previously mentioned piers and assumed that no cofferdams would be necessary but later found that they had to be used?

10. Black contracted with White to build a certain number of large transmission towers for a stated price per tower. White subsequently decided to use longer spans for the wires, thereby reducing the number of towers. Is Black entitled to an adjustment in the price per tower?

11. An engineer telephoned her resident engineer to stop work on some retaining walls that were to be revised. The latter was in a conference at the time. One hour later the resident engineer sent an assistant to notify the contractor. When the assistant arrived, 10 cubic yards of concrete had been poured in the forms and 10 cubic yards more were waiting in trucks at the site. What should be done? Who should pay the bill, if any?

12. What are the advantages from the contractor's standpoint of subcontracting portions of a construction contract? Illustrate a typical case.

13. Describe one way in which the evils of "bid shopping" may be remedied.

14. Cramer subcontracted to Williams the furnishing and installation of all equipment for a large pumping station. The operation of the pumps, said the original contract, was to be guaranteed for one year. When the plant started to operate, certain defects in the pumps were discovered. To whom will the owner look for remedy—the contractor or the subcontractor? Why?

15. What is the purpose in allowing the owner to withhold a portion of partial payments due the contractor? What happens to this money when the job is completed?

16. When and how are final payments computed and made to the contractor for a lump-sum contract? A unit-price contract?

17. Explain the purpose and operation of liquidated damages.

18. What is meant by "the contractor shall indemnify and save harmless the owner in case of any claims for damages"?

19. Brown orally told Black to build him a wooden garage 25 feet long and 15 feet wide, having a concrete floor, overhead doors, and a sloping roof covered with asphalt shingles. No other specifications were stated. The agreed-upon price was $1,600. The agreement and details were not recorded in writing. Black built the garage, but she included no windows and no electric lights. Brown claimed that these two items were included in the agreement by implication. Is Brown correct in this matter?

20. If the contract is suspended by the engineer for five days because of changes that the owner wants to make, may this affect the cost to the owner?

21. A contract required the job to be completed July 15. The engineer ordered the contractor to suspend operations from May 1 to May 15, then changed the completion date to July 31. Was the change in completion data appropriate?

22. Under what conditions might the conduct of the contractor be proper cause for owner to terminate the contract?

23. If no time for starting and completion are given in the contract, is the contractor free to construct his own schedule?

24. Why may revisions in a contract justify extra compensation for the contractor?

25. What compensation should a contractor receive because of delays due to actions of his own personnel?

26. In case of a unit-price contract, (a) when will the unit prices be applicable to extra work? (b) when inapplicable or insufficient?

27. Should the engineer get and issue data regarding soil conditions at a construction site? Should he interpret them?

28. Explain when and why the contractor may reasonably claim extra compensation when the quantity of work in a unit-price contract is decreased.

29. Who should be responsible for the protection of the public during construction operations? Why?

30. Illustrate a case in which the contractor is evidently entitled to extra compensation because of a change in the quality of the work required in a unit-price contract.

31. If the contractor has completed a unit-price contract, can the engineer compel him to build some added part at the same unit prices?

chapter

13

SPECIFICATIONS FOR WORKMANSHIP

13.1 SPECIFYING PROCEDURES

The purpose of this chapter is to discuss and illustrate some specifications relating to the *quality* of the workmanship that will be required of the contractor who is to build a construction project. *Workmanship* is intended to denote the contractor's *operations* in the shop or field rather than the materials used by him in the performance of the contract.

An *independent* contractor must be free to control how the work shall be performed. When the contractor signs the contract, it becomes his duty to perform in accordance therewith, to follow carefully the plans and specifications, and to furnish proper materials and workmanship as required by them. Broadly speaking, and absent negligence on his part, the builder who follows defective or inadequate plans and specifications furnished by the owner, engineer, or architect is not chargeable for any damage or loss that can be traced to the inherent defects of the design or the specifications. Should the contract documents specify exactly how the work is to be handled, then the engineer has largely assumed responsibility for securing the desired results. This is something about which the owner and his representatives must be extremely careful.

Assume the specifications state the concrete in a structure is to have an ultimate 28-day comprehensive strength of 4,000 pounds per square inch. They also specify the amount of cement, sand, gravel, and water to be used in the mix, together with the time for mixing and the allowable slump. If the contractor follows these last instructions, as he is obliged to do, it will not be his fault should the concrete in its furnished form fail to meet the designated strength requirement. The specifications should prescribe the quality of the ingredients and the desired final result—4,000 pounds per square inch—but they should not attempt to tell the contractor exactly how he should go about attaining that result. On the other hand, it is entirely proper and probably wise to have the specifications require a certain minimum slump for the concrete and state that the contractor is (1) to submit contractor's (or subcontractor's) data for test results of his design mix of materials being proposed for use on the job site to the engineer for the latter's examination, (2) to include sieve analyses of the aggregates, and (3) to provide a number certain of concrete test cylinders to guarantee performance by test results.

In a case some years ago, the owner had provided specifications that detailed exactly how the walls should be built and waterproofing accomplished. The contractor built the walls in the prescribed fashion, and they proved not to be watertight. The court held that this was the fault of the designer of the plans rather than any fault of the contractor—who had faithfully complied with the mandatory and very precise specifications and plans.[1] The court observed that "where a contractor agrees to produce a certain result, he is responsible if the result is not produced, but, where the owner assumes to specify the manner of construction to produce the result, the owner assumes the responsibility if the work does not turn out as expected." Thus, it would have been preferable merely to (1) specify the quality of materials, (2) show all dimensions on the plans, and (3) require that the structure be watertight. Then the contractor would be liable if the work failed to meet these standards.[2]

While the rules of law are perhaps not entirely clear in this area, generally a builder need only comply with detailed specifications; having done so, he is not answerable for an imperfect result that is not attributable to improper workmanship, negligence, or his use of defective materials. On the other hand, if plans and specifications are lacking in detail or were prepared so as to leave open the methods of construction to be employed or the kind or quality of materials to be used, then the contractor—because he has freedom of choice—must select his methods and materials and exercise his discretion to produce a result that is substantially satisfactory.

There may be circumstances that make it necessary to specify in detail just what is to be done and how it is to be accomplished, thereby deliberately assuming responsibility. This is generally done in instances where the contractor probably will not be able to determine the desired or proper course himself. Here is an illustration of such a situation. A contract for the construction of an industrial plant included drawings and specifications for a dust-collecting system. All motors, cyclones,[3] piping, and other details were shown on the drawings, and the materials and required workmanship were described fully in the specifications. This was necessary because the contractor could not tell otherwise what was desired. The contractor agreed to build the system according to the plans and specifications. Whether or not the finished product was adequate for its intended service was necessarily the responsibility of the designers. Of course, if the contractor failed to do the prescribed work correctly, he could have been compelled to make any changes

---

[1]*Kuhs v. Flower City Tissue Mills Co.*, 104 Misc. 243, 171 N.Y. Supp. 688, 690–91 (Sup. Ct. 1918). (Decision subsequently modified and amended on other grounds, and then affirmed at 231 N.Y. 637.) See also *Clark v. Whitener*, 296 So.2d 393 (La. App. 1974), where a contractor of a residence was found not liable for deficiencies in items supplied and installed in accordance with plans and specifications supplied by the owner's architect; and *Kelly v. Bank Bldg. & Equipment Corp.*, 453 F.2d 774 (10th Cir. 1972) in which a contractor was absolved from liability for defects in the design of a glass curtain wall in a 32-story building that was properly installed by the contractor.

[2]Great care must be taken not to agree, for example, to make a boiler room watertight by following the plans and specifications provided, if in fact it cannot be done that way. See *MacKnight Flintic Stone Co. v. Mayor, Etc., of New York*, 160 N.Y. 72 (Ct. of App. 1899). See also, *U.S. v. Spearin*, 248 U.S. 132 (1919).

[3]Equipment utilizing centrifugal force for collecting the dust.

necessary to conform to the requirements of the contract. But that would have been the limit of his responsibility.

The danger inherent in specifying how the contractor is to secure the desired results and to do the required work is illustrated further by an instance that was reported to one of the authors. In substance, the specifications for a large housing project stated that, to remove groundwater from the excavations for the foundations, "the Contractor shall use well points," whereas the intent of the engineer had been that "the Contractor may use well points." The specifications thus became an order instead of granting a permission. The contractor did use well points and, as a result of the transportation of very fine silty material with the pumped-out water, certain neighboring buildings settled harmfully when they were, in effect, undermined. Since the project owner specified the operation, he was subject to claims for damages amounting to nearly $500,000. He could not blame the contractor for doing what the specifications required. Therefore, the owner had to face the consequences.

13.2   SAMPLE PARAGRAPHS

The following contract paragraphs illustrate how the extent of the contractor's responsibility was specified in an actual case:

Temporary Structures

The contractor shall furnish and construct all guardrails, fences, trestles, staging, shaftways, falsework, and other temporary structures in the Work, whether or not of the type enumerated. All such structures shall have adequate strength for the purposes for which they are constructed, and the Contractor shall maintain them in a condition satisfactory to the Engineer.

The designs for such structures are to be prepared by the Contractor; nevertheless, drawings showing their design and details are to be submitted to the Engineer for his approval before being used. Examination by the Engineer, however, will be in a spirit of helpfulness but will not relieve the Contractor of his responsibility for their design, construction, and use, and the Contractor shall make good all injuries to persons or things arising on account of them.

Blasting

Whenever blasting is done, the Contractor shall comply with all federal and state laws and local regulations relating to such work. Explosives used shall be only of such character and strength as may be permitted by such laws and regulations. The Contractor shall provide, at his own expense, proper magazines and storage facilities for the storage of explosives, and these are to be in such locations as may be approved by the local authorities having jurisdiction over such work. The magazines and storage facilities shall be marked with large letters *"Explosives—Dangerous,"* and they shall be kept under lock, the key therefor being kept in the possession of the superintendent or other person designated by him.

Notice that the preceding specifications require certain things to be done by the contractor but do not explicitly state how they should be done.

13.3   SPECIFYING WORKMANSHIP

The statement that an independent contractor is not supposed to work under the specific dictation of the engineer means that the contractor is to use his men and equipment under his own direction to attain the successful completion of the job. On the other hand, this does not mean that the engineer should fail to include in the contract necessary requirements affecting the quality of workmanship demanded and a carefully prepared statement regarding certain features of the conduct of the contractor's operations. The nature and scope of such statements and requirements will vary with the character of the work. One who is preparing specifications for workmanship should be thoroughly familiar with the pertinent customs, practices, and possibilities in the particular construction field involved. If the engineer is not well versed in this line he is likely to require unwise or impracticable things of the contractor and to overlook important features for which provision should be made. The result may be undue difficulty and needless expense for the owner. At the very least, the inevitable complaints made by the contractor because of unwise specifications will make the owner lose confidence in the ability of the engineer.

Assume that the motor, gear reducer, and head pulley of a 60-inch belt conveyor are to be set and grouted on concrete foundations. The equipment is "direct-connected." This means that all parts must be aligned very carefully and accurately. What should be described in the specifications for this work? The following are some of the significant considerations:

1. Require that the equipment be erected so that the center of the pully is at the elevation and in the position called for on the drawings.

2. Specify that the drive and pulley be aligned accurately and set level.

3. Call for all bearings to be supported on steel wedges temporarily for adjustment (or call for double nuts on the anchor bolts to serve as jack screws for adjustment purposes).

4. Describe what grouting is to be done.

5. State the time that must elapse after grouting before the wedges are to be removed.

6. Require that the holes left by the wedges be pointed up.

7. State whether or not anchor bolts are to be leaded "high-strength grout" in the holes in the bases before the nuts are tightened.

8. State if and how nuts on anchor bolts are to be locked to prevent loosening.

As another illustration of composition, assume that you are to specify how a large elevated steel water tank is to be fabricated. You may state that it is to be riveted and that joints are to be caulked for watertightness. You may specify the size and spacing of rivets and you may show typical details on the drawings. On the other hand, you may specify that the tank is to be welded, show the size and type of weld, and give typical details. Your drawings and specifications must be sufficiently complete and detailed to enable the fabricator to proceed satisfactorily with his shop drawing and other work. If the tank leaks and you have designated the type of construction riveted and caulked or welded—and state that the tank is to be watertight, then the contractor must make it so.

Or, assume that you, as the engineer, are to specify the finish for the concrete of the second floor of a warehouse. Here are some of the things that you would have to determine and to specify:

1. Is the floor to be poured monolithically, or is it to have a topping applied later?

2. If a topping is to be used, what is the desired material, how thick is it to be, and how soon is it to be laid after the structural floor is poured?

3. What kind of surface finish is to be required—wood float or trowel?

4. Is a surface hardener or an integral hardener to be used? If so, exactly what is it to be and how is it to be applied?

5. Is the floor to be scored?

6. Is any particular color desired?

The difficulty of thinking out and specifying all these details is obvious, but so is their importance. Here the engineer is obliged to make many decisions in composing the specifications, and he has to assume considerable responsibility for the result.

Notice that, while the items shown in the three illustrations call for specific things that the contractor must accomplish, they do not tell him in detail how he is to do them.

The following are portions of what appear to be well-written specifications for a large warehouse:

Depositing Concrete

Concrete shall be deposited only during the presence of the Inspector and by methods approved by the Owner's Engineer. All concrete shall be placed "in the dry." Should water accumulate in any place where concrete is to be poured, the Contractor shall provide and operate sufficient pumps and do whatever else is necessary to remove the water in an approved manner. Water (other than that used for curing) shall be prevented from coming into contact with concrete while it is setting.

Installation

All metal sash and doors shall be erected plumb, level, square, and at the proper elevation and location. All joints shall be tight, and members shall be securely anchored in place. Work shall be adequately braced, and the bracing shall be maintained until its removal is approved by the Owner's Engineer. Moving parts such as sash, operating mechanisms, and doors shall be installed complete with hardware fittings and accessories. Parts shall be made to operate uniformly and smoothly.

13.4   SPECIFYING THE QUALITY OF RESULTS

Consider again the conveyor drive that is discussed early in Section 13.3. Could this work be described in some other way? For example, the specifications might read as follows: "The Contractor shall erect the head pulley and its drive at the elevation and position shown on the drawings. He shall align and level them accurately, grout the base plates fully, 'high-strength grout' the anchor bolts in the bases, and adequately tighten and lock the nuts on the anchor bolts, using double nuts." In a way this requires certain actions, but it allows the contractor to perform the work as he may wish as long as he accomplishes the specified results. This is usually a better way to handle the work than by itemizing and describing every detail of procedure. Of course, the engineer's approval of all completed work is to be required in any case.

Now assume that you are to prepare the specifications for a 500,000-gallon tank for fuel oil to be supported upon firm, level ground. One good procedure is to specify as follows: "The capacity of the tank shall be 500,000 gallons; the material, welded steel; the diameter, 60 feet; the contents, fuel oil; the roof, an approved 'floating' type. All details including environmental safeguards are to be as approved by the Engineer, and the bid price is to include delivery, erection, all piping connections, and painting." Furthermore, the specifications should indicate that the tank is to be oiltight; that the tank is to be tested by being filled with water; that the foundation material is to be firm sand; that all necessary piping and connections are to be provided and erected; and that all material and workmanship are to be guaranteed to be satisfactory for one year after acceptance of the finished structure by the engineer. In addition, sizes of piping, the positions of connections, the type and material of piping, and the lengths of piping to be furnished and installed by the contractor are all items to be definitely prescribed.

A complete set of specifications for workmanship would allow the contractor to intelligently prepare and submit for approval his own design and the proposed details. He can propose whatever type of construction procedure he thinks is best and the results of which he is willing to guarantee. In many cases the engineer can use to good advantage the foregoing method of specifying work more or less in outline form. However, the usefulness of such a method is limited to items or work that the contractor is in a position to detail for himself. More complicated construction makes it necessary for the engineer to tell the contractor in considerable detail just what is required.

The following illustrates the occasional disparity between what is intended by a specification writer and what is actually said in the specifications. The clause on finishing of concrete stated, "The exposed surface of all concrete walls are to be rubbed." To the specification writer this meant the removal of all projecting fins, the filling of any holes, and the rubbing of the concrete surface with carborundum stones and water until the surface was smooth. However, according to a strict interpretation of the inadequate wording, the contractor could rub the surface a few times with a soft cloth and still fulfill the literal requirement of the specification.

The way to avoid such a situation is to define "rubbed finish" early in the specifi-cations. Then the term can be used freely thereafter.

The following acceptable paragraphs specify desired results, but they also state certain procedures that are to be used:

Concrete

Every effort shall be made to secure a concrete of maximum density and imper-meability and minimum shrinkage during setting and at the same time a concrete which can be vibrated sufficiently to be in close contact with reinforcement and embedded steelwork.

Erection of Steelwork

The steelwork shall be set in place accurately and the bolting and field welding done as the Work progresses. Each tier of columns shall be plumbed, braced if necessary, and maintained in a vertical position. Temporary bracing shall be capa-ble of taking care of all loads to which the structure may be subjected, including wind loads and loads caused by erection equipment and its operation; such brac-ing shall be left in place as long as it may be required. As erection progresses, all members shall be securely bolted with sufficient high-strength bolts to resist all dead, wind, and erection loads.

Installation of Fixtures and Wiring

The Contractor shall properly clean all conduits and remove all burrs and obstruc-tions before snaking in or pulling the wires or cables. Wherever the use of lubri-cant for pulling wires or cables is permitted by the Engineer, the lubricant shall be an environmentally approved type. All the wires to be installed in one conduit shall be pulled at the same time, and they shall have no splices between junction boxes. Sufficient slack shall be left at junction boxes and at terminals for splicing the wires and for making connections properly. Joints shall be of approved type, carefully spliced, no-lead soldered with noncorrosive flux, and properly insulated.

13.5 ITEMIZING

There is a maxim of law that reads, "*Expression unius est exclusio alterius.*" This means that the express mention of one thing implies the exclusion of another. The importance of this principle as applied to contracts is that if there is an itemized list of things or acts that are required, other things or acts not mentioned in the list are, by implication, not required. On the other hand, a very general statement that is supposed to include everything that is necessary may be too broad and cumber-some, and it may be subject to varying interpretations. Sometimes the author of a contract clause tries to cover this difficulty by stating that the contractor is to pro-vide certain things, "such as . . . "

The contract for the structural steelwork of a large industrial plant called for "fabrication and erection," and the unit-price bid was asked for on the basis of "fob the plant site." The railroad siding entered the plant's property but it was about ½ mile from the site of some of the large buildings. The contractor claimed (and received) extra for hauling the steel from the siding to the points of erection, asserting that the contract should have read "fabrication, hauling, and erection" of the steelwork.

The virtual impossibility inherent in attempting to itemize all the required incidental operations is obvious. In the foregoing case a complete list would have to include unloading the steel from the cars, sorting it, loading it on trucks, unloading it at the various positions, and arranging it for convenience in erection. If one operation is overlooked in such a listing, the omission may open up the possibility of a claim for extras. The words "fabrication, delivery, and erection" might have been a better statement than the one actually used. It can be assumed that all operations incident to the fabrication, delivery, and erection must necessarily be performed by the contractor—and for the bid price.

In another case in which faulty itemization caused difficulties, the plaintiff had taken a contract for "furnishing and delivery only" of certain machinery, and the list of equipment was itemized in his proposal. Later, the defendant telegraphed the plaintiff that other articles, such as cables, switches, and fuses, needed for *the electrical connection and installation of the apparatus furnished* had not been received. Plaintiff protested that these articles were not in his proposal and therefore not included in the contract. Upon the defendant's insistence plaintiff furnished and delivered the materials asked for, but he stated that he was doing so under protest and that he would ask reimbursement for the cost of $2,062. The materials were accepted by the defendant, but he later refused to pay for them. In ensuing litigation the court ruled in favor of plaintiff in regard to this point. The decision involved the following reasoning.

1. Where a contract is for furnishing certain machinery, the contractor is not obligated to furnish cables, wiring, switches, and other materials needed in the installation of the machinery supplied under the contract.

2. Within ten days after demand was made upon it to furnish the materials involved, the plaintiff filed a written protest against the demand, persisted in such protest at every stage of the proceedings thereafter, and, immediately upon delivery, filed claim for reimbursement. This made it clear that *the plaintiff at no time waived his right to claim compensation.*

3. The defendant accepted the materials it had ordered and received the benefit of them. In these circumstances there was an *implied promise* on the part of the defendant to pay the plaintiff the cost of extra materials, since delivery was made on that condition. The implied promise to pay, however, is limited to the actual cost of the materials and cannot be construed to include anything beyond that.

Notice that the defendant's acceptance of the proposal signified its concurrence with the list of items therein.

13.6 STANDARD SPECIFICATIONS FOR WORKMANSHIP

Construction contracts vary so much in the character of workmanship required that it is not practicable to prepare truly comprehensive workmanship specifications, such as the ASTM has done in the case of construction materials. There are, however, some workmanship specifications prepared by persons interested in a particular field of activity or in the use of a given product. Where these are applicable, reference to them at the appropriate point in the contract documents may be very desirable.

For example, assume that you are to prepare specifications for the construction of a large store that is to have framing of structural steel. It probably will be advantageous for you to state that the fabrication and erection of the steelwork are to be in accordance with the American Institute of Steel Construction's *Specifications for the Design, Fabrication and Erection of Structural Steel for Buildings.* These specifications are well known, and they are generally accepted as requiring good practice for such work. Naturally, you must provide any special instructions necessary for your job but not included in the set of standard specifications to which reference is made.

In the matter of welding, you may refer to the *Standard Specifications for Welded Highway and Railway Bridges.* These are generally recognized as authoritative and represent some of the best thinking about the requirements for good welded construction. The general engineer might do better to trust them than to attempt to compose an adequate description of such highly specialized work.

These standard specifications as well as the contract drawings, "outside" drawings, building codes, and whatever the engineer may deem advisable for a particular contract should be *incorporated by reference* in the specifications. Thus they can control in various applicable phases of the work. For example, assume that the state highway department has published a very detailed manual containing data and requirements for the construction of highways in the state. A contract for a particular piece of highway construction can refer to this publication and incorporate the same as an official part of the contract. This practice ensures uniformity in various highway projects and saves time and effort in the preparation of the contract papers. Contractors throughout the state soon become thoroughly familiar with the contract requirements of the highway department.

Standard specifications will not contain the answers for everything that is necessary. The engineer must make certain decisions on a particular basis, as illustrated by the following case. In specifying the shopwork for structural-steel fabrication, mere reference to the specifications prepared by such organizations as the American Institute of Steel Construction may not be enough. The engineer should state in the specifications whether the shopwork is to be bolted or welded, whether or not the holes are to be subpunched (or subdrilled) and reamed to metal templates, or whether the parts are to be reamed while assembled. He should also specify whether the field connections are to be bolted or welded. The standard specifications may tell how various procedures should be done, but the choice of the type of work is a duty of the engineer.

On the whole, because much of the workmanship required in construction contracts cannot be handled through so-called "standard specifications" but has to be specified or supplemented by instructions prepared for a particular job, the engineer should give this latter task careful attention. It is one of his most important duties; many dollars may be involved in work that is described in a few paragraphs of his specifications. By ensuring excellent preparation of the contract documents the engineer can do much (1) to prevent uncertainties that often lead to difficulties in dealings with the contractor, (2) to avoid mistakes or omissions that may cause the owner unexpected expenditures for the settlement of the contractor's claims, and (3) to ensure avoidance of litigation. Excellent specifications reduce the guesswork for contractors, and thus they may result in lower bids because the figure to be included for contingencies could therefore be relatively small.

Any special features that differ from the so-called "standard specifications" being employed should be described in the specifications for the job or on the drawings. If there are such features, special clauses in the specifications describing them should take precedence over the standard specifications whenever the two conflict. As an example, assume that the engineer wishes to have certain members for a complicated portion of a steel structure subpunched, then assembled, and finally reamed in the shop while thus assembled. If his instructions call for this procedure but AISC specifications do not, then the engineer's written statement governs.

The following paragraphs are illustrations of how portions of some successful specifications were worded:

Structural Steelwork

Workmanship for all structural steelwork shall conform to the AISC Specifications for the Design, Fabrication and Erection of Structural Steel for Buildings, latest edition.

Steel Roof Deck

Each piece of the steel roof deck shall be securely fastened, in accordance with the manufacturer's standard specifications, directly to all the roof purlins under it, as well as to each adjoining piece at the end and side laps.

Built-up Roofing

Roofing shall be a twenty-year bonded Barrett "Specification" roof Type "AA," 4-ply. It shall be laid in accordance with the Barrett specification for use over insulated steel-roof decks, and the work shall be performed by a contractor approved by Barrett. The roofing contractor shall furnish Barrett's Surety Bond guaranty for twenty (20) years from date of completion in accordance with Note No. 1 of said specifications.

13.7   USE OF PREVIOUS SPECIFICATIONS

Contracts prepared for comparable former projects as well as contracts written by others may readily be used as source material for the workmanship requirements of a current job, just as for the specification of materials described in the preceding chapter. Although potentially helpful, they should be used with discretion.

Nothing can replace careful thought and careful composition when one is specifying what is to be done and how it is to be done. Think of all the steps that are involved in securing a result; then be sure that what you copy out of a previous specification covers a step or steps in your particular problem clearly and adequately, add whatever is needed, and eliminate inapplicable and erroneous material.

13.8   "AS DIRECTED BY THE ENGINEER"

There are all-inclusive statements that are sometimes used in the specifications; for example, "as directed by the Engineer," "to the satisfaction of the Engineer," or "as approved by the Engineer." Such language, if interpreted and carried out properly and fairly, can be useful.

The intent of such statements is to leave many details about the conduct of the work and the quality of the results to be settled between the engineer and the contractor as the job progresses. Their utilization saves time and effort on the part of the specification writer. If the contractor knows that the engineer with whom he is to deal is an experienced and just man, he will anticipate real cooperation and understanding in their relationships. If he expects otherwise or is uncertain about it, he is likely to increase his bid to cover in his estimate the cost of any trouble that may arise during the job because of the engineer's opinions and unilateral decisions.

In many situations when the exact conditions are unknown in advance, there may be wisdom in not trying to describe with preciseness what is to be done. For example, assume that a considerable quantity of concrete is to be poured in freezing weather. The character of the structure, the severity of the weather, and the difficulty of carrying on the work greatly influence the details of proper protective measures that should be employed. It may therefore be advisable to say that concrete poured in freezing weather "is to be protected in a manner satisfactory to the engineer." The contractor then proposes a method that the engineer accepts or rejects, or with respect to which he suggests modifications.

The rejection of work by the owner or the engineer as "unsatisfactory," when it is supposed to be done to his satisfaction, should not be based upon whim or bad faith but rather upon genuine dissatisfaction. Furthermore, such action should not be taken before it can reasonably be determined that the work will not or cannot be made satisfactory.

In any construction contract it is generally advisable to have such a clause as the following, stating specifically the authority of the engineer in the conduct of the work:

The enumeration herein of particular instances in which decision of the Engineer shall control or in which work shall be performed to his satisfaction and subject to his inspection and approval shall not imply that only such matters and those of similar kind shall be so governed and performed.

13.9   FIRST-QUALITY WORKMANSHIP

It is advisable to include in the specification a statement to the effect that all workmanship is to be first class, or "of the best quality."[4] This is not very specific, but the intention is clear. Persons engaged in any particular activity, whether in the shop or in the field, will generally know what is meant. Third parties, too, can judge fairly well whether or not a given performance meets this standard.[5]

It is practically impossible to include in the contract documents a description of, or specification for, all the procedures and work that will have to be done in the providing of materials and in the performance of a large construction contract. On the other hand, a general statement requiring first-class workmanship should not be used as a catchall or as an excuse for inadequate preparation of the drawings and the specifications. The usefulness of a general clause requiring "first-quality workmanship" is shown in the case of a contract for the steelwork of a large suspended bin. The general shape is pictured in Figure 13.1*(a)*. The curved plates were to be spliced as shown in *(a)* and *(b)*. One contractor was to fabricate the steelwork; another was to erect it. The fabricator detailed the main plates with open holes, as pictured in *(c)*. The engineer who approved the shop details did not notice this deviation from normal practice. All the plates were therefore shipped "loose." The erector had assumed, when bidding on the job, that the splice plates would be riveted along one side in the shop, as shown in *(d)*, which is the customary and more economical practice. The erector sent the owner a bill for $6,000 to cover the extra riveting that he had not included in his proposal. Because of the general-workmanship clause, and because the fabricator had to admit that the omission of the shop rivets was not customary and was not first-quality workmanship, the fabricator paid the owner $6,000 to meet the extra cost of erection.

Even though every detail that will be required is not spelled out, a contract for a structure to serve a specified purpose carries the implication that the finished structure shall be reasonably suitable for the intended purpose. The more fully the

---

[4]Whatever the precise words used are, when a home builder, for example, guarantees the quality of workmanship or materials, the home owner need not prove why a failure occurred, only that it did. *Nelson v. Marchand*, 691 N.E.2d 1264 (Ind. App. 1998).

[5]"It is the duty of every contractor or builder to perform his work in a proper and workmanlike manner, and he impliedly represents that he possesses the skill necessary to do the job he has undertaken. In order to meet this requirement, the law exacts ordinary care and skill only." *Cantrell v. Woodhill Enterprises, Inc.*, 273 N.C. 490, 160 S.E.2d 476, 481 (1968). On the question of implied warranty of skill and workmanship, see *Pollard v. Saxe & Yolles Dev. Co.*, 115 Cal. Rptr. 648, 525 P.2d 88 (1974), in which the builder of an apartment house was said to have warranted that the structure was designed and constructed in a reasonably workmanlike manner. Thus the contractor was held liable when a ceiling buckled because the contractor removed center posts and installed beams inadequate to support the patio decks of the floor above. To the same effect see *Wiggins v. Overstreet*, 962 S.W.2d 198 (Tex. App. 1998).

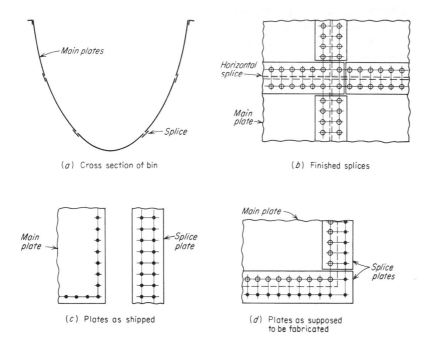

(*a*) Cross section of bin

(*b*) Finished splices

(*c*) Plates as shipped

(*d*) Plates as supposed to be fabricated

Figure 13.1   Steelwork for suspended bin.

requirements are clarified in advance, the less likely are subsequent difficulties between the engineer and the contractor.

A clause typically used in contracts is somewhat as follows:

All materials and workmanship shall be in every respect in accordance with the best modern practice. Whenever the Contract Drawings, Specifications, or directions of the Engineer admit of a reasonable doubt about what is permissible, and when they fail to state the quality of any work, the interpretation which requires the best quality of work is to be followed.

13.10   INTENT OF PLANS AND SPECIFICATIONS

It is often stated in a contract that the contractor is to carry out the "intent" of the plans and specifications. Some say that he is to perform whatever is necessary to carry out this intent, even when the particular item or procedure, though apparently intended, is not shown on the drawings or actually called for in the contract clauses or in the specifications. In some ways this is like asking the contractor to buy something sight unseen. If applied literally it would be unfair to the contractor in many cases. Such all-inclusive clauses generally have only slight value in practice and offer little protection against carelessness and ensuing mistakes on the engineer's part.

A lump-sum contract is generally quite strictly limited to what is clearly and specifically called for in the contract. Minor items that are not shown will usually be taken care of by the contractor without conflict. However, when such things cost an appreciable sum beyond what could reasonably be expected to be covered in his bid, he may properly be entitled to extra compensation.

On the other hand, omissions from the plans and contract documents seldom cause serious argument in unit-price contracts unless the extra materials and workmanship required clearly do not come under any payment item or when the underestimation of a payment item is sizable. A capable contractor is likely to have included in his estimate a margin for contingencies to cover just such omissions. As before, adequate plans and specifications should reduce the size of such cushions.

One contract referred to a certain standard specification for portland cement. The work was to be done in South America. It was the specification author's intention to limit the content of free lime in the cement to 1 1/2 percent, which is accepted as a maximum by many engineers. As it happened, a cement manufacturer in South America received the contract for furnishing all the cement. Tests of the material manufactured by him showed that the free-lime content normally exceeded the desired limit by a considerable amount. When the author tried to hold the contractor to the desired limit, he discovered to his chagrin that the standard specification did not state a limit for the free lime. What the author intended but failed to state in the specifications was not given effect. An agreement was finally made to pay the contractor an extra unit price for making the cement meet this requirement.

On the other hand, the matter of intent is considered very strongly when it can be determined with reasonable certainty by a court. Generally a decision that is based upon interpretation of intent will consider the contract as a whole, not just one part of it. Differences between the data shown on the drawings and in the contract clauses or in the specifications may make it unclear what the intent really was. Ambiguity in a language will be construed against its drafter. Even unintentional wording in the contract may cause interpretation difficulties.

13.11   PLANNING SPECIFICATIONS FOR WORKMANSHIP

This article has been prepared to illustrate how to outline and plan the specifications for the workmanship in two types of construction work. Its purpose is to outline the kind of thinking to be done, and it applies to two construction project phases that can be easily visualized: (1) clearing the site, and (2) cleaning up after construction has been completed.

A construction contract is likely to require the clearing of the site, the demolition of existing structures, and rough grading as a part of the work to be done. If so, general instructions should be given regarding such items as the following:

1. Removal and disposition of trees, stumps, shrubs, bushes, and boulders.

2. Removal and disposition of existing materials that are to be discarded or salvaged.

3. Demolition of existing structures and their foundations.

4. Removal and storage of topsoil when necessary. This may include the storage of turf for reuse.

5. Accomplishment of the rough grading—both excavation and fill.

6. Disposal of excess excavated material.

7. Designation of sources of fill to be brought in.

8. Installation of surface and subsurface drainage systems.

9. Designation and preparation of storage areas for the contractor's use.

Much of this preliminary work may have to be done by the contractor in such fashion as to meet the owner's requirements. Unless the contractor is told what these are, he cannot be expected to fulfill them and, obviously, he cannot properly evaluate them when preparing his bid. For example, consider the item of earth fill. It is not sufficient to say, "The site is to be filled in to the level shown on the contract drawings." Neither is it sufficient to state vaguely that the filling is to be done "in a satisfactory manner." In this particular problem, at least to a certain extent, the engineer should rightfully step in and describe in considerable detail such considerations as the following:

1. Removal and disposal of muck, if necessary.

2. Description of the quality and the kinds of materials that will be accepted as fill.

3. Deposition of fill in horizontal layers of some stated approximate thickness.

4. Compaction of layers of fill by means of sheep's foot rollers, rubber-tired rollers, or whatever is suitable for the job—or hand tamping if necessary.

5. Limitations in the moisture content of the soil—which limitations are to be adhered to during rolling.

6. Specification of the density of fill required after compaction.

The bid price for clearing the site and for any required demolition and rough grading is often listed as a lump-sum item in a unit-price contract. This is because such work is difficult to measure in detail. Fairness to the contractor necessitates that the engineer be careful to supply the contractor with all essential data regarding both the results to be obtained and any special means to be used in achieving such results.

Now consider cleaning up the site. Assume that you are to prepare specifications to prescribe the work to be done after the rest of a construction contract is finished. What items should be covered by your specifications? You should prepare instructions regarding such matters as the following:

1. Final grading.

2. Removal of equipment.

3. Removal and disposal of debris and excess materials.

4. Demolition and removal of temporary structures.

5. Removal of temporary facilities used for access to the site.

6. Removal of temporary power lines and other utilities that are for construction purposes only.

7. Provisions for surface drainage.

8. Completion of landscaping.

These matters, if not clarified, may cause disagreements when two or more contractors or the contractor's and the owner's forces are involved in the work. Disagreement may arise even in the case of subcontracting of portions of the job. This "cleanup" is the responsibility of the general contractor, but the requirements should be made clear in the contract wording.

13.12 SAMPLE PARAGRAPHS

The following additional paragraphs from specifications are provided to show how various pieces of information may be presented. A number of comments are included to call attention to special features. The examples are purposely taken from a variety of work.

Sequence of Work; Increase of Forces

The sequence of work done under this Contract will be left to the Contractor. Should the Engineer order the Contractor to increase his forces in order to ensure completion of the Contract within the time specified herein, the Contractor shall promptly comply with such order without additional cost to the Owner.

Notice that names are repeated in the preceding specification, the personal pronoun being used only once. This repetition of names (that is, the designations "Contractor," Engineer," and "Owner") is for the purpose of avoiding ambiguity.

The last portion of the foregoing paragraph indicates to the contractor that, if he believes overtime work may materialize, he should make allowance in his bid for such contingencies. It would seem more desirable, for all concerned, to specify that the owner compensate the contractor for the extra cost involved in such ordered overtime work unless the contractor is at fault, that is, unless the situation is the result of his negligence or delay. In any event, the engineer should have the right to order overtime work if he believes that an emergency exists or is pending, as shown in the following example.

A contractor was building a bridge pier in a shallow stream which was subject to flash floods. The forms for the pier were completed but the concrete had not been poured when a weather report came over the radio to the effect that a hurricane was likely to strike that area within two days. The engineer ordered the contractor to work overtime until the concrete was poured and danger to the structure was thus minimized.

Sanitary Regulations

The Contractor shall provide and properly maintain, for the use of all employees on the work, adequate sanitary conveniences, properly secluded from public observation. Such conveniences shall be provided at such points and in such manner as the Engineer shall approve, and their use shall be rigidly enforced.

The Contractor shall effectively prevent the committing of nuisances upon the site and upon adjacent property.

Notice that this is a performance type of specification (specifying results rather than means).

Cofferdams

The Contractor shall construct, maintain, and subsequently entirely remove suitable and efficient cofferdams in order that all work, except when expressly permitted to be done in water, may be performed by the Contractor and inspected by the Engineer in the dry.

The Contractor shall design all cofferdams, and he shall submit drawings of them for the approval of the Engineer when approval is necessary before the Contractor proceeds with the construction of the cofferdams. The Contractor shall be completely responsible for the designs and installations for strength, safety, watertightness, and sufficiency of all cofferdams, and he shall defend and hold harmless the Owner from any and all damage suits due to the construction or failure of any part or parts of the cofferdams or sheeted work. The owner's engineer will be concerned primarily with the excellence of the workmanship and materials only for the substructure of the bridge.

Field Connections

The movable span trusses, the tower trusses, the lifting frames, and the bridge portals shall be assembled in the shop, the parts adjusted to line and fit, and the holes for field connections drilled or reamed while so assembled. Holes for other field connections, except those in lateral, longitudinal and sway bracing, shall be drilled or reamed in the shop with the connecting parts assembled, or else drilled or reamed to a metal template.

An expense allowance for this connection work will be charged to the owner through the contractor's bid. The engineer endeavors to ensure, through the specifications, that the structure will fit together properly when erected in the field; otherwise the owner may have to accept delay and an unsatisfactory structure if it is necessary to apply makeshift remedies at the site.

Machinery Workmanship

All workmanship shall equal the best practice of modern machine shops. The finish shall be confined to rotating, bearing, and sliding surfaces and to wherever required to produce adequate clearance, accurate fit, and precise dimensions.

Again the contractor is made responsible for the results; the details of workmanship are to be determined by him.

Operation Tests

The complete electrical installation shall be approved carefully and signed off by the Electrical Inspector and then tested by the Contractor in the presence of the Engineer and as directed by the Engineer. All necessary corrections and adjustments shall be made promptly by the Contractor. The Contractor shall furnish an adequate supply of current at the proper voltages for making such tests, and he shall furnish the necessary instruments and appliances therefor.

Notice that such a test is one of performance, not one of materials. In the usual situation, even though the engineer may have tests of the materials used or may have had such tests made by others for him, the contractor still has to prove that the installation functions properly.

Erection

Before starting erection, the Contractor shall submit complete and detailed erection drawings and his program for erection of the steelwork, all of these being subject to the approval of the Bridge Engineer. Whenever, in the opinion of the Bridge Engineer, the proposed plans interfere with, or involve avoidable difficulties or delays in the subsequent erection of other parts of the structure by other contractors, the Bridge Engineer may order such modification either in the drawings or the program as, in his opinion, will best expedite the construction of the bridge as a whole.

The engineer thus retains the authority to see that the contractor coordinates his work with that of other contractors on the same master project.

Field Test of Mains

The work of laying the pipes and special castings, and the work of setting valves and hydrants, shall be of such character as to leave all the pipes and connections watertight.

To ensure these conditions, the Contractor shall subject all mains twenty (20) inches or more in diameter, and their appurtenances, to a proof by water pressure of not less than one hundred and twenty-five (125) pounds per square inch,[6] unless the conditions under which the main is installed make this pressure test impracticable.

Such proof of the adequacy of an installation is generally necessary before the construction is approved and accepted.

Sewers, Drains, and Their Appurtenances

The Contractor shall provide for the flow of (1) any water courses, (2) closed flumes, (3) open-joint or blind drains, and the like, which flow is interfered with during the performance of the work. He shall immediately remove and dispose of all offensive matter. A flow throughout the entire length of such sewers and appurtenances as are

---

| [6]Notice that these dimensions and figures are carefully spelled out, not given simply as "20" or "125 psi."

to be relocated or reconstructed shall be maintained until it can be transferred to the new facilities. Flows in house connections shall be maintained, properly restored, and reconnected to the old or connected to the new sewers, as required.

The phrase "as required" in the preceding paragraph is supposed to mean "as necessary to keep the facilities in service"; in fact, it would be wiser to say so. If the clause stated "as required by the Engineer," this would shift the task of determining precisely what was needed from the contractor to the engineer.

Setting Brick

Face brick shall be laid in courses of headers and stretchers, every third course being a header course with every sixth course bonded through. Face bricks shall be laid true to line with end joints not exceeding one-quarter (1/4) inch in width. Horizontal joints shall be two and five-eights (2 5/8) inches center to center. Each brick shall be well parged on the back with mortar and shall be completely embedded in mortar under the bottom and on the sides in one operation. Bed mortar shall not be furrowed. All mortar joints of the face bricks shall be tooled slightly concave.

Here the engineer specifies the results in considerable detail, but he does not specify *how* the contractor is to secure them. However, it is recognized that these matters sometimes involve a fine line of distinction.

Marking Floors

At the time the finish on the concrete floors is being floated to proper slopes, the surfaces, except in those places where the Contract Drawings show the floors to be covered with terrazzo or tiles, shall be marked off in squares of approximately four (4) feet in a pattern to be determined by the Engineer. The markings shall be cuts one-half (1/2) inch in depth, and they shall be properly rounded or chamfered with an approved edging tool.

The engineer has to determine only where the markings shall be. The contractor is to obtain this information before he can proceed with his work.

Location of Machinery

The Contractor shall erect each machine in the location indicated on the Contract Drawings.

A statement such as this is superfluous because the drawings show where each machine is to be erected, and the drawings are in themselves instructions to that effect.

Erection of Anchor Bolts

All anchor bolts for machines are to be located accurately. The bolts are to be held in place by means of wooden templates to prevent displacement during the pouring of the concrete of the machinery foundations. The location of each bolt is to be approved by the Inspector before any concrete is poured around it.

This clause is necessary because only the locations and elevations of the bolts are usually shown on the drawings. The engineer requires the use of templates in order to make certain that the bolts are held in place properly during the pouring of the concrete. The engineer insists upon inspecting for approval the locations of the bolts as a check on the contractor's work.

13.13 TYPICAL LIST OF ITEMS

Before attempting to prepare the specifications for workmanship for a project, one should compile a list of items to be covered and the types of work to be done. This will help in assuring that all necessary features and workmanship requirements are included. The following is a checklist of work and workmanship items that might have to be described in the specifications for the construction of a building. Each item may, of course, involve a number of features.

1. Demolition and clearing of site.
2. Protection of site—fences, lights, and so on.
3. Subsoil explorations, if not made in sufficient detail in advance.
4. Drainage of the site.
5. Rock excavation.
6. Earth excavation.
7. Filling, backfilling, rough grading.
8. Cofferdams.
9. Piling or caissons.
10. Concrete and reinforcement.
11. Masonry.
12. Waterproofing and dampproofing.
13. Structural steel.
14. Fireproofing.
15. Walls, siding, and partitions.
16. Flooring.
17. Roofing.
18. Insulation.
19. Stairs and railings.
20. Elevators, dumbwaiters, escalators.
21. Windows, trim and glaring.
22. Doors and trim.
23. Miscellaneous and ornamental metal.
24. Furring, lathing, plastering.
25. Carpentry and millwork.
26. Acoustical treatment.

27. Flashing and caulking.

28. Hardware.

29. Window screens and weather stripping.

30. Window shades and venetian blinds.

31. Painting and finishing.

32. Roof drainage.

33. Plumbing.

34. Heating and ventilation.

35. Power and lighting.

36. Sprinkler system.

37. Drainage of foundations and basement.

38. Landscaping.

39. Order of erection (if important).

40. Maintenance of any services.

This itemization is given to show the reader how comprehensive the preparation of specifications must be. The list will serve its purpose if it helps to emphasize the importance of adequate specifications as a means (1) of showing the contractor what is required in the line of workmanship and (2) of enabling the engineer to have data available for verifying that each part of the work is done properly.

QUESTIONS

1. What is meant by "independent contractor"?

2. Illustrate a situation in which an independent contractor is not actually independent.

3. What is the danger of itemizing in the specifications the procedures that the contractor is to follow in order to attain the required results?

4. When may the expression "as directed by the engineer" be helpful if used in the specifications? Illustrate.

5. A specification stated: "All work is to be done to the satisfaction of the engineer." (a) What does this statement mean? (b) How does the bidder know what will be required? (c) When is such a statement in the specifications useful?

6. What direct control should the engineer have over the method of construction adopted by the contractor? Under what conditions might he advise the contractor?

7. If the contractor follows specified procedures in the field, who is responsible for the results?

8. Illustrate a particular case in which it may be necessary for the engineer to specify procedures to be followed in the field.

9. The specifications stated that all joints of a steel oil tank were to be scarred and butt welded, and that the tank was "not to leak." Is this a satisfactory specification? Explain.

10. A contract for certain machines specified that all bearings should be finished to a tolerance of 0.01 inch. Is this a proper specification?

11. A contract specified that the parts of a certain large rectangular steel box should be connected by means of 1/4 inch fillet welds. When the contractor finished the job, the box was found to be badly distorted (out of shape). The contractor claimed that this result was entirely due to the required welding. What defense can be made by each party?

12. The drawings showed the positions and details of the anchor bolts for a machine but nothing was said in the specifications about how these bolts were to be erected. During pouring of the concrete, the bolts were displaced so that they were one inch too far apart. Can the engineer do anything about the situation? Would it have been proper if the specifications had required that the bolts be held by metal templates during erection? Explain.

13. Do the statements "as directed by the engineer" and "as approved by the engineer" mean the same thing? Illustrate.

14. The specifications stated that certain long girders for a bridge were to be braced laterally during erection. The contractor proposed using cables attached to the girders and to large stakes driven into the ground. If the engineer approved the idea, who should be held responsible in case the girders buckle sideways during the erection of the bridge?

15. The drawings called for sheet piling to be driven 35 feet into the ground to form a cofferdam around a deep excavation. It proved to be impossible to drive the sheet piling to the required depth. Who should pay the expense of the attempts to do so? Whose responsibility is it to devise some other method to make the excavation possible?

16. A large fan was to be supported upon steel beams in the top of a power plant. The contractor performed the work as intended. When operated, the fan caused annoying vibrations. Who is responsible for the unsatisfactory results?

17. Concrete pavement for a pier was to be screeded level and then broomed. When the work was partly done, a violent thunderstorm occurred, spoiling the finish of the completed portion. The engineer discovered the situation the next day. What possible courses of action can the engineer take?

18. A specification states that the contractor is to "carry out the intent of the plans and specifications." *(a)* When and why may such a statement be useful? *(b)* When is it not useful? *(c)* Does it make any difference whether the contract is lump-sum or unit-price?

19. What does the statement that "all work is to be of approved quality" mean?

20. What is the meaning of "best quality workmanship"? What value has this statement in a set of specifications?

21. Name some standard specifications for workmanship. Illustrate their use and explain the advantages of employing them.

22. Is it proper to specify that "the roofing is to be applied in accordance with the manufacturer's recommendations"? Explain.

23. If standard specifications, like those of the AISC, are used as reference, can any deviation from them be specified? Explain.

24. How is a court likely to determine the intent of the plans and specifications relating to workmanship?

25. A specification states that all work "shall conform to the best modern practice." Is this of value? Why? Illustrate.

chapter

14

SPECIFICATIONS FOR MATERIALS

14.1   INTRODUCTION

The specifications are to give detailed information regarding *each* and *every* thing and operation within the scope of the contract, to serve as a single and definite basis for competitive bidding, and to constitute a book of instructions for all concerned with the work. Some basic requirements for proper specifications are (1) technical accuracy and adequacy, (2) definite and clear stipulations, (3) fair and equitable requirements, (4) format such as to permit easy use during operations, and (5) careful preparation so that they will be legally enforceable.

The differing functions of the contract drawings and the specifications may be illustrated by referring to Fig. 14.1. Assume that this is a portion of a contract drawing for a large industrial plant. The parts we are interested in are the pipe tunnels. These are shown by the dotted lines in the plan view; a typical cross section is pictured in the lower view. Notice that the drawing shows the following:

1. Length of tunnels.
2. Elevations of inverts (center line of floor surface).
3. Sizes for the two types of tunnels.
4. Thicknesses of roof, floor, and walls.
5. Reinforcement required.
6. Waterproofing.
7. Open-joint pipe drains.
8. Spacing of contraction joints.

   It is left for the specification to describe the following:

1. Quality of the concrete, aggregates, and cement.
2. Workmanship required for mixing, placing, and curing the concrete, including forms.
3. Finish required for floor, roof, and wall surfaces.

Figure 14.1   Pipe tunnels.

4. Quality of reinforcement.

5. Workmanship required for placing and embedding reinforcement.

6. Quality of material for dampproofing.

7. Workmanship required for application of dampproofing.

8. Material and construction requirements for open-joint pipe drains.

9. Materials and workmanship required for contraction joints (for example, keyways, waterstops), and painting of surface with asphalt.

10. Excavation and backfilling requirements.

11. Preparation of soil foundation.

It is obvious that the specifications as well as the drawings should be carefully prepared. The engineer and the owner should never forget that if the specifications fail to show all requirements adequately, then the contractor's obligation is limited to performance of what is actually called for in such (incomplete) specifications (and/or on the drawings).

Somewhere in the contract, preferably in one of the contract clauses, there should be a statement describing the procedure to be followed if it should develop that there are discrepancies between the specifications and the drawings. In the haste with which contract documents sometimes have to be prepared, such inconsistencies unfortunately are likely to occur. They may also arise because of changes that are made in the drawings but that are not made correspondingly in the specifications, or vice versa. Again, discrepancies are likely to be caused when one statement in the specifications is changed but the called-for revision of a parallel clause relating thereto is overlooked. This is a danger that arises when the requirements for something are specified in more than one place. It is best to state definitely in the contract clauses that, in case of discrepancies between the specifications and the drawings, the engineer is to determine which of the two is to govern.

When something is called for in the specifications but is not included in the drawings, and vice versa, the contractor should furnish or perform that particular item as though it were covered in both. The contract documents must make this point clear.

At the beginning of the specifications, or perhaps at the beginning of the contract clauses, it is desirable to have a clear statement of exactly what work is to be covered by the contract. The following illustrative material is taken from the specifications for a bridge project.

This Contract shall include:

1. One (1) complete superstructure, including asphalt-paved movable span, towers, counterweights, power equipment, hydraulic jacks, signals, safety gates, barriers, machinery house, operator's cab, floormen's houses, and all miscellaneous equipment.

2. Two (2) complete abutments with pavements.

3. Two (2) complete approaches with pavements.

4. Complete removal of the substructure and superstructure of the existing bridge.

5. Removal of the piling which supports the substructure of the existing bridge and removal of all existing fender piles.

6. Dredging of the channel of the river in the vicinity of the bridge.

7. Protection of the sixteen- (16) inch water main which crosses the river at this location.

8. Maintenance of navigation and compliance with all requirements of the local United States Engineer's Office.

9. Provision for access during construction to all properties on the site of the contract for both pedestrian and vehicular traffic.

10. Operation of the bridge after completion for seven (7) days under traffic.

11. All miscellaneous items of work shown by the Contract Drawings and/or described in the Specifications.

14.2 Discretionary Power of the Engineer

There are many materials that can be used for the building of structures; for example, steel, aluminum, concrete, wood, bricks, stone, tiles, and cinder block. Similarly, there are many manufacturers of electrical, mechanical, and other equipment. These materials and products may be substituted for one another to some extent. On the other hand, some may be more suitable than others for use in specific instances. It is the engineer's duty and right to specify the one—or the alternative ones—that he believes to be best for each particular use, article, or structure. This means that he is to be the one to make the selection when the design is made. The responsibility is his alone, just as it is in the determination of the other features of the design of the structure, the machines, or whatever else the project may involve.

Without this discretionary power of the engineer there would be no end of confusion. If manufacturers of suitable materials that could be used in a project insisted that their products be included as alternatives in the contract and that competitive bids be taken before a decision were made, the choice might be made on the basis of the lowest bid price rather than the most suitable product, with obviously unsatisfactory results. Such a procedure would be very unsatisfactory. It is usually advisable and often necessary to plan a project in detail in order to ensure the use of a particular product or material. It would generally be impracticable for the engineer to try to make the drawings for a project so comprehensive as to adapt it to the use of all materials that manufacturers would like to have employed.

The engineer should make thorough studies to ascertain that the final design is the best that can be devised. Naturally, he should consider basic concepts, arrangements, and workmanship. He should also consider the relative costs of materials when making the design. Low cost alone, however, should not determine selection of materials, or of anything else for that matter. Longevity, maintenance charges, operating costs, efficiency, power requirements, safety, and general adaptability for its purpose are all important factors to be considered as well.

A threat to this discretionary power of the engineer occurred in connection with the design of the Ohio Turnpike.[1] The commissioners, upon the recommendation of the engineers, specified portland-cement concrete pavement because they believed it to be best under the circumstances. Persons who were interested in having asphalt paving included as an alternate bid brought legal action to force the commission to include this option. The Ohio Supreme Court overruled the lower court and decided that the commission (and its engineers) had the right to specify what it considered to be best, provided only that its action be taken "in good faith and not in abuse of its discretion."

---

[1] *State v. Ohio Turnpike Commission,* 159 Ohio St. 581, 113 N.E.2d 14 (1953).

14.3 STANDARD PRODUCTS

It is often both efficient and desirable to specify a standard product by trade name, catalog number, or any other suitable reference that is definite enough and is customary usage. For example, one may specify an electric motor as follows: "*X* Electric Manufacturing Company Type CSP, open, 10 hp, 1200 rpm, frame 326, 440 volt, 3 phase, 60 cycle." Thus, all concerned know exactly what is required, or they can readily find out about it.

On the other hand, this designation of one specific product is not usually permissible for government work. In such contracts it is normally a requirement that at least three alternate suitable articles be designated, any one of which will be acceptable. The purpose of this regulation is to avoid what might appear to be favoritism. It is also intended to secure adequate competition in the bidding. That is why in such contracts it is generally necessary to avoid specifying a patented product that only one producer can furnish.

Such restrictions do not apply in private work, but it is often advisable to avoid criticism and to promote competition by specifying "so-and-so or approved equal." This tells other manufacturers the kind of product or service that is desired, and it enables them to propose a similar product of their own that they consider to be just as good or better. Sometimes, unknown to the engineer, a new and better article has been developed. Usually this substitution will be advantageous. However, the engineer's approval is essential.

The following clauses illustrate the use of references to manufacturers' products in specifying plumbing and heating equipment:

A Minneapolis Honeywell T-418 B outdoor reset control with outdoor weather bulb and water bulb in a separate well shall be provided to operate the oil burner. Control shall provide 210°F water when outdoor temperature is 0°F. Provide and install the following fixtures and equipment:

Lavatories: Standard F 329 A
Tubs: Standard P 210 5T and P 2100T

This specification is intended to cover the complete installation of one (1) Electric Oil-hydraulic (electrically operated hydraulic elevator, using oil as the fluid medium) Passenger Elevator, as manufactured by Rotary Lift Company, Memphis, Tennessee, or equal as approved by the Architect.

It is important to give brand names, pattern numbers, and enough other data to make the requirements very clear and definite. It is also advisable to be sure that the article is a standard one that can be readily secured and that the manufacturer is reputable.

Another way to specify an article without resort to the use of the words "or approved equal" is to list the brand names and other information of a series of articles, any one of which will be acceptable. This procedure is more difficult, and the list, even then, may not be truly complete.

The use of these references to a standard commodity or product is, of course, much easier and safer than the preparation of detailed specifications describing all the desired qualities of the article. On the other hand, when patented or proprietary products are desired but cannot be named in the specifications, it is possible to word the specifications so that the desired product is the only one that completely meets the requirements.

The use of the phrase "or approved equal" may not be strictly correct because articles manufactured by various sources may seldom be exactly alike even though each may serve the desired purpose satisfactorily. The words "or approved equivalent" may be more technically correct. The word "substitute" does not necessarily mean the same quality, and its use is not recommended.

"Or approved equal" is a good illustration of the meaning of words as "used in the trade." A court will construe the former phrase as having its customary meaning unless some contrary statement appears in the contract. The important thing is the requirement that an article differing from the specified one may be substituted only when approved by the engineer.

On the other hand, there are cases where, for one reason or another, a specific article is alone acceptable. An example of this might be the equipment for an addition to a factory. The owner already has certain machines, motors, and other equipment in the existing plant. For the pending annex he wants more of the same ones because his maintenance people and operators are familiar with that particular type of equipment. Furthermore, he does not want to carry replacements and spare parts for a variety of equipment types and sizes. In such circumstances he is well advised to specify "more of the same."

It is frequently satisfactory to say in the specifications that a product is to be made "according to the manufacturer's standard." For a motor of a certain type and horsepower, for a truck of a specific type, model, and capacity, and for a bridge crane of some particular span and capacity, such a specification will usually be appropriate.

This may not be the case, however, if the article to be purchased has to meet various conditions of special nature. For example, a gantry crane of a particular span, height, speed, and capacity was required, and the specifications used the words "according to the manufacturer's standard" in describing it. When the drawings for the contractor's design were received, the engineer objected strenuously to certain basic features and to several details of the design because some parts were not sufficiently strong. However, he was at a great disadvantage in securing remedial measures because the manufacturer said: "This is our standard. We have built similar designs before." In this case, as in many others, the opinion of the engineer was based upon personal knowledge and experience of what would be best for long-time service. He could not prove that the manufacturer's design was unsafe, but he wished to have certain parts of the construction detailed in accordance with what he had previously found to be eminently satisfactory. The specifications should have reflected this.

It is essential that the engineer be the one to approve or disapprove any substitution. However, if the specifications state that alternative materials will be considered by the engineer, a contractor cannot be certain what the engineer will accept. Therefore, if the bidder is to play safe, he will have to base his costs upon what is specified because if he states that the bid is based upon certain stipulated substitutions, he will have changed the terms of the invitation for bids. The bidder's proposal is then likely to be rejected because it is not in proper form and because it cannot be readily compared with the proposals of other bidders. Substitutions (and any corresponding price adjustments) will usually have to be arranged after the contract is signed, if they are to be resorted to at all. After the contract is signed, it is somewhat unfair to other bidders for the engineer to accept cheaper products as substitutes for those specified, even if the contract cost is adjusted accordingly. If a contractor proposes a substitution prior to bidding, and if the engineer finds that such substitution will be in the best interest of the project, the engineer should issue an addendum to all bidders advising them that said substitution will be acceptable.

14.4 STANDARD SPECIFICATIONS FOR MATERIALS

It is a great help to refer to standard specifications—where applicable ones are available—as a means of specifying materials. The American Society for Testing Materials (ASTM) has prepared volumes of specifications for a wide variety of materials—in fact, for most of the materials used in practice. These specifications are the result of long and intensive study by experts in each field involved and are generally accepted as authoritative. The ordinary engineer cannot hope to sit down and quickly write a perfectly satisfactory specification for even a few basic materials, nor would it be advisable when such excellent ones are readily available.

For example, assume that specifications are needed for the steel to be used in a number of large castings. The engineer may state that the material is to conform to ASTM designation A 27-82, standard specification for Carbon Steel Castings for General Applications. Thus, manufacturers who wish to bid on these castings will know exactly what is required as far as quality of material is concerned. In using such a reference the engineer may add "or the latest revision thereof," if he is not sure that the reference volume designated contains the very latest revisions of the pertinent specifications.

The title used in the foregoing ASTM reference is generally descriptive; the designation is the specific reference. In this particular example the number 82 designates the year of issue of the specifications by the ASTM organization.

As the name implies, the ASTM specifications, in addition to specifying qualities, cover or set up standard procedures for acceptance tests of materials. This is an important matter. One can easily imagine the confusion that would arise if excellent specifications of the chemical and physical properties of a material were issued but organizations or users were left to devise their own methods of testing this material to ascertain whether or not a particular lot would be acceptable. Just a few of these tests as issued by ASTM are the following:

ASTM designation: E8-82 standard method of Tension Testing Metallic Materials.

ASTM designation: C151-77 standard test method for Autoclave Expansion of Portland Cement.

ANSI/ASTM designation: C88-76 standard test method for Soundness of Aggregates by use of Sodium Sulfate or Magnesium Sulfate.

Notice that the ASTM specifications do not, and should not, prescribe what material to use for a particular purpose or when to use it. These are matters for the individual engineer to determine. If he wants to make an article of cast iron instead of cast steel, the proper reference to the appropriate ASTM specifications will ensure that he is calling for good cast iron. On the other hand, if the brittleness of cast iron should prove to be a disadvantage in service, this is not the fault of ASTM. Obviously, the ASTM cannot guarantee proper design use of its data and materials.

It is clearly the responsibility of each individual engineer to be sure that he knows the contents of the section of the ASTM specifications that he uses as a reference. Anything he needs that is not covered should be specified directly. Thus the dimensions and finish of castings are generally to be given on the drawings, while requirements for annealing and any special methods to be used in making the castings are to be stated by the engineer in specifications he personally devises or are to be given through references to proper standard specifications.

The ASTM will specify only such items as the proper ultimate tensile strength, the minimum yield point, and the required minimum percent elongation. Furthermore, the ASTM does not undertake to specify unit stresses to be used for design purposes. For example, if the engineer is using structural steel, he (or some governing code) must determine what unit stress and safety factor are to be used. Again, if the engineer is using concrete, he is the one to determine whether that concrete is to have a 28-day ultimate compressive strength of 2,500 or 4,000 pounds per square inch, and so on.

Besides the ASTM specifications, there are many other materials and workmanship specifications of real help to the engineer as references. These latter are generally prepared by manufacturers of materials or by groups that are interested in particular materials. For example, the *Standard Grading and Dressing Rule for Lumber,*[2] prepared by the West Coast Lumbermen's Association, is useful when one is to prepare specifications for a timber structure; *Specifications for the Design, Fabrication and Erection of Structural Steel for Buildings,* prepared by the American Institute of Steel Construction, is very helpful in connection with building jobs, and the Building Code Requirements for reinforced Concrete (ACI 318-77) of the American Concrete Institute serve a useful purpose in certain phases of concrete work.

The fact that these specifications are prepared by those who are interested in the sales of a particular material does not mean that the specifications are untrustworthy. The manufacturers who advocate the use of their materials obviously want them used properly so that the results will be satisfactory and that credibility for future sales will be established. Design specifications and building codes do not concern the contract as such, although the structure to be built under the contract may have to be designed in accordance with their provisions.

Naturally, standard specifications must be correctly used if they are to prove valuable. It is generally better to use them in their entirety than to select pieces of them for quotation. For example, the Steel Products Manual or Hot Rolled Carbon Steel Bars, Section 8, published by the American Iron and Steel Institute in August 1952, contains, in substance, the following specification for the straightness of reinforcing bars to be used in concrete:

1.   The offset of any bar from a straight line shall not exceed 1/4 in. in any length of 5 ft.

---

[2]This rule applies to Douglas fir, Sitka spruce, West Coast hemlock, and Western red cedar.

(a) According to American Iron and Steel Institute

(b) According to specifications as written

Figure 14.2 Partial use of a specification for straightness of reinforcing bars.

2. In no case shall the offset of any bar from a straight line exceed 1/4 in. times one-fifth of the length in feet.

Both of these requirements are pictured in Fig. 14.2(a). Specifications were prepared that copied only the first of these items. Fig. 14.2(b) shows how, if only this one requirement is prescribed, the supplier may comply with it and yet ignore the equally important second item. The bars may then be curved excessively but still meet the specifications.

Notice the following advantageous uses of references to standards for electrical work:

The following industry standards shall be considered minimum requirements under this specification:

1. The standard rules of the American Institute of Electrical & Electronics Engineers.

2. The rules and regulations of the National Board of Fire Underwriters (National Electrical Code).

3. The rules and regulations of the local utility company and local Electrical Inspection Department.

4. All electrical materials and appliances shall have the listing of the Underwriters Laboratories, Inc., or shall conform to their requirements and shall be so labeled.

5. All work is to be done in accordance with all state and local regulations, and the Contractor is to obtain and pay for any charges for all permits, licenses, etc., in connection with his work.

A paragraph in another specification stated:

> All work shall be performed in accordance with the National Electrical Code, American Standard Safety Code, and such state and local codes as may be applicable. The Contractor shall obtain all necessary approvals, and he shall pay for all permits.

The following is an illustration of the use of a reference to a standard specification for plumbing work:

> All work shall meet the requirements of the National Plumbing Code, unless otherwise noted.

Standard specifications are generally prepared for use in average or ordinary conditions. When special requirements are to be met, the engineer should not trust the adequacy of standard specifications. It is his responsibility to prepare complete and accurate specifications that meet the requirements of the particular job.

14.5   USE OF PREVIOUS SPECIFICATIONS

Many products that are considered raw materials for a construction contract are really the finished product of some manufacturer, and they cannot be described adequately, if at all, by reference to standard specifications. However, use may be made of appropriate paragraphs that have been previously prepared by the engineer himself or by others. If no such paragraphs are available, original descriptive data will have to be compiled and utilized.

The use of paragraphs or clauses that have been prepared for the specifications of a preceding job may have the advantage of prior experience and testing in practice; however, previous compositions may not be completely applicable to the present case. They may contain errors or inadvisable statements, and they may fail to cover all necessary features. Often there is a statement in a former writing that refers to some feature of the previous contract that is not relevant to the present one. Again, there may be some different feature in the present contract that the copied clause does not cover at all or, at least, for which it does not prescribe the requirements correctly.

The principal lure of previous compositions is that their use relieves the engineer of the necessity of doing unnecessary original thinking and also helps to avoid overlooking some important feature. But excessive reliance upon the cut-and-paste system may lull the engineer into a false sense of security so that he does not really check to see that all necessary points are covered properly and accurately.

One way for a large organization to handle this matter of the preparation of specifications would be to compose a paragraph or series of paragraphs covering all the subjects that are likely to be applicable to its future contract, to be studied carefully by all concerned. Copies of the master document can be prepared for incorporation in future specifications, with blank spaces left for the insertion of any figures or statements that are not constant for all cases. (This procedure is likely to be safer than merely cutting paragraphs wholesale from previous specifications.) If the master set of specifications is kept up to date and if anything discovered in the course of contract work that affects these specifications is corrected, the occurrence of mistakes should be minimized. Computers afford an engineer the possibility of doing these "chores" quickly and easily.

14.6 SPECIFICATION IN TERMS OF SERVICE

In some cases, such as purchase orders, it may be satisfactory to specify materials and equipment in terms of the service required. The reason may be to secure competition in circumstances where each of several different products could serve the purpose. The engineer may use this method when he is not sure which particular material or article will be the best and the cheapest and when he wants the recommendations of, as well as prices quoted by, various manufacturers.

It seems that this *performance type* of specifications, which states what is required in the way of performance, quality, and so on, is attaining greater popularity than one that attempts to set down all the detailed requirements for a particular article. This is an especially suitable form of specification when more than one method or commodity may be used satisfactorily for attaining a particular purpose. In this case the manufacturers and contractors are permitted to make their proposals on the basis of what each one thinks is best to meet the general requirements. The engineer can then accept or reject any or all proposals if he believes that such action is desirable. If the several producers guarantee that their products will meet the requirements, then the engineer may select one on the basis of price, desirability, or other characteristics, relying upon the guarantor to make good if necessary.

Let us assume that an engineer is to specify the insulation for the flat roof of a new and very large industrial plant. This will be a separate contract that will include the material and its installation. He may specify the desired resistance to the transfer of heat or may say that the insulation is to be equivalent to a 2-inch layer of foam glass. He may also say whether or not the material is to be rigid, fire resistant, moisture proof, and/or nondecaying. The manufacturers can then propose what they recommend, what they will guarantee, and what the cost in place will be. The engineer then has to determine which one of the several possibilities proposed is the best, considering both price and quality.

Again, assume that a mechanical engineer is preparing a requisition for a bridge crane for an industrial plan. He might prepare a sketch showing the clearance diagram, the span, side and vertical clearance, distance of rails above the floor, capacity in tons, auxiliary hook (if any) and its capacity, speed of bridge travel, speed of trolley, voltage to be used for power supply, and position of cab. He might also state the date of delivery required. Various manufacturers have their own particular designs and details for such equipment, or they will make up special designs. Each may submit his proposal for the bridge crane. The engineer can then accept whichever proposal he thinks is best. The details of the proposed equipment may vary, but the guarantee of service and quality given by reputable manufacturers can be trusted.

The following specification is quoted from a contract for pumps that constituted one part of the equipment to be supplied:

Close-coupled centrifugal raw water booster pump, complete with motor, of capacity and head as given in "Design Conditions" herein, fully assembled and ready for installation.

The pump shall be designed for the following conditions and in accordance with the standards of the Hydraulic Institute.

Capacity, 20 gpm

Static head at suction, about 10 ft.

Discharge head, 195 ft.

Water temperature, approx. 35 to 700F

The final pump suction head, discharge pressure, and rotation will be given at time of approving the overall dimension drawings.

Notice that the preceding specification permits each manufacturer to propose one pump (or to design one) that is suitable for the required service without tying him down to minor mechanical details, although these must be satisfactory to the engineer.

Naturally, this method of specifying service requirements cannot be used on a wholesale basis for a large construction contract that includes a great many items. The contractor must have a fairly definite knowledge of the requirements of the contract. If the specifications have too many materials and products open to choice, the contractor cannot tell in advance just what to bid upon unless he can determine precisely what is to be used to fill each need. This sort of freedom tends to cause confusion.

On the other hand, innovation should not always be stifled. Someone may develop a new way of making something or performing some operation. It may be possible to make use of it by wording the specifications so this method may be considered provided the engineer believes it to be in the best interest of the project. Again, one should encourage participation but without making the specifications too vague.

14.7   PLANNING DETAILED SPECIFICATIONS

It is apparent that one must know a considerable amount about a material in order to write a good specification for it. One should know what qualities to expect in the material, what characteristics are needed for the special purpose, and whether or not (and, if so, how) it can obtain the desired result without undue trouble and cost.

For purposes of illustration, assume that you are to prepare specifications for the piles and timbers to be used in a wooden pier for docking colliers at a powerplant located at tidewater. Assume further that you cannot use references to standard specifications for the purpose. How would you go about accomplishing the work? Here are some of the things that you should think about and cover in your specifications:

A   Piles

1. Kind of material; that is, southern yellow pine, oak, spruce, Douglas fir, etc.

2. Variation allowed from the stipulated lengths.

3. Straightness.

4. Size range, or at least minimum sizes, of tip and butt.

5. Removal of bark.

6. Limit on knots allowed and trimming of knots.

7. Seasoning.

8. Creosoting—method to be employed and quantity of creosote to be used.

9. Limitations on cracks, shakes, and other imperfections allowed.

B   Timber for deck

1. Kind of material.

2. Variation allowed from specified lengths, especially underrun.

3. Straightness or warp.

4. Limit on knots—number, size, and position.

5. Seasoning.

6. Creosoting.

7. Amount of splits, checks, and shakes allowed; length, depth, direction.

8. Grade.

9. Chemical treatment, if any.

10. Kind of finish—rough or dressed.

11. Full trimming—no skips.

12. Character of stock—fresh, clean, no decay.

13. Grain limitations.

14. Limit on pitch streaks or pockets and on stains.

15. Allowed variation from nominal sizes.

16. Limit on worm holes.

17. Requirements if tongued and grooved.

Actually, especially with timber, the limitations generally vary somewhat with the size and general character of the material. For example, the specifications for 8-by-12 timbers will differ in some details (other than just size) from those for 1-by-6 sheathing.

As a further example of specifying a material, examine the following which applied to gravel fill at a school building:

> *GRAVEL FILL*: Gravel Fill shall consist of sound, tough, durable particles of crushed or uncrushed gravel, free from soft, thin elongated or laminated pieces and vegetable or other deleterious substances. It shall meet the sieve analysis given below, and the requirements for plasticity and the test for soft particles indicated in Connecticut State Highway Department Form 809, "Standard Specifications for Roads, Bridges and Incidental Construction," dated, January, 1963, with "Supplemental Specifications" thereto dated October, 1964, Article M-02-07, paragraphs 2 and 3.

Sieve Analysis for Gravel Fill	
Square mesh sleeves	Percent passing by weight
Pass 3-1/2 in	100
Pass 1/4 in	30–65
Pass #40	5–30
Pass #100	0–10

The difficulty of composing all these detailed specifications will soon be apparent as well as the value of standard references that can be used in preparing the required data. It must be remembered that a misstatement or an omission may cost money and may compel one to accept material that is not as good as he intended.

14.8   SPECIAL ITEMS

Seldom will an engineer or architect have to compose specifications covering material that is entirely new or a new combination of materials. However, he may desire some special qualities in, or uses for, materials. If so, he must specify them by original composition.

To illustrate, suppose that an architect wishes to use a certain unusual type, texture, color, and finish of stone for the exterior portion of the walls of a monumental building. Under the circumstances, it is necessary for him to make a study of what kinds of stone are available and suitable. He must also determine whether or not the stone of his choice can be finished in the fashion he desires. This necessitates the preparation of special specifications for this material. The architect, of course, must assume responsibility for the results of his choice.

Sometimes it is desirable to require the contractor to prepare samples of his work or product and to submit them for approval. The specifications should state that the materials furnished under the contract are to match the approved samples.

When it is necessary to specify a material in detail or to specify some commodity, it is essential for the engineer to have a thorough knowledge of the physical, chemical, and other properties of that material. He must then be careful to prepare his specifications so as to include the desired properties but to exclude or limit anything that may be undesirable. For example, sulfur may be an impurity in steel. If an excessive amount will be harmful for the intended use, the engineer should specify the maximum percentage that will be acceptable.

Provision should also be made for acceptance tests of materials. What the test should be, who should conduct it, pay for it, and approve the results should all be covered in the contract clauses or in the specifications.

The engineer should also be very careful to see that his specifications are practical and that they can be met without excessive cost and trouble.

When confronted with special cases, the engineer or architect might well go to the trouble and expense of having a competent specialist check his specifications before they are published. A misguided sense of professional pride should not be allowed to prevent this sensible extra step of precaution.

QUESTIONS

1. What are the basic requirements of proper specifications?
2. Discuss the difference in the kind of information shown in the drawings and that given in the specifications.
3. What are standard specifications? Illustrate what use can be made of them.
4. What is the special function of material specifications? Do they in any way protect the contractor?
5. When and why may one use copies of previous specifications when composing a set of contract documents? Discuss the advantages and disadvantages of this procedure.
6. What is the ASTM? How can its work product be utilized? What advantages are there for the engineer in using such available material?
7. What is a "performance" or "service" type of specification? Illustrate its use. Who is responsible for results where this type is employed?
8. When and how can the specifications use to an advantage a reference to a standard product of a particular manufacturer?
9. Why specify "or approved equivalent"? Who does the approving?
10. The drawings showed that a steel structure was to be field-bolted, but the specifications stated that it was to be field-welded. The contractor bid on the bolted work. Was he justified in so doing? What can the engineer do about the situation?
11. The specifications called for the coating with linseed oil of all "finished" surfaces of machinery. The drawings did not indicate any coating. What should the inspector require of the contractor? Explain.
12. A specification stated: "The insulation shall be 2 in. thick and of an approved type." Is this a satisfactory way to put it? Why?
13. Why is it desirable to include in the contract documents a description of the project?
14. A specification stated: "Substitutions may be submitted for the approval of the engineer." Is this a satisfactory statement? Elaborate.
15. Why is it generally inadvisable to allow bidders to make substitutions (in their proposals) for specified structural materials? Is such substitution satisfactory in the case of certain equipment?
16. Has the engineer the right to specify what he wants regardless of the opinions of the contractors?

17. Does an engineer act properly when he seeks the advice of contractors and manufacturers before preparing his specifications for some article or process? Why?

18. A specification states: "Suitable pumps shall be installed to prevent flooding of the excavation." Has the engineer control over what pumps are to be provided? If flooding occurs, who is responsible?

19. What are the advantages and disadvantages of specifying products by name and catalog number?

20. What is the purpose of public works regulations that require that at least three proposals be sought?

21. What advantages and disadvantages may there be in specifying a list of acceptable alternatives for a given purpose?

22. Under what conditions might it be desirable for the engineer to specify one and only one named product?

23. An engineer specified that a bridge crane should "have a capacity of 50 tons, with a 10-ton auxiliary, a span of 75 feet, an acceptable speed of travel, and be driven by 440-volt, 60-cycle power." Is this specification satisfactory under ordinary circumstances? Why?

24. Can a contractor propose substitutions for specified products *(a)* before the bids are received? *(b)* after the contract is awarded?

25. Can an engineer specify a material having different properties than those given in the ASTM specifications? Why?

26. Does the ASTM specify how and when a particular material (like Portland Cement, Type II) is to be used? Why?

27. As references, are standard specifications always to be used? If standard specifications are thus employed, can the engineer specify anything that differs from them?

15

DRAWINGS

15.1   INTRODUCTION

This chapter will show some of the basic requirements for the preparation of the drawings for construction contracts. The drawings, like the written provisions, will become a very important part of the contract. Between them, they are supposed to give the contractor the essential information regarding the work. The preparation of the bid will be based upon an interpretation of these papers. The details will vary with the project, but the basic principles are common to most construction contracts.

In general, the drawings made by the engineer or the architect, who are often referred to as *design professionals,* may be called *design drawings* when they are prepared for bidding purposes. When the contract is let, these drawings become known as the *contract drawings.* The *contract documents* are all the documents that comprise the building contract. These documents include working drawings, specifications, contract conditions, addenda, change orders, and the agreement or written contract. The drawings should show enough of the extent and character of the work to enable the contractor to know what is expected. For a lump-sum contract, the design drawings should be much more comprehensive and explicit than they need to be for other types. In a unit-price contract, the engineer has to make many additional drawings after the contract is let in order to show various details of the project. In almost all construction contracts it will be necessary for the contractor and/or subcontractors to provide *shop drawings* in order to make all the details clear for construction purposes.

The development of personal computers and computer-aided drafting and design, or CAD, has revolutionized the drawing process and, in turn, has an impact on the negotiation and contracting process. Not only does CAD impact the production and quality of drawings and make revisions convenient, it also changes the way drawings are delivered. Drawings created on a computer can quickly be sent across the world via e-mail, the Internet, or a network and printed at their destination without the design professional ever leaving the office. This may impact issues in the customary negotiation process, such as at what moment the contract is formed. The prevalence of CAD also brings up new legal issues for the design professional, such as licensing and copyrights. Microcad software packages, such as AutoCAD[1], are licensed products that may only be legally used after purchase of the software and a license. Applications packages that run within AutoCAD and are geared to a more specific task, such as electrical or plumbing work, are licensed products as well. Product manufacturers, such as window and fixture manufacturers, can create programs featuring their products to run with AutoCAD as well. Product manufacturers can also make this information available over the Internet. As the Internet gains more and more popularity, it will bring more flexibility and information to the design professional, as well as more legal issues.

15.2   USE OF DESIGN DRAWINGS

Design drawings are used to give the contractor needed information that can be transmitted more effectively by picture than by written description. Such data as shapes, sizes, detailed dimensions, relationship of parts, and desired locations for special features would be almost impossible to convey satisfactorily by any means other than drawings.

The preparation of design drawings is an art in itself, but in this text we are primarily interested in the functional aspect of these drawings as an important part of the contract documents. The contractor will have to provide and perform what such drawings require. When arguments arise (most likely during the course of construction) regarding contractual requirements, the key to resolving issues is what the contract drawings really show, not what they should have shown or what the engineer wanted. Considerable trouble and expense may result from drawings that fail to do the job for which they are intended. The adequacy, clarity, and detailed accuracy of the drawings, rather than their beauty, are the really important features. The vast majority of drawings are not created with CAD, but a drawing may consist simply of an amateur's freehand sketch made on a piece of wrapping paper. If so, and if made a part of the contract, the drawing would be just as binding as though created by an experienced professional with state-of-the-art CAD software and the latest computer technology.

It is ordinarily assumed that the drawings and the specifications, although prepared by the engineer, are to become the property of the owner for whom they were made and who pays for the engineering work involved. If any other "ownership" is intended, it should be agreed upon in advance between the owner and the engineer.[2] The engineer must always retain a wet-copy original of his or her design drawings for legal reasons. The owner is likewise due a wet copy because he paid for that service and deserves to know what he received. A "wet" copy means a plan marked with the design engineer's seal and signed with his handwritten name in original wet ink.

---

[1]Trademark of Autodesk, Inc., AutoCAD is by far the most widely used program.
[2]For a detailed discussion of the applicability of copyright protection of architectural plans see Chapter 24, Section 17.

15.3 TABULATION OF DRAWINGS

When they are not physically attached to the rest of the documents, the design drawings should be made an integral part of the contract through what is known as *incorporation by reference.* It is customary to have these drawings done on a computer with CAD software, then to have the drawings saved to a diskette or printed out or both.[3] With CAD, the drawing can be created in its actual dimensions rather than scaled dimensions. When a scale drawing is needed, the image is easily reduced before a hard copy is made with a printer or plotter. However, although it is possible for the computer to reduce the image to a piece of paper small enough to be bound with the written contract or specifications, it may be too small to be easily read. The prints or hard copies of the drawings in whatever size needed may be bound together and kept separate from the other contract and specification papers. On the other hand, reproductions of *small* drawings may be bound directly with the contract itself or diskettes may be attached.

It is desirable to have the incorporation-by-reference clause—which states that the design drawings are an integral part of the contract—accompanied by a table setting forth the date of the drawings, their individual numbers, and their individual titles. For example, the following hypothetical list is illustrative of one possible arrangement for the pertinent portion of a unit-price contract dealing with major highway construction:

Contract Drawings

The Contract Drawings which accompany and form a part of this Contract and of the Specifications are dated Feb. 15, 1998. They have the general title "The Connecticut State Highway Department—Route 46, Expressway—John Doe Street to City Line—Bridgeport, Connecticut—Contract No. EX-3."

The drawings are numbered and separately entitled as follows:

Drawing no.	Title
1	Location Plan and Index
2	Plan and Profile—John Doe Street to Robert Roe Avenue
6	Cross Sections
7	Robert Roe Avenue Bridge
8	West Abutment at Robert Roe Avenue
9	East Abutment at Robert Roe Avenue
14	Connection to Maple Street

[3]Before the advent of CAD, it was customary to have these drawings done on tracing paper or tracing cloth, and then to have prints made from these originals. Although 24 by 36 inches was common, drawings could be made in any size. Because of their considerable size and bulk, prints were customarily bound together and kept separate from other contract and specification papers. Reproductions of small sketches were sometimes bound with the contract itself, but suitable photostat reductions of large drawings were too costly before personal computers and desktop printers.

The contract drawings do not purport to show all the details of the work; they are intended merely to illustrate the character and extent of the performance desired under the contract. Therefore, they may be supplemented or revised from time to time, as the work progresses, by the engineer. Revisions and additional drawings are to be made by the engineer as the proper illustration of the work requires. All such supplementary and revised drawings automatically become part of the contract.

One should be very careful to see that the tabulation of pertinent drawings is complete and correct. If a drawing involving a considerable amount of work is omitted from the tabulation, this omission is as serious as the failure to put some specific written material in the contract and specifications. If the drawing is issued belatedly, the contractor can contend that such work was not covered in the contract as signed, and, therefore, the performance of the work involved is not required. If the contractor then proceeds to perform this additional work, he will be justified in making a claim for extra compensation unless the applicable unit prices cover the cost adequately.

Notice that the engineer's right to revise the contract drawings and to make binding supplementary drawings is to be specifically stated in the contract. The need to alter and amplify the original set of drawings usually arises when a unit-price contract is let on the basis of general design drawings that do not show the required work completely. It often happens that such a contract is let on the rather imprecise basis of several drawings that picture the general scope and character of the project[4] but that do not show sufficient detailed information to enable adequate performance of the work. After a contract is so awarded, the engineer may have to make from several to a few hundred supplementary drawings in order to portray all the information essential in the construction process. Such a requirement can be particularly burdensome on "fast-track" jobs because the contract to build may be awarded even before all the contract drawings are ready for construction. In such a case very close managerial control is necessary to avoid mistakes.

15.4   PRESERVATION OF CONTRACT DRAWINGS

Because revisions are frequently and easily made with CAD, the parties should retain at least one record set of the contract drawings in the form in which they

---

[4]For example, the unit-price contract for the construction of a $20 million industrial plant was let on the basis of data shown by the following design drawings only (plus, of course, specifications):

1. A general layout of the site and of the plant showing structures, transportation connections, grading, etc.
2. A topographic map of the property.
3. A foundation plan showing footings and locations of piles, plus a few typical details.
4. A floor plan showing the size, shape, and general features of the main plant.
5. Sample framing plans and sufficient details to picture the character of the work.
6. Enough architectural details to show the typical roof, wall, and floor construction.
7. Layout drawings to picture the character of the plumbing, drainage, heating, and electrical installations. After the contract was awarded, the engineer prepared over 300 supplementary drawings for the contractor's use.

were initially issued for bidding purposes for reference in the event of future disputes. A set of all the drawings, either a hard copy or on diskettes, should be preserved before any revisions are made and kept for future reference.[5] Possession of a record set of these drawings may prove to be of great value if, for example, the contractor should present claims for extra compensation. Repeatedly, this question arises: "What did he bid on?" The answer can be found by referring to the record set; by comparing these drawings with what was actually built, the validity of the contractor's claims may be ascertained.

In one case the contract drawings showed a detail for a special expansion joint in some heavy-duty crane rails. The drafter inadvertently omitted the word "thermite" from the note referring to the welding pictured. The contractor consequently assumed that ordinary electric arc welding would be satisfactory. After the contract was signed, the drawing was revised to correct the note. Since the contractor had no facilities for thermite welding, he had to engage someone else to do this extra work. He claimed payment for the extra cost. Reference was made to prints of the original contract drawings, and the contractor's claim was thereupon approved. However, this can work both ways, and numerous instances might be cited in which the record set of drawings has enabled the engineer to prove that extras claimed by the contractor were unwarranted.

Besides retaining a set of the original contract drawings, it is often desirable for the owner to require the contractor to provide a set of "as built" drawings after the work is completed, showing each part as actually constructed. They should cover all dimensions after the several parts are measured in detail in the field. These tracings may prove very useful in case of future alterations or additions to the structure. On the other hand, it should be made clear that the owner is not allowed to use any reproductions of the contract drawings or the "as built" drawings for any other purpose or project without the written permission of the design professional to do so.

15.5 SOURCES OF TROUBLE

Carelessly prepared or inadequate drawings obviously invite trouble in the performance of a contract and are a fruitful source of claims by the contractor for extra compensation. The engineer, by way of making sure the owner understands the situation, should demand sufficient time, personnel, and equipment with which to prepare really suitable drawings. In practice, the engineer is generally faced with the problem of getting the drawings and other contract documents completed for bidding purposes as fast as possible, usually under pressure from the owner and with limited resources available for performing the job. Some of these problems may be

---

[5]In the days of manual drafting, reproduced tracings made on cloth directly from the originals (before any revisions are permitted) would serve as an ideal record set of the contract drawings.

alleviated by CAD, which allows engineers to produce designs faster and with more detail. CAD also allows engineers to easily modify previous projects. Three-dimensional technology allows one to "walk through" or "fly over" the CAD drawing, which leads to more accurate representations and, thus, fewer disputes.

Sometimes unit-price proposals must be based upon preliminary drawings purporting to show in a very general way the nature and extent of the project. The advisability of this widely used approach is debatable. Subsequent development of the design almost always results in the addition of many essential features that add appreciably to the cost of the work. Some claims by the contractor to recover this excess are practically inevitable and usually justified. The owner should realize this when he lets the contract to a bidder who has had to base his proposal upon drawings that, taken as a whole, are not thorough and comprehensive.[6]

One principle to remember is that the function of drawings is to make the subject clear and definite by whatever means the drafter can devise. It is obvious that the engineer cannot afford to make the contract drawings so extensive that they show every detail of the project. Many parts may be similar in general character but different in various details. It is essential to show on the drawings enough data to describe the work sufficiently for a knowledgeable contractor to understand what is required. The engineer might label such illustrative information "typical details" or the equivalent. He should state in the specifications, or by notes on the drawings, that the data shown on the contract drawings are typical and are to describe the general nature of the work, and that the contract clauses and specifications, as well as the contract drawings and acceptable standard practices in associated fields, constitute the contract as a whole. For economic reasons, efforts should also be addressed to keeping the preparation of the drawings from becoming unduly laborious or excessively costly.

15.6   DEVELOPMENT OF DETAILS

Basically, the design drawings are intended to show the general outlines and enough detail regarding the structure, materials, and equipment to enable the contractor to bid on the job. However, seldom are these drawings entirely adequate for every need in connection with the construction work; it is necessary to enlarge upon the information that they show or imply, supplementing the engineer's drawings with what are variously called *detail drawings, shop drawings, construction*

---

[6]One large unit-price job for heavy concrete construction was undertaken on the basis of a few general drawings together with a set of prints from a previous contract—similar in a broad sense, but very different in detail. The old prints were used for the limited purposes of (1) showing the bidders some sample drawings of the type turned out by the engineer's office and (2) picturing the general nature of the construction that had been required under the earlier contract. The emerging demands of the project at hand naturally revealed many and extensive differences between the old drawings used for bidding and those "current" ones ultimately issued after the contract was awarded and actual construction was under way. The contractor's list of claims for extras reached a monetary total that was staggering. The owner blamed the engineer for the unfortunate situation, saying, "Why didn't you convince me that this would be the result?" Again, the use of CAD may have prevented this result. The prints from the previous contract could have been easily modified with CAD.

Figure 15.1 Shop details of a beam.

drawings, or *working drawings*—made by the contractor.[7] These drawings of details are intended to picture for the contractor everything needed in order to execute the work. The shop drawing for a steel beam, shown in Fig. 15.1, is as it might be made by the drafter of a steel-fabricating shop. Notice that all materials and dimensions are given so that the workers can manufacture the finished product.

The design drawings (as supplemented) might show plans for the steel framing of a building. They may consist, in part, of drawings portraying the various members by single lines, as illustrated in Fig. 15.2, which is a small portion of a drawing that depicts a steel roof truss. Each member is labeled to show the size and material required. These drawings should also reveal necessary information regarding the prescribed lengths and positions of members. Still, it is obvious that a steel-fabricating shop could not build this truss unless it was given more complete information than is available from this design (or "contract") drawing. Therefore, the contractor for the steelwork will have to put together additional drawings, giving in minute detail whatever data are needed to enable the shop to fabricate each one of the members and to build the truss. In addition, the fabricator will have to prepare erection diagrams, bills of material for computing weights, shipping bills, and any other miscellaneous papers which may prove necessary. On a large project the shop drawings and related items may be numbered in the hundreds.

---

[7]Thus, in some cases the contractor will have to make construction drawings showing designs and details for such elements as cofferdams, heavy shoring, arch centering, and other essentials for actual conduct of the work. Preparation of all these papers involves a considerable amount of labor, engineering ability, and computer expertise. When the engineer examines the drawings showing such designs prepared by the contractor for the latter's use, the engineer should make it clear that he does so only in a spirit of helpfulness and to see that, in his opinion, these plans show what seems to be suitable to accomplish the final construction required by the contract. The engineer may make suggestions (and even criticisms) if he believes that such will aid the contractor in safely performing the work involved. However, by no means should the engineer assume any responsibility for such designs and drawings by the contractor.

Figure 15.2   Truss diagram.

Going back now to the design drawings, in addition to the simple line diagram shown in Fig. 15.2, the engineer may indicate a few typical details as to the character of the work required—as illustrated in Fig. 15.3; this shows how some members are to be connected to each other. Where concrete work is involved, the engineer might prepare a design drawing somewhat like the hypothetical one in Fig. 15.4; this illustrates the general character of concrete piers and steel beams for supporting heavy equipment in an industrial plant. A careful study of this illustration will demonstrate that the contractor's workers cannot build this pier without having more information, even though the size and shape of the concrete are given, the character and sizes of reinforcement are indicated, and the sizes and spacing of the steel beams are revealed. A possible shop drawing and bar schedule for this pier are represented in Fig. 15.5.

Of course, it is possible for the engineer to prepare the shop drawings for construction purposes, but the contract should be specific on this point. If the contract contemplates that such drawings are the responsibility of the contractor, it may be desirable to clarify the following points as guidelines:

1. The standard size of drawings.

2. Any necessity for the use of printed forms for the drawings.

3. The general title to be used for all drawings pertaining to the project.

4. The printed forms to be used on the drawings for recording revisions and approval by the engineer.

5. Statement as to responsibility for the accuracy of drawings.[8]

6. Any necessity and procedure for the submission of preliminary layouts for approval by the engineer.

7. The number of prints required and the mechanics of submitting shop drawings for the approval of the engineer.

---

[8]It is desirable to provide that the contractor's drawings are to be checked by him before submission for the engineer's approval.

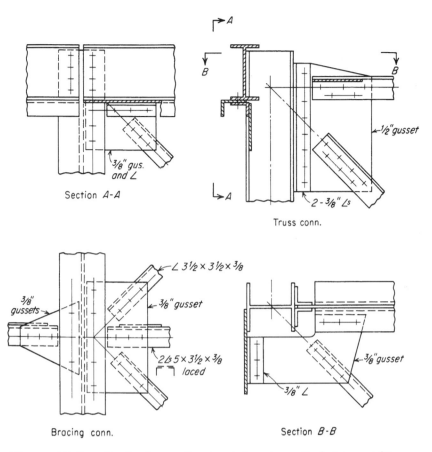

Figure 15.3 Details of connections to exterior columns (Scale 1 in. = 1 ft.).

8. The number of prints required for filing purposes by the owner and the engineer, and the number to be sent to the inspectors and to the field staff of the engineer.

9. The number of prints of erection diagrams, shipping lists, shop bills, and the like to be furnished to the engineer and his field men.

Shop drawings are ordinarily to be prepared by the contractor or by someone who is responsible to him. They are not part of the contract papers as such. In examining and approving the shop drawings, the engineer is to do so in order to see that what they show seems to be in accordance with the contract's requirements. By no means does he (or should he) assume any responsibility for their accuracy. His goal is to examine the shop drawings with reasonable care in order to ascertain that they show suitable information.

Of course, it is possible that an owner (such as an industrial concern or a governmental agency) may have a small project to perform from the planning stage through the completion of construction, using its own design professionals and other employees. In that situation, shop drawings made by the staff are still the responsibility of the owner.

Elevation

Section A-A

Figure 15.4   Portion of a contract drawing of piers and beams supporting equipment in an industrial plant.

15.7 REVISIONS

Revisions are easily made to drawings when using CAD with the *Edit* command and *Block* function. The edit commands allow extensive revision of previously created figures and can perform such sophisticated tasks as making a reverse image of a picture while leaving the accompanying text in readable form. With the block function, the design professional can reuse drawings and symbols in the same drawing or project and can also copy them from project to project. As these methods are easily employed, many ideas can be experimented with to obtain the perfect solution before approval of the drawings. As a result, CAD technology reduces the amount of revising that occurs after construction has begun. Nevertheless, there are still revisions, and whenever an original contract drawing is changed, new prints of it (or an updated diskette) should be sent to the contractor and to all other persons concerned. While the revisions are easily distinguishable from the original drawing on the computer through the use of *layers,* the computerized equivalent of overlay drafting, it is important also to enable the recipient to see easily what has been revised.[9] There are many different ways of accomplishing this, especially when using computer technology. One possibility is the revisions can be printed in a different colored ink than the rest of the drawing and keeping a detailed log or form (as in Figure 15.6) of all revisions.

15.8 NOTES

Notes on the drawings are integral parts of the drawings themselves. The notes are really "specifications" of a sort and are as effective. These notations give certain information that cannot be shown advantageously, if at all, by the pictures alone. The line work and the notes together are to describe fully the work required. Notes should be clear, specific, complete, and as carefully worded as they appeared in the

---

[9]The process of making revisions was much more complicated before microcad systems. Because the drawings could not be modified and reprinted on a computer but had to be completely redrawn, revisions were often made directly on the prior drawing. The inefficiency of this is easily seen by the methods used to keep track of revisions made to manual drawings:

1. Have a form printed on the original tracing for use in the recording of any revisions, perhaps as shown in Fig. 15.6. As a part of this form have a space available for inserting the number of the revision, the date on which it was made, the name or initials of the person who made and checked it, and a note or two regarding the nature of the change. In addition, on the drawing itself, show in a small circle at the pertinent location the number of the revision. This enables the users of the drawing to determine in what respect it has been revised and to compare the altered version (as described in the printed form previously mentioned) with the original. The encircled number should remain as a permanent record on the tracing.
2. It is possible to identify the revisions directly on the tracing (preferably using pencil) and to mark on the back of the drawing so that what is added will not interferer with the original penciled or inked information. However, this general procedure is unsatisfactory when the drawing has to be changed more than once, since earlier changes encircled on the back of the tracing become difficult to distinguish from later ones.
3. Revisions may be encircled in colored pencil on the prints of the changed drawings. However, this procedure is likely to lead to errors unless all current prints are correctly marked. Also, this system does not provide an automatic aid in locating the alterations when additional prints are taken from the tracings at some later date.

BAR SCHEDULE FOR ONE PIER - 24 required											
Type	Location	Mark	No. req'd	Bar No.	Type	A	B	C	Length	Total lin. ft.	Remarks
	Footing	S1	6	4	Str.				6'-0"	36'	
	Footing	S2	8	4	I	3'-0"			4'-0"	32'	
	Footing	S3	8	6	II	3'-0"	6"		3'-4"	27'	A vertical
		S4	2	6	II	8'-3"	2'-9"		10'-10"	22'	A vertical
		S5	2	6	Str.				12'-3"	25'	
		S6	4	6	Str.				10'-6"	42'	
		S7	4	6	Str.				7'-9"	31'	
		S8	12	4	III	1'-2"	2'-8"	2'-8"	6'-6"	78'	
		S9	6	3	III	1'-2"	1'-9"	1'-9"	4'-6"	27'	
		S10	8	3	III	1'-2"	1'-0"	1'-0"	3'-0"	24'	

Note: Standard hooks and bends; pin diam. = 6d

Figure 15.5 Details of concrete pier and reinforcement.

printed specifications. When using CAD, notes are easily incorporated into the drawings by using the CAD software and/or a word-processing program.

In the preparation of data for any contract, questions will arise about whether particular instructions should be placed in the printed specifications, shown in the form of notes on the drawings, or both. The author of the contract documents should bear in mind that, when the field personnel or those in the shop are using prints of the drawings in order to detail or construct anything, they will be more likely to see the notes if they are right on the drawings rather than buried in a set of specifications. A search through the printed specifications for detailed instructions is sometimes neglected.

In general, instructions relate to what a drawing portrays, and if these instructions are to apply to some details of that particular drawing only, it is well to place the information in the form of notes directly on the drawing in question. For example, the note about cambering the roof truss shown in Fig. 15.2 is placed on the drawing because it refers to this truss only. On the other hand, if the instructions are common to a number of drawings, the information can be placed in the specifications, where it can be made applicable to any and all affected drawings. Thus, if certain bolts in one particular connection (alone) are to be "shouldered bolts with double nuts," an appropriate note should be placed only on the drawing where details of that connection are shown. But if "all field connections are to be high-strength bolts" tightened to produce a stipulated unit stress, this information need

Figure 15.5 Continued

not be repeated on each drawing that shows connections but should appear in the specifications. However, it is often advantageous to repeat this information in a set of general notes that is recorded on one drawing but is equally applicable to all if the other drawings are each inscribed: "For General Notes, See Drawing No. ___."

REVISIONS	NO.	MADE BY	DATE	DESCRIPTION	REVISIONS	NO.	MADE BY	DATE	DESCRIPTION
	6					1			
	7					2			
	8					3			
	9					4			
	10					5			

Figure 15.6   Form for record of revisions of a drawing.

QUESTIONS

1. What kinds of information are best given by way of contract drawings?

2. Is any particular size essential for contract drawings?

3. Which are more important, the line drawings or the accompanying notes?

4. What is a "record set" of contract drawings? What is its purpose? Where should it be kept?

5. Can contract drawings be supplemented by *(a)* the contractor? *(b)* the engineer?

6. After preparation of the drawings and specifications and issuance of all contract documents to the bidders, but before receipt of any proposals, the engineer discovered that one of the drawings contained a serious error. What should he do about the matter?

7. Why should the engineer state in the contract documents that he has the right to revise and to supplement the contract drawings? If he fails to make such a statement in these documents, will he be unable to revise or supplement the drawings?

8. What relation have "shop drawings" to "contract drawings"?

9. A dimension on a drawing showed the desired length of a truss to be 75 feet, but according to the scale of the drawing, the truss measured only 70 feet. Which (if either) can the contractor assume to be correct?

10. The drawing of a basement showed no drain around the outside, but a note in one corner of the drawing said: "Provide 4-inch drain and discharge line around foundation." Is the contractor obliged to install such a drain?

11. Why might an engineer want to have in his files a copy of each of the contract drawings for a factory that he has designed?

12. What is meant by "incorporation by reference"?

13. Why is it desirable to list the contract drawings in the specifications or in some other part of the contract documents? How should the listing be done?

14. After preparation of the specifications is completed but before the contract documents are issued to the bidders, the engineer decides to add two more drawings to the list of design drawings. Can he do so? Explain how.

15. What are "preliminary drawings," and how may they be used in connection with actual construction projects?

16. Differentiate between "design drawings" and "contract drawings."

17. Does the contractor generally prepare the "shop (or detail) drawings"? Can the engineer do so if he wishes to? Explain when and why the engineer might prefer to make them.

18. When the engineer revises the contract drawings, does he have to secure the contractor's approval?

19. Jones sent a freehand pencil sketch to Smith, a builder, showing the dimensions and other pertinent data for a garage that Jones wanted to have built. Smith quoted Jones a figure of $1500 for the complete job. Jones accepted the offer. Does the free-hand sketch constitute a contract drawing in this case? Explain.

20. In what way has computer-aided drafting and design changed the substantive rules, as opposed to the mechanics, of contract drawings?

21. Should CAD-produced drawings be saved on diskettes or printed?

22. How does the advent of CAD affect the rules regarding changes in drawings?

3

SOME LEGAL MATTERS OF CONCERN TO DESIGN PROFESSIONALS

This final group of chapters is designed to acquaint the reader with some of the highlights of selected legal subjects. Of course, space limitations preclude anything approaching comprehensive treatment of these topics. Since the purpose of this part is to give design professionals a look at the principles of law in those fields that would seem to hold the most interest and significance for them, a number of areas of legal concern, for example, domestic relations, criminal law, and wills and estates, are not touched upon at all or are considered only incidentally.

16

AGENCY

16.1   DEFINITIONS AND DISTINCTIONS

Agency can be described as acting through another. One party, called the *principal,* authorizes another, called the *agent,* to represent the former in certain business dealings with outsiders. Essentially, *agency* is a consensual relationship where the agent has the power to bind the principal, and the principal has the right to control the agent.

An agent differs from a servant or employee in that the agent has been appointed to act for his principal in transactions with third parties; the servant or employee normally exercises far less discretion than an agent and is under more detailed orders from the employer about exactly how the assigned work is to be performed. Thus, in the usual situation, the servant or employee is hired to do a specified job, typically of a "ministerial" nature (action performed under a superior with little reliance on the discretion of the doer), under well-defined restrictions, and is not entitled, for example, to enter into contracts on behalf of the employer. It is possible, of course, for an employee to be authorized also to undertake the separate function of an agent. By way of illustration, a gardener regularly employed to keep a homeowner's grounds in shape could be granted the right to purchase any needed supplies directly. When exercising the latter prerogative, the employee-gardener is filling the role of agent, and his employer-principal is responsible on the contractual obligations undertaken. The true agent acts for another and under such other's general control; when such an agent proceeds within the scope of his authority, the principal is bound.

A true *independent contractor* is neither an agent nor an employee, though his status bears resemblance to each. The independent contractor is hired to do a given job in return for a set charge. The method of accomplishing the specified result is totally at his discretion, and he is subject to the employer's control only in that the end product must meet the agreed-upon specifications. Since the party employing the independent contractor has no right to control performance details, he is not liable to outsiders for harm stemming from the negligence of the contractor or his employees. Exceptions to this rule do exist, however. Where, for example, the task that the independent contractor is asked to handle is hazardous in nature, the owner cannot divest himself of potential tort responsibility. Furthermore, even where the activity involved is not inherently dangerous, if the owner contracts with someone whom he knows or should know to be incompetent, he may be held liable for injury sustained by third parties in consequence of the contractor's faulty execution of the work.[1]

The determination of the status requires an examination of both the contract between and the actions of the parties.[2]

Various factors must be considered in determining whether a person acting for another is an independent contractor or an employee. One consideration is the degree of control retained by the individual doing the hiring.

A good example is a case[3] where a subcontractor's employee sued the owner when he was injured by the collapse of a steel structure at a construction site. The plaintiff contended that a design error resulted in the specification of undersized anchor bolts and that the contractor was negligent in directing his employees and subcontractors to install them. Since the owner did not retain control beyond ensuring contract compliance, liability, if any, rested with the contractor.[4]

Another is the intent of the parties who created the relationship in question. Still another is the method of payment; if "by the job," then it is some evidence of independent-contractor status.[5] Ownership of the tools used in the work may also be significant.

16.2   TRUSTEE DISTINGUISHED FROM AGENT

The essential distinction between a trustee and an agent is that the *trustee* holds legal title to the trust property, and his acts will not expose the beneficiary of the trust to personal liability, while the agent merely represents and acts for his principal. Although in both situations a fiduciary duty is owed, the trustee normally is given much greater discretion in decision making. The trustee is expected, of course, to manage and use the trust estate in accordance with the terms of the trust instrument and to the advantage of the named beneficiaries.

---

[1] *See,* for example, *Tytell v. Battery Beer Dist.,* 608 NYS.2d 225 (App. Div. 1994) where these exceptions arose when a delivery truck backed into a bridge support, debris fell on a pedestrian, and he then sued the owner, despite the contractor's status as an independent contractor.

Duties imposed on owners and contractors by statute may also be nondelegable. See *Elezaj v. P.J. Carlin Const. Co.* 638 NYS.2d 356 (App. Div. 1996).

[2] See *Daniels v. Mead Coated Board, Inc.* 858 F. Supp. 1103 (D. Ala. 1994) applying Alabama law, where the court noted that the mere monitoring of the work of an independent contractor to ensure contract compliance is not "control" for the purpose of establishing liability of an owner.

[3] *Horner v. Hammons,* 916 S.W.2d 810 (Mo. App. 1995).

[4] A relationship analogous to owner–contractor may exist between contractor and subcontractor when the contractor does not retain control over the operations of the subcontractor. *Lillis v. City of New York,* 641 N.Y.S.2d 358 (App. Div. 1996).

[5] Thus, a roofer hired at a certain contract price was held to be an independent contractor when the owner did not control or direct the work in *Barron v. Webb,* 698 So.2d 727 (La. App. 1997) where the homeowner was sued by one who stepped on a roofing nail on the owner's premises, left there by the roofer.

16.3 IMPORTANCE OF AGENCY

The subject of agency is of tremendous importance in the modern business world and affects virtually every form of commercial undertaking. Corporate affairs are necessarily handled by agents, since a corporation, by its very nature, can act only through its officers and employees. A contract of partnership is a contract of agency, differing from what could be termed a *pure agency* only in that in the latter the agent binds his principal only, while in a partnership arrangement each of the partners doubles as principal and agent, and the acts of each are binding on all.

16.4 CREATING THE AGENCY RELATIONSHIP

Agency is created by express or implied[6] contract or, less frequently, by operation of law, estoppel, or ratification.

Where the relationship rests upon contract, the principal must intend appointment of the agent, and the latter must intend to accept the appointment and act upon it. Similarly, the other requisites of an ordinary contractual arrangement are needed. Thus, the agency must not have been created to further an unlawful purpose, and contractual capacity of the parties may have to be demonstrated. A person may handle through an agent whatever business he has the legal capacity to conduct himself.

Some jurisdictions have statutes requiring that under certain conditions the agent's authority to act be given in writing. The usual instance involves a transfer of land interests, where, for example, the agent is to sign the deed. Illustrative is this New York provision, which reads in part:[7]

> As estate or interest in real property, other than a lease for a term not exceeding one year . . . cannot be created . . . unless by act or operation of law, or by a deed or conveyance in writing, subscribed by the person creating . . . the same, or *by his lawful agent, thereunto authorized by writing.* [italics supplied].

One familiar form of written authority to an agent is the *power of attorney.* An offshoot of this is the *proxy* so frequently used in the handling of corporate affairs.

16.5 AGENCY BY ESTOPPEL OR RATIFICATION

An agency relationship may be created *by estoppel.* When Smith so conducts her affairs as to lead outsiders to believe that Jones is her accredited agent, Smith will be estopped from denying the agency when the rights of third persons become involved through acts and behavior of Jones. Agency by estoppel rests upon repre-

---

[6]The implication arises from words and conduct of the parties and from circumstances of the particular case.
[7]*New York General Obligations Law,* §5—703 (McKinney 1978).

sentations of the principal and a change of position by some third person in reasonable reliance upon such representations. In the true estoppel situation the agent will be found to have no "real" authority (express or implied) but is deemed, rather, to possess "apparent" authority that the principal has knowingly permitted him to assume. Agency by estoppel is an artificial creature that justice imposes upon the unwilling principal. It should be distinguished from *implied agency,* which is as much actual agency as if it were created by express words. The principal is fully as liable to outsiders in the case of agency by estoppel as he is in the case of implied agency, but only in the former must third persons show actual reliance on the principal's conduct.

When the word *ratification* appears in connection with a discussion of agency, it is usually employed to identify the principal's decision to endorse certain acts by the agent in excess of the latter's authority.[8] Occasionally, however, mention is made of a principal–agent arrangement being effectuated by *ratification.* Thus, it might happen that Black, without any prior commitment from White, undertakes as agent to represent White in a series of transactions. Obviously, White is free to repudiate Black's actions. If, on the other hand, she retroactively assents or, saying nothing, accepts the benefits of any contracts Black has made on her behalf, it can be said that an agency by ratification has arisen. Like agency by appointment, but unlike agency by estoppel, agency by ratification requires consent of the principal.

16.6   GENERAL AND SPECIAL AGENCY

A *general agent* is one empowered to transact all the business of his principal, all the business of a designated type, or all the business at a particular location.

The authority of a *special agent* is confined to one or more specific acts. It is often said that an agency is special when both the end and the means are specific and when no continuity of service is involved. Typically, the special agent is retained to handle a single transaction and does so in accordance with definite instructions or within restrictions necessarily implied from the nature of the act to be performed.

The terms "general agent" and "special agent" are relative, and the line of demarcation is often difficult to draw. In addition to the powers actually conveyed to him, a general agent has, by implication, incidental authority to do whatever is customary and is reasonably necessary to accomplish the purpose at hand. Consequently, outsiders dealing with a general agent are entitled to rely upon the full scope of his apparent authority. The rule does not apply when actual limitations upon the powers of the general agent are known to the third person or are contained in a writing that he realizes is intended for his inspection. Misleading conduct on the part of the principal can alter the situation at any point.

---

[8]There is a marked distinction between (1) an estoppel to deny the validity of a contract and (2) ratification in fact of such contract. In the latter instance, the principal is bound because he intended to be; in the former, he is bound against his will in order that justice may be done in regard to the innocent third party.

Third parties who contemplate doing business with a special agent must determine the precise extent of his authority, since a special agent does not have the broad powers of a general agent and the situations in which a third party is protected by reasonable reliance on his representations are more limited. A bank teller illustrates a common type of special agent with familiar and limited powers. He operates under a specific grant of authority, his duties are outlined with exactness, and his position is not such that any implication of undefined powers can legitimately arise.

Generally, neither general nor special agent can bind his principal unless such agent is acting within the confines of his authority. However, a principal is responsible for all proper undertakings by his agent, even if occasioned by a mistake, and regardless of whether the authorization is actual or apparent. Many times an agent will bind his principal through the exercise of apparent authority in spite of the fact that he violated secret instructions given him by the principal. Such conduct by the agent may render him answerable in damages to the principal.

16.7 POSITION OF THE AGENT

Every agent has certain obligations toward his principal. He must display the utmost loyalty and good faith. He must obey instructions and attempt not to exceed his authority. He is expected to utilize reasonable care and skill in fulfilling his duties, and he is obliged to account to his principal whenever the latter requests and when the agency is terminated. All profits arising from the undertaking are deemed to belong to the principal, unless otherwise agreed between the parties.

The agent is expected to communicate all information that he acquires in the course of his agency and that affects the subject matter of that agency. By no means may the agent compete with his principal. Thus, he may not profit at the principal's expense by using knowledge of the principal's business acquired while acting in a confidential capacity. Similarly, the agent is not allowed to indulge in "self-dealing." For example, an agent who is authorized to make a certain type of purchase cannot secretly buy the commodity from himself. Should this rule ever be violated the principal can rescind the transaction for fraud and recover the purchase price.

In order to bind his principal, the agent must have acted within the scope of his authority. When a particular act of the agent's is not an authorized one, the principal may elect to ratify it, thus rendering the situation the same as though the agent had possessed sufficient authority. Should the principal decline to ratify the agent's overreaching, the latter is potentially liable to any outsiders misled by his claim of authority. The principal, however, cannot repudiate his agent's action as unauthorized and yet retain for himself the fruits of such action.

The agent is generally answerable to injured outsiders for affirmative acts of negligence (that is, *misfeasance*), but not for passive negligence (that is, *nonfeasance*). An agent guilty of intentional torts of any sort is liable in damages to the victim.

16.8   POSITION OF THE PRINCIPAL

It is a fundamental proposition in law that a principal is liable on all contracts made by his agent while that individual is acting within the scope of his actual or apparent authority. Conversely, when the agent makes such a contract in the name of his principal, the principal can hold the third party to the bargain. Also, as previously noted, unauthorized acts of an agent may be ratified by the principal and thus become binding upon the latter.

Generally, the principal is charged with constructive notice[9] of facts acquired by the agent in the course of his duties, although knowledge will not be imputed when the agent is perpetrating an independent fraud or is otherwise acting adversely to his principal's interest. Additionally, information received by the agent prior to his undertaking the agency relationship will not be imputed to the principal.

The principal has certain basic responsibilities toward his agent, perhaps the most significant of which is the duty to give reasonable compensation for services rendered. Also, the principal is expected to indemnify the agent for injury suffered in the course of conducting the principal's business in line with his instructions. An agent must assume for himself the more commonplace risks, such as that of loss of personal funds through theft.

In the field of torts, the principal is liable for acts of negligence committed by the agent while the latter was operating within the scope of his authority and in furtherance of the principal's business. For nonwillful torts, it is immaterial that the agent was performing his function in an irregular manner or even contrary to explicit instructions.

Where the agent's misconduct is willful, a third party seeking to hold the principal liable must show that the tort involved is reasonably incidental to the performance of the duties assigned to the agent. This normally proves a difficult burden for plaintiff, since there is a presumption that the agent was not employed with the expectation that he would commit intentional torts.

16.9   THE UNDISCLOSED PRINCIPAL

Whenever a duly authorized agent enters into a contractual arrangement without disclosing his true role or the identity of his principal, the third party, upon discovering the facts of the situation, can hold the agent or, in most instances, may elect to hold the *undisclosed principal* liable. The doctrine works in reverse, also, and with a few exceptions the undisclosed principal may decide to reveal his interest in the contract and enforce performance by the third party. One of the exceptions comes about when the third party has previously refused to deal with the principal and the latter thereupon attempts to achieve his ends surreptitiously through an agent, who is told not to indicate for whom he is acting. In such a situation, the contract cannot be enforced by the undisclosed principal against the deceived third

---

[9] That is, he will be presumed to know, whether or not he has actual knowledge.

party. An agent is likewise liable in contract to outsiders when he pretends to represent a nonexistent principal.

16.10 SUBAGENTS

A principal selects a particular person to act as his agent, and the selection is presumably made on the basis of the agent's known competence and trustworthiness. The principal, accordingly, is entitled to have his affairs receive the personal attention of the person chosen for the job. Thus, it is said that "authority delegated to an agent cannot be further delegated by him to a subagent,"[10] assuming, of course, that the principal has not expressly empowered the agent to delegate. The prohibition, however, relates only to matters involving the exercise of discretion and does not extend to so-called ministerial acts. For example, the agent is normally free to utilize office workers to help him with such things as bookkeeping.

16.11 TERMINATION OF THE AGENCY

An agency relationship may end by (1) death of either principal or agent, (2) destruction of the subject matter of the agency, (3) fulfillment of the particular purpose for which the agency was formed, (4) expiration of a time period set in the contract, (5) supervening illegality of the agency's purpose, (6) mutual consent, and (7) unilateral termination by one party or the other.[11]

Agency is a voluntary relationship and, as such, may with reasonable notice be terminated at will by either party, without such party incurring damages for breach. However, if the contract between principal and agent has a stipulated duration, it may only be freely renounced for cause prior to the expiration of the period set. Lacking justifiable cause, the party breaching would be liable in damages. "Specific performance" of personal-service contracts will not be granted and the innocent party in a breach situation can secure damages but cannot force the other party to fulfill the precise contract obligation. But if an agent whose services are unique fails to carry out his contract with the principal, the agent may be enjoined from working during the remaining period of the breached contract for one of his principal's competitors.

An *irrevocable agency* is specifically enforceable on the ground that otherwise the injured party would be irreparably damaged. If the agency is "coupled with an interest," then it is deemed irrevocable. The "interest" referred to is an interest on the very subject matter of the agency, and not merely in the right to earn compensation or commission stemming from the exercise of the agency.

---

[10] *"delegato potestor non potest delagari."*

[11] A principal who is terminating the authority of his agent should attempt to ensure that interested third parties also receive notification.

The phrase "coupled with an interest" does not mean an interest in the exercise of the power, but rather an interest in the property on which the power is to operate.[12] The test is whether or not the agent has an interest in the subject matter of the agency independent of the power conferred.[13]

The Restatement of Agency, 2nd, Section 138, sets forth the requirements for the creation of an agency or power coupled with interest. They are (1) that the agency be held for the benefit of the agent not the principal, (2) that the agency is created to secure the performance of a duty to the agent or to protect title in the agent, and (3) that the agency is created at the time that the duty or title is created or is given for consideration.

In a case from California,[14] where the plaintiff, an architect, had been discharged by an architectural firm, these conditions were held not to have been fulfilled where the architect was not a stockholder in the firm at the time he was hired, and later acquired stock, and sued his employer, and was then dismissed when he refused to drop the suit. The plaintiff's employment, the court said, was not provided to him as a vehicle for protecting any interest he had in the company.

Let us assume that *A* has an idea of running a trucking business and gets *B* to put up the money. *A* secures a five-year contract as manager, with base salary plus a percentage of the profits. Is the arrangement irrevocable? Probably so. *A*'s argument would be that she will not make sufficient profits from the undertaking unless she is personally allowed to handle the selling end as manager. Thus she has power coupled with an interest.

The case of *French v. Kensico Cemetery*[15] will serve as a further illustration. For some years, plaintiff had paid defendant cemetery various amounts for the current care and maintenance of a plot and mausoleum. To avoid the necessity of further annual payments, plaintiff turned over to defendant $5,000, obtaining a receipt that spelled out defendant's obligation to invest the principal in securities and to use the income for perpetual care of plaintiff's plot and mausoleum. Eventually plaintiff attempted to cancel the arrangement and get back her "deposit." The Appellate Division, in holding for defendant, spoke as follows:

> Our conclusion is that the delivery of the money and the giving of the receipt constituted an agreement which created an agency (or a power) coupled with an interest in defendant and that if the agreement was founded on a sufficient consideration, it is irrevocable by plaintiff. The consideration moving from defendant was its undertaking to relieve plaintiff of the trouble and annoyance of attending to the care and maintenance of the property.
>
> Defendant's interest in the performance of the agreement is that if it is not performed as long as there is need for care and maintenance, defendant will be obliged to carry that burden, since no well-managed cemetery could depreciate its property and that of other lot owners by having on its premises a mausoleum in

---

[12]*Ogunwo v. Amer. Nat. Ins. Co.,* 936 P.2d 606 (Colo. App. 1997).

[13]*Peacock v. American Agronomics Corporation,* 422 So.2d 55 (Fla. App. 1982).

[14]*Becket v. Welton Becket & Assoc.,* 39 Cal. App.3d 815, 114 Cal. Rptr. 531 (1974).

[15]264 App. Div. 617, 35 N.Y.S.2d 826, 828–29 (2d Dept. 1942), *affirmed,* 291 N.Y. 77 (1943).

process of falling into decay and ruin upon a considerable plot, with grass uncared for and running to weeds. . .

In our opinion, the delivery of the money and the giving of the receipt created in the defendant an agency coupled with an interest, irrevocable so long as the need for care and maintenance of the plot and mausoleum continues to exist. That need is manifestly a permanent one. If plaintiff should be permitted to revoke the agency and to obtain the return of the money, defendant would be compelled to assume the duty of care and maintenance in its own interest. An agency may not be revoked where revocation would subject the agent to liability without fault of his part.

The concept of agency is very important to the professional engineer, contractor, or architect because it is a legal relationship established by the facts, regardless of the nomenclature chosen by the parties. It should be determined, therefore, whether those with whom one works are agents, employees, or independent contractors. Such a designation defines the rights, duties, and liabilities of the parties to each other as well as third persons. Knowing this in advance and structuring such a relationship with these concerns in mind may protect the professional from tort and contract liability.

Questions

1. Describe the agency relationship and how it is created.
2. What are the duties, rights, and obligations of *(a)* an agent? *(b)* a principal?
3. Distinguish between "agency," on the one hand, and "employer and employee" (or "master and servant") on the other.
4. Explain the differences between an agent and an independent contractor.
5. Distinguish between an "agent" and a "trustee."
6. Distinguish between the rights and duties of *(a)* a "general agent" and *(b)* a "special agent." Illustrate both types of agency.
7. What are implied powers in connection with an agency? Illustrate.
8. List several purposes for which an agency may be created.
9. When and how may an agency be terminated? Give illustrations.
10. May an employer discharge his employee when he wishes to do so? May a principal do likewise with his agent?
11. Does an agent have authority to use his own discretion?
12. Can a servant or employee make contracts on behalf of his employer?
13. Can a person be an employee and at the same time be appointed to act as agent?
14. How may one determine whether a given person acting for another is an employee, agent, or independent contractor?
15. In the usual case, which has more in the way of discretionary powers, an agent or a trustee?

16. Can an agency be created by implication as well as by express contract? Explain.

17. Must an agency always be created by means of a writing? Elaborate.

18. Explain and illustrate how an agency may be established through estoppel.

19. An agent does something beyond his authority. Has the principal the power to ratify the unauthorized action? If so, what would be the effect of ratification?

20. Distinguish between the principal's being bound by "estoppel" and his being bound by "ratification."

21. Explain and illustrate "agency of necessity."

22. Is the principal as much bound by acts of a general agent as he is by those of a special agent?

23. Under what conditions may an agency be irrevocable?

24. Whipple is an engineer in private practice. She appoints Monroe to act as her agent in securing business. Has Whipple this right? Can Monroe properly hire Appleton to assist? May Monroe appoint Appleton to represent Whipple as Monroe's agent? As Whipple's agent? Explain.

25. *A* is an agent for *B,* a realtor. *A* agrees to sell *C*'s house but, unknown to *B,* for a "bargain-rate" commission of $400. After the house is sold, *B* demands that *C* pay the standard commission—$500. Must *C* pay the extra $100? Give reasons.

26. Perkins, an agent for Quade, agreed that his principal would design a large store for Dunford for the sum of $2000. It soon became obvious that the job could not be done properly for anything like this figure. Is Quade bound by the arrangement made for him by Perkins? Explain.

27. If Carter has some very hazardous blasting to do, can she, by letting a contract for this work to Dawson, shift to the contractor all responsibility for possible damages to persons and property? Explain fully.

28. Suppose the agent, exceeding his authority, has made certain contracts on behalf of the principal which the latter declines to accept. Has the third party any recourse against *(a)* the principal, *(b)* the agent?

29. Blodgett is on a trip for her principal, Franklin. Just before Blodgett, as agent, signs an agreement with Gordon regarding the purchase of 20,000 tons of coal, Franklin dies. What is the legal situation; that is, is there a binding contract?

30. If an agent quits without cause and before expiration of the contract of agency, can the principal *(a)* compel specific performance; *(b)* collect damages?

17

PARTNERSHIPS

17.1 NATURE OF A GENERAL PARTNERSHIP

The Uniform Partnership Act[1] defines the ordinary partnership as "an association of two or more persons to carry on as co-owners a business for profit." Partnership arrangements, which normally are geared for a considerable period of time, feature community of interest in profits, losses, and the capital employed, as well as joint control of the operation. When a person has contracted for proprietary rights in a business, he is an *owner* thereof, and, if there are other owners of the same business, he is by definition a *partner*. Apparent intent of the parties, profit sharing, and mutual control are three factors bearing upon the existence of a partnership.

Each member of an ordinary partnership has certain rights that are specifically governed by the partnership agreement. Among them are:

1. Right to share in the management and control of the firm's operations.

2. Right to share in profits.

3. Right of co-ownership of specific partnership property. (Each partner is entitled to use the property for any *partnership* purpose. He is, however, essentially a fiduciary as respects his associates and must account to them for any personal profit realized through his private use of the firm's assets.)

4. Power to act as agent for the partnership.

5. Right of contribution from his associates in case he personally makes payments on partnership accounts.

Although it has its own assets and carries on its own business activities, a partnership, unlike a corporation, is not treated as a legal entity separate from the individuals composing it.[2]

---

[1] This act, Sec. 101 (6), originally approved by the National Conference of Commissioners on Uniform State Laws in 1914 and revised in 1994, has now been adopted in one form or another by all states except Louisiana.

[2] An exception is the Federal Bankruptcy Act, which treats partnerships as legal persons, and the firm itself may be adjudged a bankrupt, either separately or jointly with one or more of its general partners.

A most significant aspect of a partnership is the personal liability of each of the partners for debts of the enterprise, as compared with a stockholder of a corporation, whose liability is limited to his capital investment.

Each partner acts as principal for himself and as agent for his copartners. He may enter into any agreement that is within his actual or apparent authority, and the firm will be bound to honor such agreement. In other words, each partner has full power to act for the group in entering into obligations in the course of business. It can readily be seen that partnership carries with it some elements of danger. Consequently, one should exercise caution in selecting partners, and the partnership agreement should be drawn with great care. *Delectus personae* ("choice of the person") is the essence of partnership as a special form of business association; no outsider can join a partnership without first securing the consent of each of the members. Therefore, while a partner may assign his right to profits[3] and his right to share in any surplus available upon dissolution of the business, he may not effectively convey his partnership interest in the sense of entitling the assignee to a role in management of partnership affairs.

17.2   ARTICLES OF PARTNERSHIP

Unless a statute states otherwise, it is possible to form a partnership by oral agreement. However, written *articles of partnership,* signed by the parties and setting forth the terms and conditions of the agreement, provide the customary method of formalizing the agreement. An oral contract of partnership is, under the usual statute of frauds, unenforceable if it is to last more than a year. If the parties commence operations under a long-term oral contract, a *partnership at will* is deemed in effect. Such an arrangement is perfectly legal but may *without penalty* be terminated by any party at any time. Oral contracts for periods of less than a year are outside the purview of the statute of frauds. These understandings are binding and, lacking unanimous consent, can be abrogated during the contract term only at the risk of damages for breach.

Quite apart from any statutory considerations, it is advisable as a matter of common sense for the partners to have a written memorandum of agreement, fixing among themselves their respective rights, duties, and liabilities and thus reducing the likelihood of controversy. The partners may include in their formal articles any agreement they wish respecting such things as sharing of profits and losses, priorities of distribution on winding up the business, and other such details. Articles of partnership vary widely in the subjects they cover and in the degree of detail involved; much depends upon the nature and scope of the enterprise. A typical list of contents for a partnership agreement might include:

1. Name of the firm and names of the copartners.
2. Nature and location of the business to be carried on.

---

[3]See Section 17.10.

3. Date the enterprise will commence operations and intended duration of the partnership.

4. Statement of capital and the amount and nature of each partner's contribution.

5. Designation of services to be rendered by each member and statement about compensation, if any.[4]

6. Management of the business—duties and restrictions.

7. Statement of the respective shares of the several partners in profits and losses.

8. Statement about banking matters, keeping books of account, making periodic inventories, and so on.

9. Provision for arbitration of disputes, frequently "in accordance with the rules of the American Arbitration Association."

10. Designation of the rights of the parties upon dissolution and statement about the method to be employed in the final winding up. (It is particularly important to indicate what result is to follow upon the death of a partner, since, absent express agreement to the contrary, a partnership is dissolved by the death of one of its partners. Many agreements provide the surviving associate an option between purchasing the decedent's interest and liquidating the enterprise.)

At any point, any or all of the provisions in the partnership agreement can be amended, waived, or abrogated by consent of all the partners.

17.3 EACH PARTNER AS AGENT OF THE FIRM

By virtue of the partnership relation, each member has the capacity to bind his firm by all acts and representations within the scope of its business. The point is thus expressed in Section 301 of the Uniform Partnership Act:

(1) Each partner is an agent of the partnership for the purpose of its business. An act of a partner, including the execution of an instrument in the partnership name, for apparently carrying on in the ordinary course the partnership business or business of the kind carried on by the partnership binds the partnership, unless the partner had no authority to act for the partnership in the particular matter and the person with whom the partner was dealing knew or had received a notification that the partner lacked authority.

(2) An act of a partner which is not apparently for carrying on in the ordinary course the partnership business or business of the kind carried on by the partnership binds the partnership only if the act was authorized by the other partners.

---

[4]Partners are not entitled to charge each other or the firm for personal services unless there is a special agreement permitting them to do so. However, the Uniform Partnership Act, § 401(h) allows a surviving partner "reasonable compensation" for his efforts in winding up the firm's affairs.

The articles of partnership may purport to place definite limitations on the powers of a member of the firm, but such restrictions are ineffective with regard to third parties who deal with a partner unaware of any curtailment of his apparent full and complete authority to bind the partnership. On the other hand, limitations thus imposed by the partnership agreement *are* effective with such third persons who are aware of the true situation and among the partners themselves.

Since each member of the partnership acts as agent of the whole, it follows that notice of anything relating to affairs of the enterprise duly given to any one partner constitutes communication to the partnership itself. Similarly, information which a member has acquired in a partnership transaction is considered to be in the possession of the partnership.

17.4 OVERREACHING BY A PARTNER

While a partner, in his role of agent of the firm, has power to bind his copartners by any acts within his apparent authority, it is possible for him to go too far. Thus, for example, he may not properly give the firm's note in payment of a personal debt nor charge the partnership for property purchased by him for his individual use. Nor is he entitled, without the express consent of each of his copartners, to make a general assignment for the benefit of the concern's creditors or to take action of any sort which would make it impossible to carry on the ordinary business of the partnership. Where a partner has breached his obligations to his associates, the ordinary and appropriate remedy is an accounting in the course of dissolving the firm.

17.5 TORT LIABILITY

Responsibility for a partnership tort is joint and several in the sense that every member of the firm is individually liable and that the victim may proceed against all the partners jointly or against such of the partners as he chooses. Under these circumstances, recovery is obviously not dependent upon the personal wrong of the particular member against whom the claim happens to be asserted.

Whether the tort involved is truly a partnership tort, and thus one for which the various members will be liable, depends upon whether the wrong was committed within the ordinary course of the partnership's business. That a given tort is willful in nature does not necessarily preclude its having been committed in the course of the firm's business. More typically, the tortuous conduct with respect to which the partnership is sought to be charged stems from the negligent operation of a motor vehicle by one of the partners. It is often a close question whether, at the crucial time, the partner was engaged in an undertaking related to the firm's business as distinguished from his own purposes.

17.6   CONTRACT LIABILITY

Unlike the situation in regard to partnership torts, the liability of members for partnership contracts is said to be *joint* only. That is, where the alleged obligation is contractual, all partners can be said to be necessary parties. Although for most purposes a partnership is not an entity separate from its members, statutes in many jurisdictions provide that persons carrying on business as partners may sue or be sued in the partnership name.[5] Such laws amount to a recognition of partnerships as legal entities for procedural purposes.

A contractual obligation running to the partnership is regarded at common law as the joint right of the various partners. An action to enforce such must consequently be brought in the names of all the partners unless statute permits suit to be filed in the firm's name. Suits on partnership claims must be brought on behalf of the firm. A partner may not in his individual capacity recover upon obligations owed his firm.

17.7   INCOMING AND RETIRING GENERAL PARTNERS

One who is brought into a going business as a new partner is not personally liable on preexisting obligations of the firm unless he expressly assumes such personal liability.[6] On the other hand, under the Uniform Partnership Act his share in the partnership property is clearly available for the satisfaction of these old debts.

Unless there is an understanding by which the creditors agree to substitute the credit of an incoming member for that of a retiring general partner, the latter remains liable for the firm's obligations outstanding at the time of his withdrawal. Furthermore, as for subsequently incurred obligations, the former partner may find himself answerable to third parties who are unaware of his retirement and have continued to deal with the concern. To be fully effective, a retiring general partner's notice of withdrawal requires (1) personal notification to those who dealt with the firm during his tenure and (2) notice by publication to others in the area. If the associate who is retiring was a "dormant" partner, he need not give notice to creditors as a prerequisite to escaping liability for partnership debts arising in the future. A dormant partner is usually so inactive in partnership affairs that his connection with the firm is generally unknown. Nevertheless, he is in most respects a full-fledged partner and, as such, is liable for all partnership obligations incurred during his association with the enterprise.

---

[5]See, for example, New York Civil Practice Law and Rules, § 1025 (1997).

[6]In return for admission to the firm, the new member may have promised his copartners or a retiring member that preexisting claims would be paid in full. Such a promise could presumably be enforced against the incoming partner by the creditors concerned, using a third-party-beneficiary approach.

17.8   TERMINATION OF THE PARTNERSHIP

Termination is a two-step process: first comes *dissolution* of the firm, and then *winding up* of its activity.

There are a number of situations that would occasion dissolution of the ordinary partnership. Perhaps the most common of these are (1) death, bankruptcy, or withdrawal of a general partner; (2) mutual consent of the firm members; and (3) expiration of the time for which the partnership was formed.[7] Notification regarding the dissolution should go to those with whom the firm has had dealings. Dissolution in itself has no effect upon existing liabilities of the partnership.

A dissolved partnership retains its existence in the eyes of the law until the winding-up process is completed. This entails such actions as payment of debts, collection of accounts receivable, and fulfillment of commitments undertaken prior to dissolution. The surviving partner, engaged in liquidating the business, will find his powers and duties governed largely by the probate and partnership laws in the particular jurisdiction. Under the Uniform Partnership Act, the death of one partner means that his right in and to specific assets of the firm vests in the surviving partner or partners; however, the legal representative of the deceased has a right to an accounting from the surviving partner or partners from the date of death.[8] If the deceased was himself the last survivor, title passes to his legal representatives.

In reducing the partnership property to cash and distributing the proceeds, certain priorities must be recognized:

1. First come creditors of the firm other than partners.[9]

2. Next are the claims of partners for loans and advances beyond the amount of their agreed capital contributions.

3. After the foregoing categories of claims have been satisfied, under the usual partnership agreement members are entitled to a return of their respective capital contributions. If there is insufficient property available for this purpose, the loss is normally to be shared by the solvent partners in the proportions in which they were supposed to share profits. By way of illustration, assume that partners *X*, *Y*, and *Z* have subscribed, respectively, $20,000, $10,000, and $4,000 of the concern's $34,000 capital and that the articles of partnership called for sharing profits equally. Assume further that, upon dissolution and the settlement of debts, there remained $10,000, which represented a capital loss of $24,000. Equal sharing means a debit to each partner of $8,000. Therefore, *X* would get $12,000 and *Y* $2,000, while *Z* would pay in an extra $4,000 to meet the deficiency.

4. If the dissolved partnership has been a very successful enterprise, and some undistributed assets remain after the various demands outlined above are taken care of, the balance will be disposed of among the partners in the form of profits. In the

---

[7]The partners, of course, are free to ignore the fact that the winding-up date originally agreed upon has been reached and may simply carry on indefinitely. Continuance under these circumstances really amounts to an implied agreement for a *partnership at will* under the same terms as initially set.

[8]*Hansel v. Hansel,* 446 A.2d 1294 (Pa. Super. 1982).

[9]Should the firm's assets prove inadequate to meet liabilities, the individual partners must, under certain circumstances, themselves contribute to make up the difference. See the subsequent discussion in this article.

marshaling of assets, partnership creditors have priority over partnership assets but creditors of an individual partner are generally recognized as having priority with respect to that partner's individual assets. If such creditors' claims are not fully satisfied from an individual partner's personal assets, they can reach their debtor's share of whatever surplus firm assets might be left undisturbed after the firm's business has been finally settled. They have no legitimate claim against such firm assets until an accounting of the debtor-partner's interest has been made. This cross-application principle works both ways. If the partnership lacks the finances to satisfy its creditors, and one of the partners has personal assets available after paying his individual creditors, these assets can be claimed to meet the firm's needs.

17.9 LIMITED PARTNERSHIP

A limited partnership, which must be formed strictly in accordance with applicable statutes,[10] has at least one *general* partner and one or more *limited* (or *special*) partners; the latter contribute cash or property as investors but do not contribute services and have no powers of management.

The principal object of limited partnership is to protect the special partner by exempting him from general liability and placing only his invested capital in jeopardy. The limited partner has certain rights by virtue of his position. Among these are the right to share in the firm's profits and to seek return of his capital contribution upon dissolution of the business. In the absence of a definitive provision in the limited partnership agreement, the interest of a limited partner is assignable, with the assignee acquiring the right to receive the share of the profits to which the assignor would otherwise have been entitled. As long as he avoids active conduct of firm affairs, the special partner's liability for obligations of the firm is limited to the amount of his investment. Any show of management interference, however, will cost him his cloak of partial immunity and render him fully liable as a general partner. Section 303 of the Limited Partnership Act (1976) says that a limited partner who is not also a general partner does not participate in the control of the business solely by doing one or more of the following:

(1) being a contractor for or an agent or employee of the limited partnership or of a general partner or being an officer, director, or shareholder of a general partner that is a corporation;
(2) consulting with and advising a general partner with respect to the business of the limited partnership;
(3) acting as surety for the limited partnership or guaranteeing or assuming one or more specific obligations of the limited partnership;
(4) taking any action required or permitted by law to bring or pursue a derivative action in the right of the limited partnership;

---

[10]The Uniform Limited Partnership Act, was originally approved by the National Conference of Commissioners on Uniform Laws in 1916 and underwent revision in 1976. It has now been adopted in some form by all states except Louisiana.

(5) requesting or attending a meeting of partners;

(6) proposing, approving, or disapproving, by voting or otherwise, one or more of the following matters:

   (i) the dissolution and winding up of the limited partnership;

   (ii) the sale, exchange, lease, mortgage, pledge, or other transfer of all or substantially all of the assets of the limited partnership;

   (iii) the incurrence of indebtedness by the limited partnership other than in the ordinary course of its business;

   (iv) a change in the nature of the business;

   (v) the admission or removal of a general partner;

   (vi) the admission or removal of a limited partner;

   (vii) a transaction involving an actual or potential conflict of interest between a general partner and the limited partnership or the limited partners;

   (viii) an amendment to the partnership agreement or certificate of limited partnership; or

   (ix) matters related to the business of the limited partnership not otherwise enumerated [here], which the partnership agreement states in writing may be subject to the approval or disapproval of limited partners;

(7) winding up the limited partnership pursuant to Section 803; or

(8) exercising any right or power permitted to limited partners under this [Act] and not specifically enumerated [here].

Further, this enumeration does not mean that the possession or exercise of any other powers by a limited partner constitutes participation by him in the business of a limited partnership.

Like corporations, limited partnerships were unknown to the common law and are purely creatures of statute. The statutory requirements must be closely followed if the special partner is to achieve and retain his privileged status. The law in many jurisdictions requires each limited partnership to file a certificate setting forth all substantive provisions of the limited-partnership agreement.

In various respects a *lender* is in a better position than a limited partner. The lender often finds it possible to exercise some measure of control over the firm that is indebted to him, while the limited partner must leave the control to others. Moreover, upon dissolution of the partnership and distribution of its assets, the lender (as a general creditor of the firm) enjoys the highest priority.

17.10   SUBPARTNERSHIP

A *contract of subpartnership* is an agreement between a partner and an outsider, called a *subpartner,* whereby the latter is to share on an agreed basis (with the partner) profits and losses arising from such partner's association with the firm. That is, the subpartner agrees to participate in the contracting partner's share only.

The subpartner performs no active function, nor has he any power of control over the partnership affairs. Since his contract is on a purely personal basis with an individual partner, the "sub" is not directly liable to partnership creditors as a co-obligor on the firm's commitments. He is in no sense a member of the firm and has no contractual relationship with partners other than the one with whom he has made the profit-and-loss arrangement.

QUESTIONS

1. What are the fundamental rights and privileges and the potential liability of ordinary partners?

2. Explain the difference between a general partnership and a partnership. Illustrate.

3. What are the rights and obligations of an underage partner?

4. Are partnerships subject to the same governmental supervision as corporations?

5. How can the existence of a true partnership arrangement be proved or disproved?

6. List the several points that should be covered in the average partnership agreement.

7. What is the usual procedure for bringing new partners into a firm?

8. How and for what reasons may a partnership be terminated?

9. If a partnership is liquidated, how are its assets disposed of? What are the respective priorities of creditors of the firm and of creditors of an individual partner?

10. What are the powers, rights, and liabilities of *(a)* a general partner? *(b)* a limited partner? *(c)* a subpartner?

11. When several persons are contemplating formation of a partnership, how important is it for each to consider the character and personality of his prospective associates?

12. If one has entered into a partnership, is he bound by the acts of his copartners?

13. What is the purpose of the Uniform Partnership Act?

14. Is a partner an agent for his copartners?

15. Why is it desirable to have written articles of partnership?

16. What is the procedure in connection with a partner's retirement?

17. What is a subpartner, and what in general are the rights and obligations that go along with that role?

18. What are the advantages of a limited liability partnership? How does one differ from a limited partnership?

19. Black, Brown, and White were partners and carried on a small business manufacturing precast-concrete products, cinder blocks, and such. Black, without the knowledge of her partners, agreed to sell the business to Gray. Can Brown and White block the sale, and why? If Black's deal were to sell Gray $10,000 worth of blocks for $8,000, what could Brown and White do about the matter?

20. The partnership of Duncan, Howard, and Kearny was in debt for $100,000. What courses of action could the creditors pursue? With firm assets insufficient, can individual assets of the several partners be moved against?

21. *A, B,* and *C* formed a partnership to conduct certain business for five years. What steps, if any, are necessary to continue the relationship beyond the period originally stipulated?

chapter

18

CORPORATIONS

18.1   TYPES OF CORPORATIONS

Although the private stock corporation for the purpose of conducting business is the most common, corporate organizations are of different types and are formed to serve a variety of purposes. The basic distinction lies between *public* and *private* corporations. Public corporations are founded by a governmental unit and belong to it. Both a municipal corporation (that is, a city or a town) and an incorporated school district typify this category. The creating authority confers whatever powers and imposes whatever restrictions the public may require upon such corporate entities.

Corporations that are not truly public are considered *private.* However, there are also corporations popularly called "quasi-public," examples of which are the telephone, water, and power companies. Quasi-public corporations are subject to particularly strict regulation because their operations directly affect the public interest. Normally, however, public utilities are conducted for private gain and are properly classed as private rather than as public corporations despite the fact that they are commonly vested with certain powers of a public nature, such as that of eminent domain.

Within the broad category of private corporations are those with and without capital stock. The latter are known as *membership corporations* and include the bulk of the charitable, social, and educational organizations.

Professional Corporations   Until relatively recently, anyone, subject to age and residence requirements, could form a corporation for any lawful purpose *except for conducting a profession,* as it was felt that the highly personal and confidential relationship between a lawyer and client or doctor and patient imposed a standard not consistent with the ordinary commercial relationship. Today most jurisdictions allow persons engaged in the practice of professions to form professional corporations.[1] Some states require only a license for professional activity to qualify to form

---

[1] *See,* for example, Calif. Corp. Code § 13400–13410 (1997). Sec. 13401 specifically permits professional incorporation of persons licensed by the California Board of Architectural Examiners.

a professional corporation while others confer "professional" status on vocations not ordinarily considered professions and not usually requiring a license.

The majority of states require that the shareholders be licensed to render the service offered by the corporation. A few states also require the stockholders to be employed by the corporation.

Aside from tax and retirement advantages available in some circumstances, professional incorporation may offer attractive limits on professional liability, although not always to the extent of the ordinary corporation. The majority of states provide that the shareholder is liable for his own torts and those of employees directly under his supervision. A minority of states provide that all shareholders of a professional corporation are personally liable for the torts of all members, thus nullifying all aspects of limited liability enjoyed by ordinary corporations.

The majority rule with respect to contract liability is that liability is unchanged from that in a partnership. Some jurisdictions impose contract liability on the corporations for corporation debts and obligations, thus limiting the shareholders' liability to the capital invested. A minority view holds the shareholder personally liable in the corporation's contract obligations if he participates in the transaction.

"Foreign" Corporations   Frequently a corporation organized in and authorized by state *A* desires to extend its activity to states *B* and *C* as well. In that event, it must secure a "certificate of authority" or other document of permission from each of these other jurisdictions and must meet whatever requirements they impose upon such a "foreign" corporation in return for its enjoying the privilege of doing business within their confines. Normally, this will entail such things as filing a copy of the articles of incorporation, designating a local resident (typically the secretary of state) as agent for service of process, and paying fees.

18.2   DEFECTIVELY FORMED CORPORATIONS

When a corporation is created in accordance with any and all applicable requirements of law, the corporation is referred to as one of de jure. It sometimes happens, though, that compliance with the pertinent laws, while substantially complete, is defective in some regard. Where the deviations are relatively minor, the corporation will be treated as one "in fact," or de facto, and its right to operate can be attacked only in a direct proceeding brought by the state. Four prerequisites are commonly cited to test a defectively formed corporation claiming de facto status:

1. Existence of an enabling act or valid law under which the particular type of corporation involved might be organized.

2. "Colorable compliance" with such law, meaning a bona fide attempt to incorporate thereunder (as by filing the necessary papers with the Secretary of State, etc.).

3. Good-faith belief on the part of the prime movers in the enterprise that incorporation has indeed been achieved.

4. Actual operation of the corporate franchise.

In the eyes of the law, a de facto corporation differs from a de jure one only in that the former alone is vulnerable to a direct ouster proceeding at the instance of the state.

Recently, however, some states have by statute abolished the doctrine of de facto incorporation in favor of joint and several liability for debts and liabilities for those who act as a corporation without authority to do so.[2]

18.3 CHARACTERISTICS OF THE PRIVATE STOCK CORPORATION AS A FORM OF BUSINESS ASSOCIATION

While the impetus comes from the organizers themselves, a corporation is technically a creature of the state and operates within the tight framework of its own articles of incorporation or charter and applicable laws. The corporation's powers are limited to those enumerated in the incorporating document (or necessarily implied therefrom) approved by the appropriate government authority.

The corporate device enables individuals to pool their invested funds on a limited-risk basis in a profit-seeking business operation to be conducted by management of their choice. The corporation as a distinctive type of business association has several significant advantages, not the least of which is the fact that shares in a large enterprise are readily transferable (shares in a small corporation with only a few shareholders may not be sold so easily). Another plus is the perpetual duration that the average corporation enjoys, in contradistinction to a partnership, which may be subject to dissolution on the death or withdrawal of a partner. Since a corporation is an entity unto itself, the death of any of its directors, officers, or stockholders need not affect its existence or, in most cases, even cause a temporary disruption of its operations.

Perhaps the limited liability afforded its stockholders is the primary advantage of the corporate form of undertaking. Subscribers are responsible to their corporation, or to its creditors in case the corporation is insolvent, for payment in full of stock subscriptions, and satisfaction of this debt can be compelled. But the stockholder, generally speaking, has no individual liability for any indebtedness of the firm and, in the event of corporate failure, stands to lose only his investment. One exception should be mentioned. When it can be shown that a corporation has been organized to perpetrate a fraud or perhaps has set up a dummy subsidiary to evade

---

[2]*See,* for example, *Smith v. Halliburton Co.,* 879 P.2d 1198 (N.M. App. 1994) construing Section 53-18-9, N.M. Stat. Anno., which is based on Sec. 146 of the Model Business Corporation's Act.

some pertinent statute, the courts may "pierce the corporate veil" and render the responsible stockholders individually liable.

The federal income tax laws treat corporations as separate taxable units and assess them on their income before dividends. Various expenses, of course, such as reasonable salaries, are deductible by the corporation for income tax purposes. The stockholders are then taxed individually on the dividends distributed to them in cash when the total value exceeds a certain amount. A special rule pertains where *stock* dividends are involved.

Acting through their officers and agents, corporations can be guilty of at least certain torts and criminal violations.[3] Moreover, the corporation has a name and an existence of its own quite apart from that of its stockholders, who indeed may enter into contractual arrangements with it and either sue or be sued by it.

In *Granite Construction Company v. Superior Court of Fresno*[4] a construction company was found guilty of the crime of manslaughter where seven construction workers were killed in an accident at a power plant construction site. While this case turned on a construction of the language of the California Penal Code, it is clear that corporate status does not insulate from criminal responsibility. Criminal penalties against corporations, usually fines, are provided by statute.[5]

In addition to criminal liability under statutes of general application, some states also have statutes criminalizing specific corporate conduct.[6]

---

[3]The California Penal Code § 7 defines, for the purpose of the Penal Code, *person* to include corporations. Likewise, the *whoever* in a statute providing that "whoever causes the death of another human being by the negligent operation of a vehicle is guilty of a Class E felony" covers corporations as well as natural persons. *State v. Richard Knutson, Inc.*, 537 N.W.2d 420 (Wis. App. 1995), *rev. den.* 540 N.W.2d 200.

[4]197 Cal. Rptr. 3 (1983).

[5]See, for example, Cal. Penal Code § 672.

[6]See, for example, California Penal Code § 387 (1994), which provides:

Corporations; limited liability companies; managers; serious concealed dangers; disclosure; manager liability

(a) Any corporation, limited liability company, or person who is a manager with respect to a product, facility, equipment, process, place of employment, or business practice, is guilty of a public offense punishable by imprisonment in the county jail for a term not exceeding one year, or by a fine not exceeding ten thousand dollars ($10,000), or by both that fine and imprisonment; or by imprisonment in the state prison for 16 months, two, or three years, or by a fine not exceeding twenty-five thousand dollars ($25,000); or by both that fine and imprisonment, but if the defendant is a corporation or a limited liability company the fine shall not exceed one million dollars ($1,000,000), if that corporation, limited liability company, or person does all of the following:
(1) Has actual knowledge of a serious concealed danger that is subject to the regulatory authority of an appropriate agency and is associated with that product or a component of that product or business practice.
(2) Knowingly fails during the period ending 15 days after the actual knowledge is acquired, or if there is imminent risk of great bodily harm or death, immediately, to do both of the following:
(A) Inform the Division of Occupational Safety and Health in the Department of Industrial Relations in writing, unless the corporation, limited liability company, or manager has actual knowledge that the division has been so informed.
    Where the concealed danger reported pursuant to this paragraph is subject to the regulatory authority of an agency other than the Division of Occupational Safety and Health in the Department of Industrial Relations, it shall be the responsibility of the Division of Occupational Safety and Health in the Department of Industrial Relations, within 24 hours of receipt of the information, to telephonically notify the appropriate government agency of the hazard, and promptly forward any written notification received.
(B) Warn its affected employees in writing, unless the corporation, limited liability company, or manager has actual knowledge that the employees have been so warned.

18.4 PRIVATE CORPORATION'S POWERS IN GENERAL

A corporate enterprise, as a creature of law, possesses only those powers that its certificate of incorporation (framed in light of applicable statutes) confers upon it, but it includes "implied powers" that are necessary or incidental to the accomplishment of the purposes for which the organization was created.

Typical general powers of a corporation include the following: (1) to buy or sell real or personal property, (2) to sue or be sued in its own name, (3) to make contractual commitments, (4) to invest its funds, (5) to loan or borrow money for its business purposes,[7] (6) to make bylaws, and (7) to appoint officers and agents.

Most state corporation laws carry express limitations on the privileges and authority of corporate entities. For example, loans by the corporation to its directors or officers are commonly prohibited, as are dividend payments to stockholders when the effect of such payments would be to render the concern insolvent.

18.5 ULTRA VIRES ACTIVITY

A corporation may enter into only such contracts as come within the scope of its express or implied powers. Any contracts that exceed this authority are spoken of as *ultra vires*.[8] If the contract in question runs counter to a statute or to established public policy, it will normally be judicially treated as unenforceable, although some decisions have required a benefited party to pay for what he got, perhaps on a theory of estoppel or of ratification.[9] On the other hand, if the ultra vires contract is not "illegal" in the strict sense of the word but is merely "unauthorized," a more difficult question is presented. As a general proposition, the courts tend to resolve the matter as follows: (1) if the corporation has exceeded its authority in making a particular contract but there has been full performance on both sides, the courts will not interfere; (2) if the unauthorized contract is entirely executory, that is, has not been performed by either party, neither party can enforce it; (3) if the contract is partly executed, the party that received the benefit cannot urge ultra vires as a defense when pressed for counterperformance.

Stockholders may ordinarily ratify ultra vires action by management to the extent that the action in question is not utterly void because it is in contravention of statute or public policy.[10] The judicial treatment of ultra vires contracts, particularly those in category (3) above, varies considerably from one jurisdiction to the next. The defense of ultra vires is not generally favored.

---

[7]Both large and small corporations upon occasion find it necessary or desirable to borrow money, commonly issuing bonds as evidence of indebtedness. Interest on these obligations is payable to the corporation's creditors before any dividends to stockholders.

[8]*Miesch v. Ocean Dunes Homeowners' Assoc. Inc.*, 464 S.E.2d 64 (N.C. App. 1995) *rev. den.* 467 S.E.2d 717.

[9]*In re Spokane Concrete Products, Inc.*, 892 P.2d 98 (Wash. 1995).

[10]*Stroud v. Grace*, 606 A.2d 75 (Del. Supr. 1992).

It is usually held that the directors, officers, and agents who enter into ultra vires contracts on behalf of their corporation do not thereby render themselves personally liable to the other contracting party, either on a warranty of authority basis or otherwise. Further, the other party is charged with a degree of constructive notice regarding the limitations contained in the corporation's articles or imposed by statute.

The commission by a corporation of an act beyond the scope of the powers conferred upon it does not, in and of itself, put an end to the corporate existence. What it does is furnish the state's attorney general, via a *quo warranto* proceeding, with possible justification for claiming forfeiture of the document evidencing the corporation's right to do business.

A corporation is not relieved of liability for a tort simply by reason of the fact that the activity out of which the tort arose was ultra vires. The key question relates to the individual who committed the delict: Was he acting within the scope of his authority from his principal, the corporation?

18.6   FORMING THE CORPORATION

Each state has its own laws under which private business corporations are formed and operated[11] for profit.[12] Procedures and requirements of the creating process differ with the state of domicile, but most call for prescribed fees to be paid and for information to be submitted to the proper government officials. Once the law has been satisfied in other respects and the *articles of incorporation* duly filed with the appropriate state official, the latter typically certifies that the organization is officially in existence and ready to commence activity. Terminology varies and, in some quarters, this document is referred to as the "certificate of incorporation" or as the "charter." Technically, the latter term has reference to a direct legislative grant to named individuals rather than to a paper evidencing qualification under a general enabling act.

The articles of incorporation cover such items as the name[13] and location of the enterprise, the nature of its business, the amount and description of authorized capital stock, the amount of paid-in capital with which the corporation will commence its existence, and the period (if any limitation is to be set) during which the corporation expects to remain in existence.

The amount of capital stock can subsequently be changed only by vote of the stockholders supporting a formal amendment. The term *capital stock* means something far different from the term *capital*, which refers to the assets owned by the corporation.

---

[11]There are some corporate instrumentalities created by the federal government. The Tennessee Valley Authority offers an example.

[12]Special kinds of corporate organizations, insurance companies for example, are subject to a separate set of statutory provisions as are nonprofit corporations.

[13]Partly to prevent confusion to the public and partly to protect prior rights of a corporation already operating in the state, a new corporation will not be permitted to take a name identical or substantially similar to that of another corporation.

A subject mentioned in the articles of incorporation may also be treated (but in greater detail) in the *bylaws,* which are rules adopted by the corporation under which its internal affairs are to be managed. Since the process of amending the articles of incorporation generally means fulfilling several requirements that may prove burdensome, items that are subject to frequent change are generally covered in the bylaws instead.

18.7 STOCK AND STOCKHOLDERS

The sale of stock provides capital with which to operate the corporation, and the shareholders, collectively, are the owners of the enterprise. All capital stock must be authorized by the articles of incorporation, which fixes both the total amount of stock and the classes or types thereof. If par-value shares are to be utilized, the value in question will be stipulated in the basic incorporation papers. If any change in the pattern is subsequently desired, the articles must first be amended. The adoption of certain important amendments or the consummation of certain transactions (merger, for example) may invest dissenting stockholders with the right to return their stock to the corporation in exchange for payment of its fair, appraised value. In the issuance and sale of securities, federal laws administered by the Securities and Exchange Commission must be checked, along with such state provisions ("blue sky laws" primarily) as are applicable.

The two basic categories of capital stock are *common* and *preferred.*[14] Generally speaking, common stock carries voting rights and thus ultimate control of the enterprise, while preferred has preference in regard to asset distribution but lacks the control aspect. Frequently, a corporation will be authorized to issue both cumulative and noncumulative preferred stock. The distinction between the cumulative and the noncumulative is discussed in the following passage from *Day v. United States Cast Iron Pipe & Foundry Company.*[15]

> While dividends (not in liquidation) upon each can, of course, only be paid out of profits or surplus . . . the dividends upon cumulative preferred stock have at all times and for all years past and present, until paid, priority in payment over any and all unpaid dividends upon common stock, whether the net earnings for any particular past or present year were or were not sufficient to pay the stipulated cumulative dividends upon preferred stock for that year; whereas the like priority of dividends upon noncumulative preferred stock (wholly or partially as the case may be) is limited to the unpaid dividends for those years when such net earnings were sufficient (wholly or in corresponding part) to pay such dividends.

The stockholders are not, in their individual capacities, agents of the corporation, and thus can only really act for it by voting at meetings. The frequency of shareholder meetings, any relevant notice requirements, what constitutes a quo-

---

[14]Usually preferred stockholders receive dividends at a fixed rate, while the dividend rights of common stockholders are limited in the long run by the earning power of the company.
[15]96 N.J. Eq. 736, 126 A 302, 304–305 (1924).

rum, what proportion of the vote is necessary to carry certain propositions, and other matters pertaining to the conduct of meetings are set forth in the articles of incorporation, the bylaws, and the corporation statutes. The stockholders do elect the directors and thus retain a measure of control in that they can eventually unseat directors whose conduct displeases them. But the directors, by virtue of their position, are expected to exercise independent judgment in furtherance of the corporation's business, and the stockholders must not seek to influence their elected representatives. Agreements among shareholders that directly or indirectly limit the discretion of directors are usually held invalid as contrary to public policy. A director cannot bargain away his privilege of independent judgment, which he is expected to utilize for the benefit of the shareholders as a group.

The right to vote is a key element of stock ownership. Corporation laws generally provide for and regulate proxy voting; moreover, the solicitation of proxies must, in every respect, meet Securities and Exchange Commission requirements. The proxy is deemed to bear a fiduciary relationship to the stockholder appointing same, and is revocable unless coupled with an interest.

Apart from voting powers, stockholders, generally speaking, have a number of rights and privileges, chief among which are these:

1. A right to share ratably in whatever dividends are declared on the particular class of stock held (dividends, of course, are generated by profits and may, in most states, be declared and paid to the extent of *surplus*).

2. A "preemptive right," which means that, when the corporation becomes authorized to increase its outstanding capital stock by the issuance of new shares, its stockholders of record, in their respective ownership proportions, have first chance to subscribe for the additional shares. The doctrine of preemptive right of shareholders is a judicial interpretation of general principles of corporation law to the effect that existing stockholders are owners of the business and are entitled to have that ownership continued in the same proportion.[16]

3. A right to participate in the distribution of assets should the firm be liquidated.

4. A privilege of immunity from personal liability for corporate debts.

5. A right to reasonable inspection of the concern's records. Where necessary, this right can be enforced by *mandamus* proceedings.

6. A right, under certain conditions, to bring suit on behalf of the corporation.[17]

18.8   THE DIRECTORS

The business activities of a corporation and the management of its property are controlled by its board of directors, operating in accordance with its bylaws. The direc-

---

[16]*Katzowitz v. Sidler,* 24 N.Y.2d 512, 301 N.Y.Supp.2d 470 (1976). But preemptive rights do not allow shareholders the power to preclude the corporation from issuing additional shares by claiming that the issuance of such shares would coerce them into buying them to prevent dilution. *King v. Douglass,* 973 F. Supp. 707 (S.D. Texas 1996, applying Delaware law).

[17]The matter of stockholder litigation will be dealt with in Section 18.11.

tors, in turn, select a president and other administrative officers who are ordinarily removable at the pleasure of the board. The method by which the members of the original board are named varies, but thereafter the directors are elected by and are ultimately responsible to the stockholders. Broadly speaking, all matters relating to the legitimate activity of the enterprise, as outlined in its articles of incorporation (or charter), may be handled by the directors without the sanction of the stockholders. For outsiders, the directors are agents of the corporation. Accordingly, notice to or pertinent knowledge of a director will be imputed to his principal, the corporation. For the stockholder–owners and the corporation itself, the directors fill a role closer to that of trustees. Strictly speaking, they cannot be "trustees" in the full sense of the term, since a trustee is legal owner of the trust property, and title to corporate property is not vested in the directors, but rather in the corporation itself. However, it is certainly true that the directors are fiduciaries and have a substantial duty of loyalty and diligence to the interests of the corporation.

The directors cannot act individually, and generally they may exercise their powers only as a unit brought together at a properly called board meeting with a quorum in attendance. If the full board proves difficult to assemble by reason of size or geographical complications, it may be possible to provide for the delegating of some functions to an executive committee, composed of a relatively few members of the complete board.

Compensation to directors for their services may take the form of fees for attending meetings, fixed salary, or some other arrangement. Unless the bylaws provide otherwise, a director cannot be removed before the expiration of his term except when good cause is shown.

The standard of care to which directors are held is that of "reasonable persons" in their particular positions. In other words, any particular director is required to give such care and attention to the duties of the position as would corporate directors in general. This includes a duty to make reasonable inquiry. In one case,[18] in the merger context, corporate directors were held in breach of their duty where they approved a takeover of their company without adequately informing themselves of the role of the deal's advocate, were uninformed as to the intrinsic value of their company, and approved the sale upon two hours' consideration without a crisis or emergency.[19]

Ordinarily, directors acting in good faith and within the bounds of their authority are not liable for the disastrous consequences of an honest mistake in judgment. A director who absents himself from meetings does not thereby necessarily secure exemption from responsibility for actions taken by the board.

Where the facts show fraud or gross negligence resulting in a loss to the corporation, violence has been done to their "duty of care," and the errant directors are in a vulnerable position. In fact, statutes in a number of jurisdictions impose upon

---

[18]*Smith v. Van Gorkom*, 488 A 2d 858 (Del. 1985).

[19]Director liability can also be statutory. See *Witco Corp. v. Beekhuis*, 38 F.3d 682 (CA. 3 1994) where a former director who personally designed the disposal process and directed construction and maintenance of a lagoon into which chemical waste was disposed was held personally liable as an "operator" within the meaning of the Comprehensive Environmental Response, Compensation and Liability Act of 1980, (42 U.S.C. § 9601 *et seq.*).

directors personal responsibility under stated conditions of malfeasance, including such overt action as (1) paying dividends out of capital when there are no profits, (2) making loans out of corporate funds to a director or officer, and (3) authorizing publication of false financial reports.

To encourage qualified persons to serve as board members with reasonable assurance that they will not suffer financially thereby, many states have passed laws that either empower corporations to indemnify directors and officers (and sometimes certain employees) with respect to the cost of defending themselves against groundless accusations of mismanagement, or that take the form, in some cases, of affording the directors and the like a statutory right to indemnification, even if there is nothing in the bylaws or the charter and no indemnification agreement as such in existence. In most instances the individual is entitled to be indemnified (with the money perhaps provided through the medium of insurance) unless he is shown to have been guilty of bad faith or to have been engaged in substantial misconduct.

Mention has been made of the director's fiduciary capacity and of his duty of loyalty to the corporate organization. This gives rise to the common-law doctrine that if a given director's vote is needed for corporate approval of a contract in which he has a personal interest, such a contract, without regard to the fairness of its terms, is voidable at the option of the corporation. Furthermore, while a director is not precluded from selling his own property to his corporation at a profit, any such transactions are subject to careful scrutiny. On the other hand, the director (or officer, for that matter), having learned of his firm's interest in a piece of realty, cannot "race" the corporation to such property, purchase it, and then sell to the firm.

An allied problem involves the director's relationship with an individual stockholder from whom he intends to purchase shares of the corporation with which they are mutually connected. There is a divergence of opinion about whether the director is in a fiduciary position with respect to the individual stockholder such that he must disclose facts, known to him by reason of his position but presumably unknown to the stockholder, that tend to increase the apparent value of the shares that are about to change hands. Clearly, the director must refrain from active fraud or active concealment of significant information, but beyond that his duty is unclear.

18.9   THE OFFICERS

While retaining ultimate control of the corporation at the policy-making level, the board of directors will name a slate of company officers (with the principal ones likely being board members) to whom considerable administrative authority may be delegated. Some jurisdictions permit direct selection of officers by the stockholders. Officers may derive their power from statutes, articles, bylaws, or resolutions of the board. In addition to the express powers conferred upon them, the officers, especially the president, have a certain amount of "apparent authority" that stems from the nature of their position. Where a power is one which by generally accepted practice is in the domain of a particular officer rank, it is usually held that a bylaw purporting to eliminate that power is ineffective as against a stranger who has no actual notice.

The principal executive official is the president, whose function may be stated broadly as that of running the everyday operations of the corporate enterprise. This officer has at least implied authority to make such contracts as are reasonably related to the ordinary activities of the corporation. There is a rebuttable presumption of authority on his part to perform any act within the scope of the company's business. Established practice of the particular corporation will also be considered in determining his authority. Thus, if the board traditionally acquiesces when the president exceeds his delegated authority in entering into a certain type of contractual commitment, the president will be deemed clothed with "apparent authority" as regards third parties, and the corporation will be held responsible for any breach on its part of a contract so made. Whether or not a specific action taken by the president comes within some aspect of his authority is a question of fact (for a jury's determination, if need be). If there is any reasonable doubt about the president's capacity to bind the corporation to a particularly important contract in contemplation, the other party involved should request a certified copy of a board resolution granting express authority to the president to proceed.

Ordinarily, in the typical small corporate setup and with the president on hand, the vice president has no contract-making powers. The treasurer maintains financial records, prepares reports therefrom, and (under the broad supervision of the board) receives and disburses corporate funds. More often than not, the treasurer does not have express or apparent general authority to borrow money, though the board might ratify a treasurer's actions in this respect. The remaining official in the standard organizational arrangement is the secretary. He is largely a recording officer who keeps the minutes and various other official records, supervises the mechanics of stock transactions, and has custody of the corporate seal.

Corporate officers are, of course, personally responsible for crimes that they commit, regardless of whether or not they were committed at the behest of or for the benefit of the corporation.[20] While most crimes require criminal intent or knowledge, some criminal statutes impose criminal liability on corporate officers for acts or omissions in which they had a "responsible share" yet no direct knowledge or participation.[21]

All officers, or any one of them, may by and large be discharged at any time even though they hold long-term employment contracts. If the firing, however, is not "for cause," the officer involved has available against the corporation an action seeking damages for breach. An increasing number of employment contracts written for executive officers carry for their protection a liquidated-damages clause to apply in the event of their summary dismissal (for a reason other than misconduct).

---

[20]*Kelly ex rel Michigan Natural Resources Comm. v. Tiscornia*, 827 F. Supp. 1315 (W.D. Mich. 1993, applying Mich. law). *Compton v. Com.*, 473 S.E.2d 95 (Va. App. 1996).

[21]See, for example, *U.S. v. Park*, 421 U.S. 658 (1975) where the Supreme Court of the United States upheld the conviction of the president of an 874-store food market chain for violation of the Food, Drug and Cosmetic Act for sale of food contaminated by rodent excrement even without proof of his knowledge, since it was his duty to prevent or correct such violations.

18.10   STOCKHOLDER SUITS

A stockholder as an individual has no right of action against third persons, including corporate directors and officers, for damages sustained by the corporation itself, and this is so even where the stockholder in question is sole owner of the business and even where the event involved may demonstrably have resulted in reducing the value of his stock holding. If the wrong is one affecting the corporate entity and its stockholders in general, the cause of action belongs to the corporation. Should the latter, however, for one reason or another (perhaps because controlled by some of the wrongdoers) fail to proceed, suit may be filed on the corporation's behalf by one or more stockholders acting "derivatively" (this term stemming from the fact that such stockholder's privilege of bringing an action derives from the right of the corporation itself). Before assuming the role of nominal plaintiffs, such stockholders must establish either (1) that they have asked the directors to sue in the corporate name and have been refused for no justifiable reason, or (2) that it would be futile to make such a request (possibly because of alleged collusion between the directors and the prospective defendant). If and when the derivative suit is brought, any benefit flowing from the action is taken by the corporation as the real party in interest and only indirectly by the stockholder-plaintiffs.

A good example of a shareholder derivative suit is the case of *Shaffer v. Heitner*[22] in which the owner of one share of stock in Greyhound Corporation alleged that the defendants, directors, and officers of the corporation damaged it by engaging in actions that resulted in the corporation being held liable for substantial damages in a private antitrust suit and a large fine in a criminal contempt action. Although the case was dismissed on jurisdictional grounds, had the plaintiff prevailed, an award of damages would have benefited the corporation.

18.11   MISCELLANEOUS CONTROL DEVICES AVAILABLE TO STOCKHOLDERS

There are several legitimate means by which an organized minority of the stockholders can secure representation on the board and a measure of control over the corporation's destiny. One of these is the system of cumulative voting, which, when authorized, works in this fashion: Each share is entitled to as many votes as there are directors to be elected.[23] Assuming three directors are to be chosen, the stockholder has three votes per share and can cast them all for one person or can distribute the votes as desired. This device protects minority shareholders by assuring that if the minority is sufficiently purposeful and cohesive, it can gain representation on the board roughly proportional to its size.[24]

---

[22]433 U.S. 186 (1977).

[23]*In Re Woodings-Verona Tool Works, Inc.*, 157 B.R. 575 (Bkrtcy W.D. Pa. 1993), noting that under Pennsylvania law cumulative voting is the rule unless the articles of incorporation expressly provide otherwise.

[24]*CTS Corp. v. Dynamics Corp. of America*, 481 U.S. 69 (1987).

The "voting trust," where legal, is another useful stockholder device. The agreement involved separates voting power from beneficial ownership of the stock, and any applicable statutory restrictions or limitations must be considered. The essence of the voting-trust arrangement is evident in this extract from a statute[25] on the subject:

(a) One or more shareholders may create a voting trust, conferring on a trustee the right to vote or otherwise act for them, by signing an agreement setting out the provisions of the trust, which may include anything consistent with its purpose, and transferring their shares to the trustee. When a voting trust agreement is signed, the trustee shall prepare a list of the names and addresses of all owners of beneficial interests in the trust, together with the number and class of shares each transferred to the trust, and deliver copies of the list and agreement to the corporation's principal office.

(b) A voting trust becomes effective on the date the first shares subject to the trust are registered in the trustee's name. A voting trust is valid for not more than ten years after its effective date unless extended under subsection (c) of this section.

(c) All or some of the parties to a voting trust may extend it for additional terms of not more than ten years each by signing an extension agreement and obtaining the voting trustee's written consent to the extension. An extension is valid for ten years from the date the first shareholder signs the extension agreement. The voting trust must deliver copies of the extension agreement and list of beneficial owners to the corporation's principal office. An extension agreement binds only those parties signing it.

Not to be confused with the foregoing is the so-called "voting agreement," whereby a number of stockholders undertake to vote their shares as a group in some manner provided for in the understanding among them.

Once acquired, a measure of control may be perpetuated through such mechanisms as (1) using a capital-stock structure, which includes a significant percentage of preferred and of nonvoting common stock, (2) staggering the expiration dates of directors' terms of office, (3) granting long-term employment contracts to key officials, and (4) efficiently soliciting and using proxies.

18.12 SUBSIDIARY AND AFFILIATED CORPORATIONS; HOLDING COMPANIES; CONSOLIDATIONS AND MERGERS

Modern-day corporations in great numbers have established subsidiaries[26] or have established affiliations with independent concerns. Where the subsidiary is judicially determined to be merely the instrumentality of the parent corporation, the parent will

---

[25]Conn. Gen. Stat., § 33–715 amend. 1994, effective Jan. 1, 1997.

[26]Subsidiaries are organized, as a rule, to handle a given phase of the parent's business, for example, its foreign activities. Thus, the X Company, incorporated in New York, operates retail outlets in Great Britain and Ireland through X Company, Ltd.

be potentially liable for the torts and debts of its offspring. In deciding whether the subsidiary is truly a separate entity designed in all respects to be independent, the court will check for signs of (1) frequent, direct intervention by the parent in management affairs, (2) underfinancing of the subsidiary, and (3) commingling of assets as though the two ostensibly separate concerns were one and the same.

The so-called *holding company* is, in a sense, a "supercorporation"[27] created to hold such a dominant interest in one or more other companies as to be able to prescribe or, at least, to materially influence (through the medium of the voting power that attends ownership of all or most of the outstanding stock) the management policies the controlled companies will pursue.

Combination of several previously separate corporations can take the form of "consolidation" or of "merger," either process being subject to whatever statutes are relevant. When a consolidation occurs, the corporations involved lose their identities and a new concern emerges. The result is distinguishable from what happens in a merger, where one of the participating corporations survives and no completely new entity is created.

18.13   Dissolution and Winding Up; Reorganization

When financial reverses befall a corporation and insolvency impends, management may recommend and the stockholders approve voluntary dissolution of the business, following whatever steps are set forth in the applicable corporation act. This move would bring about lawful termination of the company's existence, as would involuntary dissolution pursuant to court order, or as would expiration of any limited time (for the corporation's existence) set by law or charter provision. The various jurisdictions commonly prescribe a "winding-up period" of several years in which complicated corporate affairs may be drawn to a close.

Short of dissolution or being forced into bankruptcy by its creditors, a corporation that is experiencing severe financial difficulty might, in an appropriate case, seek to avail itself of the reorganization procedure provided for under Chapter XI of the Federal Bankruptcy Act.[28] Through this avenue the struggling corporation may be able to obtain a new lease on life.

---

[27]Thus characterized in *Kelley, Glover & Vale v. Heitman,* 220 Ind. 625, 44 N.E.2d 981, 985 (1942).
[28]1 U.S.C., 1101 *et. seq.* amended (1994).

QUESTIONS

1. What are *(a)* the distinctive features of the corporate form of business organization? *(b)* its advantages? *(c)* its powers?

2. How and by whom is a corporation *(a)* authorized? *(b)* organized? *(c)* controlled?

3. Who "owns" the corporation? Who runs it?

4. What is a corporate charter? What is its function? When may a corporation be "defective"?

5. How can the ownership of a corporation be revised? How can its management personnel be changed?

6. What is a "proxy"? How does it operate?

7. How does a public corporation differ from other business corporations? Illustrate.

8. What is a subsidiary corporation? May this type of organization prove more advantageous than having a branch of the parent organization? Explain.

9. How can a corporation be dissolved? Can it be reorganized?

10. If a corporation is chartered in New York, can it do business in New Jersey?

11. Differentiate between a de jure corporation and a de facto corporation.

12. What is meant by "foreign" corporation?

13. Explain the income tax status of a corporation and of its stockholders.

14. Can a corporation be sued *(a)* by an outsider? *(b)* by one of its stockholders?

15. How can a corporation borrow money? On what security?

16. Discuss the ultra vires concept as it relates to corporate affairs.

17. Can ultra vires actions be ratified? By whom?

18. Can a corporation increase the number of shares above that authorized by its charter? If so, how?

19. Does a corporation pay dividends out of earnings or out of surplus?

20. Define directors of a corporation. What are their duties, fees, powers, responsibilities?

21. What are the duties and powers of the officers of a corporation?

22. What rights does a common stockholder have? What is cumulative voting?

23. May a director also be a stockholder of the corporation? Discuss.

24. May professionals incorporate?

25. What benefits may accrue from professional incorporation? What detriments?

26. Discuss the rights and privileges of bondholders of a corporation

27. May a corporation be convicted of a criminal offense?

28. A corporation decided to go out of business. After paying off its creditors and bondholders, the firm still had assets totaling $2 million. There were 10,000 shares of preferred stock of $50 par value and 50,000 shares of common stock

(no par value) outstanding. How much per share will each common stockholder receive as a liquidating payment?

29. The directors of a corporation voted to buy all its steel for a given year from the *XYZ* Steel Company. Can the stockholders do anything to reverse the decision? If the directors voted to sell the business outright, would the stockholders have any voice in the matter? Explain.

30. The *XYZ* Corporation went into bankruptcy. Jones owned 100 shares of the firm's common stock. Can the corporation creditors collect anything from Jones? Explain.

31. Smith owned 100 shares of General Motors Corporation common stock. What effect would Smith's death have upon *(a)* operation of the corporation and *(b)* the shares outstanding in the decedent's name?

32. Corporation *A* was chartered for the sole purpose of operating a fleet of oil tankers. Without charter amendment, can it legitimately go into the business of building tankers?

33. The president of *ABC* corporation died. Must the corporation be reorganized and, if so, what steps are necessary?

chapter

19

TORTS

19.1 DEFINITION AND SCOPE

The term *tort* is very similar in meaning to *wrong;* yet "tort" is not intended to include all wrongful acts done by one person to another, but only those for which the victim may demand legal redress. Torts may be committed intentionally or unintentionally, and with or without force. It may be said that tortuous acts consist of the unprivileged commission (or omission, as the case may be) of acts whereby another individual receives an injury to his person, property, or reputation.

A *tort* is distinguished from a *crime* in that a tort is a private injury upon which suit may be brought, while the latter is an offense against the public for which any retribution must be sought by the appropriate governmental authority. It is entirely possible for a single act to constitute at once a tort and a crime.

Contract liability (which is confined to the parties to the agreement) can likewise be differentiated from *tort liability.* Contract actions afford the innocent party a means of protecting his legitimate interest in having whatever promises are made to him fulfilled. Tort actions, on the other hand, seek to safeguard the individual from various kinds of harm.

19.2 CLASSES OF TORTS

Torts may be divided into two broad classes. The first of these is *property torts,* and this group includes all injuries to property, be it real or personal. The second is *personal torts,* embracing all harms to the victim's reputation, feelings, or physical well being.

The injuries in either category can stem from nonfeasance, misfeasance, or malfeasance on the part of the wrongdoer, who is known as the *tortfeasor*.[1]

19.3   BASES OF TORT LIABILITY

Commonly stated are three bases of tort liability:

1.   Negligence.
2.   Intentional interference.
3.   Strict liability for reasons of public policy.

To maintain a successful tort action, the wronged party must establish (1) that the defendant owed him a duty, (2) that the duty was breached, and (3) that damage[2] was suffered as a result. Where the alleged tort is founded on negligence, the plaintiff may also be required to show that he is free from any contributory negligence. This depends on whether his state has adopted comparative fault. These issues will be taken up later.

NEGLIGENCE

19.4   DEFINITION

Causing harm through negligent conduct is a basic form of tort. There is no requirement that the tortfeasor intended to occasion such an injury. It is sufficient that a reasonable man should have foreseen the harm and prevented it.

---

[1]Tort liability has traditionally been joint and several, meaning that in the case of multiple tortfeasors, each is liable for the entire amount. While contribution from other tortfeasors is possible, the doctrine encourages plaintiffs to go after the "deep pocket."

California has addressed this notion via an initiative that resulted in the following:
The People of the State of California find and declare as follows:
(a) The legal doctrine of joint and several liability, also known as " the deep pocket rule," has resulted in a system of inequity and injustice that has threatened financial bankruptcy of local governments, other public agencies, private individuals and businesses and has resulted in higher prices for goods and services to the public and in higher taxes to the taxpayers.
(b) Some governmental and private defendants are perceived to have substantial financial resources or insurance coverage and have thus been included in lawsuits even though there was little or no basis for finding them at fault. Under joint and several liability, if they are found to share even a fraction of the fault, they often are held financially liable for all the damage. The People—taxpayers and consumers alike—ultimately pay for these lawsuits in the form of higher taxes, higher prices and higher insurance premiums.
(c) Local governments have been forced to curtail some essential police, fire and other protections because of the soaring costs of lawsuits and insurance premiums.
Therefore, the People of the State of California declare that to remedy these inequities, defendants in tort actions shall be held financially liable in closer proportion to their degree of fault. To treat them differently is unfair and inequitable.
The People of the State of California further declare that reforms in the liability laws in tort actions are necessary and proper to avoid catastrophic economic consequences for state and local governmental bodies as well as private individuals and businesses.
(Added by § 3 of Initiative Measure, approved by the People, June 3, 1986.) Calif. Civil Code § 1431.1.

[2]Damages in tort actions may be either compensatory or punitive. Punitive damage awards, those intended to punish and deter rather than make whole, may violate the due process clause of the 14th amendment to the U.S. Constitution if they are excessive. See, for example, *BMW of North America, Inc. v. Gore*, 517 U.S. 559 (1996) where the Supreme Court of the U.S. found a 2 million dollar punitive damages award grossly excessive and thus in violation of due process where the compensatory award was $4,000. This highly publicized case involved BMW's practice of selling cars that had been partially repainted as "new."

The subject of negligence as a basis of responsibility in tort is a vast one. Among the various concepts involved are duty, proximate cause, contributory negligence, imputed negligence, gross negligence, assumption of risk, and last clear chance.

Broadly speaking, *negligence* consists of a failure to follow such a pattern of behavior as, under the circumstances, a reasonable person would have pursued, or, contrarily, of doing what a reasonable person would not have done. Thus negligence is conduct that is abnormally likely to cause harm to others, or which is, all circumstances considered, unreasonably dangerous, though not intentionally so.

Usually, whether one is or is not negligent is a question of fact, but there are some instances of negligence as a matter of law. Thus, when a legislature has dictated a certain procedure to be followed in a given set of circumstances, failure to comply with the statutory edict may be held to be negligence per se.

19.5 THE ELEMENTS OF NEGLIGENCE

In order to prevail in his negligence suit, the plaintiff must show that the alleged tortfeasor owed him a duty of care under the circumstances and breached that duty. Furthermore, he must prove that he suffered actual loss or injury and that there was a definite causal connection between the defendant's conduct and the damage complained of.

In the past, defendants could completely bar the plaintiff's recovery by proving that the plaintiff was contributorily negligent. However, in recent years, most states have adopted the rule of comparative fault, whereby the plaintiff's monetary recovery is reduced by the percentage of his fault. This will be discussed in more detail in Section 19.12; we need only note here that the rule is applied differently in different states.

The burden of proof is clearly on the plaintiff's shoulders to establish the wrongful conduct of the defendant and the necessary causal connection between that and the damage to plaintiff. The defendant is called upon to defend actively *only if* the court feels the plaintiff's evidence, viewed in its most favorable light, might be sufficient to warrant a finding in the latter's favor. Otherwise, the defendant would be entitled to a directed verdict dismissing the complaint.

19.6 THE STANDARD OF CARE

One of the fundamental propositions that must be sustained by the plaintiff in a successful negligence action is that the defendant, under the circumstances at the time of the alleged tort, owed a *duty of care* to plaintiff. The concept of the "normally prudent man," developed by common law over a period of many years, will be applied to the defendant's behavior to see if it conforms to a standard of reasonableness in light of the apparent risk. There are a number of ingredients that go into this "standard-of-care" yardstick: (1) so-called "normal" intellectual capacity, memory ability, and the like; (2) such minimum knowledge, skill, and experience as is deemed common to nearly everyone; (3) whatever additional or superior knowledge, skill, and experience the particular defendant may possess;[3] (4) the alleged tortfeasor's own physical traits, handicaps,[4] and so on.

Obviously the standard of an abstract "average man" is difficult to delineate, let alone apply on a uniform basis. The defendant may have conscientiously sought to do the best he could and yet find that the jury regards his behavior as falling short of the prescribed standard of intelligence and prudence that society anticipates in its members. Since some sort of external model seems the only logical thing to use, there are bound to occur some marginal cases of liability without fault (as where defendants with low IQ, slow reaction time, and the like are involved). The standard of care is the same whether it is the defendant being tested or whether, with contributory negligence an issue, the plaintiff's own conduct is under scrutiny.

In determining the proper standard of conduct in a given situation, it is not at all unusual to have considerable testimony introduced respecting the general "custom of the trade" and defendant's adherence to, or departure from, such accepted pattern.

The jury is supposed to make the ultimate decision about what the fictional "reasonable man" would have done under the set of circumstances that confronted the defendant. Directed verdicts are rare in negligence actions, and the ordinary accident case, barring settlement during trial, eventually reaches the jury room.

19.7   PROXIMATE CAUSE AND FORESEEABILITY

Though the judicial approach to *proximate cause* is not uniform throughout the country, the prevailing tendency seems to be to hold the defendant responsible even for some rather extraordinary consequences of his negligence as long as the chain of direct causation remains unbroken by an intervening cause. In other words, where it is found that the defendant was negligent and that his conduct was a *substantial cause*[5] in fact of the injuries under consideration, his vulnerability is clear, even though the precise damage that resulted was not to be anticipated. The question of liability is always anterior to the question of the measure of damages that attend the liability, but the latter remains an important question. It is difficult to delineate the "zone of danger" raised by defendant's conduct in a given situation, and there has to be a line drawn somewhere. The concept of substantial cause is supposed to preclude recovery for remote damage that defendant's conduct cannot definitely be said to have occasioned.

The landmark case respecting proximate cause is that of *Palsgraf v. Long Island R.R.*[6] A man carrying a harmless-looking package jumped aboard a moving

---

[3]Thus, in medical matters a family doctor will be held to that degree of care expected of physicians generally, while a specialist has an even higher standard to meet.

[4]The conduct of a physically disabled person will be judged in the light of the handicap and of his awareness of that impairment. The awareness is one of the circumstances that has an obvious bearing upon the reasonableness of his behavior.

[5]In this connection *substantial cause* does not necessarily mean *sole cause*.

[6]248 N.Y. 339 (1928).

train and, in so doing, lost his balance and seemed about to fall. A guard on the car, sensing the danger, reached forward to help him in and another guard on the platform pushed from behind. During these maneuvers the package became dislodged, fell to the rails, and exploded, causing some scales to be thrown down at the other end of the platform, many feet away. The falling scales struck and injured plaintiff Palsgraf, a woman on the platform intending to board the train. In the litigation that followed, the majority decision exonerated the defendant railroad, holding that the consequences befalling the plaintiff were not foreseeable and that defendant consequently could not be regarded as guilty of any negligence with reference to her. The mandate was that plaintiff must sue in her own right for wrong personal to her, if any, and not as vicarious beneficiary of a breach of duty to another. In other words, the majority opined that negligence is not actionable unless it involves the invasion of a legally protected interest, that is, the violation of a right. The conduct of defendant's guards, if tortious in relation to the holder of the package, was yet not a wrong in its relation to this plaintiff, who had been standing some distance away.

The minority view in *Palsgraf,* which appears nowadays to have become more or less the general rule, was that the railroad employee's negligence in dislodging the package from the commuter's arms was the proximate cause of the plaintiff's injuries and was therefore actionable. The dissenting judges proceeded on the theory that where there is an act that unreasonably threatens the safety of others, the doer is liable for all its proximate consequences, even where injury results to one who would generally be thought to be outside the radius of danger. Harm to some person being the foreseeable result of the negligent act, not only that one alone, but all those in fact injured may complain. In discussing proximate cause, the minority said:

> What we do mean by the word "proximate" is, that because of convenience, of public policy, a rough sense of justice, the law arbitrarily declines to trace a series of events beyond a certain point. This is not logic. It is practical politics . . .
>
> It is all a question of expediency. There are no fixed rules to govern our judgment. There are simply matters of which we may take account . . . There are some hints that may help us. The proximate cause, involved as it may be with many other causes, must be, at the least, something without which the event would not happen. The court must ask itself whether there was a natural and continuous sequence between cause and effect. Was the one a substantial factor in producing the other? Was there a direct connection between them, without too many intervening causes? Is the effect of cause on result not too attenuated? Is the cause likely, in the usual judgment of mankind, to produce the result? Or by the exercise of prudent foresight could the result be foreseen? Is the result too remote from the cause?

Mention has been made of forces that break the chain of causation and may relieve defendant of further consequences of his negligence. Such relief is afforded when the intervening force is one that defendant could not have foreseen or one that is patently not a normal incident of the risk initially created by defendant's tortuous conduct. As an example, assume that the negligence of driver *X* brings about a collision with *Y*'s automobile. *Y* steps from his car to remonstrate with *X,* slips on the icy pavement, and injures himself in falling. *X*'s negligence was the proximate cause of the collision damage to Y's car, and X is clearly liable therefor, but many courts today would likely hold that the ensuing fall by Y was not X's responsibility since Y's slipping on the ice was an intervening cause of the personal injury to him. It is apparent that "but for" the collision there would have been no occasion for Y to alight from his car at the particular time and place, but the tort by X could be deemed the remote rather than the substantial cause of Y's mishap.

While the judge in a negligence action will charge the jury on what constitutes proximate cause and related concepts, the jury must apply a broad factual test to determine whether or not the evidence indicates that there actually exists the vital causal connection between defendant's alleged tort and plaintiff's alleged injury.

19.8 VIOLATION OF STATUTE

Unexcused violation of a specific minimum standard of conduct dictated by legislation is today almost universally treated as negligence per se as long as the injury involved is of a nature that the statute was aimed at preventing and the plaintiff is within the category of persons the law sought to protect. It is open to the defendant to show that he did the best he could to obey the statute or to show by way of excuse that the violation was necessary in order to further some public policy, as, for example, deliberately crossing a solid highway line in an effort to avoid hitting a child who had suddenly run onto the road.

Relatively few jurisdictions deviate from the negligence per se concept. The minority position is that statutory violation is some evidence supporting an allegation of negligence but is not conclusive by itself. The jury must weigh the violation along with other factors.

Not all statutory provisions, of course are framed in terms of precise standards of conduct. The typical reckless driving provision is an elastic one and requires interpretation in the light of a particular fact situation to determine whether or not there has been a violation.

19.9 GROSS NEGLIGENCE

The term *gross negligence,* which connotes recklessness or wanton disregard for the rights of others, represents the conscious failure to exercise diligence in an effort to prevent an injury that the situation indicates is very likely to occur in the absence of special precautions. Contributory negligence will not be a successful defense where the defendant has committed gross negligence.

19.10 IMPUTED NEGLIGENCE

As the term implies, *imputed negligence* is, in effect, charging Peter with Paul's delict. Under certain circumstances, the neglectful conduct of *A* will be attributed to defenseless *B* and will bind *B* in his own capacity as plaintiff or defendant, as the case may be. The most common illustration is the imputing of a servant's negligence to the master or principal, respectively.

A plaintiff will be barred from recovery through having imputed to him the negligence of a third person only if their relationship is such that, as respects harm caused to others, the plaintiff, as a defendant, would have been liable for the negligence in question. Thus, the negligence of the operator of one of two vehicles in an accident will not generally be imputed to his passenger so as to prejudice the latter's action against the driver of the other car. If it can be shown, however, that the passenger and his driver were engaged in a so-called *joint venture,* the driver's negligence may very well be imputed. Much depends, of course, upon the pertinent statutes and common law of the particular jurisdiction.

19.11 CONTRIBUTORY NEGLIGENCE

In the past, there was a general proposition that any negligence on the plaintiff's own part that contributed to the injury of which he complained would bar recovery of any damages. A fairly commonplace example of contributory negligence would be the plaintiff's failure to take a reasonable alternate route rather than a route of obvious danger. In one actual situation, a general contractor was erecting the steelwork of a building. As the crane operator was attempting to swing a heavy girder into place (attached by means of a sling), a workman very foolishly walked underneath. At that moment the hook holding the sling broke, and the girder fell on the workman, killing him instantly. The wife of the deceased sued the contractor for damages. In deciding the question of liability, the court considered such points as these: (1) the crane had successfully erected two similar girders before the accident occurred; (2) the load slightly exceeded the rated capacity of the crane; (3) the hook had been properly tested for a 50 percent overload by the crane manufacturer; (4) no one ordered the workman to walk under the girder, but no one tried to stop him either. The court concluded that, although the contractor did slightly overload the crane, the workman was undoubtedly guilty of contributory negligence and this fact precluded any recovery under the circumstances.

It matters not how slight such contributory negligence may be in relation to the defendant's wrongful conduct. However, in most states the doctrine of comparative fault has now been adopted. The doctrine allows the plaintiff to recover even though some fault on his part is proven. Comparative fault will be discussed more fully in Section 19.12.

In the states that have not adopted comparative fault there are still several instances in which ordinary contributory negligence is not a defense. One of these is the situation wherein defendant's conduct in violating a statutory standard of care is negligent per se. Another involves gross negligence of the defendant. Parallel to this latter is defendant's tortious conduct of a willful, deliberate nature. The line of demarcation between wanton and inadvertent negligence is none too clearly drawn, and it is up to plaintiff to cause the court to look at defendant's behavior with more than mild resentment in order to obviate any possible defense of contributory negligence.

For another limitation that served to confuse the picture on contributory negligence, see Section 19.14 on last clear chance.

19.12   COMPARATIVE NEGLIGENCE

The doctrine of *comparative negligence* provides that an injured party will not be barred from any recovery by contributory negligence, but that there will be an apportionment of damages or responsibility in proportion to the relative fault of the parties involved. Thus, the "all or nothing" aspect of contributory negligence, which may work great hardship where the fault of one party is slight, is modified or eliminated.

Rejected for many years for largely administrative or inertial reasons, comparative negligence is now the prevailing rule in the majority of American jurisdictions, by means of either judicial or legislative action.[7]

In *Li v. Yellow Cab Company of California*,[8] the state supreme court, in abrogating the rule of contributory negligence, concluded that:

> (1) The doctrine of comparative negligence is preferable to the "all-or-nothing" doctrine of contributory negligence from the point of view of logic, practical experience, and fundamental justice; . . . (3) given the possibility of judicial action, certain practical difficulties attendant upon the adoption of comparative negligence should not dissuade us from charting a new course, leaving the resolu-

---

[7]For example, note the following provision of the Louisiana Civil Code.

Article 2323. Comparative Fault

A. In any action for damages where a person suffers injury, death, or loss, the degree or percentage of fault of all persons causing or contributing to the injury, death, or loss shall be determined, regardless of whether the person is a party to the action or a nonparty, and regardless of the person's insolvency, ability to pay, immunity by statute, including but not limited to the provisions of R.S. 23:1032, or that the other person's identity is not known or reasonably ascertainable. If a person suffers injury, death, or loss as the result partly of his own negligence and partly as a result of the fault of another person or persons, the amount of damages recoverable shall be reduced in proportion to the degree or percentage of negligence attributable to the person suffering the injury, death, or loss.

B. The provisions of Paragraph A shall apply to any claim for recovery of damages for injury, death, or loss asserted under any law or legal doctrine or theory of liability, regardless of the basis of liability.

C. Notwithstanding the provisions of Paragraphs A and B, if a person suffers injury, death, or loss as a result partly of his own negligence and partly as a result of the fault of an intentional tortfeasor, his claim for recovery of damages shall not be reduced. (1996).

[8]13 Cal.3d 809, 119 Cal.Rptr. 858, 861 (1975).

tion of some of these problems to future judicial or legislative action; (4) the doctrine of comparative negligence should be applied in this state in its so-called "pure" form under which the assessment of liability in proportion to fault proceeds in spite of the fact that the plaintiff is equally at fault as or more at fault than the defendant.[9]

There are various forms of comparative negligence. In the pure form the plaintiff will recover, no matter how high the percentage of fault, as long as he is not totally negligent. For example, a plaintiff whose fault is designated at 99 percent will still recover 1 percent of the total amount of damages. In the modified version, a state will designate a particular percentage as the cut-off for recovery. For example, in a state that has adopted 50 percent as the cut-off point, a plaintiff whose fault was designated at 51 percent would be unable to recover anything.[10]

19.13 ASSUMPTION OF RISK

Generally speaking, a person cannot voluntarily put himself in a position of manifest danger and then expect to collect from the defendant for the not-unexpected injuries that follow. The assumption of risk defense requires a showing that plaintiff had knowledge of the chance he was taking and yet voluntarily ignored the danger. Some adequate warning must have been given, except where the risk is so obvious that a person of ordinary intelligence would readily sense the likelihood of impending trouble. Where assumption of risk is shown, it goes only to the dangers normally associated with the undertaking. For example, a person contracting to paint a bridge assumes the risk of falling off, but not the danger of electrocution from negligently installed wiring.

There are many exceptions and limitations to the assumption-of-risk defense. For one, worker's compensation laws, as regards injuries falling within their scope, have deprived the employer of his onetime common-law defenses, including that of assumption of risk. Also, the doctrine of assumption of risk, insofar as it is but a variant of contributory negligence, is subsumed under the process of assessing liability in proportion to fault utilized in the comparative negligence system.

Related to the discussion of assumption of risk is the plight of the good Samaritan. If A is hurt or in danger and B chances upon him in his predicament, B is under no legal obligation to render assistance. If he accepts the moral responsibility, however, and takes steps to assist A, he runs the risk that his attempts to aid

[9]See also *Daly v. General Motors Corp.*, 20 Cal.3d 725, 144 Cal. Rptr. 380, 575 P.2d 1162 (1978), where the California Supreme Court held the principles announced in *Li* applicable to an action in strict liability and products liability cases. Most states hold that products liability is not a question of user's negligence, rather who may best spread the cost to society.

[10]Whether or not comparative law principles apply in the strict (nonnegligence) liability area is problematic. In *Jingle v. VW of America*, 975 F. Supp. 576 (1997) a federal court concluded that Vermont law on the question was undecided.

But, comparative negligence was held not available in the products liability context under Pennsylvania law in *Parks v. Allied Signal, Inc.*, 113 F.3d 1327 (CA 3 1997).

See Sections 19.46 and 19.47 *infra* regarding strict liability.

will prove negligent in some respect and that, despite his humanitarian intention, he will consequently be liable for any damage caused. For public policy reasons, this has been negated by statute in some states.

19.14   LAST CLEAR CHANCE

The doctrine of *last clear chance,*[11] which has been called everything from "an inherent limitation in the defense of contributory negligence" to "a thinly disguised theory of comparative negligence," undeniably plays a leading role in many a negligence case. Where both plaintiff and defendant have been guilty of conduct falling short of what would be expected of the "reasonable man" in the particular situation, last clear chance focuses attention upon the sequence of events and regards the defendant as answerable for the damage if—as between the two negligent parties—he had the last opportunity through use of due care to avoid the mishap and consequences.

If the evidence indicates that defendants indeed had the last clear chance to prevent the injury complained of and plaintiff's active negligence had ceased before the point of injury was reached, then the contributory negligence of plaintiff is not a bar to recovery, and the entire loss must be borne by defendant.

For a not-uncommon example, assume plaintiff, having imbibed freely, stumbles in the road and falls to the pavement in a drunken stupor; the stage is now set for operation of the last-clear-chance rule, since plaintiff has, by his own negligence, placed himself in a helpless position of peril. If an approaching driver sees[12] the danger in time and is in a position to avert an accident by exercising ordinary care and prudence, he will be responsible for injuries stemming from his failure to seize the opportunity. One way of putting it is that the law prefers the individual who is negligently unaware of his peril to the individual who is negligent despite having seen the danger.

One limitation ordinarily imposed on the last-clear-chance doctrine relates to the defendant's ability to avoid the harm. If defendant has noted plaintiff's helplessness and perceived the danger but is incapable by reason of some *prior* negligence of his own of averting disaster, no clear chance was his at the crucial time, and the general rule has no applicability. Thus, in the example outlined in the preceding paragraph, if defendant makes every reasonable move in an effort to avoid hitting the prostrate form but is stymied by mechanical failure, his helplessness, though brought on by neglect, is as complete as the plaintiff's and means that no real last opportunity was his.

Last clear chance is clearly related to the principle of proximate cause. Despite his own antecedent negligence, plaintiff is permitted to recover because his conduct, when tested as a cause of the injury, is seen to have been rendered "remote" by the supervening negligence of defendant, which latter wrong is then left as the

---

[11]The doctrine of last clear chance is subsumed under the general process of assessing liability in proportion to fault where the doctrine of comparative negligence has been substituted for that of contributory negligence. *Li v. Yellow Cab Company of California,* 532 P.2d 1226, 119 Cal. Rptr. 858 (1975).

[12]Or, in many jurisdictions, "should have seen."

sole proximate cause of the damage. A jury charge on last clear chance will not be forthcoming unless the judge feels the circumstances warrant belief that reasonable persons *might* find that, notwithstanding plaintiff's own negligent behavior, defendant was the party with the vital opportunity to avoid the accident. Generally speaking, the last-clear-chance test is in order primarily where plaintiff and defendant are on different levels of activity; for example, plaintiff pedestrian is struck by defendant's automobile while plaintiff is crossing the street.[13]

To sum up the essentials of last clear chance: If the jury finds that plaintiff's own negligence materially contributed to his injuries, they can nevertheless grant him damages if they find that (1) after the plaintiff's conduct had created for him a perilous situation, (2) defendant discovered (or should have discovered) not only this fact, but also that plaintiff apparently would not, without intervention, escape, (3) defendant, armed with such knowledge, had the opportunity to save plaintiff by exercising reasonable care, and (4) defendant failed to utilize the chance open to him.

19.15   *Res Ipsa Loquitur*

Literally translated, *res ipsa loquitur* means "the thing speaks for itself." This doctrine has the effect merely of laying the foundation for a permissible inference that defendant was indeed negligent as alleged. It applies where plaintiff is able to show three things:

1. The mishap was one that would not ordinarily occur unless there was negligence on someone's part.

2. The instrumentality or appliance whose careless construction or use occasioned the injury was in the exclusive possession and control of the defendant.

3. There was no voluntary, inexcusable action on plaintiff's part that contributed to the damage.[14]

Where plaintiff can successfully prove the points just listed, it is apparent that any evidence about the true cause of the injury is more than likely primarily, if not exclusively, accessible to the defendant. The plaintiff's showing of compliance with these three points entitles him to get to the jury, even though he cannot show any direct evidence of the defendant's negligence. Where plaintiff is able to set out in his complaint *specific* negligent acts or omissions of defendant, res ipsa has no applicability.[15]

---

[13]For an excellent discussion of the last-clear-chance principle against the factual background of the typical auto-pedestrian mishap, see *Correnti v. Catino,* 115 Conn. 213 (1932). See also *McNamee v. Woodbury Congregation,* 475 A.2d 262 (Conn. 1984) where the adoption of comparative negligence was said to abolish the last-clear-chance doctrine.
   But the doctrine may also play a role in a comparative negligence situation. See *Fouts v. Builder's Transport, Inc.,* 474 S.E.2d 746 (Ga. App. 1996) where the court noted that last clear chance merged into the rule of apportioning damages in the context of the doctrine of comparative negligence.

[14]*Bonventre v. August MAX,* 645 N.Y.S.2d 867 (A.D. 2 1996).

[15]See *Estate of Coleman v. Casper Concrete Co.,* 939 P.2d 233 (Wyo. 1997) where the doctrine was said to be inimical to a claim of negligence in the maintenance of a traffic signal.

By making out a res ipsa case, he has, purely by circumstantial evidence, created an inference of defendant's negligence, which the jury has the option of accepting or rejecting in the light of whatever the defendant is able to put in by way of explanation. In several states, the effect of a res ipsa case is somewhat stronger; that is, the raising of a definite presumption shifts the burden of proof to defendant. In such jurisdictions, the court will *require* the jury to make an inference of defendant's negligence and then see whether the evidence subsequently put in by defendant is sufficient to overcome that initial setback.

Defendant's rebuttal evidence in most res ipsa cases consists of showing due care on his part and on the part of his agents and servants as respects the construction, inspection, maintenance, and use of the instrumentality which is asserted to have brought about plaintiff's injury.

Two decisions illustrate use of the res ipsa loquitur doctrine. The first of these is *J. C. Penney Co. v. Livingston.*[16] Plaintiff two-year-old injured his hand when it inexplicably became caught between two steps of a store's escalator. Plaintiff, by his father, brought an action based on the res ipsa theory, and the appellate court, affirming a verdict for the plaintiff, agreed that all necessary elements were present. The closest question in the case was whether, according to common knowledge and experience, the accident would not have happened, but for some negligence. The reasoning was as follows: it is well known that children are attracted by an escalator and that the ordinary escalator is completely safe even for youngsters. Inasmuch as plaintiff's hand did become caught in the moving parts, there is a logical inference that the particular escalator was unsafe for use by children and that defendant store was consequently negligent in making the device available to such persons.

The other case was decided in Louisiana in 1973 and involved a claim of medical malpractice.[17] The plaintiff's son injured his elbow while playing in a high school football game and was taken to the hospital for treatment. Upon admission to the hospital, the son's only source of complaint was the injured elbow. The plaintiff's son was given a shot that put him to sleep while the defendant performed a closed reduction upon the injured elbow. Following the operation, the patient complained of severe leg pains, and a large lesion was found on his upper left thigh. While in the defendant's care, the patient also suffered injuries to his reproductive organs to the extent that his capacity to reproduce was destroyed. The plaintiff alleged that the injuries to his son's leg and reproductive organs resulted from an act of negligence by the hospital and the physician, the details of which were peculiarly within the knowledge and control of the defendants, and thus the doctrine of res ipsa loquitur was applicable against them.

The court held that the rule applies when the facts shown suggest the negligence of the defendant as the most plausible explanation of the injury. The court observed that the injury occurred within the confines of the special service rooms at the hospital and that, since the surrounding circumstances were peculiarly within the knowl-

---

[16]271 S.W.2d 906 (Ky. App. 1954). See also *Knight v. Otis,* 596 F.2d 84 (1979), where the applicability of the doctrine to a premature closure of an elevator door was said to be a jury question.

[17]*McCann v. Baton Rouge General Hospital,* 276 So.2d 259 (La. 1973), explained by *Zend v. Lincoln Gen. Hospital,* 404 So.2d 1337 at 1342 (1981).

edge of the defendants and were unavailable to the plaintiff, the failure to allege specific acts of the defendant producing the injury was not fatal to the complaint.

One must not succumb to the temptation to urge res ipsa loquitur in every instance, however.[18] For example, in one case[19] a patient was experiencing some problems and difficulties with his right arm and contacted the defendant, an orthopedic surgeon. The surgeon diagnosed the problem as the result of a nonunion of an old fracture and advised the plaintiff that he could perform a compression plating procedure by which the nonunion could be repaired. Following the surgery, the plaintiff experienced difficulty moving the fingers of his hand and an infection was identified. The problems persisted, requiring a number of additional surgical procedures, and the plaintiff's right arm was finally paralyzed. The plaintiff contended that the case should have been submitted to the jury under the doctrine of res ipsa loquitur, urging that the mere occurrence of the infection was sufficient to establish an issue for the jury to consider. After noting the conditions upon which the application of res ipsa loquitur is appropriate, the court stated the question to be whether an infection ordinarily does occur in the absence of negligence. The testimony showed that the hospital had a postoperative infection rate well below the national average, and the plaintiff claimed that the low incidence of infection at the hospital meant that infection does not ordinarily occur. But the court, agreeing with the defendant, found that this fact did not suggest that when an infection does occur, it is the result of negligence.

SPECIAL TOPICS

19.16   MEDICAL MALPRACTICE[20]

Negligence on the part of the family doctor in the treatment of a patient is hard to prove; plaintiff must show by *expert* medical testimony that the defendant physician failed to measure up to the standard of conduct common to his colleagues practicing in the same comparable community.[21] And those who are licensed as special practitioners, as chiropractors, for instance, are entitled to have testimony about a proper standard of care applicable to them given exclusively by members of their own particular "school" within the profession.

There is, of course, a logical explanation for any extra measure of protection afforded doctors and the like in malpractice cases. Professional people are commonly insured against liability for negligence, but it is not the possible immediate money loss that hurts the most; a doctor's reputation in the community and thus his future livelihood can be ruined as the result of one malpractice recovery against

---

[18]See *Sams v. Wal-Mart Stores, Inc.,* 491 S.E.2d 517 (Ga. App. 1997) where the court warned that res ipsa loquitur should be applied with caution and only in extreme cases.

[19]*Wilson v. Stilwill,* 309 N.W.2d 898 (Mich. 1981).

[20]While the term malpractice usually refers to medical malpractice, it can also apply to attorneys and other professionals. For a consideration of architectural or engineering "malpractice," *see* Chapter 20, *infra.*

[21]In a medical malpractice case, the use of expert testimony is allowed to establish that as a matter of common knowledge the incident in question would not have occurred had the defendant physician adhered to proper standards. *Bucklew v. Gross Bard,* 435 At.2d 1150 (N.J. 1981). Similarly, see *Bellardini v. Krikorian,* 537 A.2d 700 (N.J.,1988).

him. Furthermore, increased malpractice insurance costs are passed on to the consumer, making health care more expensive. To protect from lawsuits, the doctor might also use elaborate procedures in the treatment of a patient, and such procedures, although marginally safer, add tremendous costs to the patient.

In an effort to control medical malpractice awards and resulting high premiums for medical malpractice insurance, several jurisdictions are investigating the possibility of voluntary or mandatory arbitration of medical malpractice claims, and some have such programs in place.

19.17   STANDARD OF CARE FOR CHILDREN

Courts in most jurisdictions stand ready to give a child plaintiff every advantage[22] on the issue of contributory negligence, while normally holding a child defendant to the adult standard of reasonable care. Thus, the tender years and limited experience of the child plaintiff are factors taken into consideration when evaluating his conduct.

Parents are not responsible at common law for the negligence of their children, but some legislative bodies have altered the picture and made parents vicariously liable under certain circumstances, often on the rationale that the parents are themselves negligent in failing to control the conduct of minors resident in their households. One idea behind such legislation is that parents who have been placed in a vulnerable position financially are more likely to exert a restraining influence on the juveniles under their roofs.

As a practical matter, children are seldom sued unless there is insurance coverage in the background. Incidentally, minor defendants (unlike adults) are not vicariously liable for the torts of their employees or agents, ostensibly owing to the fact that the employer-employee and principal-agent relationships are contractual in nature and infants cannot generally be held on their contracts.

19.18   TORT INJURY TO MINORS

When an unemancipated child is hurt, two different causes of action arise against the negligent defendant. One of these is to be pursued in the injured child's name for his pain and suffering and his lost earning capacity for the years after majority is reached. The other is available to the parent[23] legally responsible for the injured child's care and the suit is to recover for medical expenses incurred and for loss of the child's services during minority. Some courts say that any contributory negligence on the child's part serves as a bar to the parent's recovery.

---

[22]Graphic examples of this arise in the unfortunate context of child sexual abuse litigation. See, for example, *J.S. v. R.T.H.*, 693 A.2d 1191 (N.J. Super. 1997), a pedophilia case, and *Gloria "X" v. Gibbs*, 659 N.Y.S.2d 349 (A.D. 1997), involving sexual abuse by a babysitter.

[23]An unusual variant on this is *Huddleston v. Infert. Center of America*, 700 A.2d 453 (Pa. Super. 1997), in which a surrogate mother sued a surrogacy clinic when the sperm donor murdered the surrogate child.

Assume that the injury to the child stemmed from an auto accident that was attributable to the combined negligence of the child's father and of the other driver. If the child sues the operator of the other vehicle, it is commonly held that the parent's contributory negligence is not a bar. However, should the parent as plaintiff seek recovery against such third person for medical expenses in connection with the treatment of the innocent child, the defense of contributory negligence would presumably prevail.

19.19   TORTS OF MENTALLY RETARDED PERSONS

The general rule is that a mentally incompetent individual is responsible for such of his torts as do not require a finding of malice, intent, and the like.[24] As far as damage resulting from negligence is concerned, the insane person or the individual of very low mental capacity is generally held to the same standard of care as would be prescribed for people of average intelligence and in good mental health. The rationale seems to be that the innocent victim should not be deprived of recovery just because the tortfeasor was mentally deficient.

Similarly, a person who is intoxicated (and who has thus temporarily impaired his mental competency) is liable for his torts. Intoxication does not excuse failure to exercise due care.

19.20   GOVERNMENTAL TORT LIABILITY

The state, or sovereign, is protected at common law by a blanket exemption from liability for negligence of the agents through whom it must act.[25] There have developed, however, some substantial limitations on this immunity, since government is free to pass laws, frequently styled "tort claims acts" permitting suit against it under stipulated conditions.[26] Because the enabling statute is in derogation of the

---

[24]This would exclude slander, libel, and so on.

[25]There is no comparable shield where the government unit is guilty of maintaining a nuisance. See Section. 19.28 on the general subject of nuisance.

[26]New York State, for example, has set up a special court of claims to handle suits brought against it. See also Article 12, Constitution of the State of Louisiana, Section 10A, which states that "neither the state, a state agency, nor a political subdivision shall be immune from suit and liability in contract or for injury to person to property."

The Louisiana Legislature, however, added the following limitations:

Limitations

A. No suit against the state or a state agency or political subdivision shall be instituted in any court other than a Louisiana state court.
B. (1) In all suits for personal injury to any one person, the total amount recoverable, including all derivative claims, exclusive of property damages, medical care and related benefits and loss of earnings, and loss of future earnings, as provided in this Section, shall not exceed five hundred thousand dollars.
(2) In all suits for wrongful death of any one person, the total amount recoverable, exclusive of property damages, medical care and related benefits and loss of earnings or loss of support, and loss of future support, as provided in this Section, shall not exceed five hundred thousand dollars. La.R.S. 13:5106 (1995).

doctrine of sovereign immunity, it should be strictly construed. However, in practice, the courts have not read it so narrowly.[27]

Municipal corporations are not "sovereign" in the strict sense, but they, like school districts, are deemed to be acting for the state and thus share its immunity as long as they are performing "governmental" functions, such as operating police and fire departments. Where, on the other hand, the city, town, village, or other municipality, acts in a *proprietary* capacity for instance, owns and operates transit systems or other public utilities, they will be responsible for torts of their agents or employees committed within the scope of their agency or employment. The line between governmental and proprietary operation is understandably difficult to draw at times. Highway defects are a fruitful source of municipal tort litigation. Maintenance of highways is generally regarded as a governmental function, but there are numerous statutes on the books waiving the common law exemption and imposing civil liability on the government unit for negligence in connection with road upkeep. These laws normally require a showing by plaintiff of the unreasonably dangerous condition of the road and of adequate notice to the proper authorities regarding the defect. A city or other unit of government cannot be sued, for example, for such things as failure to pass a regulatory ordinance, which would prohibit riding bicycles on sidewalks. This type of decision is regarded as a matter of discretion[28] and beyond the reach of the individual citizen.

19.21   NEGLIGENCE OF GOVERNMENT OFFICIALS

Government officials, while performing discretionary or quasi-judicial functions are not liable for their negligence, and they are not generally held liable for the defaults of their subordinates, irrespective of whether such defaults pertain to ministerial or discretionary functions. If officials were not granted such immunity it would be difficult to find public servants.

19.22   CHARITABLE INSTITUTIONS

In some jurisdictions, charitable institutions have complete immunity from tort liability; in other jurisdictions, the immunity pertains only where the would-be plaintiffs are nonpaying recipients of hospital services or similar benefits. There is something of an anomaly in permitting the paying patients to sue a hospital in

---

[27]See, for example, *Massengill v. Yoma County,* 104 Ariz. 514, 456 P.2d 376 (1969), where the court stated that the doctrine had been relegated "to the dust heap of history." The court now considers whether the duty was owed to the public in general or if the public entity breached the duty because of a special relationship, which may be station only constructed, established between the injured plaintiff and the state. See also *Carpenter v. Johnson,* 231 Kan. 783, 469 P.2d 400 (1982), where the court said that liability is the rule and immunity the exception under the Kansas tort claims acts.

[28]Cases affirming the doctrine of sovereign community for discretionary functions include *Thompson v. Dept. of Hwy. Safety and Motor Vehicles,* 692 So.2d 272 (Fla. App. 1997); and *State Dept. of Trans. and Public Fac. v. Sanders,* 944 P.2d 453 (Alaska 1997).

tort while denying recovery to charity patients; the latter group is presumably more in need.

Still another line of decisions has held that, as respects negligence of its "ministerial" employees (custodians, housekeepers etc.), a hospital is answerable to outsiders, such as the delivery boy who slips on defective flooring, but not to any of its patients, whether or not they are charity cases.

Apart from a consideration of the class of persons to whom the institution may be liable in tort, further distinctions have been based on the relationship that the actual tortfeasor bears to the charitable institution. Thus, a hospital may ordinarily be responsible for damage resulting from the fault of its ministerial employees, but nurses and doctors using the hospital facilities in the performance of their professional functions are deemed to be independent contractors and not agents of the institution. The hospital cannot be held for the negligence of these independent contractors, and this assumes only that the hospital exercised reasonable care insofar as it had a voice in their selection.

However, there are isolated cases that have drawn a distinction between negligence and mistakes of judgment on the part of hospital nurses, treating the institution as liable where negligence was found to be present. In one instance, a nurse, having determined that a delirious patient would be safer with sideboards on her bed, adjusted the boards in a negligent manner, and the patient ultimately was injured in a mishap directly traceable to that negligence. The court reasoned that, had the nurse made the wrong decision in the first place about the need for boards, the hospital would nonetheless be immune from liability because the nurse had simply used faulty judgment on a matter of discretion. But, once the decision was made to affix the boards, the ensuing negligence by the nurse placed the hospital in a vulnerable position.

Where it is recognized at all, the doctrine of charitable immunity extends to a variety of charitable endeavors. Thus, an aquarium operated for charitable and educational purposes has been held immune although entertainment was a part of the educational experience.[29]

But the common law immunity is construed narrowly and has been held not applicable to a juvenile rehabilitation camp whose funding came almost exclusively from the state.[30]

19.23 LIABILITY OF LANDOWNERS

In the use and enjoyment of his premises, the landowner or occupier must exercise reasonable care for the protection of those who are lawfully in the immediate vicinity, such as persons using a nearby public highway. But a landowner may not owe a duty to exercise due care to prevent injury on an adjacent highway over which it had no control where the injury was unrelated to the owner's use of his

---

[29]*Morales v. New Jersey Academy of Aquatic Sciences*, 694 A.2d 600 (N.J. Super. 1997) construing the N.J. Charitable Immunity Act, NJSA 2A:53A-7.
[30]*Ouachita Wilderness Inst., Inc. v. Mergen*, 947 S.W.2d 780 (Ark. 1997).

property.[31] With respect to those who actually set foot on his property, the owner's duty of care may vary with the characterization of the visitor as trespasser, licensee, or invitee. However, as will be discussed below, these classifications have become of less importance.

Trespasser   One who comes upon another's property without either (1) the consent of the occupier or (2) the legal privilege to enter irrespective of the question of express or implied consent, such as a police official armed with a search warrant, is called a *trespasser.* To him, the landowner or occupier owes merely a duty to refrain from willful misconduct. Thus, no traps may be set for the unwelcome visitor, nor may intentional injury be done him. There is no obligation to foresee or to seek out the presence of the trespasser and no responsibility to him for defects or conditions of natural origin existing on the land. A few courts have deviated from the norm and taken the position that, once a trespasser's presence is discovered, he is owed reasonable care for his safety.

The *attractive-nuisance doctrine* relates solely to trespassing children and amounts to a limitation on the general rule of non liability to trespassers unless intentional harm can be shown. The land occupier is vulnerable under the attractive-nuisance principle where he is harboring on his premises a highly dangerous instrumentality, or condition, of a nature likely to attract children of tender years who will not appreciate the danger involved. Part of the attractive-nuisance concept is supposed to be a weighing of the degree of risk of injury to minors against the utility to the owner of maintaining the complained-of-condition. If the latter factor assumes paramount importance, there should be no damage recovery by the child trespasser.

The attractive-nuisance doctrine was first clearly set forth in *Keefe v. Milwaukee & St. Paul Railway Co.,*[32] where a child was injured while playing on a railroad turntable. The turntable was not fastened or fenced or in any way protected, although it could easily have been locked to prevent this type of accident. The court held for the plaintiff and had this to say: "The difference between the plaintiff's position and that of a voluntary trespasser, capable of using care, consists in this, that the plaintiff was induced to come upon the defendant's turntable by the defendant's own conduct, and that, as to him, the turntable was a hidden danger, a trap." Some jurisdictions refuse to recognize the attractive-nuisance doctrine.[33]

Licensee   A tolerated intruder, or *licensee,* is distinguished from a trespasser in that he has the owner's express or implied permission to be on the premises. He is present, though, for his own purpose, convenience, or gratification and has no con-

---

[31]Thus, no duty existed when a visitor to a funeral home, finding the parking lot full, parked across the street, and was hit by a car as he recrossed the street. *Santoleri v. Knightly,* 663 N.Y.S.2d 505 (Sup. Ct. 1997).

[32]21 Minn. 207 (1875).

[33]*Richards v. Cincinnati West Baptist Church,* 680 N.E.2d 191 (Ohio App. 1996). This case also noted that the doctrine of dangerous instrumentality does not apply, however, where the dangerous instrumentality is not on or adjacent to a public place, and thus could not have lured the trespassing children onto the property. In this case a child climbed into a church yard and was injured when a water drenching machine fell on him. [See Sec. 19.47.]

tractual relationship with the owner. Reasonable care must be exercised to warn the licensee of hidden dangers of which the owner is aware. The owner or occupier is not required to take affirmative steps to protect a licensee but is under a duty to discover his presence if reasonably possible, to avoid active negligence toward him, and to refrain from willful misconduct toward him.

A good example of a licensee is the social guest in the home of his host. Firemen and policemen who enter upon private property in the discharge of their duty are typically treated as licensees unless they have been called by the owner, in which latter event they step up to the status of invitee and are consequently owed a higher standard of care.

Invitee An *invitee* (also known as a *business visitor*) is one who by invitation has entered upon the premises for some business purpose of mutual interest or benefit to him and to the owner. The store customer affords an everyday illustration, and is an invitee even though he buys nothing and, indeed, has no real intention of making a purchase. It is possible for a person to be a full-fledged invitee with respect to one part of the store building and a mere licensee (or even trespasser) with respect to others.

The proprietor must assume the affirmative duty of maintaining the establishment in a safe condition so as to avoid danger to those who come within the broad orbit of the business invitation. Thus, to avoid potential liability periodic and thorough inspections of the premises would have to be made and all indicated safety precautions taken. The owner must warn the invitee of all dangers other than those of which the latter is aware or those which are readily apparent.

The trend of the law of premises liability is clearly toward the elimination of technical status positions that protect certain classes from liability. Many jurisdictions now hold that distinctions between invitee and licensees have no logical relation to the duty owed by the possessor of the premises, and the tendency is toward the substitution of the broad test of reasonable care for the status rules.[34] The Supreme Court of California, for example, has said:[35]

> There is another fundamental objection to the approach to the question of the possessor's liability on the basis of the common-law distinctions based upon the status of the injured party as a trespasser, licensee, or invitee. Complexity can be borne and confusion remedied where the underlying principles governing liability are based upon proper considerations. Whatever may have been the historical justifications for the common-law distinctions, it is clear that those distinctions are not justified in the light of our modern society and that the complexity and confusion which has arisen is not due to difficulty in applying the original common-law rules—they are all too easy to apply in their original formulation—but is due to the attempts to apply just rules in our modern society within the ancient terminology.

[34]New York, for example. *Santoleri v. Knightly,* 663 N.Y.S.2d 505 (Sup. Ct. 1997).

[35]N. *Rowland v. Christian,* 70 Cal. Rptr. 97, 443 P.2d 561 (1968). See also *Pridgen v. Boston Housing Authority,* 308 N.E. 2d 467 (Mass. 1974), where "all lawful visitors" are grouped as a class and *Webb. v. City and Burrough of Sitka,* 561 P.2d. 731 (Alaska 1977), where the court abolished the classifications of trespasser, licensee, and invitee in relation to property owner liability. See also *Soule v. Mass. Elec.,* 390 N.E. 2d 719, (Mass. 1979), which distinguished child from adult trespassers.

Without attempting to labor all of the rules relating to the possessor's liability, it is apparent that the classifications of trespasser, licensee, and invitee, the immunities from liability predicated upon those classifications, and the exceptions to those immunities, often do not reflect the major factors which should determine whether immunity should be conferred upon the possessor of land. Some of those factors, including the closeness of the connection between the injury and the defendant's conduct, the moral blame attached to the defendant's conduct, the policy of preventing future harm, and the prevalence and availability of insurance, bear little, if any, relationship to the classifications of trespasser, licensee, and invitee and the existing rules conferring immunity.

19.24   LIABILITY OF LESSORS

Generally speaking, there is nothing in the law that would prevent an owner from leasing a broken-down piece of property as long as he reveals to the prospective tenant defects that are unknown to the latter and that are not readily discoverable upon inspection. Most courts obligate the landlord merely to give the lessee such information as is in his possession and do not hold him responsible with regard to additional defects he *should* have known about by reason of his presumed familiarity with his own property. Thus, a lessor will not during the term of the rental agreement be liable for harm occasioned the lessee or third parties in consequence of the condition of the leased premises as long as he informed the lessee about known defects.

Particularly where a multiunit dwelling is involved, the landlord will retain control over a portion of the premises, for instance, common approaches, stairways, and halls. Where tenants or third persons such as business visitors and social guests of the tenant are permitted use of such common appurtenances, it is incumbent upon the lessor to keep these parts in reasonably safe condition.

With respect to the portion of the premises exclusively under the control of the tenant, the landlord is under no obligation to repair or improve unless the lease or some other contractual arrangement requires him to take such action. If he promises to repair certain defects and fails to do so, the tenant has a contract action against him. If, on the other hand, the landlord actually attempts repair, whether or not acting pursuant to a binding promise, and carries through in such a negligent manner that the tenant or someone else on the premises in the right of the tenant is injured, the landlord's liability in tort is clear.[36] When the lessor enters the lessee's domain to correct defects or make improvements, his contractual relationship with his tenant is not a factor, and he is treated as would be any outsider there to accomplish a particular job. That is to say, his conduct will be tested by the usual standard of reasonable care. Where the landlord would otherwise be liable for his own

---

[36]Some courts draw a distinction where the repairs are gratuitous and say that the landlord's liability for negligence extends only to the tenant and the members of his family in permanent residence with him. Another approach where the repair undertaking is not pursuant to contractual obligation is to hold the defendant landlord liable only for *gross* negligence.

negligence, most courts will not permit him to absolve himself from responsibility merely by inserting an exculpatory clause in the lease agreement.

Where property is rented for a purpose known to the landlord to involve admission of the general public, a member of that public may recover against such landlord for injury traceable to defects in the property existing at the outset of the lease arrangement, whether or not the landlord was at the time actually aware of the unsafe condition. Similarly, should the lease negotiations alert the lessor that the tenant contemplated utilizing the property for obviously dangerous activities, the lessor may well be held responsible to persons in the vicinity of the premises for harm done them as the result of such activities.

19.25 LIABILITY OF VENDOR OF GOODS

In the absence of an appropriate exclusion or disclaimer, sales by tradesmen are generally subject to implied warranties to the effect that the goods involved are merchantable and fit for the purpose which the buyer is known to have in mind.[37]

Where the items for sale are obviously of a dangerous nature, the supplier has an exposure that may assume considerable proportions. One who manufactures, supplies, sells, or repairs a chattel that is either inherently dangerous such as poisons, explosives, and firearms, or will become dangerous if defectively assembled or repaired, like an automobile, owes a duty of care not only to the immediate purchaser but also to the third parties who might reasonably be expected ultimately to use the article in question. The bellwether case in point is *MacPherson v. Buick Motor Co.*[38] The facts were these: defendant, a manufacturer of automobiles, sold one of its products to a retail dealer, and the latter resold to plaintiff. While plaintiff was in the car, it suddenly collapsed, and he was thrown out and injured. One of the wheels had been made of defective wood, and its spokes crumbled into fragments. The wheel had not been made by defendant but was supplied by another manufacturer. The evidence showed that the wheel's defects could have been ascertained by reasonable inspection and that such an inspection was omitted by the defendant. In affirming judgment for plaintiff, the New York Court of Appeals included in its opinion the following:

> If the nature of a thing is such that it is reasonably certain to place life and limb in peril when negligently made, it is then a thing of danger. Its nature gives warning of the consequences to be expected. If to the element of danger there is added knowledge that the thing will be used by persons other than the purchaser and used without new tests, then, irrespective of contract, the manufacturer of this thing of danger is under a duty to make it carefully. That is as far as we are required to go for the decision of this case. There must be knowledge of a danger, not merely possible, but probable. It is *possible* to use almost anything in a way that will make it dangerous if defective . . .

[37]*The Uniform Commercial Code* covers details of these and other facets of the sale of goods.
[38]217 N.Y. 382 (1916).

Beyond all question, the nature of an automobile gives warning of probable danger if its construction is defective. This automobile was designed to go fifty miles an hour. Unless its wheels were sound and strong, injury was almost certain. It was as much a thing of danger as a defective engine for a railroad. The defendant knew the danger. It knew also that the car would be used by persons other than the buyer. This was apparent also from the fact that the buyer was a dealer in cars, who bought to resell.

We think the defendant was not absolved from a duty of inspection because it bought the wheels from a reputable manufacturer. It was not merely a dealer in automobiles. It was a manufacturer of automobiles. It was responsible for the finished product. It was not at liberty to put the finished product on the market without subjecting the component parts to ordinary and simple tests.

The decision in *MacPherson* did not extend the liability of the seller beyond the purchaser of the product. At present, the manufacturer's liability exposure extends to other users and consumers of the product and to those foreseeably within the vicinity of the product's use.[39]

19.26   GUEST STATUTES

Many states have laws that serve to place restrictions upon a car owner's liability to guests injured while riding gratis in his vehicle. Such guests must, as a prerequisite to recovery, prove willful misconduct or gross negligence attributable to the defendant. Typical of these "guest statutes" is that of Alabama.[40]

The owner, operator, or person responsible for the operation of a motor vehicle shall not be liable for loss or damage arising from injuries to or death of a guest while being transported without payment therefor, in or upon such motor vehicle, resulting from the operation thereof, unless such injuries or death are caused by the willful or wanton misconduct of such operator, owner, or person responsible for the operation of said motor vehicle.

The term "guest" as employed in the foregoing text, has been construed to mean one who accepts the invitation of the driver and takes a ride in the automobile either for his own pleasure or on his own business without conferring any benefit upon the driver other than the mere pleasure of companionship.

At least one state supreme court has held that its guest statute is unconstitutional as denying equal protection and due process of law and as impermissibly

---

[39]*The Second Restatement of Torts*, Section 395, states that "a manufacturer who fails to exercise reasonable care in the manufacturer of a chattel which, unless carefully made, he should recognize as involving an unreasonable risk of causing physical harm to those who use it for a purpose for which the manufacturer should expect it to be used and those whom he should expect to be endangered by its probable use, is subject to liability for physical harm caused to them by its lawful use in a manner and for a purpose for which it is supplied."

[40]Alabama Motor Vehicle and Traffic Code § 32-1-2.

closing courts and denying remedy by due process of law not to some but to all of the people of the state.[41]

Where the guest rider is injured in a collision brought about by the negligence of his driver and the negligence of a third party, most jurisdictions say the former's contributory negligence will not bar the guest's action against the third party.

19.27 FAMILY-PURPOSE DOCTRINE

This is another principle of tort law that the automotive age brought into being. Many courts hold the car owner responsible for damage done through the negligent driving of members of his family. The underlying theory is that the owner, by permitting his immediate relatives to operate the car for their pleasure and use, has made that purpose his business and thus rendered the driver his "servant." As long as general use of the vehicle is afforded by the family member, the mere fact that instructions by the owner about speed, distance, and so on, were ignored will not serve to relieve the owner of liability. Quite obviously, the family-purpose principle is another instance of getting at the so-called "deep pocket" of the party most likely to be able to pay for the harm.

Various states have enacted statutes that seek to make certain that there will be a financially responsible defendant available in motor-vehicle cases. One type of provision, for example, requires an adult's countersignature on the license application for a driver under eighteen, such endorser to be answerable for injuries occasioned by negligence of the juvenile operator.

19.28 NUISANCE

Nuisance is a condition, usually long-standing and of indefinite anticipated duration, whose existence is directly injurious to others. The old insistence on a showing of continuity as a condition precedent to recovery for nuisance is, however, being whittled away. A nuisance may or may not be lawful, and this is true whether it is of the *private* or of the *public* variety, and it is possible for a condition to constitute a private and a public nuisance at the same time. The term "nuisance" does not have reference to any particular type of conduct which results in the invasion of plaintiff's interests. The nuisance may stem from defendant's negligence, from his

---

[41] *Primes v. Tyler,* 331 N.E.2d 723 (Ohio 1975). The repeal and replacement of the California Guest Statute produced the following curious variation.

Owner as passenger; liability

No person riding in or occupying a vehicle owned by him and driven by another person with his permission . . . has any right of action for civil damages against the driver of the vehicle or against any other person legally liable for the conduct of the driver on account of personal injury to or the death of the owner . . . during the ride, unless the plaintiff in any such action establishes that the injury or death proximately resulted from the intoxication or willful misconduct of the driver. Calif. Vehicle Code § 17158.

employment of a dangerous instrumentality, or from conduct by which he fully intends to do harm.

A plaintiff will frame his complaint on the basis of nuisance primarily when he anticipates some barrier, such as contributory negligence, to a recovery on a standard negligence theory. Certain defenses commonly employed in negligence cases are not available when absolute nuisance is the gravamen, or significant point, of the complaint.

Private Nuisance   This type of nuisance grew as an adjustment of differences between adjacent landowners, permitting the aggrieved party recovery against the other for unreasonable and substantial interference with plaintiff's enjoyment of his own premises. A *private nuisance* is a wrong arising from the use of one's own property in such a manner as to do violence to the rights or interests of another. Frequently, maintenance of a nuisance on *A*'s property will materially reduce the value of *B*'s adjoining acreage. Technically, the harm need be nothing more than discomfort, annoyance, or inconvenience in order to be actionable.

Apart from taking the law into his own hands, the party adversely affected has open to him an action at law for damages or in equity for an injunction.

Public Nuisance   Where the objectionable condition is such that the public at large is adversely affected, the nuisance is characterized as a *public* one. Obstructing a common highway and thus impeding traffic would constitute a public nuisance. Unless some person suffers a special injury distinguishable from harm done the general public, he as an individual has no damages recovery available against the perpetrator of the public nuisance.

19.29   EMOTIONAL DISTURBANCES

The case law on the issue of whether or not damages are recoverable for emotional disturbances, such as fright, with or without accompanying physical distress, and with or without a showing of an "impact" chargeable to the defendant, has undergone substantial evolution. Many jurisdictions will not allow recovery for emotional disturbance or accompanying physical distress in the absence of actual impact.

Others bar recovery for emotional distress absent direct physical impact unless the defendant's conduct is so egregious as to justify imputing malice.[42] When the plaintiff has suffered physical impact from an external force, recovery for emotional distress may be allowed stemming from the incident during which the impact occurred, not only the impact itself.[43] Courts have shown more reluctance to allow recovery for emotional distress not accompanied by any physical distress.

[42]*Sweshun v. General Motors Corp.,* 812 F. Supp. 1218 (M.D. Fla. 1993).
[43]*Kingston Square Tenants v. Tuskegee Garden,* 792 F. Supp. 1566 (S.D. Fla. 1992).

A case from Virginia is characteristic of the existing state of the law. There, the plaintiff was standing in the doorway of her house when an automobile crashed through the front porch of the house, causing her severe fright and agitation but resulting in no contemporaneous physical contact. The evidence indicated that the plaintiff suffered from severe nervousness, chest and arm pains, and menstrual irregularities as a result of the shock of the collision. Addressing the question of physical impact, the court said:

> Many eminent scholars have considered the rule and are virtually unanimous in condemning it as unjust and contrary to experience and logic.
>
> Our research reveals that a total of 35 jurisdictions have considered the rule. Of these at least 25 have either completely rejected it or abandoned it as being unsound. Since 1929 every jurisdiction which has considered the issue, except the Supreme Court of Washington . . . has either abandoned the rule or refused to adopt it.
>
> A rapidly increasing majority of courts have repudiated or not followed the "impact rule" for the reasons that the early difficulty in tracing a resulting injury back through fright had been minimized by the advance of medical science . . .
>
> We adhere to the view that where conduct is merely negligent, not willful, wanton, or vindictive, and physical impact is lacking, there can be no recovery for emotional disturbance alone. We hold, however that where the claim is for emotional disturbance *and* physical injury resulting therefrom, there may be recovery for negligent conduct, notwithstanding the lack of physical impact, provided the injured party properly pleads and proves by clear and convincing evidence that his physical injury was the natural result of fright or shock proximately caused by the defendant's negligence. In other words, there may be recovery in such a case if, but only if, there is shown a clear and unbroken chain of causal connection between the negligent act, the emotional disturbance, and the physical injury.[44]

Courts have been generally reluctant, however, to take the final step and remove the requirements that physical injury accompany the emotional injury. But the Supreme Judicial Court of Massachusetts, in the case of *Agis v. Howard Johnson Company,*[45] has moved in that direction.

The plaintiff in the case was a waitress in a local Howard Johnson restaurant. The manager of the restaurant informed all of the employees that there "was some stealing going on," but that, since the identity of the person responsible was not known he would, until the person responsible was discovered, begin firing all the present waitresses in alphabetical order. The plaintiff was the first to be discharged. The plaintiff did not allege any bodily injury, but became greatly upset, began to

[44]*Hughes v. Moore,* 214 Va. 27, 197 S.E. 2d 214 (1973) explained by *Ruth v. Fletcher,* 377 S.E.2d 412 (1989) See also *Culbert v. Samsons Super Markets, Inc.,* 444 A.2d 433 (Me. 1982), where the court allowed a suit for emotional distress without a requirement of impact and without the plaintiff being the zone of danger. And see *Moldonado v. National Acme Co.,* 73 F.3d 642 (Sixth Cir. 1996, applying Mich. law) recognizing that Michigan had abolished both the "zone of impact" and "physical impact" rules. To the contrary is *Kun v. Finnegan, Henderson, Farabow, Garrett and Dunne,* 949 F. Supp. 13 (D.C. 1996).

[45]355 N.E.2d 315 (Mass. 1976).

cry, and allegedly sustained emotional distress, mental anguish, and loss of wages and earnings. Upholding the right to recovery, the court said:

> The most often cited argument for refusing to extend the cause of action for intentional or reckless infliction of emotional distress to cases where there has been no physical injury is the difficulty of proof and the danger of fraudulent or frivolous claims. There has been a concern that "mental anguish, standing alone, is too subtle and speculative to be measured by any known legal standard," that "mental anguish and its consequences are so intangible and peculiar and vary so much with the individual that they cannot reasonably be anticipated," that a wide door might "be opened not only to fictitious claims but to litigation over trivialities and mere bad manners as well," and that there can be no objective measurement of the extent or the existence of emotional distress.
>
> While we are not unconcerned with these problems, we believe that "the problems presented are not . . . insuperable" and that "administrative difficulties do not justify the denial of relief for serious invasions of mental and emotional tranquility . . . "
>
> In light of what we have said, we hold that one who, by extreme and outrageous conduct and without privilege, causes severe emotional distress to another is subject to liability for such emotional distress even though no bodily harm may result. However, in order for a plaintiff to prevail in a case for liability under this tort, four elements must be established. It must be shown (1) that the actor intended to inflict emotional distress or that he knew or should have known that emotional distress was the likely result of his conduct, (2) that the conduct was "extreme and outrageous" and was "utterly intolerable in a civilized community," (3) that the actions of the defendant were the cause of the plaintiff's distress, and (4) that the emotional distress sustained by the plaintiff was "severe" and of a nature "that no reasonable man could be expected to endure it."

In an emotional distress case from California, a doctor negligently and wrongly diagnosed the plaintiff's wife as a syphilitic and instructed her to advise her husband of the diagnosis, causing him serious emotional distress. Finding foreseeability on the part of the doctor of the reaction on the husband to be critical, the court held that the husband had stated a cause of action for negligent infliction of emotional distress even though the doctor had never spoken to the husband.[46]

But in a case[47] where a patient sued her physician for a misdiagnosis of ovarian cancer when in fact she was cancer free, the court said that absent physical injury, emotional distress must be "severe and debilitating," and must result from an existent peril. Finding the peril to be nonexistent (she didn't have cancer), the plaintiff was denied recovery.

It should be noted that recovery for emotional disturbance is not normally available in the usual breach of contract situation. In *Fiore v. Sears, Roebuck and Company*,[48] where the plaintiff alleged that he had undergone extreme mental anguish as a result of the defendant's failure to conform to its guarantee with respect to the installation of a roof and the multiple efforts made by him to have the

---

[46]*Molien v. Kaiser Foundation Hospitals*, 616 P.2d 813 (Cal. 1980). See also *King v. Otasco*, 861 F.2d 438 (1988), where the court held that a parent who had alleged a false arrest could state a cause of action on behalf of his children for emotional distress inflicted on them.

[47]*Williams v. Warren General Hospital*, 684 N.E.2d 730 (Ohio App. 1996).

[48]44 N.J. Superior, 74, 364 A.2d 572 (1976).

defect corrected, and the manner in which the claim had been handled and the harassment to which he had been subjected. The court said that as a matter of basic justice, when one can at the time of contracting reasonably foresee mental harm resulting from breach of contract, defendant ought to be liable in damages if his actions are either willful of reckless, but held that what was alleged in this case was nothing more or less than the normal breach of contract situation. The court added, however, that the allegation regarding the manner in which the claim had been handled involved a claim of tortious conduct for which an award for emotional disturbance might be proper, if the other conditions prerequisite to such liability were present.

19.30 SURVIVAL STATUTES AND WRONGFUL-DEATH ACTS

At common law no civil action would lie against the tortfeasor for an injury resulting in the death of the victim. The injured party, while he lived, had available a suit for damages, but the right of action abated at his demise and could not be maintained by his personal representatives. The anomaly of the common-law situation was that a fatal injury left the victim's estate and beneficiaries without recourse, while lesser hurts could be mended with damage money recoverable. Even in the latter circumstance, however, plaintiff would be thwarted by death of the wrong-doer prior to entry of judgment against him.

The common-law picture has been radically altered by statutory provisions in most jurisdictions, though the applicable laws vary widely. What is probably the prevailing pattern is to have a "survival-of-action" provision and a so-called "wrongful-death statute" complementing each other so as to afford to the parties damaged a thoroughgoing remedy for the entire loss sustained through defendant's malfeasance. Defenses such as contributory negligence, which would have been at hand for use against the deceased victim had he lived, generally continue to be available after he has left the scene.[49]

The *survival statutes* typically provide that a right of action for negligence belonging to the injured person does not terminate at his death, but an action to recover damages may be instituted or taken over by his estate.[50] Such an action would seek recompense for pain and suffering endured by the deceased, for expenses incurred, and for loss of earnings up to the time of death.

Unlike a true survival act, the wrongful-death statute creates a new cause of action and does not simply transfer to his successor in interest a right to sue possessed by the injured person before his demise.[51] In some states the new cause of

[49]See, by way of example, New York Estates, Powers and Trusts Law, § 5-4.2 (McGivney 1967).

[50]See, for example, *id*. § 11-3.2. Incidentally, the same statutory provision deals also with the other side of the story and stipulates that no cause of action for injury to person or property shall be lost because of the death of the person liable for the injury.

[51]Thus, New York Estates, Powers and Trusts Law § 5-4.1 (McGivney 1967) provides: "The personal representative . . . may maintain an action to recover damages for a wrongful act, neglect or default which caused the decedent's death against a person who would have been liable to the decedent by reason of such wrongful conduct if death had not ensued . . ."

action goes to the administrator of the deceased, while in others specific relatives are named as beneficiaries. In either case, recovery is the monetary loss sustained by the parties for whose benefit the action is brought, that is, the loss suffered through being deprived of what they figured to receive of the victim's earnings from the date of his death on through the rest of what would have been his anticipated life span. In other words, the wrongful-death action is essentially a suit for injury to the property rights of certain beneficiaries favored by the statute, and the measure of damages is the pecuniary value of decedent's life to his next of kin. Some jurisdictions, however, have adopted statutes that allow the beneficiary damages for loss of society and companionship with the deceased. Under the majority rule, wrongful-death actions do not survive the tortfeasor.

Survival acts and wrongful-death statutes perform separate functions in providing recourse for the damage done. The United States Supreme Court, in discussing the role of these complementary statutes, has put it this way.[52]

> Although originating in the same wrongful act or neglect, the two claims are quite distinct, no part of either being embraced in the other. One is for the wrong to the injured person, and is confined to his personal loss and suffering before he died, while the other is for the wrong to the beneficiaries, and is confined to their pecuniary loss through his death. One begins where the other ends, and a recovery upon both in the same action is not a double recovery for a single wrong, but a single recovery for a double wrong.

19.31   INTRAFAMILY TORTS

Briefly stated, parent and unemancipated child can sue each other for torts affecting property interests but not, as a general rule, for personal wrongs, intentional or otherwise. A parallel situation pertains where the husband-wife relationship is involved. Before the advent of what are commonly termed "married women's acts," statutes that give the wife control over her separate property and render her individually responsible for her own torts, not even property torts were actionable between spouses. The theory seems to have been that the ideal of domestic bliss could be advanced by preventing the marital partners from bringing each other into court on tort claims.

This doctrine, known as interspousal immunity, is dying a slow death.[53] The modern approach is well illustrated in a case in which a wife slipped and fell on a snow-covered driveway where the husband was in control of the premises and

---

[52]*St. Louis, I.M. & Southern R. Co. v. Craft*, 237 U.S. 648, 658 (1914).

[53]It has not, however, completely expired. See *Gordon v. State Farm Ins.*, 700 S.2d 1117 (La. App. 1997) recognizing the doctrine but concluding that it did not preclude a wife from suing the husband's liability insurer, and *Little v. Economy Preferred Ins. Co.*, 675 N.E.2d 1048 (Ill. App. 1997), recognizing the doctrine but holding that it did not bar an action for contribution by a third party.

responsible for sanding, salting, or shoveling after a snowstorm. The court termed the reasons that had supported the common-law rule of interspousal immunity "antediluvian assumptions" and negated the doctrine in the circumstances.[54]

TORTS THAT ARE USUALLY INTENTIONAL

19.32   INTRODUCTION

One who purposely commits a tortious act is answerable for any and all damage flowing from the wrong. There are, of course, a great many different types of torts normally intentional in nature.

19.33   FRAUDULENT MISREPRESENTATION

To prevail when the allegation is one of fraud, plaintiff must prove (1) that defendant made a false, material statement of fact, (2) that defendant either showed a reckless disregard for the truth or knew that what he advanced as true was actually false,[55] (3) that defendant intended to induce reliance by plaintiff, (4) that plaintiff did with justification rely upon the accuracy of the statement, and (5) that plaintiff was damaged in consequence of such reliance. Note particularly (4) in the above list; a seller, for example, is entitled to "puff" his wares to a degree, and the buyer cannot safely take all statements at their face value. The doctrine of *caveat emptor* ("let the buyer beware") in mercantile transactions has the earmarks of a contributory-negligence theory.

19.34   DEFAMATION

In general, a statement is defamatory if its natural tendency is to subject the victim to public ridicule, contempt, hatred, or the like. The court decides whether an odious interpretation could reasonably be drawn from the questioned statement, and the jury's function is to determine whether the statement was actually undertaken in the harmful way alleged by the complainant. The defamatory meaning of the wording used may be obvious or may arise only in the light of the surrounding circumstances, which the plaintiff would have to show. Thus, a statement that twins were born to Mr. and Mrs. Jones appears innocent enough, even if false, until it is shown that the declarant knew the Joneses were very recently married. It must be proved that the alleged wrongful remarks were communicated by defendant to some third person and that the statement in question clearly related to plaintiff and not merely to some large indeterminate group of which he happened to be a part.

---

[54]*Brown v. Brown,* 409 N.E.2d 717 (Mass. 1980). Also abrogating interspousal immunity are *Schlueter v. Schlueter,* 929 S.W.2d 94 (Tex. Ct. App. 1996), and *Steve H. v. Wendy S.,* 67 Cal.Rptr. 90 (1997).
[55]This prerequisite is called *scienter.*

The test is whether a fair percentage of the people who know plaintiff believe the material refers to him. Under the prevailing common law policy, truth and privilege are complete defenses in defamation suits, as will be discussed below.

Slander and Libel   Defamation is traditionally divided into slander and libel. The yardstick that measures statements for traces of slander or libel varies with the times, with the geographical location, and with other, less definite factors. Slander is oral defamation published without legal excuse, whereas *libel* takes the form of written statements, pictures, images, and the like. Hence, improper remarks about X dictated to one's secretary constitute slander. When the dictation is transcribed, libel has entered the scene. All true libel is actionable per se; that is, the law will infer that third persons have read the objectionable remarks and that damage has been done to plaintiff's reputation. In most slander cases, on the other hand, plaintiff must make a showing of actual damage. In many jurisdictions slander is actionable per se in the following four instances:

1. When defendant has imputed to plaintiff the commission of an indictable crime or of an act involving moral turpitude.
2. When defendant has asserted that plaintiff is suffering from some loathsome disease.
3. When defendant has imputed unchastity to a female plaintiff.
4. When defendant has made an assertion detrimental to plaintiff's business; for example, by claiming that he is unable to perform his job properly.

Measure of Damages   Recovery has been limited to those damages reasonably foreseeable by the person defaming and has not been extended to cover further injury resulting to plaintiff from totally unexpected repetition of the statements arousing adverse feelings toward him. If very offensive words are spoken in a public place before a large gathering of people, punitive damages may be recoverable.

Liability Varies   Much depends upon the status of the individual defending the defamation suit. For instance, the publisher of a newspaper is strictly liable if defamatory material appears in her paper, since she presumably has control over the printed contents. The corner news vendor is responsible only if he should have known the defamatory character of the publication he sells.

Defenses   Apart from *truth, privilege* is the key to a successful defamation defense. Certain positions carry with them an absolute privilege to defame, without regard for motive or for reasonableness of conduct. The judge in his courtroom (or the witness on the stand) epitomizes this category. Legislative proceedings, communications between husband and wife, and publications made with the consent of plaintiff are other situations in which *absolute privilege* applies. Verbatim reporting by a magazine of a senator's defamatory speech is as privileged as the address itself.

Qualified privilege likewise affords an adequate defamation defense. This type is conditioned upon defendant's reasonable behavior and lack of malice. Newspaper columnists, music critics, radio commentators, and various others enjoy a qualified privilege protecting their reports, comments, and criticisms. A plea of qualified privilege will not avail defendant if plaintiff can show that the privilege was abused, for example by excessive publication.

The Supreme Court decision in *New York Times Company v. Sullivan*[56] and related subsequent opinions preclude recovery for defamation by public officials in the absence of actual malice. The "public official" concept has been extended to include a wide variety of public figures other than officials, and a wide variety of well-known individuals have been denied recovery in defamation cases because of an absence of a showing of express malice.

Mitigating Damages What might be called partial defenses in mitigation of damages include such points as (1) the belief of defendant in the essential truth of his statements, (2) the bad reputation of plaintiff, and (3) prompt retraction by defendant of the defamatory remarks.

19.35 RIGHT OF PRIVACY

A person's life history, name, and likeness constitute the physical indicia of his individual existence; these things are, in a sense, "property rights" and will be protected against unprivileged invasion, particularly when the violator is motivated by commercial considerations. One is entitled to a certain amount of seclusion, far from the glare of unwanted publicity. Thus, the seeds of numerous invasion-of-privacy suits are sown when pictures of individuals, particularly in embarrassing situations, are taken and published without their consent. In suing for invasion of privacy, plaintiff need show no special damage of a pecuniary nature, recovery does not rest on defamation, and truth is no defense.

If the individual whose privacy has been violated is or was formerly a public figure, his chances of recovering damages through suit are slim. People in public life are deemed to have waived their rights of privacy, and anything of news value about them becomes a matter of legitimate interest to the man in the street and thus a proper subject for publication. For example, a government official's likeness is considered common property, and his consent to its general use presumed. Similarly, a private citizen may participate unwillingly in some event of such public concern that he cannot complain of his involvement in the attendant publicity.

| [56]376 U.S. 254 (1964)

19.36   MALICIOUS PROSECUTION

By means of an action for malicious prosecution, a person may recover for harm done his reputation, business, and so on as the result of an unsuccessful criminal proceeding brought against him maliciously and without probable cause.[57] This type of suit is not favored in the law, and plaintiff faces a heavy burden of proof. The essential things he must show are:

1. The party he now sues was responsible for the bringing of the criminal charges.

2. The criminal proceedings terminated in the tort plaintiff's favor.[58]

3. There was an absence of "probable cause" in connection with the criminal charges.

4. The tort defendant was guilty of malice or was spurred by a primary motive other than that of bringing an offender to justice. Lack of probable cause may imply malice.

Probable cause is always an effective defense in a malicious-prosecution action and is usually evidenced by showing that a grand jury indictment was returned or that the magistrate bound over the criminal defendant at a preliminary hearing. Advice of counsel, acted upon in good faith, is likewise a defense to an allegation of malicious prosecution.

19.37   FALSE ARREST AND IMPRISONMENT

Unless an unjustified arrest is followed by some sort of judicial proceedings, the victim cannot bring an action for malicious prosecution and will be restricted to a suit alleging false imprisonment. An arrest usually involves confinement, and a person who brings about the undeserved detention of another through the auspices of a policeman is as fully responsible as though he had physically taken matters into his own hands. When an arrest is made without a warrant, the moving party has gambled that a crime has been committed and that an arrest is therefore proper. Even when a crime undeniably has occurred, such party must be in a position to demonstrate that he had reasonable grounds for believing the arrested individual was responsible. Honesty of belief is alone insufficient, as are lofty motives. The rules are far different when the moving party swears out a complaint and has a valid warrant issued. Under such circumstances the element of probable cause has been passed upon by responsible authority, and the complainant is consequently

---

[57]There is a companion tort commonly called *vexatious suit* and based on the wrongful institution of civil proceedings.

[58]An acquittal is not necessary; abandonment of the prosecution will suffice. The theory underlying requirement (2) above is that disposition of the prosecution in a manner favorable to the tort plaintiff tends to indicate freedom from guilt. This factor, plus a showing that the accuser acted maliciously and without probable cause, establishes the tort, that is, the malicious and unfounded charge of crime against an innocent person.

insulated from any possible false-arrest suit, though if he acted maliciously, there might eventually prove to be a basis for a malicious-prosecution action.

False imprisonment may be defined as (1) any confinement of another within boundaries fixed by the tortfeasor (2) for any measurable time whatever and (3) irrespective of whether actual harm is caused, if (4) the action taken is intended to imprison the other person, (5) if he is aware of being confined, and (6) if the imprisonment is neither consented to nor otherwise privileged. The unlawful restraint must be total; that is to say, defendant must have closed to his victim every reasonable means of escape. On the question of whether the restraint involved is sufficient to support a false-imprisonment cause of action, much depends upon the physical circumstances. Attempted confinement of a male athlete, aged twenty, in a first-floor room with an open window in view is far different from imprisonment in the same quarters of an elderly woman of considerable girth. In general, if there is an obvious means of egress, free of danger, there may be inconvenience involved for the victim but there is no true imprisonment.

In recent years, it has become more common for private individuals to be sued for false imprisonment. An example would be a store owner who locks a suspected shoplifter in a room until the police arrive or an employer who detains an employee for questioning about missing funds. The tort of false imprisonment is not defined according to the identity of the tortfeasor, but rather the *act done* by the tortfeasor, the restraint of the plaintiff's liberty.

19.38 INTERFERENCE WITH BUSINESS RELATIONS

As a general proposition, one who induces *X* to breach a contract with *Y* is liable in tort to the latter, since the law imposes upon strangers to a contractual arrangement the duty to refrain from willful interference with its performance. Put another way, purposeful inducement to breach is a prima facie tort, actionable in the absence of privilege. A person is privileged to invade an existing contract interest when he acts in protection of an equal or superior interest, and there is a somewhat broader privilege when the interference is indirect and incidental. Some types of contracts that are "terminable at will" may be invaded under the guise of competition with relative safety.

Prospective as well as existing contracts may be intentionally interfered with in such a way as to give the injured party a right of action. Deliberate interference with a person's privilege to enter into advantageous economic relations is tortious, and plaintiff may recover probable damages unless defendant can show justification, such as engaging in bona fide competition for business.

A case from Texas[59] illustrates the potential scope and scale of liability from this type of claim. In this case, Pennzoil sued Texaco, claiming that Texaco had tortiously interfered with a contract Pennzoil had to purchase Getty Oil. The jury found that tortious interference had occurred and awarded the plaintiff 8.3 *billion* dollars.

| [59]*Texaco, Inc. v. Pennzoil Co.*, 729 S.W. 2d 768 (Texas 1987).

19.39   SLANDER OF TITLE

When plaintiff brings an action for disparagement of his goods or property or an action for slander of title, he must show the following:

1. That the defendant communicated to third persons statements, purporting to be factual, vilifying plaintiff's goods or casting a cloud of doubt on his title.

2. That the statements were untrue.

3. That in consequence of defendant's conduct plaintiff suffered actual damage, perhaps because others, believing defendant's allegations, refused to deal further with plaintiff. The damage must be real and not just speculative or potential.

There is some conflict of authority about whether defendant must also have acted maliciously and with knowledge that the statements he made were false. Most courts seem to require some showing of malice or improper motive. If defendant's words pertain to plaintiff's goods but necessarily imply his personal dishonesty, for example, an allegation that plaintiff butcher knowingly sold diseased meat, plaintiff's best vehicle for recovery is perhaps an action for defamation.

19.40   ASSAULT, BATTERY

Assault is a wrong to the person of the victim and may be defined as an intentional act that creates a reasonable apprehension that offensive bodily touching or injury is at hand. Mere words do not alone constitute an assault; there must be some physical maneuver by the tort defendant, coupled with the apparent present ability to carry out the immediate threat posed. The phrase "apparent present ability" poses a subjective test in that the important consideration is whether the plaintiff actually feels the defendant can and will follow through. The tort of assault has been committed when defendant threatens plaintiff with a revolver that the latter thinks is loaded. It matters not that the gun actually was without cartridges. Such a wrong as this occasionally results in real physical damage, as where the frightened plaintiff is a pregnant woman, or an elderly person with heart trouble. A threat of *future* violence is not actionable as an assault. A warning by defendant that he will shoot plaintiff the following week falls into this category.

Battery is the intentional and offensive touching of another, even to the slightest extent. In most instances, of course, assault and battery go together, though there are a fair number of civil suits involving assault alone.

A showing of provocation will mitigate damages in an assault and battery action: In addition, there are several typical defenses to such a suit:

1. *Self-defense or defense of a third person:* The degree of force used must be reasonable in the particular circumstances.

2. *Defense of one's property.* Again, the means employed must be reasonable.

3. *Enforcement of discipline,* as by a person *in loco parentis* (acting in the place of a parent), a schoolteacher, for example, subject to statutory limitations.

19.41   CONVERSION

This tort is committed through the unauthorized assumption and exercise of ownership rights with respect to the property of another. Conversion takes various forms, such as stealing, intentionally destroying or altering property, using property without authority, buying from a known thief or a "fence," selling goods belonging to someone else, willfully refusing to surrender a person's property upon demand, and misdelivering goods (as by a bailee).

The defendant in these cases is normally answerable for damages measured by the market value of the chattel at the time and place of its conversion, together with interest on this sum up to the time of trial. Where the property involved is something like used household furniture or books, recovery may be limited to the original cost less depreciation. On the other hand, when the misappropriated article is one of highly fluctuating value, such as a stock certificate, plaintiff may be able to recoup a sum equivalent to the highest market price reached by the converted property in a reasonable period after discovery of the tort.

When someone has wrongfully made off with his goods and plaintiff sues in conversion, he is seeking monetary recompense for the wrong. He may, though, elect to pursue a cause of action in *replevin,* which means he wants the actual chattel itself returned rather than its cash equivalent.

19.42   TRESPASS

Anyone who interferes with possessory rights in property or enters upon land without permission or privilege commits a *trespass* and is potentially liable for at least nominal damages even though the motive may have been beyond reproach. There are, of course, various instances of privileged invasion. Thus, the innocent owner of escaped animals has the right to go upon the land of another to reclaim them, though he is responsible for any removal damage done and for possible injury caused by leaving them on the land of such other person for an unwarranted period of time.

LIABILITY WITHOUT FAULT

19.43   *RESPONDEAT SUPERIOR*[60]

Under the doctrine of *respondeat superior,* let the principal answer, one person is held vicariously liable under certain conditions for the tortious conduct of another. The principle is applicable only when the relationship between the person sought to be charged for the damage done and the actual wrongdoer is shown to be that of

---

[60]For applications of this doctrine see Chapter 16, Agency, and Chapter 17, Partnerships.

(1) master and servant[61] or (2) principal and agent, and only to the extent that the tortfeasor on the occasion of the wrongful deed was acting within the scope of his employment or agency. While in fact accomplishing his ends through remote control, the master or principal is, in the eyes of the law, himself acting. The idea underlying vicarious liability is, of course, to permit the injured third party access to the "deep pocket."[62] Technically, both master *and* servant are liable to *X* for the torts of the servant, and the latter, in turn, is answerable to his master.

Persons engaged in a true joint enterprise are, without any wrongful conduct of their own, each responsible to injured outsiders for the fault of other participants in the undertaking as long as the tortious behavior occurred within the purview of the joint enterprise. To constitute such an enterprise, wherein the negligence of one participant is imputable to the others, there must be a community of interest in the purpose of the undertaking and an equal right for each affiliated individual to govern the conduct thereof.

19.44   Nondelegable Duties

As a rule, when *A* (perhaps a building owner or a prime contractor) hires *B* to perform certain tasks in the capacity of an *independent contractor*,[63] *A* cannot be held for *B*'s torts unless there is proof of clear negligence in the selection of *B* or a showing that the work in prospect was of such a nature as to be inherently dangerous to others.

Certain tasks and duties are of such import or nature that they cannot be delegated to the extent necessary to relieve *A* of his potential tort responsibility. Thus, the obligation of a property owner to keep his premises safe for invitees cannot be transferred to an independent contractor employed to effect repairs; under normal circumstances, negligence of the latter will render the owner, though personally blameless, liable to injured business visitors.

19.45   Worker's Compensation Acts

The worker's compensation acts, now existent in all states, permit recovery for personal injuries and certain diseases arising out of and in the course of employment. Several occupational groups, such as domestic and agricultural workers, are presently excluded from coverage under most worker's compensation acts.

---

[61]That is, employer and employee, and similar relationships.

[62]Respondeat superior is normally inappropriate with respect to minors; they cannot be held for the wrongs of their servants.

[63]As the term "independent contractor" is used here, *A* (the owner) controls only the final result and not the means by which it is accomplished; *A* is not privileged to interfere with the details of performance.

The basic test of liability under the statutes is work connection rather than fault. If the requisite work connection is found, the employer pays despite the absence of any wrongful conduct on his part. The employer can, of course, ensure his burden of compensation liability. In return for the readily available compensation-act benefits, the employee and his dependents surrender (as regards any injury covered by the act) their common-law right to sue the employer for damages.

While worker's compensation legislation varies from one jurisdiction to the next, the typical pattern expressly excludes from coverage injuries that are self-inflicted or that stem from willful misconduct on the part of the employee claimant.

19.46   EXTRAHAZARDOUS ACTIVITY

Broadly speaking, a person who engages in an activity that is inherently dangerous to others is held strictly accountable for the natural consequences. Such a person is under strict or absolute liability for the damage he causes, and the fact that he took all reasonable precautions will not relieve him of ultimate responsibility. He is, to all intents and purposes, regarded as an insurer of the safety of outsiders, and this is true even though the activity involved may be entirely lawful, proper, and even necessary.

Perhaps the example most pertinent for engineers[64] is afforded by the innumerable damage-from-blasting cases.[65] Some decisions have drawn a distinction between (1) damage done by rocks or other substances propelled as the result of the dynamiting and (2) damage occasioned purely by the concussion, imposing liability without negligence in the first instance but not in the second. The trend today, though, appears to be toward repudiating any such distinction and holding the defendant responsible in every such blasting case regardless of the fault element. An Oregon decision[66] is illustrative of what seems to be the general pattern. The following passages are of particular significance.

> This is a case of first impression in this court. It presents the question whether damages may be recovered for injury to real property caused by concussion or vibration from blasting operations where it is neither pleaded nor proven that the defendant was negligent in the conduct of such operations . . . We are satisfied that . . . the rule of liability should be the same whether the blaster injures his neighbor's land by casting rocks, debris or other material on it or by setting in motion concussions or vibrations of the earth or air. In neither case is it necessary for a plaintiff to allege and prove negligence.

---

[64]The application of the *strict liability* doctrine has been greatly extended in recent years, but not to engineers in general. See *Sweet v. Gribaldo, Jones & Assoc.*, 40 Cal. App.3d 573, 115 Cal. Rptr. 99 (1974) and *LaJolla Village v. Superior Court of San Diego*, 212 Cal. App. 3d 1131 (1989) to the same effect regarding subcontractors. See also, Chap. 20, Professional Liability.

[65]See *Clay v. Missouri Highway and Transportation Comm.*, 951 S.W.2d 617 (Mo. App. 1997).

[66]*Bedell et ux v. Goulter et al.*, 199 Ore. 344, 261 P.2d 842 (1953).

. . . Our recent decision in *Brown v. Gessler*, 191 Ore. 503, 512; 230 P.2d 541, 545; 23 A.L.R.2d 815, definitely places this court on the side of the courts of this country that have adopted as law the rule of *Rylands v. Fletcher*. Justice Blackburn in I Exch. 278 stated the rule as follows: "We think that the true rule of law is, that the person who for his own purposes brings on his lands and collects and keeps there anything likely to do mischief if it escapes, must keep it in at his peril, and, if he does not do so, is prima facie answerable for all the damage that is the natural consequence of its escape. He can excuse himself by showing that the escape was owing to the plaintiff's default; or perhaps that the escape was the consequence of *vis major*, or the act of God; but as nothing of this sort exists here, it is unnecessary to inquire what excuse would be sufficient.

It requires very little extension of this doctrine to apply it to the facts of the present case. And there is slight difficulty in holding that one who engages in blasting operations which set forth in motion vibrations and concussions of the earth and air which reach to another's land, no matter how far distant, and shatter his dwelling, commits a trespass no less than one who accomplishes the same result by the propulsion of rocks or other material . . .

19.47   DANGEROUS INSTRUMENTALITY

One who harbors, maintains, or utilizes anything commonly regarded as a *dangerous instrumentality,* for example, firearms or explosives, will be held to the very highest standard of care, amounting really to strict liability for whatever injurious consequences befall those within the circle of danger. If Smith keeps a wild animal, dangerous by nature, on her place, and there ensues injury to neighbor Jones, Smith's negligence is presumed, and she is under absolute liability. The same situation pertains if the animal is a domestic one but its owner knows that it has vicious propensities. Some jurisdictions have done away with this requirement of scienter, or knowledge, and have imposed absolute liability even where a dog owner, for instance, is not aware of the animal's shortcomings. Ordinary contributory negligence of the harmed person, as in all instances of "strict liability," is no defense. However, there is a real question when plaintiff, knowing the dog was inclined to fits of anger, deliberately provoked him.

19.48   NO-FAULT INSURANCE

A number of jurisdictions, dissatisfied with the application of the negligence system to automobile accident cases, have adopted plans that to some degree provide for reparation of auto accident losses without regard to fault.[67]

No-fault plans vary considerably in detail but generally have in common two features: (1) regardless of fault an injured insured motorist receives recompense from his own insurer; (2) tort liability is abolished at least to the extent of benefits

---

[67]See, for example, 39 NJSA 6A-1 *et seq.;* Annotated Laws of Massachusetts, Chap. 90, Section 34A et seq. Massachusetts was the first state to enact a no-fault scheme (in 1970).

received. A few programs eliminate or curtail the payment of benefits for pain and suffering but most retain conventional tort liability as the basis for recovery in cases of serious injury.

The constitutionality of no-fault schemes has been upheld.[68]

QUESTIONS

1. Define "tort"; differentiate between tort and crime.
2. Distinguish "contract liability" from "tort liability."
3. Define and illustrate "negligence."
4. Define and illustrate "contributory negligence."
5. Define and illustrate "comparative negligence."
6. What is the meaning of *(a)* the "standard of care"? *(b)* the "normally prudent man"?
7. Define and illustrate "proximate cause."
8. Distinguish among "negligence," "gross negligence," "assumption of risk," and "last clear chance."
9. Explain and illustrate the doctrine of res ipsa loquitur.
10. In general, are minors and mentally retarded persons legally responsible for their negligent actions? Elaborate.
11. What is the liability status of governmental officials in respect to their negligence? Of government itself? What is the trend of the law in this regard?
12. Name one circumstance that might result in tort liability for *(a)* a landowner, *(b)* a lessor of land, *(c)* a lessee of land.
13. Differentiate among "trespasser," "licensee," and "invitee." What degree of care does the landowner owe to each?
14. Has a vendor of goods any special tort liability? Explain.
15. What is *(a)* a "public nuisance"? *(b)* a "private nuisance"?
16. What is the difference between "libel" and "slander"? What elements would support a suit for defamation? What defense is often presented? What if the plaintiff is a public official or well-known personality?
17. What is the tort of "conversion"?
18. Explain the doctrine of *respondeat superior.*
19. Can torts stem on occasion from inaction as well as from improper action?
20. Can there be several wrongdoers involved in a single tort? Can plaintiff bring action against one, or must he include all?
21. In what circumstances may recovery be had for emotional distress?
22. What duties may there be that a property owner cannot with impunity delegate to an independent contractor who is doing some work for the former?

| [68]*Frazier v. Liberty Mutual Ins. Co.,* 374 A.2d 1259 (N.J. Super. 1977).

23. What is "worker's compensation"? How does the system operate?

24. Hart had a dog that was known to be vicious, and Hart was ordered to keep him on a leash. One day the dog broke away and bit the mail carrier, who had come to make her customary delivery. Can the latter expect to collect damages from Hart?

25. Varney operated one of two 5-ton cranes in a factory. Both cranes were to act simultaneously in lifting a 9-ton machine. The other operator was busy elsewhere, so Varney, who was in a hurry, tried to lift the machine with his crane alone. The cable broke after the load was 10 feet above the floor, and a worker who happened to be walking under the crane but who had nothing to do with the operation was injured. Has the worker a valid cause of action against Varney?

26. Perkins was about to make a contract with Green. Murray persuaded him not to do so, but to engage Black. Green brought action against Murray. What do you think of Green's prospects in court?

27. *X* was shingling the roof of *Y*'s house under a contract. *X* accidentally dropped his hammer. It rolled down the roof and injured a neighbor's child who was playing nearby. Is *X* legally responsible? How about *Y*?

28. Horton's manager, Garnett, was guilty of negligence in connection with certain behavior that endangered Horton's property. Fortunately, the trouble was detected before Horton suffered actual injury. Do you think that Horton could sue and expect to collect anything? Explain.

29. In the preceding case, assume that Garnett's negligent act caused a fire that damaged $5,000 worth of Horton's property, and that the latter brought suit. Upon whom does the burden of proof fall?

30. Jackson was driving a loaded truck, gross weight 15 tons. He was on his way from his sand pit in the country to the neighboring city. He started to cross an old bridge that was posted "10 tons maximum," and he had been over this structure many times with excess loads. However, this time the bridge collapsed. The town authorities sued Jackson for damages. What will be the probable result?

31. *A* rented a suburban house and lot from *B*. Having no garage, *A* customarily parked her automobile under a large tree (on *B*'s property) bordering the driveway. During a severe ice storm, a large branch broke off the tree and fell on *A*'s car, causing $300 worth of damages. *A* tried to collect from *B*. What do you think of *A*'s case?

32. Vines, a plumbing contractor, sold Wilson a 40-gallon hot-water tank and installed it in Wilson's basement. Four days later the tank burst, flooding the basement and ruining some goods that Wilson had stored there. Can Wilson collect for the cost of replacing the goods as well as of replacing the tank?

33. On Tuesday, Farmer Jones bought three of Holley's cows and delivery was made that afternoon. A week later, Jones discovered that one cow had a serious growth which later caused its death. Jones claimed that Holley had defrauded him. What would plaintiff Jones have to prove in order to substantiate his charge?

20

PROFESSIONAL LIABILITY OF ARCHITECTS AND ENGINEERS

20.1   SCOPE OF THE PROBLEM

The work of architects and engineers affects countless people, some directly and others indirectly. The work of architects and engineers is multifaceted; they may perform as designers, inspectors, supervisors, employers, or employees, and the extent of their liability usually depends upon their function. When there has been negligence and damage as a result of that negligence, the courts have had to determine the precise nature and limits of the obligations assumed by architects and engineers.

In many cases these obligations are the same for the architect and the engineer, in that they perform the same function. While there are discernible differences in the functions of the respective professions, the fact remains that the architect on a job often doubles as his own engineer, and vice versa. Thus, where only one party serves the owner as plan designer and supervisor of construction, it does not matter in a court of law whether that party is called the "architect" or the "engineer." The situation becomes more complex when both an architect and an engineer are on the job, with separate areas of responsibility, or where one is employed by the other.

To what standard of care and skill is an architect or engineer to be held? To whom is a duty owed and under what circumstances is that duty breached so that compensatory damages should be recoverable? May an architect or engineer be held liable without a showing of fault on his part? How long after a project is completed may an architect or engineer be held liable for damages? Such questions have proved to be a frequent source of litigation over the years. Currently, it can hardly be said that the central issues are thoroughly resolved and concise rules of law established. Decisions continue to go off in diverse directions and often depend on the specific facts of a case; however, some general guidelines can be set forth with reasonable assurance. It should be kept in mind that many of the acts or omissions that may give rise to professional liability for the architect and engineer are classified as torts, and the rules set forth in Chapter 19 are applicable to those situations.

20.2   DEFINITIONS AND DISTINCTIONS

An architect is one whose occupation entails the utilization of expertise in the formulation of designs, detailed plans, and specifications for use by a contractor in the erection or alteration of a building. The practice of architecture may likewise include, as an adjunct to the designing function, the supervision of construction under such plans from excavation to project completion. By way of comparison, one definition of a "professional engineer" is the following, appearing in § 6701 of the California Business and Professions Code (1978): " . . . a person engaged in the professional practice of rendering service or creative work requiring education, training and experience in engineering sciences and the application of special knowledge of the mathematical, physical and engineering sciences in such professional or creative work as consultation, investigation, evaluation, planning or design of public or private utilities, structures, machines, processes, circuits, buildings; equipment or projects, and supervision of construction for the purpose of securing compliance with specifications and design for any such work."

As a planner, the architect is generally an independent contractor, but as an inspector, his role is more that of agent for the owner. In his inspection capacity, the architect or engineer is supposed to guard against substandard workmanship and to prevent material deviations from the plans and specifications; in short, he assumes the duty (within limitations)[1] of seeing to it that the owner receives the building for which he bargained.

It is not at all unusual for the architect to employ engineers of one type or another. Their responsibilities may include the preparation of specialized plans, destined to become part of the architect's composite scheme, and also supervision of certain portions of the work so that construction proceeds according to plans and specifications.

20.3   THE ARCHITECT'S UNDERTAKING

The employment of an architect, and the setting of his fee (often expressed as a percentage of the cost of construction), are matters of contract, and it is that document that sets forth his rights, duties, and obligations. In a typical situation the architect might undertake to render the following professional services involved in the erection of a proposed building:

---

[1]The American Institute of Architects in its 1987 form of owner–architect agreement has incorporated these provisions, clarifying areas of responsibility during the construction phase:

> 2.6.5. *The Architect shall visit the site at intervals appropriate to the stage of construction or as otherwise agreed by the Owner and Architect in writing to become generally familiar with the progress and quality of the Work completed and to determine in general if the Work is being performed in a manner indicating that the Work when completed will be in accordance with the Contract Documents. However, the Architects shall not be required to make exhaustive or continuous on-site inspections to check the quality or quantity of the Work. On the basis of on-site observations as an architect, the Architect shall keep the Owner informed of the progress and quality of the Work, and shall endeavor to guard the Owner against defects and deficiencies in the Work. (More extensive site representation may be agreed to as an Additional Services, as described in Paragraph 3.2.)*

1. Participating in necessary conferences and preliminary studies.

2. Interpreting physical restrictions as to the use of the land.

3. Examining the site of the construction.

4. Preparing and/or interpreting soil, subsoil, and hydrologic data.

5. Preparing drawings or verifying and interpreting existing drawings of existing facilities or construction.

6. Assisting in procuring financing for the project.

7. Assisting in presentation of a project before organizations possessing approval–disapproval power.

8. Preparing drawings and specifications for architectural, structural, plumbing, heating, electrical, and other mechanical work.

9. Assisting in the drafting of forms of proposals and contracts.

10. Preparing cost estimates and controls.

11. Obtaining bids from contractors.

12. Letting contracts with owner's written approval.

13. Inspecting the contractor's work on a regular basis, including the checking of shop drawings[2] (but without dictating the method or means by which the contractor seeks to accomplish the desired results).

14. Interpreting for the contractor the meaning of the drawings and specifications.

15. Ordering the correction or removal of all work and materials not in strict conformity with specifications.

16. Keeping accurate books and records.

17. Preparing as-built drawings that show construction changes and final locations of mechanical and electric lines.

18. Issuing certificates of payment.

20.4   THE REQUISITE DEGREE OF SKILL

In antiquity, the architect-engineer was a combination of designer and builder and was exposed to liability that was most severe. For example, the Code of Hammurabi[3] required: "If a builder builds a house for a man and does not make its construction firm, and the house which he has built collapses and causes the death of the owner, that builder shall be put to death." Similar liabilities attached to lesser forms of damage.

---

[2]Be sure that the contract states that the checking of the shop drawings (and the approval of any samples of materials) by the design professional is only to see that they conform to the intent of the design. The contract drawings are to show the final desired result, whereas the shop drawings are to show how specific parts are to be fabricated and installed—matters for which the contractor should be responsible.

[3]Set of laws once considered the oldest promulgation of laws in human history, prepared by the Babylonian king, 1792–1750 B.C.

Today, the services of experts are sought because of their special competence, and an individual who practices a given profession represents to those who deal with him that he possesses and will use the knowledge and skill commonly attributed to those engaged in that calling. Thus, an architect or engineer, whether in designing a building, inspecting the work, or issuing a payment certificate, owes to the person retaining him a duty to use his best judgment and to exercise the skill normally employed by architects of good standing working on comparable projects in the same locality.

On the other hand, those who hire architects or engineers are not justified in expecting infallibility; they purchase service, not insurance. The design professional, whether technically an architect or an engineer, does not usually guarantee perfect plans, flawless judgment, or satisfactory results. In the absence of special agreement, the prevailing view is that the designer's undertaking is to exercise ordinary professional skill and diligence and to conform to accepted professional standards. A breach of this obligation will render him liable to the owner for any damage or expense that the latter consequently incurs and will also militate against any right to full compensation for services rendered.

Liability may also result from the breach of a statute or ordinance, without the necessity of proving a lack of reasonable care. For example, a design engineer who violates a state building code may be held negligent "per se" if his violation results in an injury, even if the violation did not result from any negligence.

In a 1988 case,[4] an owner appealing a lower court judgment in favor of an architect argued that the AIA Handbook of Professional Practice is the controlling authority to establish an architect's duty, and any deviation from the standards in the handbook should be deemed negligence "per se." The Supreme Court affirmed the lower court's use of the handbook standards as evidence of a duty on the part of the architect, but refused to accept the contention that a violation of the standards constituted negligence per se on the part of the architect.

20.5   DUTY TO THE OWNER-EMPLOYER

Perhaps the paramount duty an architect or engineer owes to the person who engages his services is that of good faith and loyalty. Thus, fraudulent issuance of a payment certificate will subject the architect to liability for all *resulting* damages.

Apart from fraud, actionable transgressions arise from negligence. An architect renders himself liable to his employer when he breaches his duty to exercise the requisite care and expertise. Claims against him may be alleged upon such diverse shortcomings as (1) preparing defective plans, (2) delaying construction by tardy completion of plans, (3) significantly underestimating costs, or (4) specifying inferior materials. An action by the owner to recover damages may follow upon one or more of these errors, or litigation may stem from the reluctance of the owner to pay the architect's fee. In either event, in order to prevail the owner must

---

[4]*Taylor, Than et al v. Cannaday* 749 P.2d 63 (Mont. 1988).

demonstrate that the architect fell below the appropriate standard of care. For instance, preparation of defective plans that were substantially followed: hence the defective structure came about by reason of the plans and not as the result of poor work on the contractor's part. Once it is established that the architect's performance was below accepted standards, the claimant must prove a causal connection between the negligence of the architect and the injury sustained.

20.6   MEASURE OF DAMAGES FOR DEFECTIVE PLANS OR INSPECTION

Where the architect or engineer is answerable to the owner for negligence in preparation of plans or in supervision of construction, there are two distinct rules by which damages may be measured. Where the effect is such that it lends itself to correction without undue expense, difficulty, or delay, the cost of repair is regarded as the proper damages indicator. On the other hand, where the defect is not capable of correction and a remedy would entail tearing down and rebuilding, the appropriate measure of damages is usually the difference between the value of the impaired building as it stands and the value it would have enjoyed if it had been correctly designed and constructed. This measure would apply, for example, where a warehouse was supposed to have 100,000 square feet of usable floor space, but somehow the plans were drawn and a structurally safe warehouse was built with only 95,000 square feet and it is not feasible to add to the building.

The application of this rule may work a hardship on the owner if the building as constructed is completely unsuitable for his purposes or where the building is unsuitable for his purposes and the cost of constructing a suitable building has risen substantially during the original construction or during the litigation. In some jurisdictions, damages for the delay or loss of business may be awarded.

20.7   LIABILITY TO THIRD PARTIES

In the past, courts usually took the position that an architect's exposure in damages for negligent performance of his duty extended only to the parties to the contract and not to "third persons." In other words, no one could recover damages unless he could demonstrate some connection ("privity") with the underlying contract.

The strictures of the Code of Hammurabi, for example, applied only when the owner or a member of his family was killed or injured. Courts today generally reject that rationale[5] and hold architects, engineers, and contractors liable to persons lawfully on the premises[6] (not trespassers) for injuries the "proximate cause" of which

---

[5]Privity, however, is not dead. In *Fleischer v. Hellmuth, Obata, and Kassabaum, Inc.,* 870 S.W.2d 832 (Mo. App. 1994) the lack of privity between an architect on a ship renovation project and the project's construction manager was held fatal to the manager's attempt to recover for malpractice by the architect who had been hired by the ship's owner.

[6]For example, see *Francisco v Manson, Jackson & Kane, Inc.,* 377 N.W. 2d 313 (Mich. App., 1985).

is the defendant's negligence. For example, in a 1986 wrongful death case[7], a general contractor did not put limit stops in the windows of a hospital, and a psychiatric patient committed suicide by jumping from a hospital window. The jury found that the contractor's failure to install the window stops was a proximate cause of the patient's death and imposed liability. Generally, an architect's failure to exercise the ordinary skill of his profession may create liability for damage claims brought by third persons where there is a direct causal connection between the negligent performance or nonperformance of duty, such as planning or inspection, and the foreseeable harm suffered by the plaintiff. Third parties may include business visitors to the property, passersby, or employees of the contractor, although in the last instance, some jurisdictions require the contractor's employee to prove the architect committed an affirmative act of negligence as opposed to an omission.

The liability to third persons may also include adjoining property owners. For example, an architect was held liable when an adjoining landowner suffered damage as a result of improper drainage of sewage water from a construction, which resulted from a design defect. The architect's argument that the designs were formulated to provide adequate drainage upon completion of the project, not during the construction stage, was rejected.[8] In another case, a condominium development had an artificial system designed to collect surface water that resulted in an increased flow of water onto an adjacent property which exceeded the capacity of that drainway. The condominium developer and its consulting engineer were held liable for the increased flow of surface water onto the adjacent property.[9] However, other cases have declined to hold the architect or engineer liable for damage to adjacent property. For instance, in *Div-Com, Inc. v. F.J. Zeronda, Inc.*,[10] the owner of a building adjacent to a parking lot claimed that the negligent construction of the parking lot caused a water seepage problem in the basement of the building. The court found there was insufficient evidence to prove this claim and dismissed the building owner's claim against the contractor. Liability has also been assigned for damage to property which was not adjoining. In one case, an engineer was held liable where he prepared plans that failed to disclose a water main, which was then broken by the contractor, causing the plaintiff's home to be damaged when the water rushed into it under abnormal pressure.[11]

Lawsuits against architects by employees of the contractor sometimes arise as a result of the failure of worker's compensation benefits to cover an injured employee's damages fully. Recovery under worker's compensation plans is usually limited to medical expenses and to fixed amounts for disabling injuries and lost wages. Also, the employee relinquishes his common-law rights to sue his employer for the injury, although the right to sue third persons whose negligence caused the injury is retained.

[7]*Honey v. Barnes Hospital*, 708 S.W. 2d 686 (Mo. App. 1986).
[8]*McCarthy v. J.P. Cullens & Son, Corp.*, 199 N.W.2d 362 (Iowa 1972).
[9]*Concannon v. Hanley Development Corp.*, 769 S.W. 2d 183 (Mo. App. E.D., 1989).
[10]523 N.Y.S.2d 687 (N.Y. A.D. 3 Dept. 1988).
[11]*Crockett v. Crothers*, 285 A.2d 612 (Md. 1972).

The current majority rule on liability to third persons for negligent performance of professional duties is shown clearly in *Council of Co-Owners Atlantis Condominium, Inc. v. Whiting-Turner Contracting Co.*[12] The plaintiff condominium owners' association brought suit against the general contractor, the developer, and the architects of the condominium building. The plaintiffs claimed that the building was not constructed in accordance with the plans, and consequently the building did not comply with the applicable building code. The court held that privity was not required for the builders to have a duty to the plaintiffs; rather, "the duty of builders and architects to use due care in the design, inspection, and construction of a building extends to those persons foreseeably subjected to the risk of personal injury because of a latent and unreasonably dangerous condition resulting from that negligence." The court also found that when a dangerous condition is discovered before it causes an injury, the builders are liable for "the reasonable cost of correcting the condition."

A more recent case utilized the same standard of care but emphasized the foreseeable use of the building and persons or property that might be injured thereby. The building involved in this case was designed as an apartment house but had been converted into a hotel. The plaintiff, a guest of the hotel, was injured when he walked through an inner glass door next to which a registration desk had been placed without the knowledge of the original architect. The conversion of the building to a new use was found not to be foreseeable, and no liability for the plaintiff's injuries attached to the architect. But a design professional may be liable for the foreseeable consequences of a failure to exercise reasonable care in the preparation of designs for a particular structure.[13] Additionally, the courts have recognized that, realistically, liability cannot be extended to *all* foreseeable losses;[14] other factors besides foreseeability must be taken into account when determining negligence.[15]

20.8 THE TREND TOWARD LIABILITY WITHOUT FAULT

There is also a trend in personal injury law toward the imposition of liability without a showing of negligence or fault.

The doctrine of strict liability in tort as set forth in the *Restatement of Torts 2d*, § 402A, states, "A person engaged in the business of selling or manufacturing a product is liable, notwithstanding the exercise of due care, for harm or damage caused by a defective condition present in the product when it leaves the hands of

---

[12]517 A.2d 336 (Md. 1986). See also *Mallow v. Tucker, Sadler and Bennette,* 245 Cal. App. 2d 700, where an architect was found liable in negligence when he failed to show in his plans high-voltage underground lines, called for excavations at the site, and a workman was electrocuted.

[13]*Simon v. Drake Construction Co.,* 621 N.E.2d 837 (Ohio App. 1993); motion overruled, 617 N.E.2d 688.

[14]*Sandarac Ass'n, Inc. v. W.V. Frizzell Architects, Inc.,* 609 So.2d 1349 (Fla. App. 2 Dist., 1992).

[15]Unfortunately, the court did not discuss these other factors.

the seller or manufacturer, if the defective condition renders the product unreasonably dangerous or unsafe to the user or customer." For the plaintiff to recover he must prove that his injury or damage resulted from a condition of the product, that the condition was an unreasonably dangerous one, and that the condition existed at the time the product left the manufacturer's control.

Many courts have found that strict liability theory is applicable to building or construction by considering it to be the end product of a manufacturing process. In contrast, other courts reject the products liability approach because they feel strict liability should not extend to transactions whose primary objective concerns a contract for professional services.[16] Similarly, architectural designs and building systems that are not mass produced or standardized have been held not to give rise to strict liability.[17]

It seems a simple step to extend the strict liability theory to ill-designed structures. Indeed, at least one case, *Shipper v. Levitt and Sons, Inc.*,[18] found a designer-developer-builder of mass-produced houses strictly liable where an injury resulted when a defective plumbing system discharged scalding water onto the purchaser. However, the court focused on the defendant's role as the developer-builder rather than as the designer of the structure, so the case is less than definitive. The effect of this case does seem to be limited to this fact pattern. In *Campbell v. Randville Construction Corp.*,[19] the court rejected the strict liability theory of implied warranty seen in *Shipper.* Homeowners brought suit against the builders of the home for death of the trees on the property and for settling and erosion of the land. As there was no express warranty or proof of the builder's negligence, the court found the builder not liable.

In another case, strict liability was claimed, but, although it rejected the claim, the court did not provide a definitive statement on the issue either. In *LaRossa v. Scientific Design Company*[20] the court declined to apply strict liability to an engineer who designed a chemical plant where a workman was exposed, during the plant's startup, to carcinogenic dust from a chemical catalyst. The court found proof of negligence on the part of the defendant. Because negligence was found here, the court could avoid addressing the more controversial issue of strict liability. However, strict liability is often imposed when negligence is impossible to prove.

Implied warranty, a doctrine from the law of sales, has also been applied, which further broadens the design professional's liability. A few courts have held that an engineer or an architect who furnishes specifications and plans for a con-

---

[16]*McClanahan v. American Gilshote*, 494 F.Supp 1334 (D. Colo. 1980), where it was said that a plaintiff injured in a refinery explosion could not recover against the architect in strict liability because the refinery wasn't a product within the meaning of strict liability theory. Likewise, in *Pennington v. Cecil N. Brown Co., Inc.*, 371 S.E.2d 106 (Ga. App. 1988), a church member who fell on accumulated ice in the church parking lot brought suit against the contractor who built the lot. The contractor was not found to be the manufacturer of defective property but, instead, the builder of improvements to property and, thus, not strictly liable.

[17]*Sime v. Tvenge Assoc. Architects and Planners, P.C.*, 488 N.W.2d 606, (N.D. 1992), involving a case of carbon monoxide poisoning from an allegedly poorly designed ventilation system.

[18]44 N.J. 70, 207 A.2d 314 (1965).

[19]172 N.J. Super 93 (1980).

[20]402 F.2d 937 (3rd Cir., 1968), applying N.J. law.

tractor thereby warrants or guarantees their sufficiency for their intended purpose. However, this is not the majority view. Thus, a California court said:

> [T]he well settled rule in California is that where the primary objective of a transaction is to obtain services, the doctrines of implied warranty and strict liability do not apply. Those who sell their services for the guidance of others in their economic, financial, and personal affairs are not liable in the absence of negligence or intentional misconduct.
>
> This rule has been consistently followed in this state with respect to professional services [citations omitted].
>
> Those who hire such services are not justified in expecting infallibility, but can expect only reasonable care and confidence. They purchase service, not insurance.[21]

Even if an architect or engineer's work is found to be subject to an implied warranty of fitness, it does not run to third persons but only to the architect's employer. Thus, an action by a hotel guest against an architect when the guest fell down a spiral staircase was unsuccessful, the court stating that the architect is only charged with the duty to exercise reasonable care, technical skill, and ability in the performance of the contract.[22]

Where an innocent plaintiff is injured and a well-off or highly insured design professional is the defendant, an unofficial doctrine known to lawyers as the "deep pocket theory" may be applied, thereby resulting in essentially the imposition of strict liability, though phrased in terms of a relaxation of the strict negligence standard. Thus, courts occasionally find a violation of the negligence standard (reasonable care) even where the breach of duty has been small in an effort to compensate a completely innocent plaintiff. Whether or not the design professional is insured against personal liability is theoretically irrelevant in the determination of his liability for the plaintiff's injuries, but it can hardly be doubted that widespread knowledge that professional people are usually well insured has contributed to the increasing frequency of courts' judgments against them.

An Oregon case[23] points up several of the principal issues that play a part in many lawsuits brought against architects or engineers by injured third parties. A pedestrian, hurt when winds caused a masonry wall to collapse upon him, sued the architect, the owner, and the contractor.[24] The trial court rendered judgment against the architect alone, and he appealed. In affirming, the Supreme Court of Oregon held that the architect, who was paid for assuming overall responsibility for designing the building (of which the wall in question was a part), had a nondelegable duty to meet building-code design provisions, including structural engineering requirements.[25] Although the consulting engineer retained by the architect was

---

[21] *Allied Properties v. John Blume & Assoc. Engineers*, 25 Cal.App.3d 848, 102 Cal Rptr. 259 (1972).

[22] *Gravely v. Providence Partnership*, 549 F.2d 958, (4th Cir. 1977), applying Virginia law.

[23] *Johnson v. Salem Title Co.*, 425 P.2d 519 (Ore. 1967).

[24] This is a common trial technique. By bringing an action against several defendants, the plaintiff can often get each of them to blame the others for the injury, thus making negligence seem widespread and acute.

[25] See *Whitfield Const. v. Commercial Development Corp.*, 392 F. Supp 982, 998 (DVI 1975), which distinguishes nondelegable duty from that of an engineer as an independent contractor held liable for his own faulty design.

the party who actually performed the faulty design work that failed to comply with a city building ordinance, the architect was held to be responsible in damages to the pedestrian for injuries sustained when the wall failed.

The appellate court dealt with three basic questions. The first of these was whether the plaintiff had proved negligence on the part of the designers of the building; the trial court had correctly instructed the jury that, if the wall was not designed so as to comply with the city code, such a violation would represent statutory negligence. The second question was whether there existed a causal connection between the alleged design defect and the injuries plaintiff received. The defendant had argued that the hurricane-force wind gusts on the critical day were of such unprecedented velocity as to amount to an "act of God." Despite an instruction to that effect, the jury chose to believe that a proper wall would have stood up to unusual winds. The supreme court found that there was evidentiary support for the verdict on this issue.

The final question was whether an architect can avoid liability for faulty design by delegating the planning function to an independent consulting engineer, incorporating the latter's work into the comprehensive set of drawings, and putting his signature upon the package. Recognizing the general rule to be that the employer (here the architect) of an "independent contractor" (here the consulting engineer) is not liable for such contractor's negligence, the opinion notes that there are significant exceptions to the rule in that the employer remains liable when the work involved is "inherently dangerous" or when as a matter of law an employer's duty cannot be delegated. Plaintiff in this case contended, and persuasively, that the architect was under a nondelegable duty to design the wall in conformity with the building code. The following extract is taken from the supreme court opinion:

> This exception to non-liability has been adopted by the American Law Institute:
>
> > "One who by statute or by administrative regulations under a duty to provide specified safeguards or precautions for the safety of others is subject to liability to the others for whose protection the duty is imposed for harm caused by the failure of a contractor employed by him to provide such safeguards or precautions . . ."
>
> > The question, therefore, is whether an architect is required to comply with the building-code provisions concerning the structural engineering of walls in designing a building. If he is, then he cannot avoid responsibility by subcontracting that part of his work to others . . . [26]
>
> > The evidence below showed that the architect assumed and was paid for assuming the over-all responsibility for designing the building. He contracted with the owner to provide all the drawings and specifications necessary for the construction of the building. The engineers were strangers to the owner. The building permit was issued upon the architect's plans, and the building was constructed according to those plans. Any engineering work incorporated in the plans became a part of the architect's design. Since the defendant assumed the benefits and burdens of designing the building, he assumed the responsibility of meeting the building-code design provisions, including the structural engineering requirements. His duty to meet the minimum safety standards of the building code was, therefore, nondelegable.

| [26]*Restatement (Second), Torts* §424 (1965).

The defendant argues that, as a professional man, the standard of care applicable to him is measured by the practices of the reasonably prudent architect in the same locality. Since it is the custom of architects in Salem to refer engineering work to consulting engineers, he argues, his only obligation was to select a reliable engineering firm. This he did, thereby fulfilling, according to his view, his duty of exercising due care.

Defendant's reliance on local customs among his fellow professionals is misplaced. Selecting a competent engineering firm only indicates that the defendant himself was not negligent. It begs the question of vicarious liability . . .

A similar case from a different jurisdiction[27] involved as defendants licensed mechanical and professional engineers who had designed a supermarket pylon that fell during a windstorm, struck plaintiff, and rendered her a paraplegic. She was endeavoring to enter the store during a severe thunderstorm accompanied by hail and high winds.

The complaint alleged that (1) defendants prepared architectural drawings and specifications for a building that they knew was to be erected for public use as a retail grocery store; (2) construction was performed in substantial conformity with such plans; (3) defendants knew that the concrete-block pylon would be located over the main entrance and that any defects would not be discoverable by the public; (4) defendants failed to exercise the care that should be employed by reasonably well-qualified engineers planning a similar building, in that defendants failed to design a proper pylon and they knew or should have known that (a) the pylon as planned was structurally unsound, (b) it was incapable of withstanding the wind-load force reasonably to be expected at the building site, and (c) it was of an aerodynamic shape that rendered it "eminently dangerous" in high winds; (5) the collapse of the pylon and the injury to plaintiff were the direct and proximate result of the defendants' negligence.

The defendants' answer specifically denied the allegations of negligence and proximate cause, and affirmatively argued that the cause of the collapse was an act of God for which defendants were not responsible. They further contended that their sole duty was to prepare the plans and specifications and check them for structural adequacy, and that they had no supervisory obligations in connection with the actual construction.

At the trial an expert witness testified to his opinion that the pylon would not withstand winds in excess of 75 miles per hour because of the use of lightweight concrete block. Another expert stated that the wind experienced on the day the pylon fell was unusually intense but was still within the range of winds to be expected at the location involved.

In light of the evidence, the court found that the jury was justified in finding that the defendant failed to particularly specify that the standard heavy concrete block should have been used in the construction of the pylon rather than the lightweight aggregate concrete block. The lightweight block was designated for use in other portions of the building but its inappropriate use in the pylon resulted in a pylon with strength inadequate to withstand severe winds. Because of the failure, it

---

[27]*Laukkanen v. Jewel Tea Co.*, 78 Ill.App.2d 153, 222 N.E.2d 584 (1966).

was found that defendants did not exercise the degree of skill ordinarily and customarily used under similar circumstances by members of their profession. The opinion states as follows:

> The defendants can escape liability for this occurrence as a matter of law only if the duty which they had to furnish adequate plans and specifications for the construction of this building did not extend to plaintiff as a member of the general public. Defendants contend that the duty extended only to the party who contracted for their services, and since the plaintiff was neither a party to the contract nor in privity with someone who was she cannot recover directly from them. Defendants point out that they were not hired to supervise the construction of the building they designed. They say light-weight block was not the building material they intended for the pylon. They desired standard, heavy-duty blocks to be used and they say their lack of opportunity to observe the construction or object to the use of light-weight blocks in the pylon insulates them from direct liability to the plaintiff.
>
> We do not believe the privity of contract is a prerequisite to liability . . . The building in question was certified as structurally adequate. It was to be occupied and used by the public for business purposes, and the defendant knew it . . . We conceive that the defendants owe a duty to respond in damages to those members of the general public who can be reasonably anticipated to be present in the structure they designed when negligence in design is a causal factor in injuries sustained through collapse of the building.
>
> The parties agree that the legal duty of the defendants here is the same as the duty imposed upon an architect under the same circumstances. That duty is described in 5 Am. Jur.2d, Architects sec. 23, at 686–87, as follows:
>
> > "Liability rests only on unskillfulness or negligence, and not upon mere errors of judgment, and the question of the architect's negligence in the preparation of plans is one of fact and within the province of the jury . . . "
>
> While these defendants did not supervise construction of the building, the jury here found it to be their plan that was defective, not the *construction* . . .
>
> We believe that the evidence in this case created a question of fact for the jury on the issues of negligence and proximate cause, and that the jury was justified in concluding that the defendants were negligent in designing a building containing the pylon at the location chosen by defendants to be constructed of light-weight concrete block, and that the injury to the plaintiff was foreseeable and was proximately caused by the defendant's breach of duty to members of the public.

However, it should be noted that this decision has not been extended to contract claims and is only applicable to tort claims. The theory under which liability was imposed in the *Laukkanen* case should be limited to personal injuries incurred by members of the general public.[28]

---

[28]*Inland Real Estate Corporation v. Tower Construction Co.*, 174 Ill.App.3d 421 at 426 (1988).

20.9 DEFENSIVE POSTURE

An architect or engineer is not helpless when an injured party seeks to hold him legally responsible for damage allegedly caused by professional negligence. Frequently asserted defenses include contributory negligence and assumption of risk on plaintiff's part. A decision of the Louisiana Supreme Court[29] illustrates other defensive contentions which proved compelling. In that case the architects had approved a subcontractor's shop drawing that failed to specify a pressure-relief valve for a hot-water boiler. Ultimately an explosion killed plaintiff's husband, an employee of the subcontractor in question. The defendant architects argued that the shop drawing was not intended to include all equipment required for installation of the system; furthermore, the subcontractor did not rely on the shop drawing while installing the boiler, so approval of such drawing by the architects could hardly be regarded as the "proximate cause" of the explosion and attendant tragedy. In the process of finding for the defendants the court pointed out that the architects could not be charged under the supervision phase of their contract with a duty to inspect the *methods* employed by subcontractors; it follows that, without a duty, there could be no actionable breach.

A slightly different twist to the "proximate cause" issue is to be found in a leading case decided in 1957 by the New York Court of Appeals.[30] The case stands for the proposition that neither the architect nor the contractor is liable to outsiders in connection with faulty designs, once the structures are accepted by the owner, where the danger is obvious or readily discoverable upon inspection. The basic theory is that the owner's acceptance and subsequent maintenance of the defective property breaks the causation chain and relieves the architect of responsibility to injured third parties.[31]

Additionally, the builder has been found not to be the proximate cause of an injury, and therefore, not liable for the injury, when he did not design, manufacture, distribute, or sell the product that caused the injury but merely purchased the product and incorporated it into the building. For example, in *Serna v. New York State Development Corporation*[32] the plaintiff was injured when an elevator stopped several inches below ground level, causing her to trip upon exiting. The court limited the products liability claim to "those who, in some fashion, are within the manufacturing, selling or distribution chain of a particular product."

Some courts have held that an architect's liability to third parties for supervisory oversight is limited to situations of active wrongdoing as distinguished from a mere failure upon inspection to detect a contractor's error. Knowingly permitting material deviation from the established plans or intentional overlook of improper workmanship will, as might be imagined, pave the way to a verdict in favor of the plaintiff.

---

[29]*Day v. National Radiator Corp.,* 241 La. 288, 128 So.2d 660 (1961).

[30]*Inman v. Binghamton Housing Authority,* 3 N.Y.S.2d 137, 164 N.Y.S. 2d 699.

[31]However, note *Cubito v. Kreisberg,* 419 N.Y.S.2d 578, 582 (1979), which stated that in such a circumstance the architect's liability turns on whether the architect exercised due care in preparing his plan, not on the test of patent or latent defect.

[32]586 N.Y.S. 2d 413 (1992).

Contributory negligence has occasionally been successful as a defense in actions against architects and contractors. For example, in one case a construction worker engaged in the construction of a school building was killed when he fell while climbing in a "dead space" in the ceiling of the school gymnasium in order to reconnect a sprinkler pipe. There was testimony by co-workers to the effect that work on suspended pipes was customarily accomplished from below and that the deceased walked across a 15-inch beam that was 36 feet from the floor without a safety rope. On this evidence, the court reversed a trial judge's decision that the deceased was not contributorily negligent as a matter of law.[33]

A statute of limitations may also be a defense available to the architect or engineer, as architects and engineers are professionals for the purpose of statutes of limitations in malpractice actions.[34] For example, in the case of *Borman's Incorporated v. Lake State Development,*[35] the court, after rejecting a contention that an architect is a warrantor of his plans, found that the statute of limitations begins to run from the moment of the discovery of the defect. Many states have statutes that bar suits after a specified period, often 10 years, has elapsed since the "omission complained of."

The Supreme Court of Oregon has held that a statute of limitations begins to run at the moment the defendant's negligent act occurs,[36] thus possibly decreasing the period in which a suit might be brought against the architect. However, some states are questioning the constitutionality of a statute that discriminatorily provides protection to contractors and architects but not to materials manufacturers or owners.

In response to the waning of the privity requirement, many states have now enacted statutes of limitations specifically applicable to the third party liability of architects and engineers, and the constitutionality of these statutes has been upheld in several instances. In one case,[37] a statute barred actions against architects and engineers for injuries that occurred more than six years after the time of occupancy of the completed structure. This statute was upheld, the court saying that the power of the legislature to determine under what conditions a right may accrue and the period within which it must be exercised cannot be doubted and that if the legislature can abrogate a common-law right, it can surely provide that a particular right be barred if not brought within a specific period of time.

Defenses based upon statutes of limitations are of substantially less use in cases where the suit is brought by a third person who has suffered physical injury. In such cases the statute of limitations does not ordinarily begin to run until the injury has been suffered, even though the negligence of the architect or engineer

---

[33]*Bartak v. Bell, Galyardt and Wells,* 629 F.2d 523 (4th Cir. 1980), applying South Dakota Law.

[34]*Sime v. Tvenge Assoc. Architects and Planners, P.C.,* 488 N.W.2d 606, (N.D., 1992).

[35]230 N.W.2d 363 (Mich. App. 1975).

[36]*Joseph's Inc. v. Burns and Co., Inc.,* 491 P.2d 203 (Ore. 1971), where a roof constructed by the defendant collapsed 17 years later and the action was commenced within two years of the collapse. The court held the action barred by a statute imposing a 10-year limit measured from the completion of the work. Followed by *Delay v. Marthon LeTourneau Sales,* 630 P.2d 836 (1981). But see *Galbraith v. Vongas, Inc.,* 655 P.2d 119, 122 (Idaho App. 1982) where the period in which to file suit was held to run from the time of the injury, where an allegedly defective water heater exploded 18 years after installation; *McClanahan v. American Gilsonite Co.,* 494 F.Supp. 1334 (D. Colo. 1980).

[37]*O'Brian v. Hazelet and Erdal,* 410 Mich. 1, 299 N.W.2d 336 (1982).

might have taken place many years before. On the other hand, the period in which a lawsuit may be brought in tort cases is typically much shorter than that which applies in contract cases, and many states require that court actions be brought within one year of the date of the injury.

As a defensive measure, the design professional should attempt to ensure that the contract specifications and drawings are not to be used by the owner or anyone else for any purpose outside of the original project without written permission of the design professional. The reader should remember that the drawings are stamped with the seal of the architect or engineer, or both. That means that these persons are legally responsible for the safety of their design. Use of such material on any other project may not yield a safe and satisfactory result.[38] If such use is desired by the owner, he should be required to engage and pay the original design professional for all additional services and for use of the original papers, or he should secure the latter's written permission for such use. Claims for liability resulting from any such subsequent use of the plans and specifications can be traced back to the original design professional.

20.10   MEASURE OF DAMAGES FOR PERSONAL INJURY

When a plaintiff sustains a personal injury, he is entitled to recover an amount of money that will compensate him for his losses. These amounts include the money he would have earned had he not been injured and also an amount to compensate him for pain and suffering, disfigurement, medical expenses, decreased life expectancy, and the like. Except in the case of damages for pain and suffering, however, compensatory damages must be capable of measurement in dollars and be capable of estimation with a pecuniary standard. Although compensation in tort cases is intended to put the plaintiff in the same financial position he was in prior to the tort, such theories would seem to have limited applicability where damages are awarded for pain and suffering. In an action to recover for personal injuries, the plaintiff must recover in one suit for both past and prospective injuries, including future pain and suffering, cost of medical services, and impaired earning capacity.

20.11   PROBLEMS OF PROOF

The preceding materials have discussed the legal theories upon which professional liability may rest in civil actions against architects and engineers. It is important to

---

[38]There are likely to be various circumstances or site conditions that make reuse of the original material unsuitable for the proposed project unless various modifications are made.

remember, however, that liability requires proof that the requisite standard of care, however it is defined, be breached.

In the typical case, a breach of the standard of care to which a design professional is held must be established by the testimony of experts.[39] The presence of expert testimony, alone, of course, is inadequate to establish liability, and expert testimony may also be introduced by the defense.[40]

If, however, the question at trial involves a matter that is readily understandable by the typical juror, expert testimony on that issue may not be needed. In one case, for example, an architect had designed a showroom that proved susceptible to flooding. Since the evidence showed that the architect was aware that the area had flooded on prior occasions and had not taken that fact into account in his design, expert testimony was held not necessary to establish his negligence.[41]

20.12   A REPRESENTATIVE CASE

In this chapter there has been some discussion of a number of concepts that relate to the professional liability of architects and engineers for damages stemming from imperfect work with which they have been connected. Recognizing that the courts have adopted varying points of view and that it is not entirely appropriate to pinpoint any single decision as "representative," it would seem, nonetheless, that *Miller v. DeWitt*[42] could be cited as a useful review of some common problems and theories.

The negligence action was brought by three employees of the contractor against the architects and against the owner for injuries sustained as the result of the collapse of the roof of a school gymnasium during remodeling operations. The defendant architects filed a third-party complaint against the contractor, seeking indemnity for any liability. The state supreme court determined that the evidence supported a finding that the architects had a right to interfere and halt the work if the contractor was shoring the roof in an unsafe and hazardous manner. The court concluded that the architects were negligent in failing to watch over the shoring operation, a major part of the remodeling job. However, they also found that the third-party complaint against the contractor should not have been dismissed before the presentation of evidence because a jury could have found that the plaintiffs' injuries resulted directly from improper construction methods and techniques of the contractor. Under this scenario, the architects would be liable to plaintiff employees only for their "passive" fault of failing to stop the work, but the architects could recover on their third-party demand for the contractor's "active" fault.

[39]For a discussion of the nature of expert testimony, *see* Section 26.4. The design professional's role in the litigation process, regardless of who the defendant is, is the subject of Chapter 26.

[40]See, for example *Paxton v. County of Alameda*, 259 P.2d 934 (Cal. App. 1953), an action for personal injury following the collapse of a building, where expert testimony of many types, for both plaintiff and defendant, was introduced, and the defendant architect prevailed.

[41]*Seiler v. Levitz Furniture Co. of the Eastern Region, Inc.*, 367 A.2d 999 (Del. Sup. 1976).

[42]59 Ill.App.2d 38, 208 N.E.2d 249, modified at 37 Ill.2d 273, 226 N.E.2d 630 (1967).

The central issue in the case concerned the obligations of design professionals who undertake both the planning and inspection functions.[43] The defendant architects took the position that their responsibility consisted of drafting plans and specifications and of performing such inspection of the actual construction as would assure the owner that the contractor had complied with the drawings and specifications; the finished product would accordingly be architecturally pleasing, constructively sound, and functionally useful. It was maintained that supervising architects have neither the right nor duty to direct or in any manner control the methods or means by which the contractor accomplishes the desired results. Plaintiff insisted that under the facts of the case the architects had a clear duty to prevent the builder from carrying out his work in a faulty manner; the power of architects to stop is tantamount to a power of economic life or death over the contractor, and that authority, exercised in such a relationship, carries commensurate legal responsibility.

The owner–architect contract had this to say regarding supervision of the work:

> The Architect will endeavor to guard the Owner against defects and deficiencies in the work of contractors, but he does not guarantee the performance of their contracts. The supervision of an Architect is to be distinguished from the continuous personal superintendence to be obtained by the employment of a clerk-of-the-works.

The owner–contractor agreement, in its turn, contained a number of provisions, including several on supervision, that proved important in the lawsuit:

> The Contractor shall take all necessary precautions for the safety of employees on the work . . .
> The Architect and his representative shall at all times have access to the work wherever it is in preparation or progress and the Contractor shall provide proper facilities for such access and for inspection . . .
> The Contractor shall keep on his work, during its progress, a competent superintendent and any necessary assistants, all satisfactory to the Architect . . .
> The Contractor shall promptly remove from the premises all work condemned by the Architect as failing to conform to the Contract . . .
> The Architect shall have general supervision and direction of the work. He is the agent of the Owner only to the extent provided in the Contract Documents . . . He has authority to stop the work whenever such stoppage may be necessary to ensure the proper execution of the Contract . . .
> The Contractor shall provide all bracing, shoring, and sheeting as required for safety and for the proper execution of the work . . .
> Existing structural steel shall be carefully shored and braced as required for installation of new connection steel. Existing truss reused shall be carefully removed, revised and reerected as called for . . .

[43]If an architect or engineer is not expected to perform continual inspection of field operations, that fact should be made evident in the contractual arrangement with the owner. On the other hand, if it is understood that the architect or engineer is indeed to personally supervise the conduct of fieldwork, his compensation from the owner should reflect this function and cover the cost of any additional personnel whom the architect or engineer may have to engage to assist him.

The appellate court affirmed the judgment entered below on a jury verdict for plaintiffs against defendant architects. In the process of arriving at its decision to affirm, the court noted these points.

1. The terms of architects' employment are governed by contract provisions, and in this instance their duties were not limited to preparation of plans and specifications;

2. In contracting for their services, the architects implied that they possessed sufficient skill to enable them to perform the required services at least ordinarily and reasonably well, and that they would exercise such skill without neglect;

3. They held themselves out as experts in their line of work and were retained because they were believed to be such;

4. The efficiency demonstrated by particular architects in their planning function is tested by the yardstick of the skill usually attributed to one in that profession;

5. Architects must guard against defects in the plans as to design, materials and construction, and must keep abreast of the improvements of the times;

6. Absent special agreement, architects do not undertake perfection in plan or satisfaction in results, and they are liable only for failure to employ reasonable care and expertise;

7. Liability rests on unskillfulness or negligence, not upon mere errors of judgment, and the question of the architects' negligence is one of fact and within the province of the jury;

8. Architects' liability or negligence resulting in the erection of an unsafe structure, and consequently in personal injuries to individuals lawfully and foreseeably on the premises, may be based upon their supervisory activities or upon faulty plans or both;

9. Their exposure is not limited to the owner who employed them, and privity of contract is not a prerequisite to liability;

10. There can be no recovery against the architects unless it be established that they were negligent and that this was the proximate cause of the injuries in suit;

11. Under these documents and factual circumstances, the position and authority of the architects were such that they necessarily labored under a duty to supervise the project with due care. With respect to the general contractor, too much control rested with the architects for them not to be placed under a duty imposed by law to perform without negligence their several functions, including supervision and direction of the work;

12. The architects were to be paid, in part, to use their best efforts to guard against the contractor's doing such things as erecting inadequate and unsafe temporary supports and shoring.

13. Both the contractor and the architects by virtue of their positions and their commitments to the owner were required to exercise care and skill for the protection of employees on the job.

When the case reached the Supreme Court of Illinois, that tribunal upheld the finding of actionable negligence on the part of defendant architects. It was clear from the evidence, the court noted, that the architects did not prepare detailed specifications for the temporary shoring of the gymnasium roof, nor did they compute on the plans the load that would be placed upon the shores, nor did they provide the contractor with a safety factor to be used in the shoring, nor did they oversee and inspect the shoring as used. The court reasoned that any finding of negligence must be based upon one or more of these omissions. Despite their argument that the shoring here was a method or technique of construction over which they had no control, the architects were held to have had the contractual right to interfere with and halt the work if the contractor began shoring operations in an unsafe and hazardous manner in violation of its written agreement with the owner. While conceding that the defendant architects were under no duty to specify the precise method the contractor should use in shoring, the supreme court concluded this would not obviate the architects' right and obligation under the contracts to insist that whatever method was selected be a safe and adequate one:

> From a careful examination of the record we conclude that, if the architects knew or in the exercise of reasonable care should have known that the shoring was inadequate and unsafe, they had the right and corresponding duty to stop the work until the unsafe condition had been remedied . . . If the architects breached such a duty they would be liable to these plaintiffs who could foreseeably be injured by the breach.
>
> Here it appears that the shoring and removal of part of the old gymnasium roof was a major part of the entire remodeling operation and one that involved obvious hazards. We think the shoring operation was of such importance that the jury could find from the evidence that the architects were guilty of negligence in failing to inspect and watch over the shoring operation.

20.13 SMALL THINGS MAY PROVE IMPORTANT

An error or miscalculation need not be of dramatic size in order to lead to significant damage; even a seemingly small and unimportant detail may prove to be the cause of serious trouble, as the following example shows.

The architect on a store-building job engaged an engineer to design the structural work and to check the shop drawings of structural steel and reinforcement, but it was understood that he was not to have the function of inspecting the project during construction. Fig. 20.1(a) shows a marquee or canopy over the entrance to the large store building, *ABC*. The marquee *BD* was held at *B* by a connection to the steelwork of the building at structure. At *D*, it was supported to two tie rods *CD* fastened to the building at *C*. This last connection failed suddenly during a snowstorm shortly after completion of the structure. In the ensuing collapse of the marquee, a pedestrian rightfully on the premises was severely injured, and the question naturally arose as to who (among architect, engineer, and builder) was to blame.

The contract drawings for the structural design showed an eyebolt at *C,* which was to be connected to the structural steel frame of the building somewhat as shown in Fig. 20.1(b). Here it is obvious that the pull *P* of a tie rod will cause a horizontal force P_h that tries to pull the eyebolt horizontally. *P* also causes a verti-

Figure 20.1   Example of structural failure.

cal force P_v acting downward so as to produce bending in the eyebolt. The vertical force must be resisted by a reaction R in the wall of the building. Furthermore, the tie rod was to be connected to the eyebolt by means of a bolt through a clevis as illustrated in sketch *(c)*. This clevis would cause one-half of the pull P to be applied equally on both sides of the eyebolt.

When the structure was built, a rod with a long loop at the end, similar to that shown in sketch *(d)*, was substituted for the eyebolt in *(b)*. It is obvious here that the force P now acts at a point much farther from the wall, causing greater bending in the rod where it goes into the wall. Furthermore, a similar loop was used at the top end tie rod. The two loops were connected side by side by means of a bolt as shown in *(e)*, resulting in a tendency for the force P to twist the horizontal loop about the reaction R. With the magnitudes of all forces remaining practically unchanged, the bending moment applied now in the rod near point C was much larger than before and, in addition, a large twisting moment was created. Furthermore, the looped rod was, for some obscure reason, threaded clear up to point E, about 1 inch inside the outer face of the masonry wall. The threads automatically reduced the cross section of the steel rod at this point. These rods failed suddenly at point E in sketch *(d)*, and the masonry of the wall spalled under the rods at the outer face of the brickwork.

An investigation after the accident revealed that:

1. The engineer knew nothing about the substitution of the looped rods for the eyebolts called for in his design and was unaware of the omission of the clevis. Apparently the shop drawings had not been revised for his approval. As stated previously, the engineer was given no opportunity for field inspection, which might have enabled him to make sure that his design was executed as he intended.

2. Moreover, the architect had not been consulted about the substitution of the looped rods for the eyebolts and clevises. Although he had kept watch over the project as a whole and may even have seen the looped rods, he was unaware that a significant substitution had been effected.

3. The contractor for the steelwork either had the looped rods on hand or found he could more readily procure them than have the eyebolts and clevises manufactured. He was apparently not conscious of any danger in the circumstances, and seemingly did not bother to consult anyone before making the unfortunate substitution.

The foregoing situation points up several principles to bear in mind:

1. An architect who is not also an engineer should engage a competent engineer to assist in complicated technical work. He should hold the latter responsible for engineering matters and allow adequate opportunity for attention to all such matters.

2. The architect should have the engineer examine important engineering features during construction. In the case above outlined, if there had been an inspection opportunity, the engineer was the logical one to have noticed the substitution and realized its significance. The architect should not be expected to cope with such engineering technicalities.

3. A contractor should not change structural features without consulting the architect or engineer, as the case may be. He should obtain approval of any such changes before following through with them.

4. It is important for all concerned with structural safety to be careful and conservative, even in regard to what appear to be minor details. Economy is desirable, but only as tempered by the exercise of good judgment.

5. Before any job is undertaken, a knowledgeable attorney should be consulted to draw up the various contracts. These contracts should clearly delineate the rights and duties of the parties. These contracts should include indemnification clauses, discussed below.

20.14   INDEMNIFICATION CLAUSES AND THE THIRD-PARTY DEMAND

Indemnity provisions of one type or another have found their way with increasing frequency into contracts for both public and private work. Where fault occurs during the performance of the construction work and is not brought about by design errors or by the architect's or engineer's failure to transmit important instructions, there appears to be considerable logic in the argument that the contractor, in the role of the active tortfeasor, should indemnify and hold harmless both the owner and the architect or engineer in any litigation which may take place. Contract formulation is discussed more fully in Chapter 3.

The third-party demand can be used whether or not there is an indemnity clause. When a suit is filed a defendant will usually return with a general denial of liability. He may also file a third-party demand claiming that the third-party defendant is the real party at fault and, should the original defendant be required to pay, the third-party defendant must reimburse him.

For precautionary reasons, it would be wise to request indemnification from other responsible parties for damages the other parties may cause. Indeed, some states have passed laws that allow a contractor to require indemnification by a subcontractor for damages caused by the subcontractor's negligence.[44] However, clauses that require indemnification for injuries not necessarily caused by other parties are generally thought to be against public policy and are, therefore, invalid.[45] The obligation to indemnify must be limited to situations in which there is a causal connection between the indemnifying party's work and the injury.

---

[44]See Massachusetts' G.L. c. 149, S 29C.

[45]For example, in *Harnois v. Quannapowitt Dev., Inc.,* 35 Mass.App.Ct. 286, 288–289, 619 N.E.2d 351 (1993), an indemnification clause was deemed void by the court as it required the subcontractor to indemnify the general contractor for damage that was not necessarily the fault of that subcontractor or its agents and employees.

20.15   A CASE TO THINK ABOUT[46]

A disastrous accident occurred in a major hotel in Kansas City. Two levels of a skywalk suspended in an atrium collapsed, killing 114 people and injuring another 185. The atrium was approximately 117' × 145' and 50' high. The suspended walkways were on the second, third, and fourth levels. The walkway on the third floor was suspended from the atrium roof. The second floor walkway was suspended from the walkway on the fourth floor, which was suspended from the roof. The walkways from the second and fourth floors were the ones that fell, causing the deaths and injuries. The collapse was found to be caused by the inadequate design of the box beam hanger rod connection. But the issue of who was at fault was the important question for the engineers, contractors, architects, and fabricators involved.

Inspection revealed the inadequacy of the design of the steel-to-steel connections. The connection was of the "special" kind, meaning it fell between the simple and complex on a scale of load capacity.

Here are some pertinent questions relating to the case:

1. Did the engineer indicate on the structural engineering drawings the type and design of the box beam hanger rod to be used, or did he leave that responsibility to the steel fabricator?

2. If he did not design the rod, did he indicate on the drawings the features that made the connection "special"?

3. Did he review the shop drawings to see that they accorded with the level of safety required for the walkways?

4. Did the structural engineer who placed his seal on the shop drawings adequately review them?

5. Was the architect adequately familiar with the type of rod being used to determine whether it posed a risk of danger when connected to the atrium roof?

6. Was the contractor?

In this case, who will the decedents' family members sue? Will they sue the project engineer, structural engineer, architect, contractor, fabricator, or owner? Will they sue all of them hoping to collect from someone? From the example, one can clearly see how important it is to delineate the duties of each professional. One

---

[46]The case described was an actual event. All lawsuits were settled, so the case was not reported. However, the Missouri Board for Architects, Professional Engineers and Land Surveyors brought suit against the engineer involved to subject them to discipline. The engineers' certifications of registration were subsequently revoked or suspended. See *Duncan v. Missouri Board for Architects, Professional Engineers and Land Surveyors*, 744 S.W. 2d 524 (Mo. App. 1988). For a detailed discussion of the suit, see Comment, 55 *UMKC Law Rev.* 108 (1986). Both the project and structural engineer were found to have been grossly negligent and to have engaged in misconduct and unprofessional conduct.

License revocation in "gross negligence, incompetence, or misconduct in his practice" was also held appropriate in *Wright v. State Board of Engineering Examiners*, 250 N.W.2d 412 (Iowa 1977), where the building code required that a roof be able to support a "snow load" of 30 pounds per square foot and the engineer's specifications for the structure specified such capability, but actually called for support capability of only 17.5 pounds per square foot, and the engineer knew that the plans were misleading and would be relied on.

may also note that contract formulation including the use of indemnification clauses will prove vitally important in restricting and allocating liability.

QUESTIONS

1. Explain why both architects and engineers are concerned with the matter of professional liability.

2. List the customary duties of an architect or engineer in connection with a construction project.

3. Discuss the normal inspection duties of architects and engineers in connection with construction operations in the field.

4. Discuss the normal responsibility of architects and engineers in connection with their designs.

5. What is meant by "requisite degree of skill"? Is the architect or engineer to be infallible?

6. What duty does the architect or engineer owe to the owner or employer?

7. Upon what grounds might an owner or employer make claims against an architect or engineer?

8. Discuss two customary measures of damages in cases of negligence associated with structural failures or deficiencies.

9. May architects or engineers be liable for damages to third persons in case of negligence? Illustrate.

10. Does liability for negligence necessarily cease after completion of a contract?

11. In case of injury claimed to be due to negligence, why may the injured party sue the owner, architect, engineer, and contractor? What can the architect and engineer do? Who must prove the negligence?

12. Can an architect or engineer shift responsibility for his design if he hires someone else to help and uses the latter's designs in his own drawings?

13. What is meant by "nondelegable" duty?

14. If a designer adheres to an applicable building code, has he done all that is essential to avoid liability for his design?

15. Discuss the meaning of a "reasonably prudent" architect or engineer.

16. Discuss the idea of claiming an "act of God" in defending against claims of negligence relating to a structural failure.

17. Discuss possible claims in which the "privity of contract" is a prerequisite to liability.

18. What may be the result of a breach of a statute or ordinance by a design professional?

19. What are the elements of damage for personal injury?

20. Discuss the trend toward liability without fault.

21. What is the applicability of implied warranty to construction defects?

22. When does a statute of limitations begin to run?

23. Discuss "defective plans" versus "defective construction."

24. Discuss "contributory negligence" and "assumption of risk" as defenses for the architect and engineer against claims by third parties.

25. Should the designer be responsible for methods of construction used by the contractor? Explain.

26. Discuss "active wrongdoing" versus "failure upon inspection to detect the contractor's error."

27. Discuss "passive fault" versus "active negligence."

28. If the designer is to supervise field operations, (a) what duties may this involve? (b) what authority? (c) what liability?

29. If the designer is to be responsible for safety of fieldwork, should he or she be paid extra for such responsibility? Discuss this matter.

30. Referring to the case described in Section 20.11, discuss the situation of the architect and the possible expenses to be met by him.

31. Discuss the possible use of indemnification clauses. Illustrate.

21

INSURANCE AND BONDS

21.1 INTRODUCTION

The manifold hazards to which business enterprises and personal affairs are subject have led to the development of a great many different types of insurance and bonds, each with its own purpose and characteristics. New forms—exemplified by insurance against atomic and other environmental perils and sexual harassment claims—are constantly being developed to meet emerging demand.

One need distinguish between insurance contracts and bonds. Insurance contracts involve two parties: the policyholder and his carrier; if the exposure insured against materializes, the insurance company must, within policy limits, make good the loss. Bonds, however, are tripartite contracts among the insured (called "the obligee"), the individual (called "the principal") who is under obligation to the insured, and the bonding company (called "the surety"). If a loss occurs *and* the principal defaults, then the surety pays, and, under terms of the bond, looks to the principal for reimbursement.

21.2 NATURE OF INSURANCE

An insurance contract is an agreement whereby one party (the insurer) undertakes for a stipulated consideration (the premium) to indemnify the other party (the insured) against pecuniary loss arising from the particular peril described in the policy and to pay to the insured or his nominee a stated or ascertainable sum of money or its equivalent on the occurrence of the event against which the insurance was afforded. Insurance represents contractual security against anticipated potential damage or liability. It is a device for shifting the exposure, or risk, from the insured to his carrier. By accepting from many policyholders, similarly situated, premiums paid into a general fund, the insurance company is able to underwrite each separate risk at a charge that is a small fraction of the exposure being assumed

371

on that particular risk. The technique of insurance is to utilize the statistical and actuarial laws of large numbers. By assuming a moderate amount of liability upon each of a great number of risks, ample room is allowed for the operation of the law of averages, so that the element of chance is minimized and the degree of uncertainty reduced. Predicting future experience figures is much more of an accurate proposition when many separate risks are involved in the calculation.

21.3   THE POLICY IS A CONTRACT

The insurance policy is the document that sets forth the agreed-upon limits of the liability the issuing company has contracted to assume and the conditions or terms under which they will be paid. Agreements between insured and insurance company are subject to various statutory provisions and to the general principles of contract law, noteworthy among the latter being the rule of interpretation that holds that ambiguities in the language of an agreement are to be construed strictly against the drafter (the insurer in this instance).

21.4   INSURABLE INTEREST

A valid contract of insurance presupposes a so-called "insurable interest" on the part of the applicant. The term refers to an interest of such a nature that, should the subject matter be destroyed or damaged, it would mean actual money loss for the individual involved. In life insurance, the insurable interest must exist at the time the policy is issued, not thereafter. Every person is recognized as having an unlimited insurable interest in his own life. When insuring the life of another, however, there must be indication that the applicant would have reason to desire the continuation of the life of the would-be insured.

Where property coverages are concerned, the picture is somewhat different. Here the policyholder must be able to demonstrate an interest in the subject matter of the insurance such that he would suffer financial loss at the time property damage occurs.

A contractor who has agreed to construct or repair a building has an insurable interest in it, at least where he is obligated by the contract to complete the job after the damage to it.[1] Also, those furnishing materials for use in a building's construction have an insurable interest in it.[2]

---

[1]*American Ins. Co. v. Bateman*, 186 S.E.2d 547 (Ga. App. 1971).
[2]See *National Fire Ins. Co. v. Kinney*, 141 S. 350 (Ala. 1932). Also, *All Phase Constr. Corp. v. Federated Mut. Ins. Co.*, 340 N.E.2d 835 (Ind. App. 1976).

21.5   GOVERNMENTAL REGULATION

In a celebrated case in 1944,[3] the Supreme Court of the United States re-examined its previous position[4] and held that the business of insurance, when conducted across state lines, is interstate commerce and, as such, is subject to whatever degree of regulation the Congress deems advisable for the national welfare. In an effort to resolve the resulting confusion, the McCarran-Ferguson Act[5] was passed by Congress in 1945. It declared the continued regulation and taxation of the insurance business by the several states to be in the public interest. With certain provisos regarding applicability of federal antitrust laws and several other statutes, McCarran-Ferguson stipulated that no act of Congress shall be construed to invalidate or supersede any state law regulating or taxing the business of insurance unless such federal enactment specifically related to insurance. Thus, states have the primary responsibility for regulating the insurance industry.[6] But not all state laws touching on insurance practices are laws regulating the insurance business.[7]

Each of the states has an insurance supervisory official, commonly with the title of superintendent (or commissioner or director), whose department administers the insurance code—a comprehensive set of statutory provisions dealing with all phases of this complicated business. Among others, there are sections imposing restrictions with respect to investments and dealing with the setting up of reserves for both known and contingent liabilities. Insurance companies are required to file detailed annual statements showing assets, liabilities, premium and claim figures, and other financial data, and they are subject to periodic examination by insurance departments of the states in which they operate. A substantial portion of governmental regulation is directed toward assuring carrier solvency.

Some portions of the insurance laws of a given state will relate to domestic companies only, while others pertain as well to foreign companies licensed to do business in the jurisdiction. Similarly, some provisions regulate a particular type of insurance organization (for example, a stock company or a fraternal society) and not others, or perhaps a stated line of insurance (such as accident and sickness coverage). Suffice it to say that an insurance company entered in all or even a majority of the states is faced with an imposing array of different laws and regulations with which it must comply.

---

[3]*United States v. South-Eastern Underwriters Association*, 322 U.S. 533.

[4]Many years ago a Virginia statute regulating foreign insurance companies was found not to offend the commerce clause of the federal constitution because "issuing a policy of insurance is not a transaction of commerce." *Paul v. Virginia*, 8 Wall 168 (1869).

[5]15 U.S.C. §§ 1011–1015.

[6]*Barnhardt Marine Ins., Inc. v. New England Intern. Sur. of America, Inc.*, 961 F.2d 529 (5th Cir.1992).

[7]*Fuller v. Olson*, 907 F. Supp. 257 (W.D. Mich. 1995), stating the criteria to be : (1) whether the practice has the effect of transferring or spreading policyholder's risk, (2) whether the practice is an integral part of the policy relationship between insurer and insured, and (3) whether the practice is limited to entities within the insurance industry.

21.6   SOME TYPES OF INSURANCE COVERAGE

There is no shortage of different lines or types of insurance. Among them are:

1. *Life Insurance.* This coverage may be afforded on either an individual or a group basis and further subdivides itself into a variety of special formats. For instance, it may be written as *whole life, declining term, paid up,* or participating. Actuarial studies and mortality tables, which form the cornerstone of the life insurance business, are founded on the law of averages and thus on probabilities.

2. *Annuities.* Traditionally, annuities involved repetitive benefit payments of a fixed amount each, but in recent years the *variable* annuity has achieved considerable popularity. As with policies of life insurance, annuities come in a variety of forms. One common type is the *annuity certain,* which calls for payments during the annuitant's lifetime, but with the further guarantee that, notwithstanding his early demise, payments will continue (to his named beneficiary) during the unexpired portion of the "certain" period. Quite different is the *life annuity,* under which payments cease upon the death of the annuitant, irrespective of how soon that may occur.

3. *Health Insurance.* Included in this category are hospital, surgical, and medical coverages, disability, loss-of-income protection, and others. The policies involved may or may not include a noncancelable or a guaranteed renewable feature and may be written in the individual, group, or blanket form.

Despite strong presidential support in the early 1990s, the United States has no general system of national health insurance. Comprehensive public health insurance is common in other countries, and in the United States for the elderly through programs such as Medicare.

4. *Property Insurance.* Damage to one's own property from such diverse causes as fire and theft is commonly insured against.[8] The two most familiar forms are automobile and homeowner policies. In the first of these, protection for the insured with respect to loss of or damage to his own car by collision or assorted other perils is normally combined with protection against liability to others for causing them bodily injury or property damage. The typical homeowner's policy, which includes comprehensive personal liability coverage along with insurance against loss of the owner's house and contents from a variety of possible misfortunes, illustrates the modern trend toward broad, multiperil, "package" policies.

5. *Title Insurance.* Here the carrier undertakes to indemnify to a stated extent against loss arising as the result of defects in title to real estate in which the policyholder has an insurable interest.

---

[8]An unusual case is *Davis v. United Services Auto. Asso.,* 51 Cal.Rptr.2d 566 (1996) in which an all-risk property policy that did not specifically exclude contractor negligence, but did contain an exclusion for earth movement, was held not to exclude coverage for contractor negligence for failure to properly prepare subgrade soils and reinforce a foundation slab. The court found that but for the contractor negligence, the earth movement would not have caused the loss.

6. *Insurance against Legal Liability.* Anyone may, in the daily course of his private life or of his business or professional activities, inadvertently injure the person or property of another. Various types of liability insurance have been designed to protect the policyholder from his exposure to damage recoveries stemming from accidents attributable to him. To put it another way, the insurance company providing liability protection promises to pay on behalf of the policyholder damages for which such policyholder becomes legally obligated by reason of injuries to other persons or their property. Previously mentioned was one well-known example of liability insurance—the usual automobile policy which, with stated limits, indemnifies the insured against loss that he would otherwise sustain when through his negligent operation of a motor vehicle others are injured or killed and their property is harmed or destroyed. A liability insurance policy is not identical to an indemnity policy. Unlike a policy of liability insurance an insurer's obligation to pay an indemnity policy usually arises only when the insured sustains a loss by reason of payment to an injured third party.[9] There are any number of specialized liability insurance contracts, such as those created for *(a)* physicians and *(b)* architects and engineers.

7. *Worker's Compensation Insurance.* Generally, accidental personal injuries and certain occupational diseases arising out of and in the course of employment are compensable to the affected employee under worker's compensation laws enacted in the several states. Public and private employers subject to such laws,[10] some of which are "compulsory" and others "elective," may insure their obligations through a government-operated fund (where such is available), or through a carrier licensed in their state to write worker's compensation insurance, or they may furnish evidence of adequate financial ability of their own. Only employers with rather extensive resources are positioned to self-insure, and many of these prefer to avoid that alternative; the vast majority of those employers subject to worker's compensation laws purchase insurance.

8. *Reinsurance.* This involves a contract under which an originating carrier (called "the ceding insurer") procures coverage for itself in a second carrier (variously called "the reinsurer" or "the assuming insurer") with respect to part or all of an insurance risk of the originating carrier.[11]

---

[9]*Selcke v. Duncavage*, 639 N.E.2d 168 (Ill. App. 1994). See also, *Alex Robertson Co. v. Imperial Casualty and Indem. Co.*, 10 Cal.Rptr.2d 165 (1992) where this distinction was fatal to a general contractor's claim that he was an "insured" under an architect's professional liability policy.

[10]Excepted employments vary with the jurisdictions but normally include farm workers, domestics, and "casual" employees.

[11]So defined in Oregon Revised Statutes, Chap. 731.126.

21.7   PROFESSIONAL LIABILITY INSURANCE FOR ARCHITECTS AND ENGINEERS[12]

It is not surprising that appropriate insurance protection, despite its cost, has come to be regarded by a great many practicing architects and engineers as a virtual necessity, particularly in the light of the tendency of plaintiffs to "sue everybody in the hope of collecting from somebody." Premium rates are adversely affected to the extent that frequent and liberal verdicts against architects and engineers are encountered. Also a strong motivating factor in the decision to purchase professional liability insurance is the high cost of legal defense that is usually covered by the policy, regardless of the merits of the claim.

In addition to the prospective financial outlay, an architect or engineer as defendant in what amounts to a malpractice suit finds his "stock in trade," his professional reputation, in jeopardy.

Typical policy "exclusions" would embrace such claims as those arising out of (1) failure to complete drawings or specifications in timely fashion, (2) liability of others contractually assumed by the insured, and (3) losses intentionally caused by the insured. To avoid an inordinately high premium, a deductible feature, which provides for a specified reduction from any loss payment due, is customarily included. Above such deductible, and not to exceed a figure shown as the "aggregate amount payable" during a given policy period, the insurer undertakes to make certain liability payments on behalf of the insured and to defend any suit (groundless or otherwise) against the insured complaining of negligence in the performance of professional services.

By way of example, here is the insuring clause and a portion of the exclusions from the professional liability policy involved in *Runyan v. Continental Casualty Co.*[13]

I. Coverage

To pay on behalf of the insured all sums which the insured shall become obligated to pay by reason of the liability imposed upon the insured by law for damages resulting from any claim made against the insured arising out of the performance of professional services for others in the insured's capacity as Architects and/or Engineers, and caused by any error, omission or act of the insured or of any person employed by the insured, or of any others for whose acts the insured is legally liable . . .

---

[12]For a consideration of the liability of design professionals, as opposed to insurance coverage of that liability, see Chapter 20.

[13]233 F. Supp. 214, 217 (D. Ore. 1964). See also, United States v. United States Fidelity and Guaranty Company, 601 F.2d 1136 (10th Cir. 1979), which contains an appendix providing examples of coverages and exclusions that specifically refer to architects and engineers.

See also *Comstock Ins. Co. v. Thomas A. Hanson & Associates, Inc.,* 550 A.2d 731 (Md. App. 1988) in which a "cost estimate" exclusion was held inapplicable to an architect's erroneous determination that a motel could be built within an existing warehouse structure at a cost of $12,500 per unit. The court found that the loss on the project did not result from errors in cost estimating itself, but rather from an underlying design defect and the decision that the construction could take place within the existing structure.

V. Exclusions

The company shall not be liable with respect to any claim made against the insured: . . .

f) for injury to, or destruction of property resulting from any error, omission or act of the Named insured, his agents or employees, not arising out of the customary and usual performance of professional services for others in the insured's capacity as Architect and/or Engineer and including the failure or omission on the part of the insured to effect or maintain insurance, or any required bonds . . .

Litigation between insured and insurer does materialize upon occasion, normally triggered by the insurer's declination of a claim as outside the scope of the coverage afforded. One such case[14] involved a policy insuring the architect against liability "because of injury to or destruction of tangible property, including the loss of use thereof, all in direct consequence of any negligent act, error or omission of the Insured resulting in accident." The decision ultimately turned on the interpretation of the word "accident."[15] The contractor on a school building project had, with the approval of the architect, used inferior or defective concrete (which failed to meet the specifications of the building contract) in constructing certain bents. It proved necessary to repair them, and the contractor sought to recoup his out-of-pocket cost from the architect. The latter, confronted with his insurer's denial of responsibility, compromised the outstanding claim and took legal action against the carrier, which interposed a defense that plaintiff's loss was not within the coverage of the policy because no "accident" had resulted from any error or omission of the insured. The appellate court refused to accept the defendant's argument and reversed the lower court's holding, which had been adverse to the plaintiff architect. An "accident" is an occurrence that is unforeseen and unexpected and undesigned, reasoned the appellate court and that test was met by the use of inferior concrete in constructing bents and their incorporation into the building—all of which was caused in part by the fault of the architect in approving defective material:

Whether a building has been injured by the use in its construction of defective material is ordinarily a question of fact, but it is a question of law if the fault is unquestionably so great as to materially depreciate the value of the building or create a condition which demands correction. And we cannot doubt that in the present case the incorporation into a school building of the defective bents caused injury and damage to the structure through the creation of an intolerable condition.

---

[14]*Gogerty v. General Accident, Fire and Life Insurance Corp.,* 238 Cal.App.2d 574,48 Cal.Rptr.37 (1966).

[15]A number of words may give rise to dispute. See, for example, *United States v. Security Management Co., Inc.,* 96 F.3d 260 (7th Cir. 1996), "occurrence"; *Travelers South Insurance Co. v. C. J. Gayfers and Company Insurance,* 366 So.2d 1199 (Fla. App. *1979),* "completed operations"; *C. Raymond Davis & Sons, Inc. v. Liberty Mutual Insurance Co.,* 467 F. Supp. 17 (E.D.Pa. 1979), and *Auto Owner's Ins. Co. v. Jensen,* 667 F.2d 714 (8th Cir. 1981),"expected"; *Burgess v. Pocrnich,* 672 N.E.2d 1334 (Ill. App. 1996) "structure"; *Cargill, Inc. v. Liberty Mutual Insurance Company,* 488 F. Supp. 49, affirmed 621 F.2d 275 (D. Minn. 1979), "business risk," "property damage;" *Guillory v. Foster,* 634 So.2d 1372 (La. App. 1994), "structural damage."

21.8 OWNER'S PROTECTIVE LIABILITY INSURANCE

Like the design professional and the contractor, the owner too can take out insurance. While he ordinarily is not liable for the negligence of a contractor selected with reasonable care, there are instances where responsibility may nevertheless be ascribed to the owner, as where an accident occurs through omission of a duty that the law does not allow to be delegated. An example might be injury resulting from faulty excavation under a street, where the city (as owner) has the duty of keeping that street in safe condition for traffic, a duty which cannot successfully be delegated to a contractor.

The owner's protective liability policy affords insurance against liability for damage arising out of operations performed for the insured by independent contractors or attributable to omissions or negligent supervision by the insured owner in connection with such operations.

21.9 CONTRACTOR'S LIABILITY INSURANCE

Policies are commonly issued to contractors[16] insuring them against liability to members of the public for damages or injuries stemming from the performance of contracts. The insuring provisions vary with the carrier. One type of policy in general use undertakes, subject to specified exclusions,[17] to pay on behalf of the insured contractor all sums that he shall become obligated to pay by reason of the liability imposed upon him for damages because of injury to or destruction of property caused during the policy period by accident and arising out of defined hazards.

The outcome of lawsuits involving the proper interpretation of contractor's liability policies generally rides on the word "accident" and whether or not the facts surrounding a given loss render it accidental and thus within policy coverage. Three examples will demonstrate the point. In the first of these, a building occupant brought an action against a subcontractor participating in remodeling operations, basing the complaint on allegations of the subcontractor's negligence in permitting quantities of dust and plaster to be deposited on such occupant's merchandise. Ultimately the insured subcontractor sued his carrier for wrongful refusal to defend on his behalf the prior action. The subcontractor held a policy covering liability for property damage caused by "accident." The decision was that

---

[16]Subcontractors also are very likely to be policyholders. It is certainly not unusual to find liability insurance protecting the subcontractor against its contractual obligation to indemnify the general contractor "against liability imposed upon the contractor by law for damages because of injury to or destruction of property caused by accident due to any act or omission of the subcontractor, his agents or employees, arising out of and during the prosecution of the work of the type subcontractor as contemplated under this agreement."

[17]Contractor's liability insurance policies often exclude coverage of "pollutants" or "contaminant" discharge. A claim by a contractor's customer to the effect that her hypersensitivity to chemicals caused her to be injured by fumes from standard paint and glue was thus held excluded from coverage. *Amer. States Ins. Co. v. Nethery*, 79 F.3d 473 (5th Cir.1996). And, in *Board of Regents of Univ. of Minn. v. Royal Ins. Co.*, 503 N.W.2d 486 (Minn. App. 1993) the court found an exclusion of coverage for discharge of pollutants "into the atmosphere" to include those into air within a building.

the insurer had no duty to defend; where harmful conduct is reasonably calculated to cause substantial damage of the very sort that materializes, the damage is not the result of an "accident."[18]

A similar problem arose where an insured removed several water hydrants from property it claimed under a quitclaim deed. The property was also claimed by someone else whose deed predated the insured. After a finding that the property was not his, the insured paid damages to the real owner and then sued its accident insurer to recover the damages paid. In this case, the court held that where the injury resulted from a mistaken belief on the part of the insured, there was no accident within the meaning of the policy since the insured acted intentionally.[19]

The same issue, but opposite result, can be found in *O'Rourke v. New Amsterdam Casualty Co.*[20] A sudden and unpredicted rain in Albuquerque in October, a normally dry month, was deemed an "accident" within a roofing contractor's liability policy, and the insurer was therefore liable to pay for rain damage to a house, the roof of which had not been completed.

Similarly, where an insured mismanufactured precast concrete walls and they had to be removed, refabricated, and re-erected at the manufacturer's expense it was held that the definition of "accident" is "an unexpected, unforeseen, or undesigned happening or consequence from either a known or unknown cause, and that under that definition the manufacturer's unintentional and unexpected error was an accident entitling them to recover."[21]

Another case arose under a "manufacturers and contractors schedule liability policy" issued to a painting contractor.[22] It seems that, during the course of painting the wood gables on a large number of houses in a building development, paint accidentally (and almost inevitably) splashed on the shingle siding of some 52 houses, and extensive repainting of such siding became necessary at considerable cost to the painting contractor. In entering judgment for the insurer, the appellate court found that the damage was not caused by "accident" and hence was outside the purview of the policy. The opinion is almost entirely devoted to a discussion of the proper meaning of the word "accident" in the context of this fact situation, and the court quotes with approval from various earlier decisions. Here are some extracts that put the problem well in focus:

---

[18]*Casper v. American Guarantee & Liability Insurance Co.*, 408 Pa. 426, 184 A. 2d 247 (1962). But also see *Moffat v. Metropolitan*, 238 F. Supp 165 (MD. Pa. 1964), where damages to property caused by an emanation of destructive gases caused by oxidation were held to be the result of an "accident" despite the fact that the culm banks were created and maintained within the general custom and practice of the anthracite industry.

[19]*Foxley & Co. v. U.S. Fidelity & Guaranty Co.*, 277 N.W.2d 686 (Neb. 1979). And see *Lewis v. Easley*, 614 So.2d 780 (La. App. 1993) where a roofer's faulty repair work was held not to be an accident within the meaning of a contractor's general liability policy.

[20]68 N.M. 409, 362 P.2d 790 (1961).

[21]*Yakia Cement Products Co. v. Great American Insurance*, 680 P.2d 69 (Wash. App. 1984). Also see *Medina v. Transamerica*, 680 P.2d 69 (1984), where a negligent issuance or revocation of a building permit was held to constitute an accident.

[22]*Schnoll & Son v. Standard Accident Insurance Co.*, 190 Pa. Super. 360, 154 A.2d 431 (1959).

The word "accident" is not defined in the policy, and the term must therefore be interpreted in its usual, ordinary and popular sense. Webster has defined it as "an event that takes place without one's foresight of expectation; an undesigned, sudden, and unexpected event; chance, contingency." . . . It seems clear that an accident is the antithesis of something likely to occur, foreseeable in due course. If an occurrence is the ordinary and expected result of the performance of an operation, then it cannot be termed an accident. To constitute an accident, the occurrence must be "an unusual or unexpected result attending the operation or performance of a usual or necessary act or event . . .

Schnoll's evidence clearly established that the dripping of paint was an expected occurrence in the course of the operation. In fact, the secretary-treasurer of the firm testified that "it is almost impossible to keep the drippings from falling." . . . To hold that the resulting damage was caused by accident within the meaning of the policy would be, in effect, to constitute appellant a guarantor of perfect performance. Such liability was never intended . . .

It is true that courts construing insurance contracts have differed in judgment whether the fact that the responsible cause is an intentional act suffices in itself to preclude the resulting injury from being "accidental" damage. . . . But if, in addition to being intentional, the harmful conduct is reasonably calculated to cause substantial damage of the very sort that occurs, all courts seem to recognize that the damage is outside of the insured risk.

21.10   BUILDERS' RISK POLICIES

Builders' risk policies are available to contractors or owners to protect against pecuniary damage to their separate property interests during the construction or renovation of a building. From the time materials or equipment arrive at the construction site, the owner and contractor are vulnerable to loss from a number of exposures, such as vandalism and the elements. This type of policy may be limited so as to cover loss resulting from certain stipulated causes only, such as fire, or it may be much broader in scope. Sometimes a single policy covering a building in process of construction will be issued in the names of both the owner and the contractor. In that event, and assuming that no explicit policy provision covers the point, the rights of the respective parties to any claim proceeds recoverable would seem to depend upon the relative interests of each at the time of the loss.

Where separate policies cover owner and contractor, difficult questions arise. In many instances the construction agreement obligates the contractor to assume the risk of damage occurring to the structure or its contents during the building process. Under these circumstances, court decisions are not uniform on whether or not the owner may recover from *his* "builders' risk" carrier for loss that manifests itself while construction is yet continuing. In at least the large majority of those cases where this matter has been argued, the contractor had not (at the time the owner–insurer litigation commenced) fulfilled his commitment to bear the loss. If the contractor, by reason of his obligation to repair damage arising before the structure is finished and turned over to the owner, actually does assume the cost (presumably through his insurance company), it is normally contended that the owner has suffered no damage and has no valid claim against his insurer.

Lititz Mutual Insurance Co. v. Lengacher[23] is an illustration of a lawsuit involving builders' risk insurance. The policy protected the contractor's interest in a dwelling, during its construction, against loss through fire. Meanwhile, the owner, obliged by a provision of the building contract to do so, independently procured a "fire and extended coverage insurance policy in an amount sufficient to fully protect these improvements at all times during construction." After work had reached an advanced stage and the contractor had been paid about four-fifths of the agreed price, there was a fire, and substantial damage resulted. The contractor effected the necessary repairs, as he was legally obligated to do, and sought to recoup his cost from his insurance carrier. The owner, who had sustained no loss, did not file a claim under his policy. It was held that the contractor's insurance company was primarily liable and was not entitled to have the loss prorated between it and the owner's insurance company, notwithstanding the owner's duty to procure insurance protection. The two companies insured separate and distinct interests in the same property.

St. Paul Fire and Marine v. Murray Plumbing and Heating Corporation[24] also presents a situation involving a builders' risk policy. A building under construction had suffered severe water damage when a 4-inch cast iron pipe broke, causing extensive flooding. The alleged cause was negligence on the part of the subcontractor. The insurance company reimbursed the contractor and then sought to recover against the subcontractor through its right of subrogation. However, the subcontractors had been listed as additional insureds under the policy. The insurance company argued that the policy did not extend coverage to them for the loss so as to prevent subrogation against them and that they were contractually obligated to indemnify the general contractor under the provisions of the subcontract. Finding in favor of the subcontractors, the court rejected the contention that the policy provided only property coverage and not liability coverage, thus creating a right of subrogation against the subcontractors. The policy was said to have been procured by the contractor for the mutual benefit of himself and the subcontractors. The court noted that, since subrogation exists only with respect to rights of the insurer against third persons to whom the insurer owes no duty, no right of subrogation could arise in favor of the insurance company against the subcontractor.

Builders' risk policies are often subject to coverage exclusions and how those exclusions are interpreted can be critical. In one case, a builder's risk policy excluded coverage for collapse of "foundation." Finding *foundation* to refer only to the concrete at the base of the building wall, the court said a basement

---

[23]248 F.2d 850 (7th Cir. 1957).

[24]135 Cal. Rptr. 120 (Cal. App. 1976). See also, *J. F. Shea Co., Inc. v. Hydes Plumbing and Heating,* 619 P.2d 1207 (Nev. 1980), where an employee of the subcontractor caused a fire while welding. The court there found that the contractor could recover under his builder's risk insurance for his losses as well as the subcontractor and his employee. The contractor's insurer was not entitled to subrogation against the subcontractor's insurer, as the liability for this type of risk fell under the builder's risk policy of the contractor and not under the public liability or property damage insurance of the subcontractor. This case was followed by *National Union Fire Ins. v. Engineering Science,* 884 F. 2d 1208 (9th Cir. 1989), where the court used the same logic in not allowing the insurance company to subrogate against one of its policyholders if they insured both parties under separate policies.

wall was covered by the policy.[25] Other common exclusions in builders' risk policies exclude those for "water below the surface of the ground,"[26] "damage caused by earth sinking, rising, and shifting," and "earthquake, volcanic action, and mud flow."[27]

21.11   BONDS IN GENERAL

There are hundreds of different kinds of bonds grouped into two broad categories: fidelity and surety. The risk of dishonesty is an element common to all bonds, but those in the surety class normally involve as well the risk of nonperformance, whether because of incapacity, inefficiency, or some other cause.

21.12   FIDELITY BONDS

These are instruments executed by the principal as well as the surety, or *underwriter* and designed to indemnify the named third party, *obligee,* or *insured,* against loss occasioned by a dishonest act committed by the principal. The usual fidelity bond protects an employer against employee wrongdoing, such as larceny, embezzlement, or forgery;[28] typically, an employer will pay the premium on such bond.

Fidelity bonds are written for commercial concerns, schools, clubs, and a whole host of other entities.

21.13   SURETY BONDS

Under such a bond, which again is executed by both principal and underwriter, the latter guarantees performance by the principal and is responsible for compensating the insured for any pecuniary loss sustained through the principal's failure to fulfill his contractual obligation. It matters not whether the difficulty is due to incompetence, dishonesty, or just plain bad luck. In other words, the surety has assumed responsibility for the principal's ability, trustworthiness, and financial strength. Breach by the principal gives rise to a remedy for the obligee against both principal and surety. Obviously, the quality and financial standing of the surety are matters of considerable importance to the obligee (owners), who may well require the bidding contractor to submit for approval the name of his intended surety. If the owner does not feel that he can accept that particular surety, he may demand the

---

[25]*Turner v. State Farm Fire & Casualty Co.,* 614 So.2d 1029 (Ala. 1993).
[26]See *Henning Nelson Constr. Co. v. Fireman's Fund Am. Life Ins. Co.,* 383 N.W.2d 645 (Minn. 1986).
[27]*Loretto-Utica Properties Corp. v. Douglas Co.,* 642 N.Y.S.2d 117 (Sup. Ct. App. Div. 1996).
[28]See, for example, *Central National Ins. Co. v. Ins. Co. of North America,* 522 N.W.2d 39 (Iowa 1994).

substitution of another one or may reject the bid outright. After a designated surety has been approved, the contractor should not be allowed to effect a change without the owner's consent.

It may be wise for the engineer to insert in the contract documents a provision that the contractor shall secure a satisfactory replacement surety if the original one gives indication of financial difficulties before the building project is completed. In very large contracts it is not unusual to specify that multiple sureties shall be involved in the bonding arrangements.

Surety bonds are classified as either common law or statutory. The former type is an obligation "voluntarily" undertaken, and the underwriter is free to insert such limitations and restrictions on its liability as it chooses. Statutory bonds, on the other hand, are those required by law in certain circumstances—as, for example, where contractors are engaged in government projects. Generally such bonds must comply strictly with the terms of the pertinent statutory provision and are conditioned to protect the public body as well as suppliers of material and labor.

21.14   BONDS IN PUBLIC WORK

A further word is in order regarding distinctions in the bonding picture between public and private work. In the case of private work, any requirement for bonding is a matter for owner–contractor negotiation. It is not uncommon for an owner to insist upon surety bonds to protect himself against the contractor's breach and against claims of laborers and materialmen.[29] However, a substantial percentage of private construction work is still not bonded. It is possible to allow the contractor to substitute (for the performance bond) cash or approved securities, depositing them with the owner or to his credit until the contractor has completed the work and the owner has accepted the end result. This alternative procedure, however, is seldom desirable and is rarely used. For one thing, the possible loss or misplacement of money or securities presents a danger from the owner's standpoint, since he will be responsible for the safekeeping. Also, stocks and bonds may decline in value during the life of the contract, and if trouble develops, the securities may have to be sold under adverse market conditions. The owner would then lose part of the protection afforded by the collateral. It is easy to see that, if the contract is breached, the handling of the deposit may cause difficulties and arguments. Furthermore, not every contractor is in a position to deposit collateral without impairing his financial ability to complete the contract.

Generally speaking, statutes now mandate some form of surety bond or bonds in connection with any kind of public works contract. At the federal level the Miller Act[30] requires that, before any contract for the construction, alteration, or

---

[29]Except where some specialized instrument is stipulated by law, the so-called "AIA forms" are in general use for both public and private construction work. It is understood that these bond forms were the product of cooperation between surety companies and the American Institute of Architects.

[30]40 U.S.C., starting with § 270(a) amend. (1994).

repair of any public building or public work of United States is awarded to any person, such person shall furnish to the United States:

1.   A performance bond with a surety or sureties satisfactory to the officer awarding such contract, and in such amount as he shall deem adequate, for the protection of the United States.

2.   A payment bond with a surety or sureties satisfactory to such officer for the protection of all persons supplying labor and material in the prosecution of the work provided for in said contract for the use of each such person. Whenever the total amount payable by the terms of the contract shall be not more than $1,000,000, the said payment bond shall be in a sum of one-half the total amount payable by the terms of the contract. Whenever the total amount payable by the terms of the contract shall be more than $1,000,000 but not more than $5,000,000, the said payment bond shall be in a sum of 40 percent of the total amount payable by the terms of the contract. Whenever the total amount payable by the terms of the contract shall be more than $5,000,000 the said payment bond shall be in the sum of $2,500,000.

Appropriate bond forms may be secured from the General Services Administration of the federal government.

Similar legislation, sometimes called "little Miller Acts," has been adopted rather uniformly in the states, requiring surety bonds to be furnished by contractors engaging in works projects for the states. The purpose is the dual one of assuring completion of the construction and remuneration to those who furnish labor and materials. The standard pattern seems to be to require all builders seeking public contracts to file bid bonds—with the successful bidder having then to execute a performance bond and a payment bond (occasionally termed a "labor and materials bond"). Claimants' rights and remedies under these bonds vary according to applicable local law and the conditions of the surety's obligation assumed in line with such law.

While it is the general contractor who must furnish bonds to the public body, a good portion of the actual work is let out on subcontracts. Accordingly, the general contractor, in his turn, may find it wise to require performance and payment bonds from his various subcontractors; these bonds, of course, are meant to protect the general contractor against loss in the event a sub fails to fulfill his commitments.

21.15   CONTRACT BONDS

Contract bonds are essentially credit risks; the underwriter will do well to consider in advance the contractor's financial status as well as his technical competence, experience, current work schedule, and the adequacy of his bid.

This group of suretyship obligations subdivides itself into bid bonds, performance bonds, payment bonds, and maintenance bonds.

Bid Bonds   A surety company issuing a *bid bond* thereby guarantees that the named contractor (as "principal") will, if his bid prevails, sign the contract document and furnish any requisite performance and payment bonds; its limited function does not include assurance of satisfactory completion of the project itself. In other words, the bid bond could be said to insure the good faith of the contractor in entering his bid. Should he fail to accept the contract as awarded and supply the required further bonds at that juncture, the surety must be prepared to answer in damages. These could include (1) the expense to the obligee of again putting the job out to bids, and (2) the out-of-pocket loss of the difference between the original low bid and the price at which a contract is ultimately signed. The typical bid bond penalty is perhaps 10 percent of the contract amount.

This particular bond terminates when the principal signs a contract and supplies further bonding protection or when the contract is awarded to some bidder other than the designated principal.

Instead of a bid bond to accompany each proposal, a deposit (perhaps of a certified check) is normally acceptable. The engineer or the owner will call for a deposit of such size as would seem to afford adequate protection for the owner. It is not unusual for the sum to be calculated in terms of a stated percentage of the bid price.

Performance Bonds   This bond makes certain that, should the principal fail to perform any of the terms and conditions of the contractual undertaking, the owner, variously referred to also as the insured or obligee, is protected by the surety against loss up to the amount of bond penalty. Often required in an amount equal to 100 percent of the contract price, the performance bond shifts from the owner much of the risk of damage arising from default by the contractor.

The manner in which the owner is made whole depends on the precise terms of the surety's commitment,[31] but the latter must in some fashion (1) promptly remedy the principal's failure, or (2) itself complete the contract, or (3) assist the owner to get the contract relet and fulfilled and then pay to the owner the extra cost to him of the substituted completion.[32]

Notice that the bond is not intended to provide a means for the owner to make a profit. It is designed to prevent, or at least to reduce, extra cost to him in case the contractor fails to perform.

---

[31]An example is afforded by the following quotation from "Document No. A-311 (Formerly 107) 1963 Edition," as approved by the American Institute of Architects: "Whenever Contractor shall be, and declared by Owner to be in default under the Contract, the Owner having performed Owner's obligations thereunder, the Surety may promptly remedy the default or shall promptly

(1) Complete the Contract in accordance with its terms and conditions, or

(2) Obtain a bid or bids for submission to Owner for completing the Contract in accordance with its terms and conditions, and upon determination by Owner and Surety of the lowest responsible bidder, arrange for a contract between such bidder and Owner and make available as work progresses (even though there should be a default or a succession of defaults under the contract or contracts of completion arranged under this paragraph) sufficient funds to pay the cost of completion less the balance of the contract price, but not exceeding, including other costs and damages for which the Surety may be liable hereunder, the amount set forth in the first paragraph hereof. The term 'balance of the contract price,' as used in this paragraph, shall mean the total amount payable by Owner to Contractor under the Contract and any amendments thereto, less the amount properly paid by Owner to Contractor."

[32]See *Continental Realty Corp. v. Andrew J. Crevolin Co.*, 380 F. Supp. 246 (S.D. W.Va. 1974).

Assume that a contractor secured a lump-sum contract for the building of a store. The contract price was $1,000,000; the bond was $500,000. After a little over one-half of the work was completed, the contractor was forced into bankruptcy. The owner had paid him a total of $450,000. The surety and the owner then agreed to engage another contractor to finish the job on a cost-plus-fixed fee basis. The cost of completing the store was $600,000, making a total out-of-pocket cost to the owner of $ 1,050,000. That is, of course, $50,000 more than the original contract figure. Under these circumstances, the surety would be obligated to pay only the extra $50,000 and not the entire face amount of the bond.

On the other hand, assume that the amount of the bond had been but $100,000 and that the cost of completing the structure in the preceding case was $700,000, bringing the total cost to $1,150,000 (that is, $450,000 plus $700,000). The cost above the contract price was thus $150,000. The surety was therefore liable for the full $100,000 of the bond, and even this did not make the owner "whole"—all of which shows that it is unwise to call for too small a performance bond.

If the surety had agreed to take over the foregoing store job and to have the work done under whatever plan he thought best, the owner would be expected to pay the original contract price, and the surety would still make good on any excess up to the limit of the bond.

If the payment to the owner under the bond does not fully reimburse him for the extra expense occasioned by the contractor's breach, the owner may try to recover from the defaulting contractor. But the chances of success are slim because the latter is probably in financial straits. Breach by the contractor generally creates a bad situation and leaves the whole construction job in difficulty. For one thing, a contractor who is about to default will seldom exert himself to make things easy for his successor. It is apparent that the owner should be extremely careful at the outset to see that the contractor he selects is capable, reliable, and solvent. Even though he holds a performance bond as some protection, one of the things the owner dreads is the financial failure of his contractor.

Release of Surety   There are circumstances in which the surety will be relieved of its liability, as where the obligee, without the consent of the surety, violates a condition of the bond. For example, the obligee might ignore a requirement that he advance no sums to the principal (contractor) except in exchange for sworn statements from all persons who had done work on the job or furnished material, to verify that these persons had been paid.

A case illustrating an obligee act which served to release the surety is *Mauney v. Hartford Accident and Indemnity Co.*[33] The bond in suit provided that:

---

[33]68 Ga. App. 515, 23 S.E.2d 490 (1942). See also *Airtol Eng. Co., Inc., v. U.S. Fidelity & Guaranty Co.,* 345 So.2d 1271 (La. App. 1977) where the plaintiff made payments in derogation of the contract, which called for payments to be made after materials were in place. Payment had been made for some shop drawings and some materials that the evidence indicated had not yet been installed. The court found that since these payments were in derogation of the job-site-installed clause, they were not covered by the bond and thus the surety was not liable.

The obligee shall, at the times and in the manner specified in the contract, fully comply with all the terms thereof, and if the obligee default in the performance of any matter or thing agreed or required in this bond, or in the contract, the surety shall thereupon be relieved of any liability hereunder.

It seems that the obligee, without obtaining the written approval of the surety as called for in the conditions of the bond, changed the terms of payment provided for in the building contract. It was held that this course of conduct on the part of plaintiff-obligee sufficed to discharge the surety from any obligation. In the process of so holding, the court rejected a contention by plaintiff that the surety had prior knowledge of the irregular payments and had waived its right to claim a release.

Payment Bonds   To guard against difficulties arising from the contractor's failure to pay for labor and materials, it is desirable to require that the contractor furnish a *payment bond* (also called *labor and materials bond*) to protect the owner against loss if the contractor should indeed fail to pay subcontractors and other suppliers. There are statutes providing that contractors engaged in public jobs shall give not only a bond to "secure" performance but also one to protect materialmen and laborers, suit upon the bond by these third persons being expressly or implicitly authorized.[34] Like the performance bond and unlike the bid bond, the payment bond is most typically written in the same amount as the full contract price.

A bond given pursuant to a statute must be read with the statute and extended as well as limited in its scope by the statute, unless violence would be done to the language of the bond by such a construction.[35]

Here is an example of how unfortunate the failure to secure a payment bond can be. An owner made plans for a new house and thought he would economize by making the drawings and preparing the contract himself instead of engaging an architect to do so. He let the construction contract to a "friend." When the work was about 90 percent complete and when the builder had been paid that portion of the contract price, he quit. During the next few days several concerns that had furnished materials, several subcontractors who had installed plumbing and heating fixtures, and others who had done miscellaneous work appeared on the scene with claims against the owner for what was due them from the contractor. The owner was shocked when he learned that he was required under the circumstances to pay these bills. Before he was through with the construction, the job had cost approximately 40 percent more than the original contract price. His only recourse was to take action against his former friend, the builder.

---

[34]See *Fort Smith Structural Steel Co. v. Western Surety Co.*, 247 F. Supp. 674 (W.D. Ark. 1965), where a provision in a contractor's performance bond that "payment thereon shall be postponed until all claims of the Arkansas State Highway Comm. hereon have been paid in full" was held to be without legal force in view of the repeal of the statute which required the quoted language in the bond.

[35]See *Nelson Roofing & Contracting, Inc. v. C. W. Moore Co.*, 245 N.W.2d 866 (Minn. 1976), where it was held that a one-year statute of limitations was only a minimal requirement and did not preclude the parties to a public contractor's bond from agreeing to a longer period in the bond. Followed by *Westbrook State Bank v. Aetna*, 437 N.W. 2d 738 (Minn. App.1989).

A case presenting a different twist is *Parliament Insurance Co. v. L. B. Foster Co.*,[36] wherein a materialman brought suit against a surety to recover on a subcontractor's performance–payment bond executed in favor of the original contractor. Noting that all doubts in the construction of such bonds must be resolved against the surety, the court held that the subcontractor's bond inured to the benefit of the materialman and that it was irrelevant if some of the materials were furnished to the contractor prior to the execution of the bond, so long as they were used in the work that was covered by the bond.

Maintenance Bonds   Faulty workmanship and poor materials may lead to problems that do not manifest themselves until well after the completed building has been accepted by the owner. The function of the maintenance bond is to cover the owner by binding the surety and its principal to correct defects that develop belatedly. An exclusion is customarily provided for defects (1) that cannot legitimately be blamed on the contractor or (2) that are not discovered before a certain period of time elapses after contract completion.

QUESTIONS

1. Differentiate between insurance contracts and bond.
2. Explain the general nature of insurance.
3. How does the law of averages enter the picture in the case of insurance?
4. Define "insurable interest."
5. Explain how an insurance policy is a contract.
6. Discuss regulation of insurance by government.
7. Explain the basic difference between life insurance and property insurance.
8. Define and illustrate annuities (fixed and variable).
9. Define and illustrate accident and sickness insurance.
10. Discuss insurance against legal liability.
11. What is subrogation?
12. What is worker's compensation insurance and how does it function?
13. What is meant by "reinsurance"? When may it be utilized?
14. Discuss professional liability insurance for an architect or engineer. What may be protected? What might be excluded?
15. What might be the claimed effect of lack of conservatism in a design for a structure?
16. In liability insurance, what is meant by "accident"?

---

[36]533 S.W.2d 43 (Tex. Civ. App. 1975). To the same effect, see also *General Insurance of America v. Century Indemnity Co.*, 384 So.2d 1305 (Fla. App. 1980).

17. Discuss accident to a person versus damage to a structure as far as insurance is concerned.

18. Describe "owners' protective liability insurance" and what it might cover.

19. Describe "contractors' liability insurance" and what it might cover.

20. Illustrate damages to a structure that might not be termed an "accident."

21. Define and illustrate "builders' risk policy."

22. Define and illustrate "fidelity bonds."

23. Define and illustrate "surety bonds."

24. What is the difference between common-law and statutory bonds?

25. In connection with bonds, define "obligee," "principal," and "surety."

26. Define and illustrate "contract bonds."

27. What types of surety bonds are in common use in the construction industry?

28. Explain the function of a bid bond. Illustrate.

29. How is the size of a bid bond determined? When does it cease to be effective?

30. A contract required submission of a bid bond for $10,000 for each proposal. The lowest bid was $500,000 and was made by Morse. The next lowest bid was $520,000 and was made by Whipple. Morse later refused to sign the contract. The owner then accepted Whipple's proposal and awarded the contract to the latter. (a) What is the obligation of Morse's surety? (b) What does the owner gain or lose? Explain.

31. Explain the function of a performance bond. Whom is it designed to protect?

32. Who usually determines the size of a performance bond? On what do they base this determination?

33. Does a performance bond guarantee personal performance by the contractor? Explain.

34. Why should the surety have the right to object if major revisions of the contract are made?

35. What happens to the performance bond when the contract has been completed satisfactorily?

36. Should a performance bond be oral or written? Why?

37. Should a performance bond be made to cover 100 percent of the contract price? Can it do so?

38. A clause stating that the contractor is to furnish a performance bond for $50,000 specifies the required surety by name. Is this customary? Why? Should the owner have the right to approve or reject the surety?

39. A contractor furnished a performance bond having a face value of $100,000. The contract price was a lump sum of $1 million. The contractor had completed over 60 percent of the work and had been paid $540,000 by the owner. Then the contractor defaulted, leaving unpaid bills of $100,000. The owner had withheld $60,000 of partial payments due the contractor for work done prior to the default. The owner engaged another contractor to finish the job for

$475,000. Does the surety for the performance and payment bonds have to pay? If so, how much? Explain.

40. When and why might the engineer require multiple sureties?

41. Who ultimately pays the fee for a surety bond? Explain.

42. Kiley performed part of the work required by his contract with Daniels, then defaulted. Kiley's work was, in part, very unsatisfactory. By agreement with the surety, Daniels had another contractor finish the job for $15,000 additional cost, and she also had this contractor replace Kiley's defective work for $8,000. The face value of the performance bond was $25,000, and it promised "satisfactory performance by the principal." Daniels presented the surety with a bill for $23,000. Can Daniels collect this sum? Explain.

43. Is the owner expected to obtain a profit by resort to a performance bond? Why?

44. If the contract calls for multiple sureties, can one surety take over the complete obligation?

45. Does the surety take over when the contractors get into difficulties or only when they quit?

46. A surety posted a performance bond for $30,000 for a contractor who was to strengthen and repave an old bridge. A hurricane and flood carried away the bridge a week after the contractor started work. What do you think is the obligation of the surety? Explain.

47. If the lowest responsible bidder refuses to sign the contract and furnished a bid bond of $10,000 with her bid of $102,000 on the job, and if the lowest bid was $105,000, what must the first bidder's surety pay?

48. What happens to the performance bond if the owner cancels the contract?

49. Under what conditions may a surety be released?

50. What is a "labor and materials bond" and how does it function in a construction contract?

51. Define and illustrate a "maintenance bond."

22

REAL PROPERTY

22.1 NATURE OF REAL PROPERTY

Realty as distinguished from *personalty*[1] consists of the following:

1. The land itself.
2. All buildings, trees, and other fixtures of any kind thereon.
3. All rights and privileges incidental or "appurtenant" to the land, that is, used with the land for its benefit, as in the case of a watercourse or of a passage across the property of another.

Assume that you agree to buy a farm from *A*. Barring an agreement to the contrary, you will acquire the land, the structures existing thereon, and all trees, shrubs, and other long-lived vegetation growing on the premises. However, you are not automatically entitled to crops grown by *A* and ready for harvest. The dam and the 5-acre pond on *A's* farm are part of the realty as of the time of your purchase and thus become yours, but the same is not true of *A's* boat, which is regarded as personalty and that does not, therefore, pass with the land. The farm machinery, stock, poultry, and the like owned by *A* are his personal property, and title to these does not pass with the farm unless you buy these items or *A* donates them to you. On the other hand, after agreeing to sell the farm to you, *A* has no right to tell a landscape gardener that he can take 200 cubic yards of topsoil for $3 per cubic yard.

22.2 OWNERSHIP

To own property of any sort entails the rights of possession, reasonable use, and disposition. There are various kinds and degrees of ownership of real property.

---

[1]In a broad sense personal property includes everything that is the subject of ownership and that is not properly described as real estate.

Sole ownership involves only one person. *Joint tenancy* is a relationship whereby two or more people together own an interest in land, and each individual concerned has precisely the same rights in respect of that interest as have his cotenants. *Tenancy in common* is another multiple-ownership form where two or more persons have undivided but nonetheless distinct shares in a property interest.

The generic designation *real property* is usually said to be sufficiently comprehensive to embrace all estates in land, that is, estates in fee simple, estates for life, estates for years, and other forms of ownership and possessory rights. A *fee simple* is the largest estate known to the law. It is a freehold estate[2] of inheritance carrying an unlimited power of disposition. Where land is acquired by *A* and his heirs absolutely and without any end or limitation being imposed upon the estate, *A* is said to hold title in fee simple. He can, if he desires, dispose of such fee during his lifetime. Otherwise it will pass under his will or descend to his heirs if he dies intestate. A *life estate* on the other hand, is property interest whose duration is limited to the life of the person holding same or to the life of some other named individual. During his life, the tenant has the right to full enjoyment and use of the land. However, existence of a life estate necessarily means that the fee is held by someone else, and the life tenant has no power to destroy that person's interest in the property. The fee owner, known as the remainderman, is the person to whom full enjoyment and use transfers immediately upon termination of the life estate.

Ownership of realty also varies in respect to the existence and extent of encumbrances. Holding title free and clear is a pleasant situation but no more common than to have the property burdened with a substantial mortgage, with unpaid assessments for streets or sewers, or with any number of other items.

Mention should be made here of the necessity of a writing where interests in realty are concerned. Section 689.01 of Florida Statutes Chapter 9 is typical of statutes generally patterned after the famous English Statute of Frauds (29 Car II). Section 689.01 reads:

§689.01 How Real Estate Is Conveyed

No estate or interest of freehold, or for a term of more than 1 year, or any uncertain interest of, in or out of any messuages,[3] lands, tenements or hereditaments shall be created, made, granted, transferred or released in any other manner than by instrument in writing, signed in the presence of two subscribing witnesses by the party creating, making, granting, conveying, transferring or releasing such estate, interest, or term of more than 1 year, or by the party's agent thereunto lawfully authorized, unless by will and testament, or other testamentary appointment, duly made according to law; and no estate or interest, either of freehold, or of term of more than 1 year, or any uncertain interest of, in, to or out of any messuages, lands, tenements or hereditaments, shall be assigned or surrendered unless it be by instrument signed in the presence of two subscribing witnesses by the party so assigning or surrendering, or by the party's agent thereunto lawfully authorized, or by the act and operation of law. No seal shall be necessary to give validity to any instrument executed in conformity with this section. Corporations may convey in

---

[2]At common law, *freehold estates* in real property include only estates of inheritance and estates for life.
[3]Dwelling home.

accordance with the provisions of this section or in accordance with the provisions of §§ 692.01 and 692.02.

Amended by Laws 1997, c. 97-102, § 751, eff. July 1, 1997.

22.3 CONDOMINIUMS

Lack of land in congested areas, the advantages of common maintenance, tax benefits of ownership as opposed to rental, and the high cost of single-family residences have all contributed to the growth in popularity of condominiums and cooperative apartments. Every state now has a statute allowing for or regulating condominium construction and ownership.[4]

There are significant legal differences between condominium and cooperative forms of ownership. A condominium is typically a multiunit dwelling,[5] in many instances a former apartment house, each of whose residents has exclusive ownership of an individual unit and an undivided interest in the common areas (such as land, halls, foundation, lobbies) and installations for common services (such as heating, utilities, and air conditioning). Apartment maintenance is generally the province of the individual owner, but the owner's association maintains common areas and facilities. Funds for common maintenance are derived from dues or assessments on unit owners.

A cooperative apartment is a multifamily dwelling in which each resident has an interest in the entity owning the building, as opposed to the building itself, and a lease entitling him or her to exclusive use of a particular unit. The cooperative owner is thus a stockholder rather than a property owner.

22.4 ENCUMBRANCES

An encumbrance, broadly speaking, is any burden upon land that depreciates its value. An existing encumbrance is adverse to the interest of the landowner, though it does not necessarily preclude his conveying the property. If he has contracted to sell the land free and clear of all encumbrances, he must, obviously, pay up back taxes and take other steps of like nature before the closing date arrives.

The list of encumbrances is lengthy and varied. Thus, a California statute[6] stipulates that encumbrance is a term that "includes taxes, assessments and all liens upon real property."

This provision has been interpreted to include any right to or interest in land that may subsist in someone other than the owner to the diminution of the land's value,

---

[4]For example, *see* McKinney, New York Con. Laws, Real Property Law Article 9B.

[5]It should be remembered, however, that a condominium is a type of ownership interest, not a type of building.

[6]Calif. Civil Code § 1114.

but consistent with the passage of the fee.[7] An encumbrance may include whatever charges, burdens, obstructs, or impairs the use of land or impedes its transfer. Examples include a covenant running with the land, limiting the use of property; building restrictions; a reservation of a right-of-way; an easement; an encroachment; a lease; a deed of trust; or the pendency of a condemnation proceeding.

The presence of hazardous material on a property, however, has been held not to be an encumbrance on the title of property covered by a title insurance policy, despite the fact that state and federal agencies could impose liens on the property for environmental law violations.[8] It is advisable therefore to seek a land inventory search for any possible violations prior to the purchase of property.

22.5 MORTGAGES

A mortgage contract between debtor and creditor affords the creditor, by way of a security against the outstanding debt, a charge upon the land of the debtor. To be effective as against subsequent parties in interest, the mortgage should be recorded, in the same manner as a deed, in the appropriate office of the official in the county which is the situs of the realty. It is an encumbrance created to secure a debt and takes the form of a defeasible conveyance (subject to being defeated) of the realty described. The mortgage transaction gives to the grantee-creditor (the "mortgagee") a lien against the property but leaves the grantor legal title (technically, an *equity of redemption*) and all incidents of ownership. In some jurisdictions the so-called *common-law* or *title* theory applies, by which the mortgagee becomes the owner of the legal estate and would be entitled to possession unless this last right is expressly reserved by the mortgagor. The mortgagor retains, in any event, an equity of redemption conditioned upon satisfaction of the debt.

Typically, the debtor ("mortgagor") signs a bond or a promissory note along with the mortgage. This makes the debtor personally liable. If the mortgagor fails to fulfill his mortgage commitments, the mortgagee's usual recourse is to invoke the judicial proceeding known as *foreclosure,* by which the property covered by the mortgage is subject to sale and all rights of the delinquent mortgagor, including his equity of redemption, are ultimately cut off. If the foreclosure sale does not provide sufficient funds with which to liquidate the mortgage debt, the mortgagee-creditor may sue on the note and secure a *deficiency judgment* for the balance due. On the other hand, any surplus realized from the sale belongs to the mortgagor.

A mortgage and the debt for which it stands may be assigned by the mortgagee to a third party. The latter "stands in the shoes of the mortgagee" and his interest is subject to all equities that may have existed between the parties to the mortgage. Up to the time he is actually notified of the assignment, the mortgagor may safely pay to the mortgagee any sums in reduction of the outstanding obligation.

[7]*American Title Company v. Anderson*, 52 Cal.App.3d 255 (1975); *Evans v. Faught*, 231 Cal.App.2d 698 (1965).
[8]*Lick Mill Creek Apartments v. Chicago Title Ins. Co.*, 231 Cal.App. 3d 1654 (1991).

When the debt is paid and the mortgage released, whatever paper the mortgagor receives evidencing the discharge should be recorded as was the mortgage itself, so that any subsequent title search will reveal that the burden represented by the mortgage no longer attaches to the land.

22.6 SERVITUDES

Servitude designates some privilege in reference to the land and held by one other than the landowner. A servitude amounts to a charge or encumbrance on the real estate. The three categories of servitude are easement, license, and profit *a prendre*. They will be considered separately in the following sections.

22.7 EASEMENTS

An easement is a right that one person has to use the land of another for a specific purpose. It exists distinct from the ownership of the soil itself and can be created by grant, by implication, by eminent domain, or by adverse possession. The existence of an easement presupposes two distinct tenements:[9] the *dominant estate,* to which the right belongs, and the *servient estate,* upon which the easement or servitude is imposed. A deed conveying an easement must describe the land to which the use granted attaches and must detail the particular use permitted. Three conditions are essential for an easement by implication. They are (1) the ownership of the dominant and servient estate by a common grantor followed by a separation of title; (2) use of easement prior to the separation in an apparent, obvious, continuous, and manifestly permanent manner; and (3) necessity that the easement is essential to the beneficial enjoyment of the dominant estate. Implied easements may, depending upon the circumstances, run either way, in favor of grantor or grantee.[10] In *Blanchet v. Ottawa Hills Co.,*[11] the owner of a house, equipped with sanitary facilities that were served by a private underground drain, sold the lot on which the house was located and retained title to lands through which the drain ran. The court held that the purchaser of the house acquired an "implied easement" for the continued use of the drain to its outlet.

On the other hand, implied easement was held not to be a defense to a trespass action where plaintiff at closing did not have knowledge of sewage flow from defendant's property to a septic tank on plaintiff's parcel, nor should the plaintiff have been aware of the flow.[12]

---

[9]The word "tenement" comprehends everything of a permanent nature that may be held. It signifies an estate in land or some estate or interest connected with, pertaining to, or growing out of the realty.

[10]*Miller v. Schmitz,* 400 N.E.2d 488 (Illinois 1980). Also see *Shive v. Schaefer,* 484 N.E. 2d 394, (Ill. App. 1985), where no implied easement was found in favor of a seller across property that he sold.

[11]63 Ohio App. 177, 25 N.E.2d 861 (1939).

[12]*Campbell v Great Miami Aerie No. 2309, Fraternal Order of Eagles,* 472 N.E.2d 711 (Ohio 1984).

Other characteristics of the easement are as follows: (1) it is assignable; (2) it is inheritable; (3) it may be transferred independently of the land to which it is appurtenant; (4) a person cannot have an easement in his own lands.

Here is an example of the functioning of easements. An industrial corporation desired to build a high-tension power line from its new generating station on the shores of Lake Superior to its taconite plant some 70 miles inland. The contemplated power line would cross in its journey a number of pieces of private property, and easements were therefore obtained from the several owners. The owners could continue to utilize the involved property for any purpose not inimical to the existence and operation of the power line. They could not, however, change their minds and compel the corporation to remove its towers and cables. When the owners eventually sell the affected lands, the new property holders are bound by the easements previously granted.

An easement is extinguished by agreement of the interested parties or upon cessation of the need therefor. Thus, in the above example, should the industrial corporation tear down its original high-tension line in area *A* and replace it with a new one through area *B,* the easements acquired to effect passage of the line through its now-abandoned route would terminate, and new easements from property owners in area *B* must be secured.

22.8   LICENSES

A *license* amounts to an excuse for what would otherwise be a trespass. A license to use the land of another in a given way or for a stated purpose differs from an easement in that the latter confers an interest in the land and may not be terminated at the pleasure of the servient owner. A license is simply a personal, unassignable, revocable privilege, which is generally granted orally.

For example, suppose a railroad grants a trucking concern permission to use an existing private roadway crossing over the tracks on condition that the crossing be removed upon notice from the railroad and that the trucking outfit promise to indemnify the railroad against all claims arising from use of the crossing by the trucking company or its invitees. Such an arrangement constitutes a license rather than an easement.

22.9   *PROFIT A PRENDRE*

Profit a prendre is taken from the French and means, literally, "profit to take," the words "from land" being implied in supplement. A profit a prendre, popularly shortened to the single word "profit," is an interest in realty and, under some statutes, at least, must be created by a properly executed writing. In this respect it differs from a license. In a comparison of profit and easement, both of which create interests in real property, the distinguishing feature of a profit is the right to take from the land of another part of the soil or a product of it in which there is supposed value, while the distinguishing feature of an easement is the absence of any right in the privilege holder to participate in the profits of the soil.

A profit a prendre could be a right to fish in private waters, hunt or log private land, or take water from a spring. Whether or not a right to take gas, minerals, or oil from the land of another may or may not be a profit a prendre depends on the wording of the lease and laws of the state.[13]

At least one jurisdiction has concluded that, with regard to recording the property interest, there is no distinction between a profit a prendre and an easement.[14]

22.10   THE DOCTRINE OF SUPPORT

A landowner enjoys the common-law right to lateral support,[15] which is the right to have his land in its natural state supported by the adjoining land.[16] The abutting proprietor may excavate his land up to the very boundary line, and he may use the soil as he chooses, provided he replaces by artificial means the support thus removed. If an abutting owner, without making provision for substitute support, as by a retaining wall, removes the soil from his own land so near his neighbor's property that the latter's soil will crumble away under its own weight, the actor is responsible for damages. Put another way, one who withdraws the necessary lateral support of another's land must respond in damages for any substantial subsidence of such land, absent an intervening cause or some other reason occasioning relief from liability. The actionable wrong is not the excavating itself, but the allowing of the neighbor's land to fall.

A clear explanation of the highly technical and rather complicated concept of the right to lateral support is the following, taken from *Sime v. Jensen*:[17]

> The right of lateral support from adjoining land consists in having the soil in its natural condition remain in its natural position without being caused to fall away by reason of excavations or improvements made on adjacent land. . . The right to lateral support is said to be a natural one of property, arising from the fact that in a state of nature all land is held together and supported by adjacent lands by operation of the forces of nature. Ownership of land is acquired and held subject to the rights and burdens arising from that situation. Supported land has a right of lateral support from that which naturally affords it support. Supporting land is burdened with affording such support to land which it naturally supports. . .
>
> As a necessary corollary, it follows that there is no right of lateral support for land where the natural condition thereof has been altered through man's activity so as to create need for lateral support where none existed in a state of nature, as

---

[13]See *Kennecot Corp. v. Union Oil Co.*, 196 Cal.App.3d 1179 (1987).

[14]*Figliuzzi v. Cancajou Shooting Club of Lake Koshkonong*, 516 N.W.2d 410 (Wis. 1994).

[15]Of importance particularly in connection with mining operations is the companion right to *subjacent support*, this being the right of land to support from land that underlies it.

[16]*Odette's, Inc. v. Com., Dept. of Conservation and Natural Res., Bureau of State Parks*, 699 A.2d 775 (Pa. 1997).

[17]213 Minn. 476, 7 N.W.2d 325 (1942).

where owner raises his land above his neighbor's by filling. The right of lateral support "does not include the support needed because of . . . artificial alterations in the supported land. . . The measure of this right of the other and of this duty of the actor is the natural dependence of land upon land, and the right and duty are not enlarged by alterations of the natural condition." (*Restatement. Torts* §817c.) An owner who by filling raises his land above the level of adjoining land has no right of lateral support from the latter and is under the duty to keep soil used in so raising his land off adjoining land. . . The owner who by filling raises the level of his land above that of his neighbor's is bound to build a retaining wall or other structure if necessary to keep such soil within his own line. . .

A retaining wall or other structure to keep raised land from falling cannot be erected on adjoining land without invasion of the right of the owner thereof to its exclusive use and enjoyment. An owner who raises the grade of his lot must build such a wall or structure entirely on his own land. . . The adjoining owner is entitled to a mandatory injunction to compel the removal of a wall encroaching on his land. . . The adjoining owner cannot be compelled to pay any part of the cost of a structure necessary to hold the raised land of his neighbor. . . .

There are statutes that deal with the doctrine of support. One example is California Civil Code Section 832, which reads:

Each coterminous owner is entitled to the lateral and subjacent support which his land receives from the adjoining land, subject to the right of the owner of the adjoining land to make proper and usual excavations on the same for purposes of construction or improvement, under the following conditions:

1. Any owner of land or his lessee intending to make or to permit an excavation shall give reasonable notice to the owner or owners of adjoining lands and of buildings or other structures, stating the depth to which such excavation is intended to be made, and when the excavating will begin.
2. In making any excavation, ordinary care and skill shall be used, and reasonable precautions taken to sustain the adjoining land as such, without regard to any building or other structure which may be thereon, and there shall be no liability for damage done to any such building or other structure by reason of the excavation, except as otherwise provided or allowed by law.
3. If at any time it appears that the excavation is to be of a greater depth than are the walls or foundations of any adjoining building or other structure, and is to be so close as to endanger the building or other structure in any way, then the owner of the building or other structure must be allowed at least 30 days, if he so desires, in which to take measures to protect the same from any damage, or in which to extend the foundations thereof, and he must be given for the same purposes reasonable license to enter on the land on which the excavation is to be or is being made.
4. If the excavation is intended to be or is deeper than the standard depth of foundations, which depth is defined to be a depth of nine feet below the adjacent curb level, at the point where the joint property line intersects the curb, and if on the land of the coterminous owner there is any building or other structure the wall or foundation of which goes to standard depth or deeper then the owner of the land on which the excavation is being made shall, if given the necessary license to enter on the adjoining land, protect the said adjoining land and any such building or other structure thereon without cost to the owner thereof, from any damage by reason of the excavation, and shall be liable to

the owner of such property for any such damage, excepting only for minor settlement cracks in buildings or other structures.

Since a landowner has an absolute right to have his land in its natural state laterally supported by the lands of adjoining landowners, the adjoining landowners are absolutely liable for damages caused by removal of support even though they are free from any negligence. The rule is different, however, where the case involves injury to buildings caused by the withdrawal of lateral support, and liability must be based on a negligence theory since there is no absolute right to lateral support of buildings.[18] There is a contrary view. It has been held that the application of strict liability should not be based upon whether the thing damaged is natural or artificial, but rather the distinction must hinge on whether the artificial condition created on the plaintiff's land contributed to the injury, or whether the subsidence would have occurred even if the land had remained in its natural state. That is, if the weight of the building did not contribute to the subsidence, strict liability might be imposed.[19] Potential proof problems under this approach could be substantial.

The liability situation may differ in the case of subjacent support. One court has held that a defendant is strictly liable, not only for harm to land caused by subsidence resulting from defendant's mining operations, but also for harm to artificial structures damaged by the subsidence, if the subsidence would have occurred in the absence of the structures.[20]

A subsequent owner is not liable to adjacent owners for damages caused by excavations made by his predecessor.[21] But a subsequent owner has been held liable where he failed in his duty to maintain a retaining wall erected by his predecessor.[22]

22.11 RENTAL OF REAL PROPERTY

Lease or rental of realty is a contractual arrangement between two parties designated in common parlance as landlord and tenant, whereby the owner divests himself for a period of time of the possession and use of his property in exchange for a stipulated compensation in the form of rent. The lease may be granted for life, for years, "at will," and so on, but always for some period short of the time interest that the lessor has in the premises. That is to say, a lease creates a lesser estate from the greater. If the entire interest were being conveyed, the transaction would more properly be designated an assignment than a lease. At the close of the lessee's term, the owner (landlord) has the absolute right to re-enter and make full use of his property.

---

[18] *Spall v. Janota*, 406 N.E.2d 378 (Ind. App. 1980). See also *Pugel v. Monheimer*, 922 P.2d 1377 (Wash. App. 1996).
[19] *Gladin v. Von Engehn*, 575 P.2d 418 (Colo. 1978).
[20] *Breeding v. Koch Carbon, Inc.*, 726 F. Supp. 645 (1989, applying Va. law).
[21] *Keck v. Longoria*, 771 S.W.2d 808 (Ark. App. 1989).
[22] *Urosevic v. Hayes*, 590 S.W.2d 77 (Ark. App. 1979).

A lease is a contract and is governed by the same rules as other contracts. Ordinarily, the landlord assumes the expenses occasioned by taxes, insurance, and reasonable upkeep on the rented property. The use to which leased premises are put must be in line with that agreed upon between the parties. Thus, renting a structure for living purposes does not entitle one to utilize it as a store or other business establishment. Such an attempted use might well run into the additional obstacle of zoning restrictions limiting the area to residences.

A *covenant* is an undertaking to do, or, in the case of a negative covenant, *not* to do, a stated act. Certain covenants are implied in every lease. These include a covenant by the tenant to pay rent, and covenants by the landlord (1) that he has title to the property and (2) that the tenant will have "quiet enjoyment" of the premises. The latter covenant is breached by eviction, actual or constructive.

The remedy for breach of an affirmative covenant is by damages or, sometimes, by a suit for specific performance. When a negative covenant is violated, the appropriate relief is an injunction. Some covenants are personal in nature, while others "run with the land" and hence pass from one beneficiary to his successor in interest.

If the terms of the lease do not expressly preclude him, the tenant can assign or can sublet. Even where a prohibitory clause exists, the landlord may waive his right to object by accepting rent from the assignee. An *assignment* transfers the tenant's entire interest in the remaining portion of the term. The assignee is deemed to have accepted the obligations of the lease and is responsible for the rent. Without a release from the landlord, the assignor retains a secondary liability with respect to the rent; he becomes, in a sense, a surety. A *sublease* results when the tenant transfers a portion of the unexpired term but reserves some to himself. There is no relationship between landlord and subtenant, and no rent can be recovered by the landlord from the subtenant.

An oral lease for more than one year is usually unenforceable under the statute of frauds.[23] A lease of appreciable duration should be recorded so as to give prospective purchasers of the property notice of the situation.

22.12   DISPOSING OF REAL PROPERTY

Real property may pass by intestate succession,[24] or may be devised under the will of the owner. During his lifetime the owner may convey, by one of several means, the realty by way of gift or sale. Relatively infrequently, transfer of real property from one owner to another is effected on an involuntary basis. Cases of this nature include (1) forced sale for back taxes; (2) sale attendant upon foreclosure of a mortgage; (3) bankruptcy (in which event any nonexempt real property of the bankrupt passes to the trustee for the benefit of the creditors); (4) acquisition by

---

[23]See the Florida provision quoted in Section 22.2.

[24]Statutory provisions govern disposition of a decedent's property where no will is to be found. Typically, the state prescribes that the surviving spouse receive the use for life of something like one-third (of what is left after payment of debts and charges against the estate); the remaining two-thirds would go to the children.

adverse possession, a concept to be considered in some detail in Section 22.18; and (5) eminent domain, discussed in Section 22.19.

22.13   MECHANICS OF THE SALE TRANSACTION

One very common means of disposing of real estate is by sale. The ordinary sequence of events is (1) the signing of a contract of sale, which is an agreement to buy, on the one hand, and to sell, on the other, a given piece of property upon terms stated; (2) title search and mortgage arrangements by the prospective purchase;[25] (3) the closing, wherein the vendor ("seller") delivers a deed to the property in exchange for payment of the agreed-upon consideration; (4) recording of the deed and other documents in the official land records at the situs of the property.

22.14   CONTRACT OF SALE

A *contract of sale* is an executory contract for the sale of realty. It is not a transfer of title, and it is only after the would-be purchaser has fulfilled the conditions[26] of the contract that he has a right to demand delivery of the *deed of conveyance,* vesting in him title to the property. The contract of sale ordinarily covers a number of points, among them the following:

1.   Full description of the property involved.

2.   Selling price and terms of the sale.

3.   Determination of which party will pay for such items as the water bill from the date of the closing to the end of the current period for which a bill is rendered.

4.   Statement about existing encumbrances or restrictions of any sort affecting title.

5.   Statement about whether purchaser will assume any mortgage that may be outstanding or about what other disposition will be made of such obligation. Perhaps the most common arrangement is for the seller to discharge his mortgage, using a portion of the sale proceeds, and for the purchaser to bring his own bank into the picture as a new mortgagee on the property.

6.   Type of deed the seller will furnish.

7.   Escrow arrangements.

8.   Date and place for the official closing.

---

[25]The purchaser may desire title insurance, which would indemnify him in a stated amount against loss arising through defects or encumbrances affecting the title that may be in existence when the policy is issued.

[26]Primarily, payment of the indicated price. A portion of the selling price will be paid at the time the bond for deed is executed, and this down payment is recited in the instrument as part of the consideration for the seller's promise to deliver a deed. The balance of the agreed-upon price is to be forthcoming at the closing.

When the title search[27] has been completed and ambiguities of whatever sort resolved to the satisfaction of both parties, the actual closing is the next item of business. At the closing, any mortgage transactions are consummated, transfer taxes are paid, the selling price (adjusted in minor respects for amounts due purchaser or seller) is turned over, and the deed is delivered. Then the documents will be recorded, and third parties are thus put on notice that new ownership of the property is now an accomplished fact.

If the seller should renege on his promise to transfer the property, the buyer can probably secure a remedy of *specific performance*, forcing the seller to go through with his bargain. Damages would be an inadequate remedy in many cases, since each parcel of real property is regarded as unique, and the buyer is entitled to the precise land he bargained for, and not simply to its supposed monetary equivalent.

22.15   THE DEED; FUNCTION AND TYPES

A *deed* is a written instrument by which the grantor conveys to his grantee some interest, right, or title in or to the real estate described in the document. The purpose of the deed is to declare the fact of conveyance and to stand as evidence of the transfer of title. It represents the act of but one of the parties, being signed only by the grantor, and, unless a gift is intended, is drawn in fulfillment of the grantor's commitment under a previous agreement with the grantee.

The statutes prescribing the requisites of deeds vary with the jurisdiction. Every deed should contain, among other things, the names of the parties concerned, apt words of conveyance, and a full description of the property in question, indicating what buildings, appurtenances, and privileges are included with the land.

It is not unusual to find that, with reference to a particular piece of realty, a detailed map has been drawn as the outgrowth of a survey and the establishment of precise boundary lines; a sample map is shown in Fig. 22.1. Among other ways, property descriptions may be expressed in terms of lot numbers and maps, or in terms of who occupies adjoining premises, or in terms of *metes and bounds*. The last-named form is common in certain areas of the country, particularly in the northeast. The phrase "metes and bounds" refers to the boundary lines or limits of a tract, with their terminal points and angles; such boundaries may be identified by relating them to fixed objects, either natural or artificial. Here is the substance of an actual description using metes and bounds; obviously, the impermanence of certain markers, and the probable difficulty in locating them after many years have passed, are among the frailties inherent in such a description:

---

[27]An "abstract of title" may have been supplied. Such abstract (the object of which is to enable the buyer and his attorney to pass readily upon the validity of the title) is a concise and orderly statement covering all matters, such as conveyances and encumbrances, which appear on the public records and that affect title to the realty in question.

If the buyer has indeed arranged for new financing of his own, his mortgagee, if a bank, will normally have its own lawyer conduct a title search in protection of the bank's interest, and probably charge this to its customer, the buyer, who usually will not then bother to have still another search made.

Figure 22.1 Plot map accompanying deed.

Commencing at the east end of a stone wall on the southerly side of Hill Road at a point on the west line of premises of *A*, said point being the northeast corner of premises herein conveyed; thence westerly along the southerly side of said Road 1000 feet to an iron fence post on the southerly side of the Road near telephone pole marked 127/34; thence southeasterly along line of iron pins marking northeast line of other lands of Grantors, approximately 125 yards to center line of old lumber road near pile of large stones; thence southerly along other lands of Grantors, following center line of road marked by iron pins to south bank of a brook; thence westerly along south bank of brook to east line of premises of *B*; thence southerly along *B*'s east line to hilltop and north line of premises of *C*; thence easterly along *C*'s north line to stone wall on west line of premises of *D*; thence northerly along said stone wall, easterly along a fence and northerly along a fence, all along premises of *D* to stone wall on south line of premises of *A*; thence westerly along said stone wall and northerly along fence marking *B*'s west line to beginning, 100 acres more or less.

The instrument will also recite the consideration for the transfer, the quantity of interest conveyed, and any conditions, reservations, and the like. The deed must be properly executed in the presence of whatever number of witnesses the applicable statute requires and must actually be delivered to the grantee. Unlike a will, a deed is irrevocable and takes effect upon delivery, thus passing to the recipient an immediate or "present" interest.

There are two principal types of deeds in general use today:

Warranty Deed   This is the kind the buyer invariably wants. Reproduced below is the form of such deed, which appears as a sample in Section 689.02 of the Florida Real Property Law.[28]

§ 689.02 Form of Warranty Deed Prescribed

(1) Warranty deeds of conveyance to land may be in the following form, viz.:

"This indenture, made this _____ day of _____ A.D. _____, between _____, of the County of _____, in the State of _____, party of the first part, and _____, of the County of _____, in the State of _____, party of the second part, witnesseth: That the said party of the first part, for and in consideration of the sum of _____ dollars, to him in hand paid by the said party of the second part, the receipt whereof is hereby acknowledged, has granted, bargained and sold to the said party of the second part, his heirs and assigns forever, the following described land, to wit: . . .

And the said party of the first part does hereby fully warrant the title to said land, and will defend the same against the lawful claims of all persons whomsoever."

(2) The form for warranty deeds of conveyance to land shall include a blank space for the property appraiser's parcel identification number describing the property conveyed, which number, if available, shall be entered on the deed before it is presented for recording, and blank spaces for the social security numbers of the grantees named in the deed, if available, which numbers may be entered on the deed before it is presented for recording. The failure to include such blank spaces, or the parcel identification number, or any social security number, or the inclusion of an incorrect parcel identification number or social security number, shall not affect the validity of the conveyance or the recordability of the deed. Such parcel identification number shall not constitute a part of the legal description of the property otherwise set forth in the deed and shall not be used as a substitute for the legal description of the property being conveyed, nor shall a social security number serve as a designation of the grantee named in the deed.

§ 689.03 Effect of Such Deed

A conveyance executed substantially in the foregoing form shall be held to be a warranty deed with full common law covenants, and shall just as effectually bind the grantor, and his heirs, as if said covenants were specifically set out therein. And this form of conveyance when signed by a married woman shall be held to convey whatever interest in the property conveyed which she may possess.

Quitclaim Deed   By this form the grantor turns over such title and interest as he may have in the property but makes no promise whatever in the nature of a covenant. A quitclaim deed covering a piece of real estate does not purport to con-

---

[28]Title 40, Real and Personal Property § 689.02.

vey anything more than the interest of the grantor as it existed at the time the instrument was executed. As a rule, such a deed is ineffectual in transferring to the grantee any title subsequently acquired by the grantor. This type of deed is employed when a person wants to sell an interest of which he is not sufficiently sure to merit chancing a warranty deed.

A sample version of a quitclaim deed, as contained in Section 3:07 of the New York Real Property Practice Forms, Deeds and Acknowledgments, follows:

§ 3:08 Quitclaim Deed [Form]

THIS INDENTURE, made the _____ day of _____, nineteen hundred and _____ BETWEEN _____, residing at _____, party of the first part, and _____, residing at _____, party of the second part,

WITNESSETH, that the party of the first part, in consideration of ten dollars paid by the party of the second part, does hereby remise, release and quitclaim unto the party of the second part, the heirs or successors and assigns of the party of the second part forever,

ALL that certain plot, piece or parcel of land, with the buildings and improvements thereon erected, situate, lying and being in the

_____

_____

TOGETHER with all right, title and interest, if any, of the party of the first part in and to any streets and roads abutting the above described premises to the center lines thereof; TOGETHER with the appurtenances and all the estate and rights of the party of the first part in and to said premises; TO HAVE AND TO HOLD the premises herein granted unto the party of the second part, the heirs or successors and assigns of the party of the second part forever.

AND the party of the first part, in compliance with Section 13 of the Lien Law, hereby covenants that the party of the first part will receive the consideration for this conveyance and will hold the right to receive such consideration as a trust fund to be applied first for the purpose of paying the cost of the improvement and will apply the same first to the payment of the cost of the improvement before using any part of the total of the same for any other purpose.

The word "party" shall be construed as if it read "parties" whenever the sense of this indenture so requires.

IN WITNESS WHEREOF, the party of the first part has duly executed this deed the day and year first above written.

In presence of:

_____

                                       [Signature of Grantor]

_____

[Acknowledgment]

22.16 RECORDATION

Generally speaking all conveyances of real property must be recorded, typically in the office of the clerk of the city or county that is the situs of the property, in order to be effective against subsequent parties in interest. In this connection, Section 291 of the New York Real Property Law reads in part:

> Every such conveyance not so recorded is void as against any person who subsequently purchases or acquires by exchange or contracts to purchase or acquire by exchange, the same real property or any portion thereof, or acquires by assignment the rent to accrue therefrom . . . , in good faith and for a valuable consideration, from the same vendor or assignor, his distributees or devices, and whose conveyance, contract or assignment first duly recorded.

This means that a buyer who fails to record his deed has no claim to the land if his unscrupulous vendor subsequently executes another deed to the same property, and the second buyer (having made a good faith purchase without knowledge of the prior transaction) does record his deed. The initial purchaser is left with a damages action against the double-dealing vendor.

22.17   DEDICATION

Dedication is any process, formal or otherwise, by which a landowner intentionally sets his property apart for public use. Property dedicated for a particular purpose generally cannot be used for another purpose,[29] and the use of property for purposes other than those for which it was dedicated cannot be authorized by ordinance.[30]

But dedication is usually regarded as carrying with it the right of the public to utilize the land in a way that accords with changing times and conditions. Thus, real estate dedicated for public use as a highway may continue to be so employed, not only in the fashion in which streets or highways were ordinarily used as of the time of dedication, but also to accommodate the most recently invented vehicles and modern methods of travel. Thus, where a parcel dedicated to a city for use as a public street was, after 25 years, put to use as a site for an entrance to a toll freeway, the dedication was held not violated.[31]

Similarly, where a portion of a dedicated right-of-way for pedestrians might become dangerous for public use due to earth slides, a city was not required to maintain particular lanes or paths in their original condition for perpetuity.[32]

Effective dedication requires the presence of an unequivocal offer by a competent person to commit his property and a clear acceptance on the part of the intended recipient. This acceptance is occasionally shown by passage of a resolution of some sort, but is much more likely to take the form of action or conduct that unmistakably shows reliance on the offer and that is of such a nature as to indicate acceptance. An illustration might be the start of public school construction on a site dedicated for the purpose.

---

[29] *Save The Walwood Murry Mem. Library Comm. v. City Council of the City of Palm Springs,* 263 Cal.Rptr 896 (Cal. App. 1989); *Harris Bank of St. Charles v. City of Geneva,* 663 N.E.2d 483 (Ill. App. 1996).
[30] *Zumbrotta v. Strafford Western Emigration Company,* 290 N.W.2d 621 (Minn. 1980).
[31] *McCraw v. City of Dallas,* 420 S.W.2d 793, (Civ. App. Tex. 1967).
[32] *Neighbors & Friends of Viretta Park v. Miller,* 940 P.2d 286 (Wash. App. 1997).

A number of jurisdictions have statutory provisions stipulating how land may be committed to public use; *statutory dedications* are grants made in a manner conforming to such provisions. These laws are not exclusive, however, and dedications effected outside their purview are referred to as *common-law dedications.* It has been said that, under a common law dedication, the public acquires simply an easement, or such an interest in the land as is necessary for its use.[33]

22.18   ACQUIRING TITLE TO REAL PROPERTY BY ADVERSE POSSESSION

Upon occasion, title to real property, or a right in respect of such property, is acquired by a process known as *adverse possession.* If *A* occupies a parcel of land belonging to *B* without the license or consent of the latter, and such possession and utilization of the premises continues uninterruptedly for a period of years,[34] the claimant's dominion over the property is said to ripen into title, and title achieved through adverse possession is as perfect a title as one transferred by deed from the owner. To reach that state of affairs, however, the occupancy by the adverse possessor must have been open, notorious,[35] continuous, actual, exclusive, and hostile, that is, under a claim of right that runs counter to the true owner's interest. Occasional entries upon someone else's property for such a purpose as cutting timber are not adverse possession within the meaning of the law. Acquisition of title by adverse possession is not an easy matter, since the adverse possessor must overcome the presumption that his occupancy of another's land is in subordination to the title of the real owner. Thus, even a token payment of rent destroys the requisite pattern, since such a payment by the occupant acknowledges that ownership and control belong elsewhere. Also, some adverse possession statutes require that the claimant have paid all taxes on the property.[36]

Quite commonly a "right-of-way" comes about through the medium of adverse possession. Occasionally a property owner will take positive steps to assure that sort of thing does not happen in connection with his holdings. For example, a country club owns a suspension footbridge over a body of water in Connecticut. This bridge is often used by nonmembers as part of a shortcut across the lake and the golf course. Once a year the club exercises its prerogative and closes the bridge, posting a no-trespassing sign to warn outsiders to stay away. Such action is taken to destroy any continuity of use on the part of nonmembers and thus to preclude any possible contention that a right-of-way has been acquired through adverse possession.

---

[33]*North Spokane Irrigation District No. 8 v. County of Spokane,* 86 Wash.2d 599, 547 P.2d 859 (1976).

[34]The precise number depends upon the statutes of the state wherein the real estate is situated. In California, for example, the period is 5 years. Cal. Code of Civil Procedure § 325.

[35]The requirement that a would-be adverse-possession claim be manifest from the nature or circumstances of the possession is imposed so that the real owner may be informed of the possessor's apparent intent and not be misled into acquiescence in what the owner might otherwise reasonably suppose to be a mere trespass.

[36]See, for example, Nevada Revised Statutes 11:150; *Colfer v. Harmon,* 832 P.2d 383 (Nev. 1992).

22.19 EMINENT DOMAIN

The right of *eminent domain* enables the federal and state governments and those to whom the power has been lawfully delegated to take private property and appropriate it to public use. The public use requirement once acted as a serious constraint on this government action. At present, however, a wide variety of uses that serve the public, even if they do not require public possession or ownership of the property taken, are seen as within the power.

A graphic example of this is the U.S. Supreme Court case of *Hawaii Housing Authority v. Midkiff*.[37] In Hawaii land ownership had traditionally been concentrated in a few hands, and the legislature created a mechanism to condemn residential tracts and transfer ownership to existing lessees. Upholding the scheme the court said, "[w]here the exercise of the eminent domain power is rationally related to a conceivable public purpose, the Court has never held a compensated taking to be proscribed by the clause." The owner's interest is safeguarded in two ways: (1) his property can only be taken by due process of law, and (2) he is entitled to payment of reasonable compensation. Statutes of the particular jurisdiction will set forth the exact procedure that must be followed in condemning the land and in settling any dispute over the amount the owner should be paid.[38]

The right of eminent domain is an inherent and necessary attribute of sovereignty. Were it not for the existence of such a power, the government would find it difficult or impossible, short of paying truly exorbitant prices, to secure, for instance, whatever land it needs for construction of a state highway or for the site of a new school building. The proceeding enforcing the right of eminent domain is sometimes referred to as condemnation.

22.20 ZONING

The essential purpose of zoning is to rationally coordinate land-use planning to promote orderly development and preservation of property values.[39] Another court defines zoning to mean "division of a city by legislative regulations having to do with structural and architectural designs of buildings and of regulations prescribing use to which buildings within designated districts may be put."[40] Through this process a municipality is mapped out as a grouping of separate areas, in each of which only certain designated uses of land are permitted, to the end that the community may develop in an orderly manner in accordance with a comprehensive scheme and for the good of its residents as a whole. As one example, social welfare is promoted by establishing residential areas free from the offensive smoke, odors, noise, and commotion that normally are native to industrial operations. The assurance that other parcels in a given residential area will not be devoted to objectionable uses can be

---

[37]465 U.S. 1097 (1984).

[38]For an example of laws dealing with eminent domain, *see* Chap. 835, Title 48, Connecticut General Statutes amended in 1997.

[39]*Fargo Cass County v. Harwood*, 256 N.W.2d 694 (N.D. 1977).

[40]*City of Moline Acres v. Heidbreder*, 367 S.W.2d 568, 572 (Mo. 1963), quoting Black's Law Dictionary, 4th ed., and cases therein mentioned.

thought of as compensating a particular owner for his inability (because of zoning restrictions) to use his own lot for other than residential purposes.

While they are related concepts, zoning and planning are readily distinguishable one from the other. The former is concerned primarily with the use and regulation of realty and structures, while the latter term is of broader scope and significance, contemplating the evolvement of an overall program or design covering the present and future physical development of the total community and all aspects thereof (parks, streets, etc.).

Zoning regulations derive from the "police power" of the duly constituted governmental unit. Property rights are held subject to such power, and the legality of zoning has been established beyond doubt. The statutory scheme in Connecticut will serve as a reasonably typical example of the conferring of zoning powers upon local communities. Section 8-1 of the Connecticut General Statutes provides that any municipality may, by vote of its legislative body, "adopt the provisions of this chapter and exercise through a zoning commission the powers granted hereunder." Section 8-2 indicates the purpose of zoning, and tells *what* can be regulated and *how*:

§ 8-2 Regulations

(a) The zoning commission of each city, town or borough is authorized to regulate, within the limits of such municipality, the height, number of stories and size of buildings and other structures; the percentage of the area of the lot that may be occupied; the size of yards, courts and other open spaces; the density of population and the location and use of buildings, structures and land for trade, industry, residence or other purposes, including water-dependent uses as defined in section 22a-93, and the height, size and location of advertising signs and billboards. Such bulk regulations may allow for cluster development as defined in section 8-18. Such zoning commission may divide the municipality into districts of such number, shape and area as may be best suited to carry out the purposes of this chapter; and, within such districts, it may regulate the erection, construction, reconstruction, alteration or use of buildings or structures and the use of land. All such regulations shall be uniform for each class or kind of buildings, structures or use of land throughout each district, but the regulations in one district may differ from those in another district, and may provide that certain classes or kinds of buildings, structures or uses of land are permitted only after obtaining a special permit or special exception from a zoning commission, planning commission, combined planning and zoning commission or zoning board of appeals, whichever commission or board the regulations may, notwithstanding any special act to the contrary, designate, subject to standards set forth in the regulations and to conditions necessary to protect the public health, safety, convenience and property values. Such regulations shall be made in accordance with a comprehensive plan and in adopting such regulations the commission shall consider the plan of conservation and development prepared under section 8-23. Such regulations shall be designed to lessen congestion in the streets; to secure safety from fire, panic, flood and other dangers; to promote health and the general welfare; to promote adequate light and air; to prevent the overcrowding of land; to avoid undue concentration of population and to facilitate the adequate provision for transportation, water, sewerage, schools, parks and other public requirements. Such regulations shall be made with reasonable consideration as to the character of the district and its peculiar suitability for particular uses and with a view to conserving the value of buildings and encouraging the most appropriate use of land throughout such municipality. Such regulations may, to the extent consistent with soil types, terrain, infrastructure capacity and the plan of conservation and development for the community, provide for cluster development, as defined in section 8-18, in residential zones. Such regulations shall also encourage the development of housing opportunities including opportunities for multifamily dwellings, consistent with soil types, terrain and infrastructure capacity, for all residents of the municipality and the planning region in which the municipality is located, as designated by the Secretary of the Office of Policy and Management under section 16a-4a. Such regulations shall also promote housing choice and economic diversity in housing, including housing for both low and moderate income households, and shall encourage the development of housing which will meet the housing needs identified in the housing plan prepared pursuant to section 8-37t and in the housing component and the other components of the state plan of conservation and development prepared pursuant to section 16a-26. Zoning regulations shall be made with reasonable consideration for their impact on agriculture. Zoning regulations may be made with reasonable consideration for the protection of historic factors and shall be made with reasonable consideration for the protection of existing and potential public surface and ground drinking water supplies. On or after July 1, 1985, the regulations shall provide that proper provision be made for soil erosion and sediment control pursuant to section 22a-329. Such regulations may also encourage energy-efficient patterns of development, the use of solar and other renewable forms of energy, and energy conservation. The regulations may also provide for incentives for developers who use passive solar energy techniques, as defined in subsection (b) of section 8-25, in planning a residential subdivision development. The incentives may include, but not be limited to, cluster development, higher density development and performance standards for roads, sidewalks and underground facilities in the subdivision. Such regulations may provide for a municipal system for the creation of development rights and the permanent transfer of such development rights, which may include a system for the variance of density limits in connection with any such transfer. Such regulations may also provide for notice requirements in addition to those required by this chapter. No such regulations shall prohibit the operation of any family day care home or group day care home in a residential zone. Such regulations shall not impose conditions and requirements on manufactured homes having as their narrowest dimension twenty-two feet or more and built in accordance with federal manufactured home construction and safety standards or on lots containing such manufactured homes which are substantially different from conditions and requirements imposed on single-family dwellings and lots containing single-family dwellings. Such regulations shall not impose conditions and requirements on developments to be occupied by manufactured homes having as their narrowest dimension twenty-two feet or more and built in accordance with federal manufactured home construction and safety standards which are substantially different from conditions and requirements imposed on multifamily dwellings, lots containing multifamily dwellings, cluster developments or planned unit developments. Such regulations shall not prohibit the continuance of any nonconforming use, building or structure existing at the time of the adoption of such regulations. Such regulations shall not provide for the termination of any nonconforming use solely as a result of nonuse for a specified period of time without regard to the intent of the property owner to maintain that use. Any city, town or borough which adopts the provisions of this chapter may, by vote of its legislative body, exempt municipal property from the regulations prescribed by the zoning commission of such city, town or borough; but unless it is so voted municipal property shall be subject to such regulations.

The courts will insist that zoning restrictions on the rights of landowners not be arbitrary, unreasonable, or discriminatory, and that they reveal a genuine concern for the public welfare. However, a presumption of validity attaches to decisions reached by appropriate administrative bodies, and determinations by zoning authorities will not lightly be overturned.

QUESTIONS

1. Define real property; differentiate it from personal property.
2. What is a quitclaim deed? A warranty deed?
3. If a person buys some land and the deed states "in fee simple," what does this mean for the purchaser?
4. What are the essentials in a deed?
5. What is a title search? Why is one made?
6. Explain the function and operation of eminent domain.
7. How are boundaries generally recorded?
8. What is an easement? By what means is one obtained? Can the easement be *(a)* sold, or *(b)* relinquished?
9. What general limitations are there upon one's use of his own land?
10. Do water and mineral rights usually accompany the transfer of title to land?
11. What aspects of the property should one investigate before buying a given piece of real estate? Explain fully.
12. What is meant by an "encumbrance" in regard to real property? Give several illustrations.
13. What is a lease? What restrictions are normally imposed upon the use of leased property?
14. What is a license for the use of land? How is it obtained? How is it terminated?
15. What is a condominium? A cooperative?
16. Distinguish between lease and license. Illustrate.
17. What is the meaning of "profit a prendre"?
18. What is a mortgage on real property?
19. Can a mortgage be assigned? Can a lease be assigned?
20. Explain the proper steps to take if one is *(a)* to mortgage his real property, *(b)* to pay off a mortgage.
21. If a piece of real estate is sold, what of the existing mortgage thereon? Does the mortgagee have any effective objection to the sale or to the identity of the purchaser?

22. Why does a mortgagee generally require the mortgagor to sign a bond or a promissory note as well as the mortgage itself?

23. How may realty be conveyed?

24. Explain the steps to be taken in selling a piece of realty.

25. What is an "abstract of title"?

26. What are metes and bounds?

27. Where should the instrument evidencing the conveyance of real property be recorded? Why the recording?

28. If a person buys some land, what rights, broadly speaking, does he acquire regarding such land?

29. Can two or more persons own a given piece of land? If so, on what basis?

30. If two persons own a given piece of land, can one sell it despite objections by the other? Explain.

31. What is a "life estate" in real property? If a person has a life estate in land, can he sell the property itself? Why?

32. Can ownership of real property be conveyed orally? Why?

33. What is a "covenant" as the term is employed in the law of real property? Illustrate.

34. What remedies are available for breach of a covenant?

35. As regards realty, distinguish between sale and lease. Under what conditions is real property transferred without the "approval" of the owner, and very likely against his wishes?

36. What points are generally covered in a bond for deed?

37. Explain what steps are involved at the "closing" of a real estate sale.

38. On what basis is the state able to take land (needed, for example, for a new highway) regardless of the wishes of the property owners involved? What is the justification?

39. What is an "implied easement"?

40. What is the "right of lateral support"? Illustrate.

41. Distinguish between "statutory" and "common-law" dedication.

42. What is the purpose of zoning?

43. Distinguish between zoning and planning as related to land use.

44. Brown owned 25 acres of woodland situated off the highway behind Sullivan's property, and she had an easement across the latter's land for access to the woodland. Thompson offered Sullivan a handsome price for his property, intending to construct a housing development thereon. Can Sullivan (or Thompson, after the sale is consummated) terminate Brown's easement without her consent? Elaborate.

45. What is the mortgagee's situation if the mortgagor fails to pay the taxes, a sewer assessment, and insurance on the property? Explain. What steps can the mortgagee take to enforce his rights?

chapter

23

WATER RIGHTS

23.1   INTRODUCTION

This chapter explores the rights of real property owners to the use and benefit of water that is either upon, adjacent to, or under their lands. Case law and statutory provisions respecting various aspects of water rights differ with the jurisdiction, and the legislatures in those states plagued with inadequate rainfall have enacted comprehensive control measures regarding the use of water.

A "water right" has no physical form, but is a legal interest akin to real property and may be bought and sold like any other property. The holder of the interest is privileged to make reasonable use, beneficial to him, of the water involved.

23.2   DEFINITIONS AND DISTINCTIONS

In contradistinction to waters that seep or percolate through the soil or that flow in subterranean streams, *surface waters* are an accumulation of rain or melting snow. They appear upon the surface of the ground in a diffused state and follow no well-defined course. Ultimately any identifiable segment of surface water will either be absorbed by the land, will evaporate, or will reach some lake[1] or channelized stream, whereupon it ceases to be categorized as "surface water." Conversely, flood waters becoming detached from a stream swollen by excessive rainfall and spreading over the land, never to return to the main current, are generally, though not universally, regarded as "surface waters."

---

[1]The term "lake" is taken to mean a body of water whose characteristics are (1) permanency, (2) location in a depression in the earth's surface, and (3) no perceptible flow (that is, the water is basically at rest). The distinction between a lake or pond and a pool is that a pool is generally a relatively small enlargement of a stream frequently above or below a rapid or waterfall and revealing an appreciable current as water flows through it.

413

A *natural watercourse,* normally of great benefit to the land through which it flows, is described as a stream established when surface water begins to move in a definite direction and forms a regular channel or bed with discernible banks and sides.[2] Such a stream, which ultimately empties into some other body of water, enjoys a measurable flow and a regular, though occasionally diminished or interrupted, source of supply. These concepts are deeply rooted in American law and have not changed in over 100 years. "To prove the existence of a watercourse it must be made to appear that the water usually flows in a certain direction, by a regular channel with banks or sides. It need not be shown to flow continually; it may be dry at times but it must have a well defined and substantial existence."[3] The flow of water need not be continuous but, to constitute a true watercourse, the stream must be distinguishable from mere surface drainage occasioned by freshets or other extraordinary causes.[4] Whether the stream qualifies as navigable depends upon whether it is susceptible of being utilized in its natural condition as a commercial highway upon which travel or trade may readily be conducted. The terms *public waters*[5] and *navigable waters* are not infrequently treated as synonymous, with the words *private waters* being employed to denote "nonnavigable" streams and the like.[6] The other basic grouping of waters, besides those that, in one form or another, overlie the land, is referred to as *groundwater.* This grouping in turn is divided into (1) *percolating water* and (2) water flowing in *channelized subterranean streams,*[7] the existence and location of which are ascertainable from surface indications such as to belie the need for exploratory excavation. To put the distinction another way, all subsurface water that does not travel in known channels is said to be percolating water. Percolating water, deemed a part of the soil that contains it, either flows in some unknown course or simply seeps or oozes,[8] its movement through the ground being perpendicular or horizontal, or a little of each. In the absence of actual knowledge, it is presumed that underground water is percolating and not a stream.[9]

When a storm occurs, some of the precipitation falling in the area may run off promptly, some may evaporate, some may be taken up by vegetation, and some may penetrate into the ground or even into seams in the underlying rock. Percolat-

[2]*Lowe v. Loge Realty Co.,* 138 Ind.App. 434, 214 N.E.2d 400 (1966); *Johnson v. Whitten,* 384 A.2d 698 (Me. 1978).

[3]*Ullian v. Cullen,* 325 N.E. 2d 593 (Mass. App. 1975), quoting *Ashley v. Wolcott,* 11 Cush. 192 (1853).

[4]*Reed v. Jacobson,* 169 Neb. 245,69 N.W.2d 881 (1955).

[5]These are often of considerable size and commonly used for such public purposes as bathing, fishing, and navigation.

[6]It has been held that title to the beds of nonnavigable rivers lies with the riparian owners rather than with the state. *Prazzek v. Drainage District,* 237 P. 1059 (Kan. 1925).

A transfer of title of riparian land bounded by a nonnavigable water body also transfers title to the thread-line of the bed, unless such is specifically excluded. *Snake River v. United States,* 395 F. Supp. 886 (D.C. Wyo. 1975); *United States v. Vesterso,* 828 F.2d 1234 (8th Cir. 1987, applying N.D. law); *State ex rel Meek v. Hayes,* 785 P.2d 1356 (Kan. 1990).

[7]Some authorities do not agree that water moving in underground streams can properly be denominated as "groundwater." In any event, regardless of the accuracy of the terminology employed, rights and liabilities respecting subterranean streams, as distinguished from percolating water, are generally governed by the rules of law pertaining to streams on the surface of the ground.

[8]*Jones v. Home Building & Loan Assn. of Thomasville,* 252 N.C. 626, 114 S.E.2d 638 (1960).

[9]*Woodsum v. Pemberton,* 412 A.2d 1064 (N.J. 1980).

ing water may be precipitation that has slowly filtered through the soil, or it may represent moisture that has escaped through the bed or banks of a stream and thence worked its way through the ground. Artesian water, in contrast, exists under pressure in seams of rock or in porous strata of soil underlying impervious soils that prevent its escape. When a drilled hole provides an outlet channel, the water will rise in the hole until the pressures are equalized, or it may actually flow out at the surface if the pressure behind it is sufficient.

Water law is a highly statutory subject and varies greatly from state to state. Principal rules discussed in the following sections provide a general conceptual framework, but any water-right problem requires specific reference to the law of the jurisdiction in which the watercourse is found. Federal law and a variety of interstate compacts may also be germane.

23.3   RIPARIAN RIGHTS

The term *riparian rights* is probably more familiar than any other in the overall subject of water rights. Webster's *Third New International Dictionary* defines a riparian right as the right of one owning land having access to and use of the shore and water.[10] "Riparian" derives from the Latin word *riparius,* meaning belonging to the bank of a river, and thus has reference to banks but not beds of a stream.[11]

A riparian owner is one who owns land on the bank of a river, or one who is the owner of land along, bordering upon, bounded by, fronting upon, abutting or adjacent and contiguous to and in contact with a river. The riparian proprietor must own land in actual contact with water; proximity alone does not suffice and carries no benefits relating to use of the water.[12] It follows that *riparian land* is a parcel that is bounded by or includes a portion of a natural watercourse. Technically, only one whose realty abuts a *river* is a "riparian owner," and the purists would say that one whose land touches upon a *lake* is more accurately referred to as a "littoral owner." It appears, however, that "riparian" is generally regarded as an acceptable word when the land involved borders upon either river or lake.[13]

Unless the circumstances or the express terms of the transaction indicated a different intent, at common law a grant of land hugging a nonnavigable river conveyed property rights in the stream bed to the center or "thread," which is an imag-

---

[10]Webster's *Third New International Dictionary*, G. & C. Merriam Co., Springfield, Mass., p. 1960 (1981).

[11]*Mobile Dry Docks Co. v. Mobile,* 40 So. 205 (Ala. 1906).

[12]To illustrate this point, assume that a person owns a strip of land 500 feet wide and extending 1,000 feet along the east bank of a stream. He is a riparian owner with respect to that stream, whereas the owner of the property "inland from" this person's holdings is not a riparian owner because his land does not actually border the stream. It is possible, of course, that a nonriparian owner might acquire special water privileges through grant or otherwise, and it is also possible that the riparian proprietor's use of "his water" might be so negligently handled or might take such an ultrahazardous form as to occasion liability "running to" his neighbor, the nonriparian owner.

[13]If a person is contemplating the purchase of property adjacent to an artificial pond or lake, he should carefully investigate the question of just what rights he will have to the water area and its use. It may be that the one who made the pond still owns part or all of the submerged land, and can empty the pond or even remove the dam if he so desires.

inary line at the middle of the main channel,[14] with the water being measured at its lowest stage. Riparian rights can be thought of as vested property rights that are "attached to" the land and that may not legally be invaded or taken from the owner without just compensation. Such a riparian proprietor is entitled to protect his interest by seeking to enjoin any injurious interference with the stream.

To the extent that a rule of broad applicability exists in this country on the subject of the legal rights of a riparian proprietor, every riparian owner is entitled to the natural flow[15] in its accustomed channel of the content of a stream running through or along his land, subject to the reasonable use of the water by those similarly entitled, for the ordinary purposes of life. Such flow is to be undiminished in quantity (except as affected by an act of God) and unimpaired in quality. In other words, a riparian right is reciprocal in character as to other riparian rights in the same body of water. Each riparian proprietor in turn has the right, which some sources say is neither gained by use nor lost by disuse, to make reasonable use of the watercourse that abuts his property. He also has the right to any accretions (deposits of soil) that the passing stream leaves on his property. The right of any given owner is subject, however, to the equal right of all other "similarly-situated" riparian proprietors to make reasonable use of the water during its passage through or along their respective parcels of land. A corollary of this proposition is the well-settled rule that any unwarranted obstruction of the channel, or diversion of the water, or comparable move by other owners that works injury to a given riparian proprietor entitles the latter to compensatory damages or an injunction.

In a case where the defendant had initiated a stream channelization project in order to reclaim 20 acres of land for farming purposes, the plaintiff alleged that the result of the straightening of the stream was an increase in the velocity of the water causing scouring and abrasion to creek banks as well as increased flooding, thereby damaging the plaintiff through deposits of sand, silt, and extensive corrosion. Finding for the plaintiff, the court said that "although we have never specifically held a riparian owner may be liable for accelerating or hastening the flow of a water course to the injury of another, we believe permitting recovery for this type of damage is consistent with our prior decisions requiring a land owner to exercise due care for his neighbors when he avails himself of a water course."[16] An injunction is appropriate where the evidence establishes that the injury will be either con-

---

[14]Where a meandering river is involved, such as a portion of the Mississippi (whose main channel in some places is slowly being altered by erosion and sedimentation), even state boundaries are likely to be altered somewhat with the passage of time.

In a Louisiana case, *Nevels v. State,* 665 So.2d 26 (La. App., 1995) alluvian and other problems were well illustrated where the Mississippi River diverted from its original course around a bend, and cut a new channel that eventually enlarged until a portion of the flow returned to the bendway.

It might be noted that boundaries of land bordering ponds and lakes also give rise to uncertainty upon occasion. In the case of large lakes, boundaries may be set in the same terms as are usual with tidal waters, that is, the "normal highwater mark"; or they may be established by survey or by prior appropriation, or other means. At any rate, the boundary lines should be carefully ascertained, rather than merely assumed, when one intends to take any action involving lakeside properties.

[15]An interesting question about natural flow was presented in *Huff v. Smith,* 679 So.2d 259 (Ala. App. 1996) where, after noting that a riparian proprietor has a right to natural stream flow and to be protected from "unnatural" enlargement of a stream, declined to answer whether a beaver dam was a natural obstruction. The court found that any obstruction causing unnatural enlargement gave rise to a remedy.

[16]*Oakleaf Country Club Inc. v. Wilson,* 257 N.W.2d 739 (Iowa 1977). See also *Maddocks v. Giles,* 686 A.2d 1069 (Me. 1996) where the court applied the principle that a landowner cannot drastically alter the flow of a watercourse to a subterranean spring damaged by an excavation for a gravel pit.

tinuous or repetitive. For example, the issuance of an injunction was held proper where the defendant had constructed several pits on his property to collect surplus water to enable him to irrigate his farmland and where on several occasions the pit wall failed to hold and discharged water and silt onto the plaintiff's land.[17]

The concept of riparian rights seems to be an inherently difficult one, and it might be helpful to quote briefly from several of the court decisions that discuss aspects of the subject in succinct fashion:

1. We . . . reassert the riparian right to be a vested property right inhering in and a part and parcel of the abutting lands, a right not gained by use or lost by disuse, a right (qualified only by the correlative rights of other riparian proprietors) to use the entire ordinary and natural flow of the stream for all lawful riparian uses and also to have all such flow come down to the land undiminished other than by the lawful uses by upper riparian proprietors or by the rights of those who have otherwise obtained a superior claim to the use of a portion of the stream. This right to use the water of the stream we hold to be entitled to the same respect and protection at the hands of the law as any other vested property right.[18]

2. An abutting or riparian owner of a lake, suitable for fishing, boating, hunting, swimming, and other domestic or recreational uses . . . has a right to make such use of the lake over its entire surface, in common with all other abutting owners, provided such use is reasonable and does not unduly interfere with the exercise of similar rights on the part of other abutting owners, regardless of the navigable or public character of the lake and regardless also of the ownership of the bed thereof.[19]

3. In Wisconsin riparian rights vary in accordance with the nature of the body of water. With respect to the ownership of the bed of the stream, a riparian owner owns to the thread (the geographical center) of the stream. . . The title of the riparian owner is, however, a qualified one, subject to the paramount interest of the state. . . However, the owner of the land abutting a natural lake or pond owns to the waterline only, since title to the submerged lands beneath a permanent body of natural water belongs to the state. An abutting property owner on a natural lake, except for the right of access, has no more rights as a riparian than any other member of the public . . . Riparian rights include the right to use a body of water "for bathing, swimming and boating purposes." . . . An artificial lake located wholly on the property of a single owner is his to use as he sees fit, provided, of course, that the use is lawful. He may if he wishes reserve to himself or his assigns the exclusive use of the lake or water rights.[20]

4. In Washington, riparian owners of land on nonnavigable lakes hold in common and may exercise, subject to the rule of reasonableness, such rights as access, swimming, fishing, bathing, and boating. . . Thus, the rights possessed by each of the parties are (1) the ownership of land abutting on the lake, (2) the conditions and covenant contained in the deeds, and (3) the specific undivided interest in the bottom of the lake associated with each of their parcels. What must be determined on remand is whether the portion of the dock that extends into the lake is legal consid-

[17]*Delp v. Laier*, 288 N.W. 2d 265 (Neb. 1980).
[18]*Fall River Valley Irr. Dist. v. Mt. Shasta Power Corp.*, 202 Cal. 56, 259 P. 444, 448 (1977).
[19]*Flynn v. Beisel*, 257 Minn. 531, 102 N.W.2d 284, 290–91 (1960).
[20]*Mayer v. Grueber*, 29 Wis. 2d 168, 138 N.W.2d 197, 202–204 (1965).

ering the riparian rights of the parties. The test for deciding whether a given structure is legal is twofold; it must (1) constitute a riparian use and (2) be reasonable.[21]

"Reasonable use" is often mentioned with the consideration of how a riparian owner properly may utilize the water that flows past his acreage. The rather nebulous test to be applied is that, considering all the facts and circumstances of a particular situation, a use that works substantial injury to the common right among riparian proprietors is an "unreasonable" use. By way of illustration, what is regarded as "reasonable use" in agricultural territory might well differ from the standard employed where a stream flows through a suburban community. No matter what the geographical location, however, no purpose is "reasonable" that is not lawful and beneficial to the taker—or where it can be shown that his use of the quantity of water in question was motivated solely by spite against his neighbors.

In one case[22] a small creek skirted the property of riparian owner *A* and subsequently flowed past owner *B*'s land. *A* pumped a great deal of water from the creek for irrigation of his field crops and, in the process, virtually stopped the flow of water onto *B*'s land and deprived the latter owner of a supply adequate for domestic uses and for livestock. It was held that *B* had a clear right to receive his proportionate share of the water for lawful purposes and that *A*'s monopolistic employment of the limited contents of the stream for extensive irrigation constituted an "unreasonable" use under the circumstances and an invasion of *B*'s legitimate interest in utilizing some of the water.

A difficulty arises where a riparian owner substantially diverts or blocks a natural watercourse, thus damaging downstream property by depriving it of much-needed flow. One often-repeated maxim in the field of water rights is "let it flow as it has been accustomed to flow." Thus, if a land owner has in the past enjoyed the benefit of a stream flowing over or adjacent to his land, such owner cannot have his reasonable use of this water prevented or markedly curtailed without his consent or without due process of law. Similarly, he in his turn would incur liability were he to interfere with the privileges of other rightful users.[23]

---

[21] *Hefferline v. Langkow*, 15 Wash. App. 896, 552 P.2d 1079, 1081 (1976).

[22] *Great American Development Co. v. Smith*, 303 S.W.2d 861 (Civ. App. Tex. 1957).

[23] Here are two situations in which the aforementioned "flow" maxim has pertinence:

1. The water from a spring flowed across A's property, through a ditch, to a pit dug by him; thereafter it flowed underground into B's cellar, causing damage thereto. The court awarded damages to B as plaintiff, reasoning that, it A (the owner of the dominant estate) had done nothing to change the natural flow of water over or from his property, he would not be liable for any water damage to B's property, regardless of whether the water came from springs, streams, or the surface of the land. If, however, the proprietor of the upland had diverted quantities of surface water and discharged it upon the lower land without consent of the owner of the latter property, the upland owner, A, would be liable. The important question to answer is whether or not the ditch and pit were natural in origin or were artificial and created by A; only in the latter circumstance would A be responsible for the consequences. Inspection by the court, and the testimony of B's witnesses, showed that the pit, at least, was artificial and designed to receive the flow of surface water. Consequently, A was required to pay B for the cellar damage done by the escaping spring water.

2. Jones built a dam to make a small fishpond on his property but thereby caused water to flow on or across his neighbor's land, and the latter became entitled to seek compensation for any resulting damage. Similarly, if the pond had caused harm to the neighbor because of a change it occasioned in the groundwater conditions, or if the pond diverted an appreciable volume of water away from the neighbor's land so that he no longer had the use of such water as a surface stream, a spring, or a source of supply for his well, the neighbor could again institute an action for damages.

By the same token, a lower owner cannot with impunity obstruct a surface stream, thereby flooding the lands and buildings "above" him by preventing the water from moving along as it otherwise naturally would. One is not privileged to flood the property of another, absent prescriptive right to do so or a grant of privilege by such other person.

Common law riparian rights may be legislatively altered.[24] Thus, statutes may require riparian landowners to acquire irrigation permits before using water, a requirement that in effect abrogates the common law riparian right of irrigation.[25]

23.4 APPROPRIATIVE AND PRESCRIPTIVE RIGHTS

A number of jurisdictions in the arid and semiarid western portions of the country have adopted the doctrine of appropriation, and in some of these states the body of common law surrounding riparian rights coexists; that is, such states recognize both appropriative and riparian water rights.

The term *appropriation* means diverting or taking water from some stream (or other natural source of supply) in accordance with local law and with the intention of applying the appropriated water to some beneficial use, such as domestic consumption, stock watering, industrial purposes, and a variety of others.[26] Such intention must be fulfilled within a reasonable time by actual application to the designed purpose of all the water taken. In other words, appropriation of water is the intent to take, accompanied by some physical manifestation of the intent, and for a valuable purpose.[27] Thus, a Colorado decision[28] recognized that the use of water in springs and ponds for the maintenance of livestock and for other domestic needs constituted appropriation of water to beneficial use. Likewise, preservation of aesthetic values and recreational opportunities have been held a beneficial use that would support an appropriation.[29] Since one need not "appropriate" what he already owns, an "appropriator" in the legal sense is one who takes water, either by surface diversion or from underground by wells, without possessing a property right entitling him to such taking.

Loosely speaking, appropriation includes any taking of water for other than riparian or overlying uses, and unappropriated water flowing in any natural channel is subject to appropriation. In California, to give one example, the one-time practice of appropriating water in any fashion one desired by self-help was termi-

---

[24] For a graphic illustration, see *In re Waters of Long Valley Creek Stream System*, 599 P.2d 656 (Cal. 1979), where the state of California sought to statutorily adjudicate the rights of all riparian owners within the Long Valley system. There the court held that the state water resources control board was authorized to decide the priority of unexercised riparian rights but that it could not extinguish them altogether.

[25] *Omernick v. Department of Natural Resources*, 71 Wis.2d 370, 238 N.W.2d 1, 14(1976), interpreting Wisconsin Statutes Annotated 30.18 (1973).

[26] *Concerning Application for Water Rights*, 938 P.2d 515 (Colo. 1997); *Dallas Creek Water Co. v. Huey*, 933 P.2d 27 (Colo. 1997).

[27] See *Desert Irrigation, Ltd. v. State*, 944 P.2d 835 (Nev. 1997).

[28] *Town of Genoa v. Westfall*, 349 P.2d 370 (Colo. 1960).

[29] *State Dept. of Parks v Idaho Dept. of Water Admin.*, 530 P 2d 924 (Id. 1974). Likewise, see *U.S. v. Alpine Land and Res. Co.*, 503 F. Supp. 877 (D. Nev. 1950) re: fishing.

nated when the statutory method of appropriation was made exclusive.[30] A decision[31] from California describes the essential nature of appropriative and prescriptive[32] rights:

> Perhaps the most persuasive factor in our consideration of the character of the water rights here involved is that as appropriative and prescriptive rights, they are usufructuary. That is to say, there is no right to any particular water flowing in the stream, only a right to take from the stream a certain amount of flowing water; a right that does not come into being until both the means of diverting and the means of using water have been completed.

A statutory scheme may preclude the acquisition of water rights against the state by prescription. It has been held that the California water codes are a comprehensive scheme for granting appropriative rights, and prescriptive rights have been described as parasites because the only way to obtain such rights is to take water rights from someone else.[33]

A dominant distinction between riparian rights and the doctrine of appropriation is the principle of equality among riparian owners, which contrasts with the concept of time priority ("first come, first served") among appropriators.[34] The two types of rights are further distinguishable in that a riparian owner's use of water must only be measured in terms of "reasonableness," while the appropriator's use measure is predetermined, at least in its maximum. The top limit can be thought of as set by the requirement that the appropriator's use be "beneficial." Subject to that limitation, the holder of an appropriative right enjoys a priority claim to the available water. A right of appropriation is a right to a definite quantity of water; a riparian owner, by comparison, is not entitled to a specific volume of water but rather to have the stream flow to and over his land as it is naturally wont to do, and for his reasonable use.

States that have adopted appropriation principles differ as to what waters are subject to appropriation but, in one way or another, they all recognize that private rights must be subject to the important concerns of government with respect to

---

[30]See California Water Code § 1225 (West 1974).

[31]*San Bernardino Valley Mun. Water Distr. v. Meeks and Daley Water Co.*, 226 Cal.App.2d 216, 38 Cal. Rptr. 51 (1964). This was a proceeding in eminent domain to condemn the prescriptive and appropriative water rights and diversion facilities of defendant mutual water companies.

[32]Under certain conditions continuous exercise of a claimed right to divert and use water can ripen into what is known as a prescriptive right against a riparian or overlying owner, assuming either that such owner knows of and acquiesces in such adverse use or that knowledge and acquiescence will be presumed because the adverse use was so obvious and yet had gone unchallenged. Additional essential elements in prescription have been variously expressed, but they would appear to call for actual use under a claim of right by the taking party, which use is hostile and adverse (as to the property owner's interests), and continuous and uninterrupted for a considerable period of time, the length of which varies with the jurisdiction. For typical decisions discussing the acquisition of water rights by prescription, see *Sibbett v. Babcock*, 124 Cal.App.2d 567, 269 P.2d 42 (1954); *Moore v. California Oregon Power Co.*, 22 Cal.2d 725, 140 P.2d 798 (1943); and *Smelcer v. Rippetoe*, 24 Tenn.App. 516, 147 S.W.2d 109 (1940). The Moore case quotes this passage from prior opinions in the same jurisdiction: "Any person may obtain exclusive rights to water flowing in a stream or river by grant or prescription as against either riparian owners on the stream or the prior appropriation of the water by other parties. But the right acquired by prescription is only commensurate with the right enjoyed. The extent of the enjoyment measures the right."

[33]*People v. Shirocow*, 605 P.2d 859 (Cal. 1980).

[34]*Cappaert v. United States*, 426 U.S. 128 (1976); *Colorado River Conservation District v. United States*, 424 U.S. 800 (1976).

navigable waterways. As to just how and under what circumstances an appropriative right can be acquired[35] and taking of the water properly accomplished, statutes may prove very precise. By way of example Arizona has a number of statutory provisions on the subject of which the following[36] are illustrative:

APPROPRIATION OF WATER

§ 45-151. Right of Appropriation; Permitted Uses; Water Rights in Stockponds; Federal Lands

A. Any person, the state of Arizona or a political subdivision thereof may appropriate unappropriated water for domestic, municipal, irrigation, stock watering, water power, recreation, wildlife, including fish, nonrecoverable water storage pursuant to § 45-833.01 or mining uses, for his personal use or for delivery to consumers. The person, the state of Arizona or a political subdivision thereof first appropriating the water shall have the better right.

B. To effect the beneficial use, the person, the state of Arizona or a political subdivision thereof appropriating the water may construct and maintain reservoirs, storage facilities pursuant to chapter 3.1 of this title, dams, canals, ditches, flumes and other necessary waterways.

C. A water right in a stockpond, certified pursuant to article 10 of this chapter, shall be recognized as if such water had been appropriated pursuant to this article.

D. The validity of and the right to exercise a water right obtained in accordance with state law shall not be diminished, impaired or otherwise affected because other water is or may be available to the appropriator from an alternative right or source to satisfy the same use.

E. The right to water appropriated on lands owned by the United States shall be held by the person who first effects the beneficial use of the water appropriated and by the person's successor. This subsection shall not be construed to preclude the United States from being the holder of a right if the United States first effects the beneficial use.

F. A water source that is located on land owned by the United States and that has been or may be appropriated under state law may be beneficially used on any land whether or not owned by the United States.

§ 45-153. Criteria for Approval or Rejection of Applications; Restrictions on Approval

A. The director shall approve applications made in proper form for the appropriation of water for a beneficial use, but when the application or the proposed use conflicts with vested rights, is a menace to public safety, or is against the interests and welfare of the public, the application shall be rejected.

B. An application may be approved for less water than applied for if substantial reasons exist but shall not be approved for more water than may be put to a beneficial use. Applications for municipal uses may be approved to the exclusion of all subsequent appropriations if the estimated needs of the municipality so demand after consideration by and upon order of the director.

---

[35]At the other end of the line, the appropriative right may terminate under various circumstances, abandonment being one. See, for example, *Matter of Clark Fork River Drainage Area,* 908 P.2d 1353 (Mont. 1995) where a miner, by failing to use an appropriated water right for 50 years, was held to have abandoned it despite his contention that he was waiting for the mine to become profitable.

[36]Arizona Revised Statutes, Title 45, Art. 5 (1995).

C. If the director approves an application for the appropriation of water for use on land owned by the state of Arizona, a permit or certificate shall be issued as prescribed by § 37-321.01. If the director approves an application for the appropriation of water for use on land owned by the United States, a permit or certificate shall be issued as prescribed by § 45-151, subsection E.

Amended by Laws 1995, Ch. 230, § 3.

§ 45-157. Relative Value of Uses

A. As between two or more pending conflicting applications for the use of water from a given water supply, when the capacity of the supply is not sufficient for all applications, preference shall be given by the director according to the relative values to the public of the proposed use.

B. The relative values to the public for the purposes of this section shall be:
1. Domestic and municipal uses. Domestic uses shall include gardens not exceeding one-half acre to each family.
2. Irrigation and stock watering.
3. Power and mining uses.
4. Recreation and wildlife, including fish.
5. Nonrecoverable water storage pursuant to § 45-833.01.

23.5   OVERLYING RIGHTS; GROUNDWATER

All ground or subterranean water, unless qualifying as underground streams or lakes whose boundaries and course are well defined and readily ascertainable, is referred to as "percolating" water.

Rights and liabilities to subterranean streams are generally governed by the rules of law applicable to surface streams.[37] The rule in regard to percolating water seems to be slowly changing in this country from one of substantially unrestricted privilege on the part of the overlying owner to one of "reasonable use." The latter concept is that:

> Each owner of land overlying the same general underground supply of water may take such water on his own land for any beneficial use thereon, so long as such taking works no unreasonable injury to other land overlying such waters; that, if the natural supply is not sufficient for all such owners, each is entitled only to his reasonable proportion of the whole, and that each may apply to the courts to restrain an injurious and unreasonable taking by another, and to have the respective rights adjudicated and the use regulated so as to prevent unnecessary injury and restrict each to his reasonable share.[38]

---

[37] *Tehachapi-Cummings County Water Dist. v. Armstrong*, 49 Cal.App.3d 992, 122 Cal. Rptr. 918 (1975). At least one court, however, has held the rules applicable to percolating waters to be different from those applicable to either subterranean streams or surface streams. Thus, the law in Texas is that the owner of overlying land owns percolating water and can do with it as he pleases and may use it for any purpose. *Bartley v. Sone*, 527 S.W.2d 754 (Tex. App. 1975).

[38] *City of San Bernardino v. City of Riverside*, 186 Cal. 7, 198 P. 788 (1921). *See also In re Smith*, 924 P.2d 155 (Colo. 1996), stating that a landowner has an inchoate right in the nontributary groundwater underneath his land, and that this right exists by virtue of land ownership.

In *Rank v. (Krug) U.S.*[39] the court said:

> An overlying owner . . . has the right to take water, regardless of its source, from the ground underneath his land for use on his land which lies within the watershed or basin. The overlying right is . . . based on ownership of the land and is inseparably annexed to the soil. The overlying right, though the manner of its exercise may be different, is identical in law with the riparian right. These rights are absolute property rights against the world, except that as between riparian owners similarly situated, and as between overlying owners similarly situated, their rights are correlative and common with those in a like situation.

Some of the western states that apply the doctrine of appropriation with regard to watercourses are similarly disposed where groundwaters are concerned.

Groundwater is understandably important with respect to agriculture. Operations that lower the water table unduly may deprive the land of the moisture needed for the growing of crops, while activity that raises the water level too much may flood the land or render it so swampy as to be unfit for farming.

Each proprietor should be considerate of the needs and rights of others. It is obvious that a spring or a farmer's well that serves as its owner's source of water is very important to him. Generally speaking, it is improper for another person knowingly to intercept and exhaust the supply, causing the spring or well to go dry. On the other hand, when one digs or drives a well he cannot foretell exactly where the water will come from. Nor can he know, as a rule, whether trouble will ensue for someone else. In many instances, it is difficult to draw the line between the rights of the respective parties in a situation of this kind.

A contemporary and contentious example of groundwater litigation is *Chance v. B P Chemicals, Inc.*,[40] in which property owners claimed that groundwater was being polluted by a refiner's reliance on "deep well" injection technology to dispose of refinery byproducts. The property owner's suit, seeking $1 billion in damages, was unsuccessful, as their rights were held not to be absolute and they were unable to prove physical damage due to lateral migration.

The doctrine of reasonable use does not ordinarily permit percolating waters to be used off the lands from which they are pumped if thereby others whose lands overlie the common supply are injured or damaged. For example, injunctive relief was held proper where the plaintiff sued to enjoin various mining companies from transporting water off their land overlying the common water supply to other tracts of land for use in mining operations.[41]

The trend of the law, especially in the eastern half of the United States, is toward treating rights to percolating water as limited by reasonable use. In a case from Wisconsin,[42] the court said:

> It makes little sense to make an arbitrary distinction between rules to be applied to water on the basis of where it happens to be found. There is little justification for

---

[39] 142 F. Supp. 1 (SD Cal. 1956), reversed in part and affirmed in part *Cal. v. Rank*, 293 F.2d 340 (9th Cir 1961); injunction modified on rehearing 307 F.2d 96 (1962), affirmed *Fresno v. Cal.*, 372 U.S. 627 (1963).

[40] 670 N.E.2d 985 (Ohio 1996).

[41] *Farmers Investment Co. v. Bettwy*, 558 P.2d 14 (Ariz. 1976).

[42] *State of Wis. v. Michels Pipeline Constr., Inc.*, 63 Wis.2d 278, 217 N.W.2d 339, 345 (1974), rehearing denied, 219 N.W.2d 308(1974).

property rights in groundwater to be considered absolute while rights in surface streams are subject to a doctrine of reasonable use.

The other side of the picture is that, if one takes some action that results in raising the water table to the detriment of others, he may be subject to claims for damages. It is very difficult to evaluate potential damage that might be caused by a disturbance of the previously existing conditions regarding percolating water. All sorts of trouble can follow substantial interference with the groundwater level. The engineer should endeavor to anticipate what will happen as the result of his operations and take any indicated precautions.

23.6   SURFACE WATER; THE COMMON-ENEMY DOCTRINE

Surface water is a natural accumulation of precipitation that appears on the surface of the ground in a diffuse state following no well-defined course. The owner of land upon which surface water is found is normally free to seize and use it as he wishes, even though in so doing he may completely exhaust the supply at hand.

Hostile surface water (normally occasioned by long and heavy rains) is considered a "common enemy" and the consensus view seems to be that each landowner is entitled to defend himself against such enemy as best he may by operations conducted on his own land and that, if he does not exercise such right wantonly, carelessly, or unnecessarily, even to the consequent injury of others,[43] no action for damages will arise.

What would appear to be the harshness inherent in the common-enemy doctrine, which is accepted in a number of states, is ameliorated somewhat by such commonly accepted modifications as that a landowner cannot collect the offending surface water into an artificial channel and pour unnatural quantities of it upon the land of another to the latter's severe detriment. In other words, the rights afforded by the common-enemy theory must be exercised within reasonable limits so as not to do needless violence to the privileges of others. A landowner incurs liability only when his harmful interference with and alteration of the natural movement of surface water is "unreasonable."[44] This poses a question of fact to be resolved upon

---

[43]*Diblasi v. City of Seattle*, 933 P.2d 443 (Wash. App. 1997).

[44]*See Bays v. Kent State Univ.*, 684 N.E.2d 1328 (Ohio Ct. Cl. 1997), and *Kial v. Boesch*, 557 N.W.2d 597 (Minn. App. 1996) in which the court said:
    [T]he rule is that in effecting a reasonable use for a legitimate purpose a landowner, acting in good faith, may drain his land of surface waters and cast them as a burden upon the land of another, although such drainage carries with it some waters which would otherwise have never gone that way . . . if
    (a) [t]here is a reasonable necessity for such drainage;
    (b) [r]easonable care be taken to avoid unnecessary injury to the land receiving the burden;
    (c) [t]he utility or benefit accruing to the land drained reasonably outweighs the gravity of the harm resulting to the land receiving the burden;
    (d) [w]here practicable, it is accomplished by reasonably improving and aiding the normal and natural system of drainage according to its reasonable carrying capacity, or if, in the absence of a practicable natural drain, a reasonable and feasible artificial drainage system is adopted.

a reading of all the circumstances, including the amount and foreseeability of harm caused.

At least one state has formally abandoned the common-enemy doctrine and, after declaring the doctrine "rigid" and "anarchic," held that liability for a private nuisance caused by the flow of surface water from a landowner's property to that of an adjoining landowner depends on whether the landowner is making a reasonable use of his land.[45]

23.7 NAVIGABLE WATERWAYS

There are various instances in the United States of major rivers serving to mark the boundary between one state and another. The Mississippi, the Colorado, the Ohio, the Connecticut, the Hudson, and others perform this function along at least a portion of their routes to the sea. The precise location of the boundary line "within" the stream may be the subject of a dispute such as persisted for some years between the states of New York and New Jersey.[46]

In the early days of the United States there was uncertainty about whether the federal government or the states were to be responsible for the improvement and control of navigable waterways. The former ended up with the major job, and the U.S. Corps of Engineers, the U.S. Coast Guard, and the U.S. Navy have charge of such works as:[47]

1. Dredging of harbors and channels.

2. Protection of shores against erosion.

3. Establishment and maintenance of various types of signals, buoys, and the like for the aid and protection of ships.

4. Establishment of pierhead and bulkhead lines.[48]

---

[45]*DeSanctis v. Lynn Water and Sewer Com'n.,* 666 N.E.2d 1292 (Mass. 1996). See also *Johnson v. Bd. of City Cm'rs.,* 913 P.2d 119 (Kan. 1996) for an examination of expert testimony in a case involving erosion caused by alterations in a bridge.

[46]For an instance of how some perplexing questions can arise regarding exact boundary lines, consider this situation. It is asserted that governmental land grants in the eighteenth century had given Kentucky the rights to that segment of the Ohio River that flowed past its territory, with the limit of Kentucky's jurisdiction being established as the low-water mark on the *north* side of the river. When Ohio subsequently joined the Union, the state's Constitution of 1802 (Article VII, Section 6) recited that Ohio was "bounded . . . on the south by the Ohio River to the mouth of the Great Miami River."

[47]Through its control of navigable waterways the federal government can have something to say also about what activity (especially regarding projects that may affect navigation and inter-state commerce) occurs in nonnavigable streams that are tributaries of these waterways.
Federal court jurisdiction extends to cases of admiralty pursuant to the U.S. Constitution, Art. 3, § 2, cl. 1, and 28 U.S.C. § 1331(1). A curious application of this occurred in *Great Lakes Dredge & Dock Co., v. City of Chicago,* 3 F.3d 225 (7th Cir. 1993). Where a break in the roof of a freight tunnel below the Chicago River was allegedly caused by a contractor attempting to replace pile clusters known as "dolphins" at bridge sites, and serious flooding of downtown Chicago resulted.

[48]Pierhead lines are boundaries beyond which no pier construction should project toward navigable water; bulkhead lines set the riverward limit of any bulkhead or other fixed-shore development. Between the two boundaries is the area for piers and other facilities for docking ships.

5. Determination of locations, depths, and widths of navigable channels.

6. Determination of horizontal and vertical clearances for bridges.

When planning any work involving one or more of the items in the preceding list, the engineer must be sure to ascertain and comply with all applicable regulations and permit requirements.

23.8   RESERVOIRS

A municipality desiring to construct a reservoir for water supply cannot simply buy the needed land and proceed as it wishes with the building of a dam. Owners for many miles downstream have rights to the use of the water flowing from the watershed involved, and, in many cases at least, their approval of the project will have to be obtained in advance of construction of the reservoir project.

A prime example is afforded by New York City's wish to divert to its own supply system vast quantities of water from the Delaware River. Even though this stream rises in New York State, the watershed covers parts of Pennsylvania and New Jersey as well, and the river waters serve these states over a distance of many miles. New York City was not entitled to take whatever water it wished to obtain and, in the process, ignore the interests of Pennsylvania and New Jersey. The issue became one for discussion among all parties involved in an effort to arrive at a sort of treaty or compact spelling out an equitable arrangement for the allocation of the available supply.

In some instances, it may be decided that a specified minimum flow will be maintained for the benefit of those located downstream from a dam, or there may be a guarantee that water from the system will be supplied to them. Failure to fulfill this obligation would then position the victimized persons to claim damages for loss of the use of water.

The objections of a few riparian owners cannot always be allowed to prevent the construction of works that are clearly in the public interest. The exercise of the government's right of eminent domain in the taking of property, court proceedings to determine the extent of damage resulting from the taking of the water in question, or arrangements to supply those proprietors in need with water from the reservoir are some of the steps that may be resorted to in order to end disputes standing in the way of a contemplated reservoir project.

23.9   RIGHTS TO WATER POWER

The right to develop a major hydroelectric power site may be a matter of vast importance, and there will be both state and federal laws affecting the specific location. There are often complicated questions as to whether the right to develop the available power belongs to the federal government, to the state in which the site lies, to contiguous states jointly, or to private interests.

Assume that a medium-sized stream runs through private property and affords the potential for the development of a minimum of 3,000 kilowatts of electric power, the generation of which is possible even under ordinary low-water conditions. However, the property owner has not yet made any attempt to develop this natural resource. Assume further that a neighboring city proposes to build upstream a municipal reservoir that will greatly reduce the flow of the stream below the dam in dry weather. This will mean that the downstream owner cannot rely upon generating adequate power continuously at his site if he should in the future desire to exploit the resource that he had previously neglected. Has this property owner the right to claim damages for the loss to him of this potential power development? This question cannot be answered without a detailed study of the situation, but the following four points, among others, would require consideration:

1. Is the private owner's potential power development a sound project from an engineering standpoint?

2. Would it cost more to develop this power than it is worth?

3. Even at present (with no city reservoir in being) is the minimum stream flow reliable?

4. Is there a market for the sale of the prospective power, or could the private owner himself use it profitably?

If the private owner's potential project is feasible and offers a good investment, its worth would be measured primarily by the capitalized value of its estimated earnings, and this sum very possibly might be claimed by the owner as compensation for the loss of his chance to undertake future development.

23.10 MINING

Water plays an important role in some mining operations. Various rules and customs have emerged, particularly in the western states, regarding the use of water in that connection.

In the early days many mining claims, as in the so-called "gold fields," were established on public property by prospectors who subsequently secured land grants issued by the government. These prospectors, in working their claims, were well aware of the importance of an adequate water supply. The general rule for appropriation and use of water in mining operations seems to have been, at the outset, that the prior appropriator was entitled to protect himself against subsequent appropriators. In time this was modified somewhat by the introduction of the principle of "reasonable use." Ultimately, customs prevalent in the mining community regarding the utilization of water came to be recognized by the courts and even found their way into some statutory law.

Mining has occasioned its share of "water rights" litigation over the years. For one thing, it is obvious that mining shafts, tunnels, and pits are likely to disturb the previously existing condition of groundwater (and therefore of the streams) in the vicinity of the mining operations. In one case[49] a farmer brought a successful action against a gold-mining company because a drainage tunnel excavated by the latter dried up the spring-fed creek upon which the plaintiff was dependent for irrigation, domestic, and household uses.

23.11   FLOOD CONTROL

Flood control is the management of the flow in a stream in such a way that, even in times of maximum runoff from the land in the watershed, serious flooding of the land downstream can be prevented.

One recently developed means for flood control is the construction of a dam with outlets of limited capacity that are continuously open but will allow only a moderate amount of water to flow through, the effect being the temporary impounding of excessive floodwaters. Under ordinary conditions, the river water can flow as usual but, when a big storm occurs, part of the resulting water is retained behind the dam because it cannot quickly escape through the gates. After the storm is over, the impounded water will gradually flow through the gates until the reservoir is again low. This arrangement evens out the flow below the dam and inhibits flooding of any consequence.

Private work contemplated along major rivers may have to be coordinated with plans and requirements of governmental agencies, and the engineer should investigate the situation before proceeding very far.[50] The federal government has taken over more and more of the work connected with flood control on the large rivers. This was done partly because of the great cost involved and partly because such projects usually concerned more than one state.

Even flood control, seemingly an innocuous subject on the desirability of which most people can readily agree, has occasionally led to litigation. In one situation[51] a railway company had a bridge across the Snohomish River in Washington. The flood-control district, a municipal corporation, brought an action of condemnation, asking for an "order of public use and necessity" for an easement to tie its dikes into the railroad's embankment. At the same time the district sought a judicial determination as to whether it would incur any liability for damages to the railroad bridge caused by the increased water height and velocity resulting from construction of dikes along the bank, upstream from the bridge. The Supreme Court of Washington held that the district could indeed condemn what it needed of the railroad's right-of-way (while in the process compensating the latter for the

---

[49]*Eckel v. Springfield Tunnel & Development Co.,* 87 Cal.App. 617, 262 P. 425(1927).

[50]There may be legal restrictions regarding just what can be constructed along a given stream. For example, under the authority of the general statutes, the Water Resources Commission of Connecticut has established on several streams in the state "lines beyond which in the direction of the waterway, no obstruction or encroachment shall be placed by any person, firm or corporation, public or private, unless specifically authorized by the Commission." Of course, such lines are intended to prevent interference with the channel of a stream, and the restriction may be needed in areas of congested developments in order to maintain enough discharge capacity of the stream to prevent flooding of adjacent lands.

[51]*Marshland Flood Control Dist. v. Great Northern Ry. Co.,* 71 Wash.2d 365, 428 P.2d 531 (1967).

invasion of its property). However, since liability for damages is not limited to recompense for the property appropriated but also includes injury to the remainder of the property not actually taken, the district must stand ready to pay the railroad the cost of rendering its damaged bridge once again operational. The dikes were designed to keep the river water within the confines of the stream bed and thus to prevent flooding. Despite this salutary purpose, the unfortunate and unavoidable side effect of harm to the railroad's embankment and bridge entitled the injured property owner to a remedy in damages.

An interesting situation was presented in a flood control case[52] in which a landowner was allowed recovery for flood damage. The defendant, the power company, owned flood easements but had taken steps to prevent extensive flooding. The court noted that since the landowners had relied on the defendant's flood-control practices, the power company had a duty not to unnecessarily flood their land.

An unusual variation on the flood problem was presented in *AMS Salt Industries v. Magnesium Corp. of America*.[53] AMS operated a salt production business along the shores of the Great Salt Lake, and Magnesium Corp. had solar evaporation ponds several miles away from which it extracted brine used to manufacture industrial chemicals such as magnesium and chlorine, as well as to produce salt in competition with AMS. Each company had a system of dikes to keep the water in their evaporation ponds from escaping back into the lake.

Due to several years of deep snow followed by warm spring temperatures, the lake level rose and AMS and Magnesium Corp. were forced to raise their perimeter dikes. A severe storm arose and large waves breached the Magnesium Corp. dike. Informed of this, AMS raised the level of a road near its ponds, stopping the inundation of some of its ponds. As the lake refilled its natural bed, all of Magnesium Corp.'s internal dikes and some of AMS's were destroyed.

AMS sued Magnesium Corp. alleging negligence in the design, construction, and maintenance of its perimeter dikes, claiming that it had relied on Magnesium Corp.'s perimeter dike. The court found that such reliance did not give rise to a duty of care on Magnesium Corp.'s part and that it was the lake, not Magnesium Corp., that caused the foreseeable risk of harm. Nature, the court said, not Magnesium Corp., caused the lake to rise and threaten AMS's property.

Construction in flood-prone areas is dangerous, and the Federal Emergency Management Agency of the Department of Housing and Urban Development has taken steps to issue restrictions on construction in flood-prone areas along coastlines and rivers. The regulations are to force property owners in such dangerous areas to secure federal flood insurance, to flood-proof any new structures and utilities, to flood-proof existing structures and utilities, or not to build there at all. Municipalities are to make appropriate zoning regulations to control these matters in areas below the 100-year flood levels as determined by flood-hazard boundary maps to be issued by FEMA.

---

[52]*Kinz v. Utah Power & Light Co.*, 526 F.2d 500 (9th Cir. 1975).
[53]942 P.2d 315 (Utah 1997).

23.12 STATE WATER CODES

Customs and regulations regarding riparian rights and the use of water have changed as the nation developed. Throughout the country governmental authorities are endeavoring to enact laws and compose regulations or codes that will serve to meet the problems of their areas. Some of these laws and codes relate to water conservation, irrigation, pollution, obstructing the flow of streams, and industrial usage of water, some to the establishment of regulatory bodies, and some to the construction of dams and other public works destined to aid in water supply and control problems. A number of jurisdictions have provisions bearing upon the use of water in the soil as well as water above the stream or lake bed. It is probable that the increasing need for water, and for its purification and wise utilization, will bring about still more laws and regulations affecting water rights. In arid states, such as some in the southwest, water is the heartbeat of the economy. It is not surprising, therefore, to find that such states have enacted rather elaborate sets of laws[54] dealing with almost every aspect of the subject of waters.[55] To show how comprehensive these statutory treatments are, it might be noted that Title 45 of Arizona Revised Statutes (1956) lists these chapter and article headings, among others:

---

[54]Even constitutional provisions can be found that are on point. Thus, Art. X § 2 of the California Constitution reads in part:

It is hereby declared that because of the conditions prevailing in this State the general welfare requires that the water resources of the State be put to beneficial use to the fullest extent of which they are capable, and that the waste or unreasonable use or unreasonable method of use of water be prevented, and that the conservation of such waters is to be exercised with a view to the reasonable and beneficial use thereof in the interest of the people and for the public welfare. The right to water or to the use or flow of water in or from any natural stream or water course in this State is and shall be limited to such water as shall be reasonably required for the beneficial use to be served, and such right does not and shall not extend to the waste or unreasonable use or unreasonable method of use or unreasonable method of diversion of water. Riparian rights in a stream or water course attach to, but to no more than so much of the flow thereof as may be required or used consistently with this section, for the purposes for which such lands are, or may be made adaptable, in view of such reasonable and beneficial uses; provided, however, that nothing herein contained shall be construed as depriving any riparian owner of the reasonable use of water of the stream to which his land is riparian under reasonable methods of diversion and use, or of depriving any appropriator of water to which he is lawfully entitled.

[55]The aspects of the subject vary, however, with the water situation in the state. Louisiana statutes and Code provisions cover, for example, such subjects as the following:

1. Ports and harbors.
2. Canal and other water courses.
3. Navigation districts.
4. Ships and water craft.
5. Seamen.
6. Pilots.
7. Levee districts.
8. Shore of the sea or of a lake.
9. Division of alluvion.
10. Sudden action of waters.
11. Island formed by river opening a new channel.
12. Ownership of abandoned bed when river changes course.
13. Islands and sandbars in navigable rivers.
14. Ownership of beds of nonnavigable rivers or streams.

WATERS

Chapter

QUESTIONS

1. Define *(a)* "riparian rights," *(b)* "riparian lands," *(c)* "riparian owner (or proprietor)."

2. Define *(a)* "watercourse," *(b)* "surface waters," *(c)* "percolating waters."

3. What is meant by "reasonable use" of water as applied in matters relating to riparian (or water) rights?

4. How may the riparian rights of neighboring landowners vary? Explain.

5. What are the common-law principles of riparian rights? What uses of water do these common-law principles allow?

6. What is "reasonable" use as respects riparian rights?

7. What is meant by the right of use of water through "prescription"; through "prior appropriation"?

8. List (in order of probable priority) the various uses of water that may be involved in questions of riparian rights.

9. Who is likely to own the land constituting the bed *(a)* of a small creek? *(b)* of a navigable stream?

10. Is there any "legal" limit to the amount of water that a farmer may take from a watercourse adjoining his land for use in the irrigation of his land? Explain.

11. Does the owner of a hydroelectric power site have exclusive right to develop the water power at that site as he pleases?

12. What is the difference between percolating water and artesian water?

13. Who ordinarily has the right to the use of percolating waters? Within what limits?

14. Who may set up and enforce (a) a water code, (b) regulations affecting navigable waterways, (c) rules regarding prevention of pollution of streams?

15. What is meant by "floodwater"? Who can use it or guard against it?

16. What is meant by "flood control"? Who has charge of this (a) in major rivers? (b) in small streams?

17. What is the difference between a reservoir and an ordinary lake? What should the planners of the former consider regarding persons living downstream?

18. If a riparian owner possesses a site that is suitable for the development of hydroelectric power, can she sell the "power rights" without selling the land, or vice versa?

19. Carter bought some low and partially swampy land for a housing development. She filled in the land to raise the elevation of the surface approximately 5 feet. This caused the level of the groundwater to rise upgrade from Carter's land, and this rise in the water level turned Smith's meadow into a swamp. What can Smith do about the matter?

20. Turner, a farmer, cut drainage ditches to drain a swampy pond in his pasture. Bradley, a neighboring farmer, then found that his spring for watering his stock dried up. What can Bradley do about his former spring?

21. Assume that the city of Southford plans to build a reservoir on Oak Creek, using most of the water available and designing the spillway so as to divert the excess water to Roaring Brook. (a) Has the city the right to do this? (b) What steps should be taken by the city in clearing the way for construction of the reservoir? (c) What steps may be taken by riparian owners downstream along Oak Creek to protect their rights?

22. Clark built a dam in Rice Brook (entirely on his own land) and, during the months of July and August, piped all the water to his new irrigation system. Dawson, who owned a farm downstream, tried to get an injunction to require Clark to permit part of the water to reach Dawson's property. Do you think that Dawson will be successful? Explain.

23. Alton built a small dam on his own property to create a small fishpond. The overflow from the pond continued downstream in the same channel as before, crossing Braxton's land. Has Alton damaged Braxton? Explain.

24. The *X-Y* Power Co. built a power dam on Hoton River. The company agreed to limit the level of the impounded water to elevation + 520 feet. During an unusual spring thaw and rain, the spillway jammed with ice, and the water rose to elevation + 529 feet, flooding several cottages. The owners of these cottages sued the company for damages caused by this flooding. What do you think of their rights in this situation?

c h a p t e r

24

INTELLECTUAL PROPERTY

24.1 INTRODUCTION

This chapter offers an introduction to the law of intellectual property, which comprises patents, trademarks, and copyrights. The subject is almost completely statutory, and the court decisions in this field are thus subject to frequent legislative modification.

While no design professional should attempt self-help in these areas, a basic knowledge sufficient to alert one to when professional assistance is needed is highly desirable.

Because both the law and technology are evolving rapidly, one would be well served to consult an attorney with particular expertise, should an intellectual property problem arise.

24.2 DEFINITIONS AND PURPOSES

A *patent* is a right granted by the federal government to a person or persons entitling them, for a limited period of time, to exclude everyone else from making, selling, and using the process or article that they have patented.

Article I, Section 8, Clause 8 of the Constitution of the United States recognizes the need for stimulation and protection of inventions as a matter of public interest.[1] Accordingly, the patent system of the United States was developed.

The patent system was inaugurated in 1790. It is administered by the Patent Office and Trademark Office (hereinafter Patent Office), which is in the charge of a commissioner of patents and trademarks (hereinafter commissioner of patents)

---

[1] "[The Congress shall have Power] To promote the Progress of Science and useful arts by securing for limited Times to Authors and Inventors the exclusive Right to their respective Writings and Discoveries."

under the secretary of commerce. Protection of inventions under the patent law is effective throughout the United States and its territories.

A patent is essentially a contract between an inventor and the government. Courts and legislatures will treat patents as they do other contracts. The inventor is obliged to describe his invention fully through the medium of the issued patent; the government undertakes to protect the right created by the patent. Of course, a patent on a particular article or process will be granted to the first inventor only.

The "life" of a patent in the United States is 17 years from date of issue, except for "design" patents[2] (such as for a piece of jewelry), which is 14 years. The specified term of any patent can be extended only by special act of Congress. The inventor is afforded by the government the right to exclusive use of the patented device for this period. However, this privilege is conditioned upon the *complete disclosure* of all details of the invention so that, after the expiration of the patent, anyone with the necessary know-how and finances will be in a position to make, sell, and use the device. In this sense, "patent" means "opened," or "disclosed."

Issuance of a patent does not necessarily mean that the patentee has a right to manufacture the article involved. Additional governmental or other authorization may also be needed before he can do so. For example, someone else may hold a patent on certain important features incorporated in and dominating the invention. The patent itself merely grants to the holder the privilege of temporarily preventing *others* from using the process or making the article in question.

Placing a patent label and number on an article is a way of serving notice that the maker relies upon his rights under the patent and presumably will prosecute anyone who violates them. The courts will not allow a patentee who has failed to affix such label and number any damages for any period prior to formal notice to another party that the latter is infringing the patent. The words "patent applied for" have no particular efficacy at law and merely tend to deter another person from belatedly trying to get a patent on the same idea, since the first party's application would obviously be ahead of his. The second party might also be deterred by the expense of "tooling up" for production that may never materialize because the arti-

---

[2]Design patents are authorized by 35 U.S.C. § 171, which provides, "Whoever invents any new, original and ornamental design for an article of manufacture may obtain a patent therefore, subject to the conditions and limitations of this title."

An interesting case on design patents is *Best Lock Corporation v. Ilco Unican Corporation*, 896 F. Supp. 836 (S.D. Ind. 1995), in which a patent describing a key that, for purposes of making duplication at a local hardware store more difficult, was one-third wider than a standard key with a "thin-walled offset portion" was held invalid. The court concluded that the invention was not patentable because the differences between it and the prior art would have been obvious to one having ordinary skill in the subject at the time the invention was made. Persons with such "ordinary skill" included both engineers and nonengineers.

Also, a design patent is invalid if it is functional and the function dictates the design.

cle to be produced is the subject of another and prior patent application. Similarly, "patent pending" means relatively little—only that an application for a patent is being prepared, has actually been submitted to the Patent Office, or is under consideration by the Patent Office. "Application pending" means almost nothing, although the so-called "inventor" may try to use this label as a means of keeping his invention for himself, believing that the use of the quoted phrase will inhibit manufacture of the article by others. "Application pending" labels might prove helpful in this way: would-be manufacturers who may wish to become licensees might approach the inventor with some satisfactory arrangement for production mutually beneficial to the inventor (ultimate patentee) and the licensee.

A patent will accomplish nothing unless it is put to use. That use is the purpose of the system, and profit for the inventor is more or less incidental. The patent system is supposed to make inventions available to the public sooner than they might be if the inventors and manufacturers endeavored to keep all their new developments and products strictly secret for many years. By offering an opportunity for inventors to secure protection, the patent system serves to encourage investment in research and to foster competition in invention, each imaginative person trying to outdo others in the creation of better products and processes.

Infringement of a patent is the premature use of the protected invention by another person without the permission of the inventor. The infringement may be unintentional or deliberate. It is necessary for the holder of the rights to take action in order to stop the infringer's activities; mere possession of the patent alone will not do the job. If a product or process does infringe, or seems to infringe, upon a patent, the dispute between the parties is not for the Patent Office to resolve. These disputes are within the jurisdiction of the federal courts.

Prior to receipt of formal patent application, the Patent Office will not try to determine whether or not an alleged "invention" will infringe upon an existing patent. Neither will the Patent Office give advance counsel to the applicants about whether or not their articles or processes are worth patenting.

24.3 PATENT RECORDS

The Patent Office, in order to promote the progress of the arts and sciences, maintains an excellent library of data on issued patents for the use of all who wish to learn what has already been developed. The information about patents is arranged in accordance with a predetermined classification, and it includes material about foreign as well as domestic patents. Persons who think they have developed a new process or product can ascertain whether or not someone else had preceded them. Such checking frequently avoids the waste of time and money entailed in an attempt to secure a patent in connection with an article or process that, it develops, is not original.

24.4   PATENTABILITY

By no means is every new process or article patentable. Some of the fundamental principles regarding patentability[3] are the following:

1.   The new development must have the element of invention. It is not to be merely a routine improvement of some article or process. That is to say, it must be an improvement that one might reasonably expect would be made in the normal course of events by someone who is "skilled in the art."[4] An improvement, to be patentable, must reveal the exercise of unusual ingenuity—it should represent an advance that would not ordinarily be expected. The patent laws[5] state that an invention is not patentable "if the differences between the subject matter sought to be patented and the prior art are such that the subject matter as a whole would have been obvious at the time the invention was made to a person having ordinary skill in the art to which said subject matter pertains."

2.   The invention must not be frivolous, and it must not appear that it would have an injurious effect upon the morals and health of people.

3.   The invention must be useful. This requirement may, however, be met by something (for example, a design) that merely caters to a whim of the public.

4.   Broadly speaking, a person is not entitled to a patent on someone else's invention.[6]

A patent may cover such subject matter as the following:

1.   A process or way of making something—often referred to as an "art"—such as a new method of manufacturing sulfuric acid.

2.   An article of manufacture for sale or other use, such as a new type of outboard motor.

---

[3]"Conditions for patentability" are spelled out in 35 U.S.C. § 102 (1952), amended in 1972 and 1975:
A person shall be entitled to a patent unless—
   (a) the invention was known or used by others in this country, or patented or described in a printed publication in this or a foreign country, before the Invention thereof by the applicant for a patent, or
   (b) the invention was patented or described in a printed publication in this or a foreign country or in public use on sale in this country, more than one year prior to the date of the application for patent in the United States, or
   (c) he has abandoned the invention, or
   (d) the invention was first patented or caused to be patented, or was the subject of an inventor's certificate, by the applicant or his legal representatives or assigns in a foreign country prior to the date of the application for patent in this country on an application for patent or inventor's certificate filed more than twelve months before filing of the application in the United States, or
   (e) the invention was described in a patent granted on an application for patent by another filed in the United States before the invention thereof by the applicant for patent, or on an international application by another who has fulfilled the requirements of paragraphs (1), (2), and (4) of section 371 (c) of this title before the invention thereof by the applicant for patent, or
   (f) he did not himself invent the subject matter sought to be patented, or
   (g) before the applicant's invention thereof the invention was made in this country by another who had not abandoned, suppressed, or concealed it. In determining priority of invention there shall be considered not only the respective dates of conception and reduction to practice of the invention, but also the reasonable diligence of one who was first to conceive and last to reduce to practice, from a time prior to conception by the other.

[4]See also, note 2, Section 24.2.

[5]35 U.S.C. § 103 (1952), amended in 1984.

[6]But see the discussion of "assignment" in Section 24.15.

3. A piece of apparatus, such as a machine for extruding aluminum tubes.

4. A composition of matter, such as a new plastic compound.

5. An agricultural development, such as a new variety of plant.

6. A new design whose value comes from its appearance, such as a new pattern for table silverware.

24.5 APPLICATION FOR A PATENT

The preparation of an application for a patent is an exacting task. An engineer who plans to apply should consider securing the services of an experienced agent or expert who is registered at the Patent Office. Otherwise, errors of commission or omission may be made that will prove very costly in the future, perhaps even to the extent of defeating the application.

One of the first steps to be taken is a search of the files maintained at the Patent Office in Washington to see whether the idea or principle of the device involved has previously been patented. The search may also reveal that someone has come so close to the same invention that prospects of the newcomer being able to secure a patent are not bright. Of course, the inventor (or some other person, on his behalf) may make this search personally, but it is preferable for him to engage an experienced investigator if the inventor is not familiar with such searching.

A patent will be granted only when there is an application properly filed with the Patent Office. The application must be complete in every respect and accompanied by payment of fee. The application must contain complete disclosure of the invention and satisfy the requirement that the article, composition of matter, or process be new and useful. The mere submission of an idea or suggestion for an invention is insufficient.

The application for a patent is to include a petition, addressed to the Commissioner of Patents, requesting the grant of a patent, giving a designation to the device, and stating the inventor's name and address. The signed application must contain a statement to the effect that, so far as the applicant knows, he is truly the originator of the device which he seeks to patent.[7] The petition is also supposed to include specifications (description), drawings (when practicable), and "claims" regarding exactly what the invention is intended to accomplish and what the patent is to cover. Proper preparation and wording of the foregoing material are extremely important: the information given must be both comprehensive and specific. The application for a patent must be legibly printed or written in ink, and it must be in English.

Applications—each one of which can cover no more than one invention—are given numbers in the sequence in which they are received by the Patent Office. They are examined in the order of filing and are classified according to the subject matter of the invention. They are kept confidential unless written authority is given to the Patent Office by the applicant to disclose certain information to interested

---

[7] In rare cases, subsequently to be discussed, someone else would be applying in place of the actual inventor.

persons. If the subject of the invention is a matter that should be kept secret in the interest of national defense, the Commissioner of Patents, on his own initiative, may label the application "secret" and withhold any revelation whatever.

The application is to be made by the inventor personally. If two persons worked together in the development of the process or article, they must jointly apply for a patent. When there are known to be joint inventors, neither one is allowed to patent the invention exclusively. However, under one of the practice rules of the Patent Office, if one of the joint inventors refuses to sign the application papers or cannot be reached after diligent effort, the application may be made by the other inventor on behalf of both.

One who merely supplies money to enable the inventor to proceed with his endeavor cannot qualify as a joint inventor. Working independently and without knowledge of the other's efforts, developers of separate improvements in the same article or machine cannot jointly obtain a patent.

If an inventor dies before filing, an application for a patent may nonetheless be perfected by his executor or administrator, and the patent will be granted if the application meets the usual requirements. If an inventor dies after filing his application, the patent may issue to the executor or administrator, if such fiduciary files the proper papers evidencing his appointment as the representative of the decedent's estate.

Should a certain patent application conflict with someone else's somewhat similar application pending in the Patent Office, such office will conduct what is called an *interference proceeding*. An appointed board of examiners will determine from evidence submitted who is the real inventor and thus entitled to the patent. In such a situation, one can readily see the importance of keeping adequate records.

24.6   SPECIFICATIONS

In connection with a patent application, the term "specifications" denotes a written description of the invention.[8] The specifications should include illustrative drawings when these are needed for clarification. The description should cover how the device is made and how it is to be used. The data must be clear and complete, yet concise. The invention should be described in such detail that anyone skilled in the art can understand what is being said and, by following the specifications, put together the device in question. Otherwise, a patent will not be granted.

The applicant should exercise extreme care to ensure that the description of the invention is correct. He should state the suggested method for constructing the device but should be careful not to limit the ways in which it can be made, or the process accomplished. In this connection, the applicant might use alternatives. For example, he could say that a certain portion of his machine may be a casting or

---

[8]The applicant should be very careful in stating what his invention is designed to accomplish; this is often called the *statement of invention*. The inventor ought to avoid expressing aims that are either too meager or unduly comprehensive.

may be fabricated by means of welding pieces of steel together. However, the listing of alternatives can, in certain cases, prove confusing or even detrimental.

Making the *drawings* for a patent application is almost an art in itself. These drawings should be clear, neat, and so prepared as to bring out the special points that the inventor intends to emphasize. For example, the drawings depicting a mechanical device should generally show a label or number for each pertinent piece or element, so that the specifications can, through cross-reference, clearly describe each item and its function.

The requirements regarding drawings are very specific and must be complied with in every detail. Models, in lieu of drawings, will not be accepted unless the substitution has been requested by the Patent Office.

The following suggested arrangement of items is one that may be observed in framing the application:[9]

1. Preamble, stating the name and residence of the applicant and the title or designation given to the invention.
2. Abstract, or general statement of the nature of the invention.
3. Purposes.
4. Brief description of the several views shown on the drawings (if the invention lends itself to such illustration).
5. Details of the invention.
6. Claim or claims.
7. Petition.
8. Signature of applicant.

24.7 CLAIMS

The term *claims* as used in connection with an application for letters patent denotes the statements describing what the invention is expected to accomplish. The claims must clearly convey the scope and character of the invention. Usually, the first portion of the claim material constitutes a general outline of what the patent is to cover. Subsequent portions will be more specific and will relate to details of the invention. The claims must be worded very carefully and accurately. Preparation of these claims is such an important matter that it should be handled by an expert, preferably one who is a specialist in the particular field to which the subject matter of the invention relates—for instance, chemistry or mechanical engineering.

The following example illustrates a typical set of claims. All four items are shown as they might appear in the application for one patent on the device, a card table. The drawings accompanying the claims are grouped in Fig. 24.1 and are numbered so as to accord with the corresponding claims.

---

[9]The application, per 35 U.S.C. § 111 (1982), consists of a specification, a drawing, and an oath.

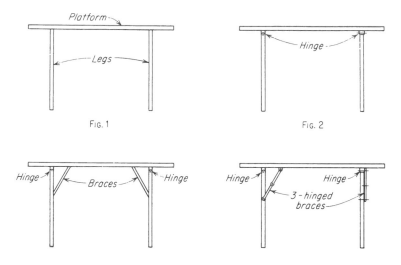

FIGURE 24.1   Drawing to accompany claims for a patent.

Claim 1 A table comprising a platform, at least one support member, and mounting means for mounting said support member to said platform.

Claim 2 In the article of claim 1, said mounting means comprises a hinge and locking means to maintain said support member in a desired position in relation to said platform.

Claim 3 In the article of claim 2, said locking means comprises a brace member having one end engaging said support member and an opposite end engaging said platform.

Claim 4 In the article of claim 3, said brace member comprises a first portion engaging said support member, a second portion engaging said platform, and said first second portions movably connected to each other.

In claim 1 (an "independent" claim), the claimed elements of the structure appear after the word "comprising," which elements are *(a)* a platform, *(b)* a support member, and *(c)* means for mounting the support member to the platform. An unauthorized person building a table with one leg or a plurality of legs might impinge upon this claim.

Claim 2, known as a "dependent" claim, contains the three elements of claim 1 with the added limitation that the mounting means is a hinge. If the first inventor did not have claim 2, another inventor might get a patent on a table with a hinge; in that case, the first inventor could not use a hinge without permission from the second inventor, and the second inventor could not make a certain type of table without permission of the first inventor. It is desirable, of course, for the first inventor to provide for as many modifications and improvements as possible in order to protect his position.

Claim 3 includes (by implication) all the elements of claim 2, but the locking means is identified as a brace. It is conceivable that another person might choose to hold the support member (leg) by means of a wing nut on the axis of the hinge—

and this arrangement would not constitute a brace. However, in the process he would run afoul of claim 2, which specifies "locking means." Claim 3 is said to be "narrower," or "limited," as compared to claim 2.

Claim 4 includes all the elements of claim 3 and is even narrower than claim 3 because it calls for the brace to have *two-part* member portions. This particular claim (number 4) could be avoided by using a one-part brace that can be hinged at one end and is slidable at the other end, but any such expedient would be unable to contend with claim 3. A three-part brace member would similarly encounter difficulty because the claim would "read on" the suggested three-part brace, which obviously has at least *two* parts. The added part (that is, added to the two) does not successfully circumvent claim 4.

From the foregoing it will be obvious that, in drafting claims, a great deal of thought must be given not only to the selection and arrangement of the words that will make up the claims, but also to the various ways someone else could avoid the claims.[10]

In general, the more elements the claim has, the more specific it becomes. One should try to make the claims broad and simple. The Patent Office will decide whether or not the claims are too broad, but it will not try to determine whether they are too narrow. If the claims are unduly narrow, the scope of the patent may be so restricted that competitors can easily come up with a slightly different device that will not infringe.

If the invention is a method of doing something, the claims should state in detail the various steps to be taken to accomplish the desired objective. Someone else who can achieve the same result in fewer steps or in different ones can assert that his invention is a new or different method and that it therefore does not infringe upon the patent of the first inventor.

One cannot add a new material to a pending patent application and at the same time preserve the original filing date. Claims can be expanded during the course of their presentation to the Patent Office *if* the original specifications mention the point involved in the attempted expansion. Of course, a new, enlarged application can be filed to replace the old, but the substituted one will necessarily bear a later date than that of the original.

If a patent is found after issue to have been based upon claims one or more of which are invalid, it may be possible for the patentee to disavow the invalid claim or claims and allow the remaining, valid claims to retain patent protection.

24.8 VALIDITY

Claims in an application for a patent are invalid if they do not meet the requirements for patentability.

---

[10]In the case illustrated, notice that the first claim listed *dominates* (for example, includes) the second, third, and fourth claims. It may be that a patent issued to cover several claims will be treated as though each claim were covered (or represented) by a separate patent.

It is entirely possible that an applicant has been unaware of prior publication or prior art concerning the substance of his "invention." Nevertheless, proof of such prior activity will cause his application to be rejected or will invalidate the patent after it has been granted. This assumes that the unlikely occurs and that there has been some oversight by, or lack of information in the hands of, the Patent Office, causing a patent to issue when it should not have.

The patent must be taken out in the name of the real inventor. If the invention is the joint product of two or more persons, proof of this circumstance will invalidate a patent issued in the name of one of the parties alone. There may be disagreement about whether an invention is *sole* or *joint*. If one inventor conceives the idea for the device and then instructs in detail other persons in the making of a drawing or working or model or in the conducting of a successful experiment, the resulting "invention" is really the product of the first individual alone. On the other hand, if the first person had merely a general conception of the prospective invention but had to depend upon the *unusual* skill and imagination of someone else to develop the article or process, this will probably be treated as a joint invention—the product of the creative efforts of both parties. If one person develops a patentable device but an assistant proposes an ingenious additional feature to add to the original scheme, the two inventions should be separately patentable. The total product is not really a joint invention because the item attributed to the first inventor is autonomous and completely separable from that produced by the second inventor.

One may have to prove the priority of his invention in order to overcome interference[11] from the other persons interested in patenting virtually the same product, and he must be able to defend his own assertion that others have not (within a certain time period) used or "published" the invention on which he seeks a patent. Any pertinent publication or use by others more than one year before an inventor submits his application for a patent will void the latter's application.

24.9   DATE OF CONCEPTION OF IDEA

If a person develops a scheme that he thinks is potentially patentable and he makes a dated record of the new proposition, such action alone will probably be insufficient to establish the *idea date* in connection with his subsequent petition for a patent. The inventor should do something beyond simply marking his records. He might, for instance, write to an outsider, giving the general outline of his idea—and do so promptly upon conceiving it. The date of the conception in the eyes of the law for the purposes of securing a patent is likely to be the date of the first *disclo-*

---

[11]In case of an "interference" proceeding (conducted under the auspices of the Patent Office to determine which of several claimants is entitled to the patent), the date of conception of an invention will be judged by such criteria as the following:
1. The date of the first verbal disclosure to someone else.
2. The date of the first written description of the invention.
3. The date of the first drawing showing the invention.
4. The date of the first reduction of the invention to practice.

sure of the idea to someone who is competent to understand it and later to verify the fact of the disclosure. This "observer" should be someone other than a person working with the would-be applicant on the invention. If such observer makes a written record of the disclosure on behalf of the inventor, and if the former signs and dates this record forthwith, the document may well be a valuable one for the inventor to have available to him.

It is apparent that, when one is developing what he hopes will be a patentable invention, he should try to establish proof of the date of conception of the idea so that he will have an "airtight case" on the point if and when needed. Letters, sketches, and tentative descriptions that have been dated, witnessed, and signed—preferably by more than one competent observer—are very useful instruments in this connection. The observers should have some understanding of the invention in case they are asked to appear in support of the inventor's claims.

24.10   REDUCTION TO PRACTICE

It is important to prove that one's invention really works in practice, not merely under ideal laboratory conditions. An inventor should have at least one witness to the fact that the invention indeed does what it is supposed to do. This testing in operation is called *reduction to practice*. Assume that *A* invents a garage door that will automatically open and roll up overhead when a car approaches it. He should build a sample of such door, install it in his garage or that of a friend, and demonstrate it to a competent observer.

Naturally, an inventor will want to maintain secrecy so that no one except his trusted friend will learn of his invention before the patent application can be submitted. This security problem is one for the inventor to work out with the aid of the friend to whom he disclosed the invention.

If the final perfection of an article or process to be patented will cost so much that the inventor cannot finance the necessary work of development, he may nonetheless file his application for a patent in order to protect his rights. This course of action is known as *constructive reduction to practice*—which means that the device described in the petition does not yet exist. The inventor then may make arrangements with someone to finance the perfection of the invention in return for a share of the benefits, on whatever terms may be mutually agreeable.

24.11   DILIGENCE

After conceiving his idea, the inventor must be "diligent" in implementing it. Exactly what will be regarded as diligence in a particular set of circumstances is hard to say. However, if nothing is done to perfect his invention within a few months of the conception of the idea, he probably will be deemed to have been dilatory. Some inventions may require years for their perfection; others may lend themselves to complete development within a few months. The reasonableness of the time period between conception of the idea and perfection of the invention to application for a patent thereon will be judged in accordance with the factual circumstances in a given case.

Let us suppose that *A* thought up the idea for an invention in January 1998, and that *B* who knew nothing about *A* or his activities, came up with the same thoughts independently in June 1998. Assume also that *A* did little to perfect his idea, whereas *B* developed the invention promptly and applied for a patent in October 1998. Shortly thereafter, *A* heard about B's application and tried to secure the patent for himself by applying in December 1998, claiming that he had the idea first. It is probable that *B* would be granted the patent because *A* had been comparatively dilatory. In one early case involving a patent in a bookbinder's press,[12] the court made the diligence point in these words:

> It is obvious from the foregoing that the man who first reduces an invention to practice is prima facie the first and true inventor, but that a man who first conceives, and, in a mental sense, first invents, a machine, art, or composition of matter, may date his patentable invention back to the time of its conception, if he connects the conception with its reduction to practice by reasonable diligence on his part, so that they are substantially one continuous act. The burden is on the second reducer to practice to show the prior conception, and to establish the connection between that conception and his reduction to practice by proof of due diligence.

Although it is advisable to proceed as quickly as possible to develop an invention, it is equally evident that the inventor's work should not be so hasty and incomplete that his claims will be disallowed because of errors, imperfections, or failure of his invention to function as advertised.

It is well for an inventor not only to have a record of the disclosure of his invention idea to at least one competent person (and preferably two or more) but also, from time to time, to have outsiders witness and verify his procedures and his progress in developing the invention. Involving *several individuals* will serve to reduce the possibility that, for one reason or another, when the need for testimony arises, no one will be available. The witnesses ought also to observe the functioning of any model of the invention, its performance under tests, and even the preparation of descriptive matter and drawings.

24.12   KEEPING NOTES ON THE INVENTION

It is very important to maintain a running record of activities once work on the invention has commenced. This record should be kept in a *bound* notebook so that others would find it difficult to claim that the inventor inserted information at a date later than was actually the case or that he deleted some pages, as would be possible with a looseleaf notebook. It is also desirable for the inventor to date and

---

| [12]*Christie v. Seybold*, 55 F. 69, 76 (6th Cir. 1893).

sign each page as he records his notes. Furthermore, at intervals he might have these notes read, dated, and signed by a trusted friend or friends, who will subsequently be able to verify the accuracy of the record. To avoid suspicion, such notes should not show erasures or alterations. If changes have to be made, it is best to add a supplementary statement correcting what was recorded previously.

The aforementioned record of the step-by-step development of the device or process should contain all relevant data, including such information as the following:

1. When the inventor first conceived the idea.

2. When and to whom he disclosed his idea.

3. What he did at each step of development.

4. What results he obtained along the way and whether such were good or unsatisfactory.

5. When he reduced the invention to practice.

6. Who has seen it work or has verified the results.

7. When the witnesses saw it work.

8. When and through whom the inventor took steps to prepare the application for letters patent.

9. Whatever else may assist in securing the patent and in establishing the inventor's precedence over some other applicant.

24.13 OWNERSHIP OF THE PATENT

Sometimes there are serious misunderstandings about who should own a patent. Here are a few principles that may serve as a guide:

1. An individual who develops his invention entirely on his own and who meets all the requirements for securing a patent is personally entitled.

2. An individual who develops his invention independently but who uses his employer's time and facilities to do so can secure the patent, but the employer may have "ship rights" to manufacture the article in question.

3. An individual who is part of a research organization is generally hired for the very purpose of inventing. As a rule, the employer of such an individual requires him to agree in advance to *assign* to the employer any patent that the employee receives in line with his regular work.

4. A member of a research organization may be individually entitled to retain a patent on an invention that he develops entirely outside his employer's field of interest and largely on his own time.

Before an engineer undertakes work, for or with others, that may result in an invention, there should be a definite and recorded agreement regarding the ownership of any resultant patent or copyright.

24.14 SECRET INFORMATION

When attempting to sell an idea, one must be careful about divulging details of an unpatented invention. By the same token, whoever receives information about such an invention should keep the data to himself. Ordinarily, a firm or individual is reluctant to accept confidential information from an inventor unless the latter—before disclosing any secrets—has patented the invention to which the information relates, has applied for a patent, or agrees to a stated compensation should his invention be accepted by the information recipient. One can easily understand the receiving party's reluctance. He would not want to be subjected to unreasonable claims by the inventor about the value of the latter's device. It is unwise to accept broad or vague ideas, the transmittal of which might position their author to claim compensation should the recipient of the disclosures later develop anything that appears to have been even remotely suggested by the volunteered information.

Negotiations regarding "secret" information may take place even when a discovery, though apparently useful, is not patentable. For example, the winner of a national cake-baking contest may sell the recipe to the sponsoring corporation in spite of the fact that the formula is not a patentable item. A different situation is created when a person with an excellent idea finds himself unable to finance the development of it; he may wish to join forces with someone who can provide the necessary money and equipment to perfect the invention. The respective rights and obligations of the several parties participating in such an arrangement should be clearly defined and the agreement reduced to writing.

Suppose a manufacturer receives from a self-styled "inventor" what appears to be an offer to disclose the idea for a new gadget of some sort. The manufacturer would do well to proceed cautiously. He should notify the sender that he has not examined the data and that he will not do so unless and until a proper agreement is reached between the parties, setting forth what the first party is to receive (if his idea proves worthwhile and of interest to the manufacturer) and what the latter is to pay for the disclosure. The arrangement may be such that the manufacturer will not be obligated to treat such information as confidential if the invention proves to be (1) unworkable, (2) nonpatentable, (3) previously disclosed to others, (4) previously known to the manufacturer, or (5) valueless for some other reason.

The following form might be used by a corporation in handling receipt from outsiders of information relating to new ideas or alleged inventions:

DISCLOSURE AGREEMENT

L-M-N Corporation:
I request that *L-M-N* Corporation consider my idea relating to

[subject matter of idea very briefly summarized here]

which idea is described in the material herewith and listed below. All additional disclosures relating to the idea submitted herewith shall be subject to the provisions of this Agreement.

I understand that no confidential relationship is established by or is to be implied from this submission or from consideration by *L-M-N* Corporation of the material, and that such material is not submitted "in confidence."

By this request and submission I do not grant *L-M-N* Corporation, or any of its subsidiaries, any right under any patents on the idea submitted. I agree that, at least unless this Agreement be superseded by a different agreement in writing, I will make no claim against *L-M-N* Corporation, or any of its subsidiaries, with respect to the idea here submitted, other than possible for patent infringement.

List of Documents and Samples [follows]:

Agreement acknowledged:
L-M-N Corporation   Signed
By   Address
Dates

It appears that, in settling disputes stemming from the disclosure of inventions, the courts give considerable weight to whether the idea was completely new to the recipient and to just how the latter made use of it. In case no agreement had been reached regarding the measure of compensation that is to be paid the inventor for utilization of his idea, the courts will try to determine what is reasonable—perhaps an amount comparable to what might have been expected in the way of royalties for use of the process or article if it had been patented.

24.15   LICENSES, ASSIGNMENTS, AND GRANTS

An inventor may assign his patent and all rights pertaining to it, or he may permit another person a license or grant[13] to "make, use, and vend" whatever is covered by *any* (or, perhaps, *all*) of the rights under the patent or under the application for patent. A license may or may not be treated as exclusive, and the agreement between the parties should clarify this point. Licensing, and possibly sublicensing, arrangements may cover manufacture of the article, its use, its sale, or some combination of these.

The licensee may make payment in the form of the royalties, the total varying with the volume of sales by the licensee. On the other hand, he may pay a lump sum for the rights, or may make any other legal arrangements agreed to by the parties.

Unless the applicable agreement provides otherwise, the license carries with it the implied right for the licensee either to sell the patented article or to make use of it himself.

---

[13]It seems that a "grant" generally affords permission on a more exclusive basis than does a "license." Both types of permit should be written or printed, properly signed, and recorded in the Patent Office.

The agreement on licensing arrangements will cover such matters as powers of the respective parties, limitations on these powers, royalties or other payments, anticipated efforts to market the device, actions that would constitute infringement by outsiders, time or territorial limits affecting the license, reports due the patentee, labeling of the article, type of use authorized, and steps designed to prevent misuse. If payment is to be on a royalty basis, the licensor will want to be sure that the licensee is going to make a sincere and adequate effort to procure and market the product involved. On the other hand, the licensee will wish to be protected in the event something occurs that may cause (1) the patent to be declared invalid or (2) use of the patented item to be declared illegal.

An assignment transfers to the assignee the inventor's interest in the patent or an agreed portion of the interest, and the assignment is effective throughout the United States. If the entire interest in an as-yet-unpatented invention is assigned, the patent will normally issue to the assignee upon application by the inventor. If the inventor declines to execute a patent application, or if he cannot be located, the assignee may apply—on behalf of and as agent for the inventor—on a showing that such action is necessary to prevent irreparable damage. If an assignee is to hold an undivided part interest in the invention, the patent will normally issue to the inventor and assignee jointly. Absent a contrary agreement, each joint owner of a patent may utilize the patented invention without accounting to the other owner or securing the latter's consent. If it is desired that the patent so issue, the assignment in either case must have been recorded with the Patent Office not later than the date of payment of the final fee for the patent.

A certificate of acknowledgment, under hand and seal of a person authorized to administer oaths, is prima facie evidence of the execution of an assignment of a patent or application for patent. Once recorded at the Patent Office, an assignment, even though bearing various conditions (regarding such things as payment to the assignor), is considered "absolute" and will remain effective unless and until abrogated by action of the parties or on an appropriate tribunal. In some instances, there may be a time limit set on the duration of an assignment.

Patent pooling is an arrangement among patent owners for the interchange of patent rights so that they each have the right to use any of such patents or to license others so to do.

Package licensing denotes an arrangement under which a patentee licenses others under more than one of his patents. If all the patents are included in a single package, this may make for simplified accounting.

Under an agreement for *cross-licensing* patentee *A* agrees to license party *B* on the understanding that *B* will reciprocate with respect to patents *he* holds.

One should not accept an assignment or seek a license privilege without first checking the pertinent patent records. Additionally, competent advice regarding exactly what is covered by the patent in question should be elicited. It is desirable to effect licensing arrangements and the like directly with the original inventor, not through some third party.

24.16 PATENTS ON NEW TECHNOLOGY

The application of a patent law system conceived in the eighteenth century to the technology of today has been predictably problematic.[14] Patent protection for such creations as genetically altered plants, animals, and computer technology, while highly desirable to encourage research and development, face political, legal, and ethical barriers. The following materials illustrate a few of these difficulties. One should note that many of the key court decisions turn on the construction of statutory language, which is always subject to change. Also, several of the most significant Supreme Court decisions in this area have been by a 5–4 vote, making them highly susceptible to changes in the Court's membership.

Plants Legislation calling for patent rights for plant-related inventions was called for as early as 1892 and endorsed by such figures as Thomas Edison and Luther Burbank. The first Plant Patent Act dates from 1930.

Plants are patentable under the Plant Patent Act,[15] which says:

> Whoever invents or discovers and asexually reproduces any distinct and new variety of plant, including cultivated spores, mutants, hybrids, and newly found seedlings, other than a tuber-propagated plant or a plant found in an uncultivated state, may obtain a patent therefor, subject to the conditions and requirements of this title.

The object is to give an exclusive right to propagate a plant invented by grafting, budding, cuttings, layering, division, and the like.[16]

Bacteria are not patentable as a "plant" under the Plant Patent Act.[17]

In the case of *Imazio Nursery, Inc. v. Dania Greenhouses*,[18] a patentee brought an infringement action against a competitor claiming violation of its plant patent for a variety of heather. The court said that the Plant Patent Act protects only the single plant and the reproduction from the one original specimen, noting the act's "asexual reproduction" requirement. Thus reproduction by "grafting, budding, cuttings, layering, division and the like" is protected, but not seeds. The key to "invention" of a new plant is the discovery of new traits plus the foresight and appreciation to take the step of asexual reproduction.

A separate federal statute, the Plant Variety Protection Act of 1970,[19] is administered by the Department of Agriculture, which issues certificates that offer patent-like protections to the "breeder of any novel variety of sexually reproduced plant (other fungi, bacteria, or first generation hybrids) who has so reproduced the variety."

---

[14]Similarly, the capabilities of even the best judges, most of whom have no technical background, are severely taxed by cases dealing with scientific and engineering matters.

[15]35 U.S.C. § 161–164.

[16]*Kim Bros. v. Hagler,*167 F. Supp. 665 (S.D. Cal.1958), aff. 276 F.2d 259 (9th Cir. 1960), an unsuccessful action for alleged infringement of a patent for nectarine trees.

[17]*In re Arzkerger,*112 F.2d 834 (Ct. Customs and Patent App. 1940).

[18]69 F.3d 1560 (Fed. Cir. 1995).

[19]7 U.S.C. 2401–2582.

Bacterium and Animals   The Supreme Court of the United States, by a 5–4 vote, held that a live, human-made, microorganism is patentable, in the case of *Diamond v. Chakrabarty*.[20] The case involved a genetically engineered bacterium capable of breaking down multiple components of crude oil. No naturally occurring bacterium has this capability. The court was called upon to decide whether the microorganism constituted a "manufactive" or "composition of matter" within the meaning of the patent statute.

Chief Justice Burger noted initially that the laws of nature, physical phenomena, and abstract ideas are not patentable. Thus, a new mineral discovered in the earth or a new plant found in the wild is not patentable. Likewise, Einstein could not have patented his equation $E = mc^2$, nor could Newton have patented the law of gravity.

The court in *Diamond,* however, found the altered life form unique and thus a patentable "new composition of matter."

Genetically engineered multicellular animals were ruled patentable in 1987,[21] and the first patent to a multicellular animal, for a mouse with a high susceptibility to cancer for use in cancer research, was granted in 1988.

One highly significant and emotion-charged area of new technology remains outside the protection of the patent law; genetically engineered human-based biotechnology products. Although the charge of the U.S. Patent and Trademark Office is to promote research and development that yield society benefits, Patent Office policy is that a claim directed to or including in its scope a human being is not patentable. This policy, apparently based on a construction of the patent statutes and concern over thirteenth amendment[22] problems, is highly contentious and may well change as technology advances.

However, a patent application's written description of the complete nucleotide sequence of a DNA coding for human fibroblast beta interferon, a protein that promotes viral resistance in human tissue along with a method for isolating that DNA, was said to be adequate for U.S. patent purposes in *Fiers v. Revel*.[23] While the case is far from the final word, since it involved a three-way interference proceeding setting forth the privity of foreign inventors who had filed U.S. patent applications, rather than the validity of a patent itself, the case harkens what is to come.

The possibility of altering, creating, and cloning animals—and maybe even humans—by genetic engineering is becoming a reality. In 1997 in Scotland, the first mammalian clone was produced. Ian Wilmut and Keith Campbell of the Roslin Institute cloned a lamb, "Dolly," from a cell of an adult ewe.[24] The implications of this scientific landmark led to much debate over the ethics of cloning humans. At the time of this writing, the lengths to which this technology can and will be extended are unknown. One thing is certain, though—future scientific advances will undoubtedly lead to changes in this legal field.

---

[20]447 U.S. 303 (1980).

[21]*Ex parte Allen,* 2 U.S.P.Q. 2d 1425 1987). The matter involved Pacific oysters, and while held patentable, the patent was denied on other grounds.

[22]Amendment XIII (1865) § 1. Neither slavery nor involuntary servitude, except as punishment for crime whereof the party shall have been duly convicted, shall exist within the United States, or any place subject to their jurisdiction.

[23]984 F.2d 1164 (Fed. Cir. 1993).

[24]*Science,* March 7, 1997, Vol. 275, No. 5305, p. 1415.

Computer Programs and Applications Intellectual property disputes involving computer software usually arise under the copyright laws[25] but their use may be subject to patent protection. The best illustration is the case of *Diamond v. Diehr*,[26] where a process for curing synthetic rubber, which included in several of its steps the use of mathematical formula and a programmed digital computer, was held patentable.

The situation involved the use of well-known time, temperature, and cure relationships to calculate, by means of the Arrhenius equation, when to open a mold press. The applicants characterized their contribution to be the process of continually measuring the temperature inside the mold with the data being automatically fed into a computer that repeatedly recalculated the cure time using the Arrhenius equation.

Clearly, the equation or algorithm itself was not patentable, but the court, again by a 5–4 vote, held that patent protection for the process of curing synthetic rubber was patentable, noting that while the process employed a well-known mathematical equation, it did not seek to preempt use of it.

Diamond v. Diehr may profitably be contrasted with *In re Trovato,*[27] which upheld a Board of Patent Appeals rejection of a patent application for an "invention" aimed at solving the problem of finding the shortest distance between two points, a subject of particular interest to students of the computer science field of graph theory. The invention in question purported to find the optimal path between two locations, whether in terms of distance, cost, capacity, time, or other criteria, by a graph called a "configuration space." The configuration space was stored in a "data structure" that arranged various information needed to solve the shortest path problem.

The court agreed with the patent examiner's conclusion that the inventor's claims, at least indirectly, recited a mathematical algorithm and did not involve physical structure or process steps beyond insignificant data-gathering steps or post-solution output. Even though the inventor contended that the invention solved a physical rather than mathematical problem and that the data structure was a physical entity consisting of electrical or magnetic signals requiring interaction between the processing and memory apparatus of a computer, the court found that unlike the invention in *Diamond v. Diehr,* the specifications provided no grasp of any underlying physical process and that no circuit diagram was revealed or hardware seriously mentioned.[28]

Computer programs written in source code, which bear at least some resemblance to writing, were problematic candidates for copyright protection under the Copyright Act of 1909, which obviously did not contemplate computers. In 1980 the adoption of the Computer Software Copyright Act[29] resolved the issue of

[25]For a discussion of the relationship between patent and copyright protection in the area of computer programs *see M. Tek Holdings v. Arce Engineering Co.,* 89 F.3d 1548 (11th Cir. 1996).

[26]450 U.S. 175 (1981).

[27]42 F.3d 1376 (Fed. Cir. 1994).

[28]For a further discussion of the ramifications of *Diamond v. Diehr,* see also *In re Alappt,* 33 F.3d 1526 (Fed. Cir. 1994).

[29]This Act amended 17 U.S.C. § 101 by adding a definition of a "computer program" and provided for lawful copying of a program by its rightful owner for use "in conjunction with a machine" or for archival purposes." 17 U.S.C. § 117.

source code, and courts since have found copyright protection to extend to material stored in object code form on Read Only Memory (ROM) chips, disks, and tapes.[30] This is so because these works are a tangible form and can be reproduced with the use of a machine. Also, operating system programs are not precluded from copyright protection as ideas, methods of operation, or processes that may more likely be the subject of patent protection.

However, a computer program menu hierarchy has been held to be a method of operation, and thus not subject to copyright protection where it provided a means by which users controlled and operated the system.[31]

Found subject to copyright protection have been nonliteral elements of programs such as structure, sequence, and organization,[32] and a program designed to solve engineering structural analysis problems[33] that conveyed information, what data the user needs to gather, and how that data should be organized for the program to run properly.[34]

24.17   Copyrights and Trademarks

A copyright is provided for in Article I, Section 8, Clause 8 of the United States Constitution. The copyright differs from the patent right in subject matter, in the protection afforded, and in other ways. Copyright law relates to literary and artistic property and is essentially inherited from English law. Copyrights are under the general supervision of the Library of Congress.

Copyrights involve no search and can be secured by the author upon complying with simple formalities and paying a nominal fee. The author's work must be *original,* and the copyright term will consist of the life of the author and extend 50 years after the author's death.[35]

The owner of a copyright has the exclusive rights to do and authorize the reproduction of the copyrighted work or to prepare derivative works based on the copyrighted item. Nevertheless, the fair use of a copyrighted work, including reproductions, is permissible for purposes such as criticism, news reporting, teaching (including multiple copies for classroom use), scholarship, or research. These activities do not constitute an infringement of copyright. In determining whether the use made of the copyrighted work in a particular case is a fair use, the factors to be considered include the following:

1. The purpose and character of the use, including whether such use is of a commercial nature or is for nonprofit educational purposes,

2. The nature of the copyrighted work,

---

[30]*Apple Computers, Inc. v. Franklin Computer Corp.,* 714 F.2d 1240 (3rd Cir. 1983).

[31]*Lotus Dev. Corp. v. Borland Int'l.,* 49 F.3d 807 (1st Cir. 1995).

[32]*Kepner-Tregol, Inc. v. Leadership Software,* 12 F.3d 527 (5th Cir. 1994).

[33]The program involved was marketed under the name STRAN. The alleged infringer was marketed as SACS IV.

[34]*Engineering Dynamics v. Structural Software,* 26 F.3d 1335 (5th Cir. 1994).

[35]For works copyrighted before January 1, 1978, the copyright term is 28 years, with the privilege of one 28-year renewal. See 17 U.S.C. § 302 (1976).

3. The amount and substantiality of the portion used in relation to the copyrighted work as a whole, and

4. The effect of the use upon the potential market for or value of the copyrighted work.[36]

A recent case illustrates contemporary copyright problems. The well-accepted assumption that computer programming languages were not subject to copyright protection because they were unprotectable ideas rather than an expression of ideas was challenged in *Lotus Development Corp. v Paperback Software, Inc.*[37] The trial court there established a precedent with wide-ranging ramifications: a recognition of proprietary rights in computer programming languages. The court found a copyright infringement where the defendant had copied the "user interface" of the plaintiff's "1-2-3" spreadsheet program. The court did not consider those components of the program to be a programming language, but added that it could not agree that a programming language, such as Pascal, was ineligible for copyright protection. The similarity that gave rise to the infringement was, the court found, in what they did and how they did it, not in their literal content.

The federal copyright law defines pictorial, graphic, and sculptural works within its coverage to include two- and three-dimensional works of fine, graphic, and applied art, and technical drawings, including architectural plans.[38] Even more important, the Architectural Works Copyright Act Protection Act of 1990[39] extended copyright protection to architectural works as well. Thus, some earlier court decisions[40] finding no infringement where the architectural plan was "used" to construct a structure, but not copied, have been superseded by statute.

Architectural plans and structures are subject to copyright protection where the author has independently created the work and the work reflects creativity, regardless of how simple the design. If a house design is sufficiently original, copyright protection is not precluded because the design is also utilitarian, since architectural works by definition are at least partly designed to serve a useful function.[41] This protection extends to the most mundane, functional products of commercial architecture so long as the minimal originality requirement of copyright law is met.

A builder may present ideas and concepts to an architect who prepares the plans, but even if the builder retains approval authority, his participation is insufficient to establish coauthorship. Ideas and concepts are not copyrightable.[42]

---

[36]17 U.S.C. 107, as amended on Oct. 19, 1976.

[37]740 F. Supp. 37 (D. Mass. 1990), later settled without appeal.

[38]17 U.S.C. § 101.

[39]17 U.S.C. § 102.

[40]See, for example, *DeSilva Constr. Corp. v. Herald*, 213 F. Supp. 184 (D. Fla. 1962).

[41]*Value Group, Inc. v. Mendham Lake Estates, L.P.*, 800 F. Supp. 1228 (D.N.J. 1992).

[42]*M.G.B. Homes, Inc. v. Ameron Homes, Inc.*, 903 F.2d 1486 (11th Cir. 1990). Also outside the scope of copyright protection are structures other than buildings and standard features such as doors and windows. 37 C.F.R. § 202.11.

Derivative works are copyrightable if they have recast, transformed, or adopted a pre-existing work and have original aspects that are more than trivial. The derivative work must not consist of actual copying and must include more than mechanical copying. In short, the work must be the original product of the derivative claimant.[43] Also, the producer of the derivative work must have the consent of the copyright holder of the pre-existing work for the creation of the derivative.[44]

Two cases in which copyrights of architectural drawings and structures were found to have been violated are instructive.

In one case, a copyright for a residential floor plan, the distinguishing characteristic of which was the placement of the family room in the front of the house, normally the location of a more formal living room, and a new exterior facade that used double-gabled roofs and other components in an original (though not particularly distinguished or imaginative) way was found to have been infringed by the construction of a nearly identical house by a builder whose former employee testified that he was told to put a rendering of the copyrighted plans into the defendant's computer while the defendant was negotiating with customers interested in the protected design.[45]

In another case[46] an architect completed the design of and drew the plans for a custom residence to be built by the defendant. During the design phase the parties faxed back and forth preliminary drawings but the final design was the work product of the architect.

The builder constructed the house in accordance with the plans with minor modifications such as enlarging windows, changing a wall height and the location of bathroom fixtures, and other minor changes of the type customarily made by a builder in the construction of a house.

Following the house's completion, the builder utilized the same floor-plan drawings to build a second house, identical to the first except for a modified front elevation, the addition of trim, and a more open entry, all without the knowledge or consent of the architect.

The court found that the changes were insubstantial and not original with the builder and that his contributions were not independently copyrightable. Nor were they copyrightable as a derivative work since no consent had been obtained from the architect. The builder was thus enjoined from further infringement of the architect's copyright on the original design.

Copyright protection has also been extended to include digital audio recording devices and media to discourage unauthorized copying of audio information, such as music, in the digital format.[47]

Trademarks come within the jurisdiction of the Commissioner of Patents. A trademark is any word, name, symbol, or the like, adopted and used by a manufacturer or merchant to distinguish his goods from a comparable product manufac-

---

[43]*L. Batlin & Son, Inc. v. Snyder,* 536 F.2d 486 (2nd Cir. 1976).

[44]*Gracen v. Bradford Exchange,* 698 F.2d 300 (7th Cir. 1983).

[45]*Richmond Homes Management, Inc. v. Raintree, Inc.,* 862 F. Supp. 1517 (W.D. Va. 1994). The defendant was not saved by the fact that the design was altered somewhat in response to customer's input.

[46]*Fred Riley Building Corp. v. Cosgrove,* 864 F. Supp. 1034 (D. Kan. 1994).

[47]Audio Home Recording Act of 1992, 17 U.S. § 1001 *et seq.*

tured by others. Trademarks may also be used to identify services and, in that connection, are generally referred to as "service marks."

Congress has enacted precise statutes covering the use of trademarks in interstate commerce, and the commissioner of patents has formulated specific rules for obtaining registration of such trademarks. A registration lasts for 10 years and may be renewed as many times as the owner can show continuation of active use in interstate commerce.[48]

A person should seek to register a trademark only on such materials as he has a bona fide intent to use. He should not attempt to obtain trademarks on each of a series of names or slogans that he thinks he may want to use at some time in the future—such a scatter-gun approach being designed to prevent someone else from using such names or slogans meanwhile. Generic words or terms cannot properly be registered as trademarks.

However, *Science* has been held not generic for a magazine devoted to scientific subjects, as it had developed through extensive use a secondary meaning that would be infringed by *Science Digest* used in a way to emphasize "science" and minimize "digest."[49]

QUESTIONS

1. What is the principal objective of the U.S. patent system?

2. On what authority is the U.S. patent system based? When was this system inaugurated?

3. What is a patent? What is its "life"?

4. What is a design patent: May plants be patented? Bacteria?

5. Are current patent laws adequate to cope with biotechnology advances? Mathematical algorithms?

6. Is a patent a contract? If so, what are the rights and obligations of the parties?

7. Who administers the patent laws of the United States?

8. What are the limits of the areas in which the U.S. patent laws are effective?

9. Does the Patent Office try to advise the patentee whether or not a patent will be a financial success?

10. List the elements that are generally necessary for patentability of an invention.

11. Describe the procedure to be followed in applying for a patent.

12. What is the meaning of the word "specifications" when referring to patent matters?

---

[48] 15 U.S.C. § 1051 *et seq.* The Trademark Law Revision Act of 1988 was the most extensive revision since the Lanham Act of 1946. While the basics remain largely unchanged, court cases or other materials produced prior to 1989 need to be checked against the new statute.

[49] *American Asso. for the Advancement of Science v. The Hearst Corp.*, 206 U.S.P.Q. 605 (D.C. 1980).

13. What is the meaning of the phrase "statement of invention" when referring to patent matters?

14. Referring to patent matters, what is *(a)* an "infringement"? *(b)* an "interference" proceeding?

15. When and why may drawings be required in an application for a patent?

16. What are the "claims" made in connection with an application for a patent? Why are they important?

17. What is meant by "complete disclosure"?

18. Differentiate between *(a)* a "sole" and *(b)* a "joint" invention.

19. Define the words "copyright" and "trademark." Illustrate how they are applied.

20. What is "fair use" of copyrighted material?

21. May computer programs be copyrighted? Patented?

22. May architectural plans be copyrighted? May ideas and concepts?

23. Of what significance is the "date of conception" of an invention?

24. What are the meaning and importance of the "date of disclosure" referring to inventions?

25. What is meant by "diligence" in matters of invention?

26. Referring to inventions, what is meant by "reduction to practice"?

27. What procedure should be followed by an inventor when developing an invention?

28. What precautions should be taken by both parties when dealing with the possible disclosure of secret information?

29. Explain and illustrate the licensing of a party to use a patent.

30. What is *(a)* a "grant" of patent rights to a party? *(b)* an "assignment"?

31. What is meant *(a)* by "patent pooling"? *(b)* by "cross-licensing" of patents?

32. What time limit is there on the life of a patent? Can this life be extended?

33. Can the Patent Office prevent the disclosure of patent data? When?

34. Why may a manufacturer stamp on an article (produced by him) the words "Patent applied for"?

35. In case of a grant of patent rights on a royalty basis, has the grantee any implied obligations with respect to the grantor?

36. If claims in an application for a patent are made extremely narrow, what may happen? If claims are extremely broad, what may happen?

37. If a patent application contains six claims and the Patent Office finds that two are invalid before issue, must the application be thrown out? What can be done?

38. Kimball was a mechanical engineer with an electric power company. Assume that she devised and built an apparatus for the disposal of coal ashes from the boilers of one of the company's plants. Two years afterward, she applied for a patent on this equipment. Do you think she could get the patent? Explain.

39. *X* was trying to develop and patent a new device for dust-collecting equipment. He had *Y*, who was in his office, assist him in perfecting the invention, and the latter showed that certain improvements, which he suggested, were vital to the successful operation of the equipment. *X* patented the invention using *Y's* suggestions, but *Y* claimed that it was a joint invention. Is *Y* justified in his claim? Explain.

40. Jones, a machinist, made and used a clever improvement in an automatic lathe, but he did not think that the device was patentable. Two years after the device was installed at the shop where Jones was employed, a visiting sales engineer saw it, had the apparatus installed on the lathes that his company manufactured, and applied for a patent on the device. Jones heard about the patent application. Could Jones attack the patent that might be issued on the device? Explain.

41. Long developed a special formula for a cough syrup, and she kept it a secret even though she manufactured and sold the medicine. Short discovered the secret formula and produced and marketed the same medicine under a different name. *(a)* Can Short patent the formula? *(b)* Can Long stop Short from making the competitive product? Explain.

42. *X* patented a special fountain pen. *Y* copied it and started manufacturing and selling the same pen. *X* appealed to the Patent Office to stop *Y's* activities. Will the Patent Office do this? Why?

43. What money damages can *X* in the preceding case collect from *Y* for goods produced before *X* learned about *Y's* activities? How can *X* stop *Y's* production?

44. Brown invented and patented a toy airplane. He later made a certain improvement in the toy and continued manufacture of the modified toy under the original patent. Is his improved device properly protected? Explain.

45. If a chemical product is made by a certain patented process, can someone else produce and sell the same material if he can manufacture the chemical by a different process?

chapter

25

EVIDENCE

25.1　EVIDENCE IN COURT GENERALLY

The rules of evidence form an integral part of our system of justice. An entire case can turn on the admissibility of a single bit of evidence offered by a litigant. The present chapter will attempt to highlight a few of the basic evidentiary principles.

Despite their great importance in the overall scheme of things, the rules of evidence, unlike, for example, the law of contracts or that of torts, can be classified as *procedural,* rather than as *substantive* law. Procedural law is so named because it addresses the procedures employed in litigation, such as how long a plaintiff has to timely file an action, the steps that must be taken to serve a party with process, what evidence is allowed in court, and so on. While many of the underlying theories of the law of evidence are universally accepted, application of some of the evidence rules will vary from one jurisdiction to another. Each state has its own code of evidence, as does the federal court system.

The *relevancy* of evidence deals with its logical connection to the fact at issue, for example, whether or not the evidence tends to prove a fact at issue in the case. The *materiality* of evidence relates to the probative value of the evidence. *Material* evidence is *relevant* evidence that is of sufficient value in the particular case to justify its consideration by the judge or jury. Thus, though evidence may be logically related to proof of a fact, that relationship may be so remote as to fail to justify its consideration. *Competent* evidence is that which is fit for its intended purpose, for example, it tends to establish the fact at issue without relying on speculation. Thus, the source of the information and form of the evidence are two factors that often render evidence incompetent. For example, hearsay evidence and oral testimony as to the written terms of a contract are normally incompetent evidence.

The two categories of probative material that may be produced in court are *testimonial evidence* and *real evidence.* Testimonial evidence can be subdivided into (1) *direct* and (2) *circumstantial. Direct evidence* is that which tends to prove a fact at issue without the necessity of proving any collateral facts. When a witness can impart knowledge about a fact in dispute that he has acquired by means of his senses, the evidence he gives is direct. Thus, a witness who personally saw or heard something relevant and material to a point in issue is in a position to give direct evidence. Very often, however, it becomes necessary for litigants to rely heavily upon another form of evidence, known as *circumstantial.* This type aims at establishing some collateral fact or set of facts from which the jury may reasonably infer the existence or nonexistence of the critical fact in contention. Examples of circumstantial evidence would be the fact of an accused's flight and related conduct being admissible as possibly pointing to his consciousness of guilt.

Real evidence involves observation by the tribunal itself. Thus, when a question arises whether a certain object is green or blue, the ideal proof of the true color would be the exhibit of the object to the jury. Real evidence is resorted to in an infinite variety of instances, one of the most familiar being the demonstration by plaintiff of the injury of which he complains.

Documentary evidence comprises (1) *public or official records* and (2) *private documents.* The former includes all writings made by government officials setting forth data that their duties require them to record. Public documents are evidence of the facts therein stated and, if properly authenticated, are normally admitted without the testimony of the officer who prepared them. Admission on this basis constitutes an exception to the *hearsay rule,* which will be discussed in detail in Section 25.5. Any writings that do not qualify as public records are private documents, and before these can be received in evidence, the party offering the evidence must prove that the paper was indeed duly executed by the person who is alleged to have executed it. There are a few exceptions under which this proof will be excused; for example, the adverse party may concede due execution of the private document in question.

Demonstrative evidence consists of things instead of assertions by witnesses about things. The possibilities are virtually unlimited but are characterized by the fact that they convey firsthand impressions to the judge or jury instead of the impressions of others. Demonstrative evidence, be it a model, a map, a photo, or something less common, is subject to the usual rules for admissibility of evidence, and, because of the unusual force it possesses to arouse emotion, is often objected to as "prejudicial." Demonstrative evidence may consist of objects that actually played a role in the case at hand or may be offered for illustrative or other purposes. If the object was involved in the case, a foundation for its admission will require testimony that the object is the same object that was involved in the incident and that its condition is substantially unchanged. If the object offered as evidence was not involved in the incident, it may be inadmissible where it does not illustrate or make clearer an issue in the case, but is admissible if it supplements a spoken description by a witness of the incident. Thus, in a case where the plaintiff sued a ladder manufacturer claiming that excessive step to side rail gaps caused rivet failure, unused exemplar ladders were admissible to illustrate an expert's testimony regarding the cause of the failure.[1]

The standard for admissibility of demonstrative evidence that is merely illustrative is somewhat less demanding, and evidence such as a model or map may be

---

| [1]*Benzel v. Keller Ind., Inc.,* 567 N.W.2d 552 (Neb. 1997).

admitted upon testimony that it is a substantially accurate representation. Any potentially misleading inaccuracies may, of course, be pointed out on cross-examination. Developments in technology, such as computer simulation and holograms, raise intriguing problems for the future of demonstrative evidence.

In a situation involving a collision between two bicycles, computer-generated evidence was required to be accurate, probative, and nearly identical to what it attempts to depict to be admissible. Thus, a computer simulation offered to illustrate expert testimony was rejected where the animation depicted a 25-mile-per-hour speed but the evidence indicated a speed of 28 to 40 miles per hour, and the animation depicted light from a street light as cast in a circle rather than diffused in an ellipse as shown by other evidence.[2]

But a computer simulation of the path of an automobile on the roadway was held properly admitted where a competent person conducted the experiment, an apparatus of a suitable kind and condition was utilized, and the experiment was conducted fairly and honestly.[3] Substantial similarity to the condition of the incident was said to be sufficient.

Experimental and scientific evidence is also an area of great significance and rapid change. Pretrial tests or experiments in such areas as paternity, blood and tissue typing, and material's strength and composition are commonplace, and their admissibility at trial depends, assuming that the normal rules on admissibility are met, upon whether their probative value is outweighed by the possibility of prejudice or confusion. A very significant element of admissibility is that the test conditions are sufficiently similar to the object or event at issue. Perfect similarity is not required and variation is often held to affect the weight rather than the admissibility of the evidence.

Experiments in the courtroom may also be used to demonstrate a scientific principle, such as a general principle of physics that is universal in application, which the judge or jury can then apply to the specifics of the case at hand. Sometimes the evidence is too technical or specialized for the layperson to analyze without additional help. In such cases, the use of an expert witness may assist the judge or jury in understanding the evidence. Testimony by expert witnesses[4] is governed by Federal Rule of Evidence 702, which provides:

> If scientific, technical, or other specialized knowledge will assist the trier of fact to understand the evidence or to determine a fact in issue, a witness qualified as an expert by knowledge, skill, experience, training, or education, may testify thereto in the form of an opinion or otherwise.

Most states have analogous provisions that are applied in state courts. The U.S. Supreme Court has interpreted Rule 702 as requiring the judge to "ensure that

---

[2]*Sommorvolo v. Grevlos,* 518 N.W.2d 733 (S.D. 1994).
[3]*Kudlacek v. Flat Spa,* 509 N.W.2d 603 (Neb. 1994). In accord see *Commercial Union Ins. Co v. Boston Edison Co.,* 591 N.E.2d 165 (Mass. 1992).
[4]See Chapter 25.

any and all scientific evidence is not only relevant, but reliable."[5] The court further emphasized that this inquiry is flexible and should focus not on conclusions, but on principles and methodology.

25.2   FUNCTION OF JUDGE AND OF JURY

In cases heard without a jury, the judge handles all phases of the trial. When there is a jury, however, it may be said that questions of fact are for the jury, and questions of law are for the court. For example, whether a defendant was present at the scene of the crime is a question of fact for the jury. Contrarily, which law applies to the situation is a question of law for the judge. As usual, there are exceptions, the primary one being that the court will decide certain "preliminary" questions of fact, such as those necessary to its determination of the admissibility of evidence or the competency of witnesses. By way of illustration, the qualifications of a would-be "expert" witness constitute a preliminary factual question for the court. Another sizable group of facts, which are treated as preliminary in nature and thus within the province of the judge, are those that are subject to *judicial notice*. *Judicial notice* is a convenient doctrine by which the judge will take official cognizance of a well-known fact without requiring the presentation of evidence. A proposition is indisputable when it has been judicially noticed. The range of things of which judicial notice will be taken is broad and includes such diverse items as the provisions of the Constitution of the United States, the existence of foreign governments, the sequence of the seasons of the year, and standard weights and measures.

The jury, for its part, decides upon the credibility of the witnesses it has heard examined and cross-examined and weighs the evidence presented. Only matters over which reasonable men could differ should be submitted to the jury. If the evidence presented by one side heavily outweighs the evidence presented by the other, such that a judge would have to set aside a verdict in favor of the party with little evidence, the judge will direct the appropriate verdict. In that case the judge directs the verdict in favor of the party with the overwhelming evidence, and the case is not submitted to the jury. If, however, submission of the case to the jury for determination appears warranted, the court will *charge* the jury. Along with instructions regarding the substantive law applicable to the controversy, the charge usually includes a reiteration of the issues of fact which have been submitted to proof, a statement about which party has the burden of proof, and a summary of the evidence on the record. The judge may not comment upon the evidence so as to give an indication of his personal opinion.

---

[5]*Daubert v. Merrell Dow Pharmaceuticals*, 113 S.Ct. 2786 at 2794 (1993). Some nonexclusive factors the court may consider in determining if the scientific evidence is reliable include: (1) testability, (2) whether it has been published or otherwise reviewed by peers, (3) known or potential rate of error, (4) maintenance of standards controlling the technique's operation, and (5) general acceptance in the scientific community. Id at 2796–2797. The Daubert factors also apply to the testimony of engineers and other experts who are not scientists. *Kumho Tire Co., Ltd. v. Carmichael*, 119 S.Ct. 1167 (1999).

25.3 PRESUMPTIONS AND EVIDENTIARY BURDENS OF PROOF

The burden of proof is the task of proving a proposition either by a "preponderance of the evidence" if the case is civil in nature or "beyond a reasonable doubt" if the action is a criminal one. While there are many exceptions, generally the rule in civil cases is that the plaintiff bears the burden of persuading the court of the truth of his allegations. Occasionally, the defendant's answer to the complaint will admit several points raised by plaintiff but will set up additional facts by way of defense. In such circumstances, the defendant has brought up the matters at issue, and the burden of proof is on him. The burden of proof does not shift from one party to the other during the course of the trial. What does vary is the duty of presenting evidence at any particular stage.

It is imperative that the jury be correctly charged or instructed as to which side has the burden of proof, since the verdict must be against that side if the evidence presented by the several parties is in equilibrium. The party having the burden of proof generally has the right to open and close the presentation of evidence and argument.

Some matters involved in a lawsuit are not subject to proof—for example, admissions, either as contained in the pleadings or made in open court. Thus, if defendant's answer admits the truth of an allegation in plaintiff's complaint, the latter need not introduce evidence in support of that allegation. Similarly, evidence is unnecessary to prove what is presumed, at least until the party adversely affected has taken steps to rebut the presumption. An example of this is the presumption of the innocence of an accused in a criminal case. He may choose to rely upon the presumption and decline to introduce evidence in his own behalf, at least until the prosecution has assembled a substantial case against him. There are several categories of presumptions, but the basic distinction is between those that are *conclusive* and those that are *rebuttable*. No evidence, however strong, will be permitted to overturn a conclusive presumption, such as that grounded upon a statute that provides that a child under a given age "is deemed incapable of committing a crime." Rebuttable presumptions are numerous; commonplace illustrations are the presumption against suicide and the presumption of innocence.

25.4 COMPETENCY OF WITNESSES AND COMMUNICATIONS EXCLUDED FROM EVIDENCE

It is part of the judge's function, in instances where a question has arisen, to decide upon the competency of prospective witnesses. Lack of mental capacity is probably the most common basis of disqualification, though the law recognizes other grounds as well. Sometimes witnesses otherwise with important knowledge to relay are not required to testify because of a relationship they have to another person.

For reasons of public policy, the law recognizes several relationships as confidential in nature and places in a *privileged* category certain information passing between the parties to such relationships. In most jurisdictions, the list includes confidential communications between husband and wife, physician and patient, clergyman and penitent, and attorney and client. For example, communications between an attorney and his client that pertain to the lawyer's professional services on behalf of the client have what amounts to a seal of silence upon them. This seal can only be broken with the client's consent. The client, however, is fully entitled to stand upon his privilege and thus to prevent the information involved from being used as evidence against him.

All of these privileges are subject to exceptions. For example, the attorney-client privilege would not apply where the client told the attorney that he was going to commit a crime likely to result in death or serious injury.

25.5   THE HEARSAY EVIDENCE RULE AND ITS EXCEPTIONS

"Hearsay" is a statement, other than one made by the declarant while testifying at the trial or hearing, offered in evidence to prove the truth of the matter asserted.[6] The hearsay rule is designed to keep out statements not tested by oath and cross-examination. Subject to a number of exceptions, hearsay evidence (whether oral or written) will be excluded upon timely objection.[7] Where testimony about the existence of a fact is not derived from the personal knowledge or observation of the witness but is based rather on a statement someone else has made, the evidence in question is hearsay.[8] As an illustration, suppose Smith sues dentist *A* for malpractice. Testimony by the plaintiff about what dentist *B* had told him as to the condition of his mouth is hearsay. The second dentist should be called to the stand for direct questioning about what he said, when the adverse party would thus have an opportunity for cross-examination.

In the average case, the hearsay rule excludes considerable testimony. It would exclude a great deal more were it not for a rather lengthy list of exceptions to the rule.[9] Illustrative exceptions include:

1. Statements for purposes of medical diagnosis.
2. Public records and reports.
3. Records of documents affecting an interest in property.
4. Excited utterances.
5. Certain declarations of pain and suffering.

---

[6]Federal Rules of Evidence Rule 801 (1997).

[7]Only in rare instances will a trial judge invoke on his own initiative a rule of exclusion.

[8]Sometimes a point in issue will be whether or not a given remark by *X* was or was not made. Under such conditions, anyone who heard the statement made can testify to the fact. Such testimony is not hearsay, since no effort is being made to establish the truth or falsity of *X*'s statement, but simply whether it was uttered.

[9]For a complete listing of the exceptions to the hearsay rule in federal courts, see Federal Rules of Evidence Rule 803 (1997).

6. Declarations against interest.

7. Book entries made in the regular course of business.

8. Dying declarations.

Spontaneous utterances and *involuntary expressions of pain and suffering* represent two out of a number of parts of the *res gestae*[10] doctrine, which constitutes a broad exception to the hearsay rule. Just what the res gestae doctrine encompasses is apparent from the following language, contained in a court decision from Hawaii:[11]

> The res gestae or excited utterance exception applies to statements relating to a startling act or event made spontaneously and without reflection while the declarant was under the stress of excitement and offered to prove the truth of the matter asserted. In order for statements to be admitted as part of res gestae, the statements must be reasonably contemporaneous with the event to which they relate: i.e., they must be such as to have been proximately caused by the exciting influence of the event without opportunity for deliberation or influence.

The general rule is that any witness who happened upon the scene of an accident can testify that the victim groaned or cried out. There is a conflict among authorities whether spontaneous declarations of a bystander are admissible along with those of a participant in the event.

Declarations against interest form a significant exception to the hearsay rule. Such declarations are admissible as a form of proof, if, at the time uttered, they were (1) against the pecuniary or proprietary interest of the since-deceased or otherwise-unavailable declarant , (2) the latter had competent knowledge of the matter on which he spoke and (3) had no real motive to misrepresent the facts.

The opposite of a declaration against interest is known in law as a *self-declaration.* The latter type is normally inadmissible when offered in favor of the party by whom made; otherwise, he would be in a position to create evidence for himself in advance of the trial. Although the foregoing is the rule in general, there are instances in which self-serving declarations are admissible—as, for example, where they are part of the res gestae. Contrarily, admissions by a party-opponent are admissible, not because they are an exception to the hearsay rule, but rather because for policy reasons, they are not considered hearsay at all. Such admission will not work to the prejudice of the party-opponent because as a party to the litigation, he is available to rebut by telling his version of the story.

By statute in some jurisdictions and under the common law in others, it is possible to put in evidence a writing or report, prepared in the regular course of business, without having to call as witnesses all those who had a hand in the writing. Thus, Rule 4518(a) of the New York Civil Practice Law and Rules[12] reads as follows:

---

[10]*Res gestae* means "things done."

[11]*State v. Messamore*, 639 P.2d 413 (Hawaii App. 1982).

[12]McKinney (1963). See also 28 U.S.C. (FRE) 803(6) (amended 1997), which provides an exception to the hearsay rule for records of regularly conducted activity, and 28 U.S.C. (FRE) 902 (amended 1988), which allows some documents, such as certified copies of public records, to be "self-authenticating."

Any writing or record, whether in the form of an entry in a book or otherwise, made as a memorandum or record of any fact, transaction, occurrence or event, shall be admissible in evidence in proof of that act, transaction, occurrence or event, if the judge finds that it was made in the regular course of any business and that it was the regular course of such business to make it, at the time of the act, transaction, occurrence or event, or within reasonable time thereafter. All other circumstances of the making of the memorandum or record, including lack of personal knowledge by the maker, may be proved to affect its weight, but they shall not affect its admissibility. The term business includes a business, profession, occupation and calling of every kind.

25.6   ADMISSIONS AND CONFESSIONS AS EVIDENCE

Where one of the litigating parties has in the past made some acknowledgment of fact or taken some action that contradicts the position he is adopting at the trial, proof will be received against him about such prior inconsistent behavior, and the proof is said to be in the form of an *admission*. The testimony relating to past conduct is introduced as probative evidence on points in dispute and in an effort to discredit the party involved by showing that he has "changed his stripes." Admissions represent still another exception to the hearsay rule. As with other forms of evidence, the weight to be given a particular admission is for the jury's determination.

25.7   THE BEST-EVIDENCE RULE

If it becomes necessary in the course of a lawsuit for one party to prove the contents of a writing, the document itself is the *best* evidence of its terms, and it must be physically produced. If extenuating circumstances are present, such as the loss or destruction of the original, the introduction of secondary evidence is permitted. The best-evidence rule aims at eliminating some errors by minimizing reliance upon copies of an original writing or upon recollections of a witness regarding the contents of the document.

The "original" of the document, and not a "copy," is to be produced. But where "duplicate originals" of a contract have been executed, all are treated as "originals," and any one of them may be produced in court. In such a situation, absence of all the duplicate originals would have to be shown to the judge's satisfaction before secondary evidence (copies or oral testimony) would be proper.

Although the best-evidence rule pertains to various kinds of writings that are sought to be used for evidentiary purposes, there are a few unusual circumstances under which the rule is inapplicable. One such exception involves judicial records and public documents. Because removal of such records would result in inconvenience to the public at large and would create the danger of loss, entries in public documents may be proved by means of certified copies.

Apart from the few situations in which the best-evidence rule does not apply, there are extenuating conditions under which production of the original document, otherwise necessary, will be dispensed with and secondary evidence allowed. Adequate excuses for inability to produce the original writing include its loss or destruction, and the fact that it is unavailable because it is outside the jurisdiction of the court or is in the possession of the uncooperative adverse party. If one of the foregoing explanations can be shown, a foundation exists for the introduction of secondary evidence, that is, (1) a copy of the instrument or (2) oral testimony from a witness who remembers what the writing says.

25.8　THE PAROL-EVIDENCE RULE

Almost invariably the parties to a written instrument will have engaged in a number of preliminary talks or negotiations which eventually culminate in the execution of the document itself. Under the *parol-evidence rule,* testimony about such prior conversations is inadmissible to contradict or vary the terms of the writing, which speaks for itself. The parol-evidence rule does not, however, exclude testimony as to a collateral, independent oral agreement between the parties, even though it may regard the very subject matter as the written contract and was made at about the same time.

Thus, the rule was held not to preclude testimony about an oral agreement as to the maximum cost of a home where an architect sued a client for his fee under a standard AIA percentage contract that made no mention of a maximum cost.[13] Similarly, the rule does not exclude oral evidence providing a new agreement (with its own consideration) intended to replace the written document or modify it in some fashion. The rule gives effect to the supposed intention of the parties and protects them from the uncertainties of oral testimony.

The parol-evidence rule has its exceptions. For one, it is not unusual for the parties to a written instrument to regard it as only part of their contract. In such circumstances, many decisions have permitted the introduction of parol evidence, not to vary the terms of the writing but to show the complete understanding of the parties. Parol evidence cannot supply any of the terms of a contract that the applicable statute of frauds requires to be in writing. Parol evidence will be admitted whenever its purpose is to show that no valid contractual obligation ever existed in the first place, perhaps because of lack of consideration, or because of fraud in the inception. The admissibility of parole evidence depends on the reason for which it is offered. If the effort is to modify or alter an admittedly valid contract, the evidence is objectionable. If the purpose is to show that the apparent contractual obligation is not binding because the agreement is invalid in law, the extrinsic evidence

---

[13]*Spitz v. Brickhouse,* 123 N.E.2d 117 (Ill. App. 1954). To the same effect see also *Wick v. Murphy,* 54 N.W.2d 805 (Minn. 1952) where a written contract for architectural services contained no agreement as to the architect's compensation if the work was abandoned.

should be admitted. By the same token, where the validity of a written document had been attacked, parol evidence sustaining the contract will not be excluded.

There are a few miscellaneous circumstances in which oral evidence is admissible to help in the interpretation of an instrument in writing. Parol evidence is proper as a means of identifying the parties to the contract and of showing the capacity in which each acts. If the language of the writing is unclear to the court—perhaps it contains technical terms or words peculiar to a certain local area—explanation by oral testimony is appropriate. Parol evidence of circumstances attending the execution of the written document may be needed to show the intentions of the parties, where identification of such intentions is important and is not made clear in the writing.

The parol-evidence rule precludes testimony that contradicts a written instrument whose terms and conditions the litigants have put in issue.

25.9   REFERENCE MATERIAL AS EVIDENCE

Generally speaking, treatises or extracts therefrom are inadmissible (under the rule precluding hearsay evidence) when offered to demonstrate the truth of what is said therein. But scientific books and similar reference materials nonetheless play an important part in many courtroom scenes. Such items may be used effectively on cross-examination for the purpose of discrediting or contradicting an opposition witness. Assume, for instance, that such a person is asked if he is familiar with a book on structural design by an X.Y. Smith. With an affirmative answer in hand, the cross-examiner may then inquire whether Smith is thought to be a reputable and capable engineer. Upon receiving a second affirmative response, the lawyer might point out that on page 210 of this published work Smith makes a statement that flatly contradicts the position the witness has taken on the point in question during his direct examination. The maneuver, of course, is designed to raise serious doubts regarding the validity and accuracy of the witness's testimony. However, during redirect examination, the attorney at whose behest the witness appeared might ask the latter if he is familiar with a book by Q.Z. Jones, who is also admittedly a well-known author in the field of structural design. Thereafter, the attorney may be positioned to bring out the fact that Jones, in his treatise, makes a statement substantiating that given by the witness and opposing that of author Smith.

It is obvious that a witness must be on guard when writings are likely to be used against him. He should be prepared to state (1) whether a particular author is regarded as being a genuine authority on the subject at issue, (2) whether the written material (to which his attention is directed on the stand) is now out of date or otherwise inapplicable to the case, and (3) whether other authors disagree with the one being quoted—with the result that the latter's statements are perhaps of questionable value.

QUESTIONS

1. What is the purpose of evidence?

2. Explain direct evidence.

3. What is circumstantial evidence? When may it be necessary? What are the weaknesses and dangers connected therewith?

4. Explain (a) how evidence may be relevant, (b) how it may be irrelevant.

5. What is the meaning of "weight" of evidence?

6. What qualities of a witness should be examined when judging his testimony?

7. What is "opinion" evidence? Under what circumstances is it admissible?

8. Who determines the weight, or credibility, of evidence?

9. What is meant by the "best" evidence? What part does the best-evidence rule play in a trial?

10. What is "secondary" evidence? Illustrate.

11. Compare written with oral (parol) evidence as respects the value of each and the role each fills.

12. What is meant by "burden of proof"? Which party assumes it?

13. What is "hearsay" evidence? When is it admissible?

14. What is meant by "competency" of evidence?

15. What is meant by "material" evidence?

16. Define "testimonial" evidence.

17. What is "real" evidence? Illustrate.

18. What is "documentary" evidence? Illustrate.

19. May a computer simulation of an event be offered as evidence?

20. What is the standard for admission of technical or scientific evidence?

21. Differentiate between the functions of a judge and a jury.

22. What is the judge's "charge" to the jury?

23. What is meant by "judicial notice"? Illustrate.

24. Who determines the "credibility" of a witness?

25. What is the significance of a "conclusive" presumption? How does it operate?

26. What is "rebuttal"? Illustrate.

27. Who passes upon the competency of a prospective witness?

28. What are "privileged communications"? Can the privileged party be forced to divulge such communications in court? May he do so voluntarily?

29. What factors might make a prospective witness incompetent?

30. List several exceptions to the hearsay rule.

31. Explain "declarations against interest" and comment on their admissibility.

32. Illustrate a situation in which a "book entry" would constitute proper evidence.

33. What purpose may admissions and confessions serve in a court case?

34. Indicate the circumstances under which an expert may testify (*a*) as to facts, (*b*) as to conclusions.

35. A witness said: "Mrs. Jones told me that her husband had willed all of his property to her." Do you think that such a statement is admissible as evidence in a suit by other relatives who claimed a share in the estate, since no will made by Mr. Jones was found?

26

THE ENGINEER'S ROLE IN A LAWSUIT BEFORE AND DURING TRIAL

26.1 INTRODUCTION: THE FUNCTION OF AN ENGINEER IN A LAWSUIT

Apart from the possibility of being a party in a lawsuit, an engineer may be retained to perform one of the following advisory functions:

1. An engineer may be hired as an *expert witness* to explain some technical matter or to give an expert opinion. This role can be thought of as aiding the court and jury in understanding technical evidence so they can make a proper evaluation of the case.

2. An engineer may assist an attorney in the preparation of the cross-examination of witnesses for the opposition, and may also assist during the actual cross-examination itself. He may do this by giving the attorney suggestions regarding the questions to be asked and weak points to be attacked in the statements of the opposing witnesses.

3. An engineer may serve as a general assistant to an attorney in the development of the case and not appear at all in the courtroom. In highly technical cases, in which it is important for the attorney to gain a considerable measure of competence in the technical field itself, this educational and advisory role may be important.

When filling one of the first two capacities, the engineer should attend the entire trial because the other witnesses' testimonies may impact what the engineer needs to bring to the attention of the court in his own testimony or indirectly through advice and suggestions to his attorneys.

26.2 THE ENGINEER AS EXPERT WITNESS

Engineers are frequently asked to appear in court as *expert witnesses.* An expert witness is "a witness who is qualified as an expert by knowledge, skill, experience, training or education to assist the court when specialized knowledge is needed to understand the evidence or determine a fact at issue."[1] Unlike an ordinary witness, a qualified expert witness can testify as to both fact and opinion. Experts are in demand in many types of lawsuits, and engineers who testify frequently may find their reputations and career potential affected by how well they conduct themselves on the witness stand.

Engineers may also be asked for testimony and statements of opinion in (1) arbitration proceedings, (2) commission hearings, (3) legislative committee hearings, (4) conferences pertaining to contract disputes, (5) hearings to establish valuations of property and rates for services, (6) hearings before zoning boards, (7) public or private meetings to consider matters relating to building codes, and many other proceedings.

Engineers and architects are often called upon to express expert opinions of whether a building was constructed in conformance with code requirements. Such questions may arise in both injury[2] and breach of contract cases.[3]

However, not every lawsuit involving architects or construction requires expert testimony. In one case,[4] construction company employees were injured when stairs collapsed. They sued the project architect for failing to detect and correct errors in shop drawings for the stairs. The court held that since the complaint alleged negligence in supervision rather than negligence in preparation, expert testimony on the appropriate standard of care was not required. The court recognized that usually there can be no finding of liability against an architect without expert testimony to support it but concluded that a "common knowledge" exception exists in negligent supervision cases.

This exception also may apply where the facts are such as to negate the assumption that laymen are unable to understand highly technical architectural requirements without hearing other architects testify as to those requirements.[5]

Expert witnesses are usually subpoenaed in by one or another of the contesting parties. Theoretically, it would seem preferable to have nonpartisan experts called by the court itself, either on its own initiative or that of a party, as divorcing expert testimony from the source of compensation would help ensure the impartiality of the witnesses involved.

While it is generally thought that courts have the inherent power to select experts to give evidence, several jurisdictions have enacted statutes expressly authorizing trial judges to appoint expert witnesses, to fix their remuneration (sub-

---

[1] Federal Rule of Evidence 702 (1975).

[2] See, for example, *Thomas v. Dixson*, 363 S.E.2d 209 (N.C. App. 1988), where a customer in a store fell down stairs that allegedly were not in compliance with the state building code.

[3] In *LaGasse v. Gardner*, 298 S.E.2d 393 (N.C. App. 1982), a breach of contract action against a contractor who assembled a modular home, two experts in construction were allowed to testify that window and door lintels did not conform to the code, and that an 8-inch retaining wall was used instead of the 12 inches required by the state building code.

[4] *Jaeger v. Heningson, Durham & Richardson, Inc.*, 714 F.2d 773 (8th Cir. 1983).

[5] In *Jaeger, supra,* the court found the exception to prevail where the specifications called for landing pans to be made from 10-gauge steel with angle stiffeners, but the shop drawing provided for 14-gauge steel without stiffeners or supports.

ject to any statutory maximum), and to treat the fees as costs of the lawsuit. An example of this is California Evidence Code § 730 (West 1998). Section 733 states that: "Nothing contained in this article shall be deemed or construed to prevent any party to any action from producing other expert evidence on the same fact or matter mentioned in Section 703; but, where other expert witnesses are called by a party to the action, their fees shall be paid by the party calling them and only ordinary witness fees shall be taxed as costs in the action."

26.3 THE EXPERT WITNESS'S COMPENSATION

If the engineer is testifying as an expert at the request of a litigating party, there should be an understanding in advance that he is to be paid for his services, especially if the engineer is required to do research or other extensive preparation. Payment under the usual agreement is made regardless of the outcome of the case. It is customary for the expert to base his total charges primarily upon the amount of time involved in preparation for his court appearance as well as at the trial itself. The rate normally approximates charges for comparable consulting work. The relative importance of the expert's prospective role in the court proceedings will undoubtedly influence the precise rate. If he figures to be the key person in resolving the principal question at issue, and particularly if his professional reputation is on the line, the measure of his compensation may well reflect this. Occasionally an expert witness will have been asked to testify on a "contingent fee basis," meaning that he would be paid only in the event the party who called him wins. The disadvantage to a contingent fee arrangement is that it gives the expert witness a pecuniary interest in the lawsuit, and, consequently, makes the expert appear partial to one side. This problem arises because the witness will probably be questioned about his compensation by the opposing counsel during the cross-examination. However, in some situations an individual with great expertise is asked merely to testify to facts that have come within his observation. In this case, the person is subpoenaed as an ordinary witness and is paid only the statutory witness fee and travel allowance.

26.4 QUALIFICATION OF WITNESS AS "EXPERT"

Sometimes the evidence is too technical or specialized for the layperson to analyze without additional help. In such cases, the use of an "expert witness" may assist the judge or jury in understanding the evidence. Testimony of expert witnesses[6] is governed by Federal Rule of Evidence 702, which provides:

| [6]See Chapter 25.

If scientific, technical, or other specialized knowledge will assist the trier of fact to understand the evidence or to determine a fact in issue, a witness qualified as an expert by knowledge, skill, experience, training, or education, may testify thereto in the form of an opinion or otherwise.

Most states have analogous provisions that are applied in state courts. The U.S. Supreme Court has interpreted Rule 702 as requiring the trial judge to act as a sort of gatekeeper to "ensure that any and all scientific evidence is not only relevant, but reliable."[7] The court further emphasized that this inquiry is flexible and should focus not on conclusions, but on principles and methodology. The relevancy of the expert's proposed testimony is determined by whether it has any logical connection to a fact at issue. Some nonexclusive factors the court may consider in determining if the scientific evidence is reliable include: (1) testability, (2) whether it has been published or otherwise reviewed by peers, (3) known or potential rate of error, (4) maintenance of standards controlling the technique's operation, and (5) general acceptance in the given scientific community.[8] The determination of whether to allow expert testimony is almost exclusively within the trial judge's discretion. An appellate court will only overrule a District Court's decision to admit or exclude expert testimony if they find an "abuse of discretion" by the lower court.[9]

When an engineer-witness takes the stand, he (like any other witness) will give his name and address and will be sworn in. Then he will be asked for information about his background and qualifications. The usual questions relate to education, practical experience, writings, accomplishments in the profession, and technical organizations with which he is connected. It is helpful if the witness can state that he is licensed as a professional engineer (or architect) in one or more states. The public recognizes that the licensed engineer has had to pass licensing examinations and that he is bound by codes of ethics to conduct himself in accordance with proper moral and professional principles.

Here are some of the questions asked by an attorney during the "qualification" of an engineer as an expert in a suit involving waterworks.

What is your occupation?

What college did you attend?

What degree or degrees have you received?

Are you a licensed professional engineer?

In what states do you hold a license?

To what professional societies do you belong?

Where and by whom are you employed?

What is the title of your position?

What is the general nature of your duties in that position?

---

[7]*Daubert v. Merrell Dow Pharmaceuticals,* 113 S.Ct. 2786 at 2794 (1993).
[8]*Id.* at 2796–2797.
[9]For a more detailed discussion of appellate review of expert testimony rulings, see *General Electric Company v. Joiner,* 118 S.Ct. 512 at 515 (1997).

Will you state briefly an outline of your professional experience?

What are some of your other activities in your profession?

Have you written any books on engineering subjects?

If so, what are they?

Have you written any articles for engineering periodicals?

If so, to what subjects do they apply in general?

Have you ever worked on the construction of waterworks?

Has that work been in the office or in the field?

Please explain in some detail the character of this work and your responsibilities in connection with it.

It is not required that the witness's expertise coincide exactly with the problem at hand. For example, where a plaintiff was injured in the collapse of a scaffold, a supervisor of construction and training management for a state industrial safety department testified as to whether a platform was capable of being "secured" as required by state law. The admission of this testimony was upheld[10] on appeal.

Likewise, a mechanical engineer with a special expertise in the safe design of farm equipment was allowed to testify that the dangers associated with the clean-out door of a combine, which amputated the plaintiff's arm when he tried to clean residual wheat from the vertical auger, would "exceed the expectation of the owners and operators of such combines."[11] The defense contention that the expert witness had no expertise in consumer sampling was rejected, the court finding that inherent in the safe design of mechanical equipment is some anticipation of how such equipment will be perceived and used by customers.

It is not required that an expert witness always possess formal academic credentials. Indeed, a witness with extensive practical experience can be very convincing, especially to a jury. For example, in a U.S. Court of Appeals case[12] involving a rare colon cancer allegedly caused by exposure to nickel/cadmium in a battery factory noted that,

> The Advisory Committee Note accompanying [federal] Rule [of Evidence] 702 reads the broad language of the note to permit expert testimony not only by experts carrying formal credentials such as university degrees and professional memberships but also by so-called skilled witnesses, whose experiences permit them to testify with authority on a given topic.

Likewise, in one federal case,[13] a hotel guest fell on a spiral stairway and was injured. He sued the architect, claiming negligent design and supervision of con-

---

[10]*Eagan v. Marr Scaffolding Co.*, 442 N.E.2d 743 (Mass. App. 1982). See also *Coursey Building Asso. v. Baker*, 301 S.E.2d 688 (Ga. App. 1983) where a structural engineer was allowed to testify as to the standard of care expected of a *contractor* who was sued by a homeowner when a basement wall in a house built by the contractor collapsed.

[11]*Wheeler v. John Deere Co.*, 935 F.2d 1090 (10th Cir. 1991). This case also describes several other cases in which engineers were allowed to testify on matters somewhat beyond the scope of their formal training.

[12]*Christophenson v. Allied Signal Corp.*, 939 F.2d 1106 (5th Cir. 1991), abrogated on other grounds by *Daubert v. Merrell Dow Pharmeceuticals, Inc.*, 509 U.S. 579, 113 S.Ct. 2786, 125 L.Ed. 469 (1993).

[13]*Gravely v. Providence Partnership*, 549 F.2d 958, (4th Cir. 1977).

struction. The court allowed the president of the manufacturer of the spiral stair-case to testify that the degree of safety of spiral and conventional stairways was relatively equal. The court weighed the president's qualifications, 26 years of experience in stairway construction, as "well justifying an opinion."

The apparent qualifications of the expert will have considerable bearing on the weight his opinion carries with the trier of the facts. The opposing attorney may challenge the standing of an expert witness on the basis (1) that he has not had adequate training in the particular field concerned, (2) that he is too young to have had satisfactory experience, (3) that he is too old (perhaps retired) and out of touch with the most recent developments in the particular field, (4) that his training is too broad on the one hand or too specialized on the other, (5) that he is too closely connected with the case to have an unbiased opinion, or (6) of his record as an expert witness.[14]

The importance of the relative qualifications of expert witnesses may be demonstrated by considering the jury's problem in judging the weight of opposing testimony given as "opinion" evidence in connection with the failure of a bridge during its erection. The attorney for the plaintiff asked his witness, "In your opinion what was the cause of this failure?" The witness replied, "I believe that the timber piles under the erection bent were not properly braced in a lateral direction. This allowed the erection bent to 'jackknife,' which means that it buckled side-wise at the top of the piles." The second expert witness, called by the opposition, stated in reply to similar questioning that he believed the temporary steel erection frame or post on top of the piles failed, thus causing the structure to fall, and that the piles were braced properly. The jury was thus faced with conflicting expert opinions. Since it was impossible, after the structure had fallen, to obtain absolute, factual proof of the cause of the collapse, the jury's finding would depend in large part upon its estimate of the qualifications and credibility of the respective experts.

26.5   KNOWLEDGE OF SUBJECT

Above all things, a person should not attempt to act as expert witness regarding a matter about which he is not well informed. If he does so, the opposing lawyers and their engineering advisers will be likely to detect his shortcomings, and the result may be the discrediting of his testimony.

A witness on the stand is fair game for opposing counsel and is in no position to try bluffing. A witness should avoid making broad assertions unless he is sure of

---

[14]Courts are well aware of professional experts or what are sometimes called "legal prostitutes," and an expert can be precluded from testifying for this reason. As a Federal Court of appeals put it, "experts whose opinions are available to the highest bidder have no place testifying in a court of law. Our message to able trial colleagues: it is time to take hold of expert testimony." This court further stated that two indications that an expert may be available to the highest bidder are (1) the expert is not willing to subject his opinions to peer review and (2) the expert spends most of his time consulting with attorneys and testifying in court. *Eymard v. Pan American World Airways,* 795 F.2d 1230 at 1234, (5th Cir. 1986).

his ground. When a witness is asked for a fact rather than an opinion and he cannot answer with assurance, it is best to say that he does not know. There have been cases wherein the supposed "expert" witness actually weakened his side by ill-advised answers on the stand. In one instance, a witness had testified to certain facts. The opposing lawyer then asked him about related things that were really matters handled entirely by another man. In trying to answer without prior study of the points in question, the witness made a statement that he subsequently had to admit was in error. This episode gave the cross-examiner an opportunity to criticize the witness severely and thus to cast doubt upon his credibility.

It is also obvious that a witness should check his facts before attempting to base any conclusions thereon. For example, an engineer testified that certain equipment and expense would be necessary if a dam was to be built in the river adjoining a particular industrial plant. He offered this opinion without having seen the final plans for the proposed construction. Later, the plans were presented in court, and they proved to be much different from what he had assumed was the case. His testimony was made to appear ridiculous in light of the actual situation.

Thorough examination of the situation and the circumstances involved in a proposed suit are usually vital before an engineer agrees to serve as an expert witness. Such preliminary investigations may be helpful to the owner and his lawyer as well as the engineer. This is exemplified by the case where an owner of a large multistory building planned to bring suit for damages against the contractor because large vertical cracks had occurred in the concrete foundation walls. After making careful measurements, the engineer found that there were no differential settlements of adjacent parts of the foundation, showing that the soil had not yielded unevenly. However, he was convinced that the cracking of the long foundation walls had been caused by the lack of vertical contraction joints that would have been essential in order to allow for horizontal shrinkage and thermal contraction of the concrete. This lack was the responsibility of the designer. The cracks were simply nature's way of showing what should have been provided. Therefore, the engineer, because of his careful investigation, had enabled the owner to avoid the expense of suing the wrong party.

26.6 NECESSITY FOR HONEST ADVICE

When assisting an attorney in the study or preparation of a case, an engineer should be absolutely honest in giving opinions and advice. The engineer and the attorney have different areas of knowledge and must rely upon each other to a considerable extent. Even though the engineer's professional opinion may not be what the lawyer wants to hear, the engineer should nevertheless give his honest opinion. If any serious flaws in the case can be found, it is better to detect them in advance (even if it means dropping the suit) than to have them brought out by the opposition at the trial.

By way of illustration, consider the following example involving a cinder-block house built about 3/4 of a mile from a stone quarry. By the time two years had elapsed, the front porch and one corner of the house had settled and cracked badly. The interior plastered partitions had settled near the center of the structure, and also were badly cracked. The owner engaged a lawyer to sue the quarry operators for damages, claiming that the cracks were caused by the blasting of rock. The attorney called in an engineer to assist in the case. The engineer carefully studied the situation and learned that the owner had built the house himself, without engineering or architectural aid and without the assistance of a contractor. The porch and corner that settled had been founded upon newly filled-in soil, the subsequent compaction of which had evidently caused their subsidence. The floor in the center of the house was supported upon a central wooden beam that had shrunk at least 1/4 inch in drying out, thus causing the partitions to sag at the center, whereas they were supported upon unyielding masonry walls at the outer edges. When the engineer advised the owner and the attorney of his findings, it was decided to forgo the suit. The engineer's advice had saved the owner considerable money that would otherwise have been spent in fruitless litigation.

In another instance, the construction of a power dam was, without doubt, going to cause the flooding of a portion of a valuable industrial-plant site. Since direct negotiations between the parties had failed to effect a settlement, the owners of the plant site brought a "friendly" suit against the power company in order to have the court determine the payment that the power company should make to the owners of the property to compensate them. The attorneys for the power company called in an engineering firm to design protective works for the site, intending to offer the plant owners the estimated cost of these works as a settlement. The engineers insisted that, although complete protection would cost more than a less effective construction job, they would not present to the court a plan that they could not defend wholeheartedly. Their reasoning was that if their plan was proved inadequate by the opposition, the power company might have to pay even more than the cost of protective facilities. The lawyers for the power company finally approved this idea. Subsequently, the hearings revealed the wisdom of this course, because the opposing attorneys would have been able to prove that anything less than the measures the engineer had suggested to the power company would constitute inadequate protection for the plant owner. A settlement substantially equal to the estimated cost of the proposed works was ordered by the court.

26.7   DISCOVERING AND PRESERVING THE FACTS BY DEPOSITION

A *deposition* is sworn testimony taken in writing, pursuant to notice, upon oral or written interrogatories, and with opportunity afforded for cross-examination. Sometimes depositions are taken for the purpose of "discovery" of information material to the issues in the case, and sometimes for the purpose of making certain that a person's testimony will be available at the trial. In this connection there are circumstances in which a prospective witness will be, for good reasons, such as physical disability, prevented from appearing in court. Arrangements may then be made to have his or her testimony recorded under oath outside the courtroom. Examination will be conducted by the respective attorneys, as though the witness were giving evidence in a courtroom. This recorded testimony is termed a *deposition,* and it will be available for reading in open court so that the judge and jury may hear all the questions and answers. Of course, such a reading may not prove as impressive as would the same testimony given in person to the court, but it is certainly better than losing altogether the benefit of what the witness has to say. A litigant may also use the deposition of the testifying witness to impeach that witness's testimony.

Statutory provisions vary with the jurisdiction, and the applicable laws would have to be consulted to determine in what situations a deposition is appropriate, who may take it,[15] and what formalities are to be observed.

Under the typical deposition procedure, the attorneys may object to certain questions as they are put to the witness. There being no judge present at that stage to rule upon the admissibility of the disputed evidence, unresolved issues of this nature will remain to be settled by the judge when the deposition is read in court. The official stenographer will have recorded in the deposition transcript the various objections and the reasons presented in support of them so that the court can make rulings as the reading proceeds. Thus, the witness whose deposition is being taken will answer questions for transcript purposes despite opposing counsel's objection, but the judge, if he eventually sustains such objection, will have the answer stricken from the records of the case.

26.8   COMMENCING A SUIT

The attorney for a would-be plaintiff in an action may want the help of an engineer in preparing a formal complaint outlining allegations that the plaintiff will be prepared to prove. Preparation of this important document entails a thorough study of the entire situation and of the evidence available. Even at this early juncture, the expert advice of engineers and other technicians can help the attorney in deciding what prospective evidence is and is not of value in establishing relevant and complicated engineering points.

Once a suit is filed expert advice will be sought by the defendant also. The following sections are equally applicable to witnesses employed by the defense.

---

[15]In California, for example, the deposition of a witness or party may be handled by any justice or judge. See California Code of Civil Procedure, § 179 (1982).

26.9 Preparing to Testify

It is essential that the engineer who is to act as witness should first become thoroughly familiar with the overall case and particularly with his special part in it. This normally involves close advance cooperation with the attorneys for his side. There should be a definite understanding about what the expert will be asked, what information he is in a position to give, and what his knowledge or experience limitations may be. The prospective witness should also prepare for cross-examination by imagining that he is on the opposing side and that he is trying to counteract the very testimony that he plans to give on direct examination. This exercise will help him get ready to meet anticipated attack from the opponents.

When in the courtroom, a witness should act with dignity and confidence. An expert witness should give an impression of knowledge, competency, honesty, accuracy, and fairness. An engineer should not attempt to be an expert witness for a party whose general position—at least on the matter about which expert testimony is desired—he cannot honestly support.

During questioning, the witness should look directly at the interrogator. While answering, the witness should maintain eye contact with the trier of fact, be it the judge or a jury. If the opposition lawyer tries to overpower him with rapid-fire questions, the witness may ask for the repetition of each question and may answer each one individually. A witness must not allow himself to become angry or intimidated. If she is sure of her position, she need not be afraid of opposing counsel, because she knows more about the subject than the opposing counsel does. The witness should not allow opposing counsel to wrest control of the situation from her to the extent that she will make some untrue, inconsistent, or self-contradictory statement. If the cross-examiner becomes abusive, the attorney who called the witness may object.

A witness should not blindly accept unproven facts as true or indicate agreement with counsel's statements unless he believes them to be correct. The witness should be on guard against leading questions.[16] When a question cannot be answered with a direct "yes" or "no," the witness should state that he cannot make an unqualified answer, but would like to answer with an explanation. If the witness is not positive regarding his answer, it is best to say, "to the best of my knowledge."

A witness should not try to make an answer cover so many fine points that it will be confusing to the judge and jury. Witnesses should try to emphasize the important points, and, if necessary, arrange for the attorney to ask additional questions that will bring out desired details. Generally speaking, it is dangerous for a witness to volunteer more information than the questions require. In doing so, witnesses may thereby unwittingly give the opposition something to attack or to use as a "red herring" to divert the attention of the judge and jury from the really pertinent information.

---

[16]*Leading questions* are those that are worded so as to suggest their own answers. For example: "When you inspected the site, did you notice the fine, water-bearing sand running into the excavation?" This type of query virtually puts words in the mouth of the witness. The question in a nonleading format would be: "When you inspected the site, what did you see?" Leading questions may be acceptable in direct examination regarding preliminary matters and in cross-examination, but not at other times.

The witness should not be unduly partisan when on the stand. It is human nature for the expert to experience some feeling in favor of the side for which he is appearing, but it is important to maintain a sense of balance and not say anything that is incorrect or misleading. If a witness inadvertently does so, a correction at the earliest opportunity is indicated. False evidence given with knowledge of its falsity amounts to perjury.

Before and during the actual court proceedings the expert witness will do well to remember that the lawyers on her side are trying, partly through her testimony, to bring out certain points relating to the issues in order to tip the scales in favor of the client they represent. The opposing lawyers, of course, will be trying either to preclude the recording of any damaging expert testimony in the first place or in some fashion to attack its accuracy or value once it has been admitted.

26.10 PRESENTATION OF INFORMATION

When giving evidence in a trial, a witness should remember that the court stenographer is taking down everything that is said and that the written record must be depended upon for future reference and as the foundation for a possible appeal to a higher tribunal. Therefore, witnesses should try to speak slowly and distinctly so that the record will be intelligible. To illustrate a related point, assume that a witness is making reference to a map that shows in red the location of a certain pipeline. The map has previously been placed in evidence and bears a certain exhibit number. Suppose that the witness points to a location on the map and says, "The pipeline is here." Those present in the courtroom will understand his testimony, but the record would mean nothing. Presumably, the lawyers will move to clarify the record, but it would have been preferable for the witness to have said something like this: "The pipeline is shown on Exhibit K by the red line extending eastward from the water tank to the northwest corner of the building designated on this map as No. 3."

Furthermore, an expert witness should bear in mind that hearings on engineering matters will doubtless involve technical terminology with which the court stenographer is not familiar. It is courteous for the witness to spell out such words as he thinks necessary, and this will ensure that they are recorded correctly. When an engineer is trying to explain or illustrate some involved matter to a judge or jury, he should remember that their background and experience are probably much different from his own. What is commonplace to him may be utterly unknown to them. Terminology and examples should be chosen with this in mind.

In one instance, a lawyer asked an expert witness to explain what he meant when he said that a certain piece of cast iron "probably failed because of fatigue." The witness replied: "Let us assume that we have a 2 by 10 plank about 18 feet long lying flat on two blocks 15 feet apart. A man who weighs 150 pounds steps on the center of the plank. It sags 3 or 4 inches but does not fail. Now, if the man steps on and off the plank time and time again, it may be that eventually the plank seems to get tired out and finally breaks under the weight of the man whom it supported safely so many times before. In a way, that is what I mean by "fatigue." The example selected was sufficiently "down to earth" that the average layman could readily see the point.

The use of maps, charts, models, and similar materials is often helpful in illustrating a point. These aids should be simple, attractively prepared, and readily understood. They should be large enough to be visible at a distance or in such a form that they can be passed around to all persons entitled to see them. A witness will not make a favorable impression on the court if he tries to illustrate points by reference to visual aids that are not easily seen and understood by the judge and jury.

The engineer must be sure that all materials that he intends to use in court are correct to the most minute detail and are consistent with one another. In one instance of litigation resulting from a contract, an engineer expert witness discovered that there was a reference in the specifications to something that had been removed from the drawings that were in the record as exhibits. During a recess, the witness told the attorney about the discrepancy. The latter took the initiative and immediately brought the matter to the court's attention. The opposing attorneys attempted to show that the inconsistency between specifications and drawings was evidence of poor preparation of the contract documents. However, they accomplished little or nothing compared to what they might have achieved if the other lawyer had not voluntarily exposed the situation.

If a witness can use some statements made by the opposition's witnesses to prove his point, this is helpful in that the other side cannot very well attack the validity of their own source of information. This is one of the reasons a witness may benefit if he attends all the trial sessions preceding the giving of his own testimony. In one case, witness *A* had stated that the building of a proposed dam would cause sufficient flooding of part of the plaintiff's land to destroy its use (and, therefore, sale value) as a site for a future industrial plant or for other structures. He claimed that this flooding would cause a decline of at least $50,000 in the value of the property in question. Witness *B,* appearing for the defendant, showed the court certain records that revealed that the land in question had been flooded many times in the past when severe freshets occurred in the adjacent river. Witness *B* pointed out that if flooding caused by the proposed dam would injure the sale value of the land, the similar and frequent flooding of this land by the river would cause similar loss of value of the property. Furthermore, since (without the dam) flooding of this land would undoubtedly recur many times in the future by reason of the river alone, the construction of the proposed dam could not be regarded as likely to have an appreciable detrimental effect on the value of the land. Thus, witness *B* was able, in a way, to use the statement by *A* to show that the asserted loss was not a factor.

In many cases it is necessary to present to the court the ultimate results of detailed calculations or even to explain the calculations themselves. One should be very careful to avoid making hasty mental or written computations while on the stand. Under pressure, a witness may make errors that will later be pointed out by the opposition. It is best to have these sets of figures complete and in proper form so that they can be placed in evidence as exhibits. Upon being offered for the record, prospective exhibits have to be submitted for the perusal of the judge and of opposing counsel who will doubtless show them to his engineering experts or other technical advisers on hand.

26.11 TESTIFYING DURING THE DIRECT EXAMINATION

When an expert witness first takes the stand, the attorney who hired him will conduct what is called the *direct examination*. The attorney will ask questions designed to bring out certain points he believes will be relevant and helpful in establishing the client's case. The substance of what the witness can be expected to say on direct should be no secret to his attorney. The principal function of the witness will be either (1) to bring out technical information or opinions in support of his side or (2) to present involved facts or expert opinion that tends to refute statements made by witnesses for the opposition.

When the expert has not actually observed the facts on which his attorney would have him base an opinion, the lawyer may have to get his conclusions by asking one or more hypothetical questions that will enable the witness, through his answers, to make the desired statements.

A witness should be certain that he understands the question before he tries to answer it. To illustrate: a pumping station was to be installed by the power company for the benefit of the plant owner, and it was to be operated by the latter. The witness had been told in advance that his attorney would ask him if this pumping equipment would be *inexpensive* to operate. Actually the question as asked was: "Will this pumping equipment be *expensive* to operate?" The expert, being a bit inattentive, replied: "Yes, we designed it that way." To the embarrassment of the witness, the lawyer said, "I believe that you misunderstood my question." Then he repeated it, and allowed the witness to correct himself.

To the extent possible, the expert should give his testimony in generally understood language, rather than in highly technical terms. One should aim at being easily understandable by the judge and jury and, accordingly, should try to keep statements (and any illustrations which he uses) within the range of common experience.

There may be considerable difference in the best way for a witness to present engineering matters to a jury or court. As juries are usually composed of persons without a technical background, all information should be given in a way that they can be reasonably expected to understand. If the case is presented before a judge, he will have excellent knowledge of the legal matters but may not grasp the technicalities of engineering as readily; hence the need for simplification is just as great. An expert witness, no matter how knowledgeable, must be careful not to patronize the jury or judge by his words or tone. If the case is before an arbitration board composed of experienced engineers, the witness can be free to present his testimony in technical terms.

Here is one illustration of how a witness presented a technical matter to a lay jury. The case involved serious diagonal cracking of masonry walls in a large building. The opposition had claimed that the cracking was produced by a wedging action of part of the structure settling with respect to adjacent portions. The witness, having heard this testimony, prepared to counteract it. To do so, he made a wedge of wood; then he placed two bricks side by side on a table in front of the jury. Next, he inserted the wedge vertically between the bricks, causing them to separate horizontally. However, he showed that a vertical force had to be applied to the wedge to cause it to move, that the wedge had to move downward appreciably in order to separate the bricks, and that the wedge had to be in contact with the sides of the bricks because it could not exert a lateral pressure through an air space. He pointed out that no such downward force existed in the structure, that there had been no permanent downward movement of one part of the structure with the respect to the next, and that there was an air space at each crack. The jury could see that the claimed wedge action could not have produced the existing cracking of the walls.

After cross-examination of the expert by the opposing side, an attorney may find it advantageous to recall him to the stand to explain or contradict points brought out by the opponent. This type of return appearance is called *redirect*.

26.12 TESTIFYING DURING THE CROSS-EXAMINATION

After completion of direct testimony by a witness, the opposing attorney will conduct his *cross-examination.* Naturally, this attorney's objective is to break down or nullify the effect of the direct testimony given by the witness. The attorney may try in various ways to discredit the "expert" and will likely ask questions intended to confuse him, to get him to contradict his previous statements, and to find any discernible weakness in the position he took on direct examination. Questions regarding the amount of the fee paid to the witness are allowable and should be answered candidly and without embarrassment.

Undergoing cross-examination can be an ordeal, since the witness is very much alone on the stand, apart, of course, from such help as the attorney who called the witness can afford through objections to improper questions. If the cross-examiner can prove, through the interrogated witness or through other witnesses, that even a small part of the direct testimony given by the expert was inaccurate, the jury's confidence in the witness is likely to be shaken.

The expert should guard against being drawn into an argument with the opposing attorney. He should also endeavor to keep from making irrelevant statements that may cloud the issue or serve as openings for the opposing lawyer to challenge the witness effectively.

The following episode illustrates the role of cross-examination in discrediting a witness. A financial expert had been asked on direct examination to testify regarding the interest rate that should be used in estimating the capitalized value of certain annual expenses that a manufacturer could expect to incur in the future. He stated that a yield of 5 percent was the maximum obtainable from really prudent investments. Under cross-examination the witness admitted that he was trustee of certain funds and that these monies were currently invested so as to earn interest and dividends ranging from 7 to 8 percent a year. The witness-trustee was thereupon asked if he considered the money prudently invested, and he naturally had to admit that such was the case. Thus, his previous statement that 5 percent was a maximum return on a "prudent" investment was made to appear foolish.

Absolute honesty under cross-examination is essential even though it may occasion temporary embarrassment. A witness, testifying in a suit for damages, was asked by the opposing attorney if he had seen a certain 24-inch pipeline to which he had supposedly been close. In an attempt to trip the witness, the attorney inquired, "Didn't you see that big pipeline lying there on the ground?" The witness replied, "No, I was examining the topography and water levels to the south of that area." This admission may appear to show a lack of keen observation on the part of the witness, but, if he had made a blind guess at the actual condition and had answered in the affirmative (which is really lying under oath), his honesty and reliability would obviously have been open to question when independent evidence later established that the pipeline was buried underground and could not have been seen.

It is customary for the engineers assisting attorneys to pass notes as the trial proceeds, suggesting questions that should be asked of a particular expert on cross-examination (or suggesting that one of them should be called to counter some aspect of the other side's evidence). Before the cross-examination of any expert is finished, the opposing lawyers will be satisfied that they have impaired the effect of his direct testimony or that they cannot succeed in such an endeavor.

If a witness is asked questions that he cannot at once answer completely, it is sometimes possible for him to ask for the privilege of consulting his attorney, other engineers, or available data, in order to make sure that he will be answering correctly. One may also ask for a reading of certain previous testimony in order to refresh his memory. Such devices are especially useful when complicated figures, or statements made earlier in the trial, are involved.

26.13 OBJECTIONS TO THE QUESTIONING

While a witness is under examination by the attorney for his side, opposing counsel will be paying close attention so that he may raise objections to questions he finds improper or to answers that he wishes to have stricken from the record. Under the rules of evidence there are a number of grounds upon which to base possible objections. Should the judge overrule the objection, of course, the question concerned will stand as originally asked (or, perhaps, as rephrased), and the witness will be directed to answer.

In a typical case a witness was asked his opinion of the construction work on a certain dam. The opposing lawyer objected, asserting that the witness was not experienced in the design of dams and knew nothing about the one in question. A series of further questions by the first attorney sufficiently established the qualification of the witness respecting the subject under discussion, and the objection was not sustained.

Having a number of objections raised during his appearance may prove very disconcerting to the witness who had planned to make certain statements in reply to anticipated questions. The problem for the attorney questioning the witness becomes one of rephrasing those questions to which valid objections are interposed, so as to bring out the desired information in such form as will meet with the court's approval. Most often, objections will be raised regarding the admissibility of the statements under the rules of evidence.

QUESTIONS

1. Define the meaning of the term "expert witness."

2. In what kinds of proceedings may an engineer have an important part as an expert witness?

3. Describe in what capacities an engineer may aid in court proceedings.

4. Why may "expert" opinion be admissible at a trial when opinion evidence in general is not? Explain.

5. Explain the difference in an engineer's situation (*a*) when acting as a witness for one of the litigants and (*b*) when rendering service strictly as an adviser to one of the attorneys.

6. Illustrate the procedure that may be followed in court in qualifying a witness as an expert.

7. What facts may greatly affect the weight of an expert witness's testimony in court?

8. Explain the difference between direct examination and cross-examination of an expert witness.

9. How may visual aids be used in connection with the presentation of testimony by an expert witness?

10. Explain when and how references may be used by an expert witness in connection with presentation of his testimony.

11. Can an engineer be compelled to give testimony in court? How?

12. If an engineer is asked to serve as an expert witness, should he investigate the case before accepting? Why?

13. What may happen if a witness makes a statement on the stand and then, under cross-examination, has to admit that he erred?

14. How can the court decide upon the relative value of opposing testimony presented by various expert witnesses?

15. Why might an engineer who is to help the attorney for plaintiff in a lawsuit be asked to assist in the preparation of the complaint?

16. If an engineer sees that a case in which he is asked to help an attorney is weak or has weak points in it, what should he do about it?

17. Why is it customary for a lawyer to go over in advance the general character of the questions that he will ask an expert witness on direct examination?

18. In preparation for direct examination, is it proper for the prospective witness himself to suggest questions that the attorney might well ask him? Explain.

19. Can an expert witness generally be recalled to the stand after he has undergone both direct and cross-examination? Why?

20. What is the purpose of making a stenographic copy of all proceedings during a hearing or court session?

21. If an expert witness is not sure of a question asked him, what should be do?

22. Can an expert witness, who is on the stand, ask for an opportunity to refresh his memory before answering a specific question?

23. When may an expert witness make use of books to prove technical points he made in his testimony?

24. May an expert witness properly be questioned about his fee?

25. Can book data, used to substantiate statements made by an expert witness, be placed in evidence as exhibits?

26. If a witness refers to computations and figures when giving his testimony, will such data be made a part of the record?

27. On the stand, an expert witness was asked: "Exactly what was the speed of the truck when it crashed through the railing of the bridge?" The witness answered: "I don't know." (*a*) Does that answer discredit the other testimony of the witness? (*b*) Should the witness try to make a specific answer? (*c*) Would the situation be different if the question were: "In your opinion, what was the approximate speed of the truck when it crashed through the railing of the bridge?"

28. Lawyer *A* came to engineer *B* to ask the latter to serve as expert witness. As the result of a discussion of the matter, *B* found that he could not agree with much of *A*'s position and claims. Should *B* accept the job nevertheless? Why?

chapter

27

ARBITRATION OF DISPUTES

27.1 FUNCTION OF ARBITRATION

The engineer or architect is frequently empowered to settle disputes between the contractor and the owner, especially regarding disputes concerning contractor's performance arising from the quality of the materials used or the interpretation of the plans and specifications. The AIA's standard form governing general conditions of the contract for construction provides that "claims shall be referred initially to the architect for action." A claim is defined as "a demand or assertion by one of the parties seeking . . . adjustment or interpretation of contract terms, payment of money, extension of time or other relief with respect to the terms of the contract." Claims also encompass other "disputes and matters in question between the owner and contractor arising out of or relating to the contract," including those alleging an error by the architect. Thus, arbitration is also frequent, where the contract so provides, when the dispute is between the owner and the architect or engineer.

Disputes between the contractor and the owner that cannot be settled satisfactorily by the engineer or architect should be resolved, if possible, without resort to litigation. One method of accomplishing this is an agreement to submit claims and disputes to arbitration. Consistent with this, the procedure for dispute resolution recommended by the AIA provides that if other party is dissatisfied with a decision made by the architect (or if the architect fails to render a decision within 45 days of a claim being made), arbitration may be demanded. The stipulation for and description of this procedure are properly a part of the contract documents.

27.2 DEFINITION OF ARBITRATION

Arbitration, or alternative dispute resolution, is the submission of a dispute to a disinterested person or persons for the final decision. Arbitration has been described as:[1]

| [1] *Barcon Associates, Inc. v. Tri-County Asphalt Corp.,* 430 A.2d 214, 86 N.J. 179 (1981).

A substitution, by consent of the parties, of another tribunal for the tribunal provided by ordinary process of law, and its object is the final disposition, in speedy, inexpensive, expeditious and perhaps less formal manner, of controversial differences between the parties.

Arbitration can attain its goal of providing final, speedy and inexpensive settlement of disputes only if judicial interference with process is minimized; it is, after all, meant to be a substitute for and not springboard for litigation.

Notice that arbitration is an extrajudicial determination of a controversy. Its purpose is to avert court action by either party. However, litigation also often arises where a dispute arises over the applicability or meaning of the arbitration clause itself, and in some situations only a part of the dispute may be within the arbitration agreement. Arbitration is a summary, businesslike, and relatively inexpensive method of settling disputes. The decision, however, may involve large sums of money, and the outcome of the proceedings is thus of great importance to the parties. The chance of having an arbitration award overturned by the legal system is highly unlikely. Arbitration is generally favored by the courts, which will only overturn an award on carefully circumscribed grounds. When arbitration has arisen due to an arbitration clause in an agreement, "there is a presumption of arbitrability that may only be overcome by 'forceful evidence' of an intent to exclude the claim."[2] In essence, an arbitration award is as binding as the ruling of a court.

27.3   DISTINCTIONS

Miscellaneous arrangements that leave to third parties the making of decisions that may be necessary regarding prices, values, quantities, qualities, and amounts are not really submissions to arbitration, and such third persons are not properly called "arbitrators." *Appraisement* is often confused with arbitration. Arbitration presupposes a controversy and is designed to resolve it, whereas appraisement is a stipulated procedure to prevent future disputes and to set a value, a price, or the like.[3] Arbitration is a quasi-judicial procedure usually involving a hearing, whereas appraisement generally implies decisions by a third-party expert upon the basis of his own knowledge and investigation without necessity of formal hearings.

A *referee* differs from an arbitrator in that a referee is appointed by a court as its officer and acts under its direction. An arbitrator is selected by the disputants. If the parties are not willing or able to appoint an arbitrator when time comes to do so, a court can make the appointment, but such an appointment is based upon prior agreement of the parties to arbitrate.

[2]*Steelworkers v. Warrior & Gulf Navigation Co.*, 363 U.S. 574, 582–83
[3]As it was put in *Sanitary Farm Dairies v. Gammel*, 195 F.2d 106, 113 (8th Cir. 1952): "In general, where parties to a contract, before a dispute and in order to avoid one, provide for a method of ascertaining the value of something related to their dealings, the provision is one for an appraisement and not for an arbitration." See also, *Bailey v. Tempore*, 75 Ill.2d 539 (1979), where it was said that the Uniform Arbitration Act is not directly applicable where a lease calls for an appraisement by an arbitrator.

27.4 THE DEMAND OR SUBMISSION

Most matters are brought to arbitration as a result of the parties having agreed in advance by inserting an arbitration clause in their contract. Such an agreement is commonly enforced under federal or state laws. Where there is an agreement, the moving party may file a *demand* or otherwise initiate the proceeding in accordance with the specific terms of the contract. In other cases, it will be necessary for the parties to execute a *submission* to arbitrate after the dispute arises. The agreement to submit should cover everything that is necessary to give the arbitrators the power to make a binding determination.

It is customary in agreements to arbitrate as contained in construction contracts, or in connection with existing contract disputes, to refer to the *Construction Industry Arbitration Rules* of the American Arbitration Association (AAA).

27.5 RESORT TO ARBITRATION

Arbitration may be resorted to even while work under the contract is progressing. Utilization of this medium avoids both the costs of litigation and the delays resulting from crowded court dockets. Because it can proceed with relative speed, the arbitration procedure is especially beneficial if the dispute is such that it has caused or may cause performance under the contract to be suspended pending a settlement. In that situation, the arbitrator should be authorized to direct that work under the contract is to continue during the arbitration process if such an order is in the best interest of the project.

It is quite possible that arbitration will be needed to settle disagreements that materialize after performance of some portion of the work but prior to final winding up of accounts. It may also happen that disputes arising during construction are held to be resolved subsequently. For example, a contractor was making a large excavation strictly accordingly to the plans. One side of the cut caved in and caused serious settlement of some adjoining construction. The engineer and the contractor agreed that the latter should take immediate remedial steps to save the structure, keeping account of all expenses involved. They agreed that the question of responsibility for the failure and thus the question of which side must assume the cost was to be settled by arbitration later on.

Even though a contract does not require arbitration the parties can nevertheless agree to settle questions in this manner. In other words, they can submit the questions to arbitration even though such action is not mentioned in the contract. The law does not, however, provide for arbitration where the parties have not agreed to it.[4]

---

[4]See *Kline v. Oak Ridge Builders, Inc.*, 656 N.E.2d 992 (Ohio App. 1995), a case involving a contract for construction of a private dwelling where the owner and construction corporation had agreed to arbitrate, but the corporation's proprietors, in their individual capacities, had not.

The arbitrator customarily resolves disputes involving such matters as (1) what is or is not included in the contract, (2) the proper interpretation of drawings and specifications, (3) the extent of monetary adjustment for mistakes made and poor workmanship performed by the contractor, (4) claims for liquidated damages, (5) determination of the computed quantities to which the bid unit prices are to be applied, (6) claims for delays, and (7) extras and allowances.

The American Arbitration Association maintains a variety of arbitration rules for the conduct of such proceedings. The *Construction Industry Arbitration Rules* are uniquely applicable to disputes of an engineering nature. The association does not itself act as an arbitrator, nor does it give legal advice. However, for a specified fee it will handle the entire administration of the case: (1) preparing a list of persons considered to be competent to act as arbitrators in the type of situation involved; (2) furnishing rules for the guidance of the arbitrators; (3) appointing an arbitrator or arbitrators, if this is desired; and (4) assisting in various administrative capacities. If the parties elect to conduct the arbitration under these rules, both sides are bound thereby throughout the proceedings.

The association suggests that, if a construction contract is to require arbitration under AAA rules, the following clause should be inserted in such contract:

Standard Arbitration Clause:

Any controversy or claim arising out of or relating to this contract, or breach thereof, shall be settled by arbitration in accordance with the Construction Industry Arbitration Rules of the American Arbitration Association, and judgment upon the award rendered by the Arbitrator(s) may be entered in any Court having jurisdiction thereof.

Not all arbitration clauses use such expansive language, and while the law encourages arbitration, it is a creature of contract, and thus the words used are generally controlling.

Some courts have found that the standard arbitration clause language is sufficiently broad to include a dispute framed as a tort.[5] Others have concluded that while language such as "because of the wrongful act or neglect of the other party" is sufficient to encompass tort claims, that "arising out of or relating to the agreement or its breach" is not.[6]

Efforts have been made to educate people to the advantage of arbitration so that disputants will resort to this device in lieu of bringing suit. As a result, the federal government and most states have passed legislation designed to facilitate enforcement of arbitration clauses in contracts and to provide judicial support for the arbitration process. By way of illustration, consider the United States Arbitra-

---

[5]*Southern Oklahoma Health Care Corp. v. JHBR-Jones-Hester-Bates-Riek, Inc.,* 900 P.2d 1017 (Okla. App. 1995), involving a claim of unprofessional services by an architectural firm in a hospital renovation.
[6]*Hazelton Area School Dist. v. Bosak,* 671 A.2d 277 (Pa. Comm. 1996), where a school district sued an architect and engineer when the roof of a new school collapsed.

tion Act of 1925, as amended.[7] Key provisions of the act were characterized by the Supreme Court[8] in this fashion:

> Section 2 provides that a written provision for arbitration "in any maritime trans-action or a contract evidencing a transaction involving commerce . . . shall be valid, irrevocable, and enforceable, save upon such grounds as exists at law or in equity for the revocation of any contract." Section 3 requires a federal court in which suit has been brought "upon any issue referable to arbitration under an agreement in writing for such arbitration" to stay the court action pending arbitration once it is satisfied that the issue is arbitrable under the agreement. Section 4 provides a federal remedy for a party "aggrieved by the alleged failure, neglect, or refusal of another to arbitrate under a written agreement for arbitration," and directs the federal court to order arbitration once it is satisfied that an agreement for arbitration has been made and has not been honored.

Among the other important provisions of the said act is Section 9 which says, in part:

> If the parties in their agreement have agreed that a judgment of the court shall be entered upon the award made pursuant to the arbitration, and shall specify the court, then at any time within one year after the award is made any party to the arbitration may apply to the court so specified for an order confirming the award, and thereupon the court must grant such an order unless the award is vacated, modified, or corrected as prescribed in sections 10 and 11 of this title. If no court is specified in the agreement of the parties, then such application may be made to the United States court in and for the district within which such award was made.

Section 10 permits a federal court to vacate an award in cases

1. Where the award was procured by corruption, fraud, or undue means.

2. Where there was evident partiality or corruption in the arbitrators, or either of them.

3. Where the arbitrators were guilty of misconduct in refusing to postpone the hearing, upon sufficient cause shown, or in refusing to hear evidence pertinent and material to the controversy; or of any other misbehavior by which the rights of any party have been prejudiced.

4. Where the arbitrators exceeded their powers, or so imperfectly executed them that a mutual, final, and definite award upon the subject matter submitted was not made.

5. Where an award is vacated and the time within which the agreement required the award to be made has not expired the court may, in its discretion, direct a rehearing by the arbitrators.

In a similar vein, Section 11 lists instances in which an award may properly be modified or corrected, as for example "where there was an evident material mis-calculation of figures."

---

[7] 9 U.S.C. §§ 1–14 (1990) as amended. "This legislation overruled longstanding judicial precedents which had refused to enforce agreements to submit justiciable controversies to arbitration on the grounds that they were contrary to public policy." *National R.R. Passenger Corp. v. Missouri Pacific R.R. Co.*, 501 F.2d 423, 426 (8th Cir. 1974).

[8] *Prima Paint Corp. v. Flood and Conklin*, 388 U.S. 395, 400 (1967), followed by *Hydrick v. Mgmt. Recruiters Int'l*, 738 F. Supp. 1434 (ND Ga.1990).

The United States Arbitration Act represents an exercise of the authority constitutionally delegated to Congress to regulate interstate commerce and maritime transactions. In enacting such legislation Congress was providing for those engaged in interstate transactions an expeditious extrajudicial process for settling disputes—a process that contracting parties can avoid entirely by merely refraining from including arbitration provisions in their agreements. A representative decision interpreting the act and a given arbitration provision is *Metro Industrial Painting Corp. v. Terminal Construction Co.*[9] The court held that the particular disputes that had arisen between the parties were appropriate for arbitration under a contract clause that required submission to arbitration of "any question with respect to performance, non-performance, default, compliance or non-compliance, whether on behalf of the Contractor or Subcontractor." The opinion concluded in these words:

> The grievance asserted by petitioners is that respondents failed to meet time schedules, insisted upon performance of duties not required of petitioners under the contract and failed to supply materials for petitioners. In view of the federal policy to construe liberally arbitration clauses, to find that they cover disputes reasonably contemplated by this language, and to resolve doubts in favor of arbitration . . . it is clear that these disputes can reasonably be said to fall within the category of compliance or non-compliance.

27.6   Disputes Subject to Arbitration

A great many matters or types of disputes are regarded as proper for settlement by arbitration. Issues submitted can be both factual and legal. As in virtually all matters of contract, the language of the agreement is the key, and the parties may limit the scope of the disputes subject to the arbitrator's authority.

This point is illustrated by two cases involving arbitration of liens. In *McCarney v. Wearing, Staats,* [10] where an owner sued an architect for negligence and the contractor sued the owner for money allegedly owed, an arbitration clause that covered "any controversy or claim" was held broad enough to cover a claim arising from the waiver of a mechanic's lien.

But the court in *Insignia Homes, Inc. v. Hinden*,[11] found an arbitration provision to specifically exclude from arbitration claims of liens by a contractor. Of course, illegal transactions cannot be the subject of arbitration because such transactions are not enforceable, and a "fine print" clause coupled with irregularity of bargaining power may result in an unenforceable contract of arbitration.[12]

---

[9] 287 F.2d 382 (2d Cir. 1961). *cert. denied* 368 U.S. 817. See also, *American Home Assurance Co. v. Vecco Concrete Construction Co.,* 629 F.2d 961 (4th Cir. 1980), where the contract stated that "If any question of fact shall arise under this contract . . . then either party hereto may demand an arbitration by reference to a Board of Arbitration."

[10] 866 S.W.2d 881 (Mo. App. 1993).

[11] 675 So.2d 673 (Fla. App. 1996), J. Sharp concurring.

[12] *U.S. Home Corp. v. Seifert,* 699 So.2d 787 (Fla. App. 1997).

27.7 SCOPE OF ARBITRATOR'S AUTHORITY

A question of the authority of the arbitrators can be decided by those individuals themselves or by a court. An effort will be made to give effect to the intent of the parties. A liberal interpretation of the extent of the arbitrators' powers is usually made by the courts, but any matter not included in the submission cannot properly be settled by the arbitrators.

27.8 REFERENCE TO COURTS

If the contracting parties have agreed that certain disputes, should they arise, will be submitted to arbitration, the United States Arbitration Act and other modern arbitration statutes provide for enforcement of the agreement to arbitrate. For example, the New York Arbitration Law provides: "A party aggrieved by the failure of another to arbitrate may apply for an order compelling arbitration."[13] This is a typical statute requiring courts to enforce an obligation to arbitrate and thereby making the arbitration clause a meaningful part of the contract.

Modern arbitration laws give the courts power to enforce arbitration agreements and to exercise supervision of the process. For example, if the agreement fails to designate a method for selecting the arbitrator, either party has the right to apply to a court for a designation. However, the *Construction Industry Arbitration Rules* of the American Arbitration Association, referred to in many of the form contracts used in the construction industry, provide a self-contained arbitration procedure so that ordinarily it is not necessary to resort to the courts for procedural matters. This reduces the cost and delay for the parties involved.

Where an owner, has, for example, an arbitration clause in a contract for the purchase of a new home with an insurance backed warranty, it has been held that arbitration and litigation are mutually exclusive. Thus, a buyer may submit a claim to arbitration or litigation, but not both.[14]

If there is not a bona fide agreement to arbitrate, it is possible under modern arbitration legislation to apply to the courts to stay an arbitration.[15] For example, in *S&M Constructors, Inc., v. Foley Company*,[16] a subcontractor on a government project petitioned the court to stop arbitration proceedings, claiming that the parties intended the Contract Disputes Act to precede arbitration. However, a federal appellate court would not even stay the proceedings pending the subcontractor's appeal because the court thought it unlikely the subcontractor would succeed on the merits of his claim.

---

[13]Art. 75, New York Civil Practice Law and Rules, § 7503(a) (McKinney 1980).

[14]*Marchak v. Claridge Commons, Inc.*, 633 A.2d 531 (N.J. 1993).

[15]See, for example, § 7503(b), New York Civil Practice Law and Rules (McKinney 1980).

[16]959 F.2d 97 (8th Cir. 1992).

27.9   ROLE AND QUALIFICATIONS OF AN ARBITRATOR

An *arbitrator* may be defined as a private judge chosen by the parties and endowed by them with power to decide a matter in dispute.

Any disinterested person may act as an arbitrator unless he lacks qualifications prescribed in the agreement or in some applicable statute. He must be impartial and nonpartisan, and he must not be financially interested in the dispute. He should also be knowledgeable with respect to the general subject matter involved. Engineers, architects, and contractors are, by the nature of their work, in a good position to arbitrate disputes arising from construction contracts, other than those with which they have some connection.

27.10   SELECTION OF AN ARBITRATOR

Ordinarily, when arbitration is provided for, the contract will specify the procedure for selecting the arbitrator or arbitrators.

Perhaps the most common arrangement is to refer the matter to the American Arbitration Association so that administration can proceed under the *Construction Industry Arbitration Rules.* A list of experts in the industry will then be sent to the parties for their consideration so that arbitrators agreeable to both sides can be appointed. The AAA then handles the details of the arbitration process.

A less desirable procedure is for the owner to select one arbitrator, the contractor to choose another, and the two arbitrators to select a third. This system is cumbersome and leads to an occasional impasse in selection of the third arbitrator.

Where three arbitrators are deemed desirable, it is preferable that each arbitrator be entirely impartial. By mutually selecting the arbitrators from a list prepared by an outside agency, the parties can obtain such a panel. Where three neutral arbitrators hear a case, one of them is ordinarily designated as the chairman and may rule on minor procedural matters. Otherwise, a majority decision is necessary unless the arbitration agreement requires unanimity.

27.11   PROCEDURE IN ARBITRATION

If the arbitration agreement stipulates certain rules that are to govern the process, such rules must be followed. Otherwise, the arbitrators have considerable latitude in their procedure. For instance, they need not follow technical rules of evidence, but proceedings must nevertheless be conducted with honesty and fairness. The arbitrators should hold a hearing within a reasonable time after their appointment and can utilize statutory subpoena power to compel the attendance of witnesses.

Both parties have the right to be notified of any pending hearing and to present evidence. In the usual situation, an award made without a full and proper hearing may be invalid unless the losing party waived his right to be heard or refused to attend. There may be some cases in which the arbitrators are appointed as experts and specifically authorized to decide the dispute upon the basis of their own knowledge, dispensing with testimony of outsiders.

The subject matter and scope of the dispute to be resolved should be made entirely clear to the arbitrators. Their function is to settle the question at issue completely, but their decision should not go to the extent of covering matters beyond the range of the submission.

When a hearing is held before the arbitrators, it is customary for representatives of both contesting parties to present evidence somewhat as though it were a court proceeding. In major cases the lawyers on either side will conduct the presentation of the evidence. Engineers normally act as expert witnesses in the course of the arbitration, and they may help in the preparation of facts and figures to substantiate whatever point of view they represent in the argument. Direct examination and cross-examination of witnesses may take place. The arbitrators will play the role of judges in determining whether evidence is or is not relevant and admissible. There may be no fixed procedure for the presentation of evidence and arguments by the opposing parties. Normally, the entire affair is relatively informal. Each side should conduct itself in a dignified manner and each will try to present its case in as favorable a light as possible. The arbitrators are supposed to be given all available data. They may ask for additional material from either or both parties if they think the information offered is inadequate to enable them to determine the matter. When a decision is rendered, it will be final, unless fraud or some other element is present that would support a contention that the award should be vacated or modified.

27.12 THE AWARD

An *award* is the decision or judgment made by the arbitrators. Unless abandoned by both parties, it supersedes any claims that were submitted for arbitration.

An award will usually stand up in a court of law if it represents the honest judgment of the arbitrators. The latter must have acted fairly, reasonably, and within any time limit on their powers. The award must cover every point included in the submission and should fix responsibility for the costs of the arbitration unless the handling of such costs has been the subject of an arrangement between the respective parties.

An award should be complete and definite, thus leaving no room for future doubt or confusion on the points involved. Even though an award may seem excessive, the courts are generally reluctant to invalidate it absent clear indication that the arbitrators exceeded their authority or were guilty of some impropriety. A valid award, made pursuant to a prior agreement to submit to arbitration, can be enforced through the judicial process.

The arbitrators are to reach their decision on the basis of their judgment as to what constitutes a proper and fair conclusion, considering all the data available to them. They need not explain to the parties exactly how or why they arrived at a given determination, though they may wish to do so at the mutual request of the parties.

27.13 ALLOCATION OF COSTS OF ARBITRATION

Arbitrators upon occasion serve without compensation, or they may be paid a reasonable sum. Sometimes the amount of compensation is stated in the agreement to arbitrate. *The Construction Industry Arbitration Rules* authorize the AAA to fix an appropriate daily rate and to outline other arrangements for submission to the parties at the outset. The rate of compensation should be fair and adequate in the light of the service rendered. If there are several arbitrators, they should generally be compensated equally.

Unless the contract clarifies the matter, a question may arise about who pays the cost of arbitration proceedings. If the owner is obligated by the contract to pay the arbitration bills, the contractor could cause him considerable expense by insisting upon submitting some petty issue at every opportunity. Dividing the expense of arbitration equally between the owner and the contractor may help to prevent needless resort to arbitration by either party. It is often desirable to empower the arbitrators, as a part of their decision, to allocate costs; they can then in appropriate cases "penalize" a party who has been unreasonable in bringing to arbitration a minor issue that should have been settled amicably without the intervention of outsiders.

27.14 MEDIATION

Related to arbitration is the method of alternative dispute resolution known as mediation. Mediation is a type of assisted negotiation that differs from arbitration in that the ultimate decision-making power remains with the parties, and it is the mediator's task not to resolve the issue for the parties but to help them find their own solution. While an arbitrator acts rather like a judge in that he or she decides the case on the facts and arguments presented by the parties, the mediator may offer creative recommendations in the mediation process.

When the parties to a dispute have a good-faith desire to resolve their differences, mediation may offer significant advantages, not the least of which is a quicker and less costly proceeding. Mediation may also be appropriate where the parties have a desire to preserve the working relationship they enjoy and to ensure continued performance while the dispute is settled.

Mediation is usually voluntary and may be the result of agreement between the parties after a problem has arisen, or it may be written into the contract that gives rise to the party's relationship. Construction and enforceability of a mediation clause or agreement are governed by the general law of contracts. In some states mediation in particular circumstances may be mandated by statute.[17] In federal civil litigation the courts are authorized to "take appropriate action with respect to settlement and the use of special procedures to assist in resolving the dispute when authorized by statute or local rule."[18]

If a mediation effort is successful in resolving a dispute, the mediated agreement itself is enforceable under the rules of contract law and may not be enforced if an essential element of a contract is missing; the agreement is subject to the usual contract law defenses such as lack of consideration or capacity.

QUESTIONS

1. What is arbitration? What is its purpose?

2. Is an agreement to arbitrate necessarily a part of a contract? If such an agreement is part of a contract, can this bind the parties to submit a future dispute to arbitration before the difference arises? Why might this be desirable?

3. Can an agreement to arbitrate be made after a contract is in operation? How?

4. Does an agreement to arbitrate preclude subsequent resort to court proceedings?

5. What is the difference between (a) arbitration and appraisement? (b) an arbitrator and a referee?

6. What is a "submission" and what does it constitute?

7. Can an agreement to arbitrate be revoked or waived? Can these things be done if the agreement is a part of the signed contract?

8. Who may decide whether a dispute is to be heard by one or by more than one arbitrator?

9. How are arbitrators generally chosen?

10. Can arbitration be resorted to only after completion of a contract? Why?

11. What is the American Arbitration Association, and what are its purposes and functions?

12. What is an "award"? How is an award arrived at?

13. Must the reasons for the magnitude and nature of the award be publicized? Why?

14. Will an arbitration award be likely to have any effect in subsequent litigation? Why?

15. From whom do arbitrators get their authority to make an award?

---

[17]See for example, Calif. Fam. Code § 3170 *et seq.*, mandating mediation in child custody and visitation disputes.

[18]Federal Rule of Civil Procedure 16(c)(9). The Advisory Committee comment to this rule specifically includes mediation. A federal court may also have inherent powers to compel parties to participate in a settlement conference, although it may not force a party to agree to a settlement. See *G. Heileman Brewing Co. v. Joseph Oat Corp.*, 871 F.2d 648 (7th Cir. 1989).

16. Does the submission indicate intended compliance with the future award?

17. What information should an arbitration agreement contain?

18. Is it customary to name the membership of a board of arbitration before a contract is started? Why?

19. Does arbitration have to proceed immediately after a dispute arises? Why?

20. Should the contract or agreement to arbitrate specify the allocation of costs for arbitration?

21. A dispute arose between Black, the owner, and Brown, the contractor, over the interpretation of a clause in the specifications. Is this a suitable subject for arbitration? Why?

22. A contract contained a clause requiring arbitration of disputes. During progress of the work, a serious fire occurred. The owner and contractor could not agree upon the size of, and responsibility for, the resultant damages; therefore the owner brought suit against the contractor. Is this proper procedure? Will the court be likely to hear the case?

23. Jones, the contractor, claimed $10,000 compensation from Smith, the owner, because of extra work done under the contract. There was no arbitration clause in the contract. Jones demanded that the dispute be submitted to arbitration. Smith refused. Can Jones force Smith to arbitrate? Why?

24. According to the terms of a certain contract, one member of a board of arbitration is to be selected by the owner, one by the contractor, and one by these two appointees. Is this better than having one person as the sole arbitrator? Explain.

25. What assistance can be rendered by the American Arbitration Association? Will it, as an organization, arbitrate disputes?

26. How does mediation differ from arbitration? What advantages does mediation offer?

28

FEDERAL LAW OF IMPORTANCE TO DESIGN PROFESSIONALS

28.1   INTRODUCTION

The expansion of federal law, both in areas of traditional federal concern and into new areas, has been dramatic and unprecedented in recent years. The largely federal law of intellectual property was considered in Chapter 24, and there are literally hundreds of other federal laws that may impact the work of design professionals. This chapter will offer an introduction to the sources and nature of federal law and then a brief look at several federal laws of particular significance. It should be remembered that these statutes and the interpretations placed on them are quite extensive and generalizations are difficult. Also, federal statutes and regulations are subject to modification, and any reference to them must be updated frequently.

28.2   SOURCES OF FEDERAL LAW

The overwhelming majority of federal law is in the form of federal statutes. While these statutes are the subject of court interpretation, there is little if any federal common, or court-made, law in the way that it exists at the state level.

Federal statutes, the products of Congress, must find as their basis a power enumerated in the Constitution of the United States. In other words, Congress does not have a generalized authority to pass laws but must rely on some provision of the Constitution that authorizes it to act. Article 1, §8 of the Constitution lists eighteen specific "powers," or areas, in which Congress may act.[1] By far the most significant today is the power "to regulate commerce with foreign nations, and among the several *states,* and with the Indian Tribes. . . . " This language is commonly referred to as the "Commerce Clause." This clause, which was intended to empower Congress to remedy attempts by the states to set up barriers to commerce that might slow the

---

| [1]Other sources of congressional authority also may be found in various places within the Constitution.

integration of the country into a coherent economic unit, was given a rather narrow construction until the Great Depression of the 1930s. However, in 1937, the Supreme Court of the United States, under considerable pressure for invalidating much of the "New Deal" legislation, reversed its course. In a rapid series of decisions, the court reached the conclusion that Congress's power to regulate interstate commerce extended to the regulation of anything, commerce or not, that, either by itself or in combination with other factors, might *substantially affect* commerce (i.e., in a nontrivial way).[2] With this as the test, Congress's authority to legislate under the Commerce Clause was subject to few limits except those of the political process, and the specific limitations that the constitution may impose.[3] However, it appears that the Supreme Court may be starting to limit Congress's Commerce Clause power. In 1995, in the landmark case of *U.S. v. Lopez*[4], the Court for the first time in decades held that a piece of legislation exceeded Congress's commerce clause authority. The court found the Gun Free School Zones Act, which made possession of a firearm in a school zone a federal offense, was not a regulation of economic activity that "substantially affected" interstate commerce.

| **28.3** LIMITATIONS ON FEDERAL POWER

Limits on the powers of Congress are sometimes characterized as internal or external. If the source of the power, for example, is the Commerce Clause, and the Court ruled that the activity regulated was not commerce, or not interstate, as the Court did in *U.S. v. Lopez,* the statute would be said to have run afoul of an internal (to the power's source) limit. Given the very pliable construction placed on the language and meaning of the commerce clause since 1937, internal limits on it are not easy to identify.

This is not to say, however, that Congress is free to do what it will, since the Constitution itself sets up some barriers to Congressional excess. These external (to the power's source) barriers may be illustrated by a simple example. Suppose Congress passes a statute that forbids the interstate transportation of newspapers. By virtually any definition, such a statute would fall within the scope of interstate commerce and would thus be constitutional if no reference to external limits is made.

---

[2]The case that opened the door was *N.L.R.B. v. Jones & Laughlin Steel Corp.*, 301 U.S. 1 (1937). By 1942 the Court had approved federal regulation, under the Commerce Clause, of a market quota of wheat assigned to a single farmer who grew a small amount, primarily for consumption on his own farm. *Wickard v. Filburn*, 317 U.S. 111 (1942).

[3]For a recent example of the use of the Commerce Clause to justify legislation that is not a regulation of interstate commerce in the ordinary sense, note the following language of the Americans with Disabilities Act (29 U.S.C. § 651, *infra*):
29 U.S.C. § 651. Congressional statement of findings and declaration of purpose and policy.
(a) The Congress finds that personal injuries and illnesses arising out of work situations impose a substantial burden upon, and are a hindrance to, interstate commerce in terms of lost production, wage loss, medical expenses and disability compensation payments.
(b) The Congress declares it to be its purpose and policy, through the exercise of its powers to regulate commerce among the several States and with foreign nations and to provide for the general welfare, to assure so far as possible every working man and woman in the Nation safe and healthful working conditions and to preserve our human resources—.

[4]*U.S. v. Lopez,* 514 U.S. 549.

The First Amendment, however, says "Congress shall make no law . . . abridging the freedom of speech, or of the press." If this language is held to apply in this situation then Congress will be restrained by this external limit on its power.[5]

Likewise, the Supreme Court has ruled on two recent occasions that Congress, acting pursuant to the Commerce Clause, may not order state legislatures or officials to take regulatory action, thus deflecting from itself any negative political consequences.[6]

28.4 FEDERAL STATUTES AND REGULATIONS

When a statute is passed by Congress and signed into law by the President, or becomes law when a presidential veto is overridden, it is assigned a public law number, such as PL 102-10. This, for example would mean that this is law number 10 of the 102nd Congress. The various public laws are then placed in one of the 50 titles of the United States Code, which is organized by subject matter.

Federal statutes often authorize or require that one of the government's administrative agencies or cabinet-level departments issue regulations detailing how the statute is to be complied with and setting forth the requirements in considerable detail. These regulations, which have the force of law, are published in the Federal Register as they are issued and are then codified in the Code of Federal Regulations. Like the U.S. Code, the C.F.R. is divided into titles by subject matter.

28.5 RELATIONSHIP TO STATE LAW

The Constitution of the United States proclaims in Article VI, Section 2 that "This Constitution, and the Laws of the United States which shall be made in Pursuance thereof; and all Treaties made, or which shall be made under the Authority of the United States, shall be the supreme Law of the Land; and Judges in every State shall be bound thereby, any thing in the Constitution or Laws of any State to the Contrary notwithstanding."

Thus, a constitutional federal statute supersedes contrary state law.[7] If Congress, in a federal statute, states that it intends it to be the sole law on the subject,

---

[5]It should not be assumed that even apparently unequivocal language, such as "no law," means what it says. Defamation and pornography, for example, are not protected speech and Congress's regulation of them under the Commerce Clause would not likely run afoul of First Amendment limits.

[6]*New York v. U.S.*, 505 U.S. 144 (1992), in which the Supreme Court rejected legislation declaring that a state that fails to provide for the disposal of all internally generated low-level radioactive waste must take title to and possession of it and become liable for damages suffered by the generator as a result of the state's failure to promptly take possession of it; and *Printz v. U.S.*, 117 S.Ct. 2365 (1997) where the Brady Handgun Violence Protection Act commanded *local* law enforcement officers to conduct background checks on prospective handgun purchasers.

[7]It should be remembered that in most cases the Constitution authorizes, but does not mandate, federal action. Likewise, a grant of power to the Congress usually does not specifically forbid the states from acting in the same area.

the federal law is said to "preempt" the state law. The situation becomes less clear, however, when the federal law is silent on the preemption issue. One might think that a silence on the subject indicates an intention by Congress not to preempt the states, but a preemptive intent is sometimes found to have been manifested by the particularly federal nature of the problem, such as immigration, or by the fact that the federal scheme is so pervasive that a court finds that Congress must have intended to preempt the field.

A different problem arises where Congress has the power to act, but has not done so. Occasionally, a state statute is held to violate this "dormant" power even though the grant of power says nothing about precluding state action. A recurring example of this problem involves the validity of state laws that regulate the length of truck trailers, or that ban double or triple trailers. If Congress were so inclined, it could doubtless regulate this matter pursuant to its power to regulate interstate commerce. Since it has not done so, the question becomes whether the mere existence of the power to do so, unused, limits the authority of the states.

In the case of *Kassel v. Consolidated Freightways Corp.*,[8] for example, a divided Supreme Court of the United States invalidated an Iowa law that prohibited 65-foot double trailers, on the grounds that it unconstitutionally burdened interstate commerce. Among the factors to be examined in such cases are the degree of the burden, any discrimination against the products of other states, and the significance of the interest the state is attempting to protect.[9]

Labor Law

28.6   Introduction

The field of labor law is an extremely complicated one and includes a wide variety of topics that define or influence the employer–employee relationship. Unions, collective bargaining, unfair labor practices, wage–hour problems, and labor disputes are all components. A complete treatment of this subject would require many volumes.

The present labor law has developed from the host of legislative and administrative schemes and years of experience. In the future, it may be subject to many changes caused by the operation of political and economic forces.

The basic statutory matrix of labor law is formed by the Labor Management Relations Act of 1947,[10] which includes as its subchapter II the National Labor Relations Act (NLRA) of 1935.[11] The purpose of the National Labor Relations Act

---

[8]450 U.S. 662 (1981).

[9]See also *City of Philadelphia v. New Jersey*, 437 U.S. 617 (1978) where similar logic was used to invalidate a New Jersey statute that prohibited the importation of solid or liquid waste that originated or was collected outside the state.

Likewise, state statutes attempting to protect local producers of products such as milk and apples from out-of-state competition are often invalidated. *Baldwin v. G.A.F. Seelig, Inc.*, 294 U.S. 511 (1935); *H. P. Hood & Sons v. DuMond*, 336 U.S. 525 (1949), milk; *Hunt v. Washington State Apple Advertising Commission*, 432 U.S. 333 (1977), apples.

[10]29 U.S.C. 141.

[11]29 U.S.C. 167.

is to protect interstate commerce[12] by guaranteeing rights to organize, to bargain collectively through chosen representatives, and to engage in concerted activities such as strikes. The act is also intended to promote fair settlement of disputes by peaceful procedures, and to place unions and employers in an equal position in bargaining and labor relations matters. The Labor Management Relations Act has been held to be a proper exercise of congressional authority under the Commerce Clause of the United States Constitution, since labor disputes in industries involved in interstate commerce so burden such commerce as to bring labor matters within the power of Congress.

Managerial and supervisory employees are excluded from NLRA coverage and are not protected employees. Engineers engaged in installing, repairing, or servicing equipment manufactured by the employer, and engineers assigned to technical supervision projects have been held not to be protected employees.[13] Supervisory status has been accorded a field engineer who was the sole person on the job site with authority to act for the employer, and to one in charge of an engineering department with authority to hire and fire.[14]

Architects may be supervisors or administrators where they check and correct the work of draftsmen.[15]

But engineers are not supervisors where they give technical advice to their employer's customers who are themselves supervised by their own foremen.[16]

28.7 LABOR ORGANIZATIONS

A labor union is an employee's organization designed to further the interest of its members with respect to matters such as wages, working conditions, and seniority rights, and to organize unified and concerted action to accomplish those goals.

The right of employees to organize is a fundamental one expressly protected by the National Labor Relations Act. It should be noted, however, that the right of organization granted by the NLRA is a right of employees, not a right of unions or employers.

The representatives selected for the purpose of collective bargaining by a majority of employees must, under the Labor Management Relations Act, be the exclusive representatives of all employees in the unit. But the "right to work" provisions state that the act does not authorize enforcement of any agreement mandating membership in a labor union as a condition of employment if state law prohibits such agreements. This provision, amended by section 14(B) of the Taft-Hartley Act, is subject to periodic legislative and political attack.

---

[12]Interstate commerce within the contemplation of federal labor relations laws may include building construction and activities. In *Plumbers, Steamfitters, R.P.F. and A. v. County of Door*, 359 U.S. 354 (1958), a labor dispute at a $450,000 building project, approximately half of which was the cost of materials brought from outside the state, was held to have a sufficient effect on commerce to be within the jurisdiction of the National Labor Relations Board.

[13]*Westinghouse Electric Corp.*, (1967) 163 NLRB 723.

[14]*Warren Rural Electric Co-op, Inc.*, (1974) 209 NLRB 325; American Steel Buck Corp. (1953) 107 NLRB 554.

[15]*Laudadio v. White Const. Co.*, 163 F.2d 383 (2nd Cir., 1947).

[16]*Westinghouse Electric Corp. v. NLRB*, 424 S.2d 1151 (7th Cir., 1970).

28.8   THE NATIONAL LABOR RELATIONS BOARD

The National Labor Relations Board (NLRB) has exclusive jurisdiction over proceedings under the Labor Management Relations Act. The five members of the NLRB are appointed by the President, upon consent of the Senate, for five-year terms. One member is appointed by the President to serve as chairman.

The NLRB serves two basic functions: prosecution and adjudication of unfair labor practices cases. The prosecution staff is administered by the NLRB General Counsel, appointed for a four-year term by the President, upon consent of the Senate.

The prosecution of unfair labor practices cannot be instigated by the NLRB until some private organization makes a complaint. The filing of the complaint triggers the NLRB investigation, and the charge may be withdrawn only with the consent of the NLRB Regional Director with whom it was filed. If the investigation warrants further action, the NLRB or its agent may issue and serve a formal complaint on the alleged violator, stating the charges and giving notice of a hearing. The alleged violator has the right to file an answer to the complaint. In effect, an answer is mandatory because NLRB regulations state that, if no such answer is filed, the complaint is deemed true. The answer must address itself specifically to each allegation in the complaint.

Usually, prehearing conferences are held with the charged party, and the NLRB has authority to settle the dispute without the consent of the complaining party. Once the hearing is commenced, settlement is still a possibility. However, at this stage, a formal settlement is normally required, subject to NLRB approval and containing a court decree enforcing the order. At the hearing, testimony of witnesses may be presented either in person or, if necessity requires, by deposition. NLRB subpoena power may be invoked to facilitate the appearance of witnesses. The hearing is conducted by an administrative law judge, and the burden of proof rests on the NLRB General Counsel.

The decision of the administrative law judge is filed with the NLRB. If exceptions are filed, the NLRB may: 1) decide the case upon the record, 2) decide the case after oral argument, 3) reopen the case to receive further evidence, or 4) close the case, adopting the administrative law judge's recommendations.

The NLRB does not have the power to enforce its orders, but it may petition the appropriate United States Court of Appeals to act. The Court of Appeals is also the proper review body regarding the order.

28.9   FAIR LABOR STANDARDS

The regulation of hours and wages of employees engaged in commerce or the production of goods for commerce and the prohibition of oppressive child labor are the purposes of the Fair Labor Standards Act,[17] commonly referred to as the Wage and Hour Law. Thus, this Act specifies minimum wages and rules for overtime compensation.

| [17]29 U.S.C. §§ 201–219.

Under certain conditions, learners and apprentices, full-time students, handicapped workers, and administrative, professional, executive, and outside sales personnel are excluded from the minimum wage and/or the overtime pay provisions of the Fair Labor Standards Act. The wage and hour provisions of the Fair Labor Standards Act also do not apply to employees engaged in agriculture if certain conditions are met.

Employees protected by the act cannot relinquish that protection by contract with their employers, since the act's purpose is of public interest. The FLSA is administered by the Wage and Hour Division of the Department of Labor and the administrator of the Wage and Hour Division issues regulations that are used as guidelines to the meaning of the FLSA.

Independent contractors, as opposed to employees, are exempt from the FLSA. Architects are normally independent contractors in the preparation of detailed plans from original plans, the design of arrangements of various construction components, or preparation of schedules of bills of materials.[18]

28.10 UNFAIR LABOR PRACTICES

The topic of unfair labor practices is an immense one, and the following materials are intended only to serve as examples of the types of employer and union activity that may violate the unfair labor sections of the Labor Management Relations Act.

An employer commits an unfair labor practice when it interferes with or coerces employees in the exercise of their right to organize labor organizations and bargain collectively. The employer may not interfere with the rights of employees engaged in concerted activities such as strikes and may not dominate or interfere with formation of labor organizations or contribute financial or other support to it. It is also an unfair labor practice to encourage or discourage membership in a union by discrimination in hiring or tenure of employment, to discharge or discriminate against an employee because he has filed charges or given testimony under the Labor Management Relations Act, to refuse to bargain collectively and in good faith with the representatives of his employees, or to refuse to hire a job applicant because he once gave testimony against a former employer in an NLRB proceeding.

The First Amendment guarantee of freedom of speech is implemented by the Labor Management Relations Act in that it is not an unfair labor practice for an employer to make antiunion statements that do not contain threats of reprisal or force or promise of benefit. It is an unfair labor practice for an employer to announce employee benefits shortly before a representation election where the intent is to induce employees to vote against the union. In the case of an economic strike, an employer may communicate with striking employees and solicit them to return to work as long as no coercion or threats are included. An employer does commit an unfair labor practice by employing labor surveillance, photographing pickets for the purpose of interfering with picketing, banning the wearing of union insignias, and recognizing two or more rival unions where there is a legitimate ques-

---

| [18]*Dolan v. Day & Zimmerman, Inc.,* 65 F. Supp. 923 (D. Mass. 1946).

tion of representation. A plant or factory relocation hastened or motivated by antiunion sentiments is an unfair labor practice, but relocation for economic reasons such as lower plant rent, lower cost of operation, or a more stable labor force is not.

Labor unions may also be guilty of unfair labor practices. In general, the Labor Management Relations Act forbids union tactics involving violence, intimidation, and reprisals or threats thereof. Strikes and peaceful picketing are not unfair labor practices, but coercing a nonmember to join the union, either by physical assault or threats thereof, or threatening loss of employment are unfair labor practices, as is a union's acceptance of exclusive bargaining authority at times when it lacks the support of the majority of the employees. A union commits unfair labor practice when it coerces employees to strike by threats, but it is not an unfair labor practice for a union to fine a member for failing to perform picket line duty during a strike or to impose fines against members who cross a union picket line and work during an authorized economic strike against an employer.

As is the case with employers, it is an unfair labor practice for labor organizations to refuse to bargain collectively. A union also may not engage in a secondary boycott, which is union pressure directed at a neutral employer to induce him to cease doing business with another employer with whom the union is involved in a labor dispute.

28.11   OCCUPATIONAL HEALTH AND SAFETY

The Occupational Safety and Health Act of 1970[19] was enacted in an effort to provide the nation's workers, so far as possible, with safe and healthful working conditions. The Occupational Safety and Health Administration (OSHA) was created in 1971 to administer the act, which empowers the secretary of labor to issue mandatory health and safety standards designed to assure healthful and safe working conditions. These standards set forth in considerable detail requirements with respect to such industrial and occupational matters as hazardous materials, personal protective equipment, fire protection, and control of health and environmental conditions, including air contaminants, noise exposure, ventilation, and radiation.

One should note that OSHA regulations are not performance standards; that is, they do not set forth the goals to be met and leave the method of attaining the goals to the employer. Instead, the regulations set out in great detail how the job is to be done.

Appendix 1 at the end of the chapter contains OSHA regulations setting forth the general requirements for scaffolds.[20] In addition to the general requirements presented, there are fourteen pages of specific requirements for wood poll scaffolds, tube and coupler scaffolds, tubular welded frame scaffolds, outrigger scaffolds, mason's adjustable multiple-point suspension scaffolds, and several other types.[21]

Inspection and enforcement of OSHA is carried out through 10 regional and 49 area offices located in major cities. Unannounced inspections at industrial work

---

[19] 29 U.S.C. § 651 *et. seq.*

[20] 29 C.F.R. § 1910.28.

[21] The detail involved in regulation of scaffolds is typical. Ladders, hard hats, and a multitude of objects, chemicals, procedures and the like are subject to similar rules.

sites are conducted by compliance health and safety officers and industrial hygienists under the supervision of area directors. The secretary of labor is authorized to enter at reasonable times and without delay any factory, plant, construction site or other workplace where work is performed by employees and to inspect all pertinent conditions, structures, machines, equipment, and material therein and to privately question any employer-operator or employee.

The Supreme Court of the United States has ruled, however, that when an employer objects to an inspection, the Secretary of Labor must obtain a warrant to satisfy the requirements of the Fourth Amendment to the U. S. Constitution.[22] Probable cause in the criminal sense is not required for the issuance of a warrant, however.

In the event a compliance officer believes that an employer has violated any OSHA standard or regulation, a written citation is issued setting forth the nature of the violation and fixing a reasonable time for the abatement. Both criminal and civil penalties for violations are possible. An employer who repeatedly or willfully violates the act or any standard promulgated thereunder may be assessed a civil penalty of not more than $10,000 for each violation, and an employer guilty of a willful violation that causes the death of an employee may, upon conviction, be punished by a fine up to $10,000 or by imprisonment for up to six months, or both.

An illustration of the problem of determining a willful violation in the construction context was a case in which a construction company engaged in water and sewer line work was charged with a willful violation when four workmen were injured after a 12- to 13-foot-deep trench opening caved in on them. The contractor had failed to slope or shore the trench sides. The construction company thought mistakenly that the excavation was shale and thus not in need of shoring. The court affirmed a finding that there was no willful violation, finding instead only a serious one, since the contractor reasonably believed that the trench was exempt from the standard's requirements.[23]

28.12   EMPLOYMENT DISCRIMINATION

The Civil Rights Act of 1964[24] and the Civil Rights Act of 1866[25] prohibit employers from failing or refusing to hire, to discharge, or otherwise to discriminate against any individual in compensation, terms, conditions, or privileges of employment because of race, sex, color, religion, or national origin. Neither may an employer limit, segregate, or classify his employees in such a way as would deprive them of employment opportunities or otherwise adversely affect their sta-

---

[22]*Marshall v. Barlow's, Inc.*, 436 U.S. 307 (1978).

[23]*Donovan v. Mica Const. Co.*, 699 F.2d 431 (8th Cir., 1983).
   The applicable standard read:
   Sides of trenches in hard or compact soil, including embankments, shall be shored or otherwise supported when the trench is more than 5 feet in depth and 8 feet or more in length. In lieu of shoring, the sides of the trench above the 5-foot level may be sloped to preclude collapse, but shall not be steeper than a 1-foot rise to each foot horizontal. When the outside diameter of a pipe is greater than 6 feet, a bench of 4-foot minimum shall be provided at the toe of the sloped portion.
   29 CFR § 1926.652 (c).

[24]42 U.S.C. § 2000 e.

[25]42 U.S.C. § 1981.

tus as employees because of their sex, for example. It is also unlawful for a labor organization to exclude or expel from membership or discriminate against an individual because of sex, or to segregate or classify its membership or refuse to refer for employment an individual because of sex.

Title VII of the Civil Rights Act of 1964 is also the legal basis for workplace claims of sexual harassment. Although the statute makes no such distinctions, it has been construed to apply to cases based on carried-out threats, usually referred to as quid pro quo cases, and to bothersome attentions or sexual remarks sufficient to create a "hostile work environment," although the latter requires that the harassment be severe or pervasive.[26]

The precise scope and requirements of the law of sexual harassment are still evolving and will continue to do so for the foreseeable future, but an employee who refuses unwelcome and threatening sexual advances of a supervisor yet suffers no adverse tangible job consequences may recover against the employer without a showing of employer negligence.

Such claims, however, may be successfully defended if the employer exercised reasonable care to prevent and correct promptly any sexually harassing behavior, and the employee unreasonably failed to take advantage of any preventive or corrective opportunities provided by the employer or to otherwise avoid harm.[27]

It is not unlawful for an employer or labor organization to hire and deploy employees or classify or refer for employment individuals on the basis of sex in those instances where sex "is a bona fide occupational qualification reasonably necessary to the normal operation of that particular business or enterprise." Such exceptions are interpreted narrowly, and the burden of proving an occupational qualification is on the employer. Refusal to hire an individual based upon stereotyped characterizations of the sexes rather than on consideration of the individual's capacity is unacceptable.

In response to a series of Supreme Court decisions that were perceived as unfavorable to employment-discrimination plaintiffs, the President signed into law the Civil Rights Act of 1991[28] on November 21 of that year. The principles noted above remain intact, but procedural changes in such areas as burden of proof, availability of damages as a remedy, and trial by jury have taken a decidedly proemployee shift. New regulations and years of litigation will no doubt attempt to clarify the precise requirements of the new law.

The Age Discrimination in Employment Act,[29] which applies to individuals of at least 40 years of age, makes it unlawful for an employer to fail or refuse to hire, discharge, or otherwise discriminate against an individual who is 40 years or older because of age, or to classify such employees in a manner that would tend to deprive them of employment opportunities because of age, or to reduce the wage rate of an employee in order to comply with the act. Similar prohibitions apply to labor organizations.

---

[26]*Meritor Savings Bank v. Vinson,* 477 U.S. 57 (1986).

[27]*Burlington Industries, Inc. v. Ellerth,* 118 S.Ct. 2257 (1998); and *Faragher v. City of Boca Raton,* 118 S.Ct. 2275 (1998).
  Also actionable under Title VII is same-sex sexual harassment in the workplace. See *Oncale v. Sundowner Offshore Services, Inc.,* 118 S.Ct. 998 (1998).

[28]Pub L.No. 102-166, Stat.1071.

[29]29 U.S.C. 621 *et. seq.*

This act is the exclusive federal remedy for age discrimination in employment and applies to private business organizations engaged in commerce with at least 20 employees, and to state and local governments. A separate provision extends coverage to federal employees.

If a covered worker is terminated and replaced it does not matter whether his replacement is a member of the protected class (over 40) or not. The relevant issue is whether the termination was based on the employee's age, not the age of his replacement.[30]

28.13 AFFIRMATIVE ACTION

The issue of affirmative action arises when a federal statute mandates affirmative action by the federal government, where a state or municipality enacts or undertakes affirmative action, or where a private employer does so. Affirmative-action laws apply to educational admissions, employment, and practically all areas. Affirmative action is most often seen in the design and construction field by way of quotas and minority "set-asides" in contracts and employment. This is a difficult topic and is subject to change with the nation's political and social climate and the membership of the Supreme Court. The very contentious matter of affirmative action began as a remedy for the effects of past discrimination in employment. However, when one group derives a benefit, it follows that there is "reverse discrimination" against another group. For this reason, affirmative action schemes are strictly scrutinized by the Supreme Court.

Laws establishing affirmative action schemes have been upheld by the Supreme Court on split votes. Race-based affirmative action schemes, whether imposed by Congress or state or local government, are "strictly scrutinized" by the Supreme Court. The most recent case of importance on this topic dealt with a construction contract. In *Adarand Constructors, Inc. v. Pena,*[31] the court examined a bid for a subcontract to supply guardrails to a federal highway project. The general contractor received a financial incentive for awarding the subcontract to a minority-owned "disadvantaged business enterprise," but was not required to do so. Although the plaintiff put in the lowest bid, the general contractor awarded the contract to a minority-owned disadvantaged business enterprise. The Court held that, to be permissible, race-conscious "reverse discrimination" must be "necessary" to achieve a "compelling government interest."[32] However, the factors that are to be used in this determination have not been clearly articulated. In other words, it is unclear what objectives are considered "compelling" and what means are considered "necessary." What is clear from *Adarand* is that strict quotas will

---

[30]*O'Connor v. Consolidated Coin Caterers Corp.,* 116 S.Ct. 1307 (1996). In this case the terminated worker was 56, his replacement, 40. The court noted, however, that when a worker is terminated and replaced by one "insignificantly younger" an inference of age-based decision making could not be made, since the act prohibits discrimination based on age, not membership in the protected class.

[31]115 S.Ct. 2097 (1995).

[32]The court sent the regulation at issue in *Adarand* back to the lower courts to determine if it could withstand this scrutiny.

almost always fail and that there must be a showing of past discrimination by the entity involved, as opposed to discrimination by society in general.

At the time of this writing, the political climate and composition of the court are such that it is predicted that the Supreme Court will drastically limit, if not completely overrule, affirmative action at its next opportunity. In 1997, the Supreme Court upheld California's groundbreaking Proposition 209, which banned race and gender preference in hiring and school admissions in California. In 1998, the Supreme Court was scheduled to hear a case[33] regarding race-conscious layoffs that many expected would end affirmative action altogether. However, the case was settled before the Supreme Court had a chance to make a ruling. In any event, it is clear that the future of affirmative action is very uncertain.

28.14   AMERICANS WITH DISABILITIES ACT

In response to a finding that 43,000,000 Americans have one or more physical or mental disabilities, in 1990 Congress enacted a federal statute intended to remedy perceived discrimination.[34] Basically, the law prohibits discrimination in employment against otherwise qualified disabled individuals and requires employers to make reasonable accommodations for the disabled. The law also provides that the disabled must have reasonable access to places of public accommodation, which includes everything from restaurants to museums and day care centers,[35] except where an entity can demonstrate that it is "structurally impracticable" to meet the requirements. Furthermore, it is also considered discrimination under this act to keep "architectural barriers" in place in existing buildings where such removal is

---

[33]*Piscataway v. Taxman,* no cite.

[34]42 U.S.C. § 12101–12213.

[35]12 U.S.C. 12181 provides in pertinent part:

The following private entities are considered public accommodations for purposes of this subchapter, if the operations of such entities affect commerce—

(A) an inn, hotel, motel, or other place of lodging, except for an establishment located within a building that contains not more than five rooms for rent or hire and that is actually occupied by the proprietor of such establishment as the residence of such proprietor;

(B) a restaurant, bar, or other establishment serving food or drink;

(C) a motion picture house, theater, concert hall, stadium, or other place of exhibition or entertainment;

(D) an auditorium, convention center, lecture hall, or other place of public gathering;

(E) a bakery, grocery store, clothing store, hardware store, shopping center, or other sales or rental establishment;

(F) a laundromat, dry-cleaner, bank, barber shop, beauty shop, travel service, shoe repair service, funeral parlor, gas station, office of an accountant or lawyer, pharmacy, insurance office, professional office of a health care provider, hospital, or other service establishment;

(G) a terminal, depot, or other station used for specified public transportation;

(H) a museum, library, gallery, or other place of public display or collection;

(I) a park, zoo, amusement park, or other place of recreation;

(J) a nursery, elementary, secondary, undergraduate, or postgraduate private school, or other place of education;

(K) a day care center, senior citizen center, homeless shelter, food bank, adoption agency, or other social service center establishment; and

(L) a gymnasium, health spa, bowling alley, golf course, or other place of exercise or recreation.

"readily achievable."[36] This law is subject to some limitations, such as the exemption for private clubs and religious organizations.[37] The implication of this for design professionals, of course, is that new buildings and modifications thereto must adhere to the strict requirements of this act and that existing buildings must be modified to provide access to the disabled.

The provisions of this act are lengthy and specific. For example, the law provides that installation of an elevator is not required for buildings fewer than three stories or fewer than 3,000 square feet per story unless the building is a shopping mall or the office of a health care provider. In accordance with this, a country club was not required to install an elevator to allow access to the second floor and the basement of the club.[38] It seems that this act will also be broadly construed and strictly enforced. In *Paralyzed Veterans of America v. Ellerbe Becket Architects & Engineers*,[39] the court held that although there were wheelchair spaces available in nearly every section of the upper bowl of an indoor arena, the wheelchair spaces were not "sufficiently dispersed" because most of the spaces in the lower bowl area were in the less popular end zone sections and not in the center court sections. Thus, it is clear that the Americans with Disabilities Act will have a large impact on the design profession.

ENVIRONMENTAL LAW

28.15 INTRODUCTION

The growth in importance of federal environmental law is well illustrated by the fact that the Environmental Protection Agency has expanded since its creation in 1970 to be the largest federal regulatory agency. Indeed, it is now a rare industrial or commercial activity that is not subject to some manner of environmental constraint.

The general trend seems to be a shift from federal assistance to states to either direct federal regulation or mandatory federal guidelines for state implementation. This trend would seem to reflect both a dissatisfaction with state achievements and an awareness that many pollution problems are national or regional in scale.

While the subject is largely statutory, it should be kept in mind that many actions resulting in pollution damage may be tortious and subject to private abatement or damages under the principles discussed in Chapter 19.

---

[36]42 U.S.C. 12181(b)(2)(A)(iii) "Readily achievable" under the statute is defined as "easily accomplishable and able to be carried out without much difficulty or expense." Generally, factors that will be considered in this determination are (1) nature and cost of the required action, (2) overall financial resources of the facility, (3) overall financial resources of the entity and (4) the type of operations of the entity.

[37]42 U.S.C. 12187.

[38]*Slaby v. Berkshire*, 928 F. Supp. 613 (D.Md. 1996) affirmed without opinion 110 F.3d 60 (4th Cir. 1996).

[39]950 F. Supp. 393 (D.D.C. 1996).

28.16   NATIONAL ENVIRONMENTAL POLICY ACT

Perhaps the single most significant example of federal environmental legislation has been the National Environmental Policy Act (NEPA) of 1969.[40] NEPA instituted the encouragement of productive harmony between man and his environment as a national policy, established the Council on Environmental Quality, and required federal agencies to include an environmental impact statement in every recommendation or report on proposals for legislation and other major federal actions significantly affecting the quality of the human environment.

Although the specific holdings of the case have been superseded, the watershed NEPA case of Calvert Cliff's Coordinating Committee v. U.S. Atomic Energy Commission[41] set the tone for the voluminous NEPA litigation to follow by observing that the sweep of NEPA is extraordinarily broad, compelling consideration of any and all types of environmental impact. The court in *Calvert Cliff's* noted the requirement that all agencies must use a systematic, interdisciplinary approach to environmental planning and evaluation in decision making that may have an impact on human environment, and it required federal agencies to consider environmental issues, just as they consider other matters within their mandates, to the fullest extent possible. Congress did not, however, establish environmental protection as an exclusive goal; rather it desired a reordering of priorities, so that environmental costs and benefits will assume their proper place along with other considerations.

28.17   COUNCIL ON ENVIRONMENTAL QUALITY

The National Environmental Policy Act established the Council on Environmental Quality in the executive office of the President to assist and advise the President in the preparation of the environmental quality report required annually by NEPA, to analyze and interpret environmental information and communicate it to the President, and to review and appraise the programs and activities of the federal government in light of the environmental policy set forth in the act. As well, the CEQ is to develop and recommend to the President national policies to promote improvement of the environmental quality, to conduct investigations relating to ecological systems and environmental quality, to document and define changes in the natural environment, and to furnish such studies and reports with respect to matters of policy and legislation as the President may request.

By executive order, the Council on Environmental Quality is also authorized to prepare guidelines to aid in the preparation of environmental impact statements.

---

[40]42 U.S.C. 4321.
[41]449 F.2d 1109 (D.C. Cir. 1971).

28.18 ENVIRONMENTAL IMPACT STATEMENTS[42]

The key requirement of the National Environmental Policy Act, and the one that has resulted in the most litigation, is that federal agencies prepare environmental impact statements on all major federal actions significantly affecting the quality of the human environment. The purpose of the environmental impact statement requirement is not to produce an objection-free document, but rather to give Congress, federal agencies, and the public a useful decision-making tool. Subsequent environmental rationalizations of decisions already fully and finally made do not meet the requirement that federal agency actions be examined and environmental consequences considered "to the fullest extent possible." NEPA does not impose a permit scheme of any sort, but agency failures to comply with NEPA's procedural requirements have resulted in litigation delaying or killing many major construction projects.

Environmental impact statements are required for all major federal actions, and this requirement includes not only federal construction projects and agency proposals for legislation but also all activities that are undertaken pursuant to a federal license, permit, or financing. Federal officials are entitled to "dream out loud" without filing an environmental impact statement, but a statement is required when a proposal moves beyond the dream stage into some tangible form. Environmental impact statements must be prepared at the earliest time possible prior to the implementation of the proposed major federal action so that alternative courses of action with less severe environmental consequences can be considered. It is clear that the environmental impact statement should be prepared before irretrievable commitments are made or options precluded by agency action. It is the federal agency itself, not environmental groups or others, that is required to produce environmental impact statements. However, the collection and analysis of environmental data are often contracted to universities or other organizations.

The environmental impact statement must contain an analysis of the environmental costs and benefits of the proposed projects, including all significant primary environmental effects and all substantial secondary environmental effects. Aesthetic considerations are part of the "quality of the human environment" that must be considered in an environmental impact statement, as are future potential circumstances, mitigation methods, and reasoned analyses in response to conflicting data or opinions on environmental issues. An environmental impact statement must not be merely a catalogue of environmental facts, but also must explain its course of inquiry, analysis, and reasoning. Responsible opposing views must also be included within the environmental impact statement, but highly remote or conjectural consequences need not be discussed.

The language of the National Environmental Policy Act calls for a detailed statement, and this requirement mandates that the environmental consequences of a particular project be sufficiently spelled out to allow an executive to arrive at a reasonably accurate decision regarding the environmental benefits and detriments to

---

[42]Procedural requirements for the EIS process, which are binding on all federal agencies, are found at 40 C.F.R. Part 1502.

be expected from the project. It must also provide a record upon which a decision maker can arrive at an informed decision.

The environmental impact statement must contain a thorough discussion of alternatives to the proposed project, including the elimination of the project altogether. Also required is a presentation of the environmental risks incident to all reasonable alternative courses of action. The alternatives to be considered naturally depend upon the type of project involved. In connection with a federally funded freeway project, for example, the environmental impact statement should consider all possible alternatives to the proposed freeway, including changes in design, different systems of transportation, changes in the route, and abandonment of the project entirely.

In an environmental impact statement dealing with a proposed lease of oil and gas lands off the coast of Louisiana, alternatives considered included the elimination of oil import quotas, development of oil shale, desulphurization of coal, coal liquefaction and gasification, and development of tar sands and geothermal resources. Obviously, the distinction between a true alternative and a supplement is not always easy to draw.

Several hundred lawsuits challenging the propriety of federal action have been brought utilizing the National Environmental Policy Act, and long delays have often resulted. Such was the case with the construction of the trans-Alaskan pipeline, and these delays, combined with energy shortages and the petroleum embargo of 1973, resulted in the passage of the Trans-Alaskan Pipeline Authorization Act,[43] which specifically authorized construction without further action under the National Environmental Policy Act of 1969.

28.19   AIR POLLUTION CONTROL

Federal law directed at the problems of air pollution has existed since the passage of the Air Pollution Control Act in 1955. Numerous other statutes with the same aim have been enacted since, but until the passage of the Air Quality Act of 1967 the emphasis was upon federal assistance to state and local governments, technical assistance, and programs of research.

In 1963 the Clean Air Act provided explicit authority for federal regulatory action to abate interstate air pollution problems. Amendments in 1965 provided for greater control over automotive exhaust emissions. The Air Quality Act of 1967 established a regional framework for the enactment and enforcement of federal-state air quality standards, but it was not until the passage of the Clean Air Act Amendments of 1970[44] that a comprehensive attack on the problems of air pollution was made. In 1990 the already immense statute was amended, adding 750 pages and resulting in a monster of complexity.

[43]Sec. 28, Mineral Leasing Act of 1920, 30 U.S.C. 185.
[44]42 U.S.C. § 7401–7515.

Requirements under the Clean Air Act are often industrywide and may have substantial economic repercussions; therefore, the requirements are subject to intense political pressure. Delays and amendments are inevitable as political and economic factors make their weight felt. Attention is called to the Energy Supply and Environmental Coordination Act of 1974,[45] which amended the Clean Air Act to facilitate the burning of coal and to grant delays in compliance with motor vehicle emission requirements.

28.20   CLEAN AIR ACT; AIR QUALITY STANDARDS

The Clean Air Act Amendments of 1970 directed the Secretary of Health, Education, and Welfare to establish nationally applicable ambient air quality standards for any pollutant or combination of pollutants for which air quality criteria had been issued. Each state is designated as an air quality control region, but interstate air quality control regions may be established where necessary to deal with interstate air pollution problems.

Along with the establishment of air quality regions, primary and secondary ambient air quality standards were translated into numbers by the promulgation of National Primary and Secondary Air Quality Standards; see Appendix 2 at the end of the chapter. The states were required to submit, by January 31, 1972, implementation plans that would achieve the level of air quality established by the primary and secondary standards within specific time limitations. Problems with respect to the maintenance of ambient air quality, transportation contracts, and the regulation of complex sources all made state compliance difficult. The Environmental Protection Agency exercises its authority to substitute specific provisions where state plans are deficient.

The Clean Air Act also grants almost unlimited powers of abatement to the administrator of the Environmental Protection Agency if he determines there is "an imminent and substantial endangerment to the health of persons and that appropriate state and local authorities have not acted to abate such sources." The administrator may also establish emission standards for any type of source that emits any substance that he determines to be hazardous.

28.21   NEW STATIONARY SOURCES

The problem of major new air-polluting sources is addressed by the Clean Air Act Amendments of 1970, which authorize the administrator of the Environmental Protection Agency to establish nationally applicable standards of performance based upon the application of best system emission reduction which (taking into account the cost of achieving such reduction) has been adequately demonstrated.[46]

---

[45]15 U.S.C. 791, 792.

[46]Standards of performance have been established for approximately 60 new stationary sources. See 40 C.F.R. Part 52. The regulations exceed 1,000 pages.

State implementation plans must provide for a review of every new source prior to construction to determine the effects in all air quality regions of the state on the overall pollution control program. State implementation plans must also provide for an analysis to determine whether a plant will allow maintenance of the primary, secondary, and nondeterioration standards that are applicable.

As the supply of fossil fuel declines, the need for major centralized power plants may increase because of their probable greater efficiency compared with that of a host of small individual means of producing electricity and heat. Thus it may be that serious conflicts will develop between what is desirable and what is possible.

28.22 Nondegradation

One of the most intriguing and important issues to have arisen under the Clean Air Act is that of nondegradation, that is, whether a state implementation plan may allow significant deterioration of existing clean air areas, areas with levels of pollution lower than the secondary standard.

The case of *Sierra Club v. Ruckelshaus*[47] held that the language of the Clean Air Act stating its purpose to be "to protect and enhance the quality of the nation's air resources so as to promote public health and welfare and the productive capacity of its population" declared Congress's intent to improve the quality of the nation's air and to prevent the deterioration of that air quality, no matter how presently pure that quality in some sections of the country happened to be. Thus, an EPA regulation permitting states to submit plans that would allow a clean air area to be degraded so long as the plans were "adequate to prevent such ambient pollution levels from exceeding the secondary standard" was upset.

The 1990 amendments to the Clean Air Act also set forth a new classification known as nonattainment areas, and establish a new array of control measures, including controls on smaller sources and new categories of industrial facilities.

28.23 Mobile Sources

The administrator of the Environmental Protection Agency is authorized by the Clean Air Act Amendments of 1970 to set emission standards for all new vehicles and engines for use on the streets and highways, and for aircraft. The act called for the establishment of standards for vehicles likely to cause or contribute to air pollution endangering public health or welfare within the constraints of available

---

[47]344 F. Supp 253 (D.D.C. 1972), *affirmed* 412 U.S. 541 (1973). Followed by *Sierra Club v. E.P.A.* 540 F.2d 1114 (D.C. Cir. 1976).

technology. It also authorized the testing of vehicles or engines or those being manufactured in order to determine whether they in fact comply with emission standards. Authority is also granted to authorize the establishment of standards respecting the composition of the chemical and physical properties of any fuel or fuel additives except in the case of aviation fuels. The Clean Air Amendments of 1990 call for additional reductions in mobile source emissions and establish a new program mandating production of cleaner fuels.

28.24 NOISE POLLUTION

The Noise Control Act of 1972[48] empowers the Environmental Protection Agency to control the noise characteristics of products distributed in commerce and to control noise produced by interstate railroads and motor carriers. Unlike many federal air and water quality laws, the noise law generally endeavors to control only noise emissions at the source, rather than ambient conditions. This is true in part because noise, unlike air and water pollution, does not accumulate in the environment but dissipates within a reasonably short distance and time.

The Environmental Protection Agency is required to propose emission standards for products identified as major sources of noise if "noise emission standards are feasible" in situations where the product is either construction equipment, transportation equipment, a motor or engine, or electrical or electronic equipment. Imported products are subject to the same standards as products made in the United States, but products made solely for export are excluded.

The control of aircraft noise is complicated by the fact that the regulation of air safety is the responsibility of the Federal Aviation Administration, and the administration of the Noise Control Act of 1972 is vested with the Environmental Protection Agency. The FAA is empowered to adopt rules prescribing flight paths, and procedures, traffic patterns, and preferential runway systems for specific airports, all of which are as important in the control of aircraft noise as is the actual amount of noise emanating from the vehicle. The Noise Control Act requires that the FAA consult with the Environmental Protection Agency before adopting noise rules and before any exemptions are granted under the rules. The FAA is empowered by the Noise Control Act of 1972, section 611, to prescribe whatever rules it finds necessary to control aircraft noise, including the authority to set noise emission standards as a condition upon aircraft-type certificates.

Standards with respect to the control of noise emission by jet aircraft are under continual revision and are complicated by the fact that the "retrofit" of older equipment is extremely expensive and many of the noisier aircraft are due for replacement by quieter wide-bodied planes.

| [48]42 U.S.C. 4901–4918.

28.25   WATER POLLUTION

The federal law of water pollution control has been evolving for more than thirty years, and is presently defined by the Federal Water Pollution Control Act of 1977, commonly known as the Clean Water Act.[49]

The Clean Water Act applies to the "navigable waters" of the United States, defining navigable waters as "waters of the United States, including the territorial seas." The act therefore applies to waters of the United States without regard to traditional definitions involving commerce and navigability. The various provisions of the act authorize the establishment of standards and issuance of permits for discharges from "point sources," which include any discernible and discrete conveyance including pipes, ditches, containers, vessels and floating facilities, and other conduits from which pollutants are or may be discharged.

In 1987 the Clean Water Act was again amended and new deadlines for effluent limitations were established. New deadlines and standards will likely follow on a regular basis.

28.26   POINT SOURCE DISCHARGES

Direct discharges of pollutants are subject to both effluent standards and water quality standards under the regulatory provisions of the Clean Water Act and must comply with the stricter of the two.

Effluent Standards   Effluent standards are limitations on the amount of pollutants that may be discharged by particular classifications of dischargers and are based on the availability of pollution-control technology. Effluent standards are measured in terms of the amount of pollutant that may be discharged per period of time or unit of production. The CWA requires the Environmental Protection Agency to establish effluent standards for new sources of pollution, and each standard must reflect the "greatest degree of effluent reduction achievable through the application of the best available demonstrated control technology, processes, operating methods and other alternatives, including a standard permitting no discharge of pollutants where practicable."

Applicants for federal permits must first obtain state certification, a requirement that essentially gives the states a veto power over federal discharge permits. A state may set its standards higher than the EPA and may also establish its own permit scheme which, if approved by EPA, will supplant the EPA scheme.

Water Quality Standards   Water quality standards are rules defining required water quality for ambient water. Such standards are based on technical information regarding minimum requirements necessary to sustain the uses to which water is

---

[49]33 U.S.C. 1251 *et seq.* Amended by Municipal Water Treatment Construction Grant Agreement of 1981. Technical and administrative amendments in 1987, 1988, 1994, 1995.

put. Standards for different waters may vary, depending on uses to which the water is put and the preferences of the individual states that adopt water quality standards subject to EPA approval. Water quality standards may be required for suspended solids, dissolved solids, hydrogen ion concentration, radioactive substances, plant nutrients, dissolved oxygen, temperature, fecal coliform,[50] and the like.

28.27 NONPOINT SOURCES

The permit scheme of the Clean Water Act applies only to point-source discharges, but the control of nonpoint sources of water pollution presents a perplexing problem which is addressed in section 208 of the act. Although the line is difficult to draw with precision, nonpoint sources of pollution may be agricultural, mine-related, construction activity runoff, and saltwater intrusion into rivers and estuaries, resulting from a reduction in freshwater flow from causes such as irrigation and groundwater extraction.

The complexity of the nonpoint problem is illustrated by the fact that the amount of runoff from a construction site may depend on the type of construction, the amount of rainfall, the topography of the site, the type of soil, the amount of vegetation left undisturbed, the amount of earth moving involved, and the type of control measure utilized. Originally, proponents of the Clean Water Act believed that effective federal control over nonpoint sources of water pollution was not feasible and thus required that state or regional agencies establish regulatory programs to control nonpoint source pollution, pursuant to federal guidelines. To date, success in controlling nonpoint sources of water pollution has varied among activities and locations.

28.28 DREDGED MATERIAL

The disposal of dredged or fill material is regulated under a separate permit system established by Section 404[51] of the Federal Water Pollution Control Act. The traditional role of the Army Corps of Engineers in the dredging of navigable channels led to the establishment of a scheme by which permits are issued by the secretary of the army acting through the chief of engineers subject to the applica-

---

[50]R. 323.1062. Fecal coliform:

"Rule 1062.
  (1) Waters of the state protected for total body contact recreation shall contain not more than 200 fecal coliforms per 100 milliliters; and all other waters of the state shall contain not more than 1,000 fecal coliforms per 100 milliliters. These concentrations may be exceeded if due to uncontrollable non-point sources.
  (2) Compliance with the fecal coliform standards prescribed by subrule (1) shall be determined on the basis of the geometric average of any series of 5 or more consecutive samples taken over not more than a 30-day period."

[51]33 U.S.C. 1344.

tion of Environmental Protection Agency guidelines and a potential EPA veto. Recent legislation authorizes the states to take over Section 404 permitting in other than traditional navigable waters following EPA approval of their procedures and standards.

28.29   O IL AND H AZARDOUS S UBSTANCES

A separate regulatory scheme[52] has been established to control spills of oil and hazardous substances. The Environmental Protection Agency has promulgated a list of hazardous substances and has defined what constitutes harmful discharge of each substance and of oil. An elaborate regulatory structure provides for penalties for oil spills and for failure to notify of a spill, for assessment of cleanup costs, and for federal authority to prescribe spill prevention equipment for oil-handling facilities and for vessels.

The Administrator of the Environmental Protection Agency is also required, by Section 307a of the Clean Water Act, to set effluent standards for toxic pollutants which are defined to be any pollutant which is toxic to any organism and which may cause death, disease, or behavioral or physical abnormalities. Since almost any pollutant could be toxic to some organism if applied in sufficient quantities, the EPA is not required to set a standard for every toxic pollutant but rather is required to publish a list of toxic pollutants for which effluent standards will be established. EPA must set the standards "at a level which the Administrator determines provides an ample margin of safety," and the standard may be in the form of a prohibition.

28.30   O CEAN D UMPING

The disposal of wastes at sea is regulated by the Marine Protection, Research, and Sanctuaries Act of 1972,[53] which is also known as the Ocean Dumping Act. This legislation establishes a permit system under which an Environmental Protection Agency permit is required for the transportation from the United States of virtually all materials for dumping in ocean water, the actual dumping of materials transported from outside the United States into the territorial sea or contiguous zone, and the transportation of materials by a United States agency or official from outside the United States for the purpose of dumping in any ocean waters. No permits may be issued for radioactive, chemical, or biological warfare agents or for highly radioactive substance. The act applies to all ocean waters seaward of the land or internal waters, and the states are preempted from adopting or enforcing any regulations relating to activities covered by the act.

[52]33 U.S.C. 1321. Technical and administrative amendments 1996.
[53]33 U.S.C. 1401 *et seq.*

28.31 PESTICIDES

The negative impacts of the extensive use of pesticides—brought to public notice primarily through the cancellation by the Environmental Protection Agency of most uses of DDT—are controlled primarily by the Federal Insecticide, Fungicide, and Rodenticide Act, as amended by the 1972 Federal Environmental Pesticide Control Act.[54]

This federal statute requires the registration of pesticides. It also requires adequate labels and directions for safe use. Amendments in 1972 added a system of classifications of pesticides using two categories: general and restricted-use products. Products placed in a restricted-use category are subject to special controls and may be applied only by trained operators. Virtually all pesticides sold in the United States require registration with the EPA.

Experimental-use permits may be issued by the EPA for certain types of newly developed pesticides—as yet inadequately tested—to apply for registration. The EPA Administrator is authorized, at his discretion, to "exempt any federal or state agency from any provision of this Act if he determines that emergency conditions exist which require such exemption."

The Federal Insecticide, Fungicide, and Rodenticide Act authorizes the Administrator of the EPA to cancel registrations of insecticides where there is an unreasonable risk to people or the environment, taking into account the social and environmental costs and benefits of the use of any pesticides.[55]

In 1979, pursuant to its emergency powers, EPA ordered an emergency ban of the herbicides 2-4-5-T and Silvex because of a probability that spontaneous human abortions were related to the spraying of these herbicides. The ban was upheld when the court found that the EPA had considered all relevant factors and did not make a clear error of judgment in deciding to order the suspension of the herbicides.[56]

28.32 SOLID WASTES

The Resource Conservation and Recovery Act of 1976,[57] as amended by the Solid Waste Disposal Act Amendments of 1980, Hazardous and Solid Waste Amendment of 1984, and Medical Waste Tracking Act of 1988, provides federal regulation of hazardous waste, financial assistance to the states for solid-waste management planning, and funding for development, research, and demonstration of new technology. The Environmental Protection Agency is required to list specific sub-

---

[54]7 U.S.C. 136 amended in 1996.

[55]See *Environmental Defense Fund Inc. v. Environmental Protection Agency,* 489 F.2d 1247(1973), where the Court of Appeals for the District of Columbia upheld the cancellation of almost all registrations for the use of DDT except for limited public health and agriculture pest quarantine purposes.

[56]*Dow Chemical v. Blum,* 469 F. Supp. 892 (D. Mich. 1979). However, an E.P.A. emergency suspension order regarding pesticide products containing dinoseb was deemed arbitrary in *Love v. Thomas,* 668 F. Supp. 1443 (D. Ore. 1987).

[57]42 U.S.C. 6901–6987.

stances deemed hazardous and to promulgate regulations regarding their disposal. Permits are required of owners and operators of hazardous waste treatment, storage, or disposal facilities, but the act applies only to wastes discharged on land. Air and water discharges are covered under the Clean Air Act and the Clean Water Act.

Major responsibility for regulation of solid wastes, other than those deemed hazardous, remains with the states. The EPA is directed, however, to establish guidelines for states' solid-waste management plans, which guidelines must be complied with if a state hopes to obtain funding for the development of such plans.

The storage of nuclear waste is a problem of immense technical and legal complexity. The three major areas of concern are temporary storage of spent fuel rods, reprocessing, and permanent disposal of high-level wastes. The approximately 30 metric tons of spent fuel rods produced each year are presently stored in on-site storage pools and must be isolated from the biosphere for as much as 250,000 years. The nuclear industry intended that this spent fuel would be reprocessed and used in the now defunct breeder reactor program.

In 1980 President Carter established a radioactive-waste management program, which called upon the nuclear regulatory commission to determine whether and how nuclear waste could be disposed of safely. However, bureaucratic overlap between the EPA, the Department of Transportation, and units of state and local government with authorities over transportation and land use have so far precluded the establishment of a comprehensive nuclear-waste disposal policy.[58]

QUESTIONS

1. What is the primary source of congressional power in the U.S. Constitution? Discuss its scope.

2. Is Congress's power subject to any limits? If so, discuss them.

3. Discuss the relationship between federal and state law.

4. What aspects of labor relations are governed by federal statute? Are engineers covered by the National Labor Relations Act? Architects? How about the Fair Labor Standards Act?

5. What are the functions of labor unions and the National Labor Relations Board?

6. Give an example of an unfair labor practice.

7. Discuss whether OSHA might be improved through the use of performance standards. Does OSHA treat willful violations differently?

8. Is there any circumstance in which an employer may legally refuse to hire or terminate a potential employee because she is a female over or under a certain age?

9. How does federal law protect against sexual harassment?

[58]See *New York v. U.S.*, Note 6, Section 28.3.

10. What concerns or opportunities may arise for design professionals as a result of the Americans with Disabilities Act?

11. Discuss the factors that have led to the federalization of environmental law.

12. What were the goals of the National Environmental Policy Act?

13. What is the role of the environmental impact statement in the decision-making process?

14. Who is required by the National Environmental Policy Act to prepare environmental impact statements?

15. Discuss the elements required to be included in an environmental impact statement.

16. Discuss the problems encountered in the effort to meet National Primary and Secondary Air Quality Standards.

17. Discuss the problems inherent in the control of noise pollution.

18. Are there any special noise pollution problems in the case of aircraft?

19. What arguments might be made in favor of allowing air quality to decline until the point of safety is reached?

20. To what waters does the Federal Water Pollution Control Act apply?

21. What is a "point source" of water pollution? A nonpoint source?

22. Differentiate effluent standards from water quality standards.

23. Discuss the problems inherent in the control of nonpoints sources of water pollution.

24. Which agency is responsible for the issuance of permits for the disposal of dredged or filled material?

25. Ocean dumping permits may not be obtained for what substances? To what waters does the Ocean Dumping Act apply?

26. In general, how does federal law control the use of dangerous pesticides?

APPENDIX I

§ 1910.28 Safety Requirements for Scaffolding

(a) *General requirements for all scaffolds*

(1) Scaffolds shall be furnished and erected in accordance with this standard for persons engaged in work that cannot be done safely from the ground or from solid construction, except that ladders used for such work shall conform to § 1910.25 and § 1910.26.

(2) The footing or anchorage for scaffolds shall be sound, rigid, and capable of carrying the maximum intended load without settling or displacement. Unstable objects such as barrels, boxes, loose brick, or concrete blocks shall not be used to support scaffolds or planks.

(3) [Reserved]

(4) Scaffolds and their components shall be capable of supporting without failure at least four times the maximum intended load.

(5) Scaffolds and other devices mentioned or described in this section shall be maintained in safe condition. Scaffolds shall not be altered or moved horizontally while they are in use or occupied.

(6) Any scaffold damaged or weakened from any cause shall be immediately repaired and shall not be used until repairs have been completed.

(7) Scaffolds shall not be loaded in excess of the working load for which they are intended.

(8) All load-carrying timber members of scaffold framing shall be a minimum of 1,500 f. (Stress Grade) construction grade lumber. All dimensions are nominal sizes as provided in the American Lumber Standards, except that where rough sizes are noted, only rough or undressed lumber of the size specified will satisfy minimum requirements. (NOTE: Where nominal sizes of lumber are used in place of rough sizes, the nominal size lumber shall be such as to provide equivalent strength to that specified in tables D-7 through D-12 and D-16.)

(9) All planking shall be Scaffold Grade as recognized by grading rules for the species of wood used. The maximum permissible spans for 2- × 9-inch or wider planks are shown in the following table:

	Material				
	Full thickness undressed lumber			Nominal thickness lumber	
Working load (p.s.f.)	25	50	75	25	50
Permissible span (ft.)	10	8	6	8	9

The maximum permissible span for $1\frac{1}{4}$- × 9-inch or wider plank of full thickness is 4 feet with medium loading of 50 p.s.f.

(10) Nails or bolts used in the construction of scaffolds shall be of adequate size and in sufficient numbers at each connection to develop the designed strength of the scaffold. Nails shall not be subjected to a straight pull and shall be driven full length.

(11) All planking or platforms shall be overlapped (minimum 12 inches) or secured from movement.

(12) An access ladder or equivalent safe access shall be provided.

(13) Scaffold planks shall extend over their end supports not less than 6 inches nor more than 18 inches.

(14) The poles, legs, or uprights of scaffolds shall be plumb, and securely and rigidly braced to prevent swaying and displacement.

(15) Materials being hoisted onto a scaffold shall have a tag line.

(16) Overhead protection shall be provided for men on a scaffold exposed to overhead hazards.

(17) Scaffolds shall be provided with a screen between the toeboard and the guardrail, extending along the entire opening, consisting of No. 18 gauge U.S. Standard Wire one-half-inch mesh or the equivalent, where persons are required to work or pass under the scaffolds.

(18) Employees shall not work on scaffolds during storms or high winds.

(19) Employees shall not work on scaffolds which are covered with ice or snow, unless all ice or snow is removed and planking sanded to prevent slipping.

(20) Tools, materials, and debris shall not be allowed to accumulate in quantities to cause a hazard.

(21) Only treated or protected fiber rope shall be used for or near any work involving the use of corrosive substances or chemicals.

(22) Wire or fiber rope used for scaffold suspension shall be capable of supporting at least six times the intended load.

(23) When acid solutions are used for cleaning buildings over 50 feet in height, wire rope supported scaffolds shall be used.

(24) The use of shore scaffolds or lean-to scaffolds is prohibited.

(25) Lumber sizes, when used in this section, refer to nominal sizes except where otherwise stated.

(26) Scaffolds shall be secured to permanent structures, through use of anchor bolts, reveal bolts, or other equivalent means. Window cleaners' anchor bolts shall not be used.

(27) Special precautions shall be taken to protect scaffold members, including any wire or fiber ropes, when using a heat-producing process.

(b) *General requirements for wood pole scaffolds*

(1) Scaffold poles shall bear on a foundation of sufficient size and strength to spread the load from the poles over a sufficient area to prevent settlement. All poles shall be set plumb.

(2) Where wood poles are spliced, the ends shall be squared and the upper section shall rest squarely on the lower section. Wood splice plates shall be provided on at least two adjacent sides and shall not be less than 4 feet 0 inches in length, overlapping the abutted ends equally, and have the same width and not less than the cross-sectional area of the pole. Splice plates of other materials of equivalent strength may be used.

(3) Independent pole scaffolds shall be set as near to the wall of the building as practicable.

(4) All pole scaffolds shall be securely guyed or tied to the building or structure. Where the height or length exceeds 25 feet, the scaffold shall be secured at intervals not greater than 25 feet vertically and horizontally.

(5) Putlogs or bearers shall be set with their greater dimensions vertical, long enough to project over the ledgers of the inner and outer rows of poles at least 3 inches for proper support.

(6) Every wooden putlog on single pole scaffolds shall be reinforced with a 3/16- × 2-inch steel strip or equivalent secured to its lower edge throughout its entire length.

(7) Ledgers shall be long enough to extend over two pole spaces. Ledgers shall not be spliced between the poles. Ledgers shall be reinforced by bearing blocks securely nailed to the side of the pole to form a support for the ledger.

(8) Diagonal bracing shall be provided to prevent the poles from moving in a direction parallel with the wall of the building, or from buckling.

(9) Cross bracing shall be provided between the inner and outer sets of poles in independent pole scaffolds. The free ends of pole scaffolds shall be cross braced.

(10) Full diagonal face bracing shall be erected across the entire face of pole scaffolds in both directions. The braces shall be spliced at the poles.

(11) Platform planks shall be laid with their edges close together so the platform will be tight with no spaces through which tools or fragments of material can fall.

(12) Where planking is lapped, each plank shall lap its end supports at least 12 inches. Where the ends of planks abut each other to form a flush floor, the butt joint shall be at the centerline of a pole. The abutted ends shall rest on separate bearers. Intermediate beams shall be provided where necessary to prevent dislodgment of planks due to deflection, and the ends shall be nailed or cleated to prevent their dislodgment.

(13) When a scaffold turns a corner, the platform planks shall be laid to prevent tipping. The planks that meet the corner putlog at an angle shall be laid first, extending over the diagonally placed putlog far enough to have a good safe bearing, but not far enough to involve any danger from tipping. The planking running in the opposite direction at right angles shall be laid so as to extend over and rest on the first layer of planking.

(14) When moving platforms to the next level, the old platform shall be left undisturbed until the new putlogs or bearers have been set in place, ready to receive the platform planks.

(15) Guardrails not less than 2 × 4 inches or the equivalent and not less than 36 inches or more than 42 inches high, with a mid-rail, when required, of 1- × 4-inch lumber or equivalent, and toeboards, shall be installed at all open sides on all scaffolds more than 10 feet above the ground or floor. Toeboards shall be a minimum of 4 inches in height. Wire mesh shall be installed in accordance with paragraph (a) (17) of this section.

(16) All wood pole scaffolds 60 feet or less in height shall be constructed and erected in accordance with tables D-7 through D-12 of this section. If they are over 60 feet in height they shall be designed by a registered professional engineer and constructed and erected in accordance with such design. A copy of the typical drawings and specifications shall be made available to the employer and for inspection purposes.

(17) Wood-pole scaffolds shall not be erected beyond the reach of effective firefighting apparatus.

Table D.7 Minimum nominal size and maximum spacing of members of single pole scaffolds–light duty

	Maximum height of scaffold	
	20 feet	**60 feet**
Uniformly distributed load	Not to exceed 25 pounds per square foot	
Poles or uprights	2 by 4 in.	4 by 4 in.
Pole spacing (longitudinal)	6 ft. 0 in.	10 ft. 0 in.
Maximum width of scaffold	5 ft. 0 in.	5 ft. 0 in.
Bearers or putlogs to 3 ft. 0 in. width	2 by 4 in.	2 by 4 in.
Bearers or putlogs to 5 ft. 0 in. width	2 by 6 in. or 3 by 4 in.	2 by 6 in. or 3 by 4 in. (rough)
Ledgers	1 by 4 in.	1¼ by 9 in.
Planking	1¼ by 9 in. (rough)	2 by 9 in.
Vertical spacing of horizontal members	7 ft. 0 in.	7 ft. 0 in.
Bracing, horizontal and diagonal	1 by 4 in.	1 by 4 in.
Tie-ins	1 by 4 in.	1 by 4 in.
Toeboards	4 in. high (minimum)	4 in. high (minimum)

APPENDIX II

Following are the National Primary and Secondary Air Quality Standards: 40 C.F.R. Part 50 (1976).

§ 50.2 Scope

(a) National primary and secondary ambient air quality standards under section 109 of the Act are set forth in this part.

(b) National primary ambient air quality standards define levels of air quality which the Administrator judges are necessary, with an adequate margin of safety, to protect the public health. National secondary ambient air quality standards define levels of air quality which the Administrator judges necessary to protect the public welfare from any known or anticipated adverse effects of a pollutant. Such standards are subject to revision, and additional primary and secondary standards may be promulgated as the Administrator deems necessary to protect the public health and welfare.

(c) The promulgation of national primary and secondary ambient air quality standards shall not be considered in any manner to allow significant deterioration of existing air quality in any portion of any State.

(d) The proposal, promulgation, or revision of national primary and secondary ambient air quality standards shall not prohibit any State from establishing ambient air quality standards for that State or any portion thereof which are more stringent than the national standards.

§ 50.3 Reference conditions

All measurements of air quality are corrected to a reference temperature of 25° C. and to a reference pressure of 760 millimeters of mercury (1,013.2 millibars).

§ 50.4 National primary ambient air quality standards for sulfur oxides (sulfur dioxide)

(a) The level of the annual standard is 0.030 parts per million (ppm), not to be exceeded in a calendar year. The annual arithmetic mean shall be rounded to three decimal places (fractional parts equal to or greater than 0.0005 ppm shall be rounded up).

(b) The level of the 24-hour standard 0.14 parts per million (ppm), not to be exceeded more than once per calendar year. The 24-hour averages shall be determined from successive non-overlapping 24-hour blocks starting at midnight each calendar day and shall be rounded to two decimal places (fractional parts equal to or greater than 0.005 ppm shall be rounded up).

(c) Sulfur oxides shall be measured in the ambient air as sulfur dioxide by the reference method described in appendix A to this part or by an equivalent method designated in accordance with part 53 of this chapter.

(d) To demonstrate attainment, the annual arithmetic mean and the second-highest 24-hour averages must be based upon hourly data that are at least 75 percent complete in each calendar quarter. A 24-hour block average shall be considered valid if at least 75 percent of the hourly averages for the 24-hour period are available. In the event that only 18, 19, 20, 21, 22, or 23 hourly averages are available, the 24-hourly block average shall be computed as the sum of the available hourly averages using 18, 19, etc. as the divisor. If fewer than 18 hourly averages are available, but the 24-hour average would exceed the level of the standard when zeros are substituted for the missing values, subject to the rounding rule of paragraph (b) of this section, then this shall be considered a valid 24-hour average. In this case, the 24-hour block average shall be computed as the sum of the available hourly averages divided by 24.
[61 FR 25579, May 22, 1996]

§ 50.5 National secondary ambient air quality standards for sulfur oxides (sulfur dioxide)

(a) The level of the 3-hour standard is 0.5 parts per million (ppm), not to be exceeded more than once per calendar year. The 3-hour averages shall be determined from successive non-overlapping 3-hour blocks starting at midnight each calendar day and shall be rounded to 1 decimal place (fractional parts equal to or greater than 0.05 ppm shall be rounded up).

(b) Sulfur oxides shall be measured in the ambient air as sulfur dioxide by the reference method described in appendix A of this part or by an equivalent method designated in accordance with part 53 of this chapter.

(c) To demonstrate attainment, the second-highest 3-hour average must be based upon hourly data that are at least 75 percent complete in each calendar quarter. A 3-hour block average shall be considered valid only if all three hourly averages for the 3-hour period are available. If only one or two hourly averages are available, but the 3-hour average would exceed the level of the standard when zeros are substituted for the missing values, subject to the rounding rule of paragraph (a) of this section, then this shall be considered a valid 3-hour average. In all cases, the 3-hour block average shall be computed as the sum of the hourly averages divided by 3.
[61 FR 25580, May 22, 1996]

§ 50.6 National primary and secondary ambient air quality standards for particulate matter

(a) The level of the national primary and secondary 24-hour ambient air quality standards for particulate matter is 150 micrograms per cubic meter ($\mu g/m^3$), 24-hour average concentration. The standards are attained when the expected number of days per calendar year with a 24-hour average concentration above 150 $\mu g/m^3$, as determined in accordance with appendix K to this part, is equal to or less than one.

(b) The level of the national primary and secondary annual standards for particulate matter is 50 micrograms per cubic meter ($\mu g/m^3$), annual arithmetic mean. The standards are attained when the expected annual arithmetic mean concentration, as determined in accordance with appendix K to this part, is less than or equal to 50 $\mu g/m^3$.

(c) For the purpose of determining attainment of the primary and secondary standards, particulate matter shall be measured in the ambient air as PM_{10} (particles with an aerodynamic diameter less than or equal to a nominal 10 micrometers) by:

(1) A reference method based on appendix J and designated in accordance with part 53 of this chapter, or

(2) An equivalent method designated in accordance with part 53 of this chapter. [52 FR 24663, July 1, 1987]

§ 50.7 [Reserved]

§ 50.8 National primary ambient air quality standards for carbon monoxide

(a) The national primary ambient air quality standards for carbon monoxide are:

(1) 9 parts per million (10 milligrams per cubic meter) for an 8-hour average concentration not to be exceeded more than once per year and

(2) 35 parts per million (40 milligrams per cubic meter) for a 1-hour average concentration not to be exceeded more than once per year.

(b) The levels of carbon monoxide in the ambient air shall be measured by:

(1) A reference method based on appendix C and designated in accordance with part 53 of this chapter, or

(2) An equivalent method designated in accordance with part 53 of this chapter.

(c) An 8-hour average shall be considered valid if at least 75 percent of the hourly average for the 8-hour period are available. In the event that only six (or seven) hourly averages are available, the 8-hour average shall be computed on the basis of the hours available using six (or seven) as the divisor.

(d) When summarizing data for comparison with the standards, averages shall be stated to one decimal place. Comparison of the data with the levels of the standards in parts per million shall be made in terms of integers with fractional parts of 0.5 or greater rounding up.
[50 FR 37501, Sept. 13, 1985]

§ 50.9 National primary and secondary ambient air quality standards for ozone

(a) The level of the national primary and secondary ambient air quality standards for ozone measured by a reference method based on appendix D to this part and designated in accordance with part 53 of this chapter, is 0.12 part per million (235 $\mu g/m^3$). The standard is attained when the expected number of days per cal-

endar year with maximum hourly average concentrations above 0.12 part per million (235 $\mu g/m^3$) is equal to or less than 1, as determined by appendix H.
(Secs. 109 and 301 of the Clean Air Act, as amended (42 U.S.C. 7409, 7601))
[44 FR 8220, Feb. 8, 1979]

§ 50.10 [Reserved]

§ 50.11 National primary and secondary ambient air quality standards for nitrogen dioxide

(a) The level of the national primary ambient air quality standard for nitrogen dioxide is 0.053 parts per million (100 micrograms per cubic meter), annual arithmetic mean concentration.

(b) The level of national secondary ambient air quality standard for nitrogen dioxide is 0.053 parts per million (100 micrograms per cubic meter), annual arithmetic mean concentration.

(c) The levels of the standards shall be measured by:

(1) A reference method based on appendix F and designated in accordance with part 53 of this chapter, or

(2) An equivalent method designated in accordance with part 53 of this chapter.

(d) The standards are attained when the annual arithmetic mean concentration in a calendar year is less than or equal to 0.053 ppm, rounded to three decimal places (fractional parts equal to or greater than 0.0005 ppm must be rounded up). To demonstrate attainment, an annual mean must be based upon hourly data that are at least 75 percent complete or upon data derived from manual methods that are at least 75 percent complete for the scheduled sampling days in each calendar quarter.
[50 FR 25544, June 19, 1985]

§ 50.12 National primary and secondary ambient air quality standards for lead

National primary and secondary ambient air quality standards for lead and its compounds, measured as elemental lead by a reference method based on appendix G to this part, or by an equivalent method, are: 1.5 micrograms per cubic meter, maximum arithmetic mean averaged over a calendar quarter.
(Secs. 109, 301(a) Clean Air Act as amended (42 U.S.C. 7409, 7601(a)))
[43 FR 46258, Oct. 5, 1978]

Glossary

Technical legal terms and Latin phrases are not abundantly employed in the text. Of those that do appear, many are defined at the point used and, in order to reduce the length of this glossary, most such definitions are not repeated here.

a fortiori Literally, "with stronger reason." Thus, given fact *A*, related and more probable fact *B* must likewise exist.

aliquot A fractional part of something else, supposed to divide the latter without remainder.

alter ego Another or second self; broadly, a confidant.

assignee One to whom an assignor transfers property or rights under an assignment.

beneficiary One who is the recipient of advantage, profit, or other benefits.

breach Violation of a right, of a duty, or of law, either by an act of commission or by nonfulfillment of an obligation. Thus, breach of contract is the unexcused failure to satisfy one's contractual undertaking.

caveat emptor "Let the buyer beware." In other words, the buyer should take pains to discover for himself any obvious defects in an article he is about to purchase.

chattel An article of personal or movable property.

de facto In fact.

de jure Of right; lawful. "De facto" and "de jure" are contrasting terms. The former is used to refer to an action or state of affairs that is essentially without legal justification but that must nonetheless be accepted for all practical purposes.

de novo Anew; generally, to retry a case from the beginning.

defeasance clause A condition whose fulfillment defeats the operation of an instrument and renders it null and void.

delectus personae Personal preference, or choice of the person; thus, the right of partners to pass upon prospective members of the firm.

delegata potestas non potest delegari "A delegate cannot (further) delegate." Without authorization from his principal, an agent cannot delegate his nonministerial functions and duties to another.

delict A violation of duty, public or private; a wrong.

devisee One to whom realty is given by will.

donee The recipient of a gift.

emancipation A term used primarily with reference to the "setting at liberty" of minors. When the parents, expressly or by implication, surrender the right to the custody and earnings of their child and renounce their parental duties, such child becomes his own master and is thus *emancipated.*

estoppel A legal bar whereby one who has by his conduct induced another to act in a particular manner is precluded (*estopped*) from thereafter adopting an inconsistent position and thus causing injury to such other person. The bar is raised when the party against whom it operates has brought about such conditions as make it inequitable for him to claim a right to which he would otherwise be entitled.

expressio unius est exclusio alterius The maxim that the express enumeration (as in a list) of certain things (or persons or places) is, by implication, the exclusion of another or others not mentioned.

fee simple The largest estate known to the law; an absolute estate in which the owner is entitled to the entire property with unconditional power to dispose of same during his lifetime and that passes to his heirs if the owner dies intestate.

filum aquae   The middle line, or thread, of a stream, which divides it into two parts and often serves as the boundary between the riparian owners on each side.

fraud   An intentionally deceitful practice aimed at depriving another person of his rights or doing him injury in some respect.

grantee   One to whom real property is transferred by grant.

gravamen   The material part, or gist, of a complaint of charge.

in extremis   In the last (that is, the ultimate) illness.

infant   A person under the age of legal majority.

infra   Below, beneath; often used in this fashion: "page 6, infra."

injunction   A writ issued by a court of equity ordering a person to refrain from a given course of action.

in loco parentis   Acting in the place of a parent.

in pari delicto   In equal fault; equally to blame.

in personam   Against a person. See under *in rem.*

in rem   Against a thing. Actions *in personam* and those *in rem* are distinguishable on the ground that the former are directed against specific persons and seek personal judgments, while in rem proceedings seek to determine rights in particular property as against all the world. Similarly, rights in personam are those primarily available against certain persons, while rights in rem are good against the world at large.

inter alia   Among other things.

intestacy   The circumstance in which a person dies without leaving a valid will to indicate his wishes about the disposal of his property.

jurisprudence   Broadly speaking, the science and philosophy of law and of legal relations.

laches   Unreasonable delay in doing what in law should have been done or neglect in seeking to enforce a right at a proper time, which delay or neglect has operated to the disadvantage of another party.

lessee   The person to whom a lease is made.

lex non scripta   Unwritten, or common, law.

lien   A charge (encumbrance) imposed on specific property as security for a debt of other obligations.

liquidated damages   A fixed sum agreed upon, at the outset of a contractual arrangement, as the proper compensation to be paid to the injured party in the event of breach.

malfeasance   The performance of an act that the party has no right to do and ought not to do; the committing of an illegal act.

mandamus   A court writ issued to compel the performance of a public or official duty owed by the person to whom the order is directed.

ministerial   A term pertaining to an action done under the authority of a superior and with relatively little reliance upon the judgment or discretion of the doer.

misfeasance   The performance in a wrongful and injurious manner of an act that might have been done in lawful fashion. Thus, *misfeasance* is the doing of a lawful act in an unlawful manner, as distinguished from *malfeasance,* which is the performance of an act positively unlawful.

modus operandi   Manner of operating.

mores   Usages; folk ways; customs.

mortgagee   The person to whom property is mortgaged.

nonfeasance   Failure to do something that ought to have been done.

nullity   Invalidity; nothingness.

parol   Verbal.

per se   By itself.

post hoc   After the fact.

prima facie   On first appearance; at first view.

privity   Successive (or mutual) relationship to the same property rights; a connection between parties.

pro rata   Proportionately.

promisee   The recipient of a promise.

quantum meruit   Literally, "as much as he deserved."

quid pro quo   One thing for another; something for something. The term is used in connection with contract consideration.

quo warranto   Literally, "by what authority?" The writ by which it is sought to recover an office or franchise from the individual or entity in possession thereof. The writ requires the defendant to appear and show by what authority he maintains possession.

ratification   Confirmation; broadly, agreement by *A* (in the fact of his right to repudiate) to adopt an act performed for him by *B* or to affirm an act that *A* himself had performed earlier.

reformation   The correction of defects so as to bring an instrument in line with the actual intent of the parties, which intent had been, through inadvertence or otherwise, improperly expressed in the agreement as originally drawn.

res gestae   Things done; every circumstance and statement associated with and incident to a given transaction or occurrence.

rescission   Annulment; cancellation.

seisin   Possession with intent to claim a freehold interest.

situs   Location; position.

sovereign immunity   A doctrine holding that governments are generally not responsible in damages for their tortious actions.

statute of limitations   A statute limiting the time period in which a lawsuit may be brought.

subrogation   Substituting one person for another in regard to rights, claims, etc.

supra   Above in position; upon. "Page 6, supra" refers the reader to an earlier page in the same publication.

tenement   Broadly, everything of a permanent nature (principally realty) that may be held. The word is also used, of course, in reference to a type of dwelling place.

testator   One who has left a will to control disposition of his property upon his death.

tort   A wrongful behavior (aside from breach of contract) for which a civil action will lie; the unprivileged commission (or omission) of an act whereby another person incurs loss or injury; such breach of duty as results in damage to plaintiff.

tortfeasor   One who commits a tort.

trespass   In the term's ordinary sense, an unlawful act committed with actual or implied violence and resulting in injury to or physical interference with the person or property of someone else; in a more limited sense, an unauthorized entry upon the real property of another, frequently entailing some measure of damage to such property.

ultra vires   In the law of corporations, an act beyond the scope of corporate powers.

vendee   One to whom a sale (usually of real property) is made; a purchaser.

waiver   Voluntary abandonment, surrender, or relinquishment of a known right or privilege.

INDEX